ENOCH AND THE SYNOPTIC GOSPELS

EARLY JUDAISM AND ITS LITERATURE

Rodney A. Werline, Editor

Number 44

SBL PRESS

ENOCH AND THE SYNOPTIC GOSPELS

Reminiscences, Allusions, Intertextuality

Edited by

Loren T. Stuckenbruck and Gabriele Boccaccini

SBL PRESS

SBL PRESS

Atlanta

Copyright © 2016 by SBL Press

Library of Congress Cataloging-in-Publication Data

Names: Enoch Seminar (7th : 2013 : Camaldoli, Italy) | Stuckenbruck, Loren T., editor. | Boccaccini, Gabriele, 1958- editor.
Title: Enoch and the Synoptic Gospels : reminiscences, allusions, intertextuality / edited by Loren T. Stuckenbruck and Gabriele Boccaccini.
Description: Atlanta : SBL Press, 2016. | Series: Early Judaism and its literature ; number 44 | Includes bibliographical references.
Identifiers: LCCN 2016021816 (print) | LCCN 2016022688 (ebook) | ISBN 9780884141174 (paperback) | ISBN 9780884141198 (hardcover) | ISBN 9780884141181 (ebook)
Subjects: LCSH: Ethiopic book of Enoch—Congresses. | Bible. Gospels—Congresses.
Classification: LCC BS1830.E7 E56 2016 (print) | LCC BS1830.E7 (ebook) | DDC 229/.913—dc23
LC record available at https://lccn.loc.gov/2016021816

Printed on acid-free paper.

CONTENTS

Abbreviations

AARSR	American Academy of Religion Studies in Religion Series
AAWG	Abhandlungen der Akademie der Wissenschaften zu Göttingen
AB	Anchor Bible
ABD	*Anchor Bible Dictionary.* Edited by David Noel Freedman. 6 vols. New York: Doubleday, 1992.
AbrNSup	Abr-Nahrain Supplements
AcOr	*Acta Orientalia*
AfOB	Archiv für Orientforschung: Beiheft
AGAJU	Arbeiten zur Geschichte des antiken Judentums und des Urchristentums
Ahw	*Akkadisches Handwörterbuch.* Wolfram von Soden. 3 vols. Wiesbaden: Harrassowitz, 1965–1981.
AJP	*American Journal of Philology*
Aland	Kurt Aland, ed. *Synopsis Quattuor Evangeliorum.* 13th ed. 1985. Repr., Stuttgart: Deutsche Bibelgesellschaft, 1990.
AOAT	Alter Orient und Altes Testament
BDAG	Walter Bauer, Frederick W. Danker, William F. Arndt, and F. Wilbur Gingrich. *Greek-English Lexicon of the New Testament and Other Early Christian Literature.* 3rd ed. Chicago: University of Chicago Press, 2000.
BETL	Bibliotheca Ephemeridum Theologicarum Lovaniensium
BHS	*Biblia Hebraica Stuttgartensia.* Edited by Karl Elliger and Wilhelm Rudolph. Stuttgart: Deutsche Bibelgesellschaft, 1983.
BibInt	*Biblical Interpretation*
BibInt	Biblical Interpretation Series
BibLeb	*Bibel und Leben*
BibOr	Biblica et Orientalia
BN	*Biblische Notizen*

Brev	*Bible Review*
BSR	*Bulletin for the Study of Religion*
BTB	*Biblical Theology Bulletin*
BTS	Biblical Tools and Studies
CAD	*The Assyrian Dictionary of the Oriental Institute of the University of Chicago.* 21 vols. Chicago: Oriental Institute of the University of Chicago, 1956–2006.
CahRB	Cahiers de la Revue biblique
CAL	Comprehensive Aramaic Lexicon
CANE	*Civilizations of the Ancient Near East.* Edited by Jack M. Sasson. 4 vols. New York: Scribner's Sons, 1995.
CBQ	*Catholic Biblical Quarterly*
CBQMS	Catholic Biblical Quarterly Monograph Series
CEJL	Commentaries on Early Jewish Literature
ConBNT	Coniectanea Biblica: New Testament Series
CRINT	Compendium Rerum Iudaicarum ad Novum Testamentum
CRRAI	Compte rendu, Rencontre Assyriologique Internationale
CSCO	Corpus Scriptorum Christianorum Orientalium
CSSH	*Comparative Studies in Science and History*
CTL	*Cambridge Textbooks in Linguistics*
CTU	*The Cuneiform Alphabetic Texts from Ugarit, Ras Ibn Hani, and Other Places.* Edited by Manfried Dietrich, Oswald Loretz, and Joaquín Sanmartín. Münster: Ugarit-Verlag, 1995.
CurBR	*Currents in Biblical Research*
DCH	*Dictionary of Classical Hebrew.* Edited by David J. A. Clines. 9 vols. Sheffield: Sheffield Phoenix, 1993–2014.
DDD	*Dictionary of Deities and Demons in the Bible.* Edited by Karel van der Toorn, Bob Becking, and Pieter W. van der Horst. 2nd ed. Grand Rapids: Eerdmans, 1999.
DJD	Discoveries in the Judaean Desert
DNWSI	*Dictionary of North-West Semitic Inscriptions.* Jacob Hoftijzer and Karen Jongeling. 2 vols. Leiden: Brill, 1995.
DSSSE	*Dead Sea Scrolls Study Edition.* Edited by Florentino García Martínez and Eibert J. C. Tigchelaar. 2 vols. Leiden: Brill, 1997–1998.
EDSS	*Encyclopedia of the Dead Sea Scrolls.* Edited by Lawrence H. Schiffman and James C. VanderKam. 2 vols. New York: Oxford University Press, 2000

EJL	Early Judaism and Its Literature
EKKNT	Evangelisch-katholischer Kommentar zum Neuen Testament
ErJb	*Eranos-Jahrbuch*
EstBib	*Estudios bíblicos*
EstEcl	*Estudios eclesiásticos*
EvQ	*Evangelical Quarterly*
ExpTim	*Expository Times*
FAOS	Freiburger altorientalische Studien
FCNTECW	Feminist Companion to the New Testament and Early Christian Writings
FRLANT	Forschungen zur Religion und Literatur des Alten and Neuen Testaments
GAAL	Göttinger Arbeitshefte zur altorientalischen Literatur
HBM	Hebrew Bible Monographs
HBT	*Horizons in Biblical Theology*
HdO	Handbuch der Orientalistik
Hen	*Henoch*
HSM	Harvard Semitic Monographs
HSS	Harvard Semitic Studies
HTR	*Harvard Theological Review*
HUCA	*Hebrew Union College Annual*
ICC	International Critical Commentary
Imm	*Immanuel*
JAAR	*Journal of the American Academy of Religion*
JANER	*Journal of Ancient Near Eastern Religions*
JBL	*Journal of Biblical Literature*
JCTCRS	Jewish and Christian Texts in Contexts and Related Studies
JEOL	*Jaarbericht van het Vooraziatisch-Egyptisch Gezelschap (Genootschap) Ex oriente lux*
JGRChJ	*Journal of Greco-Roman Christianity and Judaism*
JHI	*Journal of the History of Ideas*
JJS	*Journal of Jewish Studies*
JNES	*Journal of Near Eastern Studies*
JQR	*Jewish Quarterly Review*
JR	*Journal of Religion*
JSHJ	*Journal for the Study of the Historical Jesus*
JSHRZ	Jüdische Schriften aus hellenistisch-römischer Zeit
JSJ	*Journal for the Study of Judaism*

JSJSup	Journal for the Study of Judaism Supplements
JSNT	*Journal for the Study of the New Testament*
JSNTSup	Journal for the Study of the New Testament Supplement Series
JSOTSup	Journal for the Study of the Old Testament Supplement Series
JSP	*Journal for the Study of the Pseudepigrapha*
JSPSup	Journal for the Study of the Pseudepigrapha Supplement Series
JSS	*Journal of Semitic Studies*
JTS	*Journal of Theological Studies*
KAI	*Kanaanäische und aramäische Inschriften.* Herbert Donner and Wolfgang Röllig. 2nd ed. 3 vols. Wiesbaden: Harrassowitz, 1966–1969.
KTU	*Die keilalphabetischen Texte aus Ugarit.* Edited by Manfried Dietrich, Oswald Loretz, and Joaquín Sanmartín. Münster: Ugarit-Verlag, 1995.
LCL	Loeb Classical Library
LNTS	Library of New Testament Studies
LSS	Leipziger semitische Studien
LSTS	Library of Second Temple Studies
MC	Mesopotamian Civilizations
MdB	Le Monde de la Bible
MNTS	McMaster New Testament Studies
MTSR	*Method and Theory in the Study of Religion*
NIGTC	New International Greek Testament Commentary
NRSV	New Revised Standard Version
NTM	New Testament Message
NTOA	Novum Testamentum et Orbis Antiquus
NTS	*New Testament Studies*
NTTS	New Testament Tools and Studies
OLA	Orientalia Lovaniensia Analecta
Or	*Orientalia*
OTP	*Old Testament Pseudepigrapha.* Edited by James H. Charlesworth. 2 vols. Garden City: Doubleday, 1983–1985.
PTMS	Princeton Theological Monograph Series
PTSDSSP	Princeton Theological Seminary Dead Sea Scrolls Project
PVTG	Pseudepigrapha Veteris Testamenti Graece
R&T	*Religion and Theology*

RB	*Revue biblique*
RBS	Resources for Biblical Study
Rec.	Recension
RevQ	*Revue de Qumran*
RIMA	The Royal Inscriptions of Mesopotamia, Assyrian Periods
RSV	Revised Standard Version
RVV	Religionsgeschichtliche Versuche und Vorarbeiten
SAACT	State Archives of Assyria Cuneiform Texts
SAOC	Studies in Ancient Oriental Civilization
SBLDS	Society of Biblical Literature Dissertation Series
SBLMS	Society of Biblical Literature Monograph Series
SBLSP	Society of Biblical Literature Seminar Papers
SCS	Septuagint and Cognate Studies
SHR	Studies in the History of Religions
SNTSMS	Society for New Testament Studies Monograph Series
SO	Symbolae Osloenses
SP	Sacra Pagina
STDJ	Studies on the Texts of the Desert of Judah
StPohl	Studia Pohl
StPohlSM	Studia Pohl Series Maior
StudNeot	Studia Neotestamentica
SVTP	Studia in Veteris Testamenti Pseudepigraphica
SymS	Symposium Series
TBN	Themes in Biblical Narrative
TCL	Textes cunéiform, Musée du Louvre
TDNT	*Theological Dictionary of the New Testament*. Edited by Gerhard Kittel and Gerhard Friedrich. Translated by Geoffrey W. Bromiley. 10 vols. Grand Rapids: Eerdmans, 1964–1976.
TDOT	*Theological Dictionary of the Old Testament*. Edited by G. Johannes Botterweck, Helmer Ringgren, and Heinz-Josef Fabry. Translated by John T. Willis et al. 15 vols. Grand Rapids: Eerdmans, 1974–2006.
TLG	*Thesaurus Lingue Gracae: Canon of Greek Authors and Works*. Edited by Luci Berkowitz and Karl A. Squitier. 3rd ed. New York: Oxford University Press, 1990.
TSAJ	Texte und Studien zum antiken Judentum
TUAT	Texte aus der Umwelt des Alten Testaments. Edited by Otto Kaiser. Gütersloh: Mohn, 1984–.

VC	*Vigiliae Christianae*
VCSup	Vigiliae Christianae Supplements
VTSup	Vetus Testamentum Supplements
WBC	Word Biblical Commentary
WMANT	Wissenschaftliche Monographien zum Alten und Neuen Testament
WUNT	Wissenschaftliche Untersuchungen zum Alten und Neuen Testament
ZA	*Zeitschrift für Assyriologie*
ZNW	*Zeitschrift für die neutestamentliche Wissenschaft*

1 Enoch and the Synoptic Gospels: The Method and Benefits of a Conversation

Loren T. Stuckenbruck and Gabriele Boccaccini

The essays of the present volume, which emanate from papers given at the Seventh Enoch Seminar held in Camaldoli on 21–26 July 2013, strike up a conversation between the Synoptic Gospels of the New Testament, on the one hand, and the early Enochic tradition preserved in 1 En. 1–108, on the other. The significance of the latter for assessing the diversity of Second Temple Judaism has not gone unnoticed and, indeed, has been subject to a rapidly increasing number of studies since J. T. Milik's monograph on the Aramaic fragments from Qumran Cave 4 in 1976.[1] However, our understanding of the relationship of early Enochic traditions to Christian origins, despite notable exceptions (having mostly to do with the Son of Man figure in the Book of Parables in 1 En. 37–71), is not as well developed. While this circumstance can be variously explained,[2] the need and value of drawing comparisons has long been recognized.

---

1. J. T. Milik, *The Books of Enoch: Aramaic Fragments from Qumrân Cave 4* (Oxford: Clarendon, 1976). Among numerous scholarly monographs and articles, we note those of the Enoch Seminar published since 2002; for a bibliography, see http://www.4enoch.org/wiki4/index.php?title=Enoch_Seminar_(2001-),_learned_society.

2. Two factors can be briefly noted here. The first involves the practical challenge of expertise: many scholars whose primary focus is the interpretation of the New Testament simply do not have the expertise to deal with a wide range of languages in which the Enoch tradition survives (mostly Ge'ez, with more fragmentary remains in Greek, Aramaic, Latin, Syriac, and Coptic). Second, as is the case with other collections of Second Temple texts, reference to Enoch traditions as a conversation partner for Christian origins has fallen victim to the misleading partition of New Testament writings as simply "Christian" (and therefore of an essentially different character), thereby minimizing ways they can be understood as expressions of Jewish tradition in their own right.

It was just over a hundred years ago, in 1912, that the well-known biblical scholar R. H. Charles made the following remarkable claim: "The influence of 1 Enoch on the New Testament has been greater than that of all the other apocryphal and pseudepigraphal books taken together."[3] Since then, considerable evidence has been forthcoming for Jewish tradition relating to the Second Temple and medieval periods. This development is not only noticeable through a series of new discoveries (for example, fragments and manuscripts from the Cairo Genizah, the Dead Sea Scrolls, inscriptions from the Mediterranean world, and further finds of texts in various languages copied in Christian manuscripts), but also through a burgeoning of editions, commentaries, and publications that have begun to demonstrate the impact of this material for the interpretation of texts and traditions preserved in the Hebrew Bible and the New Testament. Now, the rhetorical claim by Charles on the importance of 1 Enoch was no doubt calculated in order to draw attention to a tradition that had only been reintroduced to the broader Western world during the previous century, beginning with translations of a few passages by A. I. Silvestre de Sacy into Latin (1800), by Richard Laurence of the whole into English (1821), and by Andreas Gottlieb Hoffmann into German (1838).[4] Thus already during the nineteenth century a number of scholars could recognize the significance of 1 Enoch for recovering Jewish traditions that were circulating before the turn of the Common Era. Charles's comparative claim, however, took scholarly assessment of the relationship between the early Enochic tradition and the New Testament to a new level. Not only was he maintaining that the significance of 1 Enoch is "greater" for the New Testament than all other noncanonical (from a Protestant perspective) Jewish books

---

3. R. H. Charles, *The Book of Enoch or 1 Enoch* (Oxford: Clarendon, 1912), xcv (see further ix–xii).

4. A. I. Silvestre de Sacy, "Notice du Livre d'Enoch," *Magasin Encyclopédique, ou Journal des Sciences, des Lettres et des Arts* 6.1 (1800): 369–98. De Sacy translated 1 En. 1:1–16:3, 22:5–7, and 32:1–6. Latin was, of course, the scholarly vernacular of his day; Richard Laurence, under the full title, *The Book of Enoch the Prophet: An Apocryphal Production, Supposed for Ages to Have Been Lost; but Discovered at the Close of the Last Century in Abyssinia; Now First Translated from an Ethiopian Ms. in the Bodleian Library* (Oxford: Parker, 1821; 2nd ed. 1833); Andreas Gottlieb Hoffmann, *Das Buch Henoch in vollständiger Uebersetzung mit fortlaufendem Commentar, ausführlicher Einleitung und erläuternden Excursen*, part 2: *Uebersetzung und Commentar au Kp. 56–105, nebst Excursen* (Jena: Croeker, 1838).

taken together, Charles was more specifically describing the nature of this significance in terms of "influence."

It is not for us in the present volume to weigh whether the details of Charles's assertion are correct; that this scholar, who was so familiar with other compositions from the Second Temple period known at the beginning of the twentieth century, could venture such a claim at all is in itself perhaps more important than anything else. Hardly anyone would doubt that the authors of 1 Pet 2:18–22, 2 Pet 2:4–5, and Jude 6 and 14–15 knowingly drew on traditions from 1 Enoch, with the first three texts arguably referring to the rebellious angels tradition known through 1 En. 6–11 and the last-mentioned text citing 1 En. 1:9 directly. One can also advance the argument that these texts, whether understood as "allusions" or "quotations," presuppose some knowledge on the part of their respective audiences regarding the source traditions being used. Even if one accepts these points, however, questions emerge in how one adjudicates the influence of 1 Enoch on other New Testament texts and, indeed, whether the significance of the early Enochic tradition for reading and interpreting the same is exhausted by "influence." Of course, there are other possible ways of construing the interrelationship between texts; in this respect, terms such as *intertextuality* (when applied in a broad sense[5]) or *echoes* (as introduced by Richard Hays[6]) are frequently used. Here we may have in mind cases in which the reading of a text is enhanced by the knowledge of another text or text-tradition without necessarily having to put forth an argument for overt use on the part of the original communicator or detailed knowledge thereof on the part of the receiver. The illumination here would be *extrinsic*, that is, per-

---

5. Julia Kristeva initially coined the term to denote written communication in which readers of a text recognize that it is making use of other texts also known to them; see her *Desire in Language: A Semiotic Approach to Literature and Art*, trans. Thomas Gora, Alice Jardine, and Leon S. Roudiez (Oxford: Blackwell, 1980). Many other critics have, however, used the term to denote relationships between texts that may lie outside the consciousness of writer and reader; cf., e.g., Roland Barthes, "Death of the Author," in *Image, Music, Text*, trans. Stephen Heath (London: Fontana, 1977), 142–54; and the assessment of the problem in Mary Orr, *Intertextuality: Debates and Contexts* (Cambridge: Polity, 2003), 168–82.

6. Richard B. Hays, *Echoes of Scripture in the Letters of Paul* (New Haven: Yale University Press, 1989), 14–21, for whom "echo" constitutes a "poetic" form of "intertextuality," drawing on the work of John Hollander, *The Figure of Echo: A Mode of Allusion in Milton and After* (Berkeley: University of California Press, 1981).

ceived by interpreters removed in time (and perhaps even location) from or without direct access to an original or early communicative setting. Even beyond this, regardless of any intrinsic or remote perspective on a connection between texts, one can ask what may happen to the understanding of a text if it is simply placed in conversation with another. In this instance, without being obliged to posit a generative connection of any sort, interpreters may find themselves exploring what happens when texts, through comparison and contrast, are allowed to speak to one another, sometimes in a privileged way, sometimes within a larger web of texts that have been brought together. To be sure, the choice of conversation partners would not be entirely arbitrary; enough thought structures or language are already shared to render a comparative analysis useful. If, however, it turns out that no line of influence or generative connection can be posited, does it follow that the enterprise is of less value?

The possibilities for relating texts just discussed are of particular relevance for the present volume's focus on traditions preserved in 1 Enoch, on the one hand, and a broad spectrum of passages in the Synoptic Gospels, on the other. There is, for example, not a single instance among the New Testament gospels in which 1 Enoch is quoted in any formal way. In addition, the figure of Enoch is only once mentioned, and passingly so, in Luke 3:37. This does not, of course, have to signify that 1 Enoch has played no role in the shaping of any part of the gospel tradition, nor does this have to mean that a conversation between the two bodies of literature cannot be mutually illuminative. The Apocalypse of John provides an analogical case in point. Hardly anyone doubts that the book draws on writings from the Hebrew Bible such as Isaiah, Ezekiel, Zechariah, Daniel, and Exodus. The identification of this series of connections, though, is based at most on allusion, not formal citation that names the source text. At the same time, one can make a careful argument in certain instances that Enochic tradition, not unlike some of the Hebrew Bible books mentioned above, has played a role in shaping particular words, phrases, and motifs in the text. Even if such an argument is found unconvincing, to what extent does knowing about the existence of motifs and thought structures in 1 Enoch help us to describe the character of John's Apocalypse?[7] To what extent

---

7. Cf. Loren T. Stuckenbruck and Mark D. Mathews, "The Apocalypse of John, *1 Enoch*, and the Question of Influence," in *The Myth of Rebellious Angels: Studies in Second Temple Judaism and New Testament Texts*, WUNT 335 (Tübingen: Mohr Siebeck, 2014), 281–325.

can "influence" and intertextual perspectives in these senses be attributed to the way one interprets the Synoptic Gospels? While drawing any comparisons, for example, one has to remember that the goal and presentation of the two texts were different: whereas the Synoptics were designed to be read immediately and present the ministry of Jesus leading up to the time of his death and aftermath, the early Enoch texts were intended as a repository of secret teachings revealed to Enoch but disclosed to recipients just before the end of time.

Despite the differences of emphasis between 1 Enoch and the Synoptics and the absence of explicit evidence for the use of Enoch tradition in the Synoptics, it is understandable that we would want to look for connections or even influence in some form. Such a scholarly itinerary is supported by a plausibility structure. We know in principle that traditions in 1 Enoch shaped the thought world of a number of Second Temple writings in relation to matters such as the provenance and effects of evil, the structure of the cosmos, poverty and wealth, the bifurcation of humanity along the lines of "the righteous" and "the wicked," the partition of time and eschatology, postmortem existence, the notion of "revealed" knowledge, and early "biblical" interpretation. We also know that most of 1 Enoch was composed before the turn of the Common Era. If, within this framework, points of meaningful contact are found between the gospel tradition and 1 Enoch—which is lesser known and often less respected by Jewish and Christian scholars, students, leaders, and laity—we learn something about traditions that became markers of religious identity during the first four hundred years CE and well beyond.[8] If we wish to carve a place for a consideration of Enoch tradition (not to mention the study of Second Temple Judaism more generally) within the broader scene of the study of Near Eastern and Mediterranean antiquity, biblical studies, and indeed— for some—theology and human well-being, it is tempting to overargue the case; after all, there is a certain self-interest that makes Enoch specialists want 1 Enoch to provide a key voice within the complex milieu of traditions shaping the thought world of Judaism in its varied forms around the

---

8. See Annette Yoshiko Reed, *Fallen Angels and the History of Judaism and Christianity* (Cambridge: Cambridge University Press, 2005); and Loren T. Stuckenbruck, "The *Book of Enoch*: Its Reception in Second Temple Jewish and in Christian Tradition," *Early Christianity* 4 (2013): 7–40. For a continuously updated account of the history of reception of 1 Enoch, prepared by Gabriele Boccaccini and Pierpaolo Bertalotto, see the website www.4enoch.org.

turn of the Common Era. As much as this aim shapes and even sharpens the questions put to texts such as those of the New Testament, one
does well to beware in saying ultimately less when attempting to claim too
much. There is a place for a rhetorical presentation of ideas in order "to try
them out," but hopefully that is but a stepping-stone on the way toward a
more ultimate goal.

Thus, in line with the discussion above, the essays of this volume,
taken as a whole, are doing more than simply seeking out influences to
describe how 1 Enoch relates to traditions that emerged in written form
from the Jesus movement. In terms of meaning or significance, there is
nothing lost when saying that some traditions found in 1 Enoch contributed to the world of thought within which the convictions and ideas found
in the New Testament took shape. Indeed, formulated in this way, such
arguments give 1 Enoch texts more space to be read with integrity, that
is, without bending them to fit into readings of other texts. It also offers
space to read the New Testament writings with more integrity as well. At
the same time, we look for insights that can emerge when these respective
collections are placed in conversation with one another. To our minds, this
conversation—without claiming in each case that a given Enochic tradition supplies the only or decisive background or context for a text in the
gospels—is what the present volume seeks.

There are a number of ways in which we may be able to talk about the
relationship between 1 Enoch and the Synoptic Gospels in terms of influence. One of the areas that has been highlighted time and again, while
met with skepticism from some quarters, has had to do with the Book of
Parables (1 En. 37–71). The essays of Daniel Assefa and Lester Grabbe will
focus on this question. In brief, if the dating of the Parables can be situated
before the Common Era or even, with a later dating to sometime in the
first century CE, preserves tradition that goes back to that time, it is hard
not to think of a connection between the Son of Man figure (also called
Anointed One and Elect One) as presented there with the way a figure
with the same designation is depicted in Matthew's Gospel. In both cases,
the Son of Man denotes a heavenly figure who executes divine judgment
on behalf of God as the present age comes to a close. There is, at the very
least, a connection if the appeals to independent interpretation of the son-
of-man-like figure in Daniel (7:13–14) in common ways does not provide
a sufficient explanation. A connection, it seems, is certain. However, is this
a literary one? That is possible too, but less certain. Ideas and traditions
can be shared without positing literary dependence. On the heels of yet

more recently publications on the matter,[9] and the added use of a broader textual base (see below), the issue will continue to merit attention beyond the confines of this volume.

Having noted a possible genetic connection between early Enochic tradition and the presentation of Jesus as Son of Man in the Synoptic Gospels, we should also acknowledge that the use of material from 1 Enoch in relation to an interpretation of the gospels does not require historical claims of "influence" in order to be fruitful in some way. It suffices here to mention several areas, a couple of which are explored in more depth by the essays of this book.

First, as for example 1 En. 15–16 make clear, illness, suffering, and evil activities among humanity are linked with the influence of spirits that emerge from giants, offspring of the "sons of God" and "daughters of humanity," who, for the atrocities they committed before the great flood, were punished by being made to exist in a disembodied state. In their contributions to this volume, Henryk Drawnel and Archie Wright explore, respectively, the ancient Near Eastern background to this narrative and its impact on the gospel narratives (see further below). As the product of an unsanctioned mix between angelic and human beings, they also represented a breach of the created order. The Enochic tradition considered the spirits of the giants to be what remains of defeated powers, which, however, have not yet been destroyed; their annihilation lies in the future. This narrative throws the activity of Jesus, as presented in the Synoptic Gospels, into the spotlight as one who does not destroy unclean or evil spirits at any time,[10] relocating them instead to a position where they can be managed or remain remote. A postexorcism threat of return remains (cf. Luke 11:24–26 // Matt 12:43–45). Thus, rather than treating exorcism in the Synoptic tradition as material that celebrates the destruction of evil, the Enochic tradition places one in a better position to recognize Jesus's activity and even the exorcistic activity of others as a treatment of some forms of suffering without pretension that they are simply removed

---

9. See the volume of essays edited by James H. Charlesworth and Darrell L. Bock, *Parables of Enoch: A Paradigm Shift,* JCTCRS 11 (London: Bloomsbury T&T Clark, 2013), including "Select Bibliography on 'the Son of Man' and the *Parables of Enoch*" on 373–90 (prepared by Charlesworth and Blake Jurgens).

10. An exception is Matt 8:32, according to which, arguably, it is "the demons" (v. 31) that had entered the herd of swine that met their death in the waters; according to the parallel in Mark 5:13, the herd, numbering two thousand, drowned in the sea.

altogether or can be wished away. In this sense, one can engage the gospel tradition, beginning with some of its underlying sources, in a constructive conversation with the field of psychiatric medicine. There are, to be sure, many differences between ancient (and even contemporary) reports of exorcism and the ways mental health problems, for example, are dealt with today.[11] In neither case, however, is the discourse so much devoted to ridding sufferers of problems altogether as it is, ultimately, to managing them.

Second, we offer an observation that follows from the point just made: The Enoch tradition, mostly the Book of the Watchers (1 En. 1–36) and also to some extent the Animal Apocalypse (1 En. 85–90) and the Apocalypse of Weeks (93:1–10 and 91:11–17)—along with some Dead Sea Scrolls and related texts—can understand evil experienced by people as already defeated, for example, when God exercised power and during the great flood. The expectation that evil in all its forms will be eradicated in the end, expressed as it is in 1 En. 10:16–22, draws on terminology reminiscent of the deluge in Genesis (Gen 6:5–9:17; cf. further Isa 65:17–25; 66:22–23). Such hope, to be sure, is a matter of describing the *Endzeit* in terms of *Urzeit*. However, there is more: what God can be thought to have enacted in the *Urzeit* functions to guarantee the eschatological annihilation of evil. Many, if not a majority of, New Testament theologians have argued that the presentation of Jesus in the gospels, and the apostle Paul, although drawing heavily on an "apocalyptic" worldview, nevertheless modified it in one fundamental point: rather than adopting a framework of two eons, as Jewish apocalyptic is assumed to have forthrightly espoused, Jesus and Paul depict God as one whose activity on behalf of humans to defeat evil has moved into the sphere of the present, thus providing assurance that evil will be obliterated in the future age. For Jesus it happened, for example, through exorcisms and healings; for Paul it happened through God's activity in Jesus's death and resurrection. The claim here is that Jews of an apocalyptic persuasion would never have thought about time in this way as well. The Enoch tradition, the Book of Jubilees, and some Dead Sea texts help us recognize that the notion of evil operating as a defeated power and that such evil can, on this principle, be curbed or managed in the present,

---

11. For a comparison, see Loren T. Stuckenbruck, "The Human Being and Demonic Invasion: Therapeutic Models in Ancient Jewish and Christian Texts," in *The Myth of Rebellious Angels: Studies in Second Temple Judaism and New Testament Texts*, WUNT 335 (Tübingen: Mohr Siebeck, 2014), 161–86.

perhaps *contributed to*—rather than contrasted with—the understandings of time reflected in the gospel tradition and the writings of Paul.

There is a third way in which a conversation with demonology that emerges from the Enoch and related literature sheds light on the Synoptic presentation of Jesus. At issue is the label *unclean* when applied to the term *spirit*. As already noted above and as several recent studies have underscored, the spirits coming from the giants as they were disembodied are deemed to have been products of defilement, an unholy union of angels and humans (1 En. 15:3–4). In Mark's Gospel the suspicion that Jesus's exorcisms evince an alliance with Satan is parenthetically explained by a comment in 3:30: "for they were saying, 'He has an *unclean* spirit.'" The Gospel of Mark does not really answer this charge, except to assert the superiority of Jesus to his opponents and to reinforce this through his authority in debate; in addition, the audience of the Markan narrative would have known that Jesus had the Spirit of God since his baptism (1:10). If Matthew and Luke's Gospels knew of the charge that Jesus has an unclean spirit (as it appears in Mark, for example), they did not draw on it directly, but rather drew on a much older tradition to represent Jesus another way: as one born of the *holy* Spirit (Matt 1:18, 20; cf. Luke 1:35).[12] If read from this perspective—one that can be traced back to Enochic tradition—the role of the Spirit in Jesus's birth, whatever that may have meant in relation to claims about his divinity as it came to be understood, may have provided one way to answer the charge that Jesus was acting in league with that which is unclean, whether this was through his association with sinners (Mark 2:16 // Matt 9:11 // Luke 5:30; cf. Luke 15:2) or through his exorcisms. A plausibility structure for the notion that the adjective *holy* was intended at some stage as a contrast to *unclean* is supplied by the stories of Noah's birth found in 1 En. 106–107 and the Genesis Apocryphon (at 1Q20 II–V).

The three examples presented here in brief illustrate how a conversation with Enochic tradition can be profitable, without requiring a close-knit argument that the one tradition has had an influence upon the other. Some of the essays in this volume reflect an attempt to make such a conversation possible. This view does not obviate that in other instances influence can be more plausibly demonstrated, and several essays indeed

---

12. For a fuller argument, see Stuckenbruck, "Conflicting Stories: The Spirit Origin of Jesus' Birth," in *Myth of Rebellious Angels*, 142–60.

advance an argument to this effect. If 1 Enoch and the Synoptic Gospels are to be compared at any point, it remains to reflect on challenges that accompany such an analysis. We are, in each case, dealing with collections of texts that are not only ancient but whose precise historical contexts are at each turn not immediately apparent.

As far as the Synoptic Gospels are concerned, complications arise as one distinguishes between the time of composition of a gospel as a whole and the times in which the respective traditions they preserve initially took shape. Since the sociopolitical landscape of Judea and the eastern Mediterranean world changed significantly between the time of Jesus and the latter part of the first century CE, this distinction is important for determining the provenience of this or that tradition. Text-critical problems aside, the span of time covered by traditions transmitted through the Synoptics embraces a period of some seventy years.

Whereas the complications regarding the literary, socioreligious, and political gospels—underscored by social-scientific and historical-exegetical disciplines—are well documented (even if consensus is hard to attain), we do well to be reminded what the title "1 Enoch" describes. Here we are dealing with a collection of some twenty (perhaps more) traditions that, taken together, reflect up to four hundred years of writing, collecting, and editing activity on the part of devout Jews who did not in each case share the same milieu, wrote at different times under distinguishable sociopolitical circumstances, and were driven by contrasting motives. Whereas the Synoptic Gospels offer a narrative focusing on selected traditions about Jesus that include both deeds and teachings and that culminate in his passion and its immediate aftermath, 1 Enoch is a collection of pieces that, framed by a title or short third person narrative, are mostly written under the name of the prediluvian patriarch, while one section is formally anonymous (chs. 6–11) and a few others are attributed to Noah. In the Ethiopic manuscript tradition, the 108 chapters are clearly divided into five major sections (Book of the Watchers, chs. 1–36; Book of Parables, chs. 37–71; Book of Heavenly Luminaries, chs. 72–82; Book of Dreams, chs. 83–90; Epistle, chs. 91/92–105), followed by two shorter additions (Birth of Enoch, chs. 106–107; Eschatological Admonition, ch. 108). First Enoch therefore covers a much greater time frame than do the Synoptic Gospels, taken singly or together, even if we take a few of the later small additions into account (e.g., Mark 16:9–20; Luke 22:43–44).

In addition to the differences in form, content, and time span covered, perhaps an even greater difficulty for comparative analysis relates to the text. The text-critical work of the New Testament gospels, which today has a very large text base at its disposal, continues to develop and refine both its methods and focus for study. The result so far has been, on the whole, to establish a remarkably stable text. This situation is more than we can say for 1 Enoch. Part of the challenge might seem that our most comprehensive version of the work is preserved in Geʿez (often referred to as Classical or Old Ethiopic), for which our textual evidence dates back to around the turn of the fifteenth century.[13] The reception of the book in the Ethiopian Orthodox Tewahedo Church as Mäṣḥäfä Henok in Geʿez manuscripts reflects a series of contexts from the fifteenth through the twentieth centuries that are very different from those in which 1 Enoch was composed during the Second Temple period, not to mention those of the early fragmentary Jewish materials in Aramaic from the Dead Sea (third to first centuries BCE) and the Christian Greek, Latin, Syriac, and Coptic evidence from the fourth century CE and later.

Despite the significant headway made by scholars in relation to the earlier, non-Geʿez materials, we can and should continue to pose a number of questions; these issues relate, for example, to manuscript reconstruction, the function of texts as artifacts, and the fragments' respective codicological contexts. Since the Aramaic fragments cover only about 5 percent of text corresponding to 1 Enoch and the Greek fragments barely 20 percent, it becomes impossible to deal with anything approaching the work as a whole without reference to the Geʿez version. This is not without difficulties; indeed, those unacquainted with 1 Enoch studies would have grounds for marveling that for a text of 108 chapters stemming from the Second Temple period we should rely so heavily on manuscripts that date no further back than 1400 CE. It should be noted, however, that compared to early Jewish writings preserved through other language traditions (e.g., Greek, Latin, Syriac, Armenian, Georgian, Slavonic), Mäṣḥäfä Henok has suffered very little obviously Christianizing emendations and interpolations,[14] something that holds for the Geʿez manuscript tradition as a whole. Notwithstanding the transmission of manuscripts of 1 Enoch as they were being read and used in an avowedly Christian setting, the

---

13. The currently earliest manuscript from Daga Estifanos on Lake Tana is microfilm number EMML 8400 at the National Archives Library Agency in Addis Ababa.

14. To be sure, some manuscripts contain marginal notes by scribes that indicate the Christian context of the book's reception. For a good example, cf. EMML 2080 from Hayq Estifanos, in which such scribal notes have yet to be properly studied.

degree of overlap between the Geʿez text and its counterparts, even the Aramaic fragments from the Dead Sea, suggests that it can be studied with a view to anchoring it within a more original Jewish context.

With respect to the text itself, the last critical edition of 1 Enoch was produced by R. H. Charles in 1906, while in 1978 Michael Knibb made an important contribution by collating a number of manuscripts around the text of a manuscript from the Rylands Library in Manchester that preserves the later, more standardizing text (Eth. II).[15] Charles listed thirty-two manuscripts, of which he was able to make full use of twenty-four and partial use of others. Knibb's collations focused mostly on seven copies of the earlier, though more varied recension (Eth. I), including the important Tana 9 not known to Charles; the latter, also labeled among the Addis Ababa National Library microfilm collection as EMML 8292, served as a significant point of departure for Ephraim Isaac's translation in James Charlesworth's *Old Testament Pseudepigrapha* (1983). A number of text-critical studies underlie several translations of all or part of 1 Enoch that have since been published: Siegbert Uhlig (1984), Patrick Tiller (1993), and of course the work of George Nickelsburg and James VanderKam (2004 and 2012).[16] Today's comparative work owes a tremendous debt to these and others scholars for what they have provided us in the way of a workable text.

However, recent listings of known manuscripts, such as those provided by Uhlig and by Nickelsburg and VanderKam,[17] which number forty-nine or fifty,[18] do not account for the actual number of known manuscripts

---

15. Michael A. Knibb, *The Ethiopic Book of Enoch*, 2 vols. (Oxford: Clarendon, 1978), esp. 2:21–37 for a discussion of the Ethiopic evidence.

16. Siegbert Uhlig, *Das äthiopische Henochbuch*, JSHRZ 5/6 (Gütersloh: Gütersloher Verlagshaus, 1984), 463–780; Patrick Tiller, *A Commentary on the Animal Apocalypse of 1 Enoch*, EJL 4 (Atlanta: Scholars Press, 1993); George W. E. Nickelsburg and James C. VanderKam, *1 Enoch: A New Translation* (Minneapolis: Fortress, 2004); Nickelsburg and VanderKam, *1 Enoch: The Hermeneia Translation*, rev. ed. (Minneapolis: Fortress, 2012).

17. Uhlig, *Das äthiopische Henochbuch*, 470–77; George W. E. Nickelsburg, *1 Enoch 1: A Commentary on the Book of 1 Enoch, Chapters 1–36; 81–108*, Hermeneia (Minneapolis: Fortress, 2001), 15–17; and George W. E. Nickelsburg and James C. VanderKam, *1 Enoch 2: A Commentary on the Book of 1 Enoch, Chapters 37–82*, Hermeneia (Minneapolis: Fortress, 2012), 4–6.

18. In these lists, the slight variance depends largely on whether one counts Tana 9 and Tana 9a (both now under the siglum EMML 8292) as texts from the same manuscript or numbers them separately.

now available for study, nor do they include emerging important evidence for the text. This point aside, we now know of the existence of up to 150 manuscripts of 1 Enoch, of which over a hundred can readily be studied.[19] Of the latter group, at least twenty-six texts preserve the older, less standardized recension of the book, and among the currently known yet inaccessible manuscripts there are sure to be more. The integration of this additional evidence for the text, some of which may be reckoned among our most important textual witnesses, will provide us with readings that, in not a few places, lead to small yet significant differences in translation. Future work on 1 Enoch, whether it is taken on its own or compared with another body of texts (as in the present volume), will be in a better position to sift through evidence than up until now has been the case.

The multiple approaches to thinking about the relationship between 1 Enoch and the Synoptic Gospels outlined above put us in a better position to introduce briefly the contributions that occur in this volume. In his discussion entitled "Narrative Depictions of Altered States of Consciousness in 1 Enoch and the Synoptic Tradition," André Gagné offers a conceptual framework for reading texts that depict Enoch and Jesus undergoing religious experiences. Over against the notion that visionary travel and encounters are strictly a matter of the mind (and therefore not the body), Gagné draws on cognitive science in order to demonstrate how much what many may explain as literary creations in fact reflect a coming to terms with the web of experience that emerges from a particular sociocultural setting. Daniel Gurtner's contribution, "The Revelatory Experiences of Enoch and Jesus: A Comparison between the Book of the Watchers and the Synoptic Tradition," follows Gagné's piece with an overview and comparison that focuses more fully on the texts. Gurtner's comparison underscores that whereas Enoch's mediatorial activity in the Book of the Watchers of 1 Enoch is primarily a function of his identity as messenger to the rebellious angels, Jesus's revelatory experiences relate more immediately to his own identity as an end in itself (i.e., as "Son of God"). Neither Gagné nor Gurtner claims that 1 Enoch has influenced the Synoptic Gospels directly; instead, they underscore the common sociocultural and religious framework within which the traditions present the figures of Enoch and Jesus, respectively.

---

19. For the first of two installments that describes both known manuscripts and some of this additional material, see Ted M. Erho and Loren T. Stuckenbruck, "A Manuscript History of *Ethiopic Enoch*," *JSP* 23 (2013): 87–133.

Two essays in this volume focus on the birth narratives of the Gospels of Matthew and Luke and engage in a series of comparisons and contrasts with material from 1 Enoch. In her study on "Unusual Births: Enochic Traditions and Matthew's Infancy Narrative," Amy Richter argues what it means to read the story of Jesus's birth in Matthew's Gospel in conversation with the tradition of rebellious angels in 1 Enoch: much in contrast to the latter, Jesus's birth, which occurs without sexual interaction, introduces righteousness into the world. Holding forth the possibility that Matthew's Gospel is aware of the Enochic myth, Richter suggests that such a background "helps make sense of why Matthew told his story in the particular way he does." Anders Klostergaard Petersen argues along different lines in his piece on "Enoch and the Synoptic Birth Narratives: A Thought Experiment," by asking what it means for 1 Enoch not to offer a birth narrative for its protagonist (Enoch), while Matthew and Luke's Gospels do (Jesus). In adjusting the Weberian definition of charismatic authority, Klostergaard Petersen is able to situate 1 Enoch closer to Paul, who by analogy did not consider it significant to include a birth narrative about the center of his message (Jesus).

In "Heavenly Beings in the Enoch Traditions and the Synoptic Gospels," Kelley Coblentz Bautch focuses on the place and function of angelology. Noting the common thought world of these sources as well as the popularity of Enoch traditions in early Christian literature, she observes that Matthew's Gospel (as well as the other New Testament gospels) is circumspect with regard to the presentation of angels. In contrast to the prominent and distinctive roles accorded angels in apocalyptic literature like the Enochic booklets and other early Christian writings, the Synoptic Gospels' restraint, for example, in associating angels with the realm of the dead has to do especially with the latter's aims to secure the prominence of Jesus in the narrative. Writing on "The Parables of Enoch and Luke's Parable of the Rich Man and Lazarus," Leslie Baynes engages in a series of critical comparisons between both the Enochic tradition (esp. 1 En. 62–63) and the Si-Osiris myth to establish the complex yet arguable background that shaped Luke 16:19–31. In particular, the case for influence is strongest in parallels in Luke and the Book of Parables not shared with other literature: "the plea of the rich in direct discourse for mercy from the flame of Sheol and the reigning heavenly figure's consequence refusal."

In addition to Baynes's essay, three further studies in this volume focus on the potential significance of the Book of Parables for interpreting the gospel traditions. In "Forgiveness of Sins: An Enochic Problem, a Synoptic Answer," Gabriele Boccaccini argues that the presence in the Book of Parables (at 1 En. 51:1–5) of those who are among neither the "righteous" nor the "sinners," but who repent and receive mercy, helps unlock the background of Jesus's message of repentance to take place before the final judgment. Without claiming a literary dependence of the gospel tradition on the Book of Parables, Boccaccini argues for the possibility that the presentation of Jesus as one who extends forgiveness to his contemporaries carries out what the Enochic tradition envisions for the period just before the end.

The essay on " 'Son of Man': Its Origin and Meaning in Second Temple Judaism" by Lester Grabbe reexamines the much debated expression that is applied to Jesus in the gospels on the basis of its precursor in Dan 7, its usage in 4 Ezra 13, and its function in the Parables of Enoch. Among several conclusions, Grabbe's study supports the view that the expression in the gospel traditions is not the equivalent of "I," and is not merely the result of borrowing from Daniel; it is precisely for its titular (and messianic) use that the Enochic Parables provide evidence.

Picking up on the significance attributed to the Son of Man figure in the Book of Parables, Daniel Assefa, in "Matthew's Day of Judgment in the Light of 1 Enoch," compares the Enochic tradition with the scene of eschatological judgment in Matt 25:31–46. Following the views of several New Testament interpreters and taking the influence of 1 Enoch on the Matthean text as a point of departure, Assefa undertakes a comparison that not only underscores common features and places but also puts into sharp relief the element of surprise in Matthew's scene, which functions to exhort readers to vigilance by warning them about the unexpected.

We have already mentioned the question of the Enochic contribution to our understanding of demonology in the Synoptics. In this regard, Archie Wright, in his essay on "The Demonology of 1 Enoch and the New Testament Gospels," offers a more in-depth treatment of this topic, identifying both the Book of the Watchers of 1 Enoch and other Jewish writings (e.g., Jubilees, selected Dead Sea texts) as sources that illuminate a tradition "that influenced the demonology of the gospels" (e.g., Mark 5:1–20 // Luke 8:27–36 // Matt 8:28–34). Wright's discussion also demonstrates how much discourse on demonology in these works is bound up with a theological anthropology whose growing emergence can be already detected in 1 En. 15–16.

In a significant study entitled "1 Enoch 6–11 Interpreted in the Light of Mesopotamian Incantation Literature," Henryk Drawnel explores a heretofore much overlooked ancient Near Eastern background (the Marduk-Ea incantation) that helps to account for much of the literary structure of 1 En. 6–11. In light of this, Drawnel then examines "possible points of influence" of the Enochic myth on several passages of the Synoptics (Mark 1:27 // Luke 4:36; Matt 12:28 // Luke 11:20).

Joseph Angel offers an essay entitled "Enoch, Jesus, and Priestly Tradition." Although emphasizing that sacerdotal portrayals of Enoch in 1 Enoch cannot be said to have influenced the use of priestly traditions to depict Jesus in the Synoptic Gospels, motifs that accrued to Enoch and that were likewise associated with ideal priestly figures (e.g., 4Q541 and the Self-Glorification Hymn among the Dead Sea texts) do illuminate the Jesus tradition, including the presentation of Jesus as the eschatological revealer of divine wisdom in Matt 11:25–30.

Though not focusing on priestly tradition as such, Benjamin G. Wold's study, "Jesus among Wisdom's Representatives: 4QInstruction," places both Jesus and Enoch traditions in conversation with the presentations of an anonymous *maskil* in 4QInstruction and the Self-Glorification Hymn. The comparison affirms the degree to which exclusivist associations with wisdom by exalted figures are intertwined with claims to authority and legitimacy.

Finally, in "The Veneration Motif in the Temptation Narrative of the Gospel of Matthew: Lessons from the Enochic Tradition," Andrei Orlov engages in a study that involves early Enoch tradition stemming not from 1 Enoch but from the Slavonic or 2 Enoch, and its relation to the temptation narrative of Jesus in the wilderness, especially as set out in Matt 4:1–11. Based on a comparison with a complex web of scenarios involving refusals to venerate "pseudo-representations" of Deity in both the Primary Adam Books and Enochic tradition (2 En. 21–22), Orlov concludes that the temptation narrative deconstructs and reconfigures such a motif in order to affirm the divinity of the human protagonist, Jesus.

As editors, we would like to thank Rodney Werline, general editor of the Early Judaism and Its Literature series of SBL Press, and members of the series board for accepting the present manuscript for publication, and Nicole Tilford for her help in seeing the manuscript to publication. In addition, we would like to thank Seth Bledsoe, Elisabeth Fischer, Lina Aschenbrenner, and Anna Kellerer at Ludwig-Maximilians-Universität München for editorial assistance in preparing the manuscript.

Last but not least, we would like to thank our sponsors, the Department of Near Eastern Studies and the Institute for Humanities of the

University of Michigan, the Michigan Center for Early Christian Studies, and the Alessandro Nangeroni International Endowment. Thanks to their generous support, the Enoch Seminar, born in 2001 as an informal biennial meeting of specialists in Second Temple Judaism, has developed into a structured organization, to which new activities have been added, including the Enoch Graduate Seminars, the Nangeroni Meetings, and the online encyclopedia 4 Enoch. The present volume marks yet another significant step in an ongoing project of research to which a growing number of scholars from around the world are contributing.

Narrative Depictions of Altered States of Consciousness in 1 Enoch and the Synoptic Tradition

André Gagné

This paper is mainly a reflection on epistemology and the use of an inter-disciplinary approach in the study of ancient Jewish and Christian litera-ture. As a scholar of the Second Temple period and early Christianity, I recognize that most of these religious texts are ultimately concerned with the human condition—experienced in this lifetime or how it was believed to be in the afterlife. This is especially true when it comes to the ques-tion of "religious experiences" such as dreams, visions, soul flights, and ecstasy.[1] It is difficult to deny that a significant amount of texts that we study contain narratives depicting such experiences—usually understood as being "religious" in nature.[2] It is clearly difficult to share the presupposi-tions of the implied writers, but they themselves (or the authors of their sources) either believed to have had such experiences or were recounting past phenomena.[3] Scholars have persuasively argued that religious beliefs

---

1. James R. Davila has also extensively written on issues pertaining to religious experience, ritual praxis in the context of early Jewish and Christian literature, as well as the *hekhalot* texts; for example, see *Descenders to the Chariot: The People behind the Hekhalot Literature,* JSJSup 70 (Leiden: Brill, 2001); "Ritual in the Jewish Pseudepigra-pha," in *Anthropology and Biblical Studies: Avenues of Approach,* ed. Louise J. Lawrence and Mario I. Aguilar (Leiden: Deo, 2004), 158–83; "The Ancient Jewish Apocalypses and the *Hekhalot* Literature," in *Paradise Now: Essays on Early Jewish and Christian Mysticism,* ed. April D. DeConick, SymS 11 (Atlanta: Society of Biblical Literature, 2006), 105–25.

2. Below I will explain the use of *religious* as an adjective to describe such experi-ences.

3. Some scholars think that ancient sources sometimes depict "true" religious experiences, narrating—directly or indirectly—real past events. For example, in

and practices are shaped by people's own worldview and culture, and that religion itself is to "be understood as a cultural system and social institution that governs and promotes ideal interpretations of existence and ideal praxis with reference to postulated transempirical powers or beings."[4] The "religious" beliefs and practices of ancient writers were also grounded in their worldview. Otherworldly forces were believed to exert some influence on the state of human affairs. For example, when one reads portions of the Book of the Watchers (1 En. 1–36), the seer is said to be transported to various places (in a vision?), while being in the presence of archangels or what can be understood as "transempirical powers or beings":

> I *traveled* to where it was chaotic.... And there I saw seven of the stars of heaven, bound and thrown in it together, like great mountains, and burning in fire. Then I said, "For what reason have they been bound, and for what reason have they been thrown here?" Then *Uriel* said to me, *one of the holy angels who was with me,* and he was their leader.... From there I *traveled* to another place. And he showed me to the west a great and high mountain of hard rock.... And I said.... Then *Raphael* answered me, *one of the holy angels who was with me....* And from there I *traveled* to another place, to the west of the ends of the earth.... And I asked and said.... Then *Reuel* answered me, *one of the holy angels who was with me....*[5]

---

the case of the visionary content of 4 Ezra, Michael E. Stone ("A Reconsideration of Apocalyptic Visions," *HTR* 96 [2003]: 178), states: "Since it resonates clearly with psychological experiences and processes known to occur, it is most plausible to assume that its source is direct or mediated knowledge of religious experience. Now, once the door is opened to this factor, even in an unusual work, certain implications inevitably follow. If we accept the idea that religious experience, including alternate states of consciousness, is part, indeed a central part, of what 4 Ezra is about, then we must envisage the possibility that this factor is present also in other works of the time. They are religious works, by religious people, and we must consider religious experience when we interpret them. The traditional and stereotypical features of the visionary descriptions in other words do not gainsay this possibility, indeed likelihood."

4. Armin W. Geertz, "Brain, Body and Culture: A Biocultural Theory of Religion," *MTSR* 22 (2010): 305.

5. See 1 En. 21–23. The text of 1 Enoch is that of George W. E. Nickelsburg and James C. VanderKam, *1 Enoch: The Hermeneia Translation* (Minneapolis: Fortress, 2012), 42–44, emphasis added.

Is the writer reporting something that actually happened? It is difficult to accept some kind of transcendent reality when modern neuroscientific research has shown that people can have such cognitive experiences. As we will see, however, they do remain purely neurological in nature. Scholars need to keep in mind that such experiences do happen, but how these are interpreted, as either being religious, psychedelic, or delusional, depends on one's cultural system:

> Visions or visual (or sound and tactile) "hallucinations" can indeed be based on sensory perceptions in the absence of an actual external stimulus but that does not make them "false" perceptions. What neuroscientific research shows is that whether a hallucination (visual, tactile or sound) is called a delusion cannot be determined on the basis of the experience itself but is given by the social circumstances or cultural system. Lenz…, for example, shows that it is practically impossible to distinguish belief and delusion in their initial phases. It is only in the life and future development that such a distinction can be made. Ultimately it is within the cultural system that the decision and prescription is to be found whether a vision is true or false, whether it belongs to reality or not.[6]

All will agree that 1 Enoch is replete with stories that depict some kind of transcendent reality and that this other ontological world was *said* to have been revealed by means of a "religious" experience. In reading such texts, one needs to remember that: (1) they are significant for the one undergoing the so-called religious experience; (2) they were narrations of what is now commonly called "altered states of consciousness" (ASCs); (3) they are concerned with divine beings and transcendent realities; (4) they share a reality that was believed to be more true and real than normal everyday life.[7] Before I pursue this inquiry into ASCs, how should we actually understand "religious experience"?

---

6. See Pieter F. Craffert, "'Seeing' a Body into Being: Reflections on Scholarly Interpretations of the Nature and Reality of Jesus' Resurrected Body," *R&T* 9 (2002): 100.

7. The following points are applied to the Nag Hammadi corpus by Michael Kaler, "Talking about Religious Experience at Nag Hammadi," *BSR* 42 (2013): 2–7, esp. 2, but this is clearly applicable to Second Temple literature such as 1 Enoch and even to some New Testament texts.

Understanding "Religious Experience"

Religious experience has mainly been studied from two different perspectives. Perennialism understands that only one reality underlies both
matter and mind.[8] There is a common ground to all mystical and religious
experiences, since it is believed that each of the world's religions shares
a single and universal truth. Only the expression of this common truth
varies. From a different perspective, constructivism is the idea that culture
and assumptions shape religious experiences (i.e., Buddhists and Christians who have some kind of mystical experience do not live the same
reality). Hard constructivists completely deny a common substratum of
religious experiences.[9]

Ann Taves is of the opinion that we should be careful when speaking
of "religious experiences."[10] According to Taves, such experiences should
rather be qualified as "experiences deemed religious,"[11] since the "religious" aspect of any experience stems from the interpretation subsequent
to the event itself. One's worldview, culture, and upbringing add the "religious" to the experience, to what could have initially been an ASC. Therefore, "religious experience" as a unique category does not exist. In the case
of Second Temple literature and the Synoptic Gospels, stories reporting
visions, dreams, and so on were already understood as being "religious"
in nature.

Defining "Altered States of Consciousness"
and Their Relationship to Culture

There are many theories of consciousness, but for our purpose we can
understand consciousness as "the subjective quality of experience."[12] How

---

8. Even if this approach existed before his time, it was greatly popularized by
Aldous Huxley's comparative study entitled *Perennial Philosophy* (London: Harper &
Brothers, 1946).

9. For an in-depth discussion of these two perspectives in the study of religion,
see Robert H. Sharf, "The Rhetoric of Experience and the Study of Religion," *Journal
of Consciousness Studies* 7 (2000): 267–87.

10. Ann Taves, *Religious Experience Reconsidered: A Building-Block Approach to
the Study of Religion and Other Special Things* (Princeton: Princeton University Press,
2009), 16–17.

11. This is what Taves (ibid., 14) calls the "attributional" approach.

12. On various theories of consciousness, see, e.g., Daniel C. Dennett, *Conscious-*

then are we to define "altered states of consciousness" or "alternate states of consciousness" (ASCs)? Referencing the research of cultural anthropologist Erika Bourguignon, John J. Pilch, in his pioneering work on ASCs in biblical studies, defines such conditions as follows:

> ASCs are defined as conditions in which sensations, perceptions, cognition and emotions are altered. These are characterized by changes in sensing, perceiving, thinking, and feeling. In addition, these states modify the relation of the individual to the self, the body, one's sense of identity, and the environment of time, space, or other people.[13]

The question then would be: Who experiences such states? In order to answer this, Bourguignon studied the ethnographic literature of 488 societies throughout the world. From these societies, 437 (i.e., 90 percent) account for several forms of culturally patterned ASCs. Closer to our interests, Bourguignon examined the data from 44 circum-Mediterranean societies and concluded that altered states of consciousness are experienced by 80 percent of these societies; they are simply part of normal life.[14]

Cultural anthropologists have classified societies into two distinct categories depending on how each perceives reality. Monophasic societies are groups of individuals for whom reality is determined empirically and is experienced strictly during the "waking" phase. Alternately, polyphasic societies value different perceptual processes, meaning that reality is also perceived through nonwaking moments/experiences; this is where ASCs come into play.[15] Ancient Mediterranean societies—as is still the case today—are polyphasic in nature. Therefore, it is not surprising to find

---

ness Explained (Boston: Little, Brown, 1991); and Susan Blackmore, *Consciousness: An Introduction* (London: Hodder & Stoughton; New York: Oxford University Press, 2003). For the definition used here, see David J. Chalmers, *The Conscious Mind* (Oxford: Oxford University Press, 1996), 6.

13. John J. Pilch, "Altered States of Consciousness: A 'Kitbashed' Model," *BTB* 26 (1996): 133.

14. For more details on this, see Erika Bourguignon, *Psychological Anthropology: An Introduction to Human Nature and Cultural Differences* (New York: Holt, Rinehart & Winston, 1979).

15. For a discussion of the differences between *monophasic* and *polyphasic* cultures, see Pieter F. Craffert, *The Life of a Galilean Shaman: Jesus of Nazareth in Anthropological-Historical Perspective,* Matrix: The Bible in Mediterranean Perspective 3 (Eugene, OR: Wipf & Stock, 2008), 174–77.

stories reporting "visions," "dreams," or "soul-flights" (or, in modern par-
lance, out-of-body experiences) in early Jewish and Christian texts, since
this worldview is part of their culture. But modern scholarship struggles
with such a perspective and what is understood to be "real." Georg Luck
speaks of the modern bias when it comes to different modes of consciousness found in ancient texts: "Visions such as the theurgists claimed to have
experienced are rejected instinctively by the modern mind because of our
scientific habits of thought, but it seems impossible, considering the evidence we have, to declare all these experiences 'unreal,' or call them clev-
erly orchestrated deceit."[16]

For Pieter Craffert, who has done extensive work on the historical
Jesus and shamanism, "what is experienced as normal or ordinary consciousness is different from culture to culture."[17] But are ASCs culturally
induced? Are people wrong into thinking that they actually experienced
something? Should we disregard the stories reporting such experiences
as fanciful and unreliable? This is where *Gattungskritik* became a useful
tool for scholars to explain the similarities between various accounts in
terms of genre. It is clear that the writer of 1 Enoch is narrating stories
that people believed could be true. The same could be said of events in
the life of Jesus as depicted by the gospel writers. Episodes such as the
theophany at his baptism (Mark 1:9–11 // Matt 3:14–17 // Luke 3:21–22
// John 1:29–34), his battle with the devil in the wilderness temptations
(Mark 1:12–13 // Matt 4:1–11 // Luke 4:1–13), or his transfiguration (Mark
9:2–8 // Matt 17:1–8 // Luke 9:28–36), depict events that ancient societies
thought to be real. Their worldview and culture provided the epistemo-
logical framework to sustain such ideas. This is why we can conclude that
Enoch's and Jesus's ASC experiences are to be explained intertextually, in
echo with other similar texts. Ancient authors used this conventional way
of writing to express their ideas. As a result, it is believed that stories of
ASCs are not necessarily describing "true" experiences but exist in order to
communicate a worldview.[18] This is how narrations of otherworldly jour-

---

16. Georg Luck, "Theurgy and Forms of Worship in Neo-Platonism," in *Religion, Science, and Magic in Concert and in Conflict,* ed. Jacob Neusner, Ernest S. Frerichs, and Paul Virgil MacCraken Flesher (New York: Oxford University Press, 1989), 214.

17. Pieter F. Craffert, "Shamanism and the Shamanic Complex," *BTB* 41 (2011): 156.

18. See Martha Himmelfarb, *Ascent to Heaven in Jewish and Christian Apoca-lypses* (Oxford: Oxford University Press, 1993).

ALTERED STATES OF CONSCIOUSNESS IN 1 ENOCH

neys, ecstatic trances, and visions are to be understood as they pertain to "experiences deemed religious."

This being said, even if people did not actually visit otherworldly spheres of existence, was it possible for people to have such cognitive experiences that were then written as if such experiences had occurred? Oxford classicist E. R. Dodds noted that both "waking" visions and dreams reflect traditional cultural beliefs and patterns. What is culturally engrained— what we can call the cultural pattern—helps the dreamer or visionary identify the figures and other elements encountered during the experience. For Dodds, culturally patterned dreams and visions were an integral part of the "religious experience" of people at that time.[19] In a nutshell, what the visionary believes is what he or she sees or dreams, and what the visionary sees or dreams is what he or she believes. With respect to literary genre, ASC reports could have been stylized according to the writing conventions of the times. It is possible that writers adapted such experiences and eventually used them as literary motifs. Building on an idea proposed by Freud, Dodds described this process as a "secondary elaboration," where, after a given visionary experience (in this context, that of healing), "the secondary elaboration will have operated, without conscious deception, to bring the dream or vision into closer conformity with the traditional culture-pattern."[20] Dodds even allowed for the possibility of a "tertiary elaboration" through the priestly cast or fellow members of a given community. On the same issue, John Pilch has shown in his study of sky journeys "that literary forms are grounded in social experiences; they give verbal shape to culturally recognized human experiences."[21] This is not to say that people did not have certain experiences but rather that we should be aware of how language is used to explain the experience. But how are ASCs even possible? Here is where neurobiological research on cognitive processes can provide some answers to this thought-provoking question.

---

19. E. R. Dodds, *The Greeks and the Irrational* (1951; repr., Berkeley: University of California Press, 1963), 108.

20. Ibid., 114.

21. John J. Pilch, "The Ascension of Jesus: A Social Scientific Perspective," in *Kultur, Politik, Religion, Sprache—Text,* ed. Christian Strecker, vol. 2 of *Kontexte der Schrift: Für Wolfgang Stegemann zum 60. Geburtstag* (Stuttgart: Kohlhammer, 2005), 79.

How Are ASCs Induced?

Cognitive scientists know that ASCs can result from various physical conditions. For example, it has been documented that people in solitary confinement, where the stream of sensory input is denied, will eventually experience hallucinations. Other ritual practices such as meditation, sleep deprivation (through vigils and solitary prayer), fasting, chanting, drumming, dancing, and singing, as well as spiritual pilgrimages to shrines, deserts, mountains, pillars, and caves, to name a few, can all contribute to the cultivation of ASC experiences.[22] Stanley Krippner has identified over twenty kinds of common ASCs experienced by people: dreams, daydreams, nightmares, sleeping, drowsiness before sleep (hypnagogic), semiconsciousness preceding waking (hypnopompic), hallucinations, illusions, visions, loss of the sense of self or of reality (depersonalization and derealization), sexual ecstasy, mystical ecstasy, hysteria, trance, stupor, coma, and expanded consciousness.[23] Some of these states can be induced by drugs or result from cranial accidents or diseases. Certain bodily conditions are sometimes responsible for ASCs, such as illnesses (e.g., fever) and religious practices (e.g., rituals). They sometimes can be induced deliberately (e.g., meditation), accidentally (e.g., highway hypnosis), or artificially (e.g., drugs).[24] Pieter Craffert quotes Newberg, d'Aquili, and Rause, who speak of the alteration of consciousness as being triggered from the body up (bottom-up) or from the brain down (top-down): "The same neurological mechanisms triggered by the physical behaviors of ritual from the bottom-up can also be triggered by the mind working in top-down fashion—that is, the mind can set this mechanism in motion, starting with nothing more substantial than a thought."[25]

---

22. See Craffert, "Shamanism and the Shamanic Complex," 155. Dan Merkur has also convincingly shown how mourning, prayer, and even Scripture meditation in early Jewish and Christian texts serve as catalysts to trigger visions; see Merkur, "The Visionary Practices of Jewish Apocalyptists," *Psychoanalytic Study of Society* 14 (1989): 119–48; "Cultivating Visions through Exegetical Meditations," in *With Letters of Light: Studies in the Dead Sea Scrolls, Early Jewish Apocalypticism, Magic, and Mysticism in Honor of Rachel Elior*, ed. Daphna V. Arbel and Andrei A. Orlov, Ekstasis 2 (Berlin: de Gruyter, 2010), 62–91.

23. Stanley Krippner, "Altered States of Consciousness," in *The Highest State of Consciousness*, ed. John White (Garden City, NY: Doubleday, 1972), 1–5.

24. Craffert, "Shamanism and the Shamanic Complex," 155.

25. Citation from Andrew B. Newberg, Eugene G. D'Aquili, and Vince Rause,

Is this not what happens to Enoch when he experiences a vision and is transported into heaven after reading and pleading for the forgiveness of the Watchers (1 En. 13:6–10)?[26] The seer is lifted upward and transported into heaven, where he visits the heavenly temple (14:8–9). Later, in 1 En. 17–18, the prophet is given a tour of heaven by angels and is shown the punishment of the wicked souls, angels, and stars after death.[27] Comparatively, in the Synoptic Gospels, Jesus hears the heavenly voice and is spirit-possessed[28] after going through a baptism ritual (Mark 1:9–11; Luke adds that Jesus was praying prior to the event, Luke 3:21). Then comes the wilderness episode (Mark 1:12–13 // Matt 4:1–11 // Luke 4:1–13), where the devil encounters Jesus to test him. This clearly parallels what was previously noted: living in isolation, without food for an extended period of time, can trigger ASC visionary experiences. The temptation story also gives a description of a soul flight, where Jesus is transported from one place to another, from the wilderness to the pinnacle of the temple in Jerusalem. Then, in another soul journey, the devil takes Jesus to a high mountain, where he is shown all the kingdoms of the earth. The mountain will also become a place of encounter for the disciples with the transfiguration episode (Mark 9:2–8 // Matt 17:1–8 // Luke 9:28–36). There Peter, James, and John see Jesus transformed into a being of light. Morton Smith goes so far as to think that this story reports a heavenly ascent, an event that some might have believed was experienced by the disciples.[29] John Ashton,

Why God Won't Go Away: Brain Science and the Biology of Belief (New York: Ballantine, 2001), 97.

26. See Crispin H. T. Fletcher-Louis, "Religious Experience and the Apocalypses," in *Inquiry into Religious Experience in Early Judaism and Early Christianity,* vol. 1 of *Experientia,* ed. Frances Flannery, Colleen Shantz, and Rodney A. Werline; SymS 40 (Atlanta: Society of Biblical Literature, 2008), 125–44, esp. 137–39.

27. Ioan P. Couliano, *Out of This World: Otherworldly Journeys from Gilgamesh to Albert Einstein* (London: Shambhala, 1991), 158–59.

28. It seems clear from the Lukan account (4:1) that Jesus was spirit-possessed after his baptism, since he was "full of the Holy Spirit" (4:1) and led into the desert to be tempted by the devil; see Craffert, *Life of a Galilean Shaman,* 214–15.

29. Indeed, Morton Smith ("Ascent to the Heavens and the Beginning of Christianity," *ErJb* 50 [1981]: 421) argues the following: "So we have here a folk tale about Jesus and his disciples. But what was the basis for the folk tale? People are to some extent characterized by stories told about them. Nobody would have told such a folk tale about Jesus' distinguished contemporary, the emperor Caligula, though he, too, claimed to be a god. Why, then, was this told about Jesus? For what purpose would Jesus take three disciples apart, up a mountain, and why would they see him in glory,

commenting on this particular episode, even states, "the heavenly journey is a motif that Jewish apocalypticism has in common with shamanism.... Jesus' ability to transform himself into a heavenly being by donning angelic clothes is a final indication of his own shamanism."[30] Even if these stories are literary creations, they nevertheless depict how humans experience ASCs and where "the self, the body, one's sense of identity, and the environment of time, space, or other people"[31] is modified. When viewed from a cultural-anthropological perspective, such ASC experiences as depicted above would be cognitively possible.

CONCLUSION

Jewish and Christian literature from late antiquity is replete with examples of rituals and meditative practices that promise an encounter with the transcendent realm. In the end, one might still ask: Are these special events "real" or are they all happening in the brain? Are people actually visiting "places" from another dimension or are these experiences simply in the mind? Is there a difference between the brain and consciousness? In his work on otherworldly journeys, Ioan Couliano asks these same questions: "Where did those people who pretended to travel to another world actually go? What is the reality of these worlds that countless people pretend to have visited? Are they part of our physical world? Are they parallel universes? Are they mental universes? And, in all these cases, how was access to them obtained?"[32]

Neuroscience has now clearly demonstrated that reports of out-of-body experiences (OBE) and/or near-death experiences (NDE) are products of the brain. There is no evidence for the existence of nonphysical modes of being and realities as expressed in ancient ASC stories. Some would argue, however, that since quantum physics hypothesizes on the existence of other realities or parallel universes, this confirms a mind/body dualistic perspec-

---

with supernatural beings? When we recall the prophecies attacking kings who were said to have gone up into the mountain of the gods, above the clouds, and there been clothed with precious stones and become gods (Ezekiel 28 and Isaiah 14), the sort of practice that gave rise to the folk tale is not hard to guess."

30. John Ashton, *The Religion of Paul the Apostle* (New Haven: Yale University Press, 2000), 71.

31. See Pilch, "Altered States of Consciousness," 133.

32. Couliano, *Out of This World*, 2.

tive.[33] But the use of quantum theory in relation to the problem of consciousness should be carefully assessed.[34] One cannot assume that there is a connection between quantum physics and consciousness just because both work in mysterious ways! Cognitive science has shown that the mind—or what some call "consciousness" or "soul"—is not distinct from the brain, but rather is embodied in it, meaning that all of our experiences are in the flesh. The mind as an epiphenomenon is the product of the brain, which in turn receives physical (material world) and psychosocial inputs (culture, language, etc.). As George Lakoff and Mark Johnson have intimated, that which can be perceived and reasoned is inevitably tied to one's bodily experience in the world:

> Reason is not disembodied, as the tradition has largely held, but arises from the nature of our brains, bodies, and bodily experience. This is not just the innocuous and obvious claim that we need a body to reason; rather, it is the striking claim that the very structure of reason itself comes from the details of our embodiment. The same neural and cognitive mechanisms that allow us to perceive and move around also create our conceptual systems and modes of reason. Thus, to understand reason we must understand the details of our visual system, our motor system, and the general mechanisms of neural binding. In summary, reason is not, in any way, a transcendent feature of the universe or of disembodied mind. Instead, it is shaped crucially by the peculiarities of human bodies, by the remarkable details of the neural structure of our brains, and by the specifics of our everyday functioning in the world.[35]

---

33. Some would argue that since quantum mechanics hypothesizes the existence of other "realities" or "parallel universes," it confirms the mind/body dualism theory; see, e.g., Jeffrey M. Schwartz, Henry P. Stapp, and Mario Beauregard, "Quantum Physics in Neuroscience and Psychology: A Neurophysical Model of Mind-Brain Interaction," *Philosophical Transactions of the Royal Society B: Biological Sciences* (2005): 2–19; and Charles T. Tart, "On the Scientific Study of Nonphysical Worlds," in *Body, Mind, Spirit: Exploring the Parapsychology of Spirituality,* ed. Charles T. Tart (Charlottesville: Hampton Roads, 1997), 214–19, esp. 215–17.

34. For an important critique of the use scholars make of physics, see Jim Baggott, *Farewell to Reality: How Modern Physics Has Betrayed the Search for Scientific Truth* (London: Constable & Robinson, 2013); and Peter Woit, *Not Even Wrong: The Failure of String Theory and the Search for Unity in Physical Law* (New York: Basic Books, 2006).

35. George Lakoff and Mark Johnson, *Philosophy in the Flesh: The Embodied Mind and Its Challenge to Western Thought* (New York: Basic Books, 1999), 4.

It is no different when it comes to cognitive experiences such as trances, OBEs, or NDEs. Whether or not stories of ASCs recounted in 1 Enoch and the Synoptic Gospels are a reflection of "true" experiences, cognitive science can now explain how they are created. The writers of "experiences deemed religious" shared a common worldview, where transempirical forces were believed to have an active role in shaping the lives of early Jewish and Christian communities.

The Revelatory Experiences of Enoch and Jesus: A Comparison between the Book of the Watchers and the Synoptic Tradition

Daniel M. Gurtner

The scope of the present essay is to examine the revelatory experiences of select aspects of the experiences of Enoch (in the Book of the Watchers) and Jesus (in the Synoptic tradition) for the purposes of comparative examination. Such "revelatory experiences" would include, of course, dreams, visions, and soul flights, but these experiences seem to be the means to a revelatory end; they are the vehicles by which the divine disclosure, mystery, or revelation is made known to the visionary. I differentiate means and end in this manner not to separate them but to bring attention to the relationship between them. The revelatory experiences of the visionary provide a context for the revelation itself, which serves a role in the overall account of the work in question.[1]

I will begin by surveying the revelatory experiences of Enoch in the Book of the Watchers, then turn to those of Jesus in the Synoptic tradition, before making some comparative observations. A comparison of select aspects of each visionary's revelatory experiences begins with the setting in which the experience occurs. Next, comparisons will be made between the means by which the revelatory experiences are presented. Then some attention will be given to the activities of the respective visionaries: in what manner he is active or passive in the accounts. Finally, comparisons will be made between the natures of the revelatory experiences, specifically their focus and role in the context of the work in which they are included.

---

1. Here I am taking revelatory experiences as an aspect of what is sometimes called "religious experience." See Mark Batluck, "Religious Experience in New Testament Research," *CurBR* 9 (2010): 339–63.

Collectively, comparing these facets of the revelatory experiences of Enoch and Jesus will serve as important data for observing similarities and differences between their traditions.

THE REVELATORY EXPERIENCES OF ENOCH
IN THE BOOK OF THE WATCHERS

The first of Enoch's visions (1 En. 1–5) gives no indication of the setting in which it takes place, but introduces the key theme of the coming of God's judgment on all humanity,[2] as well as themes repeated elsewhere in the Book of the Watchers.[3] Here Enoch has his eyes opened and receives a vision concerning the elect of a future generation who will experience the day of tribulation (1:1–2).[4] Though the remainder of the introduction to the Book of the Watchers in chapters 1–5 and the account of the rebellion of angels and their ensuing judgment in chapters 6–11 contain considerable visionary material, little (if anything) is said about the revelatory experiences of Enoch himself in these chapters.

Indeed, Enoch does not return to the account until chapter 12, which begins an extended section (chs. 12–16) reiterating, confirming, even interpreting the message of chapters 6–11.[5] Here Enoch is an intercessor for the fallen Watchers, with access to God, and commissioned to announce

---

2. George W. E. Nickelsburg, *1 Enoch 1: A Commentary on the Book of 1 Enoch, Chapters 1–36; 81–108,* Hermeneia (Minneapolis: Fortress, 2001), 129.

3. Ibid., 132; citing Lars Hartman, *Asking for a Meaning: A Study of 1 Enoch 1–5,* ConBNT 12 (Lund: Gleerup, 1979), 139–41.

4. The introduction (chs. 1–5) announces the coming judgment, disclosed to Enoch by revelation and transmitted to the chosen righteous living at the last days (the author's own time). The language reflects Deut 31:1 (blessings of Moses) and Num 23:3–4 (an oracle of Balaam) to set the visionary within the prophetic tradition of the Hebrew Bible (cf. also Mic 1; Zech 14:5; Isa 65). See Nickelsburg, *1 Enoch 1,* 137–39. It dates perhaps as early as the first half of the second century BCE; see George W. E. Nickelsburg, *Jewish Literature between the Bible and the Mishnah: A Historical and Literary Introduction,* 2nd ed. (Minneapolis: Fortress, 2005), 46; J. T. Milik, *The Books of Enoch: Aramaic Fragments of Qumrân Cave 4* (Oxford: Oxford University Press, 1976), 6. Chapters 1–5 likely introduce the remainder of the book, i.e., chs. 6–36 (Nickelsburg, *1 Enoch 1,* 132). Nicklesburg indicates that 1 En. 85–90 suggests that the Book of the Watchers was known before the death of Judas Maccabeus in 160 BCE and therefore dates the entire book dates before 175 BCE (*Jewish Literature,* 46).

5. Nickelsburg, *1 Enoch 1,* 229.

judgment.[6] The setting is narrated by Enoch, where he is blessing the Lord (12:3a) and called by his Watchers (12:3b; or just "Watcher," ער[י]ן, 4QEn[c] 1 v 19).[7] They charge him[8] to confront the fallen Watchers with a message of judgment concerning the Watchers themselves (1 En. 12:4–5), the giants (12:6), and Asael (13:1–2): By their union with human women the Watchers have "defiled themselves with great defilement upon the earth" (12:4b), and together with their offspring will have neither peace nor forgiveness (12:5–6; 13:1–2). Enoch relates the message to them all together (13:3a; the phrase is omitted in Codex Panopolitanus). Their collective response is one of fear and trembling (13:3b), and an appeal for Enoch's composition of a memorandum of petition (ὑπομνήματα τῆς ἐρωτήσεως, 13:4–6).[9]

As in his call by the Watchers (12:3), Enoch is in prayer when he is commissioned by God himself (13:7–8).[10] While interceding in prayer Enoch falls asleep (13:7; cf. 14:2) and experiences a dream (ὄνειροι) and visions (ὁράσεις, 13:8a; ὅρασις, 14:1), the object of which is to reprimand the children of heaven (13:8b). Nickelsburg observes that such epiphanies can occur in settings as an answer to prayer (cf. Dan 9:21; 4 Ezra and 2 Baruch passim; 3 Bar. 1; Tobit), though here the petition is refused.[11] When he awakens, Enoch carries out his charge (1 En. 13:9–10) and summarizes God's rejection of their petition (14:1–7). The remainder of this section (14:8–16:4) constitutes a detailed account of Enoch's heavenly commissioning, much of which resonates with Ezek 1–2 and perhaps is modeled after Ezek 40–44.[12] It begins with Enoch's heavenly ascent and travels through God's throne room (1 En. 14:8–23). In his vision the clouds and fogs call to him (14:8a) and the winds are the cause of his flight heavenward (ἄνεμοι ἐν τῇ ὁράσει μου ἐξεπέτασάν με, 14:8c). He enters the sanctuary and observes the throne and the "Great Glory" (ἡ δόξα ἡ μεγάλη, 14:9–23), who commissions him to assure the Watchers of their doom (14:24–15:7).

6. Ibid.

7. Milik, Enoch, 190.

8. Here they address him as a "scribe of righteousness" (ὁ γραμματεὺς τῆς δικαιοσύνης).

9. Nickelsburg (1 Enoch 1, 237) underscores the irony: the Watchers ask Enoch to perform an angelic duty they are now incapable of performing (cf. 14:2).

10. Ibid., 248.

11. Ibid., 249.

12. Ibid., 254.

The remainder of the book (chs. 17–36) describes Enoch's tour of the mythical world guided by seven archangels. Beginning in Enoch's journey to the northwest (chs. 17–19), we find a pattern of heavenly ascent by which the angelic figures serve as agents to what Enoch sees. They lift him up and take him (17:1 [Ethiopic omits the second verb]), lead him (17:2, 4) to where he sees (17:3, 6, 7, 8; 18:1, 2a, 2b, 3, 4, 5a, 5b, 9, 10, 11a, 11b, 12, 13) the content of the visions of judgment. Throughout the remaining journeys to the eastern edge of the world (20:1–33:4), and to the four corners of the earth (34:1–36:4), Enoch goes places (23:1; 24:1, 2; 26:1a; 28:1a; 29:1; 30:3; 32:2, 3; 33:1; 34:1; 35:1; 36:1, 2) and sees things (23:2; 26:1b, 2, 3; 28:1b; 29:2; 30:1, 2, 3; 31:1, 2; 32:1, 3; 33:2; 34:1, 2; 35:1a, 1b; 36:1b, 4), but little is said about his mode of transportation or what things were "shown" to him throughout the visions (21:1–36:4). Enoch here becomes an active figure within his revelatory experiences.

The exception is found in Enoch's final journey to the four corners of the earth (chs. 33–36) where the gates of heaven are introduced as a revelatory device. Uriel shows Enoch these gates (33:3, 4) which will open for Enoch as a means of revelatory disclosure (33:2). Through these opening heavenly gates Enoch sees the coming out of the stars of heaven (33:3–5) and the blowing through of both good and evil things (34:2; 35:1; 36:1, 2). In this respect the otherwise active figure is a recipient of revelatory disclosures.

The Revelatory Experiences of Jesus in the Synoptic Tradition

I confine this discussion of Jesus's revelatory experiences to the baptism, temptation, and transfiguration.[13] At the baptism Jesus sees the heavens torn open and the spirit descending upon him. Then the voice from heaven declares Jesus to be his beloved son in whom he is well pleased (Mark 1:11). In the Matthean account (Matt 3:13–17) the heavens are not torn but opened (3:16). In Luke (3:21) Jesus is praying when the heavens are opened, and the vocal declaration of Jesus's sonship is announced to him rather than those present (Luke 3:21–22). From here Jesus heads to the wilderness for the temptation (Mark 1:12; Matt 4:1; cf. Luke 4:1).

---

13. The choice of these scenes is determined by the scope of André Gagné's paper in this volume.

The temptation account is quite different (Mark 1:12–13; Matt 4:1–11; Luke 4:1–13). Mark's two verses are notoriously thin. Jesus is driven to the wilderness by the spirit, tempted by Satan for forty days, accompanied by wild animals, and attended by angels. No further particulars of the experience are evident. Matthew and Luke are both expansive at key points. First, in Matthew Jesus is led to the wilderness for the purpose of being tempted (Matt 4:1; cf. Luke 4:1) and is explicitly said to be fasting (Matt 4:2; a noted Matthean act of righteousness, 6:16–18). In a flurry of Mosaic typological allusions, Jesus is attentive to words proceeding from the mouth of God (4:4), to not putting God to the test (4:7), and to worshiping God alone (4:10). Throughout both Matthew's and Luke's accounts we find Jesus curiously passive. He is led by the spirit (Matt 4:1; Luke 4:1), taken by the devil to the Holy City (Matt 4:5a), stood up by the devil on the pinnacle of the temple (Matt 4:5b; cf. Luke 4:9), taken to a high mountain (Matt 4:8a), shown the kingdoms of the world (Matt 4:8b; Luke 4:5), and attended by angels (Matt 4:11). He declines certain active roles, such as turning stones to bread (Matt 4:4; Luke 4:3–4), bowing to the devil (Matt 4:10; Luke 4:8), and throwing himself from the temple (Matt 4:7; Luke 4:12). Yet Jesus is assertive in his responses, drawn almost exclusively from Israel's Scriptures (Matt 4:4, 7, 10; Luke 4:4, 8, 12). The outcome in all the Synoptic accounts is the beginning of Jesus's public ministry (Mark 1:14; Matt 4:12; Luke 4:14).

In some respects the Synoptic transfiguration accounts are similar to the baptism pericopes (Mark 9:2–8; Matt 17:1–8; Luke 9:28–36). Here Jesus takes Peter, James, and John to a high mountain (Mark 9:2; Matt 17:1), which Luke alone indicates is for the purpose of prayer (Luke 9:28). Jesus is transfigured before them (Mark 9:2; Matt 17:2a), though Luke alone indicates it is while praying that the appearance of his face changes (Luke 9:29). His garments become white (Mark 9:3; Matt 17:2b; Luke 9:29b) and his face shines (Matt 17:2; cf. Luke 9:29). Elijah and Moses appear and speak with him (Mark 9:4; Matt 9:3), with Luke telling us their conversation pertained to Jesus's departure to Jerusalem (Luke 9:31). Peter makes an unintelligible offer to build tabernacles (Mark 9:5–6; Matt 17:4; Luke 9:33), with Luke adding a strange comment about the disciples being overcome by sleep yet fully awake when they see Elijah and Moses (Luke 9:32). A cloud forms and a voice from heaven speaks (Mark 9:7a; Matt 17:5a; Luke 9:34–35a) audibly, "This is my beloved Son, listen to him!" (Mark 9:7), to which Matthew adds, "with whom I am well pleased" (Matt 17:5), and Luke adds, "my chosen one" (Luke 9:35b). In Matthew alone

the disciples respond to the voice in fear (Matt 17:6–7). When the visionary event is over the disciples are alone with Jesus, who instructs them to
say nothing of what they saw until the Son of Man is raised from the dead
(Mark 9:8–9; Matt 17:8–9; Luke 9:36; though Luke does not indicate this
as an instruction by Jesus).

COMPARATIVE ANALYSES OF THE
RESPECTIVE REVELATORY EXPERIENCES

Placing some revelatory experiences side by side allows us to make a few
comparative observations between the Book of the Watchers and the Synoptic Gospels. By focusing on particular aspects of the revelatory experiences of the central figures, one can more readily address questions of similarities and differences. The aspects we will compare involve the settings
in which the revelatory experiences take place, the means by which they
take place, the active and passive depictions of the central figure within
them, and the nature of the scenes in which they occur.

Settings

With respect to settings of the respective revelatory experiences, nothing
is said of Enoch's posture or setting for the opening vision, save that his
eyes were opened (1 En. 1:1–2), blessing the Mighty One. He receives
such experiences while standing, blessing the Lord (12:3a),[14] interceding
in prayer (12:3), and asleep (13:7b, ὡς ἐκοιμήθην; cf. 14:2; 83–90). He is
also found in a posture of fear, falling on his face (14:14a),[15] in the sanctuary (12:3; 14:9–23),[16] and by a river (ἐπὶ τῶν ὑδάτων, 13:7; cf. Ezek 1:1;
Dan 10:2–12:11). These are often indicative not only of the setting of his
revelatory experience, but explicitly of Enoch's call and commission for
his role in the Book of the Watchers.

---

14. This is a common posture for prayer; cf. 1 Kgs 8:22; Pr Azar 2; Mark 11:25;
Matt 6:5; Luke 18:11, 13; and the discussion in Nickelsburg, *1 Enoch 1*, 235.

15. Ethiopic; Codex Panopolitanus omits "upon my face"; cf. Dan 8:18; 10:15;
LAE 26:1; 27:1.

16. The setting of 12:3 is not entirely clear (cf. 13:7, 9). Regardless, Nickelsburg
(*1 Enoch 1*, 234–35) observes that such commissionings typically occur in sacred or
cultic settings (citing Gen 28:10–22; Exod 3–4; Isa 6; Luke 1:5–23).

The revelatory experiences of Jesus occur in only a few settings. The first is at his baptism (Matt 3:13–17; Mark 1:9–11; Luke 3:21–22; Aland §18), which takes place at the Jordan River (τὸν Ἰορδάνην, Matt 3:13; Mark 1:9) with others present (ἅπαντα τὸν λαὸν, Luke 3:21). Luke adds that this happens while Jesus is praying (προσευχομένου, 3:21). The temptation (Matt 4:1–11; Mark 1:12–13; Luke 4:1–13; Aland §20) initially occurs in a deserted place (εἰς τὴν ἔρημον, Matt 4:1; Mark 1:12 [twice]; ἐν τῇ ἐρήμῳ, Luke 4:1; with wild animals, καὶ ἦν μετὰ τῶν θηρίων, Mark 1:13), but also continues in Jerusalem (εἰς τὴν ἁγίαν πόλιν, Matt 4:5; εἰς Ἰερουσαλήμ, Luke 4:9) at the temple (ἔστησεν ἐπὶ τὸ πτερύγιον τοῦ ἱεροῦ, Luke 4:9) and on a very high mountain (εἰς ὄρος ὑψηλὸν λίαν, Matt 4:8; cf. ἀναγαγὼν, Luke 4:5). Matthew is explicit that Jesus is fasting (νηστεύσας, Matt 4:2; Luke 4:2 reads, οὐκ ἔφαγεν). The transfiguration (Matt 17:1–9; Mark 9:2–10; Luke 9:28–36; Aland §161) likewise occurs upon a high mountain (εἰς ὄρος ὑψηλὸν, Matt 17:1; Mark 9:2; καταβαινόντων αὐτῶν ἐκ τοῦ ὄρους, Matt 17:9; Mark 9:9; Luke 9:28) in the presence of Peter, James, and John (Matt 17:1; Mark 9:2; Luke 9:28), with an appearance by Moses and Elijah (Matt 17:3; Mark 9:4; Luke 9:30).

Means

The means of Enoch's disclosures include dreams (1 En. 13:8a, 10; κατὰ τοὺς ὕπνους μου, 14:1–2[17]) and visions (ὅρασις, 1:2; 13:8a, 10; 14:1, 2, 8a, c, 14b). He also experiences heavenly ascent (14:8c, 25; 15:1; 17:1, 2, 4; cf. 18:14–19:3) and the opening of the gates of heaven (33:2–5). The means of Jesus's revelatory experiences include the opening of heaven (ἠνεῴχθησαν οἱ οὐρανοί, Matt 3:16b; cf. Mark 1:10b; Luke 3:21). Jesus also sees (the spirit, εἶδεν τὸ πνεῦμα, Mark 1:10; Matt 3:16c; Luke 3:22) and is shown (the kingdoms, τὰς βασιλείας, Matt 4:8; Luke 4:5). Finally, a voice speaks (φωνὴ, Matt 3:17a; 17:5; Mark 1:11; 9:7; Luke 3:22; 9:36).

Passive Role

There are particular ways in which Enoch is passive in his revelatory experiences in the Book of the Watchers. This includes his physical move-

---

17. Cf. 4QEn[c] 1 vi 10; Milik, *Enoch*, 193, 197: בחלמא די אנה]חלמת ובחזיתא דא חזית אנה בחמי ...

ment, communicative activities, and visual experiences. In his physical movements, Enoch experiences heavenly ascents and travels throughout his visions. He is brought (προσήγαγέν, 14:25) and taken (ἐλήμφθη, 12:1; εἰσήνεγκάν, 14:9; παραλαβόντες, 17:1a; ἐξεπέτασάν με, 14:8c). He is led away (ἀπήγαγον, 17:1a [omitted in Ethiopic], 2a, 4a), hastened (κατεσπούδαζον, 14:8c) and sped along (ἐθορύβαζόν, 14:8c).[18] He is raised up (ἤγειρέν, 14:25), made to stand (ἔστησέν, 14:25), even made to fly upward (14:8c Ethiopic, "made me fly").[19] In his communicative activities something is written down for him (33:4a, b), but these mostly entail audial experiences. He hears everything *from* the words of the Watchers and the holy ones (1:2c; ἀπὸ λόγων in Codex Panopolitanus, otherwise παρ' αὐτῶν; מלי ומן, 4QEnᵃ 1 i 3;[20] repeated in 1 En. 1:2d) and a voice *comes to* him (ἦλθεν φωνὴ, 13:8b). He is called by Watchers (ἐκάλουν, 12:3b), by the clouds and fogs (14:8a, b, ἐκάλουν), and by the Lord (14:24, ἐκάλεσέν), and cried out to by the mists (14:8b, ἐφώνουν). Enoch is once asked (ἠρώτησαν, 13:4) but more often answered (ἀποκριθεὶς, 15:1; ἀπεκρίθη, 21:9; 22:3, 7, 9; 23:4; 24:6; 25:3; cf. 27:2; 32:6) and spoken to (εἶπέν, 15:1; 18:14; 19:1; 21:5, 9, 10; 22:3; 25:1; λέγων, 22:7, 9; 25:3; cf. 27:2; 32:6).

Enoch is sometimes passive with respect to visual aspects of his revelatory experiences. His eyes are opened (ἀνεῳγμένη ἦν, by God, 1:2b),[21] and he is shown visions (ἔδειξέν, 1:2 [by God, Codex Panopolitanus; or by angels, Ethiopic]; 22:1;[22] 24:1; ἐδείχθη, 14:4a, 8a; אחזיאת, 31:2a [4QEnᶜ 1 xii 27];[23] cf. 1 En. 33:3b). Dreams come upon him (ἐπ' ἐμὲ ἦλθον), and visions fall upon him (καὶ ὁράσεις ἐπ' ἐμὲ ἐπέπιπτον, 13:8a). Finally, in some unique texts, which fit none of the above categories, Enoch is passive in that he was created (ἔκτισεν) and given (ἔδωκεν) words to reprimand the

---

18. Nickelsburg (*1 Enoch 1*, 257) notes the support for ἐθορύβαζόν by Codex Panapolitanus and Ethiopic Abbadian 35. From the Ethiopic (cf. Nickelsburg, who suggests a Greek *Vorlage* of σπουδάξω). His translation ("speeding me along") is an emendation that supplies an expected parallelism (cf. R. H. Charles, *The Book of Enoch or 1 Enoch* [Oxford: Clarendon, 1912], 33).

19. Nickelsburg, *1 Enoch 1*, 257.

20. Milik, *Enoch*, 142.

21. So Codex Panopolitanus and Ethiopic.

22. Nickelsburg (*1 Enoch 1*, 304) posits a mistranslation of the Aramaic, which could read "And I saw" (cf. 21:1, 7; 23:2; 24:2; 26:1, 2, 3; 29:1; 30:1, 3; 32:1, 3; 33:1, 2, 3; 34:1, 2; 35:1; 36:1, 2, 4) or "I was shown" (cf. 31:2).

23. Milik, *Enoch*, 201: "I saw" (ἴδον, Codex Panopolitanus; *re'iku,* Ethiopic); cf. Nickelsburg, *1 Enoch 1*, 321.

Watchers (14:3), and in one revelatory experience doors are made to open before him (θύρα ἀνεῳγμένη κατέναντί μου, 14:15).

In the Synoptic tradition, Jesus is passive in a number of respects, including physical and verbal passivity. Regarding the physical, Jesus is baptized (ἐβαπτίσθη, Mark 1:9; cf. Matt 3:13; 3:16a; Luke 3:21). He is led (by the Spirit; ἀνήχθη, Matt 4:1; cf. Mark 4:12; Luke 4:1), taken (by the devil; παραλαμβάνει, Matt 4:5, 8; cf. Luke 4:5, 9), and stood up (by the devil; ἔστησεν αὐτὸν, Matt 4:5; Luke 4:9). He is attended by angels (διηκόνουν αὐτῷ, Matt 4:11; Mark 1:13) and perhaps borne up by them (ἐπὶ χειρῶν ἀροῦσίν σε, Matt 4:6; Luke 4:11). Jesus is left by the devil (Matt 4:11; Luke 4:13), and later transfigured (μετεμορφώθη, Matt 17:2; Mark 9:2; cf. Luke 9:29); the spirit comes upon him (Mark 1:10; Matt 3:16; Luke 3:22), the heavens are opened (to him) (ἠνεῴχθησαν [αὐτῷ], Matt 3:16; cf. Mark 1:10; Luke 3:21), and he will be raised from the dead (ἐκ νεκρῶν ἐγερθῇ, Matt 17:9; cf. Mark 9:9).

In a verbal respect, Jesus is passive in that he is spoken to (Mark 1:11; 9:4, 5; Matt 3:14; 4:6, 9; 17:4; Luke 3:22; 4:3, 6, 9; 9:30, 33) and spoken about (οὗτός ἐστιν ὁ υἱός μου ὁ ἀγαπητός, Matt 17:5; Mark 9:7; Luke 9:35). He is also deterred (διεκώλυεν, Matt 3:14) and even commanded (Matt 4:3, 6, 9; Luke 4:3, 7, 9). The visual passivity of Jesus is rather limited in the Synoptic tradition in that Jesus is shown the kingdoms (δείκνυσιν, Matt 4:8; cf. Luke 4:5) and seen by disciples (εἶδον, Matt 17:8; Mark 9:8; Luke 9:32, 36). Finally, Jesus is passive—at least grammatically—in that he is tempted by the devil (Mark 1:13; Matt 4:1; Luke 4:2) and is the object of God's pleasure (Mark 1:11; Matt 3:17; Luke 3:22).

Active Role

Though often passive in his revelatory encounters, Enoch is also active in the Book of the Watchers with respect to his physical movement, communicative activities, and visual experiences. With respect to his physical movements, Enoch comes (ἤλθομεν, 17:5a; 18:6, παρῆλθον; Ethiopic adds "toward the south") and goes (πορευθείς, 13:3a, 7a; ἦλθον, 13:9; εἰσῆλθον, 14:9, 10, 13), he arrives (κατήντησα, 17:6b) and departs (ἀπῆλθον, 17:7a; ᾠχόμην, 30:1a). Enoch travels (ἐφώδευσα, 21:1;[24] 26:1a; 32:2), proceeds

---

24. The term can be rendered "to make the rounds" and occurs here for the first of six or seven times (21:7a; 22:1a; 23:1 [Codex Panopolitanus; ḥorku, Ethiopic; אובלת);

(ἐπορεύθην, 24:2a; 28:1a [Ethiopic adds "to the east"; cf. 29:1; 30:1, 3; 32:2]; 29:1; cf. 33:1a; 34:1a; 35:1a; 36:1a, 2a), and draws near (ἤγγισα, 14:9, 10). Enoch also passes over the Red Sea (32:2b, καὶ διέβην ἐπάνω τῆς ἐρυθρᾶς θαλάσσης), crosses over the darkness (32:2c, καὶ ᾠχόμην ἐπ᾽ ἄκρων), and passes by paradise (32:3a, ἦλθον πρὸς τὸν παράδεισον τῆς δικαιοσύνης).[25]

In his communicative activities, Enoch is an active figure in that he speaks (εἴρηκα, 13:3a; λαλεῖν, 13:10; εἶπεν, 21:4a; εἶπον, 21:8a; 22:2c; 24:5; 27:1; 32:5; εἶπα, 22:14) and writes (ἔγραψα, 13:6a; 14:4a; cf. 33:3b). He asks (ἠρώτησα, 22:6a, 8a; 23:3; ὧν πυνθανομένῳ, 18:14a) and answers (ἀπεκρίθη, 21:9; ἀπεκρίθην, 25:2). Finally, Enoch recites (ἀνήγγειλα, ומללת [4QEn^c 1 vi 7; Ethiopic], 13:10; cf. 14:1–16:4), blesses the Lord (εὐλογητός, 22:14; 25:7; 27:5; cf. 36:4), and marvels (ἐθαύμασα, 26:6 [twice] cf. 22:2; 24:5; 32:5). Most of all, however, Enoch is an active agent in his visual experiences of looking[26] and seeing.[27] Importantly, at the outset of the book readers know that Enoch understands what he sees (1:2e, ἔγνων ἐγὼ θεωρῶν). All of these are, of course, in the context of Enoch's revelatory experiences.

Jesus's active roles in his revelatory experiences are primarily physical and verbal in nature. The physical activity mainly involves movment, where he travels (Mark 1:9; Matt 3:13; 17:7) and returns (ὑπέστρεψεν, Luke 4:1). He ascends (Matt 3:16; ἀναβαίνων, Mark 1:10; cf. Matt 3:16) and descends (καταβαινόντων, Matt 17:9; Mark 9:9). He also involves others in his physical movement when he takes his disciples (παραλαμβάνει, Matt 17:1; Mark 9:2; cf. Luke 9:28) and brings them up a mountain (ἀναφέρει αὐτοὺς, Matt 17:2; Mark 9:2). In one instance Jesus touches some disciples (ἁψάμενος, Matt 17:7).

4QEn^d frag. 1 i 3. Milik (*Enoch*, 218) translates, "I was transported"; cf. 14:8; 26:1; 32:2; see Nickelsburg, *1 Enoch 1*, 298.

25. Enoch also sits (ἐκάθισα, 13:7a) and counts (33:3b).

26. So ἐθεώρουν (14:14b, 18a).

27. Thus ἴδον (17:6a, 7b, 8a; 18:1a, b, 2a, b, 3a, 4a, 5a, b, c; 18:6, 9, 11a, 12a, 13; 19:3 [twice]; 26:1b, 3a; 28:1b; 29:2; 30:1b, 3; 31:1a, 1b; 32:3b), εἶδον (14:18b; 17:3a), ἑώρακα (21:2b), τεθέαμαι (21:3a, 7b; 22:5a; 32:1), ἐθεασάμην (21:2a; 23:2; 24:2b; 26:2a); cf. also 33:1b, 2a, 3a (ליד, 4QEnoch^e frag. 3 21; Milik, *Enoch*, 232, 235; "toward," πρός, Codex Panopolitanus; *westa*, Ethiopic); 34:1b (*reʾiku*, Ethiopic; "I was shown" [אחזית]; 4QEnoch^e frag. 4 21; Milik, *Enoch*, 235), 2a; 35:1b, c; 36:1b, 2b, 4. At one point Enoch is unable to describe (14:16, μὴ δύνασθαί με ἐξειπεῖν ὑμῖν) and even unable to see (14:19b, καὶ οὐκ ἐδυνάσθην ἰδεῖν; cf. Tg. Ezek 1:27). Nickelsburg (*1 Enoch 1*, 258) notes that the Ethiopic of Tana 9 reads the third plural here: "they were unable" to see.

At times Jesus declines certain active roles (e.g., turning stones to bread) while being active only in his short verbal responses, drawn largely from Deuteronomy. Jesus answers (ἀποκριθεὶς, Matt 3:15; 4:4; Luke 4:4, 8, 12) and speaks (εἶπεν, Matt 3:15; 4:4; 17:7; Luke 4:8, 12; cf. Matt 4:7, 10; 17:9) and issues commands (ὕπαγε, Matt 4:10; cf. Luke 4:12 ἐγέρθητε καὶ μὴ φοβεῖσθε, Matt 17:7; ἐνετείλατο, Matt 17:9; διεστείλατο, Mark 9:9). There is little stated active visual experience by Jesus in that he is only said to see at the baptism (εἶδεν [τὸ] πνεῦμα, Matt 3:16; εἶδεν σχιζομένους τοὺς οὐρανοὺς, Mark 1:10). Yet Jesus is active in his acts of piety in these contexts, including fasting (νηστεύσας, Matt 4:2; cf. Luke 4:2) and praying (προσεύξασθαι, Luke 9:28, 29; cf. Luke 3:21).[28]

Nature

With respect to the nature of their revelatory experiences, both have experiences that in part lend credibility to their respective messages (both in the story line and the readership). Enoch's pertain to his charge to communicate judgment upon the Watchers (1 En. 1:1–2; 12:4b–6; 13:8b). His experiences are aspects of his role as messenger of someone else's message, and readers always know the content of the message within the context of the revelatory experience itself.

The nature of Jesus's revelatory experiences seem to only partly resemble those of Enoch. Like Enoch, Jesus is in some sense a messenger with a commission from God. This is seen at the transfiguration (Mark 9:7a; Matt 17:5a; Luke 9:34–35a), where the voice from heaven speaks, "This is my beloved Son," familiar from the baptism account, but here adds the imperative, "listen to him!" (Mark 9:7). Here the declaration that Jesus is one to whom disciples are to listen seems to be grounded in his identity as the "beloved Son," and the announcement seems to be for the benefit of the disciples.

The importance of Jesus's identity is likewise borne out in all three revelatory experiences, where his identity as Son of God is a central concern in the voice from heaven at the baptism (Mark 1:11; Matt 3:17; Luke 3:22) and transfiguration (Matt 17:5; Mark 9:7; Luke 9:35), as well as for Satan in the temptation narrative (εἰ υἱὸς εἶ τοῦ θεοῦ, Matt 4:3, 6; Luke 4:3,

---

28. Notably, Mark's account of the temptation gives no evidence of an active role by Jesus.

9). Jesus is also said to be the object of God's good pleasure (Matt 17:5; Luke 9:35). Other remarkable occurrences are described that draw attention to Jesus's identity, such as his physical appearance being transformed[29] and the presence of Moses and Elijah (Matt 17:3; Mark 9:4; cf. Luke 9:30–33). There is also a response of fear (ἐφοβήθησαν σφόδρα, Matt 17:6; cf. Luke 9:34; Matt 17:7) and other supernatural displays in such contexts.

It may also be telling to note what Jesus may (or may not) do with his status as Son of God.[30] In each instance Satan implores Jesus to do something, and the presumption seems to be that Jesus is more than able to do so. Yet in each instance Jesus's refusal is accompanied by a citation from the Scriptures of Israel (γέγραπται, Matt 4:4, 7, 10; Luke 4:4, 8; εἴρηται, Luke 4:12). Moreover, the citations indicate aspects of Jesus's sonship: his concern is less with the physical sustenance of bread than that which is achieved by the words of God (παντὶ ῥήματι ἐκπορευομένῳ διὰ στόματος θεοῦ, Matt 4:4; Luke 4:4). He refuses to put the Lord to the test (οὐκ ἐκπειράσεις κύριον τὸν θεόν σου, Matt 4:7; Luke 4:8) and advocates the exclusive worship of Israel's God (Matt 4:10; Luke 4:12).[31]

Conclusion

The subject of revelatory experiences provides a case study of sorts, bringing to our attention a shared component for comparing Enoch and Jesus. The aspects they have in common, such as accounts of a revelatory nature within a narrative framework and the conveyance of a heavenly revelation from the supernatural world, are not unique to the Enochic and Synoptic traditions. Instead, these traits have come to form the foundational definition of an apocalypse,[32] and its features are found in other genres as well,

---

29. Jesus is transfigured (μετεμορφώθη, Matt 17:2; Mark 9:2; cf. Luke 9:29). His countenance is like the sun (ἔλαμψεν τὸ πρόσωπον αὐτοῦ ὡς ὁ ἥλιος, Matt 17:2; cf. Luke 9:29). His garments are as light (τὰ δὲ ἱμάτια αὐτοῦ ἐγένετο λευκὰ ὡς τὸ φῶς, Matt 17:2; cf. Mark 9:3).

30. For example, to turn stones to bread (εἰπὲ ἵνα οἱ λίθοι οὗτοι ἄρτοι γένωνται, Matt 4:3; Luke 4:3), cast himself downward (βάλε σεαυτὸν κάτω, Matt 4:6; Luke 4:9), and worship the devil (ἐὰν πεσὼν προσκυνήσῃς μοι, Matt 4:9; Luke 4:7).

31. Notably, though Jesus refuses to call upon angels to bear him up—and so put God to the test—the scene concludes with Jesus attended by angels (ἄγγελοι προσῆλθον καὶ διηκόνουν αὐτῷ, Matt 4:11; Mark 1:13).

32. See John J. Collins, ed., *Apocalypse: The Morphology of a Genre*, Semeia 14 (1979).

such as gospels. Among apocalypses one finds such features in Daniel, 4 Ezra, 2 Baruch, the Apocalypse of Abraham, 3 Baruch, 2 Enoch, T. Levi 2–5, to name but a few.[33] It seems then that while similarities between the revelatory experiences of Enoch and Jesus exist, there are also substantial differences. Aside from the difference in genre between the Book of the Watchers and the Synoptic Gospels, the role of the respective figures seems quite distinct. The role of Enoch pertains to his identity as a messenger to the fallen Watchers for his role as a heavenly intermediary, whereas with Jesus each instance pertains to his identity, seemingly as an end in itself, as Son of God. Since the similarities between the respective accounts are common among other apocalyptic traditions, and the differences seem to portray their central figures unlike one another, it would seem unwise to speak of the Enochic account having influence upon the Synoptics. Perhaps it is best to speak of similarities in terms of their shared employment of apocalyptic facets of Second Temple Judaism.

---

33. John J. Collins, *The Apocalyptic Imagination: An Introduction to Jewish Apocalyptic Literature*, 2nd ed. (Grand Rapids: Eerdmans, 1998), 5.

Unusual Births:
Enochic Traditions and
Matthew's Infancy Narrative

Amy E. Richter

Did the author of Matthew's Gospel make use of Enochic motifs or themes, particularly as we know them from the collection now called 1 Enoch, in his composition?[1] If so, did he do so intentionally? To respond to these questions, I undertake an experiment. I will focus on two of the most prominent features of Matthew's nativity narrative to see how reading Matthew in light of the Enochic story of the fall of the Watchers and its aftermath brings into focus the Matthean Jesus as the repairer of the effects of the Watchers' rebellion. The two features I will examine are the conception of the child Jesus by Mary and the Holy Spirit and Joseph's suspicions about the pregnancy of his betrothed.

I do not claim that there is a literary dependence by Matthew on the texts we now know as 1 Enoch or on other texts that tell the story of the Watchers' rebellion and its consequences. Matthew does not quote 1 Enoch,[2] cite 1 Enoch, or retell stories from 1 Enoch. Nor is positing an Enochic background the only way to explain features unique to Matthew's Gospel (scholars have been doing just fine for centuries without entertaining such a possibility). However, looking at Matthew's Gospel in light of

---

1. For the sake of convenience I will refer to the person responsible for the Gospel according to Matthew as Matthew. I will also refer to 1 Enoch without meaning to imply that the collection existed as we now have it at the time of the writing of the works of the New Testament.

2. Unless David Sim is correct that Matt 22:13a makes use of 1 En. 10:4a. See David Sim, "Matthew 22.13a and 1 Enoch 10.4a: A Case of Literary Dependence," *JSNT* 47 (1992): 3–19.

the Enochic story yields interesting and fruitful results for understanding Matthew's portrayal of Jesus.

But on what grounds may one undertake such a comparison? Is holding these two texts in conversation more than a random exercise in comparison and contrast?

My experiment proceeds as follows. I will first briefly address the possibility that Matthew used Enochic motifs and themes, either intentionally or unintentionally. I will next address the idea that it is conceivable that Matthew did so, using the literary device of parody as a model for examining one story in light of an earlier story. I will then turn to the specifics of the Enochic Watchers story and Matthew's infancy narrative, comparing the two stories to see how reading Matthew in light of Enoch's Watchers story elucidates Matthew's story.

It is important to note that I am not addressing either Matthew's Gospel or 1 Enoch using a traditional source-, tradition-, redaction-, or other historical-critical approach, as important as these are for critical scholarship. Neither does my approach disavow or disparage these methods. I will simply use the stories as we find them in two critically edited forms[3] as "complete" stories, rather than concerning myself in this exercise with the background and development of each of the texts we now call 1 Enoch and the Gospel according to Matthew. By holding the two stories in conversation, I will explore whether reading Matthew's story with the Enochic story as background brings insights into Matthew's Gospel that fit well within the overall arc of Matthew's story and theology as well as illuminating some aspects of Matthew's Gospel not completely addressed without an appeal to the Enochic story. To put it another way, if one reads Matthew after having read the story of the Watchers, do some aspects of Matthew's Gospel become clearer, get explained, or take on additional meaning—or not?

---

3. Unless otherwise noted, in this paper I use the text and translation of 1 Enoch by George W. E. Nickelsburg and James C. VanderKam, *1 Enoch: A New Translation* (Minneapolis: Fortress, 2004). For the Greek text of Matthew I use Eberhard Nestle et al., eds., *Novum Testamentum Graece,* 27th ed. (Stuttgart: Deutsche Bibelgesellschaft, 1993).

READING MATTHEW IN LIGHT OF 1 ENOCH—POSSIBLE OR PLAUSIBLE? AN EXPLORATION

First, it is possible, based on the date of the Watchers story, that Matthew made use of motifs and themes found in the Enochic story of the Watchers. It is well established that the Watchers story existed in a written form before Matthew's lifetime, and that other writers of works now in the New Testament refer to Enoch and motifs from 1 Enoch.[4]

It is also possible that Matthew made use of motifs and themes found in 1 Enoch without his knowing that 1 Enoch is a source, or the source, of an idea or way of describing it. Several scholars include references to 1 Enoch in their commentaries on Matthew's Gospel that show a theme, motif, or phrase common to both 1 Enoch and Matthew, without making the claim that Matthew knows that 1 Enoch also uses the theme, motif, or phrase. Rather, the commentator provides a passage from 1 Enoch to provide context for Matthew, showing that something in Matthew finds company in prior Jewish texts. For example, W. D. Davies and Dale Allison cite 1 En. 10:13, the pronouncement of the confinement and torture of the rebel angels in the fiery abyss that will be their prison, comparing their lot with that of the unrighteous in Matt 25:31–46, the judgment of the nations by the Son of Man.[5] Davies and Allison also cite 1 En. 93:1–10 and 91:12–17 as among Jewish apocalypses that place "the epoch of the exile immediately before the epoch of redemption."[6] Likewise, Ulrich Luz cites 1 En. 93:1–10 and 91:12–17 as providing an example of the conception that there is "a divine plan in history."[7] Donald Hagner cites the same passages as possible background for Matthew's reckoning of generations.[8]

---

4. Heb 11:5–6; Jude 6, 14–15; 1 Pet 3:19–20; 2 Pet 2:4, 9. See James C. VanderKam, *Enoch: A Man for All Generations* (Columbia: University of South Carolina Press, 1995), 169–72.

5. W. D. Davies and Dale C. Allison Jr., *A Critical and Exegetical Commentary on the Gospel according to Saint Matthew,* 3 vols., ICC (London: T&T Clark, 1988–1997), 3:431. They also cite 1 En. 10:13 as an example of dialogue between judge and judged in their exegesis of the same passage (418).

6. Ibid., 1:187.

7. Ulrich Luz, *Matthew 1–7: A Commentary,* trans. James E. Crouch, Hermeneia (Minneapolis: Fortress, 2007), 86.

8. Donald A. Hagner, *Matthew 1–13,* WBC 33A (Dallas: Word, 1993), 6. Also, see Hagner's comments on Matt 8:29 in which he cites 1 En. 15–16 as another place where unrighteous powers (demons in Matthew; rebellious Watchers in 1 Enoch) under-

Luz cites 1 En. 58:2, "Blessed are you, you righteous and elect, for glorious shall be your lot," in his discussion of the Matthean beatitudes to show that, as in Matthew, 1 Enoch also has an example of a wisdom beatitude formulated in the second person, in contrast to the usual use of the third person.[9] J. Andrew Overman cites both 1 En. 24–27 and 92–105 in a brief discussion of the development of the belief in existence after death in his comments on Matt 22:23–33 in which the Sadducees seek to test Jesus by asking him about a woman who is predeceased by six husbands.[10] In even just these examples, we see that passages from 1 Enoch are used to provide context and points of comparison with Matthew's Gospel; in none is 1 Enoch proposed as the source for what Matthew writes, or that Matthew knows that he has things in common with 1 Enoch.

In response to the question of whether Matthew made use of Enochic material, perhaps the safest claim to be made is that writings of 1 Enoch help shape the world in which Matthew lived and wrote. That is, Matthew is not necessarily intentionally using 1 Enoch, but 1 Enoch is one of several contributors to the literary world in which the evangelist wrote. Enochic works are among the contributors to the worldview of Matthew's time and are not being used intentionally by Matthew.

We know from our own experience that an author can make use of a phrase with a rich background without needing to know the source of the phrase or intending to make allusions to the phrase's background. If I use the phrase "red herring" in a story, I may expect that readers of the story will know that I am indicating something meant to throw the reader off track, without the readers' needing to know the origins of the phrase "red herring." The likelihood of the readers' understanding the meaning of the phrase increases if the story I am writing is a mystery story and the readers of my story have read other mystery stories and are therefore familiar with "red herring" referring to a false clue introduced by the writer to send readers and/or detectives off in directions that do not lead to the

stand "that at the eschatological judgment they will experience God's judgment and the end of their power" (227).

9. Luz, *Matthew 1–7*, 187.

10. J. Andrew Overman, *Church and Community in Crisis: The Gospel according to Matthew* (Valley Forge, PA: Trinity Press International, 1996), 315. See also his description (205) of scribes in Matt 13:51–52; cf. 1 En. 72–82.

true solution to the mystery.[11] If the reader does not know the meaning of "red herring," he or she can find it in a dictionary or infer it from the context and understand its meaning without needing to know its origins. The phrase is just a part of the world in which we live and its meaning is known to many of us. It may or may not interest us to learn that the phrase may have originated in a short piece of fiction written by a British journalist in the 1800s about fox hunters leading hunting dogs astray by dragging strong-smelling fish across the fox's path to distract the dogs. The commentator used the story about distracted dogs to criticize the press of his day.[12] We may be happy to know the background of the phrase; it may satisfy our curiosity about how such a phrase came to be, but knowing the origin does not add to our understanding of a mystery writer's story. Knowing whether the author who uses the phrase is aware of the origins of the phrase, let alone making use of the origins in some way, is likewise unimportant to one's comprehension of the story.

What if, however, we wish to examine the possibility that one text read in light of another brings additional understanding of the first text, as I do in the case of Matthew and 1 Enoch? Are there examples of stories that are comprehensible on their own, but when an earlier story is held up in comparison, it becomes apparent that the author of the second (later) story is responding to the earlier story? In these cases, through the comparison of the two stories, not only does the second author's knowledge of the first story become apparent, but so does the second author's use of it in crafting the second story.

The literary device of parody fits this pattern: the meaning of the second work is understandable, at least to some degree, without knowledge of the earlier work. That is, one may read a parody without realizing that it is a parody. The story may not be fully satisfying or may leave the reader wondering about some of the details, but the story may be basically understandable to the reader. However, when one is also familiar with the earlier work, the meaning of the second work is enhanced. Not only does the reader understand that the author of the second work must have been familiar with the first, but also that the author of the second work is intentionally responding to the first. In the case of parody, the

---

11. P. M. Carlson, "Clues, Red Herrings, and Other Plot Devices," in *Writing Mysteries,* ed. Sue Grafton, 2nd ed. (Cincinnati: Writer's Digest, 2002), 160–65.

12. Heidi Stevens, "Catching a Red Herring: What's the Origin of This Ubiquitous Phrase?" *Chicago Tribune,* Lifestyles, http://tinyurl.com/SBL3544a.

second author may criticize or ridicule the earlier work and its ideas, or, by twisting some element of context or detail from the earlier story, make the second work humorous. The degree of similarity between the two stories (for example, in words, phrases, themes, or narrative arc) or the inversion of details may be clues that the second author is using the first work.[13]

Let's briefly consider some examples. One can read, understand, and enjoy *Don Quixote* without knowledge of prior romantic tales of knights errant, which Cervantes was mocking in his work.[14] If one, however, reads the now lesser known *Amadis de Gaula*, or Ariosto's *Orlando Furioso*, both of which inspired Cervantes to write *Don Quixote*,[15] the comparison becomes apparent and the comedy of Cervantes heightened. Likewise, Shakespeare's Sonnet 130 includes the lover's appraisal, "And in some perfumes is there more delight / Than in the breath that from my mistress reeks."[16] The reader can understand the meaning of the statement—the woman's breath is not pleasant smelling—without knowing there is a genre of love sonnets in which mistresses' attributes are praised beyond what is humanly possible.[17] When one knows about the genre to which Shakespeare responds, one can see the humor and tenderness in his description of his mistress as being rather normal or even uncomely, "And yet, by heaven, I think my love as rare / As any she belied with false compare."[18] My point here is that one can look at a piece of literature and derive meaning from it, even if one does not realize that something more is going on. When one realizes that there is an earlier specific work or genre to which a later author is responding or using, the reader gains additional understanding and enjoyment of the second text.

Now let us return to Matthew and Enochic motifs and themes. If we can demonstrate that there are motifs and themes in common between

---

13. On parody, see Robert P. Falk and William Beare, "Parody," *Princeton Encyclopedia of Poetry and Poetics,* ed. Alex Preminger, enl. ed. (Princeton: Princeton University Press, 1974), 600–602.

14. Ibid., 601.

15. Frederick A. De Armas, "Cervantes and the Italian Renaissance," in *The Cambridge Companion to Cervantes,* ed. Anthony J. Cascardi (Cambridge: Cambridge University Press, 2002), 43.

16. William Shakespeare, *Shakespeare's Sonnets,* ed. Stephen Booth, Yale Nota Bene Edition (New Haven: Yale University Press, 2000), 112.

17. Ibid., 452–55.

18. Ibid., 112.

Matthew's Gospel and 1 Enoch—and since we know that the Watchers story in 1 Enoch predates Matthew's Gospel—it is fair to ask the question of whether Matthew knowingly or unknowingly makes use of Enochic themes in his gospel. Is Matthew making use of something that originated in the Enochic literature but has no idea of its origin and therefore also has no intention of alluding to Enochic themes or responding to them in some way (as I could use the phrase "red herring" today without necessarily needing as an author to be aware of its origins, or assuming that you, as reader, would be aware of its origins)? Or is something more along the lines of parody going on in Matthew's Gospel? That is, Matthew can be read and understood to a great extent without a reader's being aware that there is a story that predates it and that contains similar motifs and themes. However, is it possible that when Matthew is read in light of the Enochic story of the Watchers, we will find that Matthew could be making use of Enochic themes and motifs, and using or inverting them in such a way as to respond to the Enochic story or make use of it for his own purposes? What would be necessary to make the case that such a relationship exists?

In order to be persuasive, one would have to show that beyond merely a similar collection of motifs and themes in both Matthew and 1 Enoch there exists a pattern in 1 Enoch that also appears in Matthew and makes some sense within Matthew's project. For instance, the presence of angels in both 1 Enoch and Matthew does not show that Matthew knows there are angels in 1 Enoch or talks about angels in his story because it will somehow connect for his audience with 1 Enoch. However, both 1 Enoch and Matthew have heavenly beings who interact with human women and produce offspring. Now I am interested. Further, a judgment is made about the offspring in each. In 1 Enoch the offspring are terrible and lead to violence and disaster. In Matthew the offspring is righteous and leads to hope and salvation. Now I am even more interested. I will address this subject in greater detail below.

It would be more helpful to make the case that Matthew's relationship to 1 Enoch is akin to what happens in parody if one could be sure that Matthew knows 1 Enoch and knows, too, that his readers do. Neither of these will be proven by my experiment. As mentioned above, Matthew does not quote 1 Enoch nor tell us stories from 1 Enoch, and his story may be read and understood without prior knowledge of 1 Enoch. If Matthew knows the stories from 1 Enoch and also wants his audience to recognize these elements within his narrative, he must also think his audience shares this knowledge and needs no reminding or instruction about the Enochic background.

So, am I, as the author of this chapter, dragging a red herring across the Enoch-free trail Matthew is actually on and throwing us off the track of responsible inquiry?

I believe that when we put the two stories, the Enochic Watchers story and Matthew's infancy narrative, in conversation we will see more than just the presence of motifs and themes from 1 Enoch occurring in Matthew's Gospel. We will also see a narrative arc in which the Enochic elements are used by Matthew, but to a different end. The elements of the Enochic story will be subverted by Matthew so that his story will have a different thrust and call forth a response from his audience that would have them understand that Matthew's story is the one in which they should put their trust and hope. If one reads Matthew's story with the Enochic story as background, Matthew's story makes sense in a way that it does not without Enoch in the background, in a similar way that a story, once it is understood as a parody—that is, a story with a specific story or genre in the background that the author is using for his or her own critical or comedic purposes—makes more sense to the reader and elicits a specific response (laughter, delight, ridicule). I am not claiming that Matthew's Gospel is a parody of 1 Enoch. My hope is that in framing the inquiry in this way we may better understand Matthew's Gospel and what Matthew hoped his readers would gain by reading it.

Reading Matthew's Infancy Narrative in Light of 1 Enoch

As noted above, I will focus on Matthew's telling of the conception of Jesus by Mary and the Holy Spirit and Joseph's suspicions about Mary's pregnancy, showing points of connection and contrast with events from 1 Enoch, particularly the Book of the Watchers (1 En. 1–36). Because the infancy narrative sets the stage for the rest of the gospel, I also provide examples of how what we see in the divine-human origin of Jesus is developed in narratives of the adult Jesus and continues to show the repair of the Watchers' transgression. First, however, I give a brief overview of the elements of the Enochic story of the Watchers' rebellion that, when seen as a backdrop for Matthew's infancy narrative, become the materials from which Matthew will show Jesus's repair of the consequences of the Watchers' fall.

The basic elements of the Enochic story of the fall of the Watchers in 1 Enoch addressed in this paper are these: Watchers—meant to dwell in heaven, attending God, overseeing the functions of creation, and guarding the righteous[19]—transgress the boundary between heaven and earth in order to mate with mortal women; the women give birth to a hybrid race of giants, who engage in violence and bloodshed against humanity, other constituents of creation, and one another; in response to the complaint raised against the Watchers and their terrible offspring, the Deity sends archangels to punish the Watchers and a flood to purge the earth of evil and violence; however, although the giants will be destroyed, their spirits will plague humankind until "the great judgment" (1 En. 16:1).

In the Matthean birth narrative, the birth of Jesus overturns the effects of the Enochic Watchers' rebellion by using the very elements of their rebellion. The birth of Jesus, according to Matthew, redresses the Watchers' transgression. We can see the Enochic story of the Watchers behind the Matthean birth narrative when we examine the following details: Joseph's suspicion of Mary's pregnancy and the resolution to his suspicion, namely, the revelation that Mary is pregnant by the Holy Spirit. Significantly, the child is the product of the heavenly (Holy Spirit) and earthly (Mary), but without sexual union between the heavenly Holy Spirit and earthly Mary. When we examine the tradition that the Holy Spirit may have been identified as an angelomorphic celestial being at the time the evangelist wrote the gospel account, we can see further parallels, and the important distinctions, between the two stories.

The Fifth Woman

Mary is the fifth woman named in Matthew's genealogy[20] (Matt 1:16). Many have noted that with the mention of Joseph, Mary, and Jesus, the pattern of the genealogy changes.[21] All of the other men named in the genealogy become the subject of the next use of the aorist active of ἐγέννησεν (from γεννάω, "fathered," "begot"). For example, in 1:2 we see Ἀβραὰμ ἐγέννησεν

---

19. George W. E. Nickelsburg, *1 Enoch 1: A Commentary on the Book of 1 Enoch, Chapters 1–36; 81–108*, Hermeneia (Minneapolis: Fortress, 2001), 140–41.

20. For my argument that the stories of the first four women named in Matthew's genealogy recall elements of the Watchers' transgression narrative but foreshadow the redemption of the evil introduced by the Watchers, see *Enoch and the Gospel of Matthew*, PTMS (Eugene, OR: Pickwick, 2012), 42–126.

21. See, e.g., Davies and Allison, *Matthew*, 1:184–85; and Daniel J. Harrington, *The Gospel of Matthew*, SP 1 (Collegeville, MN: Liturgical Press, 1991), 32.

τὸν Ἰσαακ, Ἰσαὰκ δὲ ἐγέννησεν τὸν Ἰακωβ. When we come to Joseph, Mary, and Jesus in 1:16, the pattern of repeated uses of ἐγέννησεν between fathers and sons is broken. Joseph is the object of the verb ἐγέννησεν of which his father, Jacob, is the subject. But for the next male in the sequence, Jesus, ἐγεννήθη (aorist passive) is used. Called the "divine passive,"[22] the form is used again in 1:20, 2:1, and 2:4, and means "was conceived" or "was born."[23] The use of the divine passive separates Joseph, named in the genealogy as the husband of Mary, from the child Jesus. It is actually Mary "from whom was born Jesus, who is called Messiah" (ἐξ ἧς ἐγεννήθη Ἰησοῦς ὁ λεγόμενος Χριστός, 1:16). Joseph is called "husband of Mary," and the son named in connection with him he does not father. A yet-to-be-named divine progenitor behind the birth is hinted at by the presence of the passive voice.

Whose Child Is This?

While Joseph may not share with his forefathers the right to the verb γεννάω in the active mood, he does share with some of those who came before him a mood about a pregnancy in his family, namely, suspicion. Joseph finds out that Mary, to whom he is engaged, but with whom he has not had sexual relations, is pregnant (Matt 1:18). Because Joseph is a righteous man and does not wish to disgrace Mary publicly, he makes plans to divorce her quietly (1:19). So far, then, Joseph has done two things: he has noticed the pregnancy of Mary, his betrothed, and made a reasonable assumption about how she got that way—by another man. But the reader knows what Joseph does not yet know, that Mary is pregnant by the Holy Spirit (ἐν γαστρὶ ἔχουσα ἐκ πνεύματος ἁγίου, 1:18). This is the first of Matthew's assertions about the actor behind the divine passive in the genealogy. At this point in the story, though, Joseph believes that his betrothed has been unfaithful to him.

Joseph shares this suspicion of sexual infidelity—or better, in Joseph's case, certainty, since he knows the child is not his—with some of his forebears. We hear in the genealogy that Joseph's family tree includes women involved in sexual scandal and efforts to avoid it: Tamar, accused of pregnancy by "whoredom" (Gen 38:24 NRSV); Rahab, a woman who earns her living as a prostitute (Josh 2); Ruth, a woman involved in efforts to

---

22. Davies and Allison, *Matthew*, 1:184.
23. Ibid.

avoid suspicions of illicit sexual behavior (Ruth 3:7–14); and the wife of Uriah, pregnant by a man (David) who commits murder in order to cover up his illicit paternity (2 Sam 11:1–27). Concerns about married women engaging in sexual relations with strangers also figure in the narratives of Abram and Sarai (when Pharaoh takes an interest in Sarai, whom Abram has introduced as his sister rather than wife, Gen 12:10–20; and again, as Abraham and Sarah, with Abimelech, Gen 20:1–18), as well as in the story of Isaac and Rebekah (same issue, with Abimelech, Gen 26:6–16). Since all of these stories have happy endings, perhaps Joseph should not have worried so much. Tamar is vindicated and called "righteous" (Gen 38:26); Rahab is a prostitute, but her "infidelity" is to her own king and kind as she makes it possible for Israelite spies to enter the land of Canaan; Ruth's midnight encounter with Boaz convinces him to act as her redeemer and they become the great-grandparents of David (Ruth 4); Bathsheba is the mother of Solomon, and through her machinations he becomes David's successor (1 Kgs 1:11–40); Abraham leaves Pharaoh and Abimelech more wealthy than before he lied about his relationship with Sarah (Gen 12:16, 20:14); and Isaac and Rebekah receive protection from Abimelech in the version of the passing-wife-as-sister story in which they feature (Gen 26:11). Despite the favorable outcomes for his predecessors, one can sympathize with Joseph's predicament, however, since the one thing he knows for certain is that he is not the father of Mary's baby.

Joseph's story points us to yet another ancestor who suspects his wife of infidelity. This time the concern is not just infidelity or questionable paternity, but also the birth of a savior figure. We look now at the story of Lamech, father of Noah, and his wife in 1 Enoch and note the similarities and differences between their story and the story of Mary and Joseph.[24]

The story of the birth of Noah is presented in 1 En. 106–107. Although Gen 5:28–29 mentions the birth of Noah, the Enochic version is an expansion on the brief passage in Genesis.[25] In 1 Enoch, Lamech is married and

---

24. Similarities and differences between the Matthean infancy narrative and the story of Noah's birth in 1 Enoch have been noted by George Nickelsburg in "Patriarchs Who Worry about Their Wives: A Haggadic Tendency in the Genesis Apocryphon," in *George W. E. Nickelsburg in Perspective: An Ongoing Dialogue of Learning*, ed. Jacob Neusner and Alan J. Avery-Peck, 2 vols., JSJSup 80 (Leiden: Brill, 2003), 1:177–99.

25. Ibid., 177. First Enoch is not the only expanded version of the story. The story is also told in the Genesis Apocryphon (1QapGen), which is, as Nickelsburg (180) states, "a massive expansion of a brief notice in Gen 5:28–29." For more on the

his wife gives birth to a son (Noah). However, the child is born with an unusual appearance and atypical abilities. His body appears "whiter than snow and redder than a rose, his hair was all white and like white wool and curly" (1 En. 106:2).[26] He has a glorious countenance and his eyes emit light like the light of the sun. Although a newborn, he is able to stand and praise God (106:2–3).

After seeing the infant Noah, Lamech fears that the child is not his; he suspects that one of the Watchers must have impregnated his wife, and the child is the offspring of that union (1 En. 106:5–6). What else could explain the child's odd appearance and proclivities? Knowing the Watchers' earlier-noted sexual interaction with women and the strange offspring produced by those unions, Lamech believes that his wife has been unfaithful with a rebellious angel. But, as in the Matthean narrative of the birth of Jesus, the reader knows what the man involved does not: "she conceived from him [Lamech] and bore a child" (106:1). Still ignorant of the truth of the situation, Lamech goes to Methuselah to ask him to ask Enoch to discover the truth of the unusual child's paternity (106:4–7).[27]

Enoch provides Methuselah with much information about his grandchild's origin and destiny. Enoch affirms that Noah is the child of Lamech

---

Genesis Apocryphon, see Nahman Avigad and Yigael Yadin, *A Genesis Apocryphon: A Scroll from the Wilderness of Judaea* (Jerusalem: Magnes, 1956); Moshe J. Bernstein, "Divine Titles and Epithets and the Sources of the *Genesis Apocryphon*," *JBL* 128 (2009): 291–310; Joseph A. Fitzmyer, *The Genesis Apocryphon of Qumran Cave 1 [1Q20]: A Commentary*, 3rd ed., BibOr 18B (Rome: Pontifical Biblical Institute, 2004); Jonas C. Greenfield and Elisha Qimron, "The Genesis Apocryphon Col. XII," in *Studies in Qumran Aramaic*, ed. Takamitsu Muraoka, AbrNSup 3 (Leuven: Peeters, 1992), 70–77; Elisha Qimron, "Toward a New Edition of 1QGenesis Apocryphon," in *The Provo International Conference on the Dead Sea Scrolls: Technological Innovations, New Texts, and Reformulated Issues*, ed. Eugene Ulrich and Donald Parry, STDJ 30 (Leiden: Brill, 1999), 106–9.

26. Nickelsburg and VanderKam, *1 Enoch*, 164.

27. The version in 1 Enoch does not have the episode included in 1QapGen in which Lamech first goes to his wife, here named Bitenosh, confronting her about the unusual nature of the child and his suspicions about the child's origins. Bitenosh swears an oath that Noah is Lamech's child, and begs him to recall their pleasure in the sexual relations through which Noah was conceived (1QapGen II 3–18). The "heat" and "pleasure" to which Bitenosh refers are evidence of conception according to Greek medical thought of the fourth century BCE. See Dorothy M. Peters, *Noah Traditions in the Dead Sea Scrolls: Conversations and Controversies of Antiquity*, EJL 26 (Atlanta: Society of Biblical Literature, 2008), 117.

and not of any Watcher (1 En. 106:18). Further, Enoch informs Methuselah about the coming flood (106:15), and how Noah will play a role in the
judgment against the Watchers and "will cleanse the earth from the corruption that is on it" (106:17).[28] Enoch also tells Methuselah, "this child
will be righteous and blameless" (106:18),[29] and that the child should be
named Noah. He also reveals the name's significance: because of Noah's
role in the incipient flood, "he will be your remnant, from whom you will
find rest" (106:18).[30] Another etymology for "Noah" is given in 107:3, "he
who gladdens the earth from destruction."[31] Methuselah takes the information back to Lamech (107:3).

In 1 Enoch, then, there is a chain of messengers who inform Lamech
of what heavenly beings know. However, Lamech cannot know the situation for certain without revelation from the heavenly sphere to the earthly.
Enoch, who has been given privileged access to heavenly secrets, tells
Methuselah, who tells Lamech what is really going on. The child Noah
does have unusual attributes, but these are not due to his progenitor. Noah,
as Enoch assures Methuselah, is the child of mere mortals, and Lamech is
his father. Noah's unusual appearance denotes not unfaithfulness on the
part of Bitenosh, but rather Noah's "divine beauty" and is fitting for one
with a divinely appointed function.[32]

In the case of Joseph, he too harbors suspicions, but not that Mary's
child has supernatural origins. There is nothing to indicate that the child
Mary carries has a celestial being for a father. Joseph likely suspects infidelity of the pedestrian, human kind. However, as in the case of Lamech,
heavenly revelation sets the paternal record straight. An angel comes to
Joseph in a dream and informs him that the child is of the Holy Spirit

---

28. Nickelsburg and VanderKam, *1 Enoch*, 166.

29. Ibid.

30. Ibid.

31. Ibid., 167. How does "he who gladdens [εὐφραίνω = חדי] the earth from
destruction" relate to "Noah" (נח or נחם)? Nickelsburg suggests that the ח found in
both חדי and נח is alliterative and that joy is related to rest or consolation. Another
possibility is that the Greek reflects an Aramaic textual corruption from חדת ("to
renew") to חדי ("to gladden"). Noah will "renew the earth from destruction" because
he will repopulate the earth following the flood. Noah's renewing of the earth would
provide an *inclusio* to the beginning of Enoch's speech to Methusaleh, "The Lord will
renew his commandment upon the earth" (1 En. 106:13). See Nickelsburg, *1 Enoch 1*,
549–50.

32. Nickelsburg, "Patriarchs Who Worry," 183.

(Matt 1:20). As in the case of Noah, this child also has a divinely appointed purpose: "he will save his people from their sins" (1:21 NRSV). As in the case of Lamech, Joseph is to give the child the name indicated by the heavenly messenger, a name that signifies the child's salvific function (1:21). Both Lamech and Joseph had suspicions about the children carried by their wives; both received information from a heavenly messenger about the reality of the infants' origins and purpose.[33]

The Matthean birth narrative, therefore, bears some similarity to the story of Noah's birth in 1 Enoch, but with one important difference. Lamech suspects that his child is of celestial origin—but Noah is not; Joseph does not suspect that Jesus is the product of a union between the human Mary and a celestial being—but Jesus actually is. The other important difference is that in the Matthean narrative there is no indication that sexual relations play any role in the conception of Jesus. Mary has not had sexual relations with a celestial being in order to become "with child by the Holy Spirit." Neither has she had sexual relations with the man to whom she is betrothed. Indeed, an effort is made to expunge the possibility of any sexual relations whatsoever between Mary and Joseph while Mary is pregnant. Joseph "did as the angel of the Lord commanded him; he took her as his wife, but had no marital relations with her [οὐκ ἐγίνωσκεν αὐτὴν]" until after the child is born (Matt 1:25 NRSV). Mary's virginal status is further reflected in the fulfillment formula quotation in Matt 1:23. Matthew's statement is the same as the LXX text of Isa 7:14, "Look, the virgin [ἡ παρθένος] shall conceive and bear a son," rather than reflecting the Hebrew עלמה, which would be better translated as νεᾶνις, "young girl." The child Jesus is in fact the product of the union of earthly and heavenly beings. Jesus is one who crosses the boundaries between earthly and heavenly, but without sexual relations taking place between beings of the two realms. Jesus's existence as a mix between the earthly and heavenly, and as one who crosses the boundaries between the two, is reflected in his name, "Emmanuel, which means, 'God is with us'" (Matt 1:23 NRSV).

---

33. Noah and Jesus share one more aspect in common, although not in the Enochic materials. Like Jesus's story, Noah's story also begins with a genealogy (Gen 5:1–31). In 1 Enoch, however, Enoch receives his information for a "generation … that is distant" (1 En. 1:2; trans. Nickelsburg and VanderKam, *1 Enoch*, 19). First Enoch is concerned with passing information from one generation to the next and to some unspecified generation in the future. Even if 1 Enoch does not include a genealogy, the work is concerned with maintaining a connection among the generations.

God Is with Us Now

Matthew makes a point of showing Jesus as Emmanuel, "God is with us," as an eschatological reality later in his narrative of events in the life of the adult Jesus. Matthew specifically refers to this identity of Jesus as Emmanuel, "God is with us," through his inclusion of the stories of the healing of the hemorrhaging woman who touches the fringe of his garment (τοῦ κρασπέδου τοῦ ἱματίου αὐτοῦ; Matt 9:20–22) [34] and the healing of those in the crowd who touch the fringe of his garment (Matt 14:36).[35] The fringe, κρασπέδον, is the equivalent in the LXX of the tassels the Israelites are commanded to wear on their garments in Num 15:38–39 and Deut 22:12 (ציצת in Num 15:38; גדלים in Deut 22:12). The tassels serve to remind the people of the commandments of God and their identity as a holy people (Num 15:40).

In Zech 8:23 (LXX), however, the tassels take on an eschatological significance, pointing to the time when the nations will come to Jerusalem to worship God: "In those days ten men from all languages and nations will take hold of the tassels of a Jew [καὶ ἐπιλάβωται τοῦ κρασπέδου ἀνδρὸς Ἰουδαίου] for we have heard that God is with you [ὁ θεὸς μεθ' ὑμῶν ἐστιν]."[36] In Zechariah, the grasping of the tassels signifies the eschatological realization of the nations that God is present with the Jews. Matthew interprets Zechariah's singular Jewish man, ἀνδρὸς Ἰουδαίου, quite literally in both Matt 9:20–22 and 14:36.

Matthew draws attention to the eschatological significance of the woman's touching the tassel on his garment, as may be seen in the differences between his telling of the incident and the way it appears in Mark and Luke. In Mark's version, the woman touches not the fringe, κρασπέδον, but Jesus's garment, ἱματίων. In Luke's version, as in Matthew's, the woman touches the κρασπέδον itself. Thus Luke's version also appeals to the eschatological significance of the woman's action. However, Matthew retains Mark's detail that "the woman was saying, 'If I may touch even his gar-

---

34. The healing of the hemorrhaging woman also appears in Mark 5:25–34 and Luke 8:43–49. As in Matthew, the healing of the woman appears within the context of the raising from the dead of the daughter of a man (called ἄρχων, "ruler or leader," in Matthew; he is named Jairus and identified as a leader of the synagogue in Mark 5:22 and Luke 8:41).

35. The healing of all who touch Jesus's κρασπέδον occurs also in Mark 6:56.

36. My translation.

ments [τῶν ἱματίων αὐτοῦ], I will be healed'" (Mark 5:28), albeit charac-
teristically clearing up the detail of the audience of the woman's speech
by adding that she was saying these words "to herself" (Matt 9:21). The
woman's statement, whether to herself or aloud, is not included in Luke's
version. Matthew has taken over the woman's musing that if she touches
Jesus's garment she will be healed, as in Mark; but Matthew adds the
eschatological detail that it is the fringe that she actually touches, as in
Luke. In Matthew's version, the woman herself may not even realize the
full implications of her action: she, perhaps even unwittingly, shows Jesus
to be Zechariah's Jew whose tassel is grasped because his presence mediates God's presence. Whether the woman fully perceives the significance
of her action or not, in Matthew's version of the story Jesus is fully aware of
her actions. Unlike Mark and Luke's accounts, in which Jesus asks, "Who
touched my clothes?" (Mark 5:30 NRSV) and "Who touched me?" (Luke
8:45 NRSV), in Matthew's version Jesus turns and sees her and speaks
directly to her, knowing that she has touched his tassels because of her
faith (Matt 9:22). Matthew, by having Jesus address the woman directly,
rather than having to ask the identity of the one who touched him, shows
that Jesus perceives the significance of the woman's actions, even if she
does not. In Luke's version, it is Jesus who appears not to grasp the entirety
of the situation: if he understands the symbolism, he does not appear to
know who is responsible for the action. In Matthew, through his statement
that the woman touches the tassel of Jesus's garment, rather than the garment alone, and Jesus's knowing who it is who touched him, Jesus appears
fully cognizant of all aspects of the situation: he is Emmanuel, "God is with
us," foretold in Zechariah and witnessed to by the hemorrhaging woman.

Later in the narrative Matthew reports that many people touch the
fringe of Jesus's garments in order to receive healing (Matt 14:36). Even
though Luke includes the detail of the fringe in the story of the woman,
it is Mark, rather than Luke, who includes the story of the crowds being
healed by touching the fringe of Jesus's garment (Mark 6:56). Matthew
includes the grasping of the κρασπέδον in both the story of the woman and
the crowd. For Matthew, Jesus is the Jew whose tassels are grasped: first
by a hemorrhaging woman, then by many people; in Jesus the presence of
"God with us" is made real, not in some future time ("in those days"), but
now.[37] Jesus's identity as Emmanuel, which begins in Matthew's infancy

---

37. Roland Deines, "Not the Law but the Messiah: Law and Righteousness in

narrative, means that eschatological righteousness has become a present reality in Jesus.

Crispin H. T. Fletcher-Louis makes use of a tradition attested to in Ezekiel to make sense of the tassels incident; he argues that Jesus saw himself as the eschatological high priest, "the physical, human embodiment of the divine Glory."[38] Fletcher-Louis's comments also highlight the eschatological nature and the manifestation of divine holiness in Jesus's interaction with the woman who touches the fringes of his garment and those in the crowds who are healed when they touch Jesus's fringes. Although Fletcher-Louis focuses on Mark's version in his explication, his point would be made even more strongly if he looked at Matthew's version. The Ezekiel passage to which Fletcher-Louis refers gives the information that the priests must not wear their sacred garments when they interact with people in the outer court of the temple. The passage says, "When they go out into the outer court to the people, they shall remove the vestments in which they have been ministering, and lay them in the holy chambers; and they shall put on other garments, so that they may not communicate holiness to the people with their vestments" (Ezek 44:19 NRSV). In other words, the holiness of the priestly garments is in a tangible sense contagious.

The idea that one may "catch" holiness by means of touching garments is also communicated in Exod 30:29, in which Moses is informed that "everything that is anointed with the oil of consecration—and that includes the priestly garments—is supercharged with holiness,"[39] so that "whatever touches them will become holy" (Exod 30:29 NRSV). The woman and the crowds who follow Jesus evidently believe that his garments, even just the fringes of them, have the same sort of "contagious" holiness.

Fletcher-Louis also thinks that the fringes Jesus wears are the ציצת of Num 15:38, but points out that "those *tsitsit* are the ordinary Israelites' equivalent of the *tsits*, the rosette that bears the Name of God on the high

---

the Gospel of Matthew—An Ongoing Debate," in *Built upon the Rock: Studies in the Gospel of Matthew*, ed. Daniel M. Gurtner and John Nolland (Grand Rapids: Eerdmans, 2008), 53–84, esp. 59–60. See also John T. Cummings, "The Tassel of His Cloak: Mark, Luke, Matthew—and Zechariah," in *Papers on the Gospels*, vol. 2 of *Studia Biblica 1978: Sixth International Congress on Biblical Studies, Oxford 3–7 April 1978*, ed. E. A. Livingstone, JSNTSup 2 (Sheffield: JSOT Press, 1980), 47–61.

38. Crispin H. T. Fletcher-Louis, "Jesus as the High Priestly Messiah: Part 2," *JSHJ* 5 (2007): 76.

39. Translation in ibid., 67.

priest's forehead."[40] Because all Israelite males wear the tassels, the entire nation is "a kingdom of priests" (Exod 19:6).[41] Fletcher-Louis continues:

> Perhaps in mediating contagious holiness through that which symbolized the whole nation's priesthood—the *tsitsit*—he was not so much interested in his own, singular, high priesthood as the fulfilment of the call that the whole of Israel be a "kingdom of priests", sharing the contagious, restorative ontology of the high priest.[42]

This emphasis on the "kingdom of priests" fits well with Matthew's emphasis on the participation of Jesus's followers in all aspects of his ministry, in particular at the conclusion of Matthew's Gospel, when even teaching, up until now restricted to Jesus alone, is included in what Jesus's followers are to do (Matt 28:19–20).[43]

In the episodes connected with the touching of the fringes of Jesus's garments, we see how Matthew's narrative of the adult Jesus builds on his claim that Jesus, as announced to Joseph, is Emmanuel, "God is with us." However, in 1 Enoch, unlike in Matthew's Gospel, the ultimate presence of righteousness and an end to postdiluvial evil is still a future event. Enoch informs Methuselah that despite Noah's role in cleansing the earth of unrighteousness, still more unrighteousness, and worse, is in store. Postdiluvial evil will continue until a final period when there will:

> arise generations of righteousness.
> And evil and wickedness will end,
> and violence will cease from the earth;
> and good things will come upon the earth to them. (1 En. 107:1)[44]

Noah will bring comfort, but the flood will not bring the final eradication of unrighteousness from the earth, as the community for whom 1 Enoch was written would have known from their own experience. In the case

40. Ibid., 69–70.

41. Ibid., 70.

42. Ibid.

43. Jesus's righteous pedagogy is another aspect of Matthew's portrayal of Jesus that stands in stark contrast to the Watchers' unrighteous pedagogy in 1 Enoch, another way in which the Watchers unleash evil into the world. See Richter, *Enoch and the Gospel of Matthew*, 196–200.

44. Nickelsburg and VanderKam, *1 Enoch*, 167.

of Jesus, however, no further period of unrighteousness is in store for people and the earth. Enoch informs Methuselah that more unrighteousness will follow Noah. The angel who informs Joseph has only good news about Jesus.

The following table shows the similarities and differences between the stories of the birth of Noah and the birth of Jesus.

	Lamech	Joseph
Husband's Suspicion	The child is the product of a union between his wife and a Watcher.	The child (unborn) is the product of Mary and another man.
Informant	Methusaleh (Lamech's father) goes to Enoch on Lamech's behalf. Enoch has taken on angelomorphic qualities and has been granted access to heavenly revelation.	An angel of the Lord comes to Joseph.
Reality	Noah is truly the son of Lamech and his wife, a human child—the product of a human sexual interaction.	The child is the product of Mary and the Holy Spirit, but no sexual interaction has taken place.
Child's Identity and Purpose	His name will be Noah. He will be righteous and blameless and participate in the cleansing of the earth from corruption. Two etymologies of his name are given: "from whom you will find rest" (1 En. 106:18); "he who gladdens the earth" (1 En. 107:3).	The child's name will be Jesus, "for he will save his people from their sins" (Matt 1:21); another name is given in Matt 1:23, Emmanuel, "God is with us."
Husband's Response	The child's name is called Noah (1 En. 107:3)	Joseph does everything the angel says, including naming the baby Jesus.

The stories of Joseph and Lamech share several similarities and have some important differences. Each man is upset because of the birth or conception of a child he has reason to think is not his own. Each receives an angelic message to put his mind at ease. The content of the message indicates that the child will play a significant role for the people of the earth, a role reflected in the name each is instructed to give the child. Each child is named according to the angelic messenger's instructions. In the case of Lamech, the child is truly his, and truly the product of human sexual interaction. In the case of Joseph, however, the child is from the Holy Spirit, and not the product of any sexual interaction. Lamech's child, Noah, will be righteous and will bring cleansing to the earth. The cleansing, however, will be temporary, and more evil will prevail until the eschatological judgment. Jesus is superior to Noah in the sense that his name indicates that "he will save people from their sins," that in him "God is with us," and that his presence means that eschatological righteousness is made a present reality.

The origin of Jesus as a product of a celestial being and a woman, but without sexual relationship between them, contrasts Jesus with not only Noah but also the angelic-human mixing in the Watchers story that led to disastrous results for the world. In his portrayal of the adult Jesus, Matthew includes teaching about illicit sexual relationships and even the avoidance of sexual relationships if possible, further distancing Jesus from the Watchers' transgression.

The Watchers' Illicit Sexual Relationships versus Jesus's Rejection of Illicit Sexual Relationships

The Watchers engage in illicit sexual relationships, but Jesus eschews illicit sexual relationships, even advocating for those who are able to become "eunuchs for the kingdom." Three examples unique to Matthew in the canonical gospels serve to highlight Jesus's teaching of abstinence from not only illicit sexual relationships but even licit sexual relationships in the cause of righteousness: the report of Joseph's abstaining from sexual relations with Mary until after Jesus is born in Matt 1:25 (as mentioned above); Jesus's advocating celibacy for some in 19:12 in his mention of those who "make themselves eunuchs on account of the kingdom of heaven"; and Jesus's teaching on adultery in 5:27–28.

Matthew gives more information than is strictly necessary to establish the nonsexual nature of Jesus's origins when he mentions the abstinence of Joseph and Mary from sexual relations until after the baby Jesus is born (1:25). Matthew has already established that the child is "conceived by the Holy Spirit" (1:20) rather than by a man, and provided the fulfillment quotation using the word παρθένος ("virgin") in 1:23. Matthew then adds the detail that Joseph οὐκ ἐγίνωσκεν αὐτὴν (lit. "did not know her," i.e., have sexual relations with her) "until she had borne a son" (1:25 NRSV). As discussed above, this detail serves to distance the birth of Jesus from any sexual activity whatsoever. It also highlights the virginal status of Mary mentioned in 1:23.[45] Matthew really wants the reader to know that no one engaged in sexual relations of any kind, ever, when Jesus was conceived.

However, Dale Allison offers the possibility that this detail also serves to link Joseph's righteous behavior with Jesus's teaching in Matt 19:10–12, which Allison describes as a "qualified defense of celibacy."[46] Jesus teaches, when he mentions that some become eunuchs for the sake of the kingdom, that "sexual intercourse need not be a duty, that sexual abstinence will be incumbent upon some."[47] Joseph, in abstaining from sexual relations with Mary, not only guarantees her virginity while she is pregnant with Jesus, but also provides an example of one who abstains from sexual relations for the sake of the kingdom. Further, Allison suggests that Joseph may exemplify proper sexual conduct within marriage according to Josephus's examples of Jewish communities,[48] for example, the Essenes, who "have no intercourse during pregnancy,"[49] and Jews generally, who consider sexual intercourse with a woman who is pregnant to be unclean.[50] The human male closest to Jesus in his infancy was a righteous man who avoided sexual relations at the command of an angelic messenger. Jesus would teach that the avoidance of sexual relations, by some, could further the kingdom.

Presumably even for those not called to celibacy, in Matt 5:27–28 Jesus expands on the commandment prohibiting adultery (Exod 20:14 and Deut 5:18, quoted by Jesus) by adding that "everyone who looks at a woman with lust has committed adultery with her in his heart" (Matt 5:28 NRSV).[51] As in the rest of this section of antitheses, Jesus teaches the

45. Hagner (*Matthew 1–13*, 21) states that this functions "as a guarantee that Jesus was virgin born." See Harrington, *Matthew*, 36; and Luz, *Matthew 1–7*, 97.
46. Dale C. Allison Jr., *Studies in Matthew: Interpretation Past and Present* (Grand Rapids: Baker Academic, 2005), 167.
47. Ibid.
48. Ibid., 171.
49. Josephus, *J.W.* 2.161 (Whiston, 607).
50. Josephus, *Ag. Ap.* 2.202 (Whiston, 806).
51. Janice Capel Anderson correctly notes that this verse, like Matt 5:32, in which Jesus teaches against divorcing one's wife except in cases of unchastity, assumes a male

upholding of the commandment in light of the perfection demanded by the kingdom.[52] The avoidance of not only adulterous acts but even lustful thoughts is an example of Jesus's teaching a righteousness greater than that of the scribes and Pharisees (5:20). It is possible, of course, that Jesus's expansion on the command by adding the notion that looking at a woman with lust is merely practical: desire may be aroused through looking, so do not do it. But perhaps there is a warning here that echoes the Watchers' transgression, which began when, looking down from heaven at the "beautiful and comely daughters" of the sons of men, the Watchers "saw them and desired them" and then hatched their plan to get wives and have children for themselves (1 En. 6:1–2).

We see, then, that unlike the Watchers who engage in illicit sexual relations with women, Jesus, born quite apart from any sexual relations, teaches a righteousness that prohibits illicit sexual relations (and even thoughts of such relations) and promotes celibacy for some of his followers.

We look next at a possibility that would bring us even closer to the repair of the Enochic Watchers' transgression. Rather than being simply the product of the nonsexual union between a heavenly being (Holy Spirit) and a human woman (Mary), it may be that Matthew had in mind a tradition that conceived of the Holy Spirit as angelomorphic when the evangelist told his story of the child Jesus being "from the Holy Spirit" and having a human mother.

---

audience; see Anderson, "Matthew: Gender and Reading," in *A Feminist Companion to Matthew*, ed. Amy-Jill Levine, FCNTECW 1 (Cleveland: Pilgrim, 2001), 29. Anthony Saldarini examines how the teaching in Matt 18–20 about household and community is addressed to men, although it has import for women as well; see Saldarini, "Absent Women in Matthew's Households," in *Feminist Companion to Matthew*, 157–70. See also Kent Brower, "Jesus and the Lustful Eye: Glancing at Matthew 5:28," *EvQ* 76 (2004): 291–309. Brower argues that Jesus puts the onus on men to regard women properly, in distinction from others who hold women accountable for attracting men's attention. This passage provides another distinction from the Enochic Watchers story in which, at least in 1 En. 8, the women cause the Watchers' transgression because of their beauty: "and they [the women] transgressed and led the holy ones astray" (1 En. 8:1); cf. Nickelsburg and VanderKam, *1 Enoch*, 25.

52. Hagner, *Matthew 1–13*, 120.

The Child Is from the (Angelomorphic) Holy Spirit

An additional link between the Enochic story with its Watchers who impregnate women and Matthew's transgression-repairing narrative is found in the angel's statement to Joseph, "The child conceived in her is from the Holy Spirit" (Matt 1:20 NRSV). It is possible that Matthew had in mind the Holy Spirit as an angelomorphic[53] figure. If this is the case, then Matthew draws out the parallels and the distinctions between the Enochic myth and the genesis of the Christ. According to the Enochic Watchers story, angels have sexual relations with women: beings from heavenly and earthly realms mix. Heavenly and earthly boundaries are transgressed, and the results are evil, unrighteousness, and death. According to Matthew's narrative, the angelomorphic Holy Spirit conceives a child by a woman, but without sexual contact. Angelic and human mix, heavenly and earthly boundaries are transgressed, but the result is salvation.

Scholars, most notably John Levison, have noted that the use of "spirit" (πνεῦμα) to denote an angelic being is recognizable in pre- and postexilic Judaism and frequent at Qumran;[54] Bogdan Bucur has established that speaking of the Spirit in angelomorphic terms remained an option in

---

53. Bogdan Bucur, in his arguments for an early Christian "angelomorphic" pneumatology, makes use of this definition of "angelomorphic" proposed by Crispin H. T. Fletcher-Louis, *Luke-Acts: Angels, Christology and Soteriology*, WUNT 2/94 (Tübingen: Mohr Siebeck, 1997), 14–15: "Though it has been used in different ways by various scholars, without clear definition, we propose its use wherever there are signs that an individual or community possesses specifically angelic characteristics or status, though for whom identity cannot be reduced to that of an angel." According to Bucur ("Hierarchy, Prophecy, and the Angelomorphic Spirit: A Contribution to the Study of the Book of Revelation's *Wirkungsgeschichte*," *JBL* 127 [2008]: 175), "The virtue of this definition is that it signals the use of angelic *characteristics* in descriptions of God or humans, while not necessarily implying that the latter are angels *stricto sensu.*" See also Bucur, "The Son of God and the Angelomorphic Holy Spirit: A Rereading of the *Shepherd's* Christology," *ZNW* 98 (2007): 120–42, esp. 125; Bucur, "Revisiting Christian Oeyen: 'The Other Clement' on Father, Son, and the Angelomorphic Spirit," *VC* 61 (2007): 381–413, esp. 409; Bucur, "The Angelic Spirit in Early Christianity: Justin, the Martyr and Philosopher," *JR* 88 (2008): 190–208, esp. 193.

54. John R. Levison, "The Angelic Spirit in Early Judaism," *Society of Biblical Literature 1995 Seminar Papers*, SBLSP 34 (Atlanta: Society of Biblical Literature, 1995), 464–93; Levison, *The Spirit in First-Century Judaism*, AGAJU 29 (Leiden: Brill, 1997). See also Charles A. Gieschen, *Angelomorphic Christology: Antecedents and Early Evidence*, AGAJU 42 (Leiden: Brill, 1998).

Christianity as late as the fourth century.[55] I will summarize some of Levison's and Bucur's evidence before returning to the subject of the Spirit by whom Mary is pregnant with the Christ child.

Levison identifies at least five sources in Jewish tradition in which the Holy Spirit is described as an angelic being. First, Levison points out that within the Hebrew Bible the Holy Spirit is described in diverse terms, including as the angel who led Israel through the wilderness. Isaiah 63:9–10 states,

> In all their distress he was distressed;
> the angel of his presence saved them.[56]
> In his love and in his pity he redeemed them;
> He lifted them up and carried them all the days of old.
> But they rebelled and grieved his holy spirit.

The "angel of his presence" was the angel sent to accompany Israel through the wilderness in Exod 23:20–23.[57] Israel was commanded not to rebel against this angel. Here, however, the prophet says that they did rebel and grieved YHWH's "holy spirit." The "holy spirit" appears to be synonymous with the "angel." Second, Levison also points out the tendency to show the spirit as angelic within the LXX, for example in Judg 13:24–25; 1 Kgs 22:19–24; Isa 63:7–14; Mic 2:7, 11; 3:8; and Hag 2:5.[58] Third, in the Dead Sea Scrolls, Levison counts approximately fifty times when angelic beings are identified as "spirits."[59] Levison's fourth and fifth sources are Philo and Josephus, both of whom identify the spirit as an angelic being

---

55. Bucur, "Revisiting Christian Oeyen," 413.

56. This is the alternative rendering in *The New Oxford Annotated Bible with the Apocrypha: An Ecumenical Study Bible NRSV,* ed. Bruce M. Metzger and Roland E. Murphy, rev. and enl. ed. (New York: Oxford University Press, 1991), 953 OT, which follows the reading indicated in *BHS* (= MT).

57. John R. Levison, "The Pluriform Foundation of Christian Pneumatology," in *Advents of the Spirit: An Introduction to the Current Study of Pneumatology,* ed. Bradford E. Hinze and D. Lyle Dabney (Milwaukee: Marquette University Press, 2001), 67. Also Levison, "Angelic Spirit," 471, although here Levison cites Isa 63:9–14, rather than 7–14. Verse 9 is where מלאך actually appears, but v. 7 is the beginning of the section.

58. Levison, *Spirit in First-Century Judaism,* 46 n. 44.

59. Ibid. See Geischen, *Angelomorphic Christology,* 115, who also notes that "angels" and "spirits" are used interchangeably in some Qumran texts. For example, in the War Scroll, "angels" and "spirits" are used as parallel terms in 1QM XII 8–9: "The

in their interpretations of the story of Balaam from Num 23–24. In Philo's interpretation, when Balaam was inspired, Balaam's rational faculties were displaced by an angelic spirit who used his vocal organs to create a prophetic utterance.[60] Philo argues that he himself is inspired by an angelic spirit when he interprets Torah, [61] and that the beings called "demons" (δαίμονας) "by the other philosophers"[62] would be better called "angels."[63] In Josephus's version of the episode in Numbers, when an angel approaches Balaam and his ass, it is the divine spirit who approaches. In his description of the event, Josephus seems to use "angel" and "spirit" interchangeably: "But on the road an angel of God [ἀγγέλου θείου] confronted him in a narrow place … and the ass whereon Balaam rode, conscious of the divine spirit [τοῦ θείου πνεύματος] approaching her…."[64] In Josephus's interpretation of the Balaam story, the angel and the divine spirit are the same. Josephus's understanding that Balaam encountered the angelomorphic divine spirit may provide a further link between the Matthean Holy Spirit from whom the child Jesus is born through the participation of Mary, but without sexual interaction, and the angels of the Enochic Watchers story who impregnate women.[65] Using the examples of the Balaam episode and others, Levison, then, makes the case that within Jewish tradition there are sources that describe the Holy Spirit as an angelic being.

Bucur examines what he calls the "angelomorphic Holy Spirit" in a number of early Christian writings and argues that various authors spoke of the Holy Spirit in angelomorphic terms, at least until the fourth century.[66] For example, the words πνεῦμα ("spirit") and ἄγγελος ("angel") were sometimes used interchangeably, or in parallel ways, such as in the Shepherd of Hermas, where Mand. 5.2.7 speaks of "the spirit of righteousness,"

---

heroes of the army of his angels [צבא מלאכים] are listed with us; the war hero is in our congregation; the army of his spirits [צבא רוחיו] with our infantry and our cavalry."

60. Levison, "The Prophetic Spirit as an Angel according to Philo," *HTR* 88 (1995): 192, referring to Philo, *Mos.* 1.274, 277.

61. Levison, "Prophetic Spirit," 200.

62. Philo, *Somn.* 1.141, on Gen 28:12; in Levison, "Prophetic Spirit," 194.

63. Levison, "Prophetic Spirit," 194.

64. Josephus, *Ant.* 4.108 (Whiston, 109).

65. For more on Balaam, whose dream visions may have influenced both 1 Enoch and Matthew, see Richter, *Enoch and the Gospel of Matthew*, 159–74.

66. In the fourth century, descriptions of the Holy Spirit in angelomorphic terms were abandoned because of the Arian and Pneumatomachian controversies; see Bucur, "Son of God," 142.

and Mand. 6.2 has "the angel of righteousness."[67] In Acts 8:26, 29, and 39, the being who guides Philip is called "angel of the Lord," "spirit," and "spirit of the Lord."[68] The Shepherd uses πνεῦμα to designate a variety of angelic beings[69] as part of an early Christian tradition that used the Second Temple tradition of the seven principal angels "in the service of Pneumatology." For example, the Shepherd describes a group of seven angelic spirits, the "first created ones" (πρῶτοι κτισθέντες), one of whom is the Son of God.[70] The description of the presence of the Holy Spirit within the Christian ascetic "is conveyed in angelomorphic terms, with a penchant for the metaphors of clothing, renewal, purification, rejuvenation, strengthening, and vision."[71] Clement brings together angels, spirits, and the Holy Spirit when he describes the seven firstborn princes of the angels (*Strom.* 6.16.142–143)[72] as the "heptad of the Spirit" (*Paed.* 3.12.87).[73] Clement also connects angels and the Spirit in *Adumbrationes* in 1 Pet 2:3 and 4:14, where he writes: "the Lord works through archangels and through angels that are close, who are called 'the Spirit of Christ.' ... He says, 'Blessed are you, because there rests upon you that which is of his glory, and of God's honor and power, and who is His Spirit.'" This "his" is possessive, and designates the angelic spirit.[74] With these and other examples,[75] Bucur makes a case for an understanding of the Holy Spirit in angelomorphic terms within early Christian thought.

We do not know if the evangelist Matthew had such an angelomorphic conception of the Holy Spirit. Clearly he distinguishes between the ἄγγελος κυρίου (angel of the Lord), who appears to Joseph to inform him that he should take Mary as his wife, and the πνεύματός ἁγίου (Holy Spirit), who is responsible for the conception of the child (Matt 1:20); they are not the same being. But might they both have been understood as having angelic characteristics? If so, then it would be even more important for Matthew to distinguish between them: the angelomorphic being who is responsible

---

67. Ibid., 122–23.

68. Ibid.

69. Ibid., 122.

70. In Vis. 3.4.1 and Sim. 5.5.3. See Bucur, "Revelation's *Wirkungsgeschichte*," 179.

71. Bucur, "Revelation's *Wirkungsgeschichte*," 142.

72. Ibid., 181.

73. Ibid., 182.

74. Bucur, "Revisiting Christian Oeyen," 402.

75. On Justin Martyr's angelomorphic pneumatology, see Bucur, "Angelic Spirit," passim.

for Mary's pregnancy is a particular holy being, rather than merely one of a company of angels who crosses the boundary between the realms of heaven and earth. If angelomorphic, the Holy Spirit who impregnates Mary, but without sexual interaction and for good purpose (the child "will save his people from their sins," Matt 1:21), provides great contrast with the angelic Watchers who impregnate women through sexual interaction for their own purposes ("to beget children for ourselves," 1 En. 6:2[76]). Even if not angelomorphic, the Holy Spirit still provides the contrast between a heavenly being who impregnates a woman and causes a child to be born for good purposes, and heavenly beings whose impregnating of women results in monstrous creatures and destruction in the world.

Conclusion

Mary is with child, but this is no ordinary pregnancy. Jesus's birth shares similar suspicious circumstances with the birth of Noah in 1 Enoch. Like Noah, Jesus will be responsible for saving people; however, Noah's salvific achievements will not be permanent. In regard to the fatherhood of the child, through a message from an angel in a dream, Joseph finds out that he has nothing to fear. The child Mary bears will be "Emmanuel" and is "from the Holy Spirit." It is possible that Matthew thought of the Holy Spirit as angelomorphic, bringing another comparison with the Enochic Watchers story: Jesus is the product of a heavenly angelomorphic being and a woman. However, as Matthew makes clear, no sexual interaction is involved in this pregnancy. The infancy narrative delivers to the narrative's stage the one who will repair the damage caused by the Watchers.

While these aspects of Matthew's infancy narrative can be understood as having theological significance and unfolding in an understandable narrative in Matthew's Gospel without knowing the Watchers tradition from 1 Enoch, reading Matthew in light of 1 Enoch heightens the meaning of Matthew's story and helps make sense of why Matthew told his story in the particular way he does: his portrayal of Jesus—conceived by a heavenly, and perhaps angelomorphic, being and a human woman, but without sexual interaction—who brings righteousness into the world, stands in direct contrast to the hybrid, monstrous offspring of the Watchers and women, whose coming into the world was the result of rebellion and evil.

---

76. Nickelsburg and VanderKam, *1 Enoch*, 23.

Enoch and the Synoptic Birth Narratives: A Thought Experiment

Anders Klostergaard Petersen

Enoch and the Birth Narratives: Procrustean Bed of Forced Comparison or Viable Avenue?

This essay has the nature of a thought experiment and is, therefore, susceptible to criticism from a wide array of fronts: empirical, methodological, and theoretical. The part of the Enochic literature that we, from a particular stage in its history of reception, have come to know as 1 (Ethiopic) Enoch neither contains an infancy narrative of the figure of Enoch nor does it provide its addressees with even bare hints as to the birth and early childhood of Enoch. Therefore, it may appear as more than a straitjacket to attempt to squeeze this body of literature into comparative vesture with the birth narratives of Matthew and Luke. Comparisons, after all, if they are not conducted in a theoretically lucid manner and within the confines of rigid methodology, frequently have a shallow nature—be they a result of parallelomania or the outcome of the fallacy of the panda's thumb.[1] Despite nuances of difference in method, both procedures amount to the same thing. In order to embark on a comparative endeavor between 1 Enoch and the infancy narratives of the Synoptic Gospels, therefore, I shall argue more extensively for the raison d'être of the enterprise.

One may, of course, turn to the remarkable birth narrative of Noah (1 En. 106). The son of Enoch, Methuselah, takes a wife for his son Lamech. She becomes pregnant and bears Lamech a son. The divine look of Noah,

---

1. The latter refers to the fact that the panda bear possesses an anatomical feature superficially similar to the thumb of human beings. In the philosophy of science the example is often used as a metaphor for the fallacy that one erroneously takes a superficial similarity for a connection in terms of essence.

however, scares Lamech, since he fears that the son may be the result of an illegitimate liaison between his wife and one of the fallen Watcher angels. Noah's body is white as snow and red as a rose. His hair and its locks are white as wool. Similarly, his eyes radiate like the glow of the sun. On behalf of Lamech, Methuselah seeks out Enoch to know the truth of the fatherhood. Enoch relieves Methuselah, who can return to Lamech and inform him how his son, Noah, on behalf of God shall perform new and great deeds.

Similarly, one may point to 1 En. 93:3 in the Apocalypse of Weeks (also belonging to the Epistle of Enoch) in which Enoch recounts from the books containing all the records that he and the accompanying angels have made on their extensive travels (cf. 33:1–2; 40:8; 74:2; 81:1–2; 82:1; 103:2): "I was born the seventh during the first week, during which time judgment and righteousness continued to endure."[2] Although the text clearly refers to Enoch as the seventh in the genealogical line of Adam, this brief and allusive reference to his birth does not really qualify as a birth narrative. In the context, the reference primarily serves to locate Enoch in a noble genealogy that dates both backward and forward in time. However, that hardly suffices as a satisfactory reason for scrutinizing the relationship between the absence of a genuine birth narrative of Enoch in 1 Enoch and the infancy narratives of Matthew and Luke. Nor does it suggest any particular relationship between the figure of Enoch and that of Jesus.

Despite the somewhat preposterous character of the comparison, I believe that four arguments may be adduced to legitimize the endeavor. First, it may be advantageous, not for historically narrow comparative reasons, to raise the question with respect to the relationship between 1 Enoch and the infancy narratives of the Synoptic Gospels. Rather than framing the question as one pertaining to a possible direct historical relationship between the Enochic literature and the gospels, it may be worthwhile to consider the question in terms of the literary staging of the two textual characters of Enoch and Jesus. Why do Matthew and Luke orchestrate Jesus by recounting a narrative of his birth, while 1 Enoch apparently can do without it with respect to Enoch? A comparison conducted on these terms may help us to cast light on the manner in which the protagonist is instantiated in each body of literature. Second, one may reasonably argue

---

2. When referring to 1 (Ethiopic) Enoch, I use the translation of Ephraim Isaac, "1 (Ethiopic Apocalypse of) Enoch," *OTP* 1:5–90.

that the absence of infancy narratives or motifs pertaining to the birth of Enoch in the Enochic literature contributes to sharpening the question that inevitably needs to be posed in the context of the Synoptic Gospels: Why do Matthew and Luke create birth narratives, when Mark apparently can do without it? In this manner, a study of the Enochic literature may help us to get a better grasp of what is at stake within the historical development of the Synoptic literature. However, such a discussion is not only interesting with respect to the early Christian literature but may also be beneficial for appreciating 1 Enoch.[3] Third, the question does not only pertain to the Synoptic literature. Seemingly Paul can also do without hardly any allusions to the birth of Jesus (see, however, Rom 1:3 and Gal 4:4).[4] To pose the question of birth narratives in the context of the early Christian literature in general, therefore, may not only shed light on this particular body of literature but may also help us to understand that different types of literature are in need of different ways of staging the central hero of their narratives or discourses.[5] Fourth, although it may appear artificial and as an imposi-

---

3. When speaking about early Christian literature I adhere to the traditional nomenclature, which is problematic by virtue of the fact that it suggests an independence of Christian vis-à-vis Jewish literature, which I consider anachronistic and erroneous. In my view there is nothing in early Christian literature that does not simultaneously belong to the wider entity Judaism. See my essays, "At the End of the Road—Reflections on a Popular Scholarly Metaphor," in *The Formation of the Early Church*, ed. Jostein Ådna, WUNT 83 (Tübingen: Mohr Siebeck, 2005), 45–72, esp. 56–62; "Konstruktionen von Geschlecht und Sexualität im Neuen Testament," *ZNW* 30 (2012): 12–23, esp. 13–15; and "Finding a Basis for Interpreting New Testament Ethos," in *Early Christian Ethics in Interaction with Jewish and Greco-Roman Contexts*, ed. Jan Willem van Henten and Joseph Verheyden, STR 17 (Leiden: Brill, 2013), 53–81, esp. 62–71.

4. Although 2 Cor 8:9 and Phil 2:6–7 are sometimes adduced as examples that may refer to the birth of Christ, I do not think they qualify. Both these instances refer to the giving up of a modally superior status for that of an inferior one that may be envisioned in the light of what Paul in his two typologies of Adam and Christ in 1 Cor 15 and in Rom 5:12–21 says with respect to Adam in the modal state of the lapsarian condition. For arguments along this line of thinking, see Karl-Josef Kuschel, *Geboren vor aller Zeit: Der Streit um Christi Ursprung* (Munich: Piper, 1990), 310–96; and James D. G. Dunn, *Christology in the Making: An Inquiry into the Origins of the Doctrine of the Incarnation,* 2nd ed. (London: SCM, 1989), 113–28.

5. In the wake of a time-honored semiotic tradition, I make a distinction between discourse and narrative. The former is formulated in first and second person singular or plural, while the latter is staged in terms of third person singular or plural. Needless to say, this differentiation does not preclude the fact that narratives may make use of

tion of "foreign" questions stemming from the early Christian literature to discuss the matter of infancy narratives and 1 Enoch, potentially we may reach a point where by raising a question that initially appears far-fetched we shall obtain new insight also with regard to this text.

To embark on my endeavor, I shall do four things that initially may look odd. First, I shall take a look at the development of the early Christian literature based on the underlying assumption that this may help us to understand why the Enochic literature is without an infancy narrative. Second, I shall analyze Paul's use of Christ in more detail, since that may be an initial key to unlock 1 Enoch's lack of an infancy narrative. Third, in order to approach a text that by virtue of its narrative genre is closer to 1 Enoch than Paul, I shall proceed to Mark and pose the question why we do not find a birth narrative here. Fourth, I move on to discuss Weber's notion of charisma, since we may use that not only as a key to understanding what is at stake in Paul's orchestration of Christ and of himself but also as a lens that may help us to interpret the figure of Enoch in 1 Enoch. In the final section I return to 1 Enoch and use the insights of the previous sections to shed light on this text. In conclusion, I return to my initial considerations how the posing of a seemingly aberrant question may help us to illuminate both 1 Enoch and the early Christian literature. The emphasis placed in the title of my essay on a thought experiment should be taken literally. The hypothesis that I advocate cannot be documented by historical facts in isolation by providing, for instance, a close and careful exegesis of 1 Enoch or the birth narratives of Matthew and Luke. That will not suffice. What I am endorsing is a type of macrohistorical method that aims to account for the presence of birth narratives in Matthew and Luke and their respective absence from 1 Enoch, Paul, and Mark. The legitimacy of this procedure is located in its ability to provide a coherent and cogent argument of a plausible historical development; but it cannot be substantiated or disproven by the historical facts in isolation.[6]

---

exchanges formulated in first and second person singular or plural, but in that case we are facing examples of embedded discourse such as is the case in the dialogues of the gospels. Similarly, discursive texts may use narrative, as is the case in Phil 2:6–11.

6. In this regard, I follow a procedure promoted by Geert Hallbäck, "The Early Jesus: Gospel Genres and Types of Authority," in *The New Testament in Its Hellenistic Context: Proceedings of a Conference of New Testament Scholars, Held at Skálholt*, ed. Gunnlaugur A. Jónsson, Einar Sigurbjörnsson, and Pétur Pétursson; Studia Theologica Islandica 10 (Reykjavík: Gudfraedistofnun—Skálholtsútgáfan, 1996), 135, whose

BRIEF SURVEY OF EARLY CHRISTIAN TYPES OF LITERATURE
FROM A WEBERIAN PERSPECTIVE

As Geert Hallbäck has argued in an essay that in the wider international context has not gained the attention it deserves, Paul's letters and the gospels differ not only in terms of basic genre but also with respect to the Christology that they espouse. Intuitively, we are inclined to take the earthly Jesus recounted by the gospels and antedate an amalgam of these figures to the situation prior to Paul, thereby conflating the earthly Jesus(es) with a historical account of Jesus. In terms of development, however, there is no doubt that the Pauline letters predate the gospels, which should also have an influence on our time-honored propensity to think of the recounted world of the gospels as predating that of Paul. The truly innovative argument of Hallbäck is to write the history of early Christianity on the basis of the history of genres of early Christian literature and thereby to pay close heed to the actual historical development of this literature.

In the wake of Max Weber's typology of different forms of authority, Hallbäck surmises that the different types of early Christian literature reflect the different stages of authority in the Weberian model of authority: (1) the charismatic, (2) the traditional, (3) and the institutional. From this perspective, the Pauline letters correspond to the charismatic stage of authority, whereas the gospels reflect a traditional type of authority.[7] Finally, the subsequent development of New Testament literature such as the Pastoral Epistles and the extracanonical letters of Ignatius mirror the institutional stage of authority. In the context of this essay, I shall focus on the two first stages only.

The Pauline letters exhibit an understanding of the early Christ-communities in which Christ is conceived of as a heavenly figure present through his acting by means of charismatic figures such as apostles and

essays on the history of the development of the New Testament genres have been a decisive influence for me; see also Hallbäck, "Den fortidige Jesus: Om evangelierne og Acta som historieskrivning," in *Bibel og historieskrivning*, ed. Geert Hallbäck and John Strange (Copenhagen: Museum Tusculanum, 1999), 186–99.

7. In "Early Jesus," Hallbäck is primarily interested in pointing out the difference between the pre-Pauline hymns (Phil 2:6–11 and Col 1:15–20) as representative of charismatic authority and the gospels as epitomizing traditional authority. In "Fortidige Jesus," he transposes that difference to a differentiation between Paul, on the one hand, and the gospels, on the other.

prophets. In the gospels, however, Christ has become not only a figure of the past but also an earthly character. This is not to say that Paul excludes the earthly dimension of Christ's fate or that the gospels ignore the heavenly aspect of Christ—on the contrary. Nevertheless, there is a conspicuous difference between the two types of literature by virtue of the overwhelming emphasis Paul places on the heavenly Christ and the similarly predominant importance attributed to the earthly Jesus in the Synoptic Gospels. This difference in accentuation corresponds closely to Weber's descriptions of (respectively) the charismatic and the traditional type of authority pertaining to religious movements at different stages in their historical development. Subsequent to the charismatic phase comes a period of consolidation, which is characterized by the mastery of the group's traditions and the recollection of its past.

In light of what we know about the average age in the first-century Roman period, it is reasonable to assume that the gospels came into existence at a period in time when the early Christ movement was confronted with the question of preserving tradition, that is, when the first transmitters of tradition such as the apostles, including Paul, had died. In such a situation the gospels were construed to secure the maintenance of tradition so that it would not fade away or dissipate. Although the gospels in terms of genre have a commonality with the mode of history writing in general and the genre of biography in particular,[8] they also represent a *novum* in terms of specific genre. The emergence of this particular type of genre or subgenre takes place at the time of the transition from the first to the second generation of Christ adherents, which development from the Weberian perspective is congruent with the change from the charismatic type to the traditional form of authority. In an essay in which Hallbäck elaborates on his argument, he eloquently summarizes his view:

---

8. For the distinction between mode and genre, see Alastair Fowler, *Kinds of Literature: An Introduction to the Theory of Genres and Modes* (Oxford: Oxford University Press, 1982). For an application of Fowler's distinctions with respect to categorizing ancient literature, see Anders Klostergaard Petersen, "The Diversity of Apologetics: From Genre to a Mode of Thinking," in *Critique and Apologetics: Jews, Christians and Pagans in Antiquity,* ed. Anders-Christian Jacobsen, Jörg Ulrich, and David Brakke; Early Christianity in the Context of Antiquity 4 (Frankfurt: Lang, 2009), 15–41, esp. 32–36.

As the heavenly Christ constituted the vertical point of anchorage of the charismatic authorities, the earthly Jesus is the natural horizontal anchorage of the traditional authority. From him the tradition emanated, which now is transmitted from the bearer of tradition to the next bearer of tradition, from generation to generation. It was first at this period in time—and really first at this point—that the need to fixate in writing who the earthly Jesus was emerged. It was this particular need which the genre of the gospels fulfilled by providing a coherent, biographical story of Jesus.[9]

Interesting as this may be, the reader may reasonably ask what it has to do with Enoch and the absence of birth narratives in 1 Enoch. In order to grasp that, we shall need to take a further look at the development of the birth traditions in the gospels. I have recently put forward the argument that we may advantageously use the study of rewritten Scripture as a focal lens for understanding what is at stake in terms of development of traditions in the gospels.[10] If we acknowledge that the Gospel of Mark was the first gospel to come into being and that both Matthew and Luke presuppose this text regardless of the question of their further dependence on the oral tradition of Q, we may see the accumulation of tradition as a literary growth along the lines of what we know from other Jewish representatives of rewritten Scripture, such as the book of Jubilees, Liber antiquitatum biblicarum (LAB), and the parts of Josephus's *Antiquities* that constitute a rewriting of authoritative Jewish Scripture.

---

9. Hallbäck, "Fortidige Jesus," 195 (my trans.).

10. See my essays: "The Riverrun of Rewriting Scripture: From Textual Cannibalism to Scriptural Completion," *JSJ* 43 (2012): 475–96; "Textual Fidelity, Elaboration, Supersession or Encroachment? Typological Reflections on the Phenomenon of Rewritten Scripture," in *Rewritten Bible after Fifty Years: Texts, Terms, or Techniques? A Last Dialogue with Geza Vermes*, ed. Joszéf Zsengellér, JSJSup 166 (Leiden: Brill, 2014), 13–48; and "From Morse to Matthew," in *Contextualising Rewritten Scripture: Different Approaches to the Phenomenon of Rewriting Scripture and the Ascription of Authority to Rewritten Works in Literature, Music and Art*, ed. Anders Klostergaard Petersen (Leiden: Brill, forthcoming).

The Riverrun of Tradition: Narrative Invention
of the Birth Traditions in Matthew and Luke

Similar to the book of Jubilees, Liber antiquitatum biblicarum, and the relevant passages of Josephus's *Antiquities*, Matthew and Luke not only fill out the narrative gaps of their *Vorlage*, but they also supply the predecessor with additional stories, just as at various points they slightly change the narrative of the antecedent. Unquestionably, Matthew and Luke did not make up their narrative by virtue of a rewriting of Mark only. Despite some who question the existence of Q,[11] I think it unlikely that Matthew and Luke, apart from their reliance on Mark, did not also draw on oral sources. However, I am skeptical toward the idea of a written Q source. Be that as it may, the existence of Q as a configuration of oral traditions does not detract from the value of my argument, which will focus on the relationship between Mark and Matthew.

In Mark, Jesus appears as a young man ready to undergo the Johannine baptism for repentance and the remission of sins. Subsequently, he is bestowed with the Spirit of God by means of the heavenly baptism. Matthew, however, by adding a birth narrative to the missing details of Mark's Gospel (Who was Jesus before he arrived as a young man at the baptism of John?), changes the function of baptism significantly. By virtue of the narrative logic, there is no point in having Jesus undergo a baptism for repentance and the remission of sins. On the contrary, if Jesus already at his birth has been bequeathed with the Spirit of God (Matt 1:18), there is no point in having him undergo baptism for the forgiveness of sins. Indeed, the whole point of John's baptism is contradictory to the status already obtained by Jesus in birth. Therefore, one may also note in Matthew's scene of baptism an interesting reply that is totally irrelevant to the question it purports to answer: "Then Jesus came from Galilee to the Jordan to John, to be baptized by him. John would have prevented him, saying, 'I need to be baptized by you, and do you come to me?' But Jesus answered him, 'Let

---

11. See, e.g., Michael Goulder, *Luke: A New Paradigm*, 2 vols., JSNTSup 20 (Sheffield: Sheffield University Press, 1989); Mark Goodacre, *Goulder and the Gospels: An Examination of a New Paradigm*, JSNTSup 133 (Sheffield: Sheffield University Press, 1996); Goodacre, *The Case against Q: Studies in Markan Priority and the Synoptic Problem* (Harrisburg, PA: Trinity Press International, 2002); and Bartosz Adamczewski, *Q or Not Q? The So-Called Triple, Double and Single Traditions in the Synoptic Gospels* (Frankfurt: Lang, 2010).

it be so now [ἄφες ἄρτι], for thus it is fitting [οὕτως γὰρ πρέπον ἐστὶν] for us
to fulfill all righteousness.' Then he consented" (3:13–15).

The problems pertaining to Matthew's understanding of baptism also
become evident from the subsequent recounting of the heavenly baptism.
Rather than having the heavenly voice direct its speech to Jesus (and to
the implied audience of the gospel) as in Mark,[12] in Matthew the heavenly voice serves to designate Jesus before the audience of the recounted
story as the Son of God. Therefore, the voice no longer communicates in
the second-person singular but in the third-person singular: "This is my
beloved Son, with whom I am well pleased" (3:17). Despite this significant
difference between Mark and Matthew in terms of the narrative instantiation of Jesus as an actualized Christ,[13] the scene of the temptation in both
gospels serves as a test case of Jesus. Insofar as Jesus is conceived to have
entered into a contractual relationship with God—whether at the heavenly
baptism (Mark) or at birth (Matthew)—the narrative of the temptation
highlights the implications of Jesus's new position by testing his ability to
comply with his newly obtained status. The only real difference between
the two is that Matthew has embellished the Markan version by amplifying
the temptation scene into a tripartite and escalating event that culminates
with the devil taking Jesus to a high mountain (Matt 4:9–11).

Similar conflations and divergences, stimulated by Matthew's amplifications of his scriptural predecessor, are pervasive in the relationship
between the two gospels; but where does that leave the former with respect
to the latter? Contrary to Jubilees (e.g., 6:22), Matthew does not refer to
Mark as the "first law." Similar to Jubilees, however, Matthew incorpo-
rates a scriptural predecessor into its narrative and thereby affirms it as
authoritative Scripture. At the same time, by virtue of being a rewritten
amplification of Mark, Matthew implicitly claims to be a more complete
and, therefore, superior version of its *Vorlage*. Had Mark sufficed, so the
underlying reasoning goes, there would have been no need for Matthew
to create a novel, improved, and considerably expanded version of Mark.
Although Matthew, implicitly by virtue of being an enhanced reconfigura-

---

12. See Ole Davidsen, *The Narrative Jesus: A Semiotic Reading of Mark's Gospel*
(Aarhus: Aarhus University Press, 1993), 266–71.

13. For the precise semiotic difference between virtualization, actualization, and
realization, see the relevant entries in Algirdas Julien Greimas and Joseph Courtés,
Sémiotique: Dictionnarie raisonné de la théorie du langage (Paris: Hachette, 1979); cf.
Greimas, *Du sens II: Essais sémiotique* (Paris: Seuil, 1983), 27–29.

tion of Mark, arrogates to itself a superior status at the expense of Mark (a fact clearly testified by the subsequent *Wirkungsgeschichte* of the two texts), it does not explicitly aspire to replace its scriptural predecessor. Yet Matthew de facto became involved in an act of textual cannibalism that literally devoured the Markan text, since it came to replace Mark as a more complete version of the gospel: a fact pertaining to both content and pragmatic function.[14]

Returning to the Weberian perspective and the emergence of the traditional phase of authority, which as we previously saw was congruent with the appearance of the gospels, we are now in a position on the basis of the example from Matthew to say something about the emergence of the birth traditions as part of the gospels. With the changes in emphasis placed on the heavenly Christ and the earthly Jesus, the present figure and the past and distant person, the emergence of the birth narratives in Matthew and Luke may be seen as a further narrative enforcement of the transition from a charismatically founded to a traditionally based type of authority. When focus is directed toward the earthly Jesus, the inescapable past of whom is conceived of to imbue the present with significance, it is understandable that traditions pertaining to the earthly staging of this figure are amplified. If we face Jesus as a young man in Mark, what is more obvious than to raise the question of the past that predated the appearance of this young man? It is this particular narrative lacuna that is filled out by Matthew and Luke by means of older and authoritative traditions of Jewish Scripture in a blend with contemporary traditions of how an ideal past of such a model messianic figure should be construed. Needless to say, by formulating my view in this manner, I do not purport to claim that the gospel authors were deliberately contemplating about their narrative amplifications in terms of the way by which I have, from an etic point of view, described the process. The riverrun of tradition—epitomized by the perpetual rewriting of Scripture—is indicative of more basic cognitive mechanisms on which we are all dependent and which the majority of us do not consciously contemplate.

As indicated by the title of this section, the riverrun of tradition is in principle without end. It may flow perpetually, but this statement needs to be qualified, since we, with respect to the birth narratives, may actually

---

14. For a far more elaborate version of this argument, see Petersen, "Riverrun of Rewriting Scripture"; Petersen, "Textual Fidelity."

reach a narrative finale. Contrary to so many open questions that we have and that we shall never be able to fully answer with respect to the emergence and development of the early Christ movement, in this case we are fortunate to know the ending. It is the culmination provided by the Gospel of John. Subsequent to the emergence of the birth traditions exhibited by Matthew and Luke, it is reasonable in terms of a plausible narrative scenario along the lines of rewritten Scripture to imagine a situation at which the question was posed: Who was Jesus prior to his birth? As is well known, this is exactly the point of departure for the opening of the prologue of the Gospel of John. With John's positioning of a peremptory beginning—the prehistory of which it does not make sense to question in terms of asking behind it, since his staging of the ultimate beginning has a definitive nature—we have come to a closure. But that, of course, does not exclude that other lacunae were open to being perpetually developed. The childhood of Jesus was a resource that could be used in the subsequent tradition for rewriting stories, just as was the period after Jesus was said to have risen from the dead and prior to his ascension into heaven, events to which John also testified.

A DETOUR TO WEBER'S NOTION OF CHARISMATIC AUTHORITY

We have reached a point where we have obtained a grasp of why Paul could do without the birth narratives of the gospels. If the traditions pertaining to the birth of Jesus really reflect a stage in the history of early Christianity that presupposes not only the existence of the gospel literature but also its reaching a fairly complex point of development, it is understandable why we do not find such traditions in our earliest written tradition. Yet it may be worthwhile to invest more energy into the question of Paul and the charismatic phase of authority if we want to use this as a stepping-stone for approaching the way Enoch is staged as a narrated figure in 1 Enoch. To do that, however, we shall take a detour around Weber's notion of charisma to see in detail what is at stake in the concept. We shall look at the concept prior to Weber's use and proceed to Weber's understanding.[15]

In many regards Weber's notion of charismatic is inherently connected to the history of Christianity. This does not necessarily reduce the explana-

---

15. Part of the argument developed in this section is taken from an earlier Danish essay: "Paulus—en antikarismatisk karismatiker," in *Fra Buddha til Beckham—karisma og suggestion i sport og religion,* ed. Poul Götke, Jonas Havelund, and Kristian Rasmussen (Odense: University of Southern Denmark Press, 2005), 45–65.

tory power of the category, but it does have some ramifications on its use. If one is not aware of this background, one risks succumbing to perceptual filters that may have a distorting influence on the analyses carried out at the empirical, textual level. Michael Ebertz has emphasized how:

> Nicht nur griff er [Weber] zur Konstruktion dieses Idealtyps auf ein Vorstellungselement zurück, das zu den zentralen "Idealen der Christenheit" gehört. Er profitierte hierfür auch von der christlich-theologischen und kirchenpolitischen Reflexion seiner Zeitgenossen und machte diesen Typus selbst wieder fruchtbar für die Erschliessung der "Christentumsgeschichte," was allerdings Fragment bleiben musste.[16]

At several places Weber points out that in his use of the concept he is dependent upon an older German theological tradition. He readily refers to the church historian Rudolph Sohm, who in his important work on *Kirchenrecht* from 1892 was among the first to make extensive use of the notion.[17] Sohm's famous dictum that the law of the church stands in glaring contrast to the nature of the church patently testifies to the ideological and religious agendas underlying the discussion.[18] On the one hand, there is the church of the spirit in which grace ($\chi\acute{\alpha}\rho\iota\sigma\mu\alpha$) reigns and freely flows. On the other hand, this is markedly different from the institutionalized constitution of the church that, by its worship of the visible church, brings grace to heel. The world of the spirit cannot be grasped with juridical concepts. The pristine church is said to cover that period in which "there was nothing that juridical eyes could see and nothing that juridical eyes could capture."[19] With the emergence of Catholicism, however, Christianity underwent a detrimental process of formalization and legalization.

---

16. Michael Ebertz, *Das Charisma des Gekreuzigten: Zur Soziologie der Jesusbewegung*, WUNT 45 (Tübingen: Mohr Siebeck, 1987), 15; cf. Max Ernst Graf zu Solms-Rödelheim, "Max Webers Religionssoziologie heute: Zum 40. Todestag des Forschers," *Deutsche Rundschau* 86 (1960): 524–30, esp. 527; and Johann Winckelmann, "Exkurs zur weltgeschichtlichen Stellung des antiken Judentums," in *Max Webers Studie über das antike Judentum: Interpretation und Kritik,* ed. Wolfgang Schluchter (Frankfurt: Suhrkamp, 1981), 219–23, esp. 222–23.

17. Cf. Max Weber, *Gesammelte Aufsätze zur Wissenschaftslehre* (Tübingen: Mohr Siebeck, 1968), 482–83; Weber, *Wirtschaft und Gesellschaft: Grundriss der verstehenden Soziologie* (1956; repr., Tübingen: Mohr Siebeck, 1972), 124, 654–55.

18. Rudolph Sohm, *Die geschichtlichen Grundlagen*, vol. 1 of *Kirchenrecht* (Berlin: Von Duncker & Humblot, 1892), 1.

19. Ibid., x.

It became *vergesetzlicht und formalisiert.* A despondent development in which the emergence of church law exhibits an "Abfall von dem von Jesus selbst gewollten und ursprünglich verwirklichten Zustand."[20] Concisely put: "Mit der Entstehung des Kirchenrechts entstand der Katholizismus, mit der Fortbildung des Kirchenrechts war die weitere Katholisierung des Christentums mit Notwendigkeit gegeben."[21]

This reconstruction is well known: initially, the pure church was sustained by the Spirit and from a particular point in history underwent a process of decline to what eventually became the visible, authority-relying, and sacramental-magical Roman Catholic Church. This development was not brought to a halt before the Lutheran Reformation, at which point the church was once again set free to a pure and innocent life of grace. Once more, however, degeneration occurred. Even the Lutheran Church had at some point by "iron-hard" necessity to succumb to the law of the church. That is the tragic paradox of the nature of the church. According to its nature, so Sohm, the church is a spiritual, charismatic *ecclesia* that constitutes neither a particular empirical entity nor a social concept.[22] In the long run, however, the church cannot be without structures and the law of the church. The interpretation of Sohm ignited a heated debate at the turn of the nineteenth century. Adolf von Harnack was among the most outspoken opponents of Sohm's understanding. Right from the beginning, Harnack makes patently clear that the discussion concerns a neutral point in Protestant self-understanding:[23]

---

20. Quoted by Adolf von Harnack, *Entstehung und Entwicklung der Kirchenverfassung und des Kirchenrechts in den ersten zwei Jahrhunderten* (Leipzig: Hinrichs, 1910), 52, without indication of the precise reference in Sohm.

21. Sohm, *Geschichtlichen Grundlagen*, 199; cf. 156, 162, 205, 256.

22. Ibid., 19.

23. In his 1910 book a whole section is devoted to the criticism of Sohm's understanding. It bears the title: "Urchristentum und Katholizismus ('Geist' und Recht): Kritik der Abhandlung Rudolf Sohm's 'Wesen und Ursprung des Katholizismus,'" and consists of 65 pages (*Entstehung und Entwicklung*, 122–86). The discussion, however, is initiated already in Harnack's *Die Mission und Ausbreitung des Christentums in den ersten drei Jahrhunderten* (Leipzig: Hinrichs, 1902); and is also echoed in an article, "Kirchliche Verfassung und kirchliches Recht im I. und II. Jahrhundert," *Protestantische Realenzyklopädie für Theologie und Kirche* 20 (1908): 508–46, in which Harnack confronts Sohm's interpretation. In a work from 1909 Sohm responds to this criticism. It is this criticism that Harnack on his side opposes in the 1910 work. Parallel with and partly related to this discussion are several contributions by the Tübingen church

Sohm beginnt mit dem Satze, den er als Concessum hinstellt, dass das Urchristentum hervorgegangen sei. Aus diesem Satze ergebe sich, dass etwas im Urchristentum gewesen sein müsse, was die katholische Entwicklung in sich schloss; aber die protestantisch-theologische Forschung habe bisher keine ausreichende Antwort auf die Frage gegeben, wo im Urchristentum der Keim gelegen habe, aus dem der Katholizismus hervorgehen musste; also sei das geschichtliche Hauptproblem, welches die älteste Entwicklung der Kirche biete, noch ungelöst.[24]

In contrast to Sohm, Harnack places emphasis on the background of church law and constitution in the traditions of the Jewish synagogue—measured by the scholarly standards of today a rather dubious assumption. The law of the church did not emerge in early Christianity as an innate part of a Catholic decline. It was, so Harnack, part of the heritage of early Christianity from Judaism. Similar to Sohm's argument, a heavy dogmatic agenda underlies his interpretation. Harnack, however, on this particular point was pragmatic and therefore had no problem in acknowledging that a church without visibility, without body, is and remains a "*numerus praedestinatorum et credentium*, die einander nichts sein können, also eine Anzahl von Parallelen, die sich erst in der Unendlichkeit schneiden."[25]

I shall leave this older discussion aside. Suffice it to say that when Weber took up his notion of charismatic, he was not stepping on neutral ground. On the contrary, in light of this brief presentation it should be clear how intrinsically connected the notion of charismatic is to historically legitimizing and identity founding elements of a Christian Protestant self-understanding. It was this debate that constituted the background for Weber's use of the concept. When Weber in *Wirtschaft und Gesellschaft* defines charismatic leadership as one "auf der ausseralltäglichen Hingabe an die Heiligkeit oder die Heldenkraft oder die Vorbildlichkeit einer

---

historian Karl Holl. In his "Kirchenbegriff bei Paulus in seinem Verhältnis zu dem der Urgemeinde," in *Gesammelte Aufsätze zur Kirchengeschichte,* 2 vols. (Tübingen: Mohr Siebeck, 1928), 2:44–67 (and less so in his *Enthusiasmus und Bussgewalt beim griechischen Mönchtum: Eine Studie zu Symeon dem neuen Theologen* [Leipzig: Hinrichs, 1898]), one also senses the importance of a tacit religious and dogmatic agenda pertaining to the true nature of Christianity: either Protestantism (particularly the Evangelical-Lutheran version) or Roman Catholicism, the allegedly spiritual upheld and charismatic sustained church over against that of authority and structure.

24. Harnack, *Entstehung und Entwicklung,* 122.
25. Ibid., 149.

Person und der durch sie offenbarten oder geschaffenen Ordnungen," it is fully compatible with Sohm's understanding.[26] With reference to Rom 12:4–8 and 1 Cor 12–14, Sohm had already argued that the Pauline notion of charisma encapsulates a social-relational phenomenon tending toward a structure of hegemony or mastery. The community is organized:

> durch die Verteilung der Gnadengaben (Charismen), welchen die einzel-nen Christen zu verschiedener Thätigkeit in der Christenheit zugleich befähigt und beruft.... Da gilt nicht abstrakte Gleichheit aller Angehöri-gen der Christengemeinde.... Da gilt Überordnung und Unterordnung, je nachdem Gott einem jeglichen die Gaben ausgeteilt hat zum Dienst in der Christenheit. Das Charisma fordert Anerkennung und, soweit es zu leitender, führender, verwaltender Thätigkeit beruft, *Gehorsams* seitens der Übrigen.[27]

In the vein of this understanding, Weber defines the charismatic as *der Führer* pure and simple.[28] Weber finds his notion of a personally sustained charismatic authority in Sohm. The exhibitor of hegemonic charisma is he who formulates "in seiner Person verkörpert gedachte Sendung."[29] The spiritually sustained charismatic acts "kraft einer ihm von Gott gege-benen, in seinem Charisma ihm *persönlich* eigenen Gewalt."[30] As with Sohm and Holl, Weber contends that it is impossible to measure the par-ticular quality of the leader in an objective manner.[31] It is solely attributed and sustained "by virtue of devotion to the revelation, worship of the hero, fidelity toward the leader [*der Führer*], freely born recognition among the governed."[32] Charisma does not only imply a relationship between the governor and the governed, nor does it solely pertain to the hegemonic structure of governance.[33] Charisma is understood as a phenomenon of contrast that is contrary to both rationality and tradition: "Die echt cha-rismatische Justiz ... ist in ihrer reinen Form der extremste Gegensatz for-

---

26. Weber, *Wirtschaft und Gesellschaft*, 124.
27. Sohm, *Geschichtlichen Grundlagen*, 26.
28. Weber, *Gesammelte Aufsätze*, 482; cf. Holl, *Enthusiasmus und Bussgewalt*, 190.
29. Weber, *Wirtschaft und Gesellschaft*, 658; cf. Weber, *Gesammelte Aufsätze*, 482.
30. Sohm, *Geschichtlichen Grundlagen*, 54; cf. Holl, *Enthusiasmus und Bussgewalt*, 151–52, 188–89, on whom Weber is also closely relying.
31. Ebertz, *Charisma*, 19.
32. Weber, *Wirtschaft und Gesellschaft*, 657; cf. 140.
33. Ibid., 55.

maler und traditioneller Bindung und steht der Heiligkeit der Tradition
ebenso frei gegenüber wie die rationalistischen Deduktionen aus abstrak-
ten Begriffen."[34] Further in the text, Weber contends that:

> Die charismatische Herrschaft ist, als das *Ausser*alltägliche, sowohl der
> rationalen, insbesondere der bureaukratischen, als der traditionalen,
> insbesondere der patriarchalen und patrimonialen oder ständischen,
> schroff entgegensetzt. Beide sind spezifische *Alltags*-formen der
> Herrschaft,—die (genuin) charismatische ist spezifisch das Gegenteil.[35]

Structurally there is no great difference between Weber's notion of charismatic and its use in Sohm and Holl. The merit of Weber lies primarily in
his systematization, elaboration, and sharpening of the concept. He refines
and clarifies the notion with respect to his predecessors Sohm and Holl,
just as there is a considerable sharpening in his use. Contrary to Sohm
and Holl, who could conceive of the category in terms of something that
was "ausseralltäglich," in Weber the concept is extended to capture what is
"anti-alltäglich." Thereby the notion is intensified to denote "eine der gros-
sen revolutionären Mächte der Geschichte."[36]

Despite the considerable explanatory power of the concept—a fact
vividly testified by the *Wirkungsgeschichte* of the notion—it has been met
with considerable criticism. One of the most frequent points of criticism
has been one of essentialism, that is, that Weber's understanding is vul-
nerable to being thought of in essentialist, psychological terms. Although
there are statements in Weber that may be taken to substantiate such a
criticism, I think, as is clear from the previous discussion, that there is
enough evidence to make manifest that Weber's understanding is founded
on a basically relational conception of charisma. Any leader only possesses
charisma to the extent that those over whom he or she is exercising governance recognize the leader's charisma. It is a crucial point that permeates
all of Weber's understanding. However others may interpret the charisma

---

34. Ibid., 550.

35. Ibid., 657. Cf. Sohm, *Geschichtlichen Grundlagen*, 26. See also Bryan R.
Wilson, *The Noble Savages: The Primitive Origins of Charisma and Its Contemporary
Survival* (Berkeley: University of California Press, 1975), 9, who notes: "The charismatic figure ... is more than a mere innovator. He is necessarily also a romantic, a
disruptor of the prevailing order, a man who abrogates and transcends convention,
who creates discord, coming, as it were, to put the world to the sword."

36. Weber, *Gesammelte Aufsätze*, 483.

of the leader, the leader is first and foremost charismatic with respect to the group that acknowledges his or her charisma.[37]

Weber has also been criticized for not satisfactorily differentiating between model and reality by conflating the charismatic type with elements in empirical reality. This criticism also appears misplaced, as Weber himself in his work often makes patently clear not only that the concept has a heuristic nature but also the character of an ideal type. As emphasized by Knut Kjeldstadli, the Weberian ideal type epitomizes a purely cultivated form and stylized exposition of a historical phenomenon.[38] With respect to empirical reality, Weber's ideal types constitute an extrapolated, synthetic abstraction the purpose of which is to summarize different features within a shared figure or category with the aim in mind to establish logical connections in an immense and messy material. It is heuristic, innovative, and thought-provoking.[39]

Weber has also been met with criticism for not stipulating the social conditions and circumstances under which charismatic movements are likely to emerge.[40] That may be partly true, but the criticism is misdirected, since Weber's primary interest was not focused on charismatic movements but toward a particular type of authority connected to a figure of leadership. The interest in charismatic movements is representative of a later phase of research in the *Wirkungsgeschichte* of the concept.[41] It is at this

---

37. Ann Ruth Willner and Dorothy Willner, "The Rise and Role of Charismatic Leaders," *Annals of the American Academy of Political and Social Sciences* 358 (1965): 79.

38. Knut Kjeldstadli, *Fortida er ikke hva den en gang var: En innføring i historiefaget* (Oslo: Universitetsforlaget, 1999), 147.

39. Cf. Helmut Mödritzer, *Stigma und Charisma im Neuen Testament und seiner Umwelt: Zur Soziologie des Urchristentums*, NTOA 28 (Freibourg: Universitätsverlag; Göttingen: Vandenhoeck & Ruprecht, 1994), 280.

40. Peter Worsley, *The Trumpet Shall Sound: A Study of "Cargo" Cults in Melanesia* (New York: Schocken Books, 1968), 270–72; Tharaileth Koshy Oomen, "Charisma, Social Structure and Social Changes," *CSSH* 10 (1967): 85–99; Robert C. Tucker, "The Theory of Charismatic Leadership," *Daedalus* 97 (1968): 731–56, esp. 742.

41. This is particularly true of Wilhelm Emil Mühlmann, *Homo Creator: Abhandlungen zur Soziologie, Anthropologie und Ethnologie* (Wiesbaden: Harrassowitz, 1962); Mühlmann, *Rassen, Ethnien und Kulturen* (Berlin: Neuwied, 1964); Mühlmann and Ernst W. Müller, *Kulturanthropologie* (Berlin: Kiepenheuer und Witsch, 1966); Johannes Fabian, "Charisma and Cultural Change," *CSSH* 11 (1969): 155–73; and Florian Deltgen, *"Bewegung" als historischer und soziologischer Begriff: Versuch einer theoretischen Präzisierung* (Cologne: Gouder, 1969). See also Tucker, "Theory of Char-

stage that the concept is modified to also include the political, not only the religious, domain.[42] Second, Weber focuses on the social conditions that enable a charismatic leader and a charismatic movement to claim authority and legitimacy. It is not the formation or emergence of a charismatic movement that has Weber's primary interest. Rather, his focus is directed toward the transformations it undergoes in close contact with changing social circumstances.[43]

Contrary to these four points of criticism, four others, in terms of critique, appear more pertinent to me. I find it problematical that Weber nowhere attempts to develop a typology that embraces different forms of charismatic authority. The criteriological background for the identification of charismatic authority in a given context is nowhere explicated. Like all presupposed and intuitively established categories, such an endeavor is ultimately unsatisfactory by virtue of its theoretical indetermination. Closely related to this point, there is a lack of clarity pertaining to the different types of authority. Runciman rightly contends that:

> First of all, the borderline between charismatic and traditional authority is harder to delimit than Weber's almost pedantic definitions would suggest. Once obedience to charismatic authority has become a habit, what does it mean to say that it is charismatic? If it means (as in the case of the church) that it retains some sort of "magical" attributes, this is equally true of many rulers who are by Weber's definition traditional. If, on the other hand, it means that it remains in some sense personal, then so, once again, can traditional authority; and to say that stability is the distinguishing criterion is to turn Weber's basic insight on this topic into a circular definition.[44]

This will take us to a third point of criticism, which notably has been put forward by Peter Berger. The charismatic person is not only situated in a discrepant relationship of contrast to tradition. The charismatic has not

---

ismatic Leadership," 737–38, who even claims, "To speak of charismatic leaders, then, is to speak of charismatic movements; the two phenomena are inseparable."

42. Cf. Deltgen, *Bewegung*, passim; Eckart Pankoke, *Soziale Bewegung, soziale Frage, soziale Politik: Grundfragen der deutschen Sozialwissenschaft im 19. Jahrhundert* (Stuttgart: Klett, 1970).

43. Ebertz, *Charisma*, 38; Mödritzer, *Stigma und Charisma*, 280.

44. Walter Garrison Runciman, *Sociology in Its Place* (Cambridge: Cambridge University Press, 1970), 160.

only a revolutionary, liminal existence, who in defiance of established order engages in an *Umwertung aller Werte*. If this were the case, he would never be acknowledged for the charisma. Weber's view is inaccurate that "Die genuine charismatische Herrschaft … verhält sich daher revolutionär alles umwertend und souverän brechend mit aller traditionellen oder rationalen Norm: 'es steht geschrieben,—ich aber sage euch.' "[45] The charismatic leader may relate to a number of traditions and institutions in a manner that turns the tables upside down, but at the same time he presupposes and acts in continuity with other maintained traditions. That is a presupposition for his ability to attain authority in the first instance in a particular group and to be acknowledged as a charismatic conveyor of tradition. Paul is, indeed, a very good example of this and so, I shall argue, is Enoch in the narrative world of 1 Enoch.

The last point of criticism pertains to the resonance that the concept of charisma has in particular material. Due to the fact that the notion has an inherent relationship to the New Testament context and later stages in the history of reception of Christianity, it is reasonable to pose the question, To what extent an *emic* category ultimately has been transposed and elevated to the status of an *etic* concept? Behind this discussion is a more profound and ideologically moot way of presenting the problem regarding the relationship between a particular scholarly discourse and a Western, Christian cultural context. I shall leave this problem aside and simply note that I find the alleged gravity of this problem overrated. After all, it is only on an essentialist presupposition that a "Western magic" or "contamination" sticks to the categories we are using. Suffice it to say that the binding of the notion to a particular empirical material does not in itself imply a delegitimization of the category. If the concept may be proven to have continuous significance, a heuristic nature, and a thought-provoking character, rather than abandon it we should analytically sharpen, nuance, and refine by confronting it with novel, empirical material. Although I am not able at this point to provide a full typological differentiation between the distinctive gradations of charismatic authority, I present a provisional definition:

---

45. Weber, *Wirtschaft und Gesellschaft*, 665.

Definitio potest fieri per genus proximum et differentias specificas

Charisma	=	genus proximum: traditional institutional authority	+	differentiae specificae	**Content wise:** Authority attained through claiming a particular commission on behalf of particularly privileged source **Formal:** textual marking of a particularly privileged exercise of authority **Pragmatical:** particular exercise of authority founded on a privileged commission which presupposes the recognition of the subordinates
definiendum		*definiens*			

From Weber and Back to Paul

I shall now take a brief look at Paul and from him move to 1 Enoch. Although we may surmise a close relationship between Paul the letter writer and Paul as he is rhetorically staged by the discoursivisation of the letters, I shall focus on the latter and refrain from making arguments about the connection between the two. For the sake of the comparison with Enoch and the lack of infancy motifs in 1 Enoch, my interest is directed toward Paul as he is instantiated by the letters. My sketch of Paul is inevitably brief and cursory. I do not pretend to give a thorough portrayal of Paul as charismatic. I only want to focus on the few elements that will enable the move to 1 Enoch.

Clearly Paul comes forward as a charismatic figure. This is not surprising given that Paul in the tradition has been recognized as the charismatic par excellence. In this sense, there is an element of circularity in the identification of Paul with the charismatic. Nevertheless, the acknowledgment makes good sense when one takes a closer look at how Paul instantiates himself in the different letters, from the earliest one in 1 Thessalonians to either Romans or Philippians as the last of his seven letters. He conceives of himself in continuity with traditions of the commissioning of prophets in the Hebrew Bible. When Paul, for instance, in Galatians retrospectively recounts his former conduct of life in Judaism (Gal 1:13–14; cf. Phil 3:4–6) and proceeds to narrate how he was commissioned by God (Gal 1:15–16), he places himself in continuity with the calling of Isaiah and

Jeremiah.[46] Yet there is also a remarkable difference. Paul was not only appointed as a prophet to disseminate the good tidings to the gentiles. He was commissioned to reveal (ἀποκαλύψαι) the Son of God. Similarly, Paul did not receive his knowledge from a human source, nor was he taught it. He received it by virtue of an allegedly direct revelation of Jesus Christ, just as he claims to have partaken in a heavenly journey that involved visions and revelations as well as auditions of unspeakable words.[47] The difference between the intertextual *Vorlage* of the traditions of Isaiah and Jeremiah and that of Paul's calling is indicative of a poignant transition in terms of development from an archaic to an axial age type of religiosity.[48]

I shall not take up this discussion in this context. Suffice it to say that the emphasis Paul placed on revelation presupposes a form of religiosity that we, in the vein of older tradition, may designate a religion of salvation or, in line with more recent nomenclature, may categorize as a utopian form of religion or a type congruent with an axial age form of religion. Be that as it may, the important thing to notice is the shift in terms of thinking between what we find in the depiction of the commissioning of Isaiah and Jeremiah, on the one hand, and that of Paul, on the other. The former presupposes a religious world in which Isaiah and Jeremiah are sent to Israel to make the people repent and return to the God of Israel. It is a religion characterized by the ontological difference between Godhead and humans. Inasmuch as the two are kept apart (architecturally conspicuously expressed in the temple and its different domains of sacredness)

---

46. Cf. Terence L. Donaldson, *Paul and the Gentiles: Remapping the Apostle's Convictional World* (Minneapolis: Fortress, 1997), 249–59.

47. See 1 Cor 12:2–4 and John J. Collins, "Introduction: Towards the Morphology of a Genre," *Semeia* 14 (1979): 1–19, esp. 11.

48. On this whole discussion, see my essays: "The Emergence of Historiography: An Axial Age Perspective," in *Historiography and Religion: Writing a Religious Past*, ed. Bernd-Christian Otto, Susanne Rau, and Jörg Rüpke, RVV 68 (Berlin: de Gruyter, 2015); "1 Maccabees from an Axial Age Perspective," in *Die Makkabäer/The Maccabees*, ed. Michael Tilly, Stefan Krauter, and Predrag Bukovec, WUNT (Tübingen: Mohr Siebeck, 2016); as well as the founding works by Robert N. Bellah on which they to a great extent rely: "Religious Evolution," *American Sociological Review* 29 (1964): 358–74; "What Is Axial about the Axial Age?" *Archives Européennes de Sociologie* 46 (2005): 69–89; *Religion in Human Evolution: From the Paleolithic to the Axial Age* (Cambridge: Harvard University Press, 2011); and "The Heritage of the Axial Age: Resource or Burden?" in *The Axial Age and Its Consequences,* ed. Robert N. Bellah and Hans Jonas (Cambridge: Harvard University Press, 2012), 447–67.

and Israel is acknowledging God as its god, the heavenly blessings in the form of different forms of fecundity will flow ceaselessly to Israel. In such a form of religiosity there is no concept of immortal life. In dire contrast, Paul's religiosity is marked by the abandonment of the ontological difference between God and humans. The whole point of life is directed toward the aim that humans should free themselves from the fetters that constrain them to this life and this earth by imitating the Godhead as much as they possibly can.[49] To the extent that one undergoes a process of transformation, whereby one obtains the nature of the Godhead, one may aspire to attain heavenly and immortal life subsequent to death.

Paul's whole religiosity is permeated by this type of thinking. Therefore, his references to the revelation of Christ are pivotal, since Paul is commissioned to reveal something that people could not by virtue of their own abilities tell themselves. In contrast, Isaiah and Jeremiah are not instantiated as pronouncing something categorically new. As we may see from, for instance, the discussions in 1 Cor 1:18–2:16 and 2 Cor 3–4, Paul is staging himself as a person with a privileged knowledge ultimately claimed to derive from God. It can only be revealed by virtue of Paul's knowledge of God's wisdom and activities as a preacher. Therefore, his addressees ought to be totally dependent upon the information they are receiving from him, since it is representative of a wisdom located in the heavenly realm. In this manner, Paul puts himself in a situation not very different from the discursive status attributed by him to Christ. As Christ is conceived of as a heavenly, present figure who by means of revelations is conveying to Paul the preaching that he should proclaim,[50] so is Paul with respect to his addressees a mediatory figure who is acting on behalf of the heavenly, present Christ. According to Paul, the relationship is upheld by the spirit of which Paul is the most profound carrier. This places Paul in the role of a semidivine figure. He is the charismatic who is acting in accordance with heavenly directives and is therefore capable of bequeathing the spirit to his

---

49. Cf. Anders Klostergaard Petersen, "Attaining Divine Perfection through Different Forms of Imitation," *Numen* 60 (2013): 7–38.

50. I find it quite indicative that when Paul is referring to things he has received from Christ he is not referring to the oral tradition of Jesus as we find it in the gospels. On the contrary, he is having recourse to Christ as a present, heavenly figure who endows Paul with revelations of what he is to think at particular points; see, e.g., the tradition of the Eucharist in 1 Cor 11:23–34 and the tradition of the resurrection of Christ in 1 Cor 15:3.

addressees in the form of privileged knowledge and access to a heavenly, spiritually borne life. Inasmuch as his addressees are absorbing his teaching and in conduct are abiding by it, they will also proceed toward the final aim of the transformation of their bodies of humiliation into bodies of glory (cf. Phil 3:21).

The type of religiosity characterizing Paul is of an axial age or utopian form, but we may specify it even more by adding that Paul is representative of an apocalyptic mode of axial age thinking. This does not put him in a radically different position than, say, those forms of Greco-Roman philosophy that are also characterized by a strong emphasis on the transcendental aspect, such as Platonism and Stoicism.[51] Yet, in contrast to colleagues who have opted for a direct historical relationship between these different entities,[52] I only claim that we are seeing different manifestations of what one may identify as convergent evolution, that is, the emergence of similar phenomena in parallel sociocultural and material contexts. Needless to say, this brief portrayal of Paul as charismatic is far from complete, but I have wanted to push my understanding of Paul as charismatic to its logical conclusion in order to prepare the way for the final comparison between Paul and Enoch.

From Paul the Charismatic to Enoch and the Absence of Birth Narratives in 1 Enoch

Although criticism has been advanced against the stipulative definition of the genre of apocalypse put forward in the famous article by John Collins, I should like to retain his definition for the purpose of my present discussion. Collins defines apocalypse as *"a genre of revelatory literature with a narrative framework, in which a revelation is mediated by an otherworldly being to a human recipient, disclosing a transcendent reality which is both temporal, insofar as it envisages eschatological salvation, and spatial insofar as it involves another, supernatural world."*[53] Within the original context of

---

51. Cf. David Sedley, "The Ideal of Godlikeness," In *Plato 2: Ethics, Politics, Religion, and the Soul*, ed. Gail Fine (Oxford: Oxford University Press, 1999), 309–28, esp. 310; Petersen, "Attaining Divine Perfection."

52. See, e.g., Engberg-Pedersen (2000, 2010), who is among the most prolific spokespersons of an understanding according to which Paul is understood to rely directly on influence from a Stoic type of thinking.

53. Collins, "Introduction," 9.

the *Semeia* volume, it was fully reasonable that Collins's focus was on the definition of apocalypse as a genre. However, we may take his understanding a step further, as Collins also eventually did, by extending it to cover apocalyptic as a worldview as well.[54] In such an understanding, *apocalyptic* comes to designate a form of thinking characterized by the notion of at least two and possibly several worlds held to belong to dualistically opposed spheres of being and doing, the heavenly and the earthly. The earthly world is utterly dependent upon the heavenly world for its existence. Life in this world is illusory, ephemeral, and determined by antidivine agents. True and everlasting life can only be granted by the heavenly world, which one may approach by being increasingly transformed into a form of being characteristic of the other world. Only agents (heavenly or earthly) having a share in the heavenly world are capable of mediating between the two and leading earthly humans from their negative attachment to the present world toward present and future transformation into the heavenly world. Although Paul is no writer of apocalypses, there is no doubt that he and 1 Enoch share an apocalyptic worldview; but does that make Enoch a charismatic figure, which has been the underlying premise for my discussion?

As is well known, 1 Enoch is an assemblage of texts that belong to different historical and possibly sociocultural strands and genres as well. At the same time, though, somebody must have thought, at some point in the first part of the first century CE, that the various parts of what now constitutes 1 Enoch could be collected together in order to form a cogent and coherent text. In saying this, I do not deny the possibility of the editorial process having already taken place in a sequence of stages.[55] But as legitimate as it is to focus on the individual parts of the book and the different layers of the redactional process and strive to interpret them in

---

54. Cf. John J. Collins, "Genre, Ideology, and Social Movements in Jewish Apocalypticism," in *Mysteries and Revelations: Apocalyptic Studies since the Uppsala Colloquium,* ed. John J. Collins and James H. Charlesworth, JSPSup 9 (Sheffield: Sheffield University Press, 1991), 25–51. One may take the definition even one step further by having *apocalypticism* designate the social component of this type of thinking, that is, as a designation for the type of social groups adhering to an apocalyptic worldview and possibly but not necessarily producing apocalypses.

55. See the standard accounts in James C. VanderKam, *Enoch and the Growth of an Apocalyptic Tradition,* CBQMS 16 (Washington DC: Catholic Biblical Association, 1984); and George W. E. Nickelsburg, *1 Enoch 1: A Commentary on the Book of 1 Enoch, Chapters 1–36; 81–101,* Hermeneia (Minneapolis: Fortress, 2002).

light of their individual sociocultural contexts of origin, it is just as justifi-able to attempt to interpret 1 Enoch in light of the point of time at which it assumed its current form. Among other things, such an approach implies that the religiosity characteristic of each of the individual sources of which 1 Enoch has been composed will have to be interpreted in light of the end result, although the form of religiosity distinguishing the particular parts of the book in terms of their own history of origin may be slightly different.[56] It is the compositional end result of 1 Enoch, however, that I shall take a closer look at, although this may, with respect to the absence of birth narratives, also have a bearing on the earliest sources of which 1 Enoch was composed.[57]

Despite the conspicuous differences between Paul and 1 Enoch, it may be worthwhile to think of the possible similarities between Paul's Christ and the figure of Enoch in 1 Enoch. After all, Enoch is said to have his dwelling place among the angels (106:7; cf. 12:1–2; 70:1–4). Although it poses serious challenges to the interpreter,[58] Enoch is also eventually iden-tified with the Son of Man, a figure referred to in the previous visions but without any apparent connection with Enoch (71:14; cf. 46:2–3). Enoch, however, is not only an earthly figure who has attained divine status. He also perpetually mediates between the heavenly and the earthly world in the particular instantiation of him in the text as an omnispatial and omnipresent person. Apart from sharing some of the same features as the

---

56. Although this is a moot point in terms of semiotics, I tend to think that there must be some ideological continuity in the sources assembled in order for them to be collected into one work. Needless to say, the historically preceding sequences of inter-pretants simultaneously contribute to pave the way for this assemblage of texts that, seen from the outside, may not be judged to belong together.

57. For this reason I shall leave the Book of Giants (only preserved in Qumran fragments and possibly some later Manichean texts) out of consideration and focus solely on the work as we have it as 1 Enoch. However, if one takes a look at the Qumran fragments (4Q201–202, 204–212, and similar texts in 1Q19; 1Q23–24; 2Q24; 4Q203; 4Q530–533; 6Q8; XQEnoch, and three further fragments from the Schøyen Collection), it is obvious that they are also without any reference to Enoch's birth or childhood.

58. Cf. James C. VanderKam, *Enoch: A Man for All Generations* (Columbia: Uni-versity of South Carolina Press, 1995), 141–42; and Loren Stuckenbruck, "The Para-bles of Enoch according to George Nickelsburg and Michael Knibb: A Summary and Discussion of Some Remaining Questions," in *Enoch and the Messiah Son of Man: Revisiting the Book of Parables*, ed. Gabriele Boccaccini (Grand Rapids: Eerdmans, 2007), 65–71, esp. 69.

heavenly, present figure of Christ in Paul, Enoch is also being used by the compiler of 1 Enoch as a figure who in terms of narrative role is functionally equivalent to the role of Paul in his letters. That Enoch in 1 Enoch is attributed the role of a charismatic figure that shares elements with both the figures of Christ and Paul in the Pauline letters is exactly the point that can account for the absence of any real interest in a birth narrative of Enoch.

One may, of course, challenge this interpretation by not only pointing to the passage discussed in the beginning of this essay (1 En. 93:3), in which we have a brief allusion to the birth of Enoch as the seventh descendant in direct genealogical line of Adam, but also by referring to the several references throughout the text to Enoch's genealogy (see, e.g., 37:1; 60:8; 67:4; 83:2; 85:2–3; 91:1–2; 106:1). I do not want to explain away the emphasis of the text placed on the family relations of Enoch. Admittedly, the addressees are told about Enoch's wife Edna, his son Methuselah, his grandson Lamech, his great-grandson Noah, and his six predecessors dating back to the progenitor Adam. Potentially, one could see the lineage information as functionally related to what takes place in the birth narratives of Matthew and Luke. James VanderKam, for instance, has suggested that the genealogy in 37:1 is meant to remedy the neglect of proper lineage information in the first part of 1 Enoch (Book of the Watchers).[59] Yet these references are not a prominent feature of the text in terms of providing any elaborate family story, nor do they imply any exhaustive account of the birth of Enoch. The reason for this, I surmise, is that Enoch is used as a charismatic, narrative figure representative of a charismatic type of religiosity in which the textual use of 1 Enoch is conceived of to provide access to the presently significant heavenly wisdom crucial for acting and thinking in the current world. It is the omnipresent and ubiquitous charismatic nature of the figure that inhibits it from being bestowed with an exhaustive birth account.

In its traditional use, the concept of charisma is applied to earthly figures only; but Enoch, of course, eludes such categorization, since he is both an earthly and a heavenly figure. Additionally, *charismatic* is not traditionally used with respect to deceased persons; but once again Enoch escapes such an understanding by simultaneously belonging to the past and to the present. In terms of my previous definition of charismatic

---

59. VanderKam, *Enoch: Man for All Generations*, 133–34.

authority, however, we find all the elements pertaining to 1 Enoch's use of Enoch. In terms of content, Enoch is understood as acting on behalf of God by having obtained a particular commission. In terms of apocalyptic form, there is a textual emphasis placed on a particularly privileged exercise of authority. Throughout the text, Enoch is depicted as standing in a special and privileged relationship to the Divine. He is a mediator of new, revealed wisdom that he, with the help of the *angeli interpretes*, is capable of transmitting to the intended audience. Pragmatically, the particular exercise of authority performed by Enoch on behalf of the textual author is founded on a privileged commission that presupposes the recognition of the intended audience of the text. In the first chapter of 1 Enoch, the narrated figure of Enoch is staged in a manner so that he is capable of speaking to all generations, since the day of tribulation both in the world of the narrative and at the level of the narration belongs to the future. Therefore, Enoch's words of blessing are relevant to the elect and the righteous not only of the past but also of the present and, insofar as the day of tribulation has not yet occurred, of the future (1:1). His teaching does not belong to the past only, nor is he conceived of as a blessed and righteous man of the Lord belonging to the past (1:2). On the contrary, his teaching has pervasive importance, just as Enoch—at the level of the narrative— constitutes to the elect at all times a means through which they may gain access to that hidden wisdom crucial to leading a life that after judgment will ultimately place them among the elect and righteous. The teaching and inculcations given by Enoch do not pertain to history. By virtue of the means of communicating in visions, the visions are attributed everlasting significance. Enoch has been allowed not only to understand the past and present situation of the world but also the end of everything (19:3; cf. 1:2). To obtain access to this wisdom, one must of necessity turn to Enoch and especially the medium that provides contact to his insight, that is, 1 Enoch.

Unlike the figure of Christ in Paul, Enoch is not understood as a savior figure in 1 Enoch. Yet he is not merely staged as somebody who functions as an emissary between the celestial and the earthly world. He is also used by the Watchers and the angels as an angelic ambassador who can communicate on behalf of both the angels and the fallen ones. Although the addressees know that Enoch's intercession for the Watchers will be in vain (12:5–6), Enoch nevertheless agrees to bring a petition forward to God on their behalf, since, due to their fall and subsequent shame, they are prevented from approaching God. In this manner, Enoch is already portrayed in the first part of the book as both visionary and scribe who by virtue of

his status as a regular visitor to the heavenly world is extremely important for humans. As regular access to Christ and his earthly representative
Paul is indicative in Paul of obtaining contact with the heavenly world
that is vital for one's salvation, so is access to the knowledge possessed
by Enoch in 1 Enoch emphasized as crucial for one's salvation.[60] Enoch,
by virtue of his particular commission on behalf of God as conveyor of
hidden wisdom, is attributed the role of a privileged source of authority,
that is, a charismatic figure. The Enoch of the heavenly world is instantiated in a role that functionally comes close to the revelatory character of
the heavenly, present Christ in Paul. In order not to be misunderstood
when it comes to this decisive point, however, let me emphasize once again
that it is in this regard only that I claim that a similarity exists between the
two figures. I am not making the argument with respect to Christ's salvific
role in Paul, although Enoch at certain points comes close to doing so (cf.
43:7; 61:8).

That Enoch is understood to communicate heavenly wisdom to the
earthly world, however, also resembles the manner in which Paul in his
letters stages himself, which is the last topic we will discuss. Enoch, of
course, is a figure belonging to the primordial history of Israel, wherefore he also holds a genealogy that connects him with his six predecessors
and his subsequent descendants down to Noah. That is one challenge to
the interpretation I propound. The other one is that in the book there are
references to Enoch as scribe (12:3–4; 15:1; cf. 92:1) and an emphasis is
placed on the medium of heavenly books that similarly points in the direction of a traditional type of authority. True as this may be, Enoch is even so
not conceived of as a past figure. The wisdom he conveys to the elect and
righteous has an omnipresent nature. As the Son of Man (46:2–4; 48:2–7;
62:5, 7, 9, 14; 63:11; 69:26–27), the Righteous One (53:6–7; cf. 1:2), the
Chosen or Elect One (39:6; 45:3; 51:3, 5; 52:6; 53:6; 55:4; 62:1), and the
Anointed One or Messiah (48:10; 52:4), he is given not only a role in the
present as mediator of heavenly wisdom, but shall also a function at the
end of days by assisting the righteous and elect to ultimate vindication.
Indeed, he will ultimately become united with God (105:2). As already
indicated, hardly anything in the text prior to Enoch's third parable in the
Book of Parables has prepared the way for the identification of Enoch with
these exalted roles. Yet in chapter 71 it becomes clear that Enoch is to be

---

60. George W. E. Nickelsburg, "Enoch, First Book of," *ABD* 2:508–16, esp. 514.

identified with these four roles, and that which pertains to each of them in the preceding text, therefore, should also be applied to Enoch.

It is Enoch, however, in his role as apocalyptic seer and transmitter of hidden wisdom that constitutes the point of similarity with Paul. As Paul has been granted the wisdom of Christ (cf. 1 Cor 2:16), so has Enoch through his visions been bequeathed the ability to reveal the heavenly cosmic order to the recipients of the book. Whereas Enoch in the very first part of the book is portrayed as a righteous person capable through the endowment with visions of not only foreseeing the future but also the end of all things, he becomes, as the text proceeds, increasingly elevated in his eschatological role and in his function of granting the addressees access to God's hidden wisdom. Enoch, however, is not able on his own to provide the earthly recipients with this wisdom. Similar to Paul's reliance on the heavenly, present wisdom of Christ, Enoch is dependent upon various *angeli interpretes* who can explain to him what he sees on his journeys around the earthly and the heavenly worlds.

In situations of uncertainty, Methuselah and Noah may consult Enoch in order to obtain certain knowledge. The same opportunity is granted to the addressees of 1 Enoch, who by means of the book can gain direct access to Enoch's eternal wisdom:

> This is the beginning of the words of wisdom which I commenced to propound, saying to those who dwell in the earth, "Listen, you first ones, and look, you last ones, the words of the Holy One, which I teach before the Lord of the Spirits. It is good to declare these words to those of former times, but one should not withhold the beginning of wisdom from those of latter days." (37:2–3; cf. 82:1–3; 92:1)

In the same vein, 1 Enoch is attributed status as the medium that gives direct access to the immense wisdom of Enoch conclusive for all time: "Again know another mystery!; that to the righteous and the wise shall be given the Scriptures of joy, for truth and great wisdom. So to them shall be given the Scriptures; and they shall believe them and be glad in them; and all the righteous ones who learn from them the ways of truth shall rejoice" (104:12–13). Enoch, of course, is no apostle like Paul, but in 1 Enoch he is attributed a role similar to the one by which Paul instantiates himself in his letters, that is, as a conveyor of heavenly, hidden wisdom. It is in this particular regard that the figures of Paul and Enoch converge. Both are attributed apocalyptic qualities. By virtue of the wisdom they possess, they are in the respective textual instantiations of them capable of granting their recipients knowledge pertaining to both the mindset and the behavior deemed pivotal for attaining salvation.

A Brief Conclusion

I began this essay by pointing to its experimental nature. I have posed a question about the Enochic literature that may, admittedly, appear as a Procrustean bed in which 1 Enoch—dependent upon one's perspective— is unnecessarily extended or truncated. Yet to pose the question of the birth narratives of Matthew and Luke and the absence of a narrative of infancy in 1 Enoch may potentially increase our understanding of both corpora. Rather than engaging in a pursuit of possible historical influences of motifs between the texts, I move in a different direction.

The sequence of argument has four stages. First, I notice that the Gospel of Mark can do without a birth narrative. In light of recent discussions of rewritten Scripture, I suggest that the emergence of birth narratives in Matthew and Luke should be seen as an obvious narrative development from Mark. Second, I move backward in time to Paul and observe that he can also do without a narrative of Christ's birth. Indeed, he has no great interest in the course of the earthly Jesus's life except concerning the one and only crucial fact on which he places all emphasis—the crucifixion. In continuity with Hallbäck and his use of Weber's typology of authority, I propose that this Pauline lack of interest is not only due to a difference in terms of genre between discourse (letters) and narrative (the gospels) but to a greater extent is a testimony of two types of authority, the charismatic and the traditional. Third, I contend that not only in terms of type of religious worldview (axial age apocalyptic type) but also with respect to the form of authority exhibited by the Pauline letters and 1 Enoch, there is a relationship between the two. Fourth, these considerations allow me to suggest that the manner in which the figure of Enoch is used in 1 Enoch shares elements with the instantiation of both Christ and Paul in the Pauline letters. Although Enoch belongs to the primordial history of Israel, he is also depicted from his appearance as the seventh descendant in the genealogical line of Adam as an omnipresent and ubiquitous figure, the access to whom provides insight into the hidden wisdom considered decisive for the mind-set and behavior that will lead to the salvation of the righteous and elect. I drive home my argument by surmising that the lack of birth narrative in 1 Enoch over against the infancy narratives of

Jesus found in Matthew and Luke is due to the fact that we are facing not only different genres of literature but also—and congruent with the genre allocation—different forms of authority. Although *charismatic* is not commonly used with respect to deceased or heavenly persons, Enoch is also a present and partly earthly person who can, therefore, function as a mediator between the celestial and earthly realms. In light of a slightly revised definition of charismatic, I show how the manner in which Enoch is used in 1 Enoch complies with charismatic authority with respect to content, to form, and to the pragmatic dimension. In this regard, 1 Enoch is closer to Paul than it is to the Synoptic Gospels. Ultimately, it is this difference that is decisive for a lack of an Enochic birth narrative in 1 Enoch.

Heavenly Beings in the Enoch Traditions and Synoptic Gospels

Kelley Coblentz Bautch

Introduction

There are many reasons why early Christianity needs to be explored along-side texts associated with Enoch. First, surveys of early Christian litera-ture make obvious the popularity of Enoch and of writings associated with the patriarch.[1] Though some late antique theologians like Augustine and Jerome express consternation about literature associated with Enoch, other Christians, as suggested by Jude 14 and the Epistle of Barnabas (4:3; 16:4), regarded early Enochic literature as authoritative.[2] Second, from Justin Martyr to Clement of Alexandria, Christians recalled the story of the angels' descent and mating of women and understood Enoch as an impor-tant witness to the theme of divine judgment. The evidence suggests that Christian employment of the fallen angel myth, so prominent in Enoch traditions, was attested throughout the Roman world and in all leading centers of the church.[3] Third, more particular points of contact have been

---

1. My appreciation to Tobias Nicklas and Michael Patella for their generosity in reading drafts of the essay and for their insights and suggestions. Special thanks are due also to Randall Chesnutt for his thorough reading of and extensive engagement with the work. Chesnutt's formal response at the seminar was both munificent and substantive, and this revised version of the essay is better for his comments and chal-lenges. See Hugh Jackson Lawlor, "Early Citations from the Book of Enoch," *Journal of Philology* 25 (1897): 164–225; and James C. VanderKam, "1 Enoch, Enochic Motifs, and Enoch in Early Christian Literature," in *The Jewish Apocalyptic Heritage of Early Christianity,* ed. James C. VanderKam and William Adler, CRINT 3.4 (Assen: Van Gorcum; Minneapolis: Fortress, 1996), 33–101.

2. Cf. also Tertullian, *Cult. fem.* 1.3, on the contentious nature of this literature.

3. See VanderKam, "1 Enoch, Enochic Motifs," 87.

examined in early Christian literature, indicating awareness of Enoch traditions on some level.[4] These confluences communicate how indebted early Christians were to very particular streams of Second Temple Judaism, communities knowledgeable in traditions related to Enoch literature.

In light of the popularity of Enochic literature among early Christians, one might well wonder whether the Synoptic Gospels also share awareness of Enochic literature and dominant motifs.[5] When it comes to depictions of heavenly beings, the angelologies of early Enoch literature and the Synoptic overlap in broad conceptual ways. Still, while examination of the otherworldly beings in these works reveal a common thought world behind the texts, ultimately the Synoptic Gospels differ in their angelol-

---

4. For example, George Nickelsburg has called attention to Petrine traditions (Matt 16, 1–2 Peter, the Gospel of Peter, and the Apocalypse of Peter) that also invoke motifs particular to Enochic literature or bear relationship to the literature in other ways; see Nickelsburg, "Enoch, Levi, and Peter: Recipients of Revelation in Upper Galilee," *JBL* 100 (1981): 575–600; Nickelsburg, *1 Enoch 1: A Commentary on the Book of 1 Enoch, Chapters 1–36; 81–108*, Hermeneia (Minneapolis: Fortress, 2001), 86, 103–4. Eric Mason ("Biblical and Nonbiblical Traditions in Jude and 2 Peter: Sources, Usage, and the Question of Canon," in *Reading 1–2 Peter and Jude: A Resource for Students*, ed. Eric F. Mason and Troy Martin, RBS 77 [Atlanta: Society of Biblical Literature, 2014], 181–200) and Chad Pierce (*Spirits and the Proclamation of Christ: 1 Peter 3:18–22 in Light of Sin and Punishment Traditions in Early Jewish and Christian Literature*, WUNT 2/305 [Tübingen: Mohr Siebeck, 2011]) explore the affinities of Enochic literature with the Catholic Epistles. Loren Stuckenbruck and Mark D. Mathews ("The Apocalypse of John, *1 Enoch*, and the Question of Influence," in Stuckenbruck, *The Myth of Rebellious Angels: Studies in Second Temple Judaism and New Testament Texts*, WUNT 335 [Tübingen: Mohr Siebeck, 2014], 281–325) examine the possible influence of Enochic traditions on John's Apocalypse and establish a list of significant parallels or affinities.

5. As essays in this volume make clear, some studies suggest awareness of Enochic literature (or traditions) on the part of the Synoptics. This is suggested also, for example, by Sverre Aalen, "St Luke's Gospel and the Last Chapters of I Enoch," *NTS* 13 (1966): 1–13; the work of Nickelsburg on Matthew and the Book of the Watchers ("Enoch, Levi, and Peter," 599) and on Luke and the Epistle of Enoch ("Riches, the Rich, and God's Judgment in 1 Enoch 92–105 and the Gospel according to Luke," *NTS* 25 [1978–1979]: 544–45), and of Michael Patella, *The Death of Jesus: The Diabolical Force and the Ministering Angel (Luke 23, 44–49)*, CahRB 43 (Paris: Gabalda, 1999), 143–44, 161, 167, 171–72, who argues that Luke echoes the scene in 2 En. 67 of the crowds watching Enoch's ascension. See also the rich collection of essays edited by James H. Charlesworth and Darrell L. Bock, *The Parables of Enoch: A Paradigm Shift*, JCTCRS 11 (London: Bloomsbury T&T Clark, 2013).

ogy, downplaying, likely for theological reasons, emphases common to the otherworldly beings in Enoch literature.

Toward juxtaposing traditions of heavenly beings in Enoch traditions and the Synoptics, we first consider angelology in the Second Temple period. This broad examination sets the stage for a discussion of heavenly beings in Enochic literature and the Synoptic Gospels. Also important to the study is a discussion of the literature and the limitations of this sort of examination. Finally, as a sort of test case or probe toward illumining distinctions among these works, the roles of angels in the realm of the dead and places associated with postmortem judgment are examined in Enoch traditions and the Synoptics. These traditions are sufficiently different and highlight aspects of the gospels' theologies that help account for the variances.

HEAVENLY BEINGS IN THE SECOND TEMPLE PERIOD

Though heavenly beings are present in various books of the Hebrew Bible (including the oldest strata)[6] interest in these personalities especially flourished in the Second Temple period.[7] In works of this period, messengers (מלאכים) and the distinctive מלאך יהוה—figures we commonly identify with angels—otherworldly figures such as seraphim (Isa 6:2–6), cherubim (Gen 3:24; 2 Sam 22:11; Ezek 10:1–22; Ps 18:11; see

---

6. These include: בני־האלהים ("sons of [the] God" or "sons of the divine beings"; Gen 6:2, 4; Job 1:6; 2:1; 38:7; οἱ υἱοὶ τοῦ θεοῦ ["sons of God"; Gen 6:2, 4 LXX] and οἱ ἄγγελοι τοῦ θεοῦ ["messengers of God"; Job 1:6 LXX]); בני־אלים ("sons of divine beings"; Pss 29:1; 89:7; υἱοὶ θεοῦ ["sons of God"; Pss 28:1; 88:7 LXX]; cf. אלים in 1QHª XV 31; XVIII 10; XXIII 23; 1QM I 10, 11; 4Q181 frag. 1 II 4), אלהים ("divinities"; Ps 82:1), and קדשים ("holy ones"; Ps 89:6; ἁγίων [Ps 88:6 LXX]; cf. 1QM I 16; XII 1). These otherworldly beings serve in various roles such as משרת ("minister"; Ps 103:21; λειτουργοί [Ps 102:21 LXX]), שר ("commander"; Josh 5:14; LXX ἀρχιστράτηγος); צבא ("host" or "army"; Pss 89:9; 103:21; δύναμις [Pss 88:9; 102:21 LXX]); and צבא השמים ("host of heaven"; 1 Kgs 22:19; LXX ἡ στρατιὰ τοῦ οὐρανοῦ). Otherworldly beings are arguably best known in the Hebrew Bible as messengers (sg., מלאך; ἄγγελος); prominent among these are "the messenger of the LORD" (מלאך יהוה; ἄγγελος κυρίου; e.g., Gen 16:7).

7. See, e.g., Hans Bietenhard, *Die himmlische Welt im Urchristentum und Spätjudentum* (Tübingen: Mohr Siebeck, 1951), 101–4; Michael Mach, *Entwicklungsstadien des jüdischen Engelglaubens in vorrabinischer Zeit*, TSAJ 34 (Tübingen: Mohr Siebeck, 1992); and Carol A. Newsom, "Angels," *ABD* 1:248–53, esp. 249, 252–53.

4Q403 frag. 1 ii 15; 11QShirShabb frag. 5 9; frag. 7 5), and living beings (חיות; Ezek 1:5–15) are depicted in the heavenly realms. Additional otherworldly beings emerge in this time that are rooted in heavenly realia of earlier biblical texts.[8] For instance, the chariot throne of Ezek 1 and 10, which consists of various components, gives rise to at least three different sorts of heavenly beings; אופנים ("wheels"; Ezek 1:16), גלגל ("wheelwork"; Ezek 10:13) and כסא ("throne"; Ezek 1:26; T. Levi 3; Col 1:16) become animate entities within the divine world. Astral bodies also are understood to be obedient servants who dwell in the heavens.[9] Angelic interpreters typically take the guise of men (Dan 8:15; 9:21) and sometimes manifest theophanic attributes (Dan 10:5–6). Otherwise, heavenly beings in the presence of God assume the extraordinary nature of the divine realm and are linked especially with fire or, if part of the heavenly sanctuary, become animate.[10] Interest in these otherworldly beings coincides with speculation concerning the natural world, astronomy and time reckoning—areas of interest to sages in ancient Israel as well as in cognate cultures.

Other designations emerge in Second Temple writings for heavenly beings. One particular type of being is known as עיר/עירין ("Watcher/s"; MT Dan 4:10, 14, 20; Jub. 4:15, 22; CD II 18; 1QapGen II 1, 16; 4Q543 8), creatures that remain awake and guard divine interests.[11] The Dead Sea Scrolls—not a homogenous collection of texts or texts reflecting a single community—also use a variety of terms for heavenly beings, draw-

---

8. So Newsom, "Angels," 249. See also Saul M. Olyan, *A Thousand Thousands Served Him: Exegesis and the Naming of Angels in Ancient Judaism,* TSAJ 36 (Tübingen: Mohr Siebeck, 1993), esp. 3–13 on the growing interest in angels and their spheres of influence in the postexilic period and the reasons for such developments.

9. See, e.g., 1 Kgs 22:19 (2 Chr 18:18); Ps 103:21; Neh 9:6; Dan 8:10; and Rev 1:16.

10. On angels having a luminous or fiery appearance, see Kevin Sullivan, *Wrestling with Angels: A Study of the Relationship between Angels and Humans in Ancient Jewish Literature and the New Testament,* AGJU 55 (Leiden: Brill, 2004), 30–31. On inanimate objects developing into heavenly beings, see, e.g., Ra'anan S. Boustan, "Angels in the Architecture: Temple Art and the Poetics of Praise in the Songs of the Sabbath Sacrifice," in *Heavenly Realms and Earthly Realities in Late Antique Religions,* ed. Ra'anan S. Boustan and Annette Yoshiko Reed (New York: Cambridge University Press, 2004), 204–5.

11. See also T. Reu. 5:6–7 and T. Naph. 3:5. *Grigori* in 2 En. 18:1 derives from Gk. γρήγοροι. See Robert Murray, "The Origin of Aramaic *ʿir,* Angel," *Or* 53 (1984): 303–17; and Nickelsburg, *1 Enoch 1,* 140.

ing especially on the language of רוחות ("spirits"; 1QH^a IX 11).[12] Greek traditions likewise communicate a variety of expressions used for heavenly beings. Paul refers to classes of otherworldly beings like ἀρχαί ("rulers"; Rom 8:38), ἐξουσία ("authority"; e.g., 1 Cor 15:24) and δυνάμις ("power"; Rom 8:38; 1 Cor 15:24). Thus the catalog of heavenly beings within early Judaism is extensive, including angels, Watchers, hosts, holy ones, cherubim, seraphim, ophannim, thrones, powers, and even astral bodies, like stars. Foremost are angels who are messengers, guides, interpreters, and overseers (cf. Jub. 2:2; 1QH^a IX 1–10).

Celestial beings also come to be identified by personal names and are organized into hierarchies (e.g., the angels of holiness, spirits, powers [Jub. 15:27, 32]).[13] These are often presented as worshiping God along with human participants and in heaven (4QBerakhot; Songs of the Sabbath Sacrifice; Rev 4).[14] As speculation about numerous heavenly strata arose

---

12. These include: including רוחי אמת ("spirits of truth"; 1QS IV 23; 1QM XIII 10), רוחות דעת ("spirits of knowledge"; 1QH^a XI 23), and רוחי גורלו ("spirits of his lot"; 1QS III 24; 1QM XIII 2, 4; 11QMelch II 12). There are also אלוהי אורים ("divinities of light"; 4Q405 frag. 46 2), and other titles combined with אלוהי הרמים and אלי ("lofty ones"; 4Q403 frag. 1 I 30). On references to heavenly beings among the Dead Sea Scrolls, see Maxwell J. Davidson, *Angels at Qumran: A Comparative Study of 1 Enoch 1–36, 72–108 and Sectarian Writings from Qumran*, JSPSup 11 (Sheffield: Sheffield Academic, 1992), 142–285; Michael Mach, "Angels," *EDSS* 1:24–27; and Cecilia Wassen, "Angels in the Dead Sea Scrolls," in *Angels: The Concept of Celestial Beings: Origins, Development and Reception*, ed. Friedrich V. Reiterer, Tobias Nicklas, and Karin Schöpflin; Deuterocanonical and Cognate Literature Yearbook 2007 (Berlin: de Gruyter, 2007), 499–520.

13. Bill Rebiger, "Angels in Rabbinic Literature," in Reiterer, Nicklas, and Schöpflin, *Angels*, 629–44, esp. 633–34. On angelic hierarchies in Jubilees, see James C. VanderKam, "The Angel of the Presence," *DSD* 7 (2000): 379.

14. For differing approaches to the topic of angelic and human worship and to the Songs of the Sabbath Sacrifice, see Carol Newsom, *Songs of the Sabbath Sacrifice: A Critical Edition*, HSS 27 (Atlanta: Scholars Press, 1985); Newsom, "'Sectually Explicit' Literature from Qumran," in *The Hebrew Bible and Its Interpreters*, ed. William Henry Propp, Baruch Halpern, and David Noel Freedman, BJSUCSD 1 (Winona Lake, IN: Eisenbrauns, 1990), 167–87, esp. 179–85; Newsom and James H. Charlesworth, "Angelic Liturgy: Songs of the Sabbath Sacrifice (4Q400–4Q407, 11Q17, Mas1k)," in *Angelic Liturgy: Songs of the Sabbath Sacrifice*, ed. James H. Charlesworth and Carol Newsom, vol. 4B of *The Dead Sea Scrolls: Hebrew, Aramaic, and Greek Texts with English Translations*; ed. James H. Charlesworth (Tübingen: Mohr Siebeck; Louisville: Westminster John Knox, 1999), 3–12; James R. Davila, *Liturgical Works*, Eerdmans Commentaries on the Dead Sea Scrolls (Grand Rapids: Eerdmans, 2000), 83–167; and

during the Common Era, heavenly beings come to be associated with particular levels of heaven (Ascen. Isa. 6:13).[15] Further, various classes of heavenly beings are assigned particular tasks that maintain the cosmos (Jub. 2:2; Dan 12:1; Ascen. Isa. 7:19–20). They might combat otherworldly opponents and fight alongside humankind in battle (e.g., Josh 5:13–15; Dan 10:13, 20–21; throughout the War Scroll; 2 Macc 3:25; 5:2; 11:6–8).[16]

Often, an individual figure has a leading role among the angels. Designations for this figure include the angel of the Presence (Jub. 1:26, 28), the angel of truth (1QS III 24), and the prince of light(s) (CD V 18; 1QS III 20; 1QM XIII 10).[17] Further, groups of angels, typically known as archangels (sg. ὁ ἀρχάγγελος) or angels of the Presence are conspicuous in Second Temple traditions, and many are given personal names (Tob 12:15; 1QM IX 15–16). Michael is among the more prominent of these and is often identified as the leader of all angelic figures (Dan 12:1; 1QS III 20; 1QM XVII 6–7; LAE 13–15).[18] Such developed portraits of heavenly beings are especially visible from the Second Temple period to late antiquity in apocalyptic, pseudepigraphal, *merkabah*, and *hekhalot* texts,[19] though they are not absent from late antique Christian works that also take up heavenly realms.[20]

Crispin H. T. Fletcher-Louis, *All the Glory of Adam: Liturgical Anthropology in the Dead Sea Scrolls* (Leiden: Brill, 2002), 252–394.

15. See J. Edward Wright, *The Early History of Heaven* (New York: Oxford University Press, 2000), 98–116, 139–84.

16. Aleksander R. Michalak, *Angels as Warriors in Late Second Temple Jewish Literature,* WUNT 2/330 (Tübingen: Mohr Siebeck, 2012); Gillian Bampfylde, "The Prince of the Host in the Book of Daniel and the Dead Sea Scrolls," *JSJ* 14 (1983): 129–34; and Davidson, *Angels at Qumran,* 212–32. See Michalak, *Angels as Warriors,* 192–205, on analogous Greek traditions of heavenly warriors or interventions of gods.

17. For a survey of these traditions, see Larry W. Hurtado, "Monotheism, Principal Angels, and the Background of Christology," in *The Oxford Handbook of the Dead Sea Scrolls,* ed. Timothy H. Lim and John J. Collins (Oxford: Oxford University Press, 2010), 546–64.

18. Darrell D. Hannah, *Michael and Christ: Michael Traditions and Angel Christology in Early Christianity,* WUNT 2/109 (Tübingen: Mohr Siebeck, 1999), 25–75.

19. See comments on angelology in Peter Schäfer, *The Hidden and Manifest God: Some Major Themes in Early Jewish Mysticism,* trans. Aubrey Pomerance (Albany: State University of New York Press, 1992), 21–36, 62–66, 81–86, 103–7, 129–34.

20. Consider the second-century Testament of Levi, which describes αἱ δυνάμεις τῶν παρεμβολῶν ("the powers of encampment"; 3:3), θρόνοι, ἐξουσίαι ("thrones and authorities"; 3:8), and οἱ ἄγγελοι τοῦ προσώπου κυρίου ("angels of the presence of the

Otherworldly Beings in Enochic Literature
and the Synoptic Gospels

The early Enoch literature showcases well Second Temple developments in angelology, providing extended discussions of heavenly beings and their responsibilities. It would be an understatement to say that heavenly beings are prominent in writings associated with Enoch.[21] Liminal beings abound in the celestial realms that are explored through this literature, perpetually worshiping and attending to the Divine in the heavenly temple (e.g., 1 En. 14:22–23; 39:12–13; 40:1, 3–5; 61:6–13). At the same time, they lead the seer to otherworldly places, overseeing particular aspects or areas of the cosmos (17–36; 72–82; 41; 43–44; 52–56; 108:6–8). Angels (also designated "Watchers" and "holy ones") appear as heroes, intervening on behalf of humankind (9–10; 47:2; 104:1) and delivering communication from God (especially as *angeli interpretes*, 17–36; 53:3–7; 108). At the same time, some rebel against God, begetting violence and imparting forbidden knowledge (6–8; 15–16; 64:1–2; 69; 86:1, 3–6). In similar manner, astral bodies appear as obedient and disobedient forces (2:1; 18:12–16; 21:3–6; 33:3–36:4; 41:5–8; 43:1–4; 74:2; 75:3; 79:6; 80:7; 86:1, 3). Enochic literature features the range of beings that would become commonplace in later *merkabah* and *hekhalot* traditions. In many of the Enochic writings, heavenly beings are at least as prominent as the seer associated with these texts.

The texts' interest in the otherworld relates to the texts' interest in the numerous sorts of beings that inhabit the divine realm and serve the Creator; at the same time, much of the Enochic literature seems familiar with and engages traditions we find also in the Hebrew Bible, including representations of the otherworld and its inhabitants (e.g., Ezekiel). The different sorts of beings noted in the Enoch literature include "sons of heaven" (1 En. 6:2; 14:3), "Watchers" (4Q206 frag. 2 II); 1 En. 10:7 [Greek]; 1 En.

Lord"; 3:5), drawing on earlier expressions given to heavenly beings. For a later example, one can consider the fifth/sixth-century *Celestial Hierarchy* of Pseudo-Dionysius, which provides a systematic approach to heavenly beings arranged according to three categories. The first hierarchy consists of seraphim, cherubim, and thrones; the second: dominions, virtues, and powers; the third: principalities, archangels, and angels. This late antique Christian work imagines a plethora of heavenly beings of varied natures and ranks, a perspective also reflected in Second Temple traditions.

21. For an overview of angels in literature attributed to Enoch found among the Dead Sea Scrolls, see Davidson, *Angels at Qumran*, 31–129.

12:2; 22:6; 2 En. 18:1),[22] "angels of the power" (1 En. 20:1; 61:10 [both Greek]), or archangels (1 En. 71:3; 79:6; 2 En. 19:3; 21:3), "the angel of peace" (1 En. 60:24), hosts (1 En. 1:4; 47:3; 60:1, 4; 61:10; 82:7), cherubim (1 En. 14:11, 18; 20:7; 61:10; 2 En. 19:6; 20:1; 21:1; 22:2), seraphim (1 En. 61:10; 2 En. 20:1; 21:1; 22:3), ophannim (1 En. 61:10; 71:7), and "angels of the principalities" (1 En. 61:10). Stars, understood as sentient beings, are included among heavenly beings as well; the extent to which these are sometimes understood as angels qua messengers is not clear. Some texts present angels governing stars.[23] In terms of hierarchies, there are named angels who belong to an elite group of four or seven angels.[24] Angels are also called "holy ones" (1 En. 1:2, 9; 60:4). Comparable to depictions of heavenly beings in the Hebrew Bible and other Second Temple period texts, these otherworldly beings may well be shape shifters and associated with fire (1 En. 17:1; 18:11; 21:7; 2 En. 20:1; 29:3; cf. 1 En. 14:11; Ps 104:4). Though they are not supposed to procreate because they are beings of spirit rather than flesh (1 En. 15:3–7, 10), these beings are capable of doing so (1 En. 6:1–2).

Turning to the Synoptic Gospels, we note that many of the roles assumed by heavenly beings in these works are also comparable to what one sees in Second Temple angelologies and also suggest indebtedness to the thought world of the Hebrew Scriptures. The evangelists most frequently refer to otherworldly beings as messengers sent from the Divine (Matt 1:20, 24; 2:13, 19; 28:5; Luke 1:11, 13, 18, 19, 26, 30, 35, 38; 2:9–10;

---

22. Enochic literature suggests that the name of this heavenly being may derive from the idea that Watchers do not sleep (1 En. 71:7) and watch over the deeds of humankind (1 En. 20:1). On the use of "Watchers" in Enochic literature, see also Nickelsburg, *1 Enoch 1*, 140–41.

23. See George Nickelsburg and James VanderKam, *1 Enoch 2: A Commentary on the Book of 1 Enoch, Chapters 37–82*, Hermeneia (Minneapolis: Fortress, 2012), 413, 445.

24. On the tradition of four and seven archangels in Enochic literature, see K. Coblentz Bautch, "Putting Angels in Their Place: Developments in Second Temple Angelology," in "*With Wisdom as a Robe*": *Qumran and Other Jewish Studies in Honour of Ida Fröhlich*, ed. Károly Daniel Dobos and Miklós Köszeghy, HBM 21 (Sheffield: Sheffield Phoenix, 2009), 174–88. In addition to groups of four and seven angels, 3 Bar. 4:7 knows five archangels. Some traditions also focus on six prominent angels (e.g., Tg. Pseudo-Jonathan to Deut 34:6). The preference for six could be rooted in the tradition of the six angels of Ezek 9:2 or be associated with Near Eastern traditions of six planetary deities. See Bietenhard, *Himmlische Welt*, 106–7.

24:23; cf. Acts 7:53; 8:26; 10:3, 7, 22; 30, 35, 38; 27:23); here they reveal and explain divine information otherwise unavailable to human beings (Luke 1:26–37; Matt 1:20). Angels also warn humans of impending danger (Matt 2:13), minister to humans,[25] and protect the righteous (Matt 4:6; Luke 4:10). Angels were thought to be heavenly warriors, who can be invoked by God's agents (Matt 26:53).

To recall court angelology, the angels in the gospels have explicit roles vis-à-vis the Divine as well. These otherworldly beings worship the Divine (Luke 2:13–14) and dwell in the heavens (Matt 28:2; cf. John 1:51[26]), where they represent the righteous as guardians or perhaps heavenly counterparts (Matt 18:10; Acts 12:15). To that end, they preserve the righteous and elect (Matt 24:31; Luke 4:10; 15:10; 16:22; 22:43; Acts 5:19; 12:11, 23) and appear in eschatological scenarios of judgment (Mark 13:27; Matt 13:39, 49; 25:31; Luke 12:8, 9). For example, they accompany the Son of Man when he comes in judgment and for recompense (Mark 8:38; Matt 16:27; Luke 9:26). Angels may have access to otherworldly realms, such as the heavenly paradise for the deceased (Luke 16:22).[27] Though they can appear as humans (Acts 12:15), they also have a distinctive countenance (Acts 6:15) and do not procreate (Mark 12:25; Matt 22:30). Moreover, otherworldly beings can also serve the devil (the devil has his angels; Matt 25:41) and be destined for punishment in eternal fire.

Outstanding commonalities shared by Enochic traditions and the Synoptics concern angels as intercessors and angels participating in eschatological contexts. As to the former, in almost all strata of Enochic works, angels serve as intercessors for humankind, especially in terms of the righteous having access to justice (cf., e.g., 1 En. 9; 39:5; 47:2; 104:1). This view of angels calls to mind Matt 18:10, which presents the idea of heavenly patrons interceding on behalf of humankind.

---

25. Does the tradition of the angels ministering to Jesus in the temptation (Mark 1:13; Matt 4:11) indicate a low Christology, where Jesus is protected and served as other righteous individuals would be, or a high Christology, where the angels are serving/fulfilling duties to Jesus as to God?

26. The angels ascending and descending in John 1:51 (alluding to Gen 28:12) also communicate a connection between the divine realm and the Son of Man, in line with John's Christology.

27. In Gos. Pet. 9:35–11:44 and Apoc. Pet. 4, angels have special access to the realm of the dead.

Angels also play distinctive roles in contexts of eschatological judgment, with several parallels between the Synoptics and Enochic traditions
appearing in the Book of Parables (1 En. 37–71) and the Epistle of Enoch
(1 En. 92–105). In the Synoptics, angels gather the elect (Mark 8:38 [//
Matt 16:27 // Luke 9:26]; Mark 13:27 [// Matt 24:31]), much as angels
in the Parables seek out the righteous dead for a blessed afterlife (1 En.
61:1–5). Angels accompany the Son of Man when he comes in glory (Matt
25:31; Luke 12:8–9; cf. 1 En. 1:3–4),[28] and the Son of Man acknowledges
people before the angels of God and attends to gathering up the wicked at
the end times for punishment (1 En. 62:11; 63:1; 100:4; cf. also 103:7). As
Loren Stuckenbruck notes, the latter motif, as found especially in 1 En.
100:4 (Epistle of Enoch) and 90:26 (Animal Apocalypse) anticipates the
harvesting or reaping angels of Matt 13:38–50 (cf. also Rev 14:18–20; and
for possible earlier precedents, see Isa 63:1–6; Lam 1:15; Joel 4:2, 12).[29]

Despite these commonalities, the numerous types of heavenly beings
and hierarchies of other Second Temple literature are absent from the New
Testament gospels. The Synoptics favor simply the designation "angel(s),"
"messenger(s)," or "angel of the Lord," though Luke also knows and names
Gabriel.[30] The absence of different sorts of heavenly beings may well be
due to the dictates of the genre (see below), with these first-century gospels
having little interest in speculation on heavenly beings and otherworldly
realms. It is also possible that the evangelists are concerned that audiences
of a Hellenistic ethos would confuse heavenly beings with Greek divinities (who could communicate with humans directly and could also be
called ἄγγελοι [Lactantius, *Inst.* 1.7.1]) or with intermediary figures like
lesser gods, heroes, and the deceased.[31] Thus the Synoptics could work to

---

28. On this text and the possibility of Matthean dependence upon the Parables,
see Grant Macaskill, "Matthew and the *Parables of Enoch*," in Charlesworth and Bock,
Parables of Enoch, 218–30; and Leslie Walck, "The *Parables of Enoch* and the Synoptic
Gospels," in Charlesworth and Bock, *Parables of Enoch,* 254–58.

29. See Loren T. Stuckenbruck, *1 Enoch 91–108,* CEJL (Berlin: de Gruyter; 2008),
434–35.

30. The terms favored are ὁ ἄγγελος (Luke 1:13, 18, 19, 30, 34, 35, 38; 2:10, 13,
21; 22:43), οἱ ἄγγελοι (Matt 4:6, 11; 13:39, 41, 49; 16:27; 18:10; 22:30; 24:31, 36; 25:31,
41; 26:53; Mark 1:13; 8:38; 12:25; 13:27, 32; Luke 2:15; 4:10; 9:26; 12:8, 9; 15:10; 16:22;
20:36; 24:23), ἄγγελος κυρίου (Matt 1:20, 24; 2:13, 19; 28:2, 5; Luke 1:11; 2:9), and
Γαβριήλ or ὁ ἄγγελος Γαβριήλ (Luke 1:19, 26). Rarely does reference to the heavenly
host, πλῆθος στρατιᾶς οὐρανίου (Luke 2:13; cf. Acts 7:42), appear.

31. Lactantius, in the third-fourth centuries, is careful, for example, in his apolo-

assuage references to angels to ensure that readers inundated with poly-theism would not mistake angels as deities. They could also help readers see how angels are, as in many of the writings of the Hebrew Bible, clearly envoys of the Lord and manifestations of God's presence.[32]

One key explanation for the differences as well concerns the Synoptic Gospels' emphasis on Jesus. As intermediary figures go, Jesus is the focus of the Synoptics; he assumes easily the various roles afforded angelic beings. Moreover, these angelic beings now attend to, defer to, and assist Jesus, accentuating his status. Understandably, the aim of the evangelists would be to amplify the divinity of Jesus and to distinguish him from other heavenly beings, which are presented as serving Jesus. As the title of Susan Garrett's monograph suggests, the Synoptic Gospels would demonstrate that Jesus is, indeed, "no ordinary angel," and the angels that appear in these works do not approximate him.[33] Ancient impulses confusing Jesus with angels are checked, for example, in the book of Revelation, which communicates that angels are not to be worshiped (19:10; 22:9).[34]

CONSIDERATIONS

As we contemplate the angelologies among the Enochic writings and the Synoptic Gospels, one should consider the distinctive foci of these respective corpora—corpora contrived for the purposes of our studies. The Synoptic Gospels (if they can be thought to reflect a certain type of genre) mean to present the public ministry, death, and resurrection of Jesus, often making clear the association of these with the traditions of Israel.[35] The Enochic writings tend to link a contemporaneous audience

---

getics to distinguish angels of Christian tradition from Greco-Roman divinities, antic-ipating confusion or incorrect assumptions on the part of his audience. Even while acknowledging that God can have ministers, Lactantius denies that the latter can also be gods. See Emil Schneweis, *Angels and Demons according to Lactantius* (Washing-ton, DC: Catholic University of America Press, 1944), 1–14.

32. My thanks to Michael Patella for this observation.

33. Susan Garrett, *No Ordinary Angel: Celestial Spirits and Christian Claims about Jesus* (New Haven: Yale University Press, 2008).

34. Loren Stuckenbruck, *Angel Veneration and Christology*, WUNT 2/70 (Tübin-gen: Mohr Siebeck, 1995), 111–39, 203–4, 245–60.

35. The New Testament gospels are often examined as Hellenistic biographies (βίοι; see, e.g., M. Eugene Boring, *Introduction to the New Testament: History, Liter-ature, Theology* [Louisville: Westminster John Knox, 2012], 507–8), though Boring

understood to live in the end times (better: end of an era or particular age) with wisdom communicated via antediluvian figures. The Enochic writings also reveal information about the cosmos and the divine order. There are, therefore, some fundamental differences among these texts that challenge comparisons.

Texts associated with Enoch and Synoptics *do* overlap in the areas of wisdom and apocalypticism.[36] With attention to a "Son of Man," also identified as "Chosen One," "Righteous One," and "Messiah," the Parables (1 En. 37–71) recall the Synoptics' concentration on a particular individual. Still, the interest is especially on this figure's heavenly existence, link to a particular community, and primordial and eschatological role. This sort of presentation of Jesus is available in the Logos traditions associated with Johannine texts and in early christological expressions;[37] with the exception of wisdom traditions and the eschatological Son of Man, the Synoptic Gospels concern especially Jesus's earthly ministry, death, and resurrection.

That is, the texts under consideration have different aims even when they share common ground.[38] Though selections may share generic resemblances, such as paraenesis, when it comes to angelologies, the Synoptic Gospels are not as interested in the heavenly realms and denizens as are many Enochic writings and, say, the book of Revelation.[39] The Synoptics

---

(509–10) also notes features that distinguish the gospel tradition from ancient biographies, for example, the kerygmatic nature of the gospels ("the act of God in the Christ event"). For a different approach to the matter of gospel and genre, see Helmut Koester, *Ancient Christian Gospels: Their History and Development* (Philadelphia: Trinity Press International, 1990), 9–48.

36. See, e.g., Charlesworth and Bock, *Parables of Enoch.*

37. See Jack T. Sanders, *The New Testament Christological Hymns: Their Historical Religious Background,* SNTSMS 15 (Cambridge: Cambridge University Press, 1971), 9–20.

38. For a comparable observation, see Christopher Rowland and Christopher Morray-Jones, *The Mystery of God: Early Jewish Mysticism and the New Testament,* CRINT 12 (Leiden: Brill, 2009), 99.

39. Especially on the matter of genre and depiction of angels, see George J. Brooke, review of *Angels at Qumran: A Comparative Study of 1 Enoch 1–36, 72–108 and Sectarian Writings from Qumran,* by Maxwell J. Davidson, *JQR* 86 (1995): 186–89, esp. 188. To paraphrase, Brooke observes (188) that all texts are not to be approached in the same manner when it comes to examining the appearance of angels in writings; that is, angels are not simply a widespread literary motif. He continues: "The way [angels] are described and used in any particular text is as much a function of that

are not formally apocalypses, though they share with Enochic literature apocalyptic imagery and perspectives.[40]

Methodological attentiveness also obliges one to recognize that Enochic writings are texts that range in date and reflect various communities and contexts. It is not possible to speak of *an* Enoch tradition or corpus in the singular. Writings affiliated with Enoch emerge over several centuries and are preserved in various languages by diverse communities.[41] Our understanding of the development of the anthology 1 Enoch is limited also. Known as the Ethiopic Book of Enoch, 1 Enoch has been preserved in Geʿez among Ethiopian Christians, but otherwise this particular anthology is unattested. As if to remind us to be cautious in reconstructing an ancient collection on the basis of a contemporary anthology, the Book of Parables has not been found among the writings associated with Enoch at Qumran. Overall, the complex nature and history of 1 Enoch militates against claims of a singular Enochic tradition, let alone an ancient Enochic corpus. While some early Enochic texts may have circulated together,[42] one cannot speak

---

text's genre as it is of any common motif"; without apocalypses, we should not expect rich descriptions of angels.

40. See Nickelsburg, *1 Enoch 1*, 37, who reports: "all the major sections of 1 Enoch and many of their component parts either provide background for (the theme of God's coming judgment and its consequences: blessings for the righteous and curses for the sinners) or elaborate on it and give it prominence." On the apocalyptic outlook of the Synoptics and other New Testament writings, see Edward Adams, *The Stars Will Fall from Heaven: Cosmic Catastrophe in the New Testament and Its World*, LNTS 347 (London: T&T Clark, 2007), 133–81; and Frederick Murphy, *Apocalypticism in the Bible and Its World: A Comprehensive Introduction* (Grand Rapids: Baker Academic, 2012), 227–378. For a recent study of apocalypticism, along with eschatology, resurrection, and messianism, in the New Testament and certain Enochic writings, see Albert L. A. Hogeterp, *Expectations of the End: A Comparative Traditio-Historical Study of Eschatological, Apocalyptic and Messianic Ideas in the Dead Sea Scrolls and the New Testament*, STDJ 83 (Leiden: Brill, 2009), esp. 342–56, 400–408.

41. See, e.g., Nickelsburg, *1 Enoch 1*, 16; and more recently, Loren T. Stuckenbruck, "The *Book of Enoch*: Its Reception in Second Temple Jewish and in Christian Tradition," *Early Christianity* 4 (2013): 7–40, who expresses well the varied nature of Enoch traditions evident in extant traditions. Most noticeably, 1 Enoch consists of distinctive booklets (the Book of the Watchers [1 En. 1–36]; the Book of Parables [1 En. 37–71]; the Astronomical Book [1 En. 72–82]; the Book of Dreams [1 En. 83–90]; the Epistle of Enoch [1 En. 91–105]; plus material related to Noah and ch. 108), sections or units of text that reveal, without too much scrutiny, seams and multiple sources.

42. Randall D. Chesnutt, "*Oxyrhynchus Papyrus* 2069 and the Composition History of *1 Enoch*," *JBL* 129 (2010): 485–505.

with confidence of a single ancient corpus or of the shape of a hypothesized corpus.

Other distinctive collections associated with Enoch, namely 2 and 3 Enoch, make clear this point as well. Second Enoch, preserved in Slavonic with portions extant in Coptic, and 3 Enoch, preserved in Hebrew, speak to additional, distinctive trajectories of Enochic traditions. Moreover, a number of texts, both Jewish and Christian, employ traditions associated with Enochic literature; the Book of the Giants and Genesis Apocryphon, for instance, include themes established in early Enoch literature in very different contexts, challenging the view of a single tradition or school.

In this respect, the Enochic writings—however one comes to associate that label with a particular text—are diverse and should be approached the way one would literature in an anthology like the New Testament. The Synoptic Gospels are complicated texts as well. These early Christian writings consist of numerous traditions—for example, miracle stories, apophthegms, logia, parables, passion accounts—that have been rigorously examined on their own terms; distinctive forms within the Synoptic Gospels remind scholars of the diverse settings behind the individual units of text or traditions (and how these might influence angelologies). As with Enochic texts, the Synoptic Gospels must also be approached as redacted works and studied diachronically, with special attention given to how they relate to one another. Acknowledging the strata in and composite nature of the Synoptic Gospels and Enochic writings, as well as the distinctive contexts out of which these emerge, one realizes the challenges in comparing angelologies.[43]

---

43. To speak of "an" angelology of even just one of the booklets associated with 1 Enoch, like the Book of the Watchers, made up of distinctive literary units betraying numerous sources, would be problematic. On distinct units within the Book of the Watchers and the source contributing to these, see Nickelsburg, *1 Enoch 1*, 7, 132, 169–70, 278, 230, 292–93. To provide but one example, the Book of the Watchers knows different sets of archangels: one set of four (1 En. 9–10) and another of seven (1 En. 20); moreover, the names and order of these archangels fluctuate. For variations in the order and names of these angels in the Aramaic, Greek, and Ethiopic manuscript traditions, see Coblentz Bautch, "Putting Angels in Their Place." All this is to say that the Enochic writings about angels reflect complex and dynamic traditions.

ANGELS AND THE REALM OF THE DEAD: A TEST CASE

While the Synoptics and Enochic literature have different literary aims, they share some common perspectives on angelology and demonology. The worldview in these writings takes for granted that angels can intervene and intercede on behalf of humans and have eschatological roles, just as demons can plague humankind. Yet heavenly beings in the Synoptic Gospels are more muted—for example, there are not the same varied classifications and titles for angels—especially when contrasted with early Enoch literature like the Book of the Watchers. Further, the angels in the Synoptics also lack distinctive functions or roles, such as being given dominion over particular spheres (e.g., the realm of the dead). This is the case even when later Christian texts, taking up topics treated by the Synoptics like the scene at the tomb, would introduce angels in more active ways (like removing the stone from the tomb or assisting Jesus in departing from the tomb). These later Christian views of angels are reminiscent of the angels one sees especially in early Enoch traditions, like the Book of the Watchers, where an archangel is associated with Tartarus or with the resurrection. Yet, in the Synoptics, heavenly beings have a very faint connection to liminal spaces.

Angels appear in Second Temple literature as attending to particular functions and governing various realms (e.g., 1 En. 20). With interest in liminal, otherworldly places, Enochic literature gives angels oversight of inaccessible places like the realm of the dead, places of punishment, and paradise.[44] As with angelology, because Enochic texts are themselves of varied backgrounds, views of liminal places are not homogenous. For example, the Book of the Watchers (fourth or third century BCE) understands the dead to await final judgment in an inaccessible place at the ends of the earth. In 1 En. 22, the realm of the dead is conceived as a mountain with pits that hold the spirits of the deceased (22:1–3); the realm is likely presented also as a place of darkness near infernal rivers (17:6), comparable to Sheol or Greco-Roman views of the netherworld.[45] The Parables, of the first century BCE or CE, present the righteous dead dwelling in

---

44. See Coblentz Bautch, "Heavenly Beings Brought Low: A Study of Angels and the Netherworld," in Reiterer, Nicklas, and Schöpflin, *Angels*, 59–75.

45. See Coblentz Bautch, *A Study of the Geography of 1 Enoch 17–19: "No One Has Seen What I Have Seen,"* JSJSup 81 (Leiden: Brill, 2003), 84–90.

heaven (39:4–5).[46] Thus these writings evince various views of the realm of
the dead and of afterlife.

In most all of these representations, though, angels play a role in attending to the deceased or the places affiliated with the afterlife. In the Book of
the Watchers, chapter 20 presents three or four angels as overseeing places
associated with the afterlife and postmortem judgment: Uriel is in charge
of Tartarus (20:2);[47] Raphael is over the spirits of men (20:3);[48] Gabriel is
in charge of paradise (20:7); and Remiel is over those who rise (Greek[Pan1]
20:8), a possible reference to resurrection.[49] This brief list does not specify
how these angels govern these realms or relate to the deceased, even while
the work is clear to associate each with some responsibility. These angels

---

46. Nickelsburg (in Nicklesburg and VanderKam, *1 Enoch 2*, 51–52) notes the
lack of uniformity and consistency in the Parables' descriptions of the places of eschatological punishment and reward. For example, in 1 En. 51:1–5 the righteous and
chosen are described as being restored from Sheol. See also Nickelsburg, "Four Worlds
That Are 'Other' in the Enochic Book of Parables," in *Other Worlds and Their Relation
to This World: Early Jewish and Ancient Christian Traditions,* ed. Tobias Nicklas et al.,
JSJSup 143 (Leiden: Brill, 2010), 55–77, esp. 58–65 on heaven as a place for the righteous dead. The Epistle of Enoch and ch. 108 seem to anticipate a period where the
righteous await justice but are later recompensed (102:4–103:8; 108:11–13). See Loren
T. Stuckenbruck, "The Other World in the Epistle of Enoch," in Nicklas et al., *Other
Worlds,* 79–93, on the relationship of the cosmology in the Epistle of Enoch to that of
the Book of the Watchers.

47. Several Ethiopic MSS associate Uriel, instead, with thunder and tremors. Other
references to Uriel in the Second Temple period associate the angel with postmortem
places of punishment and resurrection (LAE 48:1; Apoc. El. 5:5; Sib. Or. 2:215, 227–
237) in support of the Greek reading. See also R. H. Charles, *The Book of Enoch or 1
Enoch* (Oxford: Oxford University Press, 1912), 43; and James C. VanderKam, *Enoch:
A Man for All Generations* (Columbia: University of South Carolina Press, 1995), 52.

48. The name of the angel connotes "healing" (see 1 En. 40:9; Tob 3:17; 12:12–13),
though Raphael is also associated with the realm of the dead comparable to chthonic
deities. See Coblentz Bautch, "Putting Angels in Their Place," 187.

49. This verse is not included in Ethiopic MSS or in a second copy of Gr[Pan]. Perhaps related to Remiel is Jeremiel, the angel of 4 Ezra 4:36 who is in charge of the
souls of the righteous; the latter are confined to a chamber as in 1 En. 22. In Apoc.
Zeph. 6:15–17, Eremiel is the angel of the abyss and Hades. Although some understand "rising" in 1 En. 20:8 to refer to the movement of celestial bodies, others understand the expression as an allusion to resurrection. See Daniel C. Olson, *Enoch: A New
Translation: The Ethiopic Book of Enoch, or 1 Enoch, Translated with Annotations and
Cross-References* (North Richland Hills, TX: BIBAL, 2004), 54, 66; and Nickelsburg, *1
Enoch 1,* 338.

also provide the seer tours of places associated with the dead, postmortem punishment, or paradise. Uriel takes Enoch on a tour of places where rebel angels and transgressing stars are held until the time of final judgment (19:1–2; 21:1–10). Raphael leads the seer to the mountain that serves as the realm of the dead and explains the nature of the place (ch. 22). Though emending the text is required, Gabriel is likely the angel who takes Enoch to the paradise of righteousness (32:1–6).[50] In the Parables, the righteous who have died reside with the angels (39:5). The angel of peace leads the seer on a tour of the valley where the rebel angels will be retained (54:1–5). In the Epistle, the righteous dead are to become companions of the host of heaven (104:6).[51] Reminiscent of the angels in the Book of the Watchers, an *angelus interpres* takes Enoch to a fiery place where sinners and blasphemers are punished (108:5–6).[52]

These accounts are most interested in communicating to readership that places related to divine judgment are built into the cosmos, so as to reaffirm their reality for the faithful.[53] Pseudepigraphal works may well build on this tradition, featuring angels as gatekeepers of the realm of the dead, Sheol, Hades, or Tartarus (see, e.g., Sib. Or. 2.228). The Enochic texts do not take up the soul's journey and so do not present angels at work as in other pseudepigraphal texts, though they are described as having these functions. In the Testament of Abraham Recension A, for instance, the patriarch in the company of Michael sees the souls of the deceased being escorted by angels to the realm of punishment or to paradise (T. Ab. Rec. A 11–14), which anticipates angels accompanying Abraham's soul heavenward (T. Ab. Rec. A 20:10–12; T. Ab. Rec. B 14:7; cf. also T. Mos. 1:6). The Testament of Moses also features a scene where Michael and the devil contend over the body of Moses, recalling the role of angels in afterlife traditions (T. Mos. 8–10; cf. Jude 9).[54]

---

50. See, e.g., Nickelsburg, *1 Enoch 1*, 320–28.

51. Stuckenbruck (*1 Enoch 91–108*, 577) clarifies that the host of heaven are the angels with whom the righteous have been associated in 104:1–2, 4. Though missing from the Chester Beatty papyrus, Stuckenbruck and Nickelsburg accept the statement as original, likely lost through scribal error; see, respectively, *1 Enoch 91–108*, 568, 577; and *1 Enoch 1*, 512, 519.

52. In the Parables (1 En. 53:3; 56:1–3), angels appear as punishing angels. See Coblentz Bautch, "Heavenly Beings Brought Low," 470–71.

53. Coblentz Bautch, *Study of Geography*, 190, 287–89.

54. On the challenges of delineating the Testament of Moses and Assumption of Moses, see Fiona Grierson, "The Testament of Moses," *JSP* 17 (2008): 265–80.

In contrast to Enochic literature, the Synoptic Gospels do not dwell on otherworldly places or provide extended discussions on the realm of the dead and the nature of the afterlife; minor references suggest a plurality of views.[55] Even so, there are certain scenes in the Synoptics that lend themselves to the theme of angels and the realm of the dead.[56] One of these occurs in Luke 16:19–31, where Jesus tells the parable of the rich man and Lazarus.[57] In the parable are descriptions of Hades, a place of torment and flames (ᾅδης; 16:23–25), and a pleasant realm inhabited by the likes of Abraham (16:22).[58] Of interest to our discussion of angels is that the poor man is carried away by angels to his resting place (ἀπενεχθῆναι αὐτὸν ὑπὸ τῶν ἀγγέλων εἰς τὸν κόλπον Ἀβραάμ; 16:22). The rich man inquires of Abraham about a dead man returning to speak to his brothers so that they might not go to a place of torment (16:28). In these conversations, angels are not intermediaries, though they do bring the deceased to an otherworldly paradise. Here we see angels behaving as the psychopomp (ψυχοπομπός) of the ancient world in conducting the soul to its next destination.[59] This example is comparable to the view of angels in pseudepigraphical works like the Testament of Abraham (see also Apoc.

---

55. See, e.g., Claudia Setzer, *Resurrection of the Body in Early Judaism and Christianity: Doctrine, Community, and Self-Definition* (Leiden: Brill, 2004); Jaime Clark-Soles, *Death and the Afterlife in the New Testament* (New York: T&T Clark, 2006); and Adela Yarbro Collins, *Mark: A Commentary*, Hermeneia (Minneapolis: Fortress, 2007), 782–94.

56. Though not the focus of this study, one could also consider how in a dispute with the Sadducees on the matter of resurrection, Jesus suggests that the dead who have risen will be like the angels in heaven (Mark 12:25 // Matt 22:30 // Luke 20:36); the comparison recalls as well the description of the righteous dead in the Epistle of Enoch. In 1 En. 104:4, those who will shine like the luminaries will rejoice also like the angels. See also 2 Bar. 51:5.

57. On the parable in its Lukan context and also in light of Mediterranean parallels, see, e.g., John T. Carroll, *Luke: A Commentary*, NTL (Louisville: Westminster John Knox, 2012), 335–39; and Richard Bauckham, "The Rich Man and Lazarus: The Parable and the Parallels," *NTS* 37 (1991): 225–46.

58. For a detailed examination of otherworldly imagery as it relates to this parable, see Outi Lehtipuu, *The Afterlife Imagery in Luke's Story of the Rich Man and Lazarus*, NovTSup 123 (Leiden: Brill, 2007).

59. Hermes often fulfills this role. See, e.g., Homer, *Od.* 24.1–15; and Lehtipuu, *Afterlife Imagery*, 199–200.

Zeph. 4:1–7).[60] On the other hand, there is much less emphasis on the angelic beings.

The empty tomb traditions that announce Jesus's resurrection from the dead—the climactic moment for the Synoptic Gospels—also feature angels, providing additional prospects for contemplating heavenly beings and the realm of the dead. Though Mark refers enigmatically to the young man dressed in white in the tomb (νεανίσκος; Mark 16:5),[61] Matthew and Luke make clear that the figure or figures in the tomb are angels (Matt 28:2–7 [ἄγγελος κυρίου] and Luke 24:23, which identifies the ἄνδρες δύο [24:4] as angels).[62] The divine messengers communicate to the women that Jesus is not in the tomb but is resurrected from the dead.[63]

Still, the angels in the empty tomb scenes are not explicitly angels associated with the realm of the dead, angels who have guided the deceased from the tomb to the afterlife, or angels who have liberated Jesus from the realm of the dead.[64] No description of the resurrection is provided, and in Matthew and Mark there are no reflections on Jesus's whereabouts prior to resurrection, though other New Testament writings do imagine Jesus in the netherworld or paradise prior to resurrection.[65] Matthew's Gospel, for

---

60. See Anitra B. Kolenkow, "The Angelology of the Testament of Abraham," in *Studies in the Testament of Abraham*, ed. George W. E. Nickelsburg, SCS 6 (Missoula, MT: Scholars Press, 1976), 153–62.

61. For discussion of and possible rationale for Mark's reference to the young man and omission of the language of "angel" in this pericope, see Yarbro Collins, *Mark*, 795–96; and Tobias Nicklas, "Angels in Early Christian Narratives on the Resurrection of Jesus: Canonical and Apocryphal Texts," in Reiterer, Nicklas, and Schöpflin, *Angels*, 294–96.

62. Matthew also makes reference to the "angel of the Lord" in the infancy narrative (1:20, 24) and 2:13, 19.

63. Lehtipuu (*Afterlife Imagery*, 205 n. 46) observes that it is not surprising that angels are present in the resurrection narratives.

64. Cf. Nicklas, "Angels in Early Christian Narratives," 300.

65. These include Luke 23:43 (where Jesus states he will be in paradise following the crucifixion); Eph 4:8–10 (Jesus descends to the lower regions); and 1 Pet 3:18–22 (Jesus preaches to the spirits in prison [likely rebellious angels of Enochic lore]). Probably drawing upon the Gospel of Matthew, Gos. Pet. 41–42 would seem to clarify—by means of the heavenly voice asking if Jesus had made a proclamation to those who had fallen asleep—Matthew's resurrection of the saints. See Tobias Nicklas, "Resurrection in the Gospels of Matthew and Peter: Some Developments," in *Life beyond Death in Matthew's Gospel: Religious Metaphor or Bodily Reality?*, ed. Wim Weren, Huub van de Sandt, and Joseph Verheyden, BTS 13 (Leuven: Peeters, 2011), 27–41, esp. 28, 40–41.

example, depicts the angel arriving at the tomb via descent from heaven (ἄγγελος γὰρ κυρίου καταβὰς ἐξ οὐρανοῦ καὶ προσελθὼν ἀπεκύλισεν τὸν λίθον καὶ ἐκάθητο ἐπάνω αὐτου; Matt 28:2), arguing against the angel's connection to a chthonic realm of the dead.

In contrast to these examples from the Synoptics, other early Christian traditions give a more prominent role to angels in their guise as overseers or gatekeepers of the realm of the dead. For example, in the Ascension of Isaiah, Jesus is able to overcome the angel of Sheol (Ascen. Isa. 9:16; 10:8; 11:19).[66] Also noteworthy is that in some accounts the angels associated with the empty tomb scene appear to participate in liberating Jesus from the tomb. In the Gospel of Peter, two men (δύο ἄνδρας) descend from the heavens that have opened and approach the tomb; the stone rolls away on its own and the young men enter the tomb (36–37). Next two men supporting a third, all of gigantic proportions, emerge from the tomb (39–40). The descent of the men, their heavenly height, and the cross that follows the three from the tomb identify the figures as angels supporting the resurrected Jesus.[67] As Tobias Nicklas observes, the angels in this text are not functioning as interpreting angels; in fact, later an individual angel descends in order to serve as the *angelus interpres* for the women who come to the empty tomb (44, 56).[68]

Reminiscent of Luke 16:22, Codex Bobbiensis (*k*) has an addition to the Latin of Mark that follows 16:4. In this text, angels descend from heaven, and, following Jesus's resurrection, they ascend with him to heaven. The Ascension of Isaiah more explicitly ties archangels to the liberation of Jesus. In this pseudepigraphon, Gabriel and Michael open the sepulcher on the third day and carry the risen Christ on their shoulders (3:16–17). Nicklas rightly associates these accounts with traditions of angels leading the deceased to the afterlife or to paradise.[69] At the same time, Enochic

---

66. On the background of the Ascension of Isaiah, see, e.g., Richard Bauckham, "The Ascension of Isaiah: Genre, Unity and Date," in *Fate of the Dead: Studies on the Jewish and Christian Apocalypses,* NovTSup 93 (Leiden: Brill, 1998), 363–90; and Robert G. Hall, "Isaiah's Ascent to See the Beloved: An Ancient Jewish Source for the Ascension of Isaiah?" *JBL* 113 (1994): 463–84.

67. For a comparison of this account with that of the empty-tomb scenes in the Synoptics, see Nicklas, "Angels in Early Christian Narratives," 305–6.

68. Ibid., 306. Nicklas understand the angels in the Gospel of Peter to serve as escorts, accompanying Jesus to heaven, not necessarily as angels who liberate Jesus from the netherworld; see Nicklas, "Resurrection in the Gospels," 35.

69. Nicklas, "Angels in Early Christian Narratives," 307.

literature may illumine further these examples from outside the Synoptics. For example, the archangels are presented as binding and imprisoning the rebel angels in Enochic literature (cf. 1 En. 10; 54:6; 88:1–3); so too could they serve as gatekeepers or psychopomps (cf. Sib. Or. 2:214–19; Apoc. El. 5:5) who facilitate passage between liminal realms.

Examining the role angels play vis-à-vis the realm of the dead or post-mortem places of punishment and reward in Enochic literature and the Synoptic Gospels provides some insights. For example, the parable of the rich man and Lazarus in Luke 16 gives an example of angels guiding the soul of the deceased from the world of the living to a blessed afterlife. Other apocryphal traditions (as in the Gospel of Peter) present Jesus's release from the tomb in a comparable manner: Jesus is escorted by angels heavenward. The empty tomb traditions of the three Synoptic Gospels present angels delivering the news of the Jesus's resurrection, serving as interpreting angels, as one finds also in Enochic literature, as heavenly messengers reveal information otherwise unavailable to those worthy of the divine communication. The Synoptic Gospels do not address, however, particular angels governing over the realm of the dead or postmortem places, as Enochic literature and later Christian traditions do.

CONCLUSION

In light of the fact that other Christian traditions have less aversion to featuring angels in association with the realm of the dead, what might be the reason for the Synoptic Gospels to downplay this motif?

I began by sketching broadly Second Temple period angelology and the depiction of angels in Enochic literature. I noted that comparisons among the writings associated with Enoch and the Synoptic Gospels are challenged by the diverse nature of the texts associated with each. Even so, Enoch literature, apocalyptic writings that present the patriarch as possessing wisdom for the elect who read these works, and the Synoptics seem to share the same conceptual thought world; this thought world accepts messengers from the Divine who interact with humans, can wield power, and play a role in eschatological scenarios. The portraits also are indebted in various ways to portraits of angels from the Hebrew Scriptures. Still, in some key ways, there is a diminished angelology in the Synoptic Gospels. The angels of the Synoptics serve Christ, the focal point of this literature. The gospels are especially circumspect in the presentation of angels and the realm of the dead.

Would the reticence in the gospels be to underscore that Jesus the Christ is the ultimate authority over the realm of the dead?[70] Instead of Eremiel (over the abyss and Hades in Apoc. Zeph. 6:11–15) or another archangel, perhaps early Christians behind the Synoptics want to make clear that Jesus commands and controls otherworldly realms like that serving the deceased; thus, in Rev 1:18, the risen Christ, the "Living One" (ὁ ζῶν), proclaims: "I hold the keys to death and the netherworld" (ἔχω τὰς κλεῖς τοῦ θανάτου καὶ τοῦ Ἅιδου). Comparable imagery—the gates of the netherworld (πύλαι ᾅδου) and keys to the kingdom of heaven (τὰς κλεῖδας τῆς βασιλείας τῶν οὐρανῶν)—is found also in Matt 16:18–19.[71] Some early Christian traditions emphasize that Christ trumps heavenly beings (cf. Eph. 1:21; Col 2:10; 1 Pet 3:22), and thus angelic dominion over the realm of the dead might be diminished in order to make clear the supremacy of Christ or the direct association between God and Christ.[72] At the same

---

70. To put it another way, God's immanence is to be especially communicated through Jesus, rather than through other heavenly beings. See Edith Humphrey, "God and Angels," in *Jesus among Friends and Enemies: A Historical and Literary Introduction to Jesus in the Gospels,* ed. Chris Keith and Larry W. Hurtado (Grand Rapids: Baker Academic, 2011), 35–60, esp. 49–52.

71. The language of binding and loosing in Matt 16:19 also recalls how these terms have been used not only in terms of demonology, but in association with the punishment of the rebel angels. See also Beate Ego, "Textual Variants as a Result of Enculturation: The Banishment of the Demon in Tobit," in *Septuagint Research: Issues and Challenges in the Study of the Greek Jewish Scriptures,* ed. Wolfgang Kraus and R. Glenn Wooden, SCS 53 (Atlanta: Society of Biblical Literature, 2006), 371–78; and Nickelsburg, "Enoch, Levi, and Peter," 595.

72. If these traditions express a desire to tamp down angelic dominion over such realms in order to emphasize Christ's power, it might explain why Matthew excludes reference to angels at the rising of the saints. The tombs of the latter are opened and they are said to be raised at the time of the crucifixion (Matt 27:52), but interestingly, they do not ultimately come forth from their tombs until after Jesus's resurrection (Matt 27:53). This text is difficult for commentators to explain. Ulrich Luz (*Matthew 21–28: A Commentary,* trans. James E. Crouch, Hermeneia [Minneapolis: Fortress, 2005], 568–69) thinks the conclusion of Matt 27:53—that the righteous are not raised until after Jesus's resurrection—is a post-Matthean gloss. For a different reading of the resurrection of the saints in Matt 27:52 that sees the account as dependent on particular readings of Ezek 37 (in which graves are opened for eschatological resurrection of the dead) and Zech 14:4–5 (in which a mountain splits in two, the result of an earthquake), and hence not requiring angelic participation in the event, see Dale Allison, "The Scriptural Background of a Matthean Legend: Ezekiel 37, Zechariah 14, and Matthew 27," in Weren, van de Sandt, and Verheyden, *Life beyond Death,* 153–81.

time, in light of the fact that Greco-Roman traditions knew of intermediaries like Hermes and Hecate associated with the netherworld, there may have been sufficient reason for the evangelists to avoid relating particular angels to the realm of the dead.[73] With these points in mind, it is possible that the Synoptics provide reserved portraits of angels—reserved in contrast to Enoch literature—in reaction to the colorful angelology that could have potentially distracted from Jesus or confused early Christians.

73. See Schneweis, *Angels and Demons*, 9–10.

The Parables of Enoch and Luke's Parable of the Rich Man and Lazarus

Leslie Baynes

In 1966 Sverre Aalen drew attention to parallels between Luke 16:19–31, the parable of the rich man and Lazarus, and the Epistle of Enoch.[1] In 1979 and still more strongly in 2003, George W. E. Nickelsburg essentially affirmed and even augmented certain aspects of Aalen's claims, going so far as to say that the parable "is based on revelatory traditions in 1 [i.e., the Epistle of] Enoch."[2] This paper does not dispute their conclusions. Rather it argues that there may be another Enochic influence upon Luke 16:19–31, the Parables of Enoch (1 En. 62–63). In literary form, content, themes, plot, and in one instance of very specific linguistic overlap, 1 En. 62–63 resembles the Lukan parable and its immediate environs. The Epistle of Enoch, the Parables of Enoch, and Luke's parable all condemn the wealthy and envision them suffering eternal torment, in marked contrast to the fate of the poor. But only the Enochic and the Lukan parables highlight a rejected plea for relief from postmortem torment narrated in the first person. And—as Abraham tells Dives[3]—that is not all. Several

---

1. Sverre Aalen, "St Luke's Gospel and the Last Chapters of I Enoch," *NTS* 13 (1966): 1–13.

2. George W. E. Nickelsburg, "Revisiting the Rich and the Poor in 1 Enoch 92–105 and the Gospel according to Luke," in *George W. E. Nickelsburg in Perspective: An Ongoing Dialogue of Learning*, ed. Jacob Neusner and Alan J. Avery-Peck, 2 vols., JSJSup 80 (Leiden: Brill, 2003), 2:569; and in the same volume, see "Riches, the Rich, and God's Judgment in 1 Enoch 92–105 and the Gospel according to Luke," 2:521–46.

3. With the exception of one extant manuscript (P^{75}), the Greek textual tradition does not name the rich man, in contrast to its designation of the poor man as Lazarus (the only time a character is named in a gospel parable). See Kendrick Grobel, "'... Whose Name Was Neves,'" *NTS* 10 (1963–1964): 373–82. "Dives" is in fact not a name at all, but rather a "deliberate misunderstanding of the Latin," as Joseph A. Fitzmyer

related concepts, including wealth versus poverty, reversal and exclusion, and perhaps the heavenly banquet, also appear in Luke's special material (e.g., Mary's canticle) and in the redaction of his sources. That is, material that reflects the Parables of Enoch is not limited to Luke 16:19–31. If a hypothesis positing a relationship between the two texts is correct, it has important implications not only for understanding Luke's sources but also for the vexed question of the dating of the Parables and their use in the first century CE.

A PROPOSED METHODOLOGY, OR HOW TO AVOID PARALLELOMANIA

At least since the publication of Samuel Sandmel's influential article,[4] biblical scholars have tried to avoid promiscuous assertions of parallels among texts. For the most part, however, Sandmel's work serves a negative function, cautioning against what one should not do. What, then, is a legitimate procedure for identifying parallels? Surely the process will never be a science, but it is necessary to articulate some guidelines for it at the outset. Thomas Brodie's work is helpful in this regard. Here follows a summary of his positive criteria as well as principles that may be misleading in judging literary dependence, with my own additions and variations interspersed.

The first of Brodie's positive criteria is external plausibility. Obviously anachronistic lines of dependence are excluded from consideration. Second, thematic similarities are a good place to start, but not necessarily definitive on their own. I note in addition that the more themes two passages under consideration share, the stronger the argument for a relationship between them potentially becomes—if the parallels are significant and pertinent. As Sandmel writes, sheer lists of parallels profit us little, even if they are true ones; more consequential is the use to which they are put.[5] Third are similarities in plot/action, especially if they occur in the same order, or close to the same order. Brodie does not say this, but it is important to note that parallels of any sort (themes, plot/action, words and phrases) that cluster together in both texts are more convincing than

---

writes in *The Gospel according to Luke X–XXIV*, AB 28A (Garden City, NY: Doubleday, 1983), 1130. I use the name Dives here because of its ongoing presence in Christian tradition.

4. Samuel Sandmel, "Parallelomania," *JBL* 81 (1962): 1–13.

5. Ibid., 2–5.

similar material scattered throughout one or the other or both.[6] Fourth, linguistic/verbal parallels are important, but they too are not definitive. Common words and phrases by themselves are less likely to demonstrate dependence than rare ones. The essence of this criterion also has a bearing on criteria 2 and 3. Similarities in themes or plot/action that are rare in extant literature are more likely to be parallels than those that are common. Finally, differences between texts are not necessarily fatal. At issue is the intelligibility of the differences. Do they make sense in the context of what we can discern of the later author's larger purposes?[7]

Brodie's list of principles that can mislead begins with the problem of weak connections between texts (see my addendum to criterion 2 above). Weak parallels obviously never make a strong argument. Nevertheless, "that some are weak does not matter as long as there are enough that are strong."[8] The next principle is probably the one most commonly leveled against an argument for dependence: that one text does not rely on a second, but rather on a third text, a shared literary tradition that is no longer extant (e.g., Q). Closely related to this point is the possibility that an author uses an idea that is "in the air" or an oral tradition rather than a written document. The hypothetical nature of such claims can sometimes be problematic, however. Why (without other compelling factors that better explain the data at hand, e.g., re: Q) reflexively dismiss actual connections between real texts in favor of things unseen?[9] Finally, a bias, conscious or unconscious, in favor of a certain form of dependence (e.g., the Two Source Hypothesis) may prevent someone from recognizing or acknowledging anything but that particular model, when in fact ancient authors creatively used and reused texts in many different ways.[10]

---

6. Cf. Nickelsburg, "Riches," 523.

7. Thomas L. Brodie, *The Birthing of the New Testament: The Intertextual Development of the New Testament Writings*, NTM 1 (Sheffield: Sheffield Academic, 2004), 44–46.

8. Ibid., 47.

9. I, unlike Brodie, accept the Two Source Hypothesis, and all references to it and Q in this summary originate with me.

10. Brodie, *Birthing of the New Testament*, 47–49, and chs. 1–2 on ancient literary imitation.

1 Enoch 62–63 and Luke 16:19–31 as Parables

Luke 16:19–31 and 1 En. 62–63 share the same literary form, the parable. Ironically, while the Lukan pericope coheres to many modern readers' expectations of what a parable is, be those readers scholarly or lay, it does not identify itself as such.[11] The Enochic text, on the other hand, unmistakably names itself as a parable (Ge'ez *messālē*; cf. Heb. משל), but how it might fit the definition is initially unclear.

The Greek παραβολή indicates something that is placed next to something else for purposes of comparison. In all but two instances in the LXX it translates Hebrew מָשָׁל.[12] In the Hebrew Scriptures, however, the meaning of משל is more equivocal than it is among the Greek rhetoricians, as indicated by the various ways the NRSV alone has translated it: for example, "oracle" (Num 23:7), "discourse" (Job 27:1), "taunt" (Isa 14:4), and "proverb" (Ps 49:4).[13] In Pss 49:4 and 78:2, משל appears in poetic parallelism with חידה, translated by the NRSV as "riddle" and "dark saying," respectively. Thus at some points in the Hebrew Scriptures a משל does not contain a readily apparent comparison, and it takes on the same connotation that Jesus will later adopt in Mark 4:11 to describe his own parables, a μυστήριον or secret, by definition something difficult to comprehend. Understanding this, we move closer to grasping the generic essence of the apocalyptic parables in 1 Enoch's Book of Similitudes/Parables.

Just because a text labeled a parable contains no overt comparison does not mean that a comparison is absent, however. Investigating the usage of *messālē* in the Parables of Enoch, David Suter examines Ps 49, which specifically calls itself a parable, in terms of its themes. The psalm compares and contrasts the rich and the poor in this life and the next. The rich enjoy their lives (and in contrast to both 1 Enoch and Luke, the psalm never

---

11. Except in one manuscript, Codex Bezae, which reads "and he spoke another parable" at the beginning of the pericope. See Philip Comfort, "Two Illustrations of Scribal Gap Filling in Luke 16:19," in *Translating the New Testament: Text, Translation, Theology,* ed. Stanley E. Porter and Mark J. Boda, MNTS (Grand Rapids: Eerdmans, 2009), 111–13, esp. 112.

12. Friedrich Hauck, "παραβολή," *TDNT* 1:360.

13. George W. E. Nickelsburg and James C. VanderKam, *1 Enoch 2: A Commentary on the Book of 1 Enoch, Chapters 37–82,* Hermeneia (Minneapolis: Fortress, 2012), 92–93.

faults them for that), but both rich and poor alike end up in Sheol, where wealth does no one any good. A similar theme appears in 1 En. 62–63; but as an apocalyptic text, it is not satisfied, as Ps 49 apparently is, to let the righteous dead languish in Sheol in undifferentiated company with their wealthy neighbors. Instead the Parables engages in eschatological reversal, condemning the rich, whose wealth cannot save them from the flames, and exalting the poor. In combination with understanding a parable as a riddle, a mystery, or an enigma, Suter argues that the presence of material comparing and contrasting rich and poor, now and then, makes Ps 49 and 1 En. 62–63 truly parables.[14]

That 1 En. 62–63 and the parable of Dives and Lazarus share the same literary form is in and of itself insignificant, but this element does not stand alone.

1 Enoch 62–63 and Luke 16:19–31: Parallels between the Parables

The Parables of Enoch makes up 1 En. 37–71. Dating this section is notoriously difficult. The section is extant today only in Geʿez, the ancient liturgical language of the Ethiopian Orthodox Church, which considers 1 Enoch part of its canon.[15] The first chapter of this large Enochic booklet introduces the work and delineates its organization and literary form as three parables, each of which is explicitly named and numbered as such at the outset (1 En. 37:5, 38:1, 45:1, 58:1). Chapters 62–63 are part of the third parable (chs. 58–69), ostensibly dedicated to the righteous and chosen (58:1), but in actuality very much concerned with the arrogant kings and wealthy mighty ones who are the human villains in the Parables. Rather than acknowledging the name of the Lord of Spirits and thanking him for their good fortune, the kings and mighty trust in their wealth and in idols (46:5–8). They oppress and impoverish the book's protagonists, the righteous and chosen ones: "Everything that (the righteous) labor over, the sinners lawlessly devour" (53:2).[16] Unbeknownst to their oppressors,

---

14. David W. Suter, "*Māšāl* in the Similitudes of Enoch," *JBL* 100 (1981): 193–212.

15. Leslie Baynes, "*Enoch* and *Jubilees* in the Canon of the Ethiopian Orthodox Church," in *A Teacher for All Generations: Essays in Honor of James C. VanderKam*, ed. Eric F. Mason et al., 2 vols., JSJSup 153 (Leiden: Brill, 2012), 2:799–818.

16. Several Geʿez manuscripts and English translations of the Parables of Enoch have been consulted for this paper (see below). This translation is from George W.

however, the righteous poor have on their side a heavenly figure variously called the Chosen One, the Son of Man, and the Messiah.[17] In 1 En. 61–62 the Lord of Spirits sets him on his throne to judge, and the kings and mighty finally acknowledge them both (cf. Matt 25:31–46). But it is too late. The Lord of Spirits hands the formerly haughty but now protesting souls over to angels of punishment "so that they may exact retribution from them for the iniquity that they did to his children and his chosen ones" (62:11). The kings and mighty form a spectacle for the righteous, who eat with the Son of Man in the new, glorious garments of their resurrected bodies (62:12–16).[18] The poor who suffered at the hands of the rich now feast at the messianic banquet.[19]

In chapter 63 the kings and mighty launch into first person speech begging for "a little respite" (63:1, 5–6, 8) from their punishment so that they may at last bless "the Lord of the mighty and the Lord of the rich" (63:2). They have finally realized that "our lives are full of ill-gotten wealth, but it does not prevent us from descending into the flame of the torment of Sheol" (63:10). This request is denied.

There are several parallels between 1 En. 62–63 and Luke 16:19–31.[20] In addition to congruity of literary form, they share plot points and themes

---

E. Nickelsburg and James C. VanderKam, *1 Enoch: A New Translation Based on the Hermeneia Commentary,* rev. ed. (Minneapolis: Fortress, 2012).

17. The literature on this figure is vast. For more detailed information, see Gabriele Boccaccini, ed., *Enoch and the Messiah Son of Man: Revisiting the Book of Parables* (Grand Rapids: Eerdmans, 2007).

18. As Nickelsburg notes, such a viewing of one's enemies' punishment is traditional. See 1 En. 27:3; 90:26–27; Dan 12:2. Cf. Nickelsburg and VanderKam, *1 Enoch 2,* 166, 175. Fitzmyer (*Luke X–XXIV,* 1132) adds 4 Ezra 7:85, 93, and 2 Bar. 51:5–6.

19. Dennis E. Smith ("The Messianic Banquet Reconsidered," in *The Future of Early Christianity: Essays in Honor of Helmut Koester,* ed. Birger A. Pearson [Minneapolis: Fortress, 1991], 64–65) writes that it is "appropriate … to broaden the concept [of the messianic banquet] to refer to the general phenomenon in which a meal is used symbolically to present a mythological event or realities on the mythological level" without necessarily requiring the attendance of a messiah); cf. Smith, *From Symposium to Eucharist: The Banquet in the Early Christian World* (Minneapolis: Fortress, 2003), 166. In this paper, however, I do require the attendance, if not of a messiah specifically, then of some sort of heavenly being, to make a meal a messianic banquet.

20. "Luke" wrote this gospel, but did he write the parable of the rich man and Lazarus himself, or does it come from the historical Jesus? Opinions on the question vary widely. I believe that the parable is consistent with what we can recover about the

that are employed for essentially the same purposes. In Luke, Lazarus goes hungry in his earthly life while his rich neighbor, dressed in purple, makes merry. In the afterlife, their situation is reversed. Lazarus lies in the bosom (κόλπος) of Abraham, an image that may indicate that Lazarus reclines at a heavenly banquet.[21] Meanwhile, the rich man suffers flames of torment. He sees Lazarus from afar and in the first person asks Abraham, the senior heavenly figure in the scene, for mercy to cool his tongue, that is, "that part of him with which he feasted during life."[22] Dives either sees or assumes that Lazarus has access to water, just as the righteous in the Parables of Enoch are surrounded by metaphorical water in 39:5, or more likely, as the righteous souls enjoy a fountain in 1 En. 22:9.[23] But Abraham denies his request.[24]

The following chart lays out proposed similarities of theme and plot:

Luke 16:19–31	1 Enoch 62–63
There was a rich man … who made merry [εὐφραινόμενος] during his life.	The kings, rich, and mighty rule and have their way over the earth and its people (passim).
	46:7 Their power rests on their wealth.
And at his gate lay a poor man by the name of Lazarus, covered with sores and longing to satisfy his hunger with what fell from the rich man's table;	53:2 Everything that the righteous labor over, the sinners lawlessly devour.
And even the dogs would come and lick his sores.	

historical Jesus, but I will operate under the only verifiable assumption I can make: that the author of the gospel is ultimately responsible for his material.

21. Dennis E. Smith, "Table Fellowship as a Literary Motif in the Gospel of Luke," *JBL* 106 (1987): 613–38, esp. 625–26.

22. Fitzmyer, *Luke X–XXIV*, 1133.

23. Laurence W. Grensted, "The Use of Enoch in St. Luke xvi. 19–31," *ExpTim* 26 (1914–1915): 333–34; and Larry Kreitzer, "Luke 16:19–31 and 1 Enoch 22," *ExpTim* 103 (1992): 139–42.

24. There do not seem to be any parallels between 1 En. 62–63 and the remainder of the parable of the rich man and Lazarus in Luke 16:27–31.

The poor man died and was born away by the angels to the bosom of Abraham. The rich man also died and was buried.	62–63 The kings and mighty/righteous poor die and find themselves in the presence of/separated from God and the Son of Man.
The "bosom of Abraham" connotes a heavenly banquet scene?	62:14 And the Lord of Spirits will abide over them, and with that Son of Man they will eat.
In Hades, where he was in torment, he lifted his eyes and saw Abraham far away with Lazarus in his bosom.	62:3 And there will stand up on that day all the kings and the mighty and the exalted and those who possess the land. And they will see and recognize that he sits on the throne of his glory. 62:11 And he will deliver them to the angels for punishment, so that they may exact retribution from them for the iniquity that they did to his children and his chosen ones.
He called out, "Father Abraham, have mercy on me, and send Lazarus to dip the tip of his finger in water and cool my tongue; for I am in agony in this flame."	62:9 They will supplicate and petition for mercy from him [the Son of Man].
[In Hades (Ge'ez: Sheol), where he was in torment]	Three instances of imputed speech (63:5, 6, 8) asking for respite from punishment, and one more specifically for deliverance "from the flame of the torment of Sheol" (63:10).
	1 En. 39:5 And righteousness was flowing like water before [the righteous], and mercy like dew upon the earth; thus it is among them forever and ever.

Despite some significant differences (more on this topic below), the Parables of Enoch (1 En. 62–63) and Luke 16:19–31 share the following elements: (1) the literary form "parable"; (2) the rich devouring resources on the earthly plane; (3) a vignette of eschatological reversal, which may include the poor feasting with a heavenly figure at a divine banquet; (4) while simultaneously the deceased rich address an influential heavenly figure in imputed speech delivered in the first person, (5) request mercy from him, (6) ask for relief from flames/torment of Sheol, and (7) are denied.[25]

Number 1 was discussed above. Number 2 is a common plaint in Judeo-Christian literature and thus does not play a unique role here in terms of parallel themes. The most important items in the list are numbers 3–7. Number 3 proposes the idea of the poor soul/s partaking in a heavenly banquet, a scene that clearly appears in 1 En. 62:14. Does it appear in the Lukan parable as well? Does Lazarus's position in the "bosom of Abraham" (εἰς τὸν κόλπον Ἀβραάμ; Ge'ez *westa ḥeḍna 'Abrehām*) imply his reclining at table? Scholarly answers to this question have been mixed, as the evidence itself is ambiguous.[26] Standard reference works in the field reflect this ambiguity. The *Greek-English Dictionary of the New Testament* (BDAG) and the *Theological Dictionary of the New Testament* (*TDNT*) include meal imagery as part of their definitions for κόλπος, noting that one meaning of the word has to do with a diner's position near his neighbor at table. Lampe's *Patristic Greek Lexicon* and Liddell and Scott, however, do not, defining it primarily as "fold," "lap," or "inlet," the most

---

25. In addition to these elements are two less certain commonalities: first, the righteous in the Parables of Enoch receive new "garments" for the heavenly banquet, a minor overlap with/contrast to Luke's mention of Dives's purple and linen. But since the Parables never describes the attire of the rich, and Luke never discusses new attire for Lazarus, this is a weak parallel. Second, while Dives is never called a king, his purple may connote royalty. See Fitzmyer, *Luke X–XXIV*, 1130. Among the groups 1 Enoch as a whole consigns to the flames (errant angels, antediluvian humanity, "shepherds" and "sheep," several varieties of sinners, and especially the wealthy), only the Parables specifically condemns kings. In both his redaction of sources and in his special material, Luke also highlights kings.

26. Opinions range from Dennis Smith, a strong proponent of understanding Luke's "bosom of Abraham" as a heavenly meal, to Paul Haupt, who rejects it completely. See Smith, "Table Fellowship"; Smith, *From Symposium to Eucharist*; cf. John Paul Heil, *The Meal Scenes in Luke-Acts: An Audience-Oriented Approach*, SBLMS 52 (Atlanta: Society of Biblical Literature, 1999), 131–45; Paul Haupt, "Abraham's Bosom," *AJP* 42 (1921): 162–67. Others acknowledge the concept while also entertaining alternative interpretations, including Fitzmyer, *Luke X–XXIV*, 1132; François Bovon, *Luke 2: A Commentary on the Gospel of Luke 9:51–19:27*, trans. Donald S. Deer (Minneapolis: Fortress, 2013), 481–82; I. Howard Marshall, *The Gospel of Luke: A Commentary on the Greek Text*, NIGTC (Grand Rapids: Eerdmans, 1978), 636; Outi Lehtipuu, *The Afterlife Imagery in Luke's Story of the Rich Man and Lazarus*, NovTSup 123 (Leiden: Brill, 2007), 214–16.

common uses of κόλπος, without noting any connection to eating. Most
of the results of a *Thesaurus Linguae Graecae* (*TLG*) search of the word
also do not refer to eating.[27] Several references, however, lend themselves to understanding κόλπος within the context of a meal. The classic
locus is John 13:23, ἀνακείμενος εἷς ἐκ τῶν μαθητῶν αὐτοῦ ἐν τῷ κόλπῳ
τοῦ Ἰησοῦ. In LXX 2 Sam 12:3, the ewe lamb of Nathan's parable would
"eat his [owner's] bread and drink out of his cup and lie in his bosom
[κόλπος]." The Roman writers Pliny and Juvenal also evidence the concept. Pliny writes, "Nerva ate dinner with a few people; Veiento was next
to him and reclined in his bosom" (Cenabat Nerva cum paucis; Veiento
proximus atque etiam in sinu recumbebat; *Ep.* 4.22.4). Juvenal satirizes a
wedding banquet: "The contract has been signed; the benedictions have
been pronounced; a crowd of banqueters seated, the new made bride is
reclining on the bosom of her husband [ingens cena sedet, gremio iacuit
noua nupta mariti]" (*Sat.* 2.120 [Ramsay, LCL]). Although the Spanish
Jesuit Juan Maldonado (d. 1583) seems to be the first commentator on
Luke 16:22 to identify Lazarus's position in the bosom of Abraham as a
heavenly banquet,[28] ancient evidence does provide some warrant for his
doing so.[29] The narrative context of the parable also supports that interpretation: Luke highlights the rich man's merrymaking[30] while the poor
man starved. So given other roughly contemporary evidence regarding
the word κόλπος in conjunction with reclining at table, it fits very well
here as a pointed form of eschatological reversal. Because of the paucity
of ancient references to the idea, however, one must apply it cautiously.

---

27. Thanks to Kindalee De Long for running the search and to my graduate assis-
tant Austin Jacobs for his review of the material.

28. Francis E. Gigot, "Abraham, Bosom of," *The Catholic Encyclopedia,* ed. Charles
G. Herbermann et al., 15 vols. (New York: Appleton, 1907–1912), 1:55–56.

29. Johannes Maldonatus, *Commentarii in Quatuor Evangelistas,* ed. J. M.
Raich, Illustrium Theologorum in Sacras Novi Testamenti Scripturas Commentarii
2 (Moguntiae: Sumptibus Francisci Kirchheim, 1874), 283–85. Maldonatus does not
cite any ancient sources other than John 13:23 to support his assertion. To the best of
my knowledge, the early church fathers did not interpret the bosom of Abraham as
a heavenly meal. Cf. Ann W. Astell, "In the Bosom of Abraham: Saint Bonaventure,
Lazarus, and the Houses of Hospitality," in *Crisis, Call, and Leadership in the Abrahamic Traditions,* ed. Peter Ochs and W. S. Johnson (New York: Palgrave Macmillan,
2009), 139–52; Martin O'Kane, " 'The Bosom of Abraham' (Luke 16:22): Father Abraham in the Visual Imagination," *BibInt* 15 (2007): 485–518.

30. Greek εὐφραίνω, which indicates taking joy in food, among other things.

Numbers 4–7 breaks down different elements of one scene, the exact configuration of which occurs in only two extant ancient texts, 1 En. 62–63 and Luke's parable of the rich man and Lazarus: the imputed speech of wealthy souls as they beg an authoritative figure for mercy from the flames of Sheol/Hades. Imputed speech in the mouths of the rich is not rare in the Hebrew Scriptures and Second Temple Jewish literature. Indeed, as Mark Mathews demonstrates, "attributed or imputed speech becomes a widely circulated, stereotypical way of referring to people as 'rich sinners.'"[31] To the best of my knowledge, however, no characters in any ancient text address a plea for mercy to a heavenly figure (or anyone else) as they suffer in Sheol except in the Parables of Enoch 62–63 and Luke's parable. One may compare and contrast related scenes such as Ezek 28's oracle against the wealthy ruler of Tyre who, like the kings in the Parables of Enoch, does not acknowledge God. This king also ends up in the pit and in flames, but he never asks for mercy; his imputed speech is pure defiance, at least in the eyes of the biblical writer. The Epistle of Enoch attributes only boasting, cruelly haughty speech to its wealthy antagonists (1 En. 98:3; 102:6–11; 104:7). In Wis 4:16–5:23 imputed speech is given to the unrighteous rich whose pleasures include lavish eating and drinking and oppressing the poor (see Wis 2:7–10).[32] They do regret their actions in the afterlife, but they do not beg for mercy, and there is no mention of fiery torment.

The conjunction of elements in numbers 4–7 is unique to Luke and the Parables of Enoch, a fact that leads one to consider the possibility that Luke may have known the Parables. If he did, he probably would have encountered it in Greek, a now hypothetical text for which some have argued. George Nickelsburg posits the existence of such a manuscript throughout his magisterial commentary, as does Matthew Black in his.[33] Loren Stuckenbruck, too, noting Jude's description of Enoch as seventh from Adam, an enumeration that appears only in Jude and the Parables of Enoch (1 En. 60:8; cf. 37:1), writes, "Jude 14 may also point towards the circulation of the Book of Parables (or floating tradition from it) in Greek. If the Book of Parables is behind the designation for Enoch at all, we are in a position at least to consider whether a simultaneous reception of the

---

31. Mark D. Mathews, "The Function of Imputed Speech in the Apocalypse of John," *CBQ* 74 (2012): 327.

32. Wisdom 6:1 implies that these wealthy also include kings.

33. Nickelsburg and VanderKam, *1 Enoch 2*, 30–34; Matthew Black, *The Book of Enoch or 1 Enoch*, SVTP 7 (Leiden: Brill, 1985), esp. 427.

Book of the Watchers and Book of Parables suggests these Enochic writings were being transmitted in close proximity to one another."[34]

LITERARY DEPENDENCE?

Verbal parallels between two texts are much easier to discern when both texts are in the same language. Greek copies of the Epistle of Enoch have survived to compare with the Greek text of Luke, as Aalen and Nickelsburg have done, but such unfortunately is not the case for the Parables of Enoch, which is extant only in Geʻez. While the Parables of Enoch is not available in Greek, the Gospel of Luke is available in Geʻez, and so one may look for verbal parallels between the two documents in Geʻez. *If* there was a Greek text of the Parables of Enoch available to Luke, and *if* Luke was influenced by it, might the two documents have been translated into Geʻez similarly? In an attempt to investigate that question, I have consulted the Garima Gospels, the earliest Geʻez manuscript of Luke (sixth century?), along with Thomas Platt's Ethiopic New Testament, and EMML 8400 (the earliest Ethiopian manuscript of 1 Enoch; ca. 1400), EMML 1768 (sixteenth century), Rylands 23, Michael Knibb's base text (eighteenth century), and Nickelsburg and VanderKam's critical apparatus and commentary.[35] EMML 8400 and 1768 are important representatives of Eth. I manuscripts, while Rylands 23 represents Eth. II.

Concepts shared between the two narratives that might have been translated into Geʻez similarly are "rich (man)," "Sheol/Hades," "mercy/respite," "torment," and "flame." In my reading of the Geʻez manuscripts of Luke 16:19–31, I have found two exact verbal counterparts with 1 En. 62–63: (1) the use of *bāʻel* for rich (man) in 1 En. 63:2 and throughout the Lukan parable,[36] and (2) the word *siʾol* (Sheol) in both Luke 16:23 and 1

---

34. Loren T. Stuckenbruck, "The *Book of Enoch*: Its Reception in Second Temple Jewish and in Christian Tradition," *Early Christianity* 4 (2013): 15–16.

35. Many thanks to Curt Niccum for his transcription of Luke 16:19–31 from the Garima Gospels, which he provided to me. See also Thomas Pell Platt, ed., *Novum Testamentum Domini nostri et Salvatoris Jesu Christi Aethiopice* (Leipzig: Officina G. Drugulini, 1899); M. A. Knibb, *The Ethiopic Book of Enoch: A New Edition in the Light of the Aramaic Dead Sea Fragments,* 2 vols. (Oxford: Clarendon, 1978); and Nickelsburg and VanderKam, *1 Enoch 2,* 256–57. A more extensive collation of Geʻez manuscripts on these passages is a desideratum.

36. For variants on *bāʻel* among other manuscripts of the Parables, see Nickelsburg and VanderKam, *1 Enoch 2,* 256.

En. 63:10, both of which my sample manuscripts unanimously attest. From this point, however, the vocabulary differs between Luke and the Parables. When the *bāʿel* in Luke 16:24 begs Abraham to "have mercy on me," he uses a form of the verb *shahala*, whereas in the Parables (1 En. 62:9) the mighty kings supplicate for mercy using a form of the verb *maḥara*. They also repeatedly ask for "respite," *meʿerāf*, from the verb *ʿarafa*. These words hold true over all sample texts.

In Luke 16:23 the rich man is in damnation (*westa dayn*)[37] in Sheol, which he later calls a "place of torment" (*beher/a*[38] *ḥemām*; v. 28);[39] and in 16:24 he reports, "I am suffering torment in this flame" (*ḥamameki bazāti ʾesāt*).[40] The counterpart in 1 En. 63:10 to Luke 16:23–24, however, has a more complex textual tradition. In Nickelsburg's translation, the kings lament that their ill-gotten wealth will not prevent "our descending into the flame of the torment of Sheol" (*waradotana ʾemlāhbā lakebada siʾol*), a reading that appears in Rylands 23, other Eth. II, and some Eth. I manuscripts.[41] However, EMML 8400 demonstrates *ḥatana ʾemlāhbā lakebada siʾol*, "our burning from the consciousness of the torment of Sheol." EMML 1768 reads *waradotana ʾemlāhbā la-kabada siʾol*, "our descending into the consciousness of the torment of Sheol," a reading also evidenced by many other Eth. I manuscripts.[42] Tana 9 has *ʾemkebuda siʾol* ("burdensome Sheol").[43] Among the many difficulties in 1 En. 63:10, the two most pertinent concern *lāhb* ("flame") versus *lēb* ("heart, understanding, consciousness") and the meaning of *kabada* ("weight, burden, torment"), especially in light of the proposed Greek *Vorlage*. Nickelsburg and VanderKam, following earlier scholars, write that *kabada* may have translated Greek βάρος, "burden," while R. H. Charles notes that βάρος could have been a corruption of βάρις, "stronghold."[44] Relying particularly on Tana 9, Black conjectures further that βάρις may have translated בירה, "stronghold," an

---

37. Greek ἐν βασάνοις.

38. Garima, *beḥer*; Platt, *beḥera*.

39. Greek τόπον τοῦτον τῆς βασάνου.

40. Greek ὀδυνῶμαι ἐν τῇ φλογὶ ταύτῃ.

41. BL Or. 491, Abbadian 35, EMML 2080, Eth II. See Nickelsburg and VanderKam, *1 Enoch 2*, 257.

42. Nickelsburg and VanderKam, *1 Enoch 2*, 257; Olson, *Enoch: New Translation*, 118.

43. Nickelsburg and VanderKam, *1 Enoch 2*, 257.

44. Wolf Leslau, *Comparative Dictionary of Geʿez (Classical Ethiopic)* (Wiesbaden: Harrassowitz, 1987), 257.

error for בורה, "pit," and that the author of the Parables originally wrote "the pit of Sheol."[45]

In summary, therefore, the textual evidence surveyed here, oblique as it is, provides little foundation for an argument for verbal dependence between the Parables of Enoch and Luke 16:19–31. Interestingly, however, there is an exact verbal parallel between the Geʿez texts of 1 En. 63:10 and Luke 16:9, which is not part of the parable of the rich man and Lazarus but immediately precedes it. In 1 En. 63:10, the rich and mighty admit that "our lives are full of ill-gotten wealth [newāya ʿāmmaḍā], but it does not prevent our descending into the flame of the torment of Sheol." The Geʿez newāya ʿāmmaḍā, literally "wealth of unrighteousness," is the identical Ethiopic phrase that translates Luke 16:9's μαμωνᾶ τῆς ἀδικίας in the parable of the steward.[46] A *TLG* search reveals that the Greek phrase is unique to Luke 16:9 and quotations of it, and apparently the same is true of the Ethiopic.[47] The Aramaic equivalent, ממון דשקר, seems to appear only in a few targumim.[48] This particular phrase, therefore, unlike baʾel and siʾol, is uncommon. By itself it cannot prove literary dependence of Luke on the Parables of Enoch, but it does decisively link them.

Clearly there are thematic differences between the Enochic and Lukan parables as well as divergent ways they utilize thematic similarities. For instance, Nickelsburg outlines the many ways the Epistle of Enoch's treatment of wealth and poverty, rich and poor, overlaps with Luke's.[49] While the Parables of Enoch are definitely concerned with how the rich exploit the poor, and one of the stated reasons for the punishment of the rich is because of the iniquity they level against the poor, the Parables emphasizes the denial of the name (i.e., sovereignty) of the Lord of Spirits and his Chosen One much more than behavior toward the poor. Furthermore, in contrast to God/the Chosen One, the heavenly being in Luke's parable, Abraham, does not require worship, and initially there is no hint that the

---

45. Black, *Book of Enoch*, 138. In his comment on this passage Black evaluates the presence of flames in the pit of Sheol negatively, yet he maintains them in his translation.

46. Nickelsburg and VanderKam, *1 Enoch 2*, 270.

47. I am grateful to Curt Niccum for his *TLG* search. Cf. August Dillmann, *Lexicon linguae Aethiopicae cum indice Latino* (Leipzig: Weigel, 1865); Sylvain Grébaut, *Supplément au Lexicon Linguae Aethiopicae de August Dillmann (1865) et Édition du Lexique de Juste d'Urbin (1850-1855)* (Paris: Imprimerie Nationale, 1952).

48. Friedrich Hauck, "μαμωνᾶς," *TDNT* 4:88–90.

49. See Nickelsburg, "Riches"; Nickelsburg, "Revisiting the Rich."

rich man's behavior affected anyone except Lazarus. However, at the end of
the parable, readers discover that that is not necessarily the case through
(1) Dives's request to send Lazarus back from the dead to warn his brothers, and (2) Abraham's appeal to the law and the prophets, events that do
not and, indeed, cannot occur in the Parables of Enoch. The wealthy in the
Book of Parables never ask for someone to return from the dead because
in the narrative world of that text there is no need for such a thing. Enoch
himself returns and relates his visions as a cautionary tale to the living.
Furthermore, unlike Luke, the Parables of Enoch never appeals to the
Scriptures, although it continually echoes and alludes to them. Instead,
the Parables (in company with all of 1 Enoch) replaces and transcends the
authority of the Tanak with that of the apocalyptic visionary. Luke's parable, on the other hand, refuses "an apocalyptic revelation from the world
of the dead"[50] and refers its audience instead to the law and the prophets,
which are permeated with God's outrage against those who ignore, exploit,
and oppress the righteous poor.[51]

FURTHER REFLECTIONS OF THE PARABLES OF ENOCH
IN THE GOSPEL OF LUKE

Luke's "bosom of Abraham" may or may not refer to a heavenly meal, but
the Parables' conjunction of a meal, wealth/poverty, reversal, and exclusion is reflected throughout that gospel. In Enochic literature, a messianic
meal takes place only in the Parables. In the gospels, however, every meal
Jesus eats is an intimation of the eschatological messianic banquet, sometimes subtly, other times overtly. We see this especially in the Gospel of
Luke, which contains much more meal language than the other Synoptic
Gospels, as can be revealed through redaction criticism.[52] Luke contains
its own unique meal material, and when the author borrows from Mark
or Q, he often intensifies its meal language. In addition, he sometimes
rearranges his sources to the same purpose. One example that incorpo-
rates all of these strategies is Luke 22:24–30, the dispute about greatness,

---

50. Bauckham, "Rich Man and Lazarus," 246.

51. Alternatively, within the narrative world of the parable itself, Dives and his
brothers may have read a "canon within a canon" emphasizing a "prosperity gospel"
that blamed the poor for their state (e.g., Prov 6:11; 14:23). See James A. Metzger, *Consumption and Wealth in Luke's Travel Narrative*, BibInt 88 (Leiden: Brill, 2007), 151.

52. Smith, "Table Fellowship," 616.

which Luke alone places after the Last Supper, as well as adding brand new material rife with meal language.[53] This section serves explicitly to link the eucharistic meal Jesus and his disciples have just eaten with the future eschatological banquet, and it also highlights kingship and reversal. In 1 Enoch only the Parables singles out kings, and Luke, too, highlights kings in his redaction of Mark and Q and in his special material. Jesus tells his disciples that they should not lord it over one another as the kings of the gentiles do. Of the three Synoptics, only Luke uses "kings" here (οἱ βασιλεῖς; cf. Mark 10:42, οἱ δοκοῦντες ἄρχειν; and Matt 20:25, οἱ ἄρχοντες). The greatest should be as the youngest. Jesus illustrates his exhortation with the immediately relevant example of a meal: "For who is greater? The one reclining at table or the one serving? Is it not the one who reclines? Yet I am among you as one who serves" (cf. Luke 12:37–38). Joseph Fitzmyer hypothesizes that Jesus himself may have served the Passover meal,[54] and thus he practices (even embodies) what he preaches. Nonetheless, he immediately informs his disciples of yet another reversal: they themselves will become kings, sitting on thrones and judging the twelve tribes in Jesus's kingdom, where they will eat and drink at his table.

This is not the only place the evangelist juxtaposes a meal in the presence of a heavenly agent, a disparagement of kings and/or the rich and mighty, and the exaltation of the humble. At the beginning of Luke's Gospel, Mary praises the God who has "brought down the powerful from their thrones, and lifted up the lowly … filled the hungry with good things, and sent the rich away empty" (Luke 1:52–53 NRSV). Here Luke's main exemplar is Hannah's victory hymn in 1 Sam 2, and it is enlightening to observe his redaction of it.[55] Mary's Magnificat retains Hannah's reversal of the hungry and the full (1 Sam 2:5) as well as its lifting up of the poor (2:8), but only Mary reverses the status of the poor and the rich.[56] Mary

---

53. Cf. Matt 20:20–26.

54. Fitzmyer, *Luke X–XXIV*, 1418. I take no position on the historical status of the meal in Luke as a Passover meal here because it has no bearing on my argument; I simply repeat what the gospel, and Fitzmyer, write.

55. Fitzmyer, *The Gospel according to Luke I–IX*, AB 28 (Garden City, NY: Doubleday, 1981), 359. Fitzmyer notes other possible allusions on pp. 356–57. I attribute the composition of the canticle to Luke. Even if he inherited it from earlier Christian tradition, he likely redacted it to suit his own purposes. Most certainly he, and/or the original author/s, used the LXX.

56. 1 Sam 2:7 notes that God makes poor and makes rich, and 2:8 that the poor

also adds the overthrow of kings, while Hannah's song upholds them (1 Sam 2:10 LXX = βασιλεῖς).

Mary's canticle is the first of many reversals of the rich and poor that populate the Gospel of Luke, as they do the Parables and Epistle of Enoch. Only the Parables places this reversal in the context of eschatological eating, however, as Luke often does.[57] For instance, in Luke's Beatitudes Jesus proves he is his mother's son: the physically poor and hungry are blessed, but the rich and satiated receive woes (Luke 6:20–25).[58] Contrast Matthew's spiritualized blessings of the poor in spirit and those who hunger and thirst for righteousness, with no woes reversing the rich/poor and full/hungry. Immediately following Luke's woes, however, Jesus somewhat surprisingly commands his audience to be good to their enemies and to bless those who hate them, sentiments totally foreign to the Parables of Enoch, where the righteous poor rejoice over the eternal damnation of their foes, the "sinners" who repent only under duress in the afterlife. One wonders if their repentance on earth would have satisfied the righteous in the Parables. The harsh apocalyptic dualism in the text makes one suspect not.

Jesus's attitude to moneyed sinners oscillates somewhat in this gospel. The tax collector Levi, for instance, accepts Jesus's invitation to follow him, and in Luke alone fixes him a δοχὴν μεγάλην, a great banquet (Luke 5:29; in Mark 2:13–17 and Matt 9:9–13, they merely recline at table). The local scribes and Pharisees criticize Jesus's willingness to eat and drink with sinners.[59] Luke, who allegedly suffers from *Dublettenfurcht*,[60] alone introduces

---

will join princes at the gate, but neither of these includes a reversal of the poor and rich/mighty.

57. Other important examples include the sayings in Luke 14:7–24 (L material through v. 15 and scattered throughout the remainder of the section). Of special note is v. 13, where Jesus urges his listeners not to invite the rich to a banquet, but to "invite the poor, the crippled, the lame, and the blind. And you will be blessed, because they cannot repay you, for you will be repaid at the resurrection of the righteous"; and v. 21, the invitation to the poor, maimed, blind, and lame (only in Luke) in place of the original guests.

58. The "woe form" leveled against the wealthy is one of the major parallels between the Epistle of Enoch and Luke. See Aalen, "St Luke's Gospel," 6; and Nickelsburg, "Riches," 524–28.

59. For more on the categories of sinner/tax collector in the context of meal fellowship, see Smith, *From Symposium to Eucharist*, 232–35.

60. W. Bussmann as cited by Fitzmyer, *Luke I–IX*, 81.

the Q parable of the lost sheep in Luke 15:2 by repeating this sentiment (eating with sinners) with the same cast of characters in the lead roles (scribes and Pharisees scoffing, sinners and tax collectors denigrated).

People who eat together typically are or soon will be friends, and in the Greco-Roman world, at least, one of the stated purposes of sharing food was to encourage friendship.[61] There is every reason to believe that this idea would also hold true in Hellenistic Palestinian Judaism. Conversely, those excluded from table fellowship are not friends. Jesus, unlike the righteous ones in the Parables of Enoch, often eats with sinners, and so he can and does use meals to signal inclusion. Other times in the gospel he does the opposite, however, excluding from table fellowship those who do not acknowledge him in scenarios quite reminiscent of 1 En. 62–63. One of these occasions is Luke 13:22–30, the emphases of which emerge sharply when juxtaposed to its counterpart, Matt 8:5–13. Matthew uses the proclamation of eating with the patriarchs primarily to include, but Luke uses it primarily to exclude. Matthew does so by placing the saying in the context of the healing of the centurion's slave:

> When he entered Capernaum, a centurion came to him, appealing to him and saying, "Lord, my servant is lying at home paralyzed, in terrible distress." And he said to him, "I will come and cure him." The centurion answered, "Lord, I am not worthy to have you come under my roof; but only speak the word, and my servant will be healed. For I also am a man under authority, with soldiers under me; and I say to one, 'Go,' and he goes, and to another, 'Come,' and he comes, and to my slave, 'Do this,' and the slave does it." When Jesus heard him, he was amazed and said to those who followed him, "Truly I tell you, in no one in Israel have I found such faith. I tell you, *many* will come from east and west and will eat with Abraham and Isaac and Jacob in the kingdom of heaven, while the heirs of the kingdom will be thrown into the outer darkness, where there will be weeping and gnashing of teeth." And to the centurion Jesus said, "Go; let it be done for you according to your faith." And the servant was healed in that hour.

Matthew uses the promise of eating and drinking with Abraham, Isaac, and Jacob to include the centurion and the "many" as well as to exclude "the heirs of the kingdom." The many in Matthew will eat with the patri-

---

61. Smith, "Table Fellowship," 633–35.

archs, as opposed to the many in Luke 13:22–30 who will see others eating with the patriarchs while they themselves weep and gnash their teeth.

Luke sets his rendition after the teaching of the narrow door, a Q saying that in Matthew appears in chapter 7. Luke's arrangement creates utterly the opposite effect from that of Matthew:

> Jesus went through one town and village after another, teaching as he made his way to Jerusalem. Someone asked him, "Lord, will only a few be saved?" He said to them, "Strive to enter through the narrow door; for *many*, I tell you, will try to enter and will not be able. When once the owner of the house has got up and shut the door, and you begin to stand outside and to knock at the door, saying, 'Lord, open to us,' then in reply he will say to you, 'I do not know where you come from.' Then you will begin to say, 'We ate and drank with you, and you taught in our streets.' But he will say, 'I do not know where you come from; go away from me, all you evildoers!' There will be weeping and gnashing of teeth when you see Abraham and Isaac and Jacob and all the prophets in the kingdom of God, and you yourselves thrown out. Then they will come from east and west, from north and south, and will eat in the kingdom of God. Indeed, some are last who will be first, and some are first who will be last."

Luke's use of eating and drinking in the kingdom here is primarily to exclude, just as it is in the Parables of Enoch 62–63. Notable also is meal language unique to Luke, "We ate and drank in your presence," as well as the additional language of eschatological reversal, "some are last who will be first, and some are first who will be last." The latter statement is not unique to Luke, but its placement is: only Luke sets it in the context of a heavenly meal (cf. Mark 10:31 and Matt 19:30; 20:16). Exclusion from the eschatological banquet means permanent estrangement with no hope of reconciliation, both in the Parables of Enoch and the Gospel of Luke.

INFLUENCE OF LUKE 16:19–31 FROM OTHER SOURCES?

Earthly and heavenly meals, with all their nuances of inclusion and exclusion, are certainly not unique to the Parables of Enoch and Luke.[62] Neither is the motif of the reversal of rich and poor in the afterlife.[63] The most influ-

---

62. See, e.g., Isa. 11:4; 25:6–8; 65:13–14; T. Levi 18; 2 Bar. 30.

63. By the second century CE, the motif was evidently so familiar that Lucian could satirize it hilariously in his *Cataplus*, a piece that might have been based on Luke

ential of these reversal tales on the scholarship of Luke 16:19–31 has been the Egyptian story of Si-Osiris, considered a possible source for the parable at least since the publication of Hugo Gressmann's 1918 study.[64] One Demotic papyrus manuscript dated confidently to the mid-first century CE is extant, although that version is probably based on an older exemplar.[65] The relevant section of the tale is as follows: Si-Osiris, a young Egyptian boy, and his father Setme watch two funerals, one of a rich man buried in fine linen with great pomp, and the other of a poor man buried ignominiously in a straw mat. Setme exclaims that he would prefer the burial of the former to that of the latter. But his son disagrees. He is wise beyond his years, for he was actually a denizen of the underworld (Amenti) who has been reincarnated by Osiris. Little Si-Osiris takes his father on a tour of Amenti to prove his point. There they observe the rich man tormented by the hinge of a door fixed in his eye, opening and closing. The poor man, on the other hand, has been given the rich man's fine linen to wear in a place of honor next to Osiris himself. Si-Osiris then delivers the moral of the story: the rich man's bad deeds outweighed the good, but the poor man's good deeds outweighed the bad. The following chart compares and contrasts this tale to Luke 16:19–31 (differences between the two are italicized):

Luke 16:19–31	Si-Osiris
There was a rich man who was dressed in purple and linen and who made merry during his life.	A rich man receives a splendid burial shrouded in fine linen.
And at his gate lay a poor man by the name of Lazarus, covered with sores and longing to satisfy his hunger with what fell from the rich man's table;	*There is no connection between the rich man and the poor one.*

16:19–31. The dating of the respective texts decisively refutes any attempt to argue for the opposite. See Ronald F. Hock, "Lazarus and Micyllus: Greco-Roman Backgrounds to Luke 16:19–31," *JBL* 106 (1987): 447–63.

64. Hugo Gressmann, *Vom reichen Mann und armen Lazarus: Eine literargeschichtliche Studie*, Abhandlungen der königlichen preussischen Akademie der Wissenschaften phil.-hist. Kl. 7 (Berlin: Königliche Akademie der Wissenschaften, 1918). For a list of the many scholars who have accepted a strong relationship between the Egyptian story and the Lukan parable, see Hock, "Lazarus and Micyllus," 449 n. 7.

65. Grobel, "Whose Name Was Neves," 375; Bauckham, "Rich Man and Lazarus," 225.

And even the dogs would come and lick his sores.

The poor man died and was borne away by the angels to the bosom of Abraham. The rich man also died and was buried.

A poor man is buried ignominiously but receives a place of honor in the underworld (Amenti), with the ruler of the underworld, Osiris.

In Hades, where he was being tormented, he lifted his eyes and saw Abraham far away with Lazarus in his bosom.

The rich man is tormented in the underworld.

The rich man's torment is a door hinge through his eye. He does not see the poor man in Amenti, and vice versa; they are both observed by third parties, Si-Osiris and his father.

He called out, "Father Abraham, have mercy on me, and send Lazarus to dip the tip of his finger in water and cool my tongue; for I am in agony in this flame."

The rich man never begs for mercy. He does not suffer flames.

But Abraham said, "Child, remember that during your lifetime you received your good things, and Lazarus in like manner evil things; but now he is comforted here, and you are in agony.

The moral of the story: good deeds must outweigh bad in order to enjoy peace in the afterlife.*

Besides all this, between you and us a great chasm has been fixed, so that those who might want to pass from here to you cannot do so, and no one can cross from there to us."

He said, "Then, father, I beg you to send him to my father's house—for I have five brothers—that he may warn them, so that they will not also come into this place of torment." Abraham replied, "They have Moses and the prophets; they should listen to them." He said, "No, father Abraham; but if someone goes to them from the dead, they will repent." He said to

Si-Osiris has returned from the dead, but in a manner completely unrelated to any request from the tormented rich man.
Si-Osiris's father takes to heart the negative example he observed in Amenti.

him, "If they do not listen to Moses
and the prophets, neither will they be
convinced even if someone rises from
the dead."

    * All of the stories we have considered here give different rationales for the rich man/men suffering in the afterlife, a detail Luke does not explicitly articulate. Much ink has been spilled trying to explain the reason for Dives's torment, but I agree with Bauckham that it is clear, like it or not: the rich man received good in his life, and Lazarus did not. I go beyond Bauckham ("Rich Man and Lazarus," 232–33) in using internal context clues to infer that Dives's earthly treatment of Lazarus was callous—literally damning—indifference to him. We do not know if Dives built his wealth unjustly on the backs of the poor, as the rich in the Parables and Epistle of Enoch did. Active oppression of the poor is one important reason for the rich suffering the flame of Sheol in both those books, while the Parables also emphasizes arrogant refusal to acknowledge God and his Chosen One.

    As the chart demonstrates, the story of Si-Osiris is not a perfect match with Luke 16:19–31. But while it is always possible that Luke did not know this story, either in a written or an oral form, and used instead texts based on it that are no longer extant, or related ideas "in the air" of a common milieu, I believe the text we have at hand precludes the necessity to peer into the void speculating about (currently) nonexistent alternatives. Hence in addition to the Epistle and the Parables of Enoch, I think it is likely that Luke was influenced by the story of Si-Osiris as well.

CONCLUSION

Like many ancient authors, Luke used numerous sources. If we hold the Two-Source Hypothesis, we believe that he drew upon Mark, Q, and L, his "special material," which consisted of many texts and traditions both oral and written (cf. Luke 1:1–4). In this paper I have argued that one of those sources may have been the Parables of Enoch. One possible indicator of this is the single significant verbal parallel they share, the unusual "mammon of unrighteousness." Perhaps the phrase was on everyone's lips at the time of Luke, and its rarity today is an historical accident. Even if one were to discount it, however, the peculiar constellation of themes and plot points the Parables of Enoch and Luke 16:19–26 have in common remains. The strongest parallels in content, as with wording, are parallels that appear nowhere else, and thus the best argument for Luke's use of the

Parables is the plea of the rich in indirect discourse for mercy from the flame of Sheol and the reigning heavenly figure's denial of their request. In addition, a messianic banquet combined with the eschatological reversal of rich and poor appears in 1 En. 62–63, an emphasis that also significantly shapes the Gospel of Luke almost from start to finish. Evidence also supports Luke's utilization of the story of Si-Osiris, the Epistle of Enoch, and, to a lesser extent, the Book of the Watchers.

These conclusions have at least two important implications. The first regards the difficult topic of dating the Parables. Much recent research has been crystalizing around a pre-Christian date, and more specifically to one around the turn of the era.[66] If Luke was influenced by the Parables of Enoch, then one of the primary results of this research has been to help undergird this emerging consensus. Second, in working with only one small Lukan pericope, we have seen that Luke may have dipped into a panoply of Enochic literature. He seems to have an affinity for it. Did he use it elsewhere? By opening the doors of possibility to this question, we may find that he did.

---

66. Paolo Sacchi, "The 2005 Camaldoli Seminar on the Parables of Enoch: Summary and Prospects for Future Research," in *Enoch and the Messiah Son of Man: Revisiting the Parables of Enoch*, ed. Gabriele Boccaccini (Grand Rapids; Eerdmans, 2007), 499–512, esp. 511.

Forgiveness of Sins:
An Enochic Problem, a Synoptic Answer

Gabriele Boccaccini

Introduction

In the Synoptics there are no explicit references to the character of Enoch (except as a name in the genealogy of Jesus by Luke), even when, as in the episode of the transfiguration, the ancient patriarch would have fit very well in a narrative located in Upper Galilee, near Mount Hermon, where the exalted Jesus met the other exalted figures of the ancient Jewish tradition (Elijah of course, but why Moses and not Enoch?).[1] In the Synoptics there are no direct quotations from the Enoch texts (apart from the complex and controversial issue of the "Son of Man").[2] The Synoptic Gospels seem to ignore completely the existence of that written tradition mentioned in the book of Jubilees or in the Testaments of the Twelve Patriarchs, which through Enoch many Second Temple Jews believed went back to the "tablets of heaven."[3]

Nonetheless, the modern interpreter cannot help feeling a special connection between the Jesus and the Enoch movements: they share a common apocalyptic worldview, a common understanding and concerns

---

1. George W. E. Nickelsburg, "Enoch, Levi, and Peter: Recipients of Revelation in Upper Galilee," *JBL* 100 (1981): 575–600.

2. Gabriele Boccaccini, ed., *Enoch and the Messiah Son of Man: Revisiting the Book of Parables* (Grand Rapids: Eerdmans, 2007); Larry W. Hurtado and Paul L. Owen, *"Who Is This Son of Man?": The Latest Scholarship on a Puzzling Expression of the Historical Jesus*, LNTS 390 (London: T&T Clark, 2011); Leslie W. Walck, *The Son of Man in the Parables of Enoch and in Matthew*, JCTCRS 9 (London: T&T Clark, 2011).

3. Lynn R. LiDonnici and Andrea Lieber, eds., *Heavenly Tablets: Interpretation, Identity and Tradition in Ancient Judaism*, JSJSup 119 (Leiden: Brill, 2007).

about the disruptive presence of the evil spirit and the power of Satan on earth; they both hope for the coming of the kingdom of God and the redemption of the poor. The relations between the Enoch and the Jesus movements are enigmatic.[4]

The problem of the kind of Judaism from which the Jesus movement was born is inescapable. In history there is no such thing as a social group that suddenly emerges, coming from nowhere, taking a little from everywhere. The puzzle cannot be easily solved by arguing multiple (and equally relevant) influences. Origins and influences are not coincidental. Obviously, if we compare the Synoptics with what we know about any of the Jewish movements of the Second Temple period, we can only conclude that they did not belong to any. The Synoptics are not a product of "Enochic Judaism":[5] they are evidence of a stage in the formation of the Jesus movement in which the new group had already reached a conceptual and distinctive autonomy not only from the Enochic movement but from all the other Second Temple Jewish movements of the time. The Jesus movement was, according to all parameters, a Jewish messianic and apocalyptic movement, but it would be incorrect to try and label it according to any other known Jewish movement of the time (Pharisaic, Essene, Sadducean, Enochic, Zealot, or Jewish Hellenistic). The Synoptics present a new "building" centered around the figure of Jesus the Messiah, a building that stands along the other buildings to form the skyline of Second Temple Judaism, with an identical mixture of continuity and discontinuity with the previous Jewish traditions. The problem is simply ill-posed. When we ask the question of the origins of the Jesus movement, in reality we inquire about the kind of Judaism from which the early followers of Jesus devel-

---

4. See George W. E. Nickelsburg, *1 Enoch 1: A Commentary on the Book of 1 Enoch, Chapters 1–36; 81–108*, Hermeneia (Minneapolis: Fortress, 2001); and George W. E. Nickelsburg and James C. VanderKam, *1 Enoch 2: A Commentary on the Book of 1 Enoch, Chapters 37–82*, Hermeneia (Minneapolis: Fortress, 2012). Citations of 1 Enoch below have been adapted from Nickelsburg's translation.

5. On "Enochic Judaism" as a distinctive form of Second Temple Judaism, see Paolo Sacchi, *Jewish Apocalyptic and Its History*, trans. William J. Short, JSPSup 20 (Sheffield: Sheffield Academic, 1996); Gabriele Boccaccini, *Roots of Rabbinic Judaism* (Grand Rapids: Eerdmans, 2002); John J. Collins, "How Distinctive Was Enochic Judaism?" in *Meghillot: Studies in the Dead Sea Scrolls* 5–6 (2007): 17*–34*; Collins, "Enochic Judaism: An Assessment," in *The Dead Sea Scrolls and Contemporary Culture*, ed. Adolfo D. Roitman, Lawrence H. Schiffman, and Shani Tzoref (Leiden: Brill, 2011), 219–34.

oped their own interpretation of Judaism and inherited the open questions they tried to answer.

The goal of my article is to go beyond the search for quotations, allusions, parallels, and influences. I aim to explore the relationship between the Jesus and the Enoch traditions from a different angle, that of premises. Was the Enochic worldview the starting point, the necessary premise (or at least one of the fundamental premises), of the theology of the Synoptics? My exploration will focus on a central theme, that of God's forgiveness of sins.

FORGIVENESS OF SINS IN THE SYNOPTICS

There are discussions whether, how, or to what extent the theme of forgiveness of sins was part of the teachings of the historical John the Baptist and Jesus. Some scholars have suggested that it was rather a later addition of the Synoptics, but the issue here is not about the historical John the Baptist or Jesus; rather it is about the relationship between Enochic and Synoptic traditions.[6]

However, one cannot deny that in the tradition of the Synoptics, "forgiveness of sins" is (or has become) a central element: John preached a baptism for "forgiveness of sin," Jesus was the Son of Man who had the authority on earth to forgive sins, and after the death of Jesus his followers began baptizing in his name a baptism for the forgiveness of sins. In the Synoptics, God's forgiveness of sins through Jesus is a crucial piece of good news connected with the coming of the kingdom of God.

The Gospel of Mark claims that "John appeared, baptizing in the wilderness and proclaiming a baptism of repentance for the forgiveness of sins" (1:4). Mark then introduces Jesus as a man of authority, somebody who could tell the paralytic: "My son, your sins are forgiven," without committing blasphemy, since "the Son of Man has authority on earth to forgive sins" (2:1–10). Mark sees Jesus's power of healing as a manifestation of God's forgiveness: "Those who are well have no need of a physician, but those who are sick; I have come to call not the righteous but sinners" (2:17). Apart from the sin of "blasphemy against the Holy Spirit," there are

---

6. Tobias Hägerland, *Jesus and the Forgiveness of Sins*, SNTSMS 150 (Cambridge: Cambridge University Press, 2012).

no limits to God's forgiveness: "everything will be forgiven to the human children, the sins and the blasphemies" (3:28–29).

Matthew and Luke basically repeat Mark's message on these issues, with some significant additions. Matthew claims that Jesus's blood was "poured out for many for forgiveness of sins" (Matt 26:28), thus attributing a forgiving power to the death of Jesus—a theme already dear to Paul and destined to become central in later Christian traditions. Luke adds the episode of the sinful woman, who in the Pharisee's house anointed the feet of Jesus. That the episode is likely a secondary transformation of the narrative of the anointing of Jesus at Bethany does not reduce the importance of the episode. Whatever reason Luke may have had to censor the anointing at Bethany, he could have simply suppressed the narrative. Instead he decided to turn it into a new episode, which combines elements from the healing of the paralytic (i.e., the questioning by the Pharisees and the explicit declaration of authority by Jesus) with elements from the calling of the tax collector (Mark 2:13–17; Matt 9:9–13; Luke 5:27–32), where in a similar context of a banquet the recipient of the gift of forgiveness is not symbolically a sick person but explicitly a sinner. Rhetorically, the centrality of the idea of forgiveness of sins is emphasized by the creation of an episode in which Jesus himself reiterates Luke's own belief that the Messiah had "authority" to say: "Your sins are forgiven" (Luke 7:36–50). In both Matthew and Luke the tendency is thus to reiterate Mark's message on forgiveness and expand it by building new narratives around this theme or interpreting other aspects of Jesus's life (like his death on the cross) in light of it.

The way in which Acts consistently retells the life of Jesus and the message of the early church attests and confirms that the announcement of forgiveness of sins in the name of Jesus was perceived as a central belief by the new community. Peter's first speech in Jerusalem at Pentecost set the tone: "And Peter said to them, 'Repent and be baptized every one of you in the name of Jesus Christ for the forgiveness of your sins'" (Acts 2:38). The numerous references to this theme in Acts (5:31; 10:43; 13:38; 26:18) and in the letters of Paul seem to indicate that the preaching of forgiveness of sins was indeed an established practice and belief in the early Jesus movement at the time the Synoptics were composed.

Forgiveness of Sins in the Enoch Tradition

While the centrality of forgiveness of sins in the theology of the Synoptics (and in the practice of the early church) is obvious, it is more difficult to understand *why* this theme became so central, if not in Jesus himself, at least in his movement. At first the comparison with the Enochic tradition may look like an odd choice. The early Enochic literature, from the Book of the Watchers to the Epistle of Enoch, does not provide any parallel. On the contrary, not only is there no reference to forgiveness of sins but the very idea of forgiveness of sins seems to be radically denied. The first mission given to Enoch is to announce to the fallen angels that "there will be no forgiveness for them" (1 En. 12). Enoch was chosen by God not as a preacher of forgiveness, but rather as a messenger of unforgiveness. A compassionate Enoch indeed accepted to intercede on behalf of the fallen angels and "draw up a petition for them that they might find forgiveness, and to read their petition in the presence of the Lord of Heaven" (13:4–5), but only to be lectured by God. Enoch had to report back to the fallen angels that such a petition "will not be accepted." The last word of God leaves no room for any hope of forgiveness. "Say to them: You have no peace" (16:4).[7]

The result is that the best parallel provided by the early Enoch tradition is with the only passage in the Synoptic tradition where God's unforgiveness is announced against those who blaspheme against the Holy Spirit: "whoever blasphemes against the Holy Spirit never has forgiveness, but is guilty of an eternal sin" (Mark 3:29; cf. Matt 12:31–32; Luke 12:10). The Synoptics seem to have learned well from Enoch that even a tradition that proclaims that everything can be forgiven has to set a limit to God's forgiveness.

Both the Dream Visions and the Epistle of Enoch draw a clear distinction between the righteous and the sinners and make no reference to forgiveness of sins. In the Animal Apocalypse there are white sheep who open their eyes, but no black sheep becomes white. In the Epistle of Enoch the opposition between the righteous and the sinners is turned into a sociological conflict between the rich and the poor, the oppressors and the oppressed, the haves and the have-nots.[8]

Once again this is a lesson that the Synoptics seem to share, especially Luke, whose series of blessings and woes in the Beatitudes echoes the language of the Epistle of Enoch. Once again, the Enoch tradition shows no interest in any call for repentance, but rather in the good news of God's

---

7. Nickelsburg, *1 Enoch 1*, 229–75.

8. On the Epistle of Enoch, see Loren T. Stuckenbruck, *1 Enoch 91–108*, CEJL (Berlin: de Gruyter, 2007).

vengeance. We might conclude that the idea of an uncompromised opposition between God and evil and the idea of an equally uncompromised opposition between the rich and the poor is what the Synoptics seem to have learned from the early Enoch tradition, in spite of the new emphasis on forgiveness of sins.

The question then arises from where the Synoptics derived their idea of repentance and God's forgiveness. The tension between with two concepts—God's unlimited forgiveness and God's uncompromised opposition to evil—is so strong that the Synoptics feel compelled to explain why not everybody is expected to convert and repent: "To you has been given the secret of the kingdom of God, but for those outside, everything comes in parables; in order that 'they may indeed look, but not perceive, and may indeed listen, but not understand; so that they may not turn again and be forgiven'" (Mark 4:11–12, quoting Isa 6:9–10).

Should we then look at the Enochic tradition as an apocalyptic tradition that limited the Synoptics, forcing or helping them not to go too far on the path of forgiveness? Or were the Enoch texts evidence of a tradition that the early Christians had to fight against? In both scenarios, the idea of forgiveness of sins would be then a unique original development by the Synoptics, beyond the limits originally set by the Enochic tradition, perhaps the result of other influences from unidentified sources or from the heritage of the earlier prophetic tradition. But is this the case?

THE BOOK OF PARABLES

At first the Book of Parables seems to reiterate in its language and imagery the same uncompromised opposition between the oppressed and the oppressors that we have seen in the Epistle of Enoch.[9] In 1 En. 48 the emphasis is on the last judgment and the revelation of the Messiah Son of Man. The reference is explicitly to Dan 7, but contrary to the source text, the Son of Man is not the recipient of God's judgment but is now the Judge, sitting on the throne of God.

---

9. On the Book of Parables, see in particular David W. Suter, *Tradition and Composition in the Parables of Enoch,* SBLDS 47 (Missoula, MT: Scholars Press, 1979); Sabino Chialà, *Libro delle parabole* (Brescia: Paideia, 1997); Nickelsburg and VanderKam, *1 Enoch 2*; and James H. Charlesworth and Darrell L. Bock, eds., *Parables of Enoch: A Paradigm Shift,* JCTCRS 11 (London: Bloomsbury T&T Clark, 2013).

The oppressed are saved in the name of God as they are filled with good works and have hated the world of unrighteousness:

> And the wisdom of the Lord of Spirits has revealed him to the holy and righteous; for he has preserved the lot of the righteous, because they have hated and despised this world of unrighteousness, and have hated all its works and ways in the name of the Lord of Spirits: for in his name they are saved, and according to his good pleasure has it been in regard to their life. (1 En. 48:7)

An opposite destiny awaits the sinners; they will not be saved "because of the works of their hands":

> In those days, downcast in countenance shall the kings of the earth have become, and the strong who possess the land because of the works of their hands, for on the day of their anguish and affliction they shall not [be able to] save themselves. And I will give them over into the hands of my elect: as straw in the fire, so shall they burn before the face of the holy; as lead in the water shall they sink before the face of the righteous, and no trace of them shall any more be found. And on the day of their affliction there shall be rest on the earth, and before them they shall fall and not rise again: and there shall be no one to take them with his hands and raise them; for they have denied the Lord of Spirits and his Anointed. The name of the Lord of Spirits be blessed. (1 En. 48:8–10)

Then after a brief interlude (ch. 49) praising the justice of God and the elect, suddenly in chapter 50 a third group ("the others") is singled out besides the righteous and the sinners—they are "those who repent and abandon the works of their hands."

> And in those days a change shall take place for the holy and chosen, and the light of days will dwell upon them, and glory and honor will return to the holy. On the day of distress, evil will be stored up against the sinners. And the righteous will be victorious in the name of the Lord of Spirits: and he will cause the others to witness (this), so that they may repent and abandon the works of their hands. They will have <no> honor in the presence of the Lord of Spirits, yet through his name they will be saved, and the Lord of Spirits will have mercy on them, for great is his mercy. And he is righteous in his judgment, and in the presence of his glory unrighteousness will not stand: at his judgment the unrepentant will perish in his presence. "And hereafter I will have no mercy on them," says the Lord of Spirits. (1 En. 50:1–5)

In the context of the Enochic tradition, this passage is extremely important, as it for the first time introduces the idea of repentance at the time of the last judgment; yet it has not received the attention it deserves and has been mistranslated and misinterpreted even in the more recent and comprehensive commentaries on the Book of Parables by Sabino Chialà and George Nickelsburg and James VanderKam.[10]

With the majority of manuscripts and all previous translations, Chialà correctly translates verse 3 as "they will have no honor" (Eth. *kebr*), in the sense that they will have no "merit" before God. In the commentary, however, Chialà understands the verse as referring to the "righteous": "they" (not the others) are the subject of the sentence. Chialà then takes the verse as a general statement that God's judgment is based exclusively on God's mercy even for the "righteous," who cannot claim any "honor" before God. But this contradicts what the Book of Parables had said in chapter 48: the righteous have good works, while the sinners do not. Besides, here the author refers to "the others" (the ones who repent and abandon the works of their hands), as is proved by the fact that the following verses (4–5) continue the discussion about repentance, not "righteousness," to the extent that "the sinners" are now denoted as "the unrepentant."[11]

Nickelsburg correctly identifies the "others" as a distinctive group— an intermediate group between the righteous and the sinners, but understands them as a subgroup of "the righteous" who may not have the same merits but will share the same destiny: "Given the references to the righteous and their oppressors in vv. 1–2b, 'the others' mentioned in this action must be either the gentiles not included among the oppressors of the righteous or other Israelites not included among the righteous, the holy, and the chosen."[12] To reinforce his own interpretation, Nickelsburg quite arbitrarily "corrects" the text, based on the testimony of only two manuscripts against most (and previous translations, like Charles and Chialà), and suppresses the negative ("they will have *no* honor"). Like the righteous, the others will have "honor" before God and will be saved in his name. But "the others" are not defined in the text for who they are but for what they do ("they repent and abandon the works of their hands"). Nickelsburg's interpretation that the "works of their hands" is a reference to idolatry is contradicted by the fact that the text here repeats the same

10. See the bibliography in n. 9 above.
11. Chialà, *Libro delle parabole*, 224.
12. Nickelsburg and VanderKam, *1 Enoch 2*, 180–83.

phrase used in 48:8 to denote the sinners ("the strong who possess the land because of the works of their hands ... will not be saved"). "The others" are not "good gentiles" or "not-so-bad Israelites"; like the sinners, they can claim no honor before God.

Both Chialà and Nickelsburg miss the revolutionary importance of the text, which at the end of times envisions the emergence of a third group besides "the righteous" and "the sinners." The righteous have "honor" (merit, good works) and are saved in the name of God, while "the sinners" have no honor (no good works) and are not saved in the name of God. The others are not a subgroup of the righteous nor a less guilty group of sinners or gentiles, but as the text explicitly states they are rather a subgroup of the sinners who will repent and abandon the works of their hands. Like the sinners (and unlike the righteous), the "others" have no "honor" (no merit or good works) before God, but because of their repentance they will be saved in the name of God, like the righteous (and unlike the sinners).

In other words, the text explores the relation between the justice and mercy of God, a theme that we would find at the center of the Jesus movement and would be broadly discussed also in the early rabbinic movement.[13] According to the Book of Parables, the righteous are saved according to God's justice and mercy, and the sinners are condemned according to God's justice and mercy; but those who repent will be saved by God's mercy, even though they should not be saved according to God's justice. Repentance makes God's mercy prevail on God's justice. No reference is made to the traditional means of atonement related to the temple or good works; the Book of Parables refers to the time of the manifestation of God and the Messiah as a (short) time in which a last opportunity of repentance will be offered to the sinners. The time is limited: after the judgment absolutely no further chance of forgiveness will be offered to "the unrepentant." The ones who do not repent will be lost forever.

The Book of Parables does not attribute forgiveness to the Messiah, who remains the judge and destroyer of evil. Yet the text signals a radical turn in a tradition that had never paid attention to the problem of repentance or forgiveness of sin, except to exclude such a possibility. Repentance is now a central theme in the Book of Parables; it is so important that it

---

13. A survey of this debate in rabbinic literature is found in Ephraim E. Urbach, *The Sages: Their Concepts and Beliefs*, trans. Israel Abrahams (Jerusalem: Magnes, 1975), 448–61.

becomes clear why one of the four archangels (besides Michael, Raphael, and Gabriel) was said to be specifically entitled to this task: "Phanuel, who is set over the repentance unto hope of those who inherit eternal life" (1 En. 40:9). The text does not further elaborate on these points, but if we read the Synoptics about the preaching of John the Baptist and Jesus, it is like reading a midrash of 1 En. 50. Regardless of the issue of whether this interpretation reflects, "adjusts," or corrects what the historical John the Baptist and the historical Jesus "really" did or meant to do, from the view point of the Synoptics, the time of the end has come and God's Messiah has been revealed in Jesus. The prophecy of 1 En. 50 no longer belongs to the future but has become true in the manifestation "on earth" of the Son of Man Jesus and his precursor John. Their entire mission would be devoted to "the others."

READING THE SYNOPTICS IN LIGHT OF ENOCH

From the vantage point of the Synoptics, John the Baptist was not primarily the popular preacher recorded by Josephus, the "wise man" who lived in the wilderness, had numerous disciples, and was executed by Herod Antipas. John was the precursor of the Son of Man, Jesus. He came to announce (or should we now say to remind people?) that "those who repent and abandon the works of their hands" will be saved by God's mercy, even though they have "no honor" before God.

This was the mission of John the Baptist, as interpreted by the Synoptics. His mediation was essential to prepare the path for the preaching of Jesus as well as the development of his movement. The function of eschatological judge immediately connects the Messiah announced by John to the "Son of Man" of the Parables of Enoch (and not to the traditions related to the Messiah Son of David). The imminent coming of the eschatological judge, who will cleanse the earth with fire, makes urgent repentance and "forgiveness of sins" for those who in this world have "no honor." The urgency of John's call is consistent with the Book of Parables' view that at the end only a small window will be opened to repentance and there will be no time afterward.[14]

---

14. On John the Baptist as an apocalyptic preacher, see Eric Noffke, *Giovanni Battista: Un profeta esseno? L'opera e il messaggio di Giovanni nel suo contesto storico* (Turin: Claudiana, 2008).

Facing the Judge and the "fire" of judgment means certain annihilation for the sinners. The solution indicated by John the Baptist is also based on a narrative central in the Enochic tradition—the purifying value that the Enochic tradition attributed to the water. The model was that offered by the flood, when the earth had already been immersed in order to limit the spread of evil. "Be baptized with water; otherwise, you will be baptized with the fire of judgment by the Son of Man"—this seems to be in essence the original message of John the Baptist, as understood by the Synoptics, an interpretation that does not contradict the interest of the Christian authors to present it as a prophecy of Christian baptism (by the Holy Spirit). That expressed by John the Baptist was a call based on the prophecy of 1 En. 50. At the end of times God will offer the sinners a last chance. If a sinner sincerely repents and abandons the works of his or her hands, even though such a person has no honor before God, God's mercy will prevail on God's justice, and he or she will be saved in God's name. As in the Parables (and contrary to what the Synoptics would claim about Jesus), the Messiah has no part in the work of forgiveness and remains the judge and destroyer of evil.

Similar ideas find an echo also in the Life of Adam and Eve, a text also generally dated in the first century CE, in which the sinner Adam does penance for forty days immersed in the waters of the Jordan (and it is not by accident that John baptized in the "living water" of the Jordan). The first man (and first sinner) is driven by one steadfast hope: "Maybe God will have mercy on me" (LAE 4:3). His plea to be allowed back in the garden of Eden will not be accepted; but at the time of his death, his soul will not be handed over to the devil, as his crime deserved, but carried out to heaven, as God decided in his mercy, despite the complaints of Satan.[15]

While John the Baptist was the precursor who announced the urgency of repentance, Jesus is the Son of Man who had authority on earth to forgive sins, left to his disciples the power of forgiveness though baptism "with the Holy Spirit," and will return with the angels to perform the judgment with fire. The relative absence of explicit messianic statements by Jesus in the Synoptics is also not surprising. "Messiah," as it should now be evident, was in the first century an extremely vague and ambiguous term (the Parables also used it only once). The primary need and challenge for any

---

15. On the Life of Adam and Eve, see Johannes Tromp, *The Life of Adam and Eve in Greek: A Critical Edition*, PVTG 6 (Leiden: Brill, 2005).

messianic pretender in the first century was rather to clarify the characteristics of his messianic claims.[16] It then becomes even more relevant that
Jesus was assigned only and exclusively sayings that related him to the "Son
of Man." The only case in which Jesus mentions the Messiah "son of David"
is to deny the concept entirely. To the "[Pharisaic] scribes [who] say that
the Messiah is the son of David," Jesus polemically replies that it cannot
be, because "David himself calls him 'Lord': How then can he be his son?"
(Mark 12:35–37). The messianic idea that the Synoptics refer to is the same
as the Enochian belief in the "Son of Man," a preexisting heavenly figure,
whose name is "hidden" from the moment of creation to the time of the
end, when he reveals himself as the Judge, and "comes in the glory of the
Father with his angels" (Mark 8:38). With the coming of the Son of Man,
the power of the "strong man" of this world is put to end, for "someone
stronger than he" has come (Luke 11:22), one who has the power to "tie
him up" and "plunder his house" (Mark 3:27). The "blasphemy" of which
Jesus was guilty before the high priest was neither the messianic self-proc-
lamation by a prisoner without power (such proclamation would have been
a matter of pity or laughter) nor a statement of divine identity (which is
not implied in the question of the high priest nor in the answer of Jesus).
Facing the question of his messiahship, which for all Jews involved a special
father-son relationship with the Father ("Are you the Messiah, the Son of
the Blessed?"), Jesus claimed a superhuman, heavenly identity: "Yes, I am!
And you will see the Son of Man seated at the right hand of the Power and
coming with the clouds of heaven" (Mark 14:61–62).

Jesus's answer reveals the significant and scandalous variations that the
Synoptics introduced into the Enochic model, where forgiveness of sins is
promised at the end but no role is given to the Messiah in this task. From
the Synoptic perspective, the Son of Man who will come from heaven as
the eschatological Judge has already been manifested on earth in Jesus of

---

16. The complexity of messianic expectations in Second Temple studies is
emphasized by all contemporary treatments of the subject; see Jacob Neusner, William Scott Green, and Ernest S. Frerichs, eds., *Judaisms and Their Messiahs at the Turn
of the Christian Era* (Cambridge: Cambridge University Press, 1987); John J. Collins,
*The Scepter and the Star: The Messiahs of the Dead Sea Scrolls and Other Ancient Lit-
erature,* 2nd ed. (Grand Rapids: Eerdmans, 2010); Gabriele Boccaccini, ed., *Il messia
tra memoria e attesa* (Brescia: Morcelliana, 2005); and Albert L. A. Hogeterp, *Expectations of the End: A Comparative Traditio-Historical Study of Eschatological, Apocalyptic, and Messianic Ideas in the Dead Sea Scrolls and the New Testament,* STDJ 83
(Leiden: Brill, 2009).

Nazareth. The Christian uniqueness lies exactly in this: "The Son of Man has power [and the mission] on earth to forgive sins" (Mark 2:1–12; cf. Matt 9:1–8; Luke 5:17–26). The statement sounds like blasphemy for those who maintain that the Messiah (the son of David) will be the leader of Israel in the world to come, but not the savior and redeemer of the individual, whose justice is measured by God the Judge according to the Torah, but also breaks the tradition of Enoch that had presented the Son of Man exclusively as the final judge from heaven, not as the forgiver "on earth."

In this, according to the Synoptics, also lies the superiority of Jesus over John. The baptism of John was a call to the sinners to become "the others" through repentance. At the end only "the unrepentant" will be damned. But John could only express a hope, based on the prophecy of Enoch and the belief that God is good and merciful and cannot remain insensitive to the cries of anguish of sinners who, like Adam in the Life of Adam and Eve, plead to God in repentance and faith. According to his followers, Jesus offered a more concrete perspective, as the promise of forgiveness comes from the Son of Man himself. Who can have more authority to forgive than the one whom God has designated as the eschatological Judge?[17]

The Synoptics do not repeat the Enochic model of the Parables. Yet the concept of the existence of a time of repentance immediately before the judgment and the prophecy that at that point "the sinners" will divide between "the repentant" (the others) and "the unrepentant" is the necessary premise of the mission of the Son of Man on earth. Jesus was not sent to "the righteous" but to "the sinners" so that they may repent. God is like a good shepherd who searches for the lost sheep; Jesus was sent to "the lost sheep of the house of Israel" (Matt 10:6) There is no evidence in the Synoptics of a universal mission of Jesus to every person; the righteous do not need the doctor; Jesus was the doctor sent to heal the sinners (Mark 2:17; Matt 9:13), as Luke makes explicit: "I have come to call not the righteous but the sinners to repentance" (Luke 5:32).

Reading the Synoptics in light of the Book of Parables sheds light also on some parables that the Christian tradition attributed to Jesus. The parable of the lost sheep (Matt 18:10–14; Luke 15:1–7) defines the relationship between God and "the others": Luke's parable of the prodigal son (15:11–

17. See Paolo Sacchi, *Gesù e la sua gente* (Cinisello Balsamo: San Paolo, 2003); Gabriele Boccaccini and Piero Stefani, *Dallo stesso grembo: Le origini del cristianesimo e del giudaismo rabbinico* (Bologna: Dehoniane, 2012).

32) reiterates the theme but also adds a teaching about the relationship between "the righteous" and "the others," between those who have honor and are saved because they have never abandoned the house of the Father and those who have no honor and yet are saved as well since they have repented and abandoned the works of their hands. The examples could be multiplied, but no parable seems more effective to me than the one narrated by Matthew on the workers in the vineyard (Matt 20:1–16). The householder who pays the same salary for different "measures" of work gives the full reward (salvation) to the "righteous" and to the "others," as 1 En. 50 claimed that God would also do in the last judgment. God's mercy ("Am I not allowed to do what I choose with what belongs to me? Or do you begrudge my generosity?") wins over God's justice, or as the Letter of James would say, "mercy triumphs over judgment" (2:13; κατακαυχᾶται ἔλεος κρίσεως).[18]

The contrast with the rabbinic tradition could not be stronger. The rabbis freely discuss the relation between the two middot, God's measures of justice and mercy, providing flexible answers to the issue. Mishnah Soṭah (1:7–9) sticks to the principle, "With what measure a man metes it shall be measured to him again," and affirms that "with the same measure" God gives justice when punishing evil deeds and mercy when rewarding good deeds. On the other hand, the parallel text in Tosefta Soṭah (3:1–4:19) claims that "the measure of mercy is five hundred times greater than the measure of justice." But the two divine attributes are never opposed as in the Book of Parables and in the early Christian tradition; on the contrary, their necessarily complementary nature is emphasized. Not accidentally, the rabbinic version of the parables will end with different words in which God's mercy is praised but God's justice is not denied: "This one did more work in two hours than the rest of you did working all day long" (y. Ber. 2:8).[19]

CONCLUSION

Although there is no evidence of literary dependence, the Synoptic tradition reads and interprets the experience of John the precursor and Jesus the Messiah by borrowing its categories from the Book of Parables, or

---

18. See Boccaccini, *Middle Judaism*, 213–28.
19. See Boccaccini and Stefani, *Dallo stesso grembo*.

better from the traditions of the Book of Parables, to the point that the gospels could be understood almost as a midrash to 1 En. 50 in a perspective of realized eschatology: John the Baptist and Jesus have fulfilled the Enochic prophecy. At the center is the destiny of the righteous, the sinners, and "the others" now that "the end is near." The Synoptics add some new elements, which indeed differentiate the Jesus movement from the Enochic model, and yet do not separate it from the world of Second Temple Judaism at large. These elements enhance the specificity of the Jesus movement in relation not only to the Sadducees and the Pharisees, but also in relation to its Enochic roots and to the message of John the Baptist himself. In the Synoptics, Jesus becomes the protagonist of a "prologue on earth" that precedes, and prepares for, the "heavenly judgment" of the Messiah Son of Man, who is now both the forgiver on earth and the eschatological Judge. The possibility of repentance announced by the Parables of Enoch and John the Baptist as one of the signs of the end becomes the center of the activity of the Messiah Jesus, who came as the Son of Man who has authority on earth to forgive sins. In baptizing in his name the early church continues and prolongs Jesus's message of forgiveness as an instrument of God's mercy, until Jesus will return to perform the judgment, and no further time for repentance will then be allowed. The Jesus movement was not an Enochic movement but an outgrowth of the Enochic movement. The Synoptics are not Enochic texts but an answer to an Enochic problem.

"Son of Man":
Its Origin and Meaning in Second Temple Judaism

Lester L. Grabbe

The debate over the meaning and connotation of the phrase "son of man" has produced a massive stack of literature in the past forty years. No doubt, one of the main reasons has been the application of the epithet to Jesus of Nazareth, since anything to do with Jesus seems to generate hyperbolic interest. My purpose is to consider the use of the expression in Second Temple Judaism, including early Christianity, since this originated as a movement within Judaism.

Philological Discussion

The term "son" has a wide range of uses in the various Semitic languages. It is part of a set of words that are combined with other words to designate groups, including words like "son," "master" (*ba'al*), "man," and the like (the phenomenon is, of course, known in other languages; for example, in English "sons" and "daughters" are used in group names: Daughters of the American Revolution, Sons of Anarchy, Daughters of the Texas Republic). In addition to its literal reference to an actual son or even descendant, it can be used to show a more general relationship.[1]

---

1. This is perhaps best catalogued in Hebrew in the *DCH* entry "בֵן." A number of examples from general Semitic can be given. The Mari texts talk of the "sons of the South" and the "sons of the North" as a designation of certain tribal groups: "Designation of someone belonging to a family, tribe, or another community" (*DNWSI*, 194). I leave aside the debate as to whether "sons" in the name should be read as *bin*, to yield a name similar to Benjaminite, or as Akkadian *maru*; see the discussion and references in Lester L. Grabbe, *Ancient Israel: What Do We Know and How Do We Know It?* (London: T&T Clark, 2007), 46–47. In Neo-Assyrian inscriptions the word

In Aramaic the expression בר אנש occurs as early as the eighth century BCE, in the Sefire inscription, meaning "someone."[2] However, this is the only example in Old Aramaic, though the Deir ʿAlla inscription (how-

---

maru, "son" (Sumerian DUMU), was used to designate the king of a country. Note the designation of Adramu king of Hamath as DUMU *A-gu-ú-si*, Aḫunu king of Adini as DUMU *A-di-ni* , and Ḫaiiānu king of Gabbari as DUMU *Gab-ba-ri* in the Kurkh Monolith; see A. K. Grayson, *Assyrian Rulers of the Early First Millennium BC II (858–745 BC)*, RIMA 3 (Toronto: University of Toronto Press, 1996), 17–18 (A.0.102.2:15, 24, 27). This explains the usage that has puzzled many, when Jehu was referred to as a "son" (בן) of Omri, even though he was a usurper who had no genealogical connection to Omri. It now becomes clear that "*mari* Ḥumri" was simply a way of saying "king of [the kingdom of] Omri"; cf. Lester L. Grabbe, "Omri and Son, Incorporated: The Business of History," in *Congress Volume, Helsinki 2010,* ed. Martti Nissinen, VTSup 148 (Leiden: Brill, 2012), 61–83. Inscriptions of Shalmaneser show that the Sumerogram DUMU, "son of," is used in a number of cases simply to designate a citizen of a particular country (hence the translation "man of "), though the person so designated usually happens to be the king (cf. also the Aramaic inscription *KAI* 222A:16; B:3: *bny gš*, "inhabitants of Gush").

In Hebrew the expression tends to be בן אדם, "son of man (= man, human, humanity)," which is found in many biblical passages (e.g., Num 23:19; Isa 51:12; Jer 49:18, 33; Pss 8:5; 80:18; Job 16:21; Dan 8:17; and many places in Ezekiel). Also found with much the same meaning are בן איש (e.g., Lev 24:10; 1 Sam 9:1; 17:12; 2 Sam 1:13) and בן אנוש (Ps 144:3). At Qumran, the Thanksgiving Hymns have an example of "sons of men" (1QH IX 34: "[I shall report?] to the sons of man [ולבני אנוש] all the marvels that you have intensified").

In Phoenician inscriptions *bn ʾdm* means "person" or, in the plural, "men, humans"; see Charles R. Krahmalkov, *Phoenician-Punic Dictionary,* OLA 90, Studia Phoenicia 15 (Leuven: Peeters, 2000), 105. We have a Neo-Punic inscription that reads, "He *treated* every person honestly" (*KAI* 165:3: *kl bn ʾdm kn nḥr*). A Phoenician inscription has the plural (in parallel to "gods"): "in the eyes of gods and humans" (*KAI* 48:4: *lʿn ʾlnm wbn ʾdm*). More puzzling is Ugar. *bnš*, meaning "man, an individual, someone, person people, personnel," as well as "farmhand, laborer." At first, it might not seem relevant, but it has been proposed that it comes from *bn* plus (ʾ) *nš*, though this is not certain; see Gregorio del Olmo Lete and Joaquín Sanmartín, *A Dictionary of the Ugaritic Language in the Alphabetic Tradition,* trans. Wilfred G. E. Watson, HdO 1.67, parts 1–2 (Leiden: Brill, 2003), 230–32; Fritz Maass, "אנוש," *TDOT* 1:346. In any case, in the alphabetic Ugaritic texts we do have the form *bn adm*, "man," in parallel with *adm* (*CTU* 1.169:14–15), and "a man's word" (*CTU* 9.435:10 [*RSO* 14.52:10] *hwt bn nšm*; the information of *CTU* 9.435 is taken from Olmo Lete and Sanmartín, *Dictionary,* 227, since the full inscription has apparently not been published). Likewise, the plural is attested: "men" (*CTU* 1.6 II 18–19: *bn nšm* [// *hmlt arṣ,* "multitudes of the earth"]).

2. *KAI* 224:16; Joseph A. Fitzmyer, "The New Testament Title 'Son of Man' Philo-

ever one classifies its language) has "sons of men" (2:8: בני אש). There appear to be no examples so far found in the large known resources of Imperial Aramaic. In Middle Aramaic, apart from the one example in Dan 7:13,[3] the phrase occurs in several texts, though they seem mostly to come from Qumran; there appear to be no examples from other texts from the Judean Desert:[4]

1QapGen (1Q20)
VI 9, לבני אנשא, "the Most High to the sons of men [= humans]"
VI 20, בנת אנו[שא], "the Holy Ones [= angels] who [had inter-course?] with the daughters of m[en (= human women)]"
XIX 15, ובנ[י] אנוש, "And sons of man [= some people] came and were seeking to cut down and uproot the [ce]dar"
XIX 23, [כול בר אנוש], "that no [son of man (= no one)] should see her"
XXI 13, כול בר אנוש, "I shall multiply your seed like the dust of the earth that not any son of man [= no one] is able to count"

4QEnoch[a] ar (4Q201)
1 iii 18, כל בני אנשא, "the toil of all the sons of man [= the humans]"

logically Considered," in *A Wandering Aramean: Collected Aramaic Essays*, SBLMS 25 (Missoula, MT: Scholars Press, 1979), 147.

3. For some reason, Fitzmyer did not include Biblical Aramaic in his category of Middle Aramaic, but I believe that the language of Daniel belongs here.

4. Nothing is found in Naphtali Lewis, *The Documents from the Bar Kokhba Period in the Cave of Letters: Greek Papyri, Aramaic and Nabatean Signatures and Subscriptions* (Jerusalem: Israel Exploration Society, 1989); Hannah M. Cotton and Ada Yardeni, eds., *Aramaic, Hebrew and Greek Documentary Texts from Naḥal Ḥever and Other Sites, with an Appendix Containing Alleged Qumran Texts (The Seiyâl Collection II)*, DJD 27 (Oxford: Clarendon, 1997); Yigael Yadin and Yaakov Meshorer, *Masada I: The Yigael Yadin Excavations 1963–1965, Final Reports: The Aramaic and Hebrew Ostraca and Jar Inscriptions; The Coins of Masada* (Jerusalem: Israel Exploration Society, 1989); Pierre Benoit, J. T. Milik, and Roland de Vaux, *Les grottes de Murabbaʿât*, 2 vols., DJD 2 (Oxford: Clarendon, 1961); Joseph A. Fitzmyer and Daniel J. Harrington, *A Manual of Palestinian Aramaic Texts*, BibOr 34 (Rome: Biblical Institute Press, 1978); this was confirmed by a search on the Comprehensive Aramaic Lexicon (CAL) website (http://cal1.cn.huc.edu). There also seems to be a bilingual inscription from the second century CE with one example of בר אינש (*KAI* 276:9–10).

4QEnoch^e ar (4Q206)
frag. 2 II 1, כל בני אנשא, "[the sou]l of all the sons of man"

4QEnastr^b ar (4Q209)
frag. 23 8, בני אנשא, "of the earth: one of them for the sons of man [= humans] to dwell in"

4QEnoch^g ar (4Q212) v 20, [מן כל בני א[נוש], "Or who is he [from all the sons of m]an who is able…?"

4QEnGiants^c ar (4Q531)
frag. 14 4, בין בני אנש, "he did [no]t live among the sons of man [= humans]"

11QtgJob (11Q10)
IX 9 (Job 25:6), [וב]ר אנש, "and a son of man [is but] a worm"
XIII 9 (Job 28:28), לבני [אנש], "and he said to the sons of [man]"
XXVI 3 (Job 35:8), ולבר אנש, "and your justice [affects] a son of man [like yourse]lf" (parallel to איש in the Hebrew text and probably something like לגבר in the gap in the Aramaic text).
XXVIII 2 (36:25), ובני אנשא, "and all men look upon him, and the sons of man from a distance"

There are some linguistic points to notice about these passages:

1. It is clear that the idiom is not a frequent one in texts up to the end of the first century CE, with only one example occurring in pre-Qumran Aramaic texts. Although the number of examples is partly a result of the accidents of history as to which texts were preserved, the corpus is large enough to give a reasonable sample from which certain tentative conclusions can be drawn.

2. The normal generic reference to humans is the plural בני אנשא or occasionally בני אנש. Where the singular occurs, it always occurs in the absolute (unemphatic) form: בר אנוש.

The late Geza Vermes wrote an influential article on the meaning of בר נש(א) in rabbinic Aramaic literature[5] in which he surveyed the Pales-

---

5. The seminal work was Gustaf Dalman's *Words of Jesus,* trans. D. M. Kay (Edinburgh: T&T Clark)—the 1902 English translation of which was more or less a second edition—in his chapter on the "son of man" (ch. 9, pp. 234–89). As a leading special-

tinian Talmud, Genesis Rabbah, the "Palestinian Targum," and the Genesis Apocryphon.[6] Vermes argued for three primary meanings for the expression: (1) "a human being"; (2) an indefinite pronoun—"someone," "anyone," (with כל) "everyone," (with a negative) "no one," "some people," "a certain man"; (3) a circumlocution for "I." One of the main points Vermes wished to make, however, was a negative one: "not one among the hundreds of examples scrutinized by me suggests that *bar nāsh(ā)* was ever employed as a messianic designation.... On the contrary, all the available Aramaic evidence appears to point to the unsuitability of *bar nāshā* as a name or title."[7] This denial is justified for most of the philological evidence considered in this section, but there are passages that still need to be considered. They will be considered in the section below on "The Eschatological Question."

Vermes's first two definitions were hardly new, but the third one requires some comment; indeed, it has been widely rejected by Aramaists.[8] Even where בר נש(א) refers to or at least includes the speaker, it is not the equivalent to "I." The whole point of using that phrase instead of "I" is to create a particular semantic situation different from using "I." For example, a product of a British public school, who is praised for an achievement of some sort, might well say, "One does one's best." Does he mean that to be understood as, "I do my best"? Absolutely not! It goes

---

ist in Aramaic at the time, Dalman discussed the philology as it was understood from the Palestinian Aramaic linguistic material available to him, which was mainly rabbinic writings, primarily the Aramaic targumim, the Palestinian Talmud, and Midrash Rabbah.

6. This choice of literature is not without some difficulties. While it is all Western Aramaic, the reference to the "the Palestinian Targum" is problematic (see Fitzmyer and Harrington, *Manual of Palestinian Aramaic*, 18, 72–74, for further discussion), though this is perhaps primarily (if not entirely) a terminological issue. However, the Genesis Apocryphon is centuries earlier than the rabbinic material, and we cannot assume a uniform usage in the two bodies of literature. The Qumran material has already been examined above.

7. Geza Vermes, "Appendix E: The Use of בר נש/בר נשא in Jewish Aramaic," in Matthew Black, *An Aramaic Approach to the Gospels and Acts,* 3rd ed. (Oxford: Clarendon, 1967), 327–28.

8. The concept itself is not new, for Delbert Burkett (*The Son of Man Debate: A History and Evaluation,* SNTSMS 107 [Cambridge: Cambridge University Press, 1999], 86–87) shows that this interpretation has a long history. Among those rejecting this interpretation, Fitzmyer ("New Testament Title," 154) should particularly be noted; a number of others also rejecting it are catalogued by Burkett.

without specific statement that he has done his best, and he may well want with all his being to be praised and credited with the achievement. Yet by saying "one" rather than "I," he is distancing himself from his achievement. He could well have phrased it, "People do their best" or "Each participant has done his or her best," with somewhat the same connotation. But rather than being a circumlocution for "I," it is a way of drawing attention away from the speaker. It might represent false modesty, but it is a statement of modesty. To be told, "Oh, you mean that you did your best," would be to heap insult upon his head.

In my opinion, none of the examples given by Vermes demonstrates the use of (בר נש(א as a circumlocution for "I." It would take too much space to examine each example, but I shall look at one example here. Vermes seems to draw special attention to his last example (from Genesis Rabbah), concluding, "In other words, *bar nāshā* is definitely a circumlocution for 'I' in this instance at least." Here is that example, as apparently translated by Vermes himself:[9]

> Rabbi Simeon ben Yohai and his son hid in a cave for thirteen years.... At the end, he went forth and sat at the entrance to the cave. There he saw a hunter trying to catch birds. When he heard a heavenly voice saying *Dimissio*, the bird escaped, (and when he heard it say) *Specula* (execution), it was caught. He then said, Not even a bird is caught without the will of Heaven. How much less the soul of *bar nāshā* (נפש דבר נשא). So he went forth and found that affairs had quietened down. (Gen. Rab. 79:6 [ed. Theodor, 941–42])

Far from "the soul of *bar nāshā*" being a circumlocution for "I," this is plainly a gnomic saying in which the soul of a man (or a human soul) is of more concern to Heaven than that of a bird. That Rabbi Simeon ben Yohai then applies the saying to himself does not mean that that was the original meaning of the saying. We constantly apply traditional sayings to specific situations without saying that the particular situation was original intent of the saying.

Vermes's mistake is assuming that application is the same as identity. He notes, for example, that a textual variant has "my soul" instead of "soul of the son of man," but this does not make the two readings identical. On the contrary, "my soul" has a different connotation from the reading

---

9. Vermes, "Appendix E," 326.

adopted in the Theodor text. That a linguistic phrase or expression can be substituted for another in a sentence does not mean they are automatically identical. "I hit my thumb with a hammer" could read "I hit my forefinger with a hammer": "thumb" and "forefinger" have the same linguistic or grammatical function in the sentence. They also happen both to be parts of the hand, yet they are not the same thing.

Another point is that Vermes, followed by Maurice Casey and Barnabas Lindars, argued that there was no difference between the absolute (בר אנש) and emphatic (בר אנשא) forms of the Aramaic phrase.[10] This needs to be seriously challenged.[11] Casey has replied to criticisms, but inadequately, in my view. He makes some general points about linguistics, drawing on J. K. Chambers and Peter Trudgill and Christopher Lyons, which are of course valid; he refers to an excellent essay by James Barr on the Hebrew article; and he notes that one should not overly press the boundaries of the various Aramaic periods. Unfortunately, none of this proves—or even addresses the issue—that there is no difference between the absolute and emphatic forms of the Aramaic expression.

It is a sad commentary on one's argument if, in a linguistic debate, a scholar tries to rewrite the rules of grammar in order to support his hypothesis. Yet this is what Casey does. Further, he dismisses leading Aramaic scholars such as E. Y. Kutscher, Franz Rosenthal, Takamitsu Muraoka, Bezalel Porten, and Stephen Kaufman, on whom we all depend for our current understanding of the forms of Aramaic (not to mention giants such as Theodor Nöldeke and Carl Brockelmann, on whose shoulders we

---

10. Maurice Casey, *The Solution to the "Son of Man" Problem*, LNTS 343 (London and New York: T&T Clark, 2007), 59–61; Barnabas Lindars, *Jesus Son of Man: A Fresh Examination of the Son of Man Sayings in the Gospels in the Light of Recent Research* (London: SPCK, 1983), 19–20.

11. Studies that have already done so are Paul Owen and David Shepherd, "Speaking up for Qumran, Dalman and the Son of Man: Was *Bar Enasha* a Common Term for 'Man' in the Time of Jesus?" *JSNT* 81 (2001): 81–122; Paul L. Owen, "Problems with Casey's 'Solution,'" in *"Who Is This Son of Man?": The Latest Scholarship on a Puzzling Expression of the Historical Jesus,* ed. Larry W. Hurtado and Paul L. Owen, LNTS 390 (London and New York: T&T Clark, 2011), 28–49; and in the same volume the entries by David Shepherd, "Re-Solving the Son of Man 'Problem' in Aramaic," 50–60; and Peter J. Williams, "Expressing Definiteness in Aramaic: A Response to Casey's Theory concerning the Son of Man Saying," 61–77. See Casey's reply in "Aramaic Idiom and the Son of Man Problem: A Response to Owen and Shepherd," *JSNT* 25 (2002): 3–32.

all humbly stand).[12] However, he goes further by attempting to reclassify Aramaic dialects and rewrite Aramaic grammar. For example, he wants to classify Syriac not as Eastern Aramaic but as a new entity, "Central Aramaic." Grammar and linguistic description are always subject to discussion and revision, but we should be skeptical when it is written by someone with an axe to grind or a theory to prove. Trained linguists carrying out a purely descriptive task should do the job. It is true that linguistic description is not always as cut and dried or as precise as some handbooks present it. But Casey has not dealt with the main issue: West Aramaic dialects generally maintained the distinction between the absolute and the emphatic state during this time.

There is a further difficulty in that he moves into some presumed Aramaic quotations in the Greek New Testament (which raise a whole raft of questions) to argue his case. But what really amazes is his concluding statement:

> ὁ υἱὸς τοῦ ἀνθρώπου occurs no less than 14 times in Mark, and 8 times in Q: there are 69 occurrences in the Synoptic Gospels as a whole, and when all parallels are discounted, this still leaves no less than 38 independent sayings. It follows that בר (א)נש(א) was as normal in first-century Galilean Aramaic as it is in later Jewish sources and in Syriac, and that its frequency should not be guessed at by mechanical counting of earlier sources.[13]

This type of argument is astonishing, if one takes seriously Casey's position. In order to determine how frequently the phrase בר אנש occurs in Aramaic of the first century, he points us to a *Greek* phrase and its use in a very specific context—the sayings of Jesus. He then contrasts this bizarre statistical method with "mechanical counting" of the Aramaic phrase in Aramaic texts. This looks to me like desperately clutching at straws!

---

12. It defies belief that Casey so cavalierly writes off some leading contemporary Aramaists, but this is the only way I can understand his statement: "So they [Owen and Shepherd] rely on Kutscher for determination being used 'correctly,' Muraoka for deviations from 'classical usage' and apparently also for 'deviation from the expected use of the states,' and Kaufman for the two noun states being used 'quite properly.' This is especially regrettable because the discussion of these matters in existing secondary literature is not satisfactory" (Casey, "Aramaic Idiom," 15–16).

13. Ibid., 11.

Yet Casey has a point, in one sense. He has drawn the debate's attention to the issue that linguistic usage cannot easily be reduced to a cold set of logical rules. Living language is too flexible, organic, and responsive to local speech communities for it to be covered by simplistic grammatical rules. The general question of determinative versus absolute forms is relevant, but it ultimately comes down to how the specific idiom (א)בר אנש is used in specific speech acts. Since native speakers no longer exist, the best we can do for speech acts is look to contemporary texts. This is also where Vermes and others have created problems, by using examples from a later stage of Aramaic.

It is true, as Casey says, that the Aramaic language was stable over centuries, but that is unremarkable: most written languages are stable. Hebrew was stable, Greek was stable, English is stable. Aramaic was not unusual in this regard.[14] Also, appealing to this stability can be misleading since it might imply no changes, whereas we know that Aramaic changed continually through the centuries (as has been carefully catalogued by some of the Aramaic linguists that Casey so casually dismisses), with innovations in some areas and conservative retentions in others. Again, it is a mistake to speak in general terms when arguing this case: we have to look at specific texts from a specific time.

To get down to the specifics: from the first, Casey confuses matters linguistically by continually writing the Aramaic phrase as בר (א)נש(א). This begs the question still to be addressed of the absolute versus the emphatic state. Also, the form appears either as בר אנש or בר אנשא. There is no בר נש or בר נשא until later dialects. Casey argues that the initial א might not have been pronounced in Galilee. That may or may not have been the case; in any event, the *graphic form* at this time is always with the initial א, even in much of the later targumic tradition. Casey misleads by lumping together earlier and later forms, as well as the emphatic and absolute states. Until such a form as נש(א) is attested for the first century BCE or CE, it should not be assumed.

---

14. Casey notes that words such as זרע, "seed," ידע, "know," כל, "all," לא, "not," and מלך, "king" are found in both earlier and later dialects of Aramaic. This is hardly surprising, since such base words tend to persist in any language. Look at the words for "brother," "father," and other fundamental vocabulary in Indo-European that have exhibited remarkable persistence in widely spread languages over millennia of linguistic usage.

We have already looked at the material from Qumran, which is the only evidence contemporary with Aramaic usage of the first centuries BCE and CE. We saw that the plural form was generally in the emphatic state (בני אנשא), though there were one or two examples of the absolute. On the other hand, the singular (which was rather less frequent than the plural) was consistently in the absolute (בר אנש). Even though the examples were not numerically overwhelming, they were sufficient to draw some preliminary conclusions: Aramaic usage of the time favored the determined forms for the plural and the nondetermined form for the singular, and the singular was less frequent than the plural.

This preliminary conclusion is buttressed by examination of the targumic usage.[15] In Targum Onqelos, the singular does not occur at all, only the plural (10 times), which is always in the determined state. Targum Jonathan to the Prophets has only the plural determined form in the Former Prophets (sixteen times). Likewise, in the Latter Prophets the plural emphatic form is the most frequent usage; however, there are five instances of the absolute singular. Finally, there are two instances of the singular determined form, in Isa 51:12 and 56:2.[16] As it turns out, in all the targumic texts currently available on CAL's website, the only singular determined forms are the two in Isaiah and one further one in the "additional Tosefot to the Prophets." Otherwise, the emphatic forms are all plurals, and the singular forms (five in Targum Jonathan to the Prophets and one in the rabbinic Targum to Job) are all in the absolute.

A survey of "Jewish Galilean" Aramaic texts through CAL is quite interesting. It basically consists of Palestinian rabbinic texts, some quite late: Midrash Rabbah, the Palestinian Talmud, Pesiqta de Rab Kahana, Midrash ha-Gadol of Genesis, Qohelet Zuṭa, Midrash to Psalms, and a few other texts. Just under five hundred examples are found. By far the most frequent form is ברנש, with more than 375 occurrences. Much less

15. This survey is based on use of the texts and search programs available on the CALCAL website (http://cal1.cn.huc.edu), whose designers and workers I wholeheartedly thank for the excellent linguistic resource being developed here. This was supplemented by cross-checks to the concordances of Johannes C. de Moor, ed., *A Bilingual Concordance to the Targum of the Prophets*, 21 vols. (Leiden: Brill, 1995–2005); and Martin G. Abegg Jr., James E. Bowley, and Edward M. Cook, *The Dead Sea Scrolls Concordance*, 3 vols. (Leiden: Brill, 2003).

16. Shepherd ("Re-Solving," 56) argues that definiteness is already implied in that both are used as subjects of relative clauses.

frequent but still significant are the more than forty occurrences of ברנשא,
followed by בניש at nearly thirty. There are only a handful of examples of
ש(י)א בני אנשא, בר אנ(י)ש(י)א, בר א(י)ש, and בנינשא. This shows a
considerable development in comparison with Middle Aramaic. It looks as
if a development similar to that of Syriac has taken place, in which ברנש—
the singular apocopated form—has become the normal (rather than the
earlier exceptional) way of saying "a man, someone, human." Most frequent is the absolute form, but the determined form is not insignificant.

What this survey and comparison suggests is that the use of the determined or nondetermined form is not arbitrary but follows meaning: the
plural is mostly determined because that is its connotation, though it occasionally occurs in the absolute when that fits its meaning. On the other
hand, the singular is normally nondetermined because it usually expresses
a general reference. The singular is infrequent in the earlier (late Second
Temple) period, with the determined singular even less frequent than the
absolute. The singular becomes the most frequent form a few centuries
later in rabbinic texts, though the determined form is a lot less frequent
than the absolute. The transition from earlier בר אנש to later ברנש has
taken place in the rabbinic period, though some examples of the earlier
form still occur.

In anticipation of being criticized for the point just made, I should
point out that Casey argues that reliance on early examples is not sufficient
because "the Dead Sea scrolls do not contain enough Aramaic to form a
language."[17] I find this statement problematic. There is limited Aramaic
material in the scrolls from the Judean Desert, but there is also limited
Aramaic material in the Palestinian Talmud (which has a peculiar content). Each text is a *parole*, to use de Saussure's term, but it reflects a *langue*,
a language with its grammar and usage.[18] The fact is that there is a relative
abundance of examples making use of various forms of בר אנש in the
Judean Desert manuscripts. It is certainly sufficient to draw preliminary
conclusions and also provide a basis for comparing with other Aramaic
dialects. The methodological principle is, though, that we compare dialects as attested in texts. We do not just grab and lump together forms
eclectically across geographically and chronologically separated dialects.

---

17. Casey, "Aramaic Idiom," 7–8.
18. Ferdinand de Saussure, *Course in General Linguistics,* trans. Roy Harris, 3rd
ed. (Chicago: Open Court, 1972).

Conclusions on the Philology

We have not examined all the relevant texts, since a number alleged to
show a messianic title or something similar will be considered in the next
section. Thus the question of messianic/eschatological usage of the term
"son of man" has been postponed and not settled in this section. The main
conclusions of this section can be summarized as follows:

1. *The expression "son of man" does not necessarily function exactly
as "man" or other expressions in the Semitic languages.* Although various
words for "man, human," are frequent in Semitic literature, "son of man"
is not very frequent in the early period and is often a ballast variant in
Semitic poetry or parallelism.

2. *The Aramaic phrase בר אנש and its various forms are not necessarily interchangeable.* Even when they largely overlap in meaning, they may
still differ in frequency or particular literary contexts (from a linguistic
point of view, the semantic register of synonyms may be different). For
example, when the Aramaic form בר אנש occurs in the last centuries
BCE and first centuries CE, it is normally in the plural determined form
(בני אנשא, "sons of man"). The absolute form of the singular is quite
infrequent, and the emphatic form of the singular is the least frequent.
This is important because statements in secondary sources sometimes
present the different forms as if they were interchangeable, which makes
questionable several conclusions or even premises in some secondary
literature.

3. *In western Middle Aramaic the determined forms are not interchangeable with the absolute forms.* Although standard linguistic references state
generally that absolute and determined forms had separate linguistic
usage in western Middle Aramaic, our question concerns the specific
usage of בר אנש and בר אנשא. What we found was that no examples of
the determined form were attested in the Middle Aramaic writings currently available. This impression was supported by a survey of targumic
literature, which also showed only three examples of the determined form
in all the targumim presently known. Yet in the later rabbinic Aramaic literature, the singular absolute is by far the most frequent form, comparable
to Syriac.

4. *The term is not simply a way of saying "I."* Even where it includes or
refers specifically to the speaker, the semantic content is different from the
straightforward use of "I."

THE ESCHATOLOGICAL QUESTION

In the previous section we looked at a variety of texts in order to determine the normal meaning of "son of man" in the various Semitic languages. I deliberately omitted, however, several passages that have been alleged to show a messianic title or relate to matters of eschatology that I will now scrutinize. Through much of the twentieth century, the standard view was the "eschatological" one, that "son of man" was an eschatological title and was so used by Jesus, or at least by the Jesus tradition.[19]

Beginning about 1966, however, it became common to reject the eschatological explanation. This came about partly because the Parables of Enoch were not found at Qumran, partly because of the impact of Vermes's study of Aramaic usage of the term "son of man" in rabbinic literature (mentioned in the previous section), but also because of the influence of other studies, such as those of Norman Perrin.[20] My aim is this section is to consider the eschatological explanation: has it been disproved, as some argue? Also to be considered is the Greek version of "son of man" (υἱὸς ἀνθρώπου, ὁ υἱὸς τοῦ ἀνθρώπου), which is well known from the New Testament.

Daniel 7

The fount of much of the debate about "son of man" is Dan 7. Many of the later uses of "son of man" in Jewish and Christian texts have some connection with this text. After a description of the "Ancient of Days" in 7:9–10, 7:13–14 state the following:

> I was observing in visions of the night and, behold, with the clouds of heaven one like a son of man [אנש כבר] was coming, and he reached the Ancient of Days, and they brought him before him, and to him was given authority and glory and kingship, so that all peoples, nations, and tongues would serve him. His authority is an eternal authority that shall not pass away, and his kingship shall not be destroyed.

Some have claimed that the "one like a son of man" is simply a symbol for the "saints of the Most High," that is, the Jewish people.[21] There is no

---

19. See the survey in Burkett, *Son of Man Debate*, 68–70.
20. Ibid., 70–76.
21. Casey, *Solution*, 82–91.

doubt that this figure represents the Jewish people (7:18, 22, 27), but that does not stop his constituting an actual being or supernatural personage within the mythical world of the text. In this instance, there is a good case to be made that the "one like a son of man" was the archangel Michael.[22] An expression similar to the one in Dan 7:13 is found in the Hebrew text of Dan 10:16: "And, behold, one like the sons of man [כדמות בני אדם] was touching my lips." This refers to a heavenly being who is engaged in opposing the princes of Persia and Greece (10:5–6, 12–13, 16–20), perhaps Gabriel (since he is being helped by "Michael, one of the first princes," and is the only other named angelic figure in Daniel [8:16; 9:21]).[23] Note that the more frequent (in early texts) plural form of the term is used.

Parables of Enoch (1 En. 37–71)

The dating of the Similitudes or Parables has been much discussed.[24] There seems to be a clear reference to the Parthian invasion of Palestine in 56:5–57:2, but no known historical details are given.[25] The conclusion I come to is that the Parables were written either before or a good time after the Parthian invasion of 40 BCE, since the reference to Parthians and Medes seem to be to a type rather than a reference to a specific historical event. This suggests to me a date some decades after 40 BCE. If 1 En. 67:5–13 refers to Herod's visit to Callirrhoe in search of a cure shortly before his

---

22. Originally proposed, as far as I am aware, by Nathaniel Schmidt "The Son of Man in the Book of Daniel," *JBL* 19 (1900): 22–28. The most recent and thorough case has been made by John J. Collins, *The Apocalyptic Vision of the Book of Daniel*, HSM 16 (Missoula, MT: Scholars Press, 1977); idem, *Daniel: A Commentary*, Hermeneia (Minneapolis: Fortress, 1993), 304–10, esp. 310.

23. Cf. Collins, *Daniel*, 373.

24. Mostly recently, see George W. E. Nickelsburg and James C. VanderKam, *1 Enoch 2: A Commentary on the Book of 1 Enoch, Chapters 37–82*, Hermeneia (Minneapolis: Fortress, 2012), 58–63.

25. The reference to the Parthians and Medes in 56:5–57:2 is often taken to be a reference to the invasion of the Parthians in 40 BCE in which Jerusalem was captured, Aristobulus was put in control, and Herod escaped to Rome. The problem is that the wording of the passage suggests that Jerusalem was not taken and that the invaders fought among themselves and were destroyed (56:7–8). In addition, a second invasion from the east seems to be envisaged (57:1–2). Needless to say, none of this happened. Whatever the historical reality, this passage seems to be a metaphor for an eschatological defeat of Jerusalem's enemies.

death in 4 BCE, this would suggest a composition in the late first century BCE or the first part of the first century CE. This date is the one becoming widely recognized in scholarship.

The "son of man" passages are found mainly in the second parable (1 En. 45–57) and third parable (1 En. 58–69). The figure is introduced in 46:1 (*zagaṣṣu kama rə'yata sab'*,[26] "whose face [is] like the appearance of a man") and designated as "that son of man" in 46:2. First Enoch 46–47, with the Head of Days and the Son of Man, is clearly related to Dan 7:9–14, with its Ancient of Days and one like a son of man. Yet a number of present-day scholars have argued that "Son of Man" in the Parables is not a title because the figure is referred to as "this Son of Man" or "that Son of Man."

Because Ethiopic has no article, some have suggested that demonstrative pronouns used in a number of passages to designate "that son of man" are a way of expressing what would be the definite article in other Semitic languages (such as Hebrew). R. H. Charles argues that it is a rendering of the Greek phrase and is simply the Ethiopic way of showing the Greek article.[27] The problem is that all passages seem to have a demonstrative, except where the context shows definiteness, whereas it has been noted that terms such as *Chosen One* never have the demonstrative adjective.[28] Yet that is not the full story, because some of the other designations also have demonstrative (like Son of Man) or possessive pronouns. In the two passages where "the Anointed" occurs, it is "*his* Anointed" (48:10; 54:6). Indeed, although "Chosen One" does not have a demonstrative, it does have a possessive adjective in several passages: "*my* Chosen One" (45:3, 4; 51:5; 55:4). Finally, the "Head of Days," who can be none other than God himself, is called "*that* Head of Days" in a couple of places (71:12, 13), as is also "that Lord of Spirits" (62:10).

Also, a number of biblical figures and symbols have influenced and contributed to the figure of the Parables.[29] Briefly, the data of Dan 7 form

---

26. Wolf Leslau's transliteration is used; see Leslau, *Comparative Dictionary of Ge'ez (Classical Ethiopic)* (Wiesbaden: Harrassowitz, 1987), xx–xxi. Some biblical scholars favor Thomas Lambdin's transliteration found in *Introduction to Classical Ethiopic (Ge'ez)*, HSS 24 (Missoula, MT: Scholars Press, 1978), but I have been informed that this is regarded as nonstandard by *éthiopisants*.

27. R. H. Charles, *The Book of Enoch* (Oxford: Clarendon, 1913), 86–87.

28. Leslie W. Walck, *The Son of Man in the Parables of Enoch and in Matthew*, JCTCRS 9 (London: T&T Clark, 2011), 70.

29. See the discussion in Nickelsburg, "Son of Man," *ABD* 6:137–50; Nickelsburg and VanderKam, *1 Enoch 2*, esp. 113–23; Walck, *Son of Man*, 50–164.

the main basis of the description of the "son of man" in 1 En. 46, yet the figure in the Parables is much more than the "one like a son of man" in Dan 7. The figure is greatly expanded by passages and images from elsewhere in the biblical text: the servant of YHWH (Isa 42:1–4 and 49:1–6) and the David oracles, which include God's Anointed (Ps 2 and Isa 11).[30] He existed before the beginning of the world but was hidden and preserved in God's presence (1 En. 48:2–3, 6; 62:7).[31] In this case, the image drawn on is preexistent Wisdom, known from Prov 8:22–36 and Sir 24:1–3. He is a "light to the nations" (1 En. 48:4; Isa 49:6). The "servant" of Deutero-Isaiah makes an important contribution (though not the suffering aspect, which has no place here with regard to the "son of man"), in that he is also the "Chosen One" (Isa 42:1). In 1 En. 48–49 the figure is identified with the Chosen One (49:2, 4: ḫaruy) who had already appeared in 39:6 and 45:3, 4 and is additionally named in 51:3; 52:6, 9; 53:6; 61:5; 62:1. This figure also bears the name of the Davidic Messiah or Anointed One (48:10: masiḫu) who is mentioned again later (52:4). He is further designated the "Holy One" (37:2), the "Righteous One" (38:2; 53:6), and the "Chosen One of Righteousness" (39:6).[32]

The concept of the messiah in the Parables stands out from what seems the most widespread concept in Second Temple Judaism.[33] Although there is a variety of messianic types, most are not heavenly figures. Instead of an earthly (if perhaps larger than life) conqueror and champion of the Jews, the Parables put forward a heavenly messiah, hidden from before creation but revealed to the righteous (48:6–7). One could argue (as did an older scholarly generation) that these were originally separate figures, perhaps coming from separate sources, that only later became assimilated to one another.[34] Whether this was the case or not, chapter 48 seems to identify

30. Nickelsburg and VanderKam, *1 Enoch 2*, 167–72.

31. His preexistence is rejected by James C. VanderKam, "Righteous One, Messiah, Chosen One, and Son of Man in 1 Enoch 37–71," in *The Messiah: Developments in Earliest Judaism and Christianity*, ed. James M. Charlesworth, First Princeton Symposium on Judaism and Christian Origins (Minneapolis: Fortress, 1992), 169–91, esp. 179–82; and Walck, *Son of Man*, 97–99.

32. Michael A. Knibb (*The Ethiopic Book of Enoch*, 2 vols. [Oxford: Clarendon, 1978], 2:126) has the plural in this last text.

33. For a survey, with literature, see Lester L. Grabbe, *Judaic Religion in the Second Temple Period: Belief and Practice from the Exile to Yavneh* (London and New York: Routledge, 2000), 271–91.

34. See the discussion in Charles, *Book of Enoch*, 64–65.

them by referring to the Son of Man as the Chosen One (48:6) and the Messiah (48:10). The present form of the book appears to be thinking of a single figure, and the centrality of this figure to the Parables is evident.

The central figure of the Parables (apart from the "Lord of Spirits"/"Head of Days") is called by the various titles or designations mentioned above. It is not just that in the Parables "the Messiah is occasionally referred to as 'that son of man,' as an alternative to the other titles that are used for him";[35] on the contrary, "son of man" is the most frequent designation (seventeen times), in comparison with "the Chosen One" (sixteen times), "the Righteous One" (twice), or "Messiah" (twice). Also, this Son of Man is more than just a reflex of the figure in Daniel. One of the most noticeable features is that he acts as heavenly judge over both the wicked and the righteous, after being enthroned (1 En. 46:4–6; 54:4; 61:8–9; 62–63; 69:26–29), which is not one of the activities of the "son of man" in Daniel.

One of the most curious incidents within the book is that Enoch seems to be identified ultimately with the Son of Man (71:13–17). Most readers find this puzzling, since Enoch seems to see the Son of Man as a separate being in his visions; some, however, have attempted to argue that this identification was anticipated throughout the Parables.[36] Crucial in this argument is 70:1–2, for which there occurs a significant variant in the Ethiopic text.[37] The text accepted by Nickelsburg and Knibb reads, "his [Enoch's] name was lifted up, living [while he was alive], into the presence of that Son of Man," whereas the variant text would read something like, "the living name of the Son of Man was lifted up" to the Lord of Spirits. The latter fits better the denouement of the Parables in which Enoch is identified with the Son of Man, but fits less well the earlier statements about the Son of Man in 1 En. 46–69.

---

35. Lindars, *Jesus Son of Man*, 5.

36. E.g., Casey, *Solution*, 91–111.

37. For discussion of the textual differences and problems, see esp. Nickelsburg and VanderKam, *1 Enoch 2*, 315–19; Michael A. Knibb, "The Translation of 1 Enoch 70:1: Some Methodological Issues," in *Biblical Hebrew, Biblical Texts: Essays in Memory of Michael P. Weitzman*, ed. Ada Rapoport-Albert and Gillian Greenberg, JSOTSup 333 (Sheffield: Sheffield Academic, 2001), 340–54; Daniel C. Olson, "Enoch and the Son of Man in the Epilogue of the Parables," *JSP* 9 (18) (1998): 27–38; idem, "'Enoch and the Son of Man' Revisited: Further Reflections on the Text and Translation of 1 Enoch 70.1–2," *JSP* 18 (2009): 233–40; Walck, *Son of Man*; Casey, *Solution*. The variant occurs in the phrase *tala'āla səmu ḥəyāw baḥabehu lawə'atu walda 'agʷāla 'əmaḥəyāw*, in which the variant text lacks the word *baḥabehu* ("in the presence of").

Yet the question of Enoch's being identified with the Son of Man is not crucial to our analysis of the connotation of "Son of Man." Even if Enoch is finally said to be the "Son of Man," he is still a heavenly figure with characteristics far beyond the human and the natural; he is a supernatural being, whether seen as "my Chosen One," "my Anointed One," or "this Son of Man." All of these are significant designations of this heavenly being. To repeat what was noted above, the question of whether "Son of Man" is a title becomes a mere scholastic matter in the light of the way the figure has been fleshed out over twenty-five chapters. He is a heavenly messianic individual who is repeatedly referred to as "Son of Man" in the Parables. "Son of Man" has a significance going well beyond the simple meaning of "human, human being."

In sum, in this section on the Parables of Enoch we found that three different Ethiopic phrases are used for the expression "son of man" (see table on p. 187), though there seems to be general agreement that the three phrases are all translations of the Greek υἱὸς τοῦ ἀνθρώπου and are comparable in meaning, in spite of the rather different wording. Demonstrative pronouns are used in a number of passages, such as "that son of man." On the other hand, some of the other designations also have demonstrative or possessive pronouns. For example, it is sometimes "my Chosen One" (45:3, 4; 51:5; 55:4). In the two passages where "the Anointed" occurs (48:10; 54:6), it is "his Anointed." Even the "Head of Days," who can be none other than God himself, is called "that Head of Days" (71:12, 13), and also "that Lord of Spirits" (62:10).

The figure of the "son of man" is a development from the figure referred to as "like a son of man" in Dan 7:13. However, a variety of other biblical images have gone into this development, including the Davidic king, the servant of Isa 42 and 49, and the figure of Wisdom, to create an important and defined figure within the Enochic tradition. The phrase "son of man" is one of four titles applied to a central figure in the Parables, along with "the Chosen One," "the Anointed One," and the "Righteous One."[38]

The question of whether "son of man" is a title in the Parables thus becomes an academic one. There is no doubt that the "son of man" is not just a brief reference as in Daniel: this personage, with his various titles

---

38. John Collins ("Enoch and the Son of Man: A Response to Sabino Chialà and Helge Kvanvig," in *Enoch and the Messiah Son of Man: Revisiting the Book of Parables,* ed. Gabriele Boccaccini [Grand Rapids: Eerdmans, 2007], 222) is not afraid to refer to "Son of Man" as a title in the Parables.

Different Forms of "Son of Man" in Parables

	walda sab'	walda baʾsi(t)	walda ʾəgʷāla
46:2	zəku walda sab' (zəntu wəʾətu) walda		
46:3	sab' (zalotu kona sədq) wəʾəzəntu walda sab' (zarəʾika)		
46:4	zəku walda sab'		
48:2		lazəku walda baʾsit	
62:5			walda ʾəgʷāla ʾəmaḥəyāw
62:7			lazəku walda ʾəgʷāla <ʾə>maḥəyāw
62:9			zəku walda ʾəgʷāla <ʾə>maḥəyāw
62:14			zəku walda ʾəgʷāla ʾəmaḥəyāw
63:11			lawaʾətu walda ʾəgʷāla ʾəmaḥəyāw
69:26			lawalda ʾəgʷāla ʾəmaḥəyāw
69:27		waʾətu walda baʾsi	
69:29		lawaʾətu walda baʾsi	
70:1			lawaʾətu walda ʾəgʷāla ʾəmaḥəyāw

or designations, is a central feature of the Parables and a focus of this section of the 1 Enoch. He is not just "one like a son of man," that is, a figure in human form, but "this Son of Man," "that Son of Man," or just "Son of Man." Giving the designation in capitalized format in the translations of Nickelsburg and others is an appropriate way of showing its significance.

4 Ezra 13

The Apocalypse of Ezra was probably written originally in a Semitic language.[39] At some point, it seems to have been translated into Greek. Both the original and the Greek version have disappeared in the course of history; what has come down to us are two main versions, the Latin and the Syriac, plus several versions evidently based on these. It is not often noted that the "man from the sea" in chapter 13 is referred to by the phrase "son of man" (*brnš*) in the Syriac version (13:3, 5, 12, etc.). This intriguing reading might at first suggest that the original Semitic version of the writing had "son of man" where the Latin has "man" (*homo*). Two considerations, however, make this less than probable. First, the Latin New Testament passages with "son of man" are generally translated literally as *filius hominis* (e.g., Matt 8:20; Mark 2:10, 28; Luke 11:30; 12:8; John 3:13–14; Acts 7:56; Rev 1:13; 14:14). The translator of 4 Ezra might have followed a different mode of translation, but this seems unlikely. Second, the phrase "son of man" seems to have been a regular part of the Syriac translator's linguistic usage, since we find it not only in chapter 13 but also in many other passages throughout the book (3:36; 5:38; 6:10, 26, 39, 46; 7:29, 65, 78, 127; 8:6, 34, 44; 10:14, 54; 11:37; 14:9, 14). Thus "son of man" as the original description of the "man from the sea" can only be considered a possibility.

Yet, as has long been expounded, the figure is based on the "one like a son of man" in Dan 7. Probably the most thorough recent discussion has been given by Michael Stone, who argues that the author "is here writing his own interpretation to a previously existent allegory."[40] Although the

---

39. See G. H. Box, *The Ezra-Apocalypse, Being Chapters 3–14 of the Book Commonly Known as 4 Ezra (or II Esdras)* (London: Pitman, 1912), xiii–xx, for an argument that it was originally in Hebrew.

40. Originally given in his 1965 PhD thesis (published as *Features of the Eschatology of IV Ezra*, HSS 35 [Atlanta: Scholars Press, 1989], 120–33; the quote is from 124), it is also discussed in his *Fourth Ezra: A Commentary on the Book of Fourth Ezra*, Hermeneia (Minneapolis: Fortress, 1990), 381–410.

term "son of man" is probably not applied to the figure arising from the sea in 4 Ezra 13, the dependence of this figure on the "one like a son of man" of Dan 7 seems obvious, though his activities go beyond the Danielic personage. He has a number of points in common with the "Son of Man" in the Parables, including being preexistent but revealed at the end time, taking care of the righteous, being called "servant"[41] and "my son," and acting as judge.[42] Stone writes, "Therefore, it may be that in view of the title 'man' and of the cosmic imagery applied to this figure in the vision, that the Son of Man is here involved."[43] It is because of these parallels with the "Son of Man" of the Parables that the "man" of this vision in 4 Ezra 13 is evoked as a similar figure.

So why is he not called Son of Man (unless the Syriac text points to such a designation)? A look at Christian texts (such as Revelation) suggests that the term as a messianic title or designation did not continue to find favor by this time, as has been argued by Sabino Chialà.[44] Why this should be is rather puzzling, but at this point it is sufficient to note what seems to be a trend, even if we cannot yet explain it.

THE NEW TESTAMENT

As has long been recognized, the Jesus tradition has been filtered through the memory and interpretation of the early church. This raises substantial problems with trying to determine the teachings of the historical Jesus. This problem especially applies to determining the ipsissima verba of Jesus.[45] My concern in this paper, however, is not the words of the histori-

---

41. The figure in the Parables is not called "servant" directly, but he is the "Chosen One," a designation of the servant in the Servant Songs of Deutero-Isaiah. See the section above on "Parables of Enoch." The figure is called "servant" here in 4 Ezra 13 but not "Chosen One," whereas the Parables use "Chosen One."

42. Stone, *Features of Eschatology*, 120–33; Nickelsburg and VanderKam, *1 Enoch 2*, 121.

43. Stone, *Features of Eschatology*, 128.

44. Sabino Chialà, "The Son of Man: The Evolution of an Expression," in *Enoch and the Messiah*, ed. Boccaccini, 153–78, esp. 171–76.

45. Attempts have been made to reconstruct the "original Aramaic" of sayings in the gospels, for example, by Maurice Casey in a number of books—e.g., *Aramaic Sources of Mark's Gospel*, SNTSM 102 (Cambridge: Cambridge University Press, 1998); and *An Aramaic Approach to Q: Sources for the Gospels of Matthew and Luke*, SNTSM 122 (Cambridge: Cambridge University Press, 2002)—but he is only the latest in a

cal Jesus. My concern is to elucidate the meaning of "son of man," and in order to do that we have to begin with the actual linguistic data we have, not theoretical or reconstructed data. What we have are a number of sayings relating to the "son of man" in the New Testament. They are in Greek (not Aramaic), and they have a particular meaning and form in their present context. It is my purpose in this section to analyze these sayings and to draw linguistic conclusions that may, ultimately, have nothing to do with the historical Jesus. Thus, unlike some of those who have written on the "son of man" in the gospels and elsewhere in the New Testament, determination of the usage of the historical Jesus is not our objective, which is fortunate since that is an extremely complicated question in any case and would take up a minimum of a monograph rather than a short article.

The Gospels

The term "son of man" is only ever applied to Jesus, either in words ascribed to him (mostly) or in (a few) references to him by others. It is quite clear that "the Son of Man" is as much a title applied to Jesus as "Christ." Some have argued that the phrase always evokes Dan 7,[46] but this is not at all obvious. Many references to "the Son of Man" have not the slightest indication of having anything to do with Daniel. Thus, although the New Testament usage of "son of man" may possibly have its ultimate origin in the Danielic usage (a debatable point), many passages with "son of man" show not a shadow of connection with Dan 7 or any other passage in Daniel.

We can begin with what are thought to be the earliest written sources for Matthew and Luke: Mark and Q. Mark 13:26 refers to the Son of Man coming in clouds with power and glory, a clear allusion to Dan 7:13. According to Mark 2:10, the Son of Man has power to forgive sins upon earth. In Mark 8:29–31, Peter declares Jesus to be the Christ (i.e.,

---

long line of those wanting to get back to the original words of Jesus. This can be an interesting exercise, but it proves nothing. Although it is a reasonable assumption that Jesus normally taught in Aramaic, it is still an assumption, and we cannot rule out that he taught at least some of the time in Greek. Furthermore, the early disciples and Christians were Aramaic speakers in many cases and might have passed the tradition (or their understanding and interpretation of the tradition) down in Aramaic, before it was recorded in Greek by the gospel writers. Thus, being able to turn a Greek saying into Aramaic does not by itself prove we have the words of Jesus.

46. E.g., Lindars, *Jesus Son of Man*, 10–11.

the Anointed or Messiah), after which Jesus begins to teach them about the suffering of the Son of Man; his rejection by the elders, chief priests, and scribes; his being killed; and finally his rising after three days. Similar statements are found in 9:31 and 10:33–34. In 9:9 Jesus warns Peter, James, and John to tell no one their vision of Elijah and Moses until the Son of Man has risen from the dead. These all make clear that Jesus is himself the Son of Man, and this Son of Man is not just "someone" or "a person" but is a heavenly figure. This conclusion is stated explicitly in 14:61–62, where the high priest asks Jesus whether he is "the Christ, the Son of the Blessed." Jesus replies, "I am, and you will see the Son of Man seated on the right hand of power 'coming with the clouds of heaven.'" According to the picture of this passage, Jesus accepts that he is the Messiah and states that he is also the Son of Man seated on the right hand of God and coming with the clouds of heaven. Already in the sayings unique to Mark, the "Son of Man" is identified with the Messiah:

> Evidently, Jesus and the disciples, as characters in the narrative, on the one hand, and the author of Mark and his audience, on the other, have a shared understanding of the notion of the Davidic messiah and a shared assumption that "the Messiah" and "the Son of Man" are equivalent. That such information is commonly understood is clear from the fact that it needs no comment, explanation, or defense.[47]

In the hypothesized source Q, nine "son of man" sayings are preserved, according to a recent standard collection: 6:22; 7:34; 9:58; 11:30; 12:10, 40; 17:24, 26, 30.[48] Although Rudolf Bultmann thought Q was eschatological,[49] a number of recent scholars have seen the eschatological sayings as part of a later redactional layer, but this is still a debated point.[50] The term "son

---

47. Adela Yarbro Collins, *Mark: A Commentary*, Hermeneia (Minneapolis: Fortress, 2007), 69. She gives cross-references to another section of her commentary on Mark (pp. 58–63) and to a contribution to John Collins's Daniel commentary (Collins, *Daniel*, 90–112).

48. James M. Robinson, Paul Hoffmann, and John S. Kloppenborg, eds., *The Critical Edition of Q: Synopsis including the Gospels of Matthew and Luke, Mark and Thomas with English, German, and French Translations of Q and Thomas*, Hermeneia (Minneapolis: Fortress, 2000).

49. Rudolf Bultmann, *Theology of the New Testament*, trans. Kendrick Grobel, 2 vols. (New York: Scribner's Sons, 1951), 1:42.

50. Cf. Burkett, *Son of Man*, 79–80.

of man" is used by Jesus; and, in their present context, the sayings refer to Jesus himself. A good example is Q 9:58 (with Matt 8:20) in which Jesus states that foxes have holes and birds have nests, but the Son of Man has no place to lay his head. This saying (which also appears in Gos. Thom. 86) cannot be explained by the "normal" meaning of Aramaic בר אנש, since "a man," "humans," normally have houses, homes, or other places to lay their heads. Similarly, just as Jonah was a sign to his generation, the Son of Man is a sign to his generation (Q 11:30 // Matt 12:40). Jesus warns that the Son of Man will come at an hour when he is not expected (Q 12:40 // Matt 24:44). Several verses (Q 17:24, 26, 30 // Matt 24:27, 37, 39) refer to the day of the Son of Man, which is like the days of Noah and the day when fire and brimstone rained down on Sodom.

Matthew is a very interesting case. Nine of its passages are from Q, as already discussed. Many others are held in common with Mark and probably borrowed from that gospel, which Matthew used as a source. Several passages appear to be unique to Matthew and independent of other gospel sources. The interpretation of the parable of the tares in 13:36–43 (found only in Matthew) mentions that the Son of Man sows the good seed and will send his angels to gather the wicked and cast them into the furnace. Matthew 25:31 is particularly notable because it mentions that the Son of Man will come in glory with all his angels, and he will sit on a glorious throne. Matthew 26:2 notes that the Passover is in two days, when the Son of Man will be given over to be crucified.

Matthew is a particularly interesting case, in light of the recent study by Leslie Walck.[51] After a thorough examination of the "Son of Man" passages in both the Parables of Enoch and the Gospel of Matthew, he notes the considerable "similarities and distinctions," even though they do not rise to the level of proof that Matthew was literarily dependent upon the Parables.[52] Many of the characteristics of the figure in the Parables also occur in Matthew but not in Dan 7 or other early literature, including his judicial role and his revelatory role. The phrase "throne of his glory" is found only in the Parables (1 En. 69:29) and Matthew (19:28; 25:31). Walck concludes that it is "at precisely those points where Matthew has unique material" (13:36–43; 25:31–46) that the similarities with the Parables "are greatest, and the shaping of Jesus in the direction of *Par[ables of] En[och]*

---

51. Walck, Son of Man.
52. Ibid., 249.

the clearest."[53] His conclusion seems to me well founded: "Because so many features Matthew has incorporated do not appear in other contemporary literature, it is likely that he knew and used *Par[ables of] En[och]* in particular, along with his other sources for the story of Jesus."[54]

Like Matthew, Luke's Son of Man sayings are mostly taken from Mark or Q. Yet there are a couple of unique statements. Luke 18:8 asks whether, when the Son of Man comes, he will find faith on earth, and 19:10 states that the Son of Man came to save the lost. These relate to Jesus's unique mission. But 21:36 tells the disciples to watch and pray always that they can escape the coming tribulations of the end time and stand before the Son of Man (implied is that the Son of Man will be a figure, perhaps a judge, of the end time). In Luke 22:48 Jesus asks Judas whether he betrays the Son of Man with a kiss, identifying himself as the Son of Man. Finally, Luke 24:7 asserts that even while in Galilee Jesus predicted that the Son of Man would be delivered to sinners and crucified. Thus Jesus's betrayal, death, resurrection, and role in the eschaton are ascribed to his identification as the Son of Man.

The Fourth Gospel has had a special place in the discussion of the gospels, because it is so different from the Synoptics.[55] It has also usually been judged as more remote from the historical Jesus. Regardless of the truth of this latter point, the Gospel of John represents a faction of the early church and shows how the term was used in that particular environment. An explicit identification of Jesus with the Son of Man is made in John 12:32–34 (cf. 8:28). A number of the sayings talk about the Son of Man being lifted up and also being glorified, alluding to the crucifixion

---

53. Ibid., 250.

54. Ibid.

55. Recent studies include J. Harold Ellens, *The Son of Man in the Gospel of John*, NTM 28 (Sheffield: Sheffield Phoenix Press, 2010); and Benjamin E. Reynolds, *The Apocalyptic Son of Man in the Gospel of John*, WUNT 249 (Tübingen: Mohr Siebeck, 2008); idem, "The Use of the Son of Man Idiom in the Gospel of John," in *"Who Is This Son of Man?": The Latest Scholarship on a Puzzling Expression of the Historical Jesus*, ed. Larry W. Hurtado and Paul L. Owen, LNTS 390 (London and New York: T&T Clark, 2011), 101–29. Reynolds sees the Johannine Son of Man as an apocalyptic figure––a heavenly entity and the Messiah––with a strong relationship to the figure in Dan 7. Ellens argues that in John the divine Logos descends from heaven as the Son of Man and becomes incarnated in Jesus, thus differing from the concept in the Synoptic Gospels. I am grateful to both Dr. Ellens and Dr. Reynolds for kindly supplying a copy of their respective monographs to me.

but also the subsequent resurrection (3:14; 8:28; 12:23, 34; 13:31). Several passages confirm the heavenly origin of the Son of Man, speaking of his descent from heaven and his ascending back to his place of origin (3:13; 6:62; cf. 1:51). A point is made about the necessity of believing in the Son of Man (3:15; 9:35). The Son of Man will provide food that will not perish, and it will be required that followers eat his flesh and drink his blood (6:27, 53). Finally, like the Son of Man in the Parables of Enoch, the Son of Man will execute judgment (John 5:27). The heavenly origin and nature of the Son of Man is made clearer in the Fourth Gospel than in the Synoptics, showing how the community or group behind that gospel viewed matters.

Elsewhere in the New Testament

Only a few references to the Son of Man are made elsewhere in the New Testament. The plural form—which is the form most frequently found in Aramaic texts of the first centuries BCE and CE—is found Eph 3:5, while Heb 2:6 is simply a quote from Ps 8:5 (note that the Greek is anarthrous just like the original Hebrew בן־אדם). In the Stephen martyrdom episode in Acts 7, Stephen sees the heavens opened and the Son of Man standing at the right hand of God. In the book of Revelation, John sees one "like a son of man" (i.e., a human figure) in the midst of the lampstands (1:13) and, later in the vision, "one like a son of man" with a golden crown seated on a white cloud (14:14). Here the figure is described in much the same terms as the figure in Dan 7:13. The difference between this description and the Son of Man in the gospels and Acts is obvious.

Other Early Christian Texts

Some of the early Christian literature that may be contemporary with parts of the New Testament or not long afterward can be briefly summarized. Ignatius mentions that since Jesus was of the seed of David, he was both "Son of man and Son of God" (Ignatius, *Eph.* 20:2). Justin says that Jesus was called "son of man," either because he was born of the Virgin who was of the family of David and Abraham, Isaac, and Jacob, or because Adam was the father both of him and those from whom Mary descended (*Dial.* 100.3–4). Irenaeus normally agrees that "son of man" relates to Jesus's humanity, which is contrasted with his status as Son of God, though his humanity in common with other humans means that they too can become sons of God (*Haer.* 3.10.2; 3.16.3, 7; 3.17.1; 3.18.3–4; 3.19.1). One passage in Irenaeus seems to equate "son of man" with "Christ, the son of the living God" (3.19.2), but it is not clear that this makes "son of man" a messianic title. Barnabas 12:10 states that in the flesh Jesus was not "the son of man" but the Son of God. In this literature generally, "son of man" seems to be a way of referring to Jesus's humanity.

Summary of the New Testament

Several points have emerged in this section on the New Testament:

1. My concern in the present essay is not with whether the "Son of Man" sayings in the gospels are authentic words of Jesus. Sayings in the Greek text that can be retroverted back to Aramaic might be more likely to be authentic, but many members of the early church were Aramaic speakers. Sections of the gospels that might be based on Aramaic sources do not necessarily reflect the ipsissima verba of Jesus. There is also the possibility that Jesus taught at least part of the time in Hebrew or even Greek.

2. What we have are the present wording and context of the sayings, which are Greek. They might well come from a different context and be retroverted and/or adapted from an original saying that had a different connotation, but this cannot be assumed—it requires evidence. An Aramaic original needs to be demonstrated rather than assumed.

3. The arthrous and anarthrous forms of the Greek phrase are to be distinguished. The anarthrous form is used in Revelation and, in context, refers to a humanlike figure. There is also an anarthrous form as part of a quote in Heb 2:6, which translates the Hebrew literally. Otherwise, the singular arthrous form is consistently used of Jesus.

4. The expression ὁ υἱὸς τοῦ ἀνθρώπου is used in the gospels and Acts as a title, with the implication that it refers to the messianic figure of Jesus, including his divine state in heaven. It is clear that some sections of the early church considered "Son of Man" a messianic title of Jesus (whether or not Jesus himself used the term in that sense).

FINAL SUMMARY AND CONCLUSIONS

The mass of secondary literature on the "son of man" question has shown how intractable the problem has been, or at least how much scholars have disagreed. Yet, although each study has often seemed to go over much the same ground, gradually in the past few decades some new data and new arguments have come forward. A number of new points of consensus have developed out of the continuing discussion:

1. The Aramaic expression בר אנש, and the expression בן אדם that is generally its Hebrew equivalent, is used to mean "man, human" (cf. also בנת אנש, "woman"). However, in Aramaic the singular undetermined form is rather infrequent, and the determined singular is even less frequent. The form normally seen is the determined plural בני אנשא, "men, people, humans."

2. The figure of the "son of man" is a development from the figure referred to as "like a son of man" in Dan 7:13. However, it is also evident that the figure has developed, drawing on symbolism, imagery, and characteristics found in other biblical passages and even from nonbiblical traditions, including the Davidic king (Ps 2; Isa 11), the servant of Isa 42 and 49, and preexistent Wisdom (Prov 8:22–36; Sir 24:1–3), to create an important and defined figure within the Enochic tradition.

3. It is generally agreed (in spite of Vermes's claim) that the Aramaic expression is not the equivalent of "I" in the first century CE, and my investigation supports that conclusion.

4. As a number of researchers have recently argued, there is no evidence that Son of Man was a widespread messianic title in first-century Judaism, as had once been argued.

5. On the other hand, "Son of Man" clearly functioned as a title or something similar to it in some circles of late Second Temple Judaism. Its employment in the Parables of Enoch and in the gospels shows that it was so used by some groups within Judaism. The phrase "Son of Man" is one of four designations applied to a central figure in the Parables, along with "the Chosen One," "the Anointed One," and "the Righteous One."

6. Some have argued that the expression "son of man" is not a title in the Parables, since demonstrative pronouns are used in many passages in the Parables (such as "that son of man"). On the other hand, some of the other designations also have demonstrative or possessive pronouns ("his Anointed": 48:10; 54:6; "my Chosen One": 45:3, 4; 51:5; 55:4). More important, the Head of Days, who can be none other than God himself, is called "that Head of Days" (71:12, 13) and "that Lord of Spirits" (62:10). Finally, "Son of Man" is the most frequent designation for the figure in the Parables, despite other titles for him. There seems no doubt that "son of man" has taken on a messianic identity in the Parables of Enoch.

7. "Son of Man" functions as a title for Jesus in the gospels and Acts. In addition, the argument that there is direct influence of the Parables of

Enoch on the Gospel of Matthew seems to be well based and indicates that the figure of the Son of Man is not just a borrowing from Daniel.

8. Yet it is also evident that "Son of Man" as a messianic title did not persist either in Judaism or in the Jewish sect that became Christianity with that meaning. For a time it influenced some groups among the Jews but then fell into disuse or even out of favor. Why this happened is unclear, but it might explain why the messianic figure in 4 Ezra 13:1 is referred to as "the man (from the sea)" rather than the Son of Man.

Matthew's Day of Judgment
in the Light of 1 Enoch

Daniel Assefa

Introduction

Among the Synoptic Gospels, Matthew seems to be the most influenced by 1 Enoch.[1] Assuming that the motif of judgment plays an important role both in Matthew and 1 Enoch,[2] one may ask the following questions: How is judgment described in these works? Who are the righteous and who is liable to judgment in these texts? Are we dealing with the same kind of people in both texts? Do the references to the day of judgment have the same function in both texts?[3] This short paper will deal with the expres-

---

1. George W. E. Nickelsburg, *1 Enoch 1: A Commentary on the Book of 1 Enoch, Chapters 1–36; 81–108*, Hermeneia (Minneapolis: Fortress, 2001), 84. For Hagner, Matthew's Gospel, besides having an "apocalyptic orientation," is the most "apocalyptic gospel"; see Donald A. Hagner, "Apocalyptic Motifs in the Gospel of Matthew: Continuity and Discontinuity," *HBT* 7 (1985): 53–82. David C. Sim (*Apocalyptic Eschatology in the Gospel of Matthew*, SNTSMS 88 [Cambridge: Cambridge University Press, 1996], 222–43) affirms that Matthew's Gospel reveals an apocalyptic worldview whose function would be to respond to challenges and threats coming both from the Jewish community of the time and from law-free Christianity.

2. Nickelsburg (*1 Enoch 1*, 55) affirms, "The great judgment that looms in almost every major section of 1 Enoch and many of its subsections … is the *final* judgment, which will occur at the end of the old age and before the beginning of the new." Judgment is a focal point of 1 Enoch; judgment is central in 1 Enoch (see pp. 25, 37–40, 90). Daniel Marguerat has consecrated an entire book on the theme of judgment in Matthew's Gospel; see *Le jugement dans l'Evangile de Matthieu*, 2nd ed., MdB 6 (Geneva: Labor et Fides, 1995), esp. 3–4.

3. One should not forget however that 1 Enoch and Matthew do not belong to the same literary genre. Matthew's Gospel is not an apocalypse. The narrator is not telling a report of a vision. The scenes are taking place on a given space and time on

sion "on the day of judgment" (ἐν ἡμέρᾳ κρίσεως)[4] found four times in Mat-thew[5] (Matt 10:15; 11:22, 24; 12:36) but absent from Mark and Luke.[6] The aim of the paper is to show that, though close or dependent on 1 Enoch, Matthew's day of judgment innovates by introducing and emphasizing the theme of surprise with regard to the verdict of the last judgment and to the time of the end. The exhortations concerning judgment in Matthew's Gospel warn against something unexpected that will happen. Those who thought they would be compensated are not rewarded, and those who did well, without even knowing it, are rewarded. The last judgment will come suddenly and catch people by surprise.

THE EXPRESSION "DAY OF JUDGMENT" IN MATTHEW'S GOSPEL

In Matthew's Gospel, the term "day" may refer to the period between the morning and the evening.[7] Thus in Matt 6:34, worries and troubles should

---

earth, more precisely in Galilee and Judea, with much attention to the Lake of Galilee, to some mountains, synagogues, houses, and to the temple of Jerusalem. No other-worldly agent is transmitting or interpreting the message of the gospel. No description of the otherworld is given. Heaven is referred to but not as part of a setting where actions develop. God is indeed depicted as a person "who is in heaven" in the mouth of Jesus (cf. Matt 5:16, 45; 6:1; 7:11, 21; 10:32–33; 16:17; 18:10, 14). Besides, the voice that comes down from heaven in Matt 3:17 is not part of an apocalyptic imagery. What precedes and what follows, including the baptism of Jesus, is taking place on earth. The situation is quite different in 1 Enoch; several events reported in the first person take place in heaven. One reads about the "ends of the earth" and the otherworld, including the portrayal of a heavenly temple, based on otherworldly journeys. For the characteristics of an apocalypse with regard to the genre, see the various entries in *Semeia* 14 (1979).

4. According to Marc Philonenko, the expression "day of judgment" comes from the Essenes or a movement close to Qumran where "eschatological hope" has a promi-nent role; see "Au jour du jugement: Origine et diffusion d'une formule eschatologique (contribution d'une sociolecte esseno-qoumrânien)," in *Le jour de Dieu—Der Tag Gottes,* ed. Anders Hultgård and Stig Norin, WUNT 245 (Tübingen: Mohr Siebeck, 2009), 101–5.

5. Concerning the idea of judgment, Jean-Claude Ingelaere affirms that Matthew uses other sources that belong to eschatological traditions than used by Mark and Luke; see "Les jours du Seigneur dans l'Évangile de Matthieu," in Hultgård and Norin, *Jour de Dieu,* 92–98.

6. In the New Testament there are a few other references to the day of judgment (2 Pet 2:9; 3:7; 1 John 2:17), but these do not affect the main topic of this paper.

7. For the meaning of the ordinary "day" in the Scriptures, see Roger T. Beckwith,

be confined to the day (τῇ ἡμέρᾳ) and not extend to following one. "That same day Jesus went out of the house" in 13:1 (Ἐν τῇ ἡμέρᾳ ἐκείνῃ) indicates that Jesus's activity is limited to the period between the morning and evening. "That day," here and in 22:23, does not indicate incidents to happen in the more or less remote future (cf. 7:22; 24:36; 26:29) but rather a sequence of events that has taken place. Similarly, the disciples, in Matt 14, affirm that "the day is over" meaning that the crowd that listens to Jesus is now staying beyond the limit of the period called "day."[8]

However, "To this day" or "until today" in Matt 27:8 (ἕως τῆς σήμερον) and 28:15 (μέχρι τῆς σήμερον [ἡμέρας]) has the meaning of "this moment"; the expression does not refer to the period between the morning and the evening.[9]

The other important usage of the term "day" has to do with the future, more precisely with the last judgment. People will not be saved even if they say (ἐροῦσίν) that they had prophesied and had cast out demons in the name of Jesus (Matt 7:22) at the day of judgment. The dialogue at the scene of judgment according to Matthew[10] includes an imploring from the part of people who expected to be saved. Thus, "day" in the expression "on that day" (ἐν ἐκείνῃ τῇ ἡμέρᾳ) does not necessarily connote an event taking place between the morning and the evening. It indicates more the moment in which an important action will happen. It is an instant qualified by fright, more terrible than what happened to Sodom and Gomorrah (Matt 10:15).

Calendar and Chronology, Jewish and Christian: Biblical, Intertestamental and Patristic Studies (Leiden: Brill, 2001), 1–9.

8. For more examples of this usage, see Matt 16:21; 17:23; 20:6, 12, 19; 26:17, 55; 27:62; 28:1.

9. For a similar expression see 1 En. 69:9.

10. Such dialogue is absent from 1 Enoch. The fallen angels do not have any conversation with God after they committed their sins. At most, they ask for the intercession of Enoch. Even when they are sent to a place of punishment, they are bound by archangels without protest or imploration. Besides, in the Book of the Watchers, the angels who will come down to meet with women knew very well that they were to commit a grave sin. In other words, their transgression does not come as a surprise. The same is true in the Animal Apocalypse. One does not see any complaint in order to avoid the condemnation. Moreover, where the judgment of the fallen angels is a recurring motif, Matthew focuses on the judgment of human beings. Perhaps the only exception to that is Matt 25:41, which alludes to the space of punishment prepared for Satan and his angels.

In Matt 25:31–46, the theme focuses on what has been done in favor of
the Son of Man or against him.[11] Although very close to 1 En. 62:11, Matt
25:31–46 affirms that both the righteous and the wicked are surprised by
the verdict. Both affirm that they had not met the Son of Man in order to
take care of him or deprive him of attention. The Son of Man identifies
himself with the needy and the suffering and this comes as a surprise to all
who ignored the connection.

THE DAY OF JUDGMENT ACCORDING TO 1 ENOCH

The "day" is, by far, the most frequent indicator of time in 1 Enoch. The
term appears 118 times in the singular ('əlat) and 145 times in the plural
(mawā'əl).[12] The period between the morning and the evening is frequently
mentioned in the Book of Astronomy. For instance, the whole chapter 72
makes comparisons between the length of the day and the length of the
night (cf. also 1 En. 73–74). However, the divisions of the day itself are
not well described in 1 Enoch. The "midday" (qatr) is mentioned in 1 En.
69:12 in connection with an evil spirit. The "morning" (ṣbāḥ) is mentioned
in particular in 1 En. 72 (see 72:9, 11, 13).

Second, "day" refers to a given period of time. Thus, in the sentence
"they will not be judged all the days of their life" (1 En. 5:9), days are not
opposed to nights. Here, as in 1 En. 5:5, "days" are synonymous with
"years" in one's life, while in 5:9, the term "days" refers to duration, the
idea of not turning to wrongdoing for a long time (all the days of their life).
Similarly "the days of summer" in 1 En. 4 indicates the duration time of a
given season. Day, here, in the second meaning, does not denote twenty-
four hours.

Third, "day" is frequently connected with a specific time or event,[13]
namely with the last judgment. Day or days are used in order to indicate a

---

11. Cf. Nickelsburg, *1 Enoch 1*, 84.

12. "Day" (Heb. יום) is the first word analyzed by Gershon Brin in *The Concept
of Time in the Bible and the Dead Sea Scrolls*, STDJ 39 (Leiden: Brill, 2001), esp. 1,
52–57, 125–67, 309–60. It occurs 2,317 times in the Hebrew Bible. For Brin, and for
other scholars, it is one of the most important words to express time, be it the past, the
present, or the future. "That day, the previous day, the ancient day" refer to the past.
The Hebrew term יום might not always be translated by "day" in other languages. The
Ethiopic equivalent is 'əlat or mawā'əl. The Aramaic has the same root as the Hebrew,
whereas the Greek uses the word ἡμέρα.

13. In 1 En 60: 5, the angel Michael tells Enoch about "the day of mercy," which

decisive final time in the future. One observes the same usage of the "day of judgment" in both Matthew's Gospel and 1 Enoch. The day of "their distress" in 1 En. 48:8 and the day of "trouble" in 50:2 describe a time of suffering. Here too, the day of judgment does not necessarily consist of twenty-four hours. The construct form "day of judgment" ('əlata kwənanē), where 'əlata is followed by a word referring to the final judgment, even with some variation of the second term ("trouble, iniquity, distress"), is quite frequent (cf. 1 En. 1:1; 10:12; 16:1; 19:1; 22:4, 13; 54:6; 55:3; 81:4; 84:4; 96:8; 97:1; 98:8, 10; 99:15; 100:4; 104:5).

An equivalent of the Hebrew אחרון יום, badaḥāri mawāʿəl, is found at least in two places in 1 Enoch: 27:3 and 108:1.[14] In both places Charles translates the expression with "in the last days,"[15] whereas Nickelsburg has "the last times" in 1 En. 27:3.[16] One example, among many, for this usage could be Isa 30:8,"And now, go, write it before them on a tablet, and inscribe it in a book that it may be *for the time to come* as a witness forever" (RSV). Versions in some other languages drop the term "day."[17] For instance, both the RSV and the Jerusalem Bible translate אחרון יום with "for (the) time to come."

The expression "in those days" (waba'əmāntu mawāʿəl) in 1 Enoch often indicates something that happens in the future. With regard to the resurrection expressed metaphorically in terms of the earth that "returns" what has been entrusted to it, one may refer to 1 En. 51:1. Now, the resurrection, being connected with the last judgment, reflects the transition moment between this age and the following one.[18]

---

has lasted. "Day" here refers to a time of mercy that has taken place in the past and continues to exist. The dimension is not about the future but about God's mercifulness, which has already happened and continues to happen.

14. See Brin, *Concept*, 148–49.

15. R. H. Charles, *The Book of Enoch or 1 Enoch* (Oxford: Clarendon, 1912), 56 and 269.

16. Nickelsburg, *1 Enoch 1*, 317.

17. Although the term "day" appears in the LXX in Isa 30:8, the verse is slightly different as the idea of "later" does not appear.

18. Commenting on 1 En. 108:1, Stuckenbruck affirms that the theme of keeping the law "in the last days" refers to the author's own time. The last days are characterized by the faithfulness of the righteous vis-à-vis the Torah, as one may also observe in 1 En. 10:16; 90:6–15; 92:1; 93:10b; 104:12–13; 107:1; see Loren T. Stuckenbruck, *1 Enoch 91–108*, CEJL (Berlin: de Gruyter, 2007), 697.

Already the first verse of 1 Enoch 1 announces the coming of a "day of tribulation." The prediction makes a distinction between two kinds of persons. On the one hand, we have "the chosen and the righteous," and, on the other, "the wicked and the godless." The chosen and the righteous are linked with blessing, while the wicked and the ungodly are linked with removal. The blessing is an anticipated one, for it only predicts that a time will come when the wicked suffer tribulation in a distant future. Enoch blesses the righteous but does not curse the wicked; he rather announces their removal. The day of tribulation recalls "the day of judgment" or "the day of God"[19] in the Old Testament. However, "the day of judgment" (ʿalata kwunane)[20] is more frequent than "the day of tribulation" (ʿalata mandābē) in 1 Enoch.

According to 1 En. 10:12, the fallen angels are bound "until the day of their judgment." They are in prison, waiting for a lasting punishment, "until the judgment for all eternity is accomplished." In 16:1, the giants' flesh is described as being destroyed before a judgment. To which judgment does it refer? If it were to the last judgment, one would not understand the need for such a reference. It makes more sense if the text is referring to the flood, which is a model for the last judgment.[21]

---

19. For various contributions on the "day of God," see Hultgård and Norin, *Jour de Dieu*. For the scholarly debate on the "day of the Lord" in the Old Testament and for new insights on the topic, see, in the same volume: Wolfgang Oswald, "Zukunftserwartung und Gerichtsankündigung: Zur Pragmatik der prophetischen Rede vom Tag Jhwhs," 19–29; and Stig Norin, "Der Tag Gottes im Alten Testament: Jenseits der Spekulationen—Was ist übrig?" 33–42.

20. See 1 En. 1:1; 10:12; 16:1; 19:1; 22:4, 13; 54:6; 55:3; 81:4; 84:4; 96:8; 97:1; 98:8, 10; 99:15; 100:4; 104:5.

21. Listening to the cry of the earth, God acts before the last judgment in 1 En. 10:12 and 16:1. In 7:5–6, the earth cries like a person, complaining about the lawless ones who devoured one another and drink one another's blood. Here the earth, filled with blood and iniquity (cf. 9:1, 9), is not guilty but rather a victim. The earth is a place where evil is perpetrated. The motif of the earth's complaint is continued in 8:4 and 9:2, where human beings cry and where the angels express their desire to hear it grieve: "And they said to one another; 'Let the devastated earth cry out with the sound of their cries towards the gate of heaven.'" The complaint of the earth in 7:6 is explained through human beings' cry in 8:4. Similarly, it may be said that "the earth" means mainly human beings when it is said that the earth will be judged (92:1). Nevertheless, the earth, when personified here, could also refer to something more than human beings, and may include the created world in general as well. In the Hebrew Bible, heaven and earth are invoked by God as witnesses of Israel's unfaithfulness (cf.

Again, in 1 En. 54:6, a reference is made to the fallen angels in connection with judgment. The hosts of Azazel (54:5) is thrown into a burning furnace by archangels on the day of judgment. The bad influence of these angels on human beings that are lead astray is mentioned there. In 1 En. 84:4, it is affirmed that the fallen angels' sins will have an impact on humanity until the day of judgment. Such an explicit connection between the fallen angels and the situation of humanity is not visible in Matthew's Gospel.[22]

The Animal Apocalypse, being allegorical, does not use the expression "the day of judgment." It does, however, describe the judgment. In the narration of 1 En. 90:20–25, unlike in Matt 25, no spatial distinction, like the one separating some on the right side and others on the left, is made. As to the verdict, different groups are accused of different transgressions. The fallen angels, symbolized by fallen stars, are brought for punishment because of their mating with human beings and of teaching bad things. The seventy shepherds are guilty of causing an excessive destruction of Israelites. Some of the gentiles are destroyed for their hostility toward Israel. Some of the Israelites are condemned because they went astray from the right path and from God's law (note the imagery of beings having the eyes closed or open).

The day of tribulation marks the end of the present age. Just as the flood was the end of one period, the day of judgment also brings about the end of a period. However, the last judgment includes a decisive end, for it involves all the other ends. It is the end of all the events of the past. Even the flood and the events that preceded it are included. That is why, according to the Animal Apocalypse, the angels who brought about sin into the human sphere are punished. Their chastisement does not end at the time

---

Deut 4:26; 30:19; 31:28; Isa 1:2). On the other hand, the earth rejoices in 1 En. 51:5. While the cry is linked with iniquity, shedding blood, and oppression, the rejoicing is connected with the dwelling of the righteous. Another example of personification is described in 1 En. 51:1. Accordingly, the earth will give back what has been entrusted to it. This may be related to 1 En. 62:15, which refers to the resurrection.

22. However, even if the judgment of the fallen angels is not described in Matthew's Gospel, Satan's and demons' actions are described in different places. Satan tempts Jesus (Matt 4:10) and demons are cast out in 7:22; 8:31; 9:34; and 10:8. There is reference to a kingdom of Satan (12:26). Cf. Jack D. Kingsbury, *Matthew as Story* (Philadelphia: Fortress, 1988), 56. In Matthew's Gospel, the prince of the demons is Beelzebul (Matt 12:24), whereas Shemihazah/Shemiazah and Asael/Azazel, the chiefs of the fallen angels in 1 Enoch, are not mentioned.

of the flood. The end of the present age is the destruction of the causes of evil, suffering, and injustice. It is a universal judgment.[23] What happens at the day of judgment is just a "public" or universal confirmation of the verdict that had already been pronounced against the fallen angels at the time of the flood. Only the day of the "great judgment" will appease God's anger provoked by the sin of fallen angels (1 En. 84:4). The scene of the judgment, as mentioned earlier, is described in 90:20–28. For the Apocalypse of Weeks, there is a last judgment in the ninth week (91:4).

The day of judgment is a moment of truth in the sense that nothing can be hidden from the eyes of God. All the transgression is recorded by otherworldly agents, as one can see in the Animal Apocalypse (the angels who records the deeds of the shepherds; cf. 1 En. 89:70). The recording and the opening of books is not mentioned in Matthew's Gospel. One sees, however, in the gospel the motif of accountability; people will be judged even on account of what they have said on earth (Matt 12:36).

The Reasons for Judgment

Omission with regard to some duties becomes a reason for punishment in Matthew's Gospel. One is not judged for what one does only but also for what one fails to achieve. Matthew 18:23–25 affirms that the one who does not forgive will be punished. In 25:31–46, those who did not help the needy are condemned. The "tree which does not bear fruit" is thrown into fire (3:10; 7:19). Similarly, in the parable of the weeds, the throwing into the furnace by the angels of the Son of Man (13:42) is symbolized by the

---

23. The day of judgment puts an end to the oppression of the present age. It is a day of God's vengeance in favor of the righteous and the humble (1 En. 25:4). A recurrent motif in the Book of Parables, it is described as a time of affliction, distress, and pain (16:1; 19:2; cf. 45:2; 55:3; 63:8); it is not for everybody, however. The negative attributes concern the part of the people who are liable to punishment (60:6), as mentioned earlier. For the righteous, it is not a moment of affliction. It is even an occasion to join the Chosen One (the Son of Man), who sits on the throne of glory (45:3; 51:3; 60:2, 7). The nearness of the end is good news for the just as affirmed in 51:2: "for the day has come near that they must be saved." The day is also called a great day of restoration (54:6); those who were destroyed or devoured by animals come back to life (61:5). All creatures of heaven and earth will be summoned to praise God (61:10). Regarding restoration, we see a convergence with the Animal Apocalypse (90:33), which confirms the resurrection of the righteous in order to enter into the new house of God. Meanwhile the righteous and the chosen will be saved (62:13).

burning of the weeds with fire (13:40). Unlike in Matthew's Gospel, in 1 En. 62–63 the mighty and the kings are judged by the Son of Man.

According to 1 Enoch, the following will be condemned on the day of judgment: those who oppress and afflict the righteous (96:8; 99:15; 100:7), those who curse (22:11), those who deny the name of the Lord of Spirits (45:1–2; 46:7; cf. 67:10), those who do not exalt the Son of Man (46:5), and those who worship idols (19:1).

Reasons for Being Rewarded

What are the criteria for being rewarded? In Matthew's Gospel, conversion, being poor in spirit, being persecuted for righteousness (Matt 5:1–12), humility (18:1–4; 19:14), doing God's will (7:21), feeding the hungry (25:31–46), being like children (18:3), and forgiving one's brother or sister (18:35) are rewarded.

Humility goes hand in hand with righteousness in 1 Enoch, too (e.g., 5:8; 10:17; 25:4; 108:7). One may suppose that the righteous of 1 Enoch are doing the will of God. However, the motif of forgiving one's brother (Matt 18:35) is not reflected in 1 Enoch. One would say the same concerning the theme of becoming like eunuchs for the sake of the kingdom (Matt 19:12). In Matt 19:21, one is invited to go and to sell one's property in order to inherit heaven, and in 19:23 wealth is described as an obstacle for inheriting the kingdom of heaven. Trusting in one's riches and consequently forgetting the Most High becomes a cause of judgment in 1 En. 94:8. The oppression of the poor by the rich is also condemned in 96:4–8 (cf. 97:8–10). Riches will not save the wicked (100:6). According to 82:4, being righteous includes observing the "correct calendar," but such an element is absent from Matthew.

The Eschatological Judge

In 1 Enoch, there is a heavenly person called "Son of Man"[24] (1 En. 46:2, 3, 4; 48:2; 60:10; 62:5, 7, 9; 62:14; 63:11; 69:26, 27, 29; 70:1; 71:14, 17),

---

24. All the references to the Son of Man are found exclusively in the Book of Parables (1 En. 37–71). For the various debates regarding the "Son of Man" and his role in 1 Enoch and in other texts of Second Temple Judaism and of the period of the origins of Christianity, see Gabriele Boccaccini, ed., *Enoch and the Messiah Son of Man: Revisiting the Book of Parables* (Grand Rapids: Eerdmans, 2007).

with a higher status than angels but also distinct from the Lord of Spirits, who plays the role of an eschatological judge. He was hidden before the creation of the world (48:6). Righteousness (46:3) as well as the spirit of wisdom (49:3) dwell in him.[25] The righteous and the holy will rely on him (48:4). It is especially what he will do in the future that is announced.[26] He is a preexistent figure who will come to judge with God. One significant prediction is that he will sit on a heavenly throne (61:8). Other appellations are also given to him: the "Chosen One" (ḫəruy; 48:6), the "Messiah" (masiḥu) of the Lord of Spirits (48:10). First Enoch 61:5 refers to "the day of the Chosen One." The day of judgment in the Book of Parables is strongly connected with the day of the Son of Man. Similarly, in Matthew's Gospel, the Son of Man holds the position of an eschatological judge (see Matt 13 and 25).[27]

There is a close parallelism between 1 En. 62:2 and Matt 19:28, as well as between 1 En. 62 as a whole and Matt 23:22. All the verses affirm that the Son of Man will sit at the throne of glory in order to judge. The blissful state of the righteous and the elect is described in 1 En. 62:13–16. Their delight includes the Son of Man's company. The metaphors of eating, lying down, and putting on the garment of life are mentioned.

THE PERSONS WHO ARE JUDGED

The persons who are judged and condemned in the Animal Apocalypse are quite easy to identify: the fallen angels, the seventy shepherds (who

---

25. While being an inhabitant of heaven, he is also the dwelling place or space of Wisdom. It is noteworthy that Wisdom, which resides in the Son of Man, did not find a residence on earth.

26. At the end of the Book of Parables, Enoch seems to have been called Son of Man. There is, however, a lot of controversy as to the reading. Not all manuscripts support it.

27. According to Sabino Chialà, the Son of Man in Matthew—more than in Mark and Luke—has an important eschatological mission. Matthew thus would have been influenced by the contents of the Book of Parables; see "The Son of Man: The Evolution of an Expression," in Enoch and the Messiah, ed. Boccaccini, 153–78, esp. 167. Matthew's dependence on 1 Enoch with regard to the eschatological role of the Son of Man is underlined with much detail in the same volume by Leslie Walck, "The Son of Man in the Parables of Enoch and the Gospels," 299–337, esp. 328–29. The study focuses on Matt 13:41; 16:27; 19:25, 28; and the Book of Parables (more precisely 1 En. 62; 40:1; 56:1–5; 70:1). See also Sim, Apocalyptic Eschatology, 111–28.

probably represent evil angels), the gentiles who are hostile to Israel, and the unfaithful among Israel. In Matthew's Gospel the identification of those who are judged is not that easy or clear. Those who do not repent (Matt 11:20), those who do not accomplish the will of God (Matt 7:21), and those who fail in charity (Matt 25:31–46) are difficult to identify as distinct categories.

The characteristics of the day of tribulation, just mentioned above, indicate the existence of two kinds of suffering. There would be variation in terms of the nature of suffering but also in terms of the persons who would undergo the distress. Until the last judgment pain is the lot of the righteous. But from the last judgment onward suffering is the lot of the wicked. Thus, "the day of the great consummation" (1 En. 16:1) and "the great judgment day" (19:1) refer, respectively, to the suffering of evil spirits and the fallen angels.

REPENTANCE BEFORE THE LAST JUDGMENT

Repentance is more recurrent in Matthew's Gospel than in 1 Enoch. Jesus scolds the cities that did not repent despite of his miracles (Matt 11:20). According to Matt 21:32, unlike the chief priests as well as the elders and the Pharisees, tax collectors and harlots believed in John's teaching of repentance.

In 1 En. 40:9, Phanuel is the angel in charge of repentance and the source of hope for those who will inherit eternal life. It is, however, unclear to the reader of what exactly the act of repentance consists. Does it mean to join an Enochic sect? Or to be righteous? And what does "to be righteous" mean? There are, nevertheless, two interesting references to repentance in the Book of Parables. In 50:2, in connection to the "day of trouble," disaster is shown to "sinners" so that they may repent and "abandon the works of their hands." Salvation is promised to those who repent (50:3) and destruction those who do not repent (50:4). Now, the question would be to see how much this theme of repentance represents the other parts of 1 Enoch.

THE WARNINGS ABOUT THE LAST JUDGMENT

Warnings are prominent in Matthew's description of the last judgment. Behind the warnings, there is a desire to see the conversion of the wrongdoers. In both Matthew and 1 Enoch, the woes concern warnings in the

light of what will happen in the future, more specifically at the time of the
last judgment. In both cases, a danger is announced. However, 1 Enoch
does not appear to explain clearly how the danger may be avoided, whereas
Matthew's warning seems to be more explicit.

In Matthew's Gospel, there are two kinds of warnings. On the one
hand, the woes against the Pharisees and the scribes (Matt 23) are similar
to the woes against the oppressors (in the Epistle and the Book of Parables), even though the former concerns religious attitudes and the latter
deals with social justice. However, Matthew's Gospel also has warnings of
exhortation or of advice for those who wish to be rewarded but who do not
grasp the message of the kingdom of God. Thus followers of Jesus should
beware of showing up their devotion in order to attract the attention of
others lest they miss the reward of the heavenly Father (Matt 6:1).

The Aftermath of the Day of Judgment

In both 1 Enoch and Matthew's Gospel, heaven is announced as reward.
Yet, while the reality is just mentioned in Matthew, it is given much more
description in 1 Enoch. Heaven, according to Matt 5:12, is a place of recompense or reward, where the righteous become like angels (Matt 22:30).[28]
While the heavenly fire surrounding God's throne (cf. Dan 7; 1 En. 14;
71:2) is absent from Matthew,[29] the fire of punishment is mentioned both
in 1 Enoch (90:24–27) and Matthew (3:10, 12; 5:22; 13:50; cf. 25:41).

The Time of the Judgment

The parable of the good and the wicked servants (Matt 24:45–51), the
parable of the foolish and wise maidens (Matt 25:1–13), and the parable
of the talents (Matt 25:14–30) all seem to suggest the delay of the parou-

---

28. The heavenly realm is characterized by light. Thus "the righteous will shine
like the sun in the kingdom of their Father" (Matt 14:43). This is also clearly shown in
1 Enoch (cf. 1 En. 38:2; 51:4–5; 91:16; 96:3; 104:2; 108:13, 14). Thus the heavenly house
in 1 En. 14 is full of light, with walls of fire and ice. Glory and splendor are closely
linked with light in heaven. There will be an endless light after the last judgment (1
En. 58).

29. However, Matt 3:11 speaks positively of fire in connection with the baptism
with the Holy Spirit and fire.

sia.[30] Nevertheless, the time of the last judgment cannot be calculated or known in Matthew's Gospel. No one knows the time (cf. Matt 25:13, οὐκ οἴδατε τὴν ἡμέραν οὐδὲ τὴν ὥραν). This accentuates ignorance about the day of judgment.

Various parts of 1 Enoch underline that the end is near. The author of the Animal Apocalypse seems, consequently, to believe that the end is very near—that it would take place in the first century BCE—and that his generation would be a witness of the end. The Hellenistic domination (like the fourth beast of Daniel) would be a sign of the end of the present age. The Maccabean crisis might have accentuated the idea of the end.

In contrast, with regard to the time of the judgment, Matthew underlines the surprise motif. People will be caught by surprise, for they do not know when the end will happen. Perhaps more than the question of the delay of the parousia (cf. Matt 25:1–13; the parable of the foolish and wise maidens), it is the question of surprise that is emphasized. This can, indeed, be read in the light of Matt 24, where a lack of knowledge is underlined with regard to the end: thus "no one knows [οὐδεὶς οἶδεν] of the day and hour of the end" (24:36). Similarly, "before the flood they were eating and drinking, marrying … and they did not know [ἔγνωσαν] until the flood came" (24:38–39). In 24:45–51, a lack of knowledge is underlined with regard to the wicked servant. The master of that servant will come on a day when he does not expect him and at an hour he does not know (24:50).

Surprise at the Last Judgment

Matthew underlines a big difference between what one expects at the last judgment and what will, in fact, happen. In 1 Enoch, the fallen angels do not manifest any surprise when they are imprisoned until the last judgment (10:12; 22:4). Nor are giants surprised when they are punished by the flood (16:1). On the other hand, the flood, an example for the last judgment in Matt 24:39, happens suddenly: "they did not know [οὐκ ἔγνωσαν] until the flood came." The scene does not include the fallen angels. It is rather an allusion to the unexpected destruction of human beings. This might indicate two things: either Matthew's Gospel is referring to Gen 6–9 only; or, if we

---

30. Cf. Sim, *Apocalyptic Eschatology*, 6, 150–74. After a review of literature on whether Matthew's parables on the parousia (Matt 24–25) are less about the imminence of the end and more exhortative, Sim argues strongly in favor of Matthew's conviction of the end's imminence.

suppose a dependence on 1 Enoch, the gospel has voluntarily ignored or left out the motif of the fallen angels and of the giants. In Matt 24:38–39, the question is one of being ready to escape a danger. One needs to be vigilant, lest one is caught by surprise when the Son of Man comes.

For instance, even prophesying in the name of Jesus is not enough to be rewarded (Matt 7). Moreover, in contrast with those who prophesy in the name of Jesus, people who did not seem to have recognized Jesus as they were feeding the hungry are rewarded. People who did not consider themselves part of a category of the "righteous" are rewarded.

The surprise is also expressed in terms of correction, often of making the moral standard higher, that is, more difficult or more interior. For instance, in Matt 5:22, one sees an adjustment: killing was liable to judgment. Someone who would say "you fool" is now liable to "the hell of fire."

As mentioned earlier, idle speculation is excluded since "no one knows of the day and hour of the end" (Matt 24:36, 38–39, 50). In 25:31–46, the people who are judged do not seem to use the language of a sect. They do not seem to know whether they belong to the group of the elect. At least they do not refer to a certain group as their identity marker, unless one affirms that a "universal" idea of helping the needy is the identity marker of the Matthean community.

FUNCTION OF THE JUDGMENT

One may wonder why there is such a focus on the day of judgment in Matthew's Gospel. Is it in order to comfort? Is it in order to control the group? Both functions can be envisaged in 1 Enoch and Matthew's Gospel. According to David Sim, Matthew espoused an "apocalyptic-eschatological scheme" because of the "social setting of the community" that he is addressing.[31] A defensive attitude would explain such a stand. Nevertheless, the motif of surprise in Matthew's Gospel changes both the question of consolation and of controlling one's group as well.

CONCLUSION

Matthew's Gospel shares a lot of common motifs with 1 Enoch. The resurrection, life after death, judgment of the dead, punishment or individual

---

31. Ibid., 223–30.

retribution in the otherworld, and the judging role of the Son of Man are among these common themes. Both texts envisage the end of the world, something absent from the prophetic texts of the Old Testament. It is not merely the end of a period or the end of a nation's history,[32] but an end that leads into the otherworld.

This short study has tried to show that the notion of the "day of judgment," while very similar in Matthew and 1 Enoch, has some important differences, one of which is the motif of surprise, which appears only in the gospel. There the day of judgment comes suddenly, like a thief. There the criteria of righteousness are quite different from what one would normally expect. The themes of humility, interior life, doing good, and a higher standard of morality are spelled out strongly. In 1 Enoch, there is room for foreknowledge, whereas Matthew's Gospel underlines ignorance. Therefore, one needs to be prudent and avoid presumptuous speculations with regard to the day of judgment, lest one is easily deceived. False security is challenged; ignorance about the future is underlined. Now if those to be rewarded are not clearly known, does that not compromise a deterministic affirmation of the elect or the chosen ones? Similarly, if the question of reward is open and holds the motif of surprise, does that not lead to a review of a clear-cut dualism, since it is difficult to know who is righteous and who is wicked? Donald Hagner proposes four functions of apocalyptic literature: instruction, encouragement, paraenesis, and readiness.[33] It would be then interesting how one would evaluate these functions in connection with the question of surprise.

32. John J. Collins, *Apocalypticism in the Dead Sea Scrolls* (London: Routledge, 1997), 5–6.

33. Hagner, "Apocalyptic Motifs," 74–76.

THE DEMONOLOGY OF 1 ENOCH
AND THE NEW TESTAMENT GOSPELS

Archie T. Wright

INTRODUCTION

Despite the presence of demonology as a key component of many of the ancient religious cosmologies, until recently it has received little serious attention in scholarly endeavors. While mild curiosity about the unenlightened beliefs of others (e.g., belief in demons) may still be allowed, it is as if the topic had been exhausted of all but antiquarian interest. Although some may reject any demonological discussion, this does not necessitate that beliefs about demons were naïve, absurd, or juvenile. As is being shown in the ever-growing study in early Jewish literature, in particular Enochic literature and the Dead Sea Scrolls, demonology played a significant role in the worldview of Judaism and of the authors of the New Testament. It is clear that the authors of the gospels and, if we are to believe their testimony, Jesus believed in the existence of demons/evil spirits[1] and

---

1. It should be noted that several first-century CE authors were somewhat ambiguous when discussing angels, demons, and evil spirits; although, as we see in the LXX, they may all fit the common category of "evil superhuman beings," they are not necessarily the same species of being. The primary exception is Jub. 10 in which the polluted demons are identified as evil spirits in 10:3. The Apocalypse of Zephaniah and the Life of Adam and Eve do not equate angels and demons. The Apocalypse of Abraham identifies Azazel as a heavenly being who was associated with an evil spirit but is not identified as a demon. See Dale C. Allison, *Testament of Abraham*, CEJL (Berlin: de Gruyter, 2003), 31. Philo of Alexandria is one of the first writers to identify angels with demons. In *Gig.* 6–16, he states that Moses uses the term ἄγγελος in a similar manner to which other philosophers use the term δαίμων. Josephus does not connect angels and demons but does equate an evil spirit with δαίμων in the case of King Saul's affliction (see *Ant.* 6.166, 168, 211). We see a shift in the works of post–New Testa-

their ability to take possession of or oppress individuals.[2] These evil spirits are referenced multiple times in the gospels and subsequent Christian texts. What did the people believe them to be at the time? Are they human spirits, animal spirits, or something entirely different? One's initial response, if one believes in such phenomena, is that the "demons" of the gospels are "evil spirits" or "unclean spirits." It appears from the New Testament evidence that all three terms fall under the same general category of a spiritual being that existed outside the physical human realm, but at the same time interacted with humanity. But what exactly are these demons/evil spirits? The gospel writers do not tell us the origin of these spirits; however, based on extant Second Temple period Jewish literature, the concept of an "evil spirit/demon" appears to have established a strong foothold in the worldviews of significant groups in first-century Palestine.

The etymology of the term *demon* is not particularly helpful for offering a New Testament understanding of the word.[3] One can argue that demons in the ancient Mediterranean world were seldom thought to be evil but fell into the area of a vague and ambiguous power.[4] The *Iliad*

---

ment Christian authors such as Justin Martyr and Athenagoras, who acknowledge the existence of two distinct beings—the fallen angels and demons—but they are both called "evil spirits." Tatian (*Orat. ad Graec.* 7–8) and Tertullian (*Idol.* 4.2; 9.1–2; *Apol.* 22) were the first to connect demons and fallen angels.

2. See Luke 4:36: "They were all amazed and kept saying to one another, 'What kind of message is this? For with authority and power he commands the unclean spirits, and out they come!'"; and Mark 1:27: "They were all amazed, and they kept on asking one another, 'What is this? A new teaching with authority! He commands even the unclean spirits, and they obey him.'" Both of these verses seem to indicate that the people acknowledged the existence of evil/unclean spirits prior to the work of Jesus as an exorcist.

3. Philip Alexander argues that "demons, rituals and incantations ... may be 'borrowed' freely from other traditions"; cf. "Contextualizing the Demonology of the Testament of Solomon," in *Die Dämonen—Demons: Die Dämonologie der israelitisch-jüdischen und frühchristlichen Literatur im Kontext ihrer Umwelt—The Demonology of Israelite-Jewish and Early Christian Literature in Context of Their Environment*, ed. Armin Lange, Hermann Lichtenberger, and K. F. Diethard Römheld (Tübingen: Mohr Siebeck, 2003), 617: "At the level of theological reflection, however, this seems to be less true. The theology is inevitably expressed in terms of a dominant religious or philosophical worldview, and this may result in very different ontologies of demons."

4. See David Frankfurter, "Master-Demons, Local Spirits, and Demonology in the Roman Mediterranean World: An Afterword to Rita Lucarelli," *JANER* 11 (2011): 126–31, esp. 129.

and the *Odyssey* reveal that the early use of the term was synonymous with the name for God (θέος); δαίμων was thought to describe the power and activity of the god as seen in the realm of nature and its interaction with humanity. Following its use in Homeric writings, δαίμων was used to describe particular godlike beings who were understood to be inter-mediaries (primarily benevolent) between the gods and humanity. Hesiod describes the men of the *Golden Age* as δαίμονες, those appointed by Zeus to watch over and guard humanity.[5] In the later development of the con-cept, we recognize that demons were considered morally imperfect crea-tures, some being good and some being evil. Xenocrates, a student of Plato, is thought to be responsible for the development of the idea that demons were mediators between the gods and humanity. All inappropriate reports concerning the actions of the gods were now attributed to the so-called demons. Xenocrates argued for three categories of demons: the first were those that always existed as demons; the second were the departed souls of humans—both good and evil; the third type he identified as internal demons identical to the human soul or intelligence (following Plato in *Tim.* 90a).[6] The first-century Greek historian and philosopher Plutarch understood demons to be intermediaries between the gods and human-ity that existed in the realm of the air. Their primary task was to watch over humanity; however, Plutarch did not see all δαίμονες as good (e.g., *Def. orac.* 417c), nor were they immortal (*Def. orac.* 419c). He describes demons in *De Iside et Osiride* as being superhumanly strong men in whom the divine nature was joined with a soul nature and physical nature. In this sense, Plutarch's demons sound very much like the "giant offspring" of the

---

5. Zech 1:8–11 perhaps describes similar beings that were assigned by YHWH to patrol the earth watching over humanity.

6. Plato, *Tim.* 89e–90a: "We have frequently asserted that there are housed within us in three regions, three kinds of soul, and that each of these has its own motions; so now, likewise, we must repeat, as briefly as possible, that the kind which remains in idleness and stays with its own motions; necessarily becomes weakest, whereas the kind which exercises itself becomes strongest; wherefore, care must be taken that they have their motions relative to one another in due proportion. And as regards the most lordly kind of our soul, we must conceive of it in this wise: we declare that God has given to each of us, as his daemon, that kind of soul which is housed in the top of our body and which raises us—seeing that we are not an earthly but a heavenly plant up from earth towards our kindred in the heaven. And herein we speak most truly; for it is by suspending our head and root from that region whence the substance of our soul first came, from the Divine Power" (Lamb, LCL).

Enochic tradition. Josephus (*J.W.* 1.69, 613; 7.185; and *C. Ap.* 2.263) uses δαιμόνιον to refer to a "divine person" who is generally referred to as θεῖος ἄνηρ. thus comes close to the use of δαίμων among classical Greek authors: to denote a deity, as a designation for spirits or ghosts of the dead, or evil spirits (see in particular *J.W.* 8.45, in which δαίμων can mean evil spirit).[7]

A later stage in the development of demons takes place within Christian literature in which the term "demon" identifies an evil or unclean spirit rather than a divine intermediary.

As we can see, little in the Greek literature portrays demons in a similar fashion as the evil beings we find in the New Testament.[8] However, Rita Lucarelli shows in an essay that the term "demon" was used to describe both good and evil demons, in particular evil demons that were under the control of the deities.[9] This may help to explain the use of the Greek term δαιμόνιον to translate the Hebrew terms identified as demons/evil spirits in the LXX (cf. Philo, *Gig.* 16—"The common usage of men is to give the name of demon to bad and good demons alike" [Colson and Whitaker, LCL]). As such, this might explain its use by New Testament writers to describe the various evil spirits at work in the gospel pericopes. In addition, it is likely that other traditions (e.g. Near Eastern) may lend to New Testament demonology.[10]

There are several suggestive comparisons between Jewish and Babylonian demonology. Three passages stand out in the discussion of demons in the Hebrew Bible: Isa 34:14; Deut 32:23–24a; and Hab 3:5. Isaiah 34 describes the destruction of Edom by YHWH in retribution for his people. The text reads, "And desert-demons shall meet with jackals, and one hairy-goat creature will cry out to another; indeed there Lilith will come to a rest and find for herself a resting place." The author appears to compare demons and wild beasts (those that combine human and animal features).

---

7. See Carl R. Holladay, *Theios Aner in Hellenistic Judaism: A Critique of the Use of the Category in New Testament Christology,* SBLDS 40 (Missoula, MT: Scholars Press, 1977), 64.

8. Based upon this, it may be fair to say that "demonic" may be a misnomer for the type of spiritual activity we discover in the gospels. Perhaps we need to rethink what we now call "demonology of the gospels."

9. Rita Lucarelli, "Demonology during the Late Pharaonic and Greco-Roman Periods in Egypt," *JANER* 11 (2011): 109–25.

10. See Karel van der Toorn, "The Theology of Demons in Mesopotamia and Israel: Popular Belief and Scholarly Speculation," in Lange, Lichtenberger, and Römheld, *Dämonen,* 61–83.

Lilith is recognized as a demon in Akkadian texts and later Jewish traditions. She, as with other demons, dwells on the outskirts of civilization, but she is not understood as an adversary to the gods, or in Israel's case an adversary to YHWH. Deuteronomy 32 describes how YHWH will pour out his wrath upon his people for their disobedience: "I will pile up disasters against them; I will unload my arrows upon them; *they will be* exhausted from famine, being consumed by pestilence [רשף][11] and bitter destruction [קטב]."[12] Karel van der Toorn argues that Hab 3:5 contains two demons from the ancient Near East, Deber and Resheph: "Before him went a plague [דבר] and pestilence [רשף] went out before his feet."[13] According to van der Toorn, all of the creatures mentioned above operated under the authority of YHWH and are closely associated with deadly disease.[14] Both societies, Israelite and Mesopotamian, were inclined to see demons as instruments of the gods/God; both have their origins in heaven. Demons represent spiritual beings that were either cast out of heaven or descended to the earth; however, the monotheistic worldview of Judaism required the minor deities to be lower on the scale of being, and possibly understood as evil.

We also should consider the view that demons/evil spirits were understood as departed human (or animal) spirits, which view may have emerged from the religions of the ancient Near East and may have influenced the demonology of the New Testament.[15] One primary class of demon from this belief system is the Utukku, which was a disembodied human spirit (spirits of the giants?) that "could find no rest and wandered over the face of the earth."[16] It is believed they sought refuge in the desert places, cem-

---

11. Van der Toorn (ibid., 64) identifies Resheph as a "chthonic deity," known in other literature as Rashpu and Rasap, a plague god. Some scholars have equated with the Mesopotamian god of the underworld Nergal in texts from Ebla and Ugarit (see *KTU* 1.14 i 18–19 and 1.15 ii 6).

12. Van der Toorn suggests that Qeteb is the demonic creature *qẓb* in *KTU* 1.5 ii 24, in which it is an agent of destruction also found in other biblical passages; cf. Nicholas Wyatt, "Qeteb," *DDD*, 673–74.

13. Deber has been identfied as a "demon causing pestilence" (Dabir) in the Ebla texts.

14. Van der Toorn, "Theology of Demons," 64.

15. Edward Langton, "What Are Demons?" *The London Quarterly and Holborn Review* 23 (1954): 26–32. See also F. C. Conybeare, *Christian Demonology* (repr., Piscataway, NJ: Gorgias, 2007), 8.

16. See Ida Fröhlich, "Invoke at Any Time," *BN* 137 (2008): 41–74.

eteries, or the mountains. Customarily, the spirits of the dead entered the netherworld, but when the body was not buried, the spirit roamed the earth tormenting the living. It is possible that we can detect an allusion to this belief in Josephus (*J.W.* 7.180–185). He speaks of the Baaras root, used in exorcism, which, when brought to the afflicted person, drives away the demons, which he explains are the spirits of the wicked that enter into humans who are alive and kill them unless they are exorcised (see also *J.W.* 7.185, in which Josephus identifies the demons as the spirits of wicked humans; and *Ant.* 8.45–47). As can be seen from this brief review, there may well be several "demonic" traditions at work in the developing demonology of the gospels and New Testament writings.

A tradition that should not be ignored of course is the Watcher tradition from 1 En. 6–16 and that which is found in Jubilees (cf. T. Sol. 5:2, 6:2, and 17:1, which suggest the author knew of the fallen Watchers tradition). One can argue for various interpretations of this apocalyptic text,[17] but it seems clear that the Watcher tradition, whether it is from 1 Enoch or some other written or oral tradition, provides an impetus for what we discover in the various gospel pericopes concerning the affliction of human beings by demons.

The Watcher Tradition

It is not necessary to repeat here the whole story of the rebellion of the fallen Watchers in 1 Enoch and the arguably foundational story in Gen 6:1–4, but rather it is important to speak of the consequences of the angelic rebellion. The corollaries of the angelic rebellion in 1 Enoch and Genesis are described in relation to the effect upon humanity and the rest of creation. The first aspect of the aftermath of the rebellion is described in Gen 6:5 (cf. Gen 8:21), which declares that humanity has grown completely evil following the descent of the בני האלהים and the birth of their offspring: "Then the LORD saw that the wickedness of humanity was great on the earth and that every inclination [יצר] of the thoughts of their hearts were

---

17. See, e.g., David Suter, "Fallen Angel, Fallen Priest: The Problem of Family Purity in 1 Enoch 6–16," *HUCA* 50 (1979): 115–35; George W. E. Nicklesburg, *1 Enoch 1: A Commentary on the Book of 1 Enoch, Chapters 1–36; 81–108*, Hermeneia (Minneapolis: Fortress, 2001); Archie T. Wright, *The Origin of Evil Spirits*, WUNT 2/198 (Tübingen: Mohr Siebeck, 2005).

only evil continually."[18] The author of 1 En. 8:2 expresses the theme of this verse: "and there was great impiety and much fornication, and they went astray, and all their ways became corrupt."[19]

Little else is disclosed in either account about the actions of humanity. In Gen 6 the Lord was sorry that he had created humans (v. 6) and decided to remove them from the face of the earth (v. 7). This declaration may suggest that humans were to blame (v. 5) for the previous events in 6:1–4. However, 1 Enoch interprets these events from a different viewpoint. Although humans have a role in the rebellion, they are passive victims of the oppressive behavior of the fallen Watchers. If humanity is seen as corrupt (1 En. 8:1), the author links their corruption directly to the sexual encounter with Shemihazah and the other angels in 7:1 and to the teachings of Asael (the instruction motif) beginning in 8:1.[20] The author of 1 Enoch makes no mention of blame being placed directly upon humanity (see 7:6; 9:2, 3, 10); rather he identifies the reason for the corruption in 9:9 (cf. 9:1). There a scene of massive violence is attributed to the giant offspring of the Watchers and the human women ("and the women bore giants and thereby the whole earth has been filled with blood and iniquity"). The author of the Book of the Watchers clearly understood that the corruption of humanity and the earth was the fault of the angels.

Genesis 6:12 states that, for some unspecified reason, all creatures (i.e., flesh) had fallen into ruin. The author of 1 En. 7:5 picks up this theme in his description of the action of the giants: "and they [presumably the giants] began to sin against birds, and against animals, and against reptiles and against fish, and they devoured one another's flesh[21] and drank the blood from it."[22] By doing so, the author was presumably connecting

---

18. Cf. 1 En. 8:2, 4. See also Jub. 7:24 (also 5:3): "and every imagination and desire of men imagined vanity and evil continually." See also LAB 3:3, "And God saw that among all those inhabiting the earth wicked deeds had reached full measure; and because they were plotting evil all their days" (trans. D. J. Harrington, "Pseudo-Philo," OTP 2:306).

19. Translation from Knibb, *Ethiopic Enoch*, 2:81.

20. The instruction motif is missing from almost all other early Jewish and New Testament literature except for Jubilees and the Book of Parables in 1 Enoch.

21. One may question here whether the giants turned to cannibalistic practices because of the lack of food. The text seems to be referring back to the giants, but it is possible that what we have here is the beginning of prey and predator instincts in the animal kingdom.

22. Brackets are mine. See Jub. 7:24 (also 5:2), "and after this they sinned against

the reason for the flood directly to the action of the בני האלהים (i.e., the birth of the giants[23]) through his interpretation of Gen 6:5, 11, and 12. He has not only explained the flood in antiquity, but he has also identified a reason for the oppression that Israel was facing during his time: evil spirits.

EVIL SPIRITS IN THE GIANT TRADITION OF 1 ENOCH AND JUBILEES

In examining the Book of the Watchers and Jubilees, one finds a somewhat ambiguous description of the nature of the offspring of the Watcher angels and the human women. There is little argument among scholars that the offspring of the union of the Watchers and women were creatures of gargantuan stature. First Enoch 7:2 makes clear that the offspring were physically huge, "and their height was three thousand cubits."[24] It is possible that the giants were indeed superhuman "heroes," although not necessarily gigantic in physical size, but in their spiritual nature (i.e., born of an angelic spirit). The author seems to emphasize deliberately the spiritual aspects of the giant offspring alongside their physical nature. The Greek[pan] of 1 En. 15:8 identifies the spirits of the giants as πνεύματα ἰσχυρά, "strong spirits" (Greek[sync] reads πνεύματα πονηρά, "evil spirits"). This may help identify the spiritual nature of the giants. The spiritual power that resides in the spirit of an angel now occupied a physical body, thus pushing the limits of the human flesh that attempted to contain it. First Enoch 15:7 states that God did not allow angels to reproduce with women because of their spiritual nature; their place was to reside in the heavens, not in human flesh.

Because of their stature, the giants are said to have devoured all the sustenance that humanity produced until the supply ran out and they ultimately turned on the humans themselves (1 En. 7:1–3; Jub. 5:1–9). Thus, with little warrant from the Genesis passage, the authors of the Book of the Watchers and Jubilees have turned the seemingly heroic גברים of Gen 6:4 into a group of bloodthirsty cannibals. The author's description of the physical giants and their actions is quite graphic in 1 En. 7:4. They are described as murderers and cannibals. Milik's reconstructed Aramaic

---

the beasts and birds, and all that moved and walked on the earth." There is perhaps an allusion to the giants devouring humans found in Ps 14:4, "Do all the doers of evil not know, the ones eating my people *as* they ate bread, and the LORD they do not call?"

23. Gen. Rab. 26:7 identifies the giant offspring as the Nephilim (Gen 6:4a) in that they caused the "fall" of all the world.

24. See Ethiopic and Greek[pan]; see also 4Q201 1 iii 16.

fragment of 4QEnᵃ 1 iii 18, 19 reads: והוו גבריא [אנשא ו]למכל לקטלה לאנשא ו[למכל
אנון, "but the giants] conspired to kill men and [to devour them."[25] Moreover, it is possible that 1 En. 7:6 describes them as "lawless ones," though
it is unclear whether the verse refers to the giants or to their angelic parents. In the immediate context, it would appear that the expression has the
giants in view; this could then imply that the author understood they are
in violation of numerous Levitical laws concerning blood. Leviticus 3:17;
7:26, 27;[26] 17:10, 12, 14;[27] and 19:26[28] all proscribe eating (or drinking) the
blood of an animal, an injunction that is broken by the giants in 1 En. 7:5,
thus rendering them "unclean."[29] The punishment for this sin, articulated
in Leviticus, is that the person shall be cut off (נכרת) from his people.[30]
The result of this sin is described in 1 En. 10:15, "and destroy all the spirits
of lust and the sons of the Watchers, for they have wronged men."

---

25. See J. T. Milik, *The Books of Enoch: Aramaic Fragments from Qumran Cave 4* (Oxford: Clarendon, 1976), 150–51. Milik has reconstructed the beginning of the verse (supported in the Ethiopic and Greek traditions), "but the giants" and the ending, "to devour them." Cf. 4QEnᵇ 1 ii 22–23, in which Milik reconstructs the entire verse similar to that found in 4QEnᵃ 1 iii 18, 19. His reconstruction is supported in the Greekᵖᵃⁿ of 1 En. 7:4. There is a possible parallel to the giants in Sib. Or. 1:104–108; see John J. Collins, "The Sibylline Oracles," *OTP* 1:337. This passage refers to a genera-tion who were "mighty in spirit, of overbearing terrible men appeared who performed many evils among themselves. Wars, slaughters, and battles destroyed these continu-ally, men of proud heart"; see 1 En. 10:9 and 14:6. Interestingly, this generation imme-diately follows the mention of the Watchers.

26. Lev 7:26 and 27 make specific reference to drinking the blood of birds and animals, which the giants are accused of violating in 1 En. 7:5.

27. Lev 17:14 presents two interesting questions about the action of the giants: "For the life [נפש] of all flesh is its blood, it is its life [נפש]. And I said to the sons of Israel, 'You shall not eat blood of any flesh, for [the] life of all flesh is its blood; anyone who eats of it shall be cut off.'" First, we should perhaps ask if there is any significance in why the giants drank the blood of the animals. One possible answer is that they were seeking immortality through the drinking of blood. Second, were the giants cut off from the people? Anyone in violation of the law of Lev 17:14 was to be cut off from the people, which would occur in the case of the giants (1 En. 10:15).

28. Lev 19:26 describes the eating of blood alongside the sin of the practice of divination and soothsaying, two practices that could be tied to the instruction of the Watchers in 1 En. 8:2.

29. See also the concern of the author of Jubilees over the issue of eating or drink-ing blood in relation to the evil spirits in Jub. 7.

30. The verb נכרת is defined as "cut off, removed, or destroyed." See *DCH* 4:465.

The death of the giants due to their infighting (10:9) or the flood (11:20–22)[31] reveals something about the nature of their spirits. They are considered evil spirits because they were born on the earth (15:8); they are a mixed product of a spiritual being (Watcher angel)[32] and a physical human being, one whose spiritual makeup is left somewhat ambiguous in the Book of the Watchers.[33] The resulting entities are identified in 1 En. 15:8 as "strong spirits," "evil spirits," which come out of their bodies at their death.[34] We get no real sense of the spiritual nature of the Watchers' offspring, other than that they are strong or evil spirits.

References outside Hebrew tradition describe the nature of the off-spring of somewhat similar unions. Hesiod's *Catalogue of Women* frag. 1.6 describes the offspring of women and the gods as ἡμίθεοι, "half-gods," perhaps indicating a fifty/fifty mix of human and divine.[35] The Epic of Gilgamesh (I ii 1; IX ii 16) describes the Sumero-Babylonian hero Gilgamesh, who is the son of the goddess Ninsun, as two-thirds divine and one-third mortal. The latter description may better suit the spirits of the giants in 1 Enoch, as they seem to take on more of the angelic characteristics fol-lowing their death than the human side, that is, they are able to roam the earth. The spirit of the giant is in a class similar to the spirit of a Watcher, but with distinct differences.

Two main points identify important characteristics of the nature of the giants' spirits in comparison with the angelic Watchers. First, we find no evidence that upon the death of their physical body, the spirits of the giants are able to transform themselves into human form[36] in order to

---

31. See also 3 Macc 2:4; Sir 16:7; and Wis 14:6, which claim the giants died in the flood because of their arrogance or revolt.

32. See Jub. 10:5, which states that the Watcher angels were the fathers of the evil spirits that were oppressing Noah's grandchildren.

33. See also Martin L. West, *The East Face of Helicon: West Asiatic Elements in Greek Poetry and Myth* (Oxford: Oxford University Press, 1997), 117. There is a pos-sible Israelite heroic figure identified in Judg 3:31 and 5:6; he is Shamgar, the son of a Canaanite goddess called Anat.

34. There are no extant Aramaic fragments of 1 En. 15:8. Jubilees 10:1–3 identifies them as unclean demons, wicked (unclean) spirits.

35. See also the claims of Macedonian kings to divine descent in Plutarch, *Alex.* 2.1; cf. *Plutarch's Lives*, trans. Bernadotte Perrin, LCL (Cambridge: Harvard University Press, 1919), 7.

36. For reference to angelic transformation see 1 En. 17:1, "And they took me to a place where they were like burning fire; and when they wished, they made themselves

have intercourse with the women, as did their fathers.[37] The inability to transform themselves into human form may have implications in the evil spirit's desire to reinhabit a human body.[38] The second point involves the necessity for the Watchers to be bound in Tartarus in order to halt their activity, while the spirits of the giants, following the death of their physical body, are allowed to roam freely upon the earth.[39] The ability to roam about the earth links the nature of the spirits of the giants to the spiritual nature of the Watchers prior to their fall. What is not clear is why the

---

look like men." This verse is describing the action of the angels with whom Enoch is touring heaven, but the Watchers were likely in the same class. 1 En. 19:1 states: "And Uriel said to me: 'The spirits of the angels who were promiscuous with the women will stand here and they, assuming many forms, made men unclean and will lead men astray.'" See also 4Q204 frag. 5 ii 18–19: "they transgressed [the word of the Lord ... they si]nned and trans[gressed ... and] they changed [th]eir [nature] to g[o] [unto women and sin with them ...]"; T. Reu. 5:6 reads: "then they [Watchers] were transformed into human males." These texts seem to indicate that angels had the ability to transform into humans (at least in part), which is an attribute clearly missing from the spirits of the giants.

37. 4Q203 frag. 8 7–8 states that the sons of the Watchers had wives and sons of their own. Loren T. Stuckenbruck (*The Book of Giants from Qumran: Texts, Translation, and Commentary*, TSAJ 63 [Tübingen: Mohr Siebeck, 1997], 87–90) reads the fragment as follows:

7   ‏ועובדכון ודי נש...[‏
8   ‏אנון [ו]בני[הון ונ]שיא ד]י בולהון ‏

7   your activity and that of [your] wive[s and of your children and of
8   those [giants and their]son[s and] the [w]ives o[f all of them.

See also the reading in *DSSSE* 1:411:

7   ‏ועובדכון ודי נשישון [...] ‏
8   ‏אנון [ו]בני[הו]ן ונשיא ד]י בניהון [... ‏

7   and your deeds and those of you wives [. . .]
8   they [and the]ir sons and the wives o[f their sons . . .].

This would imply that the giants had sexual intercourse with human women (or female giants?).

38. Alexander ("Contextualizing," 630) argues that "demons can possess a human body: they are 'souls' and like the human soul can be, and indeed desire to be, embodied."

39. See Luke 11:24–26, which suggests that unclean spirits inhabit a human body, and when they are not, they wander the earth. Philip Alexander ("Demonology of the Dead Sea Scrolls," in *The Dead Sea Scrolls after Fifty Years: A Comprehensive Assessment*, ed. Peter W. Flint and James C. VanderKam, 2 vols. [Leiden: Brill, 1999], 2:339) suggests that the free roaming spirits of the giants (lot of Belial) are found in 1QM I 5 and IX 5–6.

giants' spirits are given that freedom. However, the Watcher tradition in Jubilees indicates that this semifreedom was required in order for them to operate under divine authority. In describing Noah's complaint about the spirits of the giants who were leading astray and corrupting humans,[40] Jub. 10:3–6 states that in order for their (the evil spirits') actions to be stopped, they must be bound up and held fast (i.e., from moving about freely on earth) in the place of condemnation, similar to the fate of their fathers (Jub. 10:5, 11; 1 En. 11–14).[41] However, Mastema asks the Lord for some of the spirits to remain free in order that he may execute his task upon the earth, perhaps an elaboration of a similar theme in 1 En. 15:11–12.[42]

A further description of the nature of the giants is given in 1 En. 10:9. The author of this verse may have been trying to connect the corrupt nature of the offspring of the angels and (human) women to Gen 6:3. Any allusion to Gen 6:3 is curiously omitted in 1 En. 6, but is possibly alluded to in 10:9–10. The author of 10:9 may be identifying the characters of Gen 6:3 as the giants: "Proceed against the bastards[43] and the adulterers[44] and

---

40. See Jub. 10:1–2, where the task of the evil spirits/demons was to make the grandchildren act foolishly, to destroy them, to mislead them, to blind them, and to kill them. Jub. 12:20 states that evil spirits rule the thoughts of people's minds. Jub. 15:30–32 suggests that each nation has a spirit ruling over it except for Israel. Jub. 19:28 states that the task of the spirits is to lead the chosen race away from the true God.

41. See Luke 8:31, in which the unclean spirits ask Jesus not to send them to "the abyss."

42. 1 En. 15:11–12 reads: "And the spirits of the giants lead astray, do violence, make desolate, and attack and wrestle and hurl upon the earth and cause illnesses. They eat nothing, but abstain from food and are thirsty and smite. These spirits rise up against the sons of men and against the women, for they have come forth from them."

43. Cf. also Greek[pan] 1 En. 10:15, which identifies the spirits of the giants as "bastards" (τὰ πνεύματα τῶν κιβδήλων), while the Ethiopic refers to them as "souls of lust and sons of the Watchers" (trans. Knibb, *Ethiopic Enoch*, 2:90).

44. Does this imply the giants also had sexual relations with married women? Based on the references to the three layers of offspring in Greek[sync] 1 En. 7:1c–2, 86:4, and Jub. 7:22, it seems possible that the giants fathered their own offspring. Alexander ("Demonology," 340) argues, based on "a sterile race of the Giants," that there is a fixed number of demons on the earth. In addition, he suggests that since 1 En. 6:6 states that there were only two hundred Watchers at the start of the rebellion, and "unless they were extremely promiscuous and their partners very fertile, we should not be thinking of countless myriads of demons." Alexander is correct in his assumption that there is a limited number of demons at work on the earth, but the number could be quite large, based on several points: (1) the Watchers could have been with more than one

against the sons of the fornicators, and destroy the sons of the Watchers from among humanity. Send them into a war of destruction, for they will not have length of days."[45] The statement, "for they will not have length of days," indicates that the giants will not live a long "human" life. At the same time, however, it does not say anything about the issue of their continued spiritual existence.

The character of the גבורים of Gen 6:4 has been clearly elaborated upon by the author of the Book of the Watchers. They no longer carry the heroic image that is implied by the language of the Genesis narrative. They have emerged as a hybrid creature that wreaks havoc upon the earth while in its physical form. Without the intervention of God to end their physical existence, they would have destroyed all of humanity. They caused the corruption of the earth that required its purification by the flood and a new beginning for humanity through Noah. Nevertheless, the physical death of the giants did not bring an end to their existence. Following their physical deaths, the author of the Book of the Watchers introduces the crux of the

---

partner; (2) the giants could also have had sexual relations with human women (or other female giants); and (3) there is a possible 120-year span of time before the flood in which all this could have repeated itself. See 3 Bar. 4:10, which numbers the giants at 409,000 at the time of the flood.

45. Cf. Jub. 5:6–11, which describes, in similar terms, the destruction of the giants: "And against their sons went forth a command from before his face that they should be smitten by the sword and removed from under heaven." The author of Jub. 5:8 has, similar to 1 En. 10:9, made a connection between the physical giants and Gen 6:3. The Jubilees author has in fact quoted the passage, "My spirit will not always abide on man, for they also are flesh and their days shall be one hundred and twenty years"; cf. also 1 En. 88.2, "and one of them drew his sword and gave it to those elephants and camels and asses and they began to strike one another." See also 1 En. 12:6, "for they will not rejoice in their sons. The slaughter of their beloved ones they will see, and over the destruction of their sons they will lament and petition for ever" (see Knibb, Ethiopic Enoch, 2:92; also 1 En. 14:6). The story of the death of the offspring is slightly different in the Animal Apocalypse. Unlike their deaths prior to the flood in the Book of the Watchers, the author of the Animal Apocalypse (89:6) states that the death of some of the offspring will occur during the flood. It appears that not only do we not have the survival of the physical giants, but also there is no reference to the survival of the spirits of the offspring. However, the author may have allowed for the survival of the spirits of the giants in the form of the seventy shepherds. The actions of the shepherds (under the influence of the spirits?) in 1 En. 89:59–90:25 perhaps allude to the actions of the spirits in Jub. 10:8, while 1 En. 90:25 could represent the final destruction of the spirits on the day of judgment (16:1).

problem of the union of the Watchers and women: the emergence of evil
spirits from the bodies of the giants (15:9).

AETIOLOGY OF EVIL SPIRITS

The Book of the Watchers' depiction of the origin of evil spirits describes
the beginning of an ongoing problem with evil spirits in the Second Temple
period. This may have resulted from the need to explain the broader issue
of the "problem of evil" and the role of YHWH (Isa 45:7) during the Persian and Hellenistic periods; that is, was there a demonic streak in the
Israelite conception of God? In addressing this issue, it is evident from a
number of references in early Jewish literature that evil spirits had taken a
place in the theological worldview of at least some strands of early Judaism.[46] This may explain, or be explained by, the aetiological use of Gen 6 in
the development of evil spirits in 1 En. 15–16 and Jubilees.

In 1 En. 15:6 God declares to Enoch the extent to which the Watchers have disrupted the cosmos. They were spiritual beings that were never
meant to cross the line of their heavenly existence and become part of the
fleshly world (15:7). The continued existence of the angels did not require
the act of procreation for which God gave women (θηλείας) to men. Therefore, by procreating through the women, the Watchers have created an
unauthorized new being, one that is a mix of the heavenly nature of the
Watchers and the body and flesh of humans: "they will be called evil spirits and they will dwell among humans" (15:8). First Enoch 15:9 helps to
clarify further the spiritual nature of the giants: "Evil spirits came out from
their bodies[47] because they originated from above,[48] and out of the holy

---

46. See, e.g., 4Q560; 4Q510; 4Q511; 4Q230; 4Q231; 11Q11; 1QapGen; 4Q544;
4Q429; and 4Q444. The evil spirits are designated as πνεύματα πονηρά, which are usually spirits that lead people to sin or they cause illness. A possible origin is found in the
Hebrew Bible in 1 Sam 16 and 18. It is also found in literature of the immediate period;
see, e.g., T. Sim. 3:5; 4:9; T. Jud. 16:1; T. Levi 5:6; 18:12; Tob 6:7; and in gospel accounts
of Luke 7:21; 8:2; 11:26; and Matt 12:43.

47. Greek[sync] reads, "They will be evil spirits, the evil spirits which have come out
from the bodies of their flesh."

48. Greek[sync] reads, "they originated from men," which is followed by Matthew
Black, *The Book of Enoch or 1 Enoch: A New English Edition with Commentary and
Textual Notes*, SVTP 7 (Leiden: Brill, 1985), 34. The Greek[pan] and Ethiopic reading
"from above" seems to make better sense. Knibb (*Ethiopic Enoch*, 2:101) argues that
"the clause explains why *spirits* came out of the flesh of the giants, not why *evil* spir-

Watchers; [this is] the origin of their creation and their foundation. They will be called evil spirits."[49] The author of the Book of the Watchers has made clear in 15:10 that, as spirits, the former physical giants are no threat to the heavenly realm; they are spirits born on the earth, who are confined to the earth. Rather, now as spirits, they continue to be perceived as a threat to humanity (15:11).

Similar to Gen 6:5–7:24, there is no clear textual evidence in the Watcher tradition that permits the survival of the גבורים (physical giants), the offspring, following the flood.[50] On the contrary, their physical destruction seemed certain in each development of the tradition (1 En. 15:12; 89:6; Jub. 7:25).[51] However, equally certain is the survival of the evil spirits that came out of their bodies upon their death (1 En. 16:1). The giants, like their human counterparts, were composed of two elements: they each had a fleshly body, which could die, and they each had an immortal spirit (in the sense that its existence continued following a physical death).[52] The

---

its came out," but it seems this is precisely the explanation. The spirits of the giants originated within the Watchers, but became eternal spirits of impurity. Nickelsburg (*1 Enoch 1*, 272–73) suggests that we should not compare the spiritual makeup of the giants with the spiritual makeup of humans. The spirit of a giant is a result of the Watchers spawning their substance onto the earth.

49. Greek[sync] 9e–10 reads, "They will be evil spirits upon the earth."

50. Loren T. Stuckenbruck suggests there were sufficient grounds for the readers of Second Temple period literature to imagine that these giants had survived the flood ("The 'Angels' and 'Giants' of Genesis 6:1–4 in Second and Third Century BCE Jewish Interpretation: Reflections on the Posture of Early Apocalyptic Traditions," *DSD* 7 [2000]: 356). He proposes two likely scenarios: (1) they escaped on the ark with Noah's family, either as part of it or otherwise (see 1 En. 106–107; 4Q204 5 ii; and 1QapGen II); and (2) the author of the biblical text omitted the specifics of how they survived the deluge, but from the many references in the biblical narrative, one may surmise their possible survival. See, in particular, the story of Nimrod as a γίγας in Gen 10:8–11. Nimrod's connection to Babylon is perhaps alluded to in Eusebius, *Praep. ev.* 9.17.2–3. The city of Babylon is founded by the giants who escaped the flood, who then built the tower of Babel (Gen 10:10; 11:3–4); see Robert Doran, "Pseudo-Eupolemus," *OTP* 2:880.

51. This is also the case in several of the Dead Sea Scrolls fragments, 4Q370 1 6; 4Q202 1 iv 5–6; 1 vi 8–10; 4Q203 5; 4Q204 1 v 2; 1 vi 15–16; 4Q531 4 5.

52. 4Q531 14 indicates a self-description by the giants that they are neither "bones nor flesh," a form from which they will be blotted out, implying they are spiritual beings; see discussion in Stuckenbruck, *Book of Giants*, 159–60. See also T. Sol. 5:3, which identifies the demon Asmodeus of Tobit as the son of an angel with a human mother, identifying him as a giant (cf. also T. Sol. 17:1).

spiritual element of the giants, however, had a slightly different nature than that of the human spirit. The giants' spirits, unlike the human spirit, were able to roam the earth unseen (1 En. 15:11), a trait inherited from their fathers. Philip Alexander suggests an important difference that exists between the giants and angels: the former, as evil spirits, are able to invade the human body.[53] This characteristic, it seems, goes beyond the description of their task as evil spirits upon the earth in 1 En. 15:11–12: "And the spirits of the giants, the nephilim,[54] inflicting harm, being corrupt, and attacking, and fighting, and dashing on the ground,[55] and they cause sorrow; and consuming nothing, but abstaining from eating and do not thirst, and they strike spirits."[56] Nonetheless, as Alexander notes, this list of characteristics does not eliminate the possibility that the spirits are also capable of "possessing" a human body.

Jubilees 10 describes a similar situation concerning the actions of the spirits of the giants following the flood. We are told that the unclean spirits began to lead humanity astray and to destroy them: "impure demons began to mislead Noah's grandchildren, to make them act foolishly, and to destroy them."[57] This ability of the evil spirits to lead humanity astray may be premised on the Watchers teaching their sons the mysteries of heaven. This idea is found initially in 1 En. 10:7: "not all the sons of men shall be destroyed through *the mystery of everything which the Watchers made known and taught to their sons*."[58] First Enoch 19:1 may suggest what exactly

---

53. See Alexander, "Demonology," 339.

54. Unfortunately, there are no Aramaic fragments of this passage. All three extant versions, Ethiopic, Greek[pan], and Greek[sync], appear corrupted and seem very disjointed. Black (*Book of Enoch*, 34) presents a good mix of the Greek versions. See discussion of the corrupt nature of this portion of the text in Knibb, *Ethiopic Enoch*, 2:101.

55. Greek[pan] reads here πνεύματα σκληρὰ γιγάντων, "hard [harsh] spirits of [the] giants."

56. See Greek[pan], καὶ προσκόπτοντα πνεύματα, "striking spirits." Knibb (*Ethiopic Enoch*, 2:102) has suggested "and are not observed"; Black (*Book of Enoch*, 34) suggests "and produce hallucinations" (from Greek[sync]).

57. Translation from James C. VanderKam, *The Book of* Jubilees, CSCO 511 (Leuven: Peeters, 1989), 58. Jub. 10:1, 2 identifies the spirits of the giants with the term "demon," which is not a term used in the Book of the Watchers to identify the spirits.

58. Trans. Knibb, *Ethiopic Enoch*, 2:88, emphasis added. This, again, is a very corrupt text that Knibb suggests was altered by Syncellus or his sources. 1 En. 16:3 explains that the instruction, which the Watchers taught humanity and their sons, was a "worthless mystery" that caused evil to increase on the earth. 1 En. 16:3 also implies

the humans were led to do that would destroy them, "[the spirits of the angels] who lead men astray so that they sacrifice to demons [δαιμονίοις] as gods."[59] Several passages in the Hebrew Bible (see, e.g., Deut 32:17 and Ps 105:37) state that humans were sacrificing to demons.[60] According to these two examples, the people were led to sacrifice to demons (Heb. שדים) as gods.[61] Although we cannot assume that these texts influenced the author

---

that it was for malevolent reasons (perhaps jealousy?) that the Watchers taught these mysteries, "in the hardness of your hearts."

59. Suggestions in the Watcher tradition imply that the spirits of 19:1 may be the spirits of the giants. Nickelsburg (*1 Enoch 1*, 268, 273) suggests this can be found in 15:11 by reading νιμόμενα ("pasturing") for Aramaic רעין, corrupt for תעין ("lead astray") or for רעין ("shatter") in v. 11a. This idea is elaborated upon in Jub. 7:27; 10:2, 7–13; 11:4; 12:20. The spirits, by implication, would carry on the activity of the giants and their fathers the Watchers based on 10:7. The Watcher tradition in Jubilees makes clear that it is the spirits of the giants who lead humans astray (10:2; 12:3), "and the sons of Noah came to Noah their father and they told him concerning the demons which were leading astray." Jubilees 10:4 implies it is these same spirits that lead humans to make idols and to worship them, "and malignant spirits assisted and seduced them into committing transgression and uncleanness." The difficulty with the extant forms of 1 En. 19:1 is that it challenges the interpretation of the judgment scene of the Watchers in ch. 10 of the Book of the Watchers and in Jub. 5. If we interpret the story as prediluvian, and there is nothing to tell us otherwise, it looks back to the time before the confinement of angels, when during their time on earth they led humanity to sacrifice to idols. Therefore, it may be plausible for one to suggest that the spirits of the giants are leading humanity to sacrifice to idols; see Nickelsburg, *1 Enoch 1*, 287. See Jub. 15:31–32, "He [God] made spirits rule over all [nations] in order to lead them astray from following him"; cf. Ps 96:4–5, "For all the gods of the nations are idols" (95:5 LXX: "For all the gods of the nations are demons [δαιμόνια]").

60. These demons (δαιμονίοις) should not be understood as the evil spirits of the giants, but rather as the spiritual powers of the principalities and nations (cf. Deut 32:8 and Sir 17:17); see Dale B. Martin, "When Did Angels Become Demons?" *JBL* 129 (2010): 667 n. 42. Jubilees suggests that when Israel is under foreign rule (1:20; 11:18–22; 48), the people suffer from the conflict, bloodshed, famine, and diseases caused by demons.

61. The Greek[pan] text of 1 En. 16:1 states that these evil spirits will corrupt humanity without judgment until the great judgment. The Ethiopic text differs significantly from the Greek texts in this verse. Siam Bhayro has suggested in a personal correspondence that the Greek[pan] text is likely the most reliable in comparison to the Aramaic original of the Book of the Watchers. The Ethiopic makes no mention of the continued destructive work of the spirits of the giants until the day of judgment. Another significant variant occurs in 16:3; the Greek describes the mysteries that the Watchers revealed as "mysteries of God," whereas the Ethiopic reads "worthless mysteries."

of the Book of the Watchers, it seems the author was aware of the practice in Israel's history.

The author of the Book of the Watchers introduced an answer to the evil in his day that the Genesis flood narrative does not address. The Genesis narrative implies that all corrupt flesh will be destroyed in the deluge (Gen 6:13). This throws the spotlight on the figure of Noah, in whom both the biblical narrative and the Enochic tradition are theologically invested. What does complete annihilation through the flood mean in relation to Noah?[62] As the rest of the story of Genesis shows, sin continues after the flood.[63] Genesis simply implies that sin survived through Noah and his family, whereas the Watcher tradition recounts the survival of the evil spirits as an explanation of why evil persists in the author's day (1 En. 16:1). However, the reader is not left without hope concerning these evil spirits. In 1 En. 16:1, the author describes their unabated oppression and affliction of humanity, but he reports that there is a limit to their dominion. The great day of judgment will end their powers over humans, and they will be judged and punished along with the Watchers and human sinners.

The Watcher tradition in 1 En. 15:12 states that the spirits of the giants "will rise against the sons of men and women because they came forth from them."[64] The context of this verse, established in 15:11, seems to indicate that little restraint is placed upon the activity of the giants' spirits; their end will come only in the eschaton. However, Jubilees presents a slightly different view of the postdeluge actions of the evil spirits. It is a perspective that perhaps brings the actions of the surviving evil spirits in

---

62. 1 En. 10:2–3 reveals that humanity will be preserved through Noah the son of Lamech: v. 3, "Teach the righteous one what he should do, the son of Lamech how he may preserve himself alive and escape forever. From him a plant will be planted, and his seed will endure for all the generations of eternity." In the Watcher tradition in Jub. 10:3, Noah's prayer following the flood implies that he is very much aware of his sinful nature and is thankful for the mercy and grace that God has shown to him.

63. Jub. 10:8 states that following the flood "great is the wickedness of the sons of men." The postflood situation seems quite the opposite in 1 En. 10:20–11:2, which suggests that "all the sons of humanity will become righteous, and all the peoples will worship [YHWH]" (v. 21).

64. This verse seems to imply the reason for the spirits' oppression of humanity is simply that they were born out of their flesh. This could indicate a need for the spirit to reoccupy flesh, i.e., possession. Alexander ("Demonology," 339) suggests that "as disembodied spirits roaming the world, like the human 'undead,' they particularly seek embodiment, with all its attendant problems for the one whom they possess."

line with the limited demonic activity we find in the Hebrew Bible. The author of Jub. 10 further develops this element of the Watcher tradition by limiting the autonomy of the evil spirits. It is possible, from Charles's reading of 10:6, that up to this point the spirits had free reign over humanity (similar to what we find in 1 En. 15:11–12), "for you [God] alone can exercise dominion over them.[65] And let them not have power over the sons of the righteous."[66] God then orders the archangels to bind all the evil spirits (10:7), but the chief of the spirits, Mastema, implores the Lord to leave some of them with him in order to carry out his task against humanity. This is a major shift from the role of the evil spirits in the Book of the Watchers; there they have no apparent leader, and there is no mention of the figure of Satan (Mastema in Jubilees). The notion of a leader over the realm of evil spirits seems to have been taken up in some of the Dead Sea Scrolls that express a demonological interest and perhaps serve as a connection between the evil spirits of the Watcher tradition and those found in the gospels; we will discuss a few of these texts below.

4QSONGS OF THE MASKIL (SAGE) SERVING AS THE BRIDGE

We have looked briefly at the origins of evil spirits in the Watcher tradition of 1 Enoch and Jubilees. Although these texts are unlikely sectarian, it appears they were a major influence in the demonology of Qumran and the overall worldview of the Qumran sect.[67] Two texts in which this is clear are 4Q510 and 4Q511, the Songs of the Maskil (Sage). I stress here that these are not the only Qumran texts that support this view, but I use them as an example of the influence of the Watcher tradition on the authors of the Qumran texts (cf. 11Q11; 4Q560). The Songs of the Maskil are dated

---

65. A similar divine sovereignty is suggested in the Mesopotamian epic Erra and Ishum in which a group of demons operates under the direction of the god of the netherworld, Erra; however, in this case the "demons" were created by the king of the gods, Anu. See van der Toorn, "Theology of Demons," 73–76.

66. Nickelsburg, *1 Enoch 1*, 287, note on Jub. 10:6. Nickelsburg argues that Charles has emended the Ethiopic without due cause, and that it should read: "for you alone know their punishment; and may they not have power over the sons of the righteous."

67. See Philip S. Alexander, "'Wrestling against Wickedness in High Places': Magic in the Worldview of the Qumran Community," in *The Scrolls and the Scriptures: Qumran Fifty Years After*, ed. Stanley E. Porter and Craig A. Evans, JSPSup 26 (Sheffield: Sheffield Academic, 1997), 318–37.

paleographically to the late first century BCE or early first century CE.[68] The content of the Songs gives a clear indication that at least some strands/ groups of Second Temple period Judaism believed in the ongoing activity of the evil spirits of the Watcher tradition (see 4Q510 1 4–8). This section of the Songs presents a prayer that was apparently being used apotropa- ically against the attack of demons upon individuals or the community as a whole. The content reflects the multifarious nature of the demonic realm in some cosmological traditions of Judaism at the time. The author incor- porates the spirits that are spoken of in Ps 91, also those in Isa 13:21, along with those of spirits of the bastard giants of the Watcher tradition. These spirits have been given permission, under the guidance of Mastema/Satan, to afflict humanity until the day of judgment.[69] This may explain the ques- tion raised by the evil spirits afflicting individuals in the gospels, "have you come to destroy us before the time?" (hinted at in 4Q510 1 6–8: "those who strike suddenly to lead astray the spirit of understanding and to hor- rify their hearts and souls during the period of the dominion of wicked- ness and the times appointed for the humiliation of the Sons of Light"). The task of the evil spirits spelled out here is to attack the minds of the individuals (see also Jub. 10:1; 1QS 3:20–24), which we may see reflected in the Gerasene/Gedarene demoniac pericopes in the gospels.[70]

Demonology of the Gospels

The canonical gospels present a plethora of demonic activity that is high- lighted in numerous pericopes about the ministry of Jesus and his disci- ples.[71] Before we discuss this material, it is important to attempt to iden-

---

68. Esther Eshel, "Genres of the Magical Texts," in Lange, Lichtenberger, and Römheld, *Dämonen*, 395–415.

69. See Michael Segal, *The Book of Jubilees*, JSJSup 117 (Leiden: Brill, 2007), 174–80.

70. At this point it should be noted that one may be limiting one's focus should one say that it is the 1 Enoch giant tradition that serves as an impetus for New Testa- ment demonology. If one considers the "evolution" of the tradition in Jubilees and the above-mentioned scrolls, which I would argue include a developing anthropology closer to the New Testament demonic pericopes, it may be more appropriate to advo- cate for the broader Watcher/giant traditions of early Jewish literature as the back- ground for New Testament demonology.

71. See, e.g., Matt 4:24; 7:22; 8:2, 3, 16, 28–33; 10:1, 8; 12:22, 26, 43, 45; 13:38, 41; 14:26; 15:22; 17:15, 18; Mark 1:23, 27, 32, 34, 39; 3:11, 15, 22, 30; 5:2, 8, 12, 15; 6:49; 7:25, 26, 30; 9:17–18, 25; 16:17; Luke 4:33, 35, 36, 41; 5:12; 6:18; 7:21; 8:2, 27, 29, 30,

tify what the authors of the gospels understood "demon" to mean. The early New Testament writers were not identifying the fallen angels with the term "demon," as this is a development from the second and third centuries CE.[72] The gospel authors use two primary designations in parallel with δαιμόνιον: "evil spirit" (τὸ πνεῦμα τὸ πονηρόν) and "unclean spirit" (τὸ πνεῦμα τὸ ἀκάθαρτον).[73] Both these parallel phrases are used in the Watcher tradition to identify the spirits of the giants following their physical death. "Evil spirit" is found in the Greek[Sync] version of 1 En. 15:8–9 ("strong spirit" in Greek[Pan]), while "unclean spirit" appears in the Watcher tradition of Jub. 10.[74]

Although used on three other occasions in the gospels (Matt 12:45; Luke 7:21; 11:26), "evil spirit" is used to clarify further the term "demon" only once in Luke 8:2: "as well as some women who had been cured of evil spirits and infirmities: Mary called Magdalene, from whom seven demons had gone out."[75] However, the phrase "unclean spirit" is equated with "demon" on several occasions in the gospels: Mark 7:26; 5:12; Luke

<hr>

33–38; 9:39, 42, 49; 11:14, 15, 20, 26; 13:11, 16, 32; 22:3; John 7:20; 8:48, 52; 10:20–21; 13:27).

72. See Martin, "When Did Angels Become Demons?" In addition, the translators of the Hebrew Bible in the LXX never translated Heb. מלאך as Greek δαίμων.

73. The apostle Paul identifies various spiritual beings including demons, good and evil spirits, and good and evil angels; see, e.g., Rom 8:38; 1 Cor 4:10; Gal 3:19; and 2 Thess 1:17. In addition, Jesus identifies "serpents and scorpions" in possible allusion to demons from Ps 91:13 (Luke 10:19 "Behold, I have given you authority to tread upon serpents and scorpions, and over all the power of the enemy, and nothing shall injure you."). Testament of Levi 18:12 offers a similar allusion to Ps 91, "And he will grant to his children authority to tread upon wicked spirits."

74. Loren Stuckenbruck has recently raised the issue as to why the gospels do not attempt to explain why the demons are identified as unclean spirits. One can only suggest that the authors were aware of the Watcher traditions of 1 En. 7:5 in which the giants are rendered "unclean" by the drinking of blood, which, upon their physical deaths, would render the giants' spirits unclean. We also see the spirits of the giants identified as unclean in Jub. 10. See Stuckenbruck, "The Human Being and Demonic Invasion: Therapeutic Models in Ancient Jewish and Christian Texts," in *The Myth of Rebellious Angels: Studies in Second Temple Judaism and New Testament Texts*, WUNT 335 (Tübingen: Mohr Siebeck, 2014), 174.

75. "Evil spirit" also parallels "demon" in Tob 6:8: "He replied, 'As for the fish's heart and liver, you must burn them to make a smoke in the presence of a man or woman afflicted by a demon or evil spirit, and every affliction will flee away and no longer remain with that person.'"

4:33 (spirit of an unclean demon); 8:28; 9:38, 42.[76] Matthew's Gospel does not draw the comparison between demon and "unclean spirit," but it does equate "unclean spirit" and "evil spirit" in Matt 19:43–45, in which the "unclean spirit" departs from a person, after wandering in the waterless places it returns with seven other spirits more evil than itself.[77] In addition, the author of Matt 8:16 states that a person who is being demonized (δαιμονίζοται) has a "spirit" that must be cast out by "a word."

As can be seen, the majority of "demonic" activity represented in the gospels is centered on the phrase "unclean spirit" (appears only once in the HB, Zech 13:2 [Heb. רוח חטמאה; LXX τὸ πνεῦμα τὸ ἀκάθαρτον], where it appears to represent a spirit that has occupied the land and the people, rather than one that is afflicting an individual).[78] The behavior and activity of the unclean spirits seems to be the same as the δαιμόνια. Demons appear to possess individuals based upon the language used; that is, the demon "entered into" (εἰσελθεῖν) the individual who was being "tormented/demonized" (δαιμονισθείς).[79] However, the more convincing evidence for

---

76. 1 Tim 4:1 parallels "demon" with the phrase "deceitful spirit": "Now the Spirit expressly says that in later times some will renounce the faith by paying attention to deceitful spirits and teachings of demons"; also Rev 18:2: "And he cried out with a mighty voice, saying, 'Fallen, fallen is Babylon the great! And she has become a dwelling place of demons and a prison of every unclean spirit, and a prison of every unclean and hateful bird.'"

77. We can see a possible parallel in Zoroastrianism in which the evil spirits possess the waterless regions of the earth.

78. Several Dead Sea Scrolls mention an unclean spirit (רוח טמאה) in relation to demonic possession (e.g., 11QPs[a] 19:15; 4Q444 1 i 8; possibly 4Q458 2 i; cf. 1QS 4:21–22, ברוח נדה). Through this purity language (cf. 1QS 3:8–9), the scrolls reflect an image within the demonology of Qumran that equates demonic possession to impurity, but at the same time does not limit impurity to demonic possession. We find similar language in the gospels. The phrase πνεύματα ἀκάθαρτα occurs 22 times in the demonic pericopes of the gospels in which unclean spirits are seen as responsible for physical possession and affliction of individuals. It is in this context that we find the clearest connection of the Watcher tradition to the demoniac story in Mark 5. There is clear language of impurity that defines both the spirit that has afflicted the person (see 5:2, 8) and the individual (5:3). Sacchi (Jewish Apocalyptic, 214) argues that impurity was a source of evil for humankind that, at times, could enter into humans.

79. See Matt 8:16; 9:33; 15:22; Luke 8:27–36. There is little evidence of demonic possession in the intertestamental literature despite the argument for such in the Genesis Apocryphon, 11Q11, the Songs of the Maskil (4Q510–511, 444), and 11Q5. Some later Jewish texts (mid- to late first century CE) include the idea of demonic posses-

possession is the exorcistic language used by the authors when the demon or unclean spirit is rebuked and told to leave the individual, hence "come out" (ἔξελθε).

Individuals who are "possessed" are described as "having a demon(s)" (ἔχων δαιμόνια). Robert Hall has rightly pointed out that the unfortunate modern concept of "possessed by a demon" has perhaps skewed the idea presented in the gospels. We must understand that in the Synoptic Gospels a demon does not "have a human being"; rather the language always seems to indicate that the individual "has a demon" (see, e.g., Matt 11:18; Mark 3:22; 5:15; Luke 4:33; 7:33; 8:27).[80] Luke 4:33–36 (// Mark 1:23–27) describes an individual who had a spirit of an unclean demon (ἔχων πνεῦμα δαιμόνιου ἀκαθάρτου; in Luke 4:36 described as "unclean spirit"). We see evidence in the pericope that perhaps points to the demonology of the Watcher tradition. The individual "cries out with a loud voice," suggesting he is being tormented by the unclean demon, one of the tasks of the spirits of the giants in 1 En. 15:11–12 (cf. Luke 9:42, in which the evil spirit crushes and throws the young boy to the ground during the exorcism). The "possessed" man asks Jesus, "what have you to do with us?" and "have you come to destroy us?"; Jesus's response is simply to rebuke the demon, which comes out of the man without harming him.

In Mark 7:25, the daughter of the Syro-Phoenician woman is said to "have an unclean spirit/demon"; after Jesus perceived her belief, the demon leaves ("goes out from," ἐξέρχομαι) the daughter and she is healed. Mark 9:17–26 (// Luke 9:39–42) describes a young boy who has a spirit of dumbness. The spirit is said to seize the boy and throw him to the ground; he is foaming at the mouth, he grinds his teeth, and he becomes stiff (as if dead). Again, we see the belief of the father playing a role in the release of the boy from the spirit—Jesus rebukes the spirit and tells it not to reenter the boy.

---

sion. See esp. Josephus, *Ant.* 8.42–49; cf. 4Q266 6 i 7–11; 1QS III 13–IV 26; and 4Q560 1 i 3–6, which provides the clearest notion of bodily possession in the Qumran library.

80. I am grateful to Robert Hall for his insight on this issue, which he offered in his response to this essay at the Enoch Seminar in Camaldoli. Hall further notes that the language of Luke in 7:21, 8:2, and Acts 5:16 indicates that an individual is healed from evil spirits in the same manner as any other infirmity; in other words, according to Hall, "in the [S]ynoptics the phrase 'to have a demon' seems precisely parallel to the phrase 'to have a disease' (cf. Matt 4:24; 8:6; Mark 1:32, 34). For the Synoptics, having a demon can be as natural and normal as having a cold" (response, p. 2).

Perhaps the most significant of the demonic pericopes in the gospels
is that of the Gerasene demoniac in Mark 5:1–20 (// Luke 8:27–36; Matt
8:28–34), which describes a man under the influence of, or possessed by,
an unclean spirit.[81] Mark 5:2 reads, "And when he [Jesus] had come out
the boat, immediately a man [Matt 8:28 has two demoniacs] from the
tombs with/having an unclean spirit met him."[82] We are told nothing of
how this man arrived at this condition, only that he has been subjected
to the affliction of an unclean spirit (only identified as a "demon" in Matthew) for some period. We are also told that he had been bound previously
in shackles and chains, but it was no longer possible to do so. Mark 5:5
implies that this action was for his own protection, "And constantly night
and day, among the tombs and in the mountains, he was crying out and
gashing himself with stones" (cf. Matt 8:29 and Luke 8:29, both of which
lack the man gashing himself with stones)—here again we see the language of torment inflicted by the demon. The assumed possession by the
unclean spirit has given the man a supernatural strength that allows him
to free himself from the chains; the language suggests he tore the chains
and shackles (Matthew lacks any mention of the demoniac being chained
and freeing himself). The unclean spirit has afflicted the man to the point
that he has chosen, or been forced (Luke notes that he was driven into
the wilderness by the demon), to live among the tombs. As such, the man
would have been considered unclean according to Torah.[83] It appears from
the narrative that the man has little choice in his actions; he gashes himself
with stones in verse 5, and it is clear in verse 7 that the spirit has the ability
to control the man's speech. Nevertheless, even though the spirit has the
ability to take control of the man's body, verse 7 implies that the authority
of God limits the autonomy of the spirit (see the role of the giants' spirits
in Jub. 11:2–6; also 10:8–9).

---

81. For discussion, see Mark McVann, "Dwelling among the Tombs: Discourse,
Discipleship, and the Gospel of Mark 4:35–5:43" (PhD diss., Emory University, 1984);
and Ken Frieden, "Language of Demonic Possession: Keyword Analysis," in *The Daemonic Imagination: Biblical Text and Secular Story,* ed. Robert Detweiler and William
G. Doty, AARSR 60 (Atlanta: Scholars Press, 1990), 41–52.

82. Brackets are mine. One may raise the question as to why the demoniac
wanted to meet Jesus, while in v. 7 he wants to dissociate from him. Perhaps it is the
spirit or soul of the man that is drawn to Jesus in an effort to find freedom from the
unclean spirit.

83. See Num 19:11, 14, 16. However, the location of the pericope, i.e., in the
Decapolis, may imply that the demoniac was a gentile rather than a Jew.

In this pericope, we are told several characteristics of the unclean spirit. First, the invading spirit causes violence and gives the individual great strength (Mark 5:3–5; Matt 8:28; Luke 8:29; cf. 1 En. 15:11, πνεύματα ἰσχυρα [Greek^{Pan}]). Second, it has the ability to possess a physical body (Mark 5:2, 8, 13; Matt 8:28, 31; Luke 8:27, 29; cf. 1 En. 15:12). Third, it recognizes the authority of God over its activity (Mark 5:7; Matt 8:29; Luke 8:28; cf. 1 En. 16:1). Fourth, it has a need, or desire, to inhabit a body of flesh (Mark 5:12; Matt 8:31; Luke 8:31, 32; cf. 11Q11 IV 4–8). What we are not told about the spirit is what happens to it when the body it occupied is killed (Mark 5:13).

In addition, the author of Mark 5 conveys several characteristics of the man while he is under the influence of the spirit and when he has been released from its affliction. First, we are told, or at least it is implied, that he has been made unclean (v. 3). Second, he has obtained great strength that we can assume he did not previously possess (vv. 3, 4).[84] Third, he became mentally afflicted to the point of self-mutilation, screaming loudly, and withdrawing from society (v. 5).[85] Fourth, he appears to lose control of his power of speech when the spirit speaks through him to Jesus (vv. 7, 9, 12).[86] Fifth, following the exorcism of the unclean spirit, the man is described as being in his right mind, fully clothed, and presumably in a state of normalcy.

Furthermore, in the Watcher tradition of Jub. 10 we find a connection to the demonic pericopes in the gospels. The author of Jub. 10 describes the request of Noah that God bind up the evil spirits of the giants in order that they cease oppressing the sons of Noah (cf. Jub. 23:11–31 in which demons cause starvation, diseases, and natural disasters). God agrees to bind them up, but he is interrupted by Mastema (heavenly being?) who asks that God leave some of the spirits free that he might use them to fulfill his task of testing humanity. God agrees to leave 10 percent of the spirits free to work under the leadership of Mastema, who is operating under the sovereignty of God. Mark 5:7 takes up the theme of the spirits being under some kind of divine decree. The unclean spirit goes as far as to

---

84. Cf. Acts 19:16 "And the man, in whom was the evil spirit, leaped on them and subdued all of them and overpowered them."

85. Cf. Mark 9:22, 26.

86. See discussion of the loss of mental control to a spirit in John R. Levison, *The Spirit in First Century Judaism*, AGJU 29 (Leiden: Brill, 2002), 30–42.

implore the name of God to prevent Jesus from prosecuting it (or them).[87] There is some indication in Mark 5:7 that the unclean spirit is attempting to bind Jesus in an oath not to destroy it by addressing him "Jesus Son of the Most High God."[88] The use of the divine title may indicate the spirit was aware that it operated under the divine authority of a group of spirits who were allowed to oppress humanity prior to the great judgment (see 1 En. 15). In addition, the spirit pleads with Jesus by the name of God that he not torment him. The use of the divine name appears to be the common practice in incantation prayers against demons (thus the use of the name of Jesus by the disciples for exorcism); it may be that the spirit is attempting to reverse the roles in this situation. Interestingly, any indication of the use of incantations by Jesus (or his disciples) in the exorcism pericopes is glaringly absent considering their apparent use in other groups in Judaism (e.g., Qumran).

A Developing Anthropology

The demonology that was developing in various Second Temple period Jewish writings offers a point of comparison between demonic and human spirits. While comparing the description of the two spirits, one is able to recognize a developing anthropology that allows for the affliction and possession of humans. As the sources show, the understanding of human nature is bound up with perceptions of evil. This is already suggested in 1 En. 15–16, which, at the same time, leaves a number of questions about human nature unanswered. Fortunately, some authors of the Dead Sea Scrolls and other early Jewish literature have taken up the Book of the Watchers' story of the origin of evil spirits to formulate an anthropology that reveals more fully the effects of the interaction of these spirits with humanity.

---

87. The use of the divine name by an individual is common practice in incantation prayers against evil spirits in several Dead Sea Scrolls. It is interesting that the spirit would try to turn this around to his benefit. The divine name was used to frighten the spirit in order to force it to stop afflicting the individual. See, e.g., 11Q11; 11Q5 XIX, "Plea for Deliverance"; possibly 4Q560 1 ii.

88. Cf. Acts 19:13. It should be noted that the use of ὕψιστος corresponds to Heb. עליון, the title used by non-Israelites when referring to the God of Israel; see Dan 3:26 and 4:2.

The author of the Book of the Watchers presents a basic picture of his anthropology in 1 En. 15 by offering a comparison of the human makeup to that of the Watchers and the giants. First Enoch 15:5 states that humans are physical beings and require physical reproduction in order to continue their species. They are described as having souls (9:10; 22:3) that cry out to heaven from the place of the dead following their demise at the hand of the giants.[89] It is implied in 15:10 that because humans were born on the earth they have spirits (cf. 20:3; 22:3, 5).[90]

The author also presents a basic picture of his "giantology" in 1 En. 15–16. The giant offspring have a mixed nature. They are similar to humans in that they are born of flesh and blood, and so, unlike their fathers the Watchers, they could die a physical death. They also shared the nature of angels; they are immortal spirits that emerged from their physical bodies at the point of death and are able to remain active on the earth (15:9). The physical and spiritual natures of the giants described in the Book of the Watchers reveal some key distinctions between the giants (and ultimately their evil/unclean spirits) and humanity. These distinctions are apparent in the notion of spirit and soul.

In the Book of the Watchers, like the physical giants, humans are confined to the earth while they are still alive. At the point of death, humans, as spirit and soul, are removed to the places of the dead (22:3).[91] The giants, however, upon death are not confined to the places of the dead, but rather their spirits roam freely upon the earth.[92] A clear difference between the

---

89. An important point to note here is the omission of any existence of the human soul or spirit outside the "places of the dead." I am unaware of any instances in the Hebrew Bible that describe the body and soul together in Sheol. Several passages state the soul (נפש) will be brought up out of Sheol; see Pss 30:3; 49:16; 86:13; 89:49; and Prov 23:14. 1 En. 22:3–5 states that all the souls and spirits of the dead are gathered to these places until the day of their judgment. This is a clear contrast to the spirits of the angels and giants that are either bound under the earth (angels) or are free to roam the earth (giants).

90. These passages seem to make no clear distinction between the human soul and spirit. They are perhaps two distinct parts of the human composition, inseparable from each other, but not from the human flesh.

91. 1 Enoch implies all souls go to Sheol to await the judgment, in 102:5 the righteous, and in 102:11 the wicked. The wicked human spirits are destroyed in the fire (98:3); cf. 99:11: they will be killed in Sheol, they will not have peace.

92. Jub. 10:7 and 11 state that in order for the evil spirits of the giants to stop oppressing humans they must be bound in the place of condemnation, i.e., with the Watchers.

anthropology and giantology of the author of the Book of the Watchers emerges; there is no evidence that the dead giants' spirits linger in the places of the dead, nor do human spirits roam freely upon the earth. This may indicate that the giants belong to the category of angelic spirits (cf. 15:10), not of human souls per se, and this difference allows this freedom.

The giantology of the Book of the Watchers raises some interesting questions concerning the nature of the giants in relation to their human component. Was there an innate incompatibility between the angelic spirit of the giant and his physical body? Is this the reason they had such a violent nature? It seems the spirits of the giants were not able to exist within a physical body without bringing about violent behavior, because they are illegitimate and not properly constituted. If one considers Gen 2:7 in the creation process ("And the LORD God formed man out of the dust of the ground, and breathed into his nostrils the breath of life [נשמת חיים]; and Adam became a living soul"), God would have played no part in the creation of these beings, as they would not have received the "breath of life."[93] In contrast to the giants, God created humans both physically and non-physically. This is a key distinction between humans and giants: God has no part in the creation of the giants (see 1 En. 15:7–12).[94]

Mark 5:4–5, in its description of the actions of the demoniac, perhaps may exhibit the influence the violent nature of the giantology of the Book of the Watchers. The presence of the unclean spirit, or "strong spirit" (1 En. 15:8), within the demoniac's body resulted in superhuman strength and a violent and destructive behavior. However, it is considerably muted in contrast with the actions of the giants in the Book of the Watchers. The spirit that now occupies the body of the man in Mark 5 is the spiritual offspring of an angel. It is clear that this affliction or possession by the spirit pushed the limits of the human flesh that attempted to contain it, resulting in the destructive actions of the man (and the pigs).

---

93. Sacchi argues that the giants have souls; see *Jewish Apocalyptic*, 56.

94. It is possible that the Watcher tradition from Jub. 5:7–10 creates some difficulty in keeping God separated from any role in the creation of the giants. In the context of discussing the Watchers and the destruction of their sons, Gen 6:3 ("my spirit shall not always abide on man; for they also are flesh and their days shall be one hundred and twenty years") is inserted into the story in reference to the slaying of the giants by the sword. The author of the Book of the Watchers makes clear that the spirits of the giants are illegitimate and therefore do not come from God, which would appear to negate any connection of the giants to Gen 6:3. The only explanation to offer is that the Jubilees tradition is a later interpretation that equated this verse to the giants.

An additional allusion to the demonology of the Watcher tradition is found in Luke's version of the Gerasene demoniac. In Luke 8:31, the author tells of the evil spirit's plea not to be sent to the abyss, an allusion to the action taken against the giants' spirits in Jub. 10. There we are told that 90 percent of the spirits of the giants have been bound up in the abyss (Tartarus) until the day of judgment. The spirit obviously is aware that at some point in time (Matt 8:29) it too would be sent there for judgment.

We discover a further allusion to the Watcher tradition outside the gospels in the book of Acts. Acts 19:13–16 tells the story of seven Jewish exorcists (sons of Sceva) who were attempting to cast out evil spirits by using the name of Jesus to rebuke the spirits.[95] This story perhaps alludes to the spirits of the giants from the Watcher tradition in that the individual is granted great strength by which he is able to overcome the seven men, strip them naked, and wound them to the point that they fled from the house. Here we also find the evil spirit speaking through the possessed man to the exorcists asking them who they were. He acknowledges Jesus and even Paul but does not bow to their misuse of the name of Jesus.

CONCLUSION

As we have seen, the Gerasene demoniac pericope, among others, provides several insights into the characteristics of the unclean spirits and humans that may assist in identifying an earlier Jewish tradition that influenced the demonology of the gospels. In the foregoing discussion I have endeavored to demonstrate a plausible progression of this earlier tradition, which, for Second Temple period Jews, I suggest originated in the Book of the Watchers (1 En. 1–36, or an earlier tradition), was further developed in the book of Jubilees[96] and a portion of the Dead Sea Scrolls, and taken up by the New Testament authors. This tradition of the presence of evil spirits evolved alongside a developing anthropology in Second Temple period Jewish literature to a place that portrayed evil spirits as invading or afflicting the human body.

---

95. In *Ant.* 8.46–48 Josephus tells of the exorcism that the Jewish exorcist Eleazar performed in the presence of Vespasian.

96. Of course, one might argue for a more nuanced relationship between the Book of the Watchers and Jubilees in which Jubilees is a later development of the Watcher tradition in the Book of the Watchers, or that it (or both) is drawing on an earlier tradition of the emergence of evil spirits in the Jewish cosmology.

1 Enoch 6–11 Interpreted in the Light of Mesopotamian Incantation Literature*

Henryk Drawnel

Introduction

The research presented below interprets the Enochic myth in the light of Mesopotamian incantation literature. The literary structure of 1 En. 6–11 is related to one of the common literary forms in Mesopotamian incantation literature: the literary pattern of the Marduk-Ea incantation. Not only do the main elements of the literary structure in 1 En. 6–11 correspond to the literary structure of the Marduk-Ea incantation, but also the main theme, that is, the elimination of demonic beings, overlaps with what one finds in Mesopotamian incantations. The demonology in 1 En. 6–11 and the authority of the God of Israel over demons constitute a firm fundament for the subsequent development of the ways of elimination of the unclean and violent spirits in Jewish tradition of the Second Temple period and in the New Testament.

1. Mesopotamian Incantation Literature

In Mesopotamian incantation literature the incantation (én[1]/*šiptu*[2]) is an oral rite, complementary to the magico-religious ritual, whose purpose is

---

* The financial means for the completion of this project were assigned by the National Science Centre, Poland, on the basis of the decision no. Dec-2013/09/B/HS1/00728. I would also like to thank Professor Markham Geller from London College University, who kindly agreed to read the paper and to comment on it. The responsibility for all the opinions expressed in this paper is mine.
    1. The "classical" formula prefixed to incantations, or added after them, is én-é-nu-ru used, with orthographic variations already in the Early Dynastic period and later

to combat evil in its various forms and to heal the patient.[3] In the incantations, evil was conjured with threats and blandishments; the help of a deity was often requested in the form of a prayer;[4] and the conjurer presented himself as the messenger of usually Enki/Ea and his son Asalluḫi/Marduk, gods of exorcism. Incantations sometimes included brief narratives in which the cosmic origins of the exorcised evil were traced.[5] The priestly *āšipu* pronounces the incantation in order to heal the patient from an illness or distress that may be caused by the gods, demons, witches, or war-

---

on in the Akkadian and Ur III periods; see Graham Cunningham, *"Deliver Me from Evil": Mesopotamian Incantations 2500–1500 BC*, StPohlSM 17 (Rome: Pontifical Biblical Institute, 1997), 9–10. In the second and first millennia én alone is written rather regularly at the beginning of the incantations. It is not clear what the expression é-nu-ru alone would mean.

2. A noun from the root *wšp*; the noun *āšipu* (G participle) comes from the same root and denotes the expert in the use of incantations. The verb *uššupum* attested in the D stem ("to effect results by means of incantations, to 'cure' by exorcism") is probably of denominative origin.

3. W. G. Lambert ("The Classification of Incantations," in *Proceedings of the 51st Rencontre Assyriologique Internationale Held at the Oriental Institute of the University of Chicago, July 18–22, 2005*, ed. Robert D. Biggs, Jennie Myers, and Martha T. Roth, SAOC 62 [Chicago: Oriental Institute of the University of Chicago, 2008], 95) defines the incantation in the following way: "An incantation is a text to be recited which brings magic power to bear, usually when recited with observation of some rite or rites. It unlocks a certain power in the universe which the person reciting either wants or needs."

4. Since incantations could also contain prayers, it was rather difficult to see, especially in the late periods of Mesopotamian history, the difference between a prayer and an incantation; many texts of that period show the literary elements that are characteristic of both genres. In the second and first millennia BCE, many Sumerian and Akkadian compositions, usually defined as prayers, were prefixed with the sign én, probably because, similar to incantations, they were recited in the course of rituals. This type of composition were called by German scholars *Gebetsbeschwörungen*, and generally defined as "ritual prayers of an individual beseecher" that may be recited within a context of a liturgical rite; see Werner R. Mayer, *Untersuchungen zur Formensprache der babylonischen "Gebetsbeschwörungen,"* StPohlSM 5 (Rome: Pontifical Biblical Institute, 1976), 10–11.

5. See, e.g., the incantation against toothache: "After Anu created heaven, heaven created earth, earth created rivers, rivers created watercourses, watercourses created marshland, marshland created the worm"; in Benjamin R. Foster, *Before the Muses: An Anthology of Akkadian Literature*, 3rd ed. (Bethesda, MD: CDL, 2005), 995. For other cosmological incantations, see Wayne Horowitz, *Mesopotamian Cosmic Geography*, MC 8 (Winona Lake, IN: Eisenbrauns, 1998), 148–50.

locks. Mesopotamian incantation literature constitutes the main source of knowledge about demons and the ways of their elimination in Mesopotamian polytheistic religion.

The oldest incantations in Sumerian from the middle of the third millennium BCE (Abu Ṣalabikh, Shuruppak, and Lagash) were mostly destined to heal the patient, but already in the Akkad and Ur III periods they are attested in different types of magical literature.[6] Until the middle of the second millennium BCE, incantations mostly contained the oral part of the rite, but later their texts developed to include also rituals.[7] In the first millennium BCE, they were regrouped into series according to the nature of the demons, the main cause of human suffering, and most of them were accompanied by the Akkadian translation.[8] The Sumerian Udug-ḫul (Akk. *Utukkū Lemnūtu;* henceforth *UL*) incantation series began to be compiled already in the Old Babylonian period,[9] but acquired its "canonical form" with Akkadian translation only in the Neo-Assyrian period.[10] The bilingual *Šurpu* ("Burning") series, whose "canonical" form is also known

---

6. For a study of the incantations stemming from the pre-Sargonic, Sargonic, Neo-Sumerian, and Old Babylonian periods, see Cunningham, *Deliver Me from Evil,* 5–159. These early texts already mention the priestly officiant of the rite, the gudu-priest in the Sumerian incantations, and the *mašmaššu* or *āšipu* in the Akkadian text; see ibid., 14–16.

7. Many separate incantations are scattered among collections with magical prescriptions and among many different rituals against any kind of suffering; for a short but clear presentation of this type of incantation in Akkadian medical texts, see Markham J. Geller, "Incantations within Akkadian Medical Texts," in *The Babylonian World,* ed. Gwendolyn Leick (New York: Routledge, 2007), 389–99.

8. The study of the Sumero-Akkadian incantations is somewhat neglected in Assyriology; see the comment by Wolfgang Schramm, *Ein Compendium sumerisch-akkadischer Beschwörungen,* Göttinger Beiträge zum Alten Orient 2 (Göttingen: Universitätsverlag, 2008), 1: "Die sumerisch-akkadischen Beschwörungen gehören noch immer zu den von der Forschung eher vernachlässigten Bereichen der babylonischen und assyrischen Literatur. Nur wenige der grösseren Beschwörungsserien liegen in einer moderner Bearbeitung vor, während andere nur teilweise oder in völlig veralteten Bearbeitungen zugänglich sind."

9. See Markham J. Geller, *Forerunners to Udug-hul: Sumerian Exorcistic Incantations,* FAOS 12 (Freiburg: Steiner, 1985), 4–5. Although the compilation process was taking place in the Old Babylonian period, there is no evidence for a fixed order of tablets, characteristic of the later series.

10. For a preliminary edition of the "canonical" version of the series, see Markham J. Geller, *Evil Demons: Canonical Utukkū Lemnūtu Incantations,* SAACT 5 (Helsinki: Neo-Assyrian Text Corpus Project, 2007).

beginning with the Neo-Assyrian period, was performed when the patient did not know what behavior caused the apparent offense of the gods or of the existing world order.[11] The bilingual series *Maqlû* ("Combustion"), stemming from the same historical period, was intended to counteract the evil machinations of witches and warlocks against the patient, and the influence of black magic was destroyed by burning the effigies of the sorcerers.[12] The incantations were used in Mesopotamian religion until the extinction of cuneiform,[13] and some Greek-Babylonian texts from the first century CE contain fragments of bilingual incantations,[14] which suggests a recourse to religious healing practices in the latest attested period of cuneiform culture.

The following notes concentrate on the relationship between 1 En. 6–11 and Mesopotamian incantation literature. That the Jewish composer of 1 En. 6–11 had access to this type of literature is attested by his description of the giants, demonic warriors, in 7:2–5. The voracious appetite of the giants and their aggression against nature, humanity, and animals are similar to the Sumero-Akkadian incantation series Udug-ḫul-a-meš (Akk. *Utukku Lemnūtu*), in which the evil demons are presented in the same manner.[15] The Enochic description of the violent behavior of the spirits of

---

11. For the edition of the text and English translation, see Erica Reiner, *Šurpu: A Collection of Sumerian and Akkadian Incantations*, AfOB 11 (Graz: Weidner, 1958).

12. The complete edition by Gerhard Meier, *Die assyrische Beschwörungssammlung Maqlû*, AfOB 2 (Berlin: Weidner, 1937), still remains the only one available. Tzvi Abusch and Daniel Schwemer ("Das Abwehrzauber-Ritual *Maqlû* ["Verbrennung"]," in *Omina, Orakel, Rituale und Beschwörungen*, ed. Bernd Janowski and Gernot Wilhelm, TUAT NF 4 [Gütersloh: Gütersloher Verlagshaus, 2008], 128–86) prepared the German translation of the text based on their new edition of the composition, which has not yet been published.

13. For an overview of the use of incantations in southern Mesopotamia in the Hellenistic and Arsacid periods, see Joachim Oelsner, "Incantations in Southern Mesopotamia—From Clay Tablets to Magical Bowls (Thoughts on the Decline of the Babylonian Culture)," in *Officina Magica: Essays on the Practice of Magic in Antiquity,* ed. Shaul Shaked, Institute of Jewish Studies: Studies in Judaica 4 (Leiden: Brill, 2005), 31–52.

14. BM 34816, paleographically dated to the first century CE; the Sumero-Akkadian text preserves an unidentified incantation, similar in content to tablet 9 of the *Utukkū Lemnūtu* series. See Markham J. Geller, "The Last Wedge," ZA 87 (1997): 76–77, pls. I–VIII. Geller argues that cuneiform could still have been read in the third century CE.

15. For a comparison of these Enochic texts with the Udug-ḫul incantation series,

the giants in 1 En. 15:11 also corresponds to what one finds in the same Mesopotamian incantation series about demonic beings. It is certain that the Jewish author of the myth did not base his description of the demonic giants in the myth on the text of the Hebrew Bible, which contains no description of demons similar to 1 En. 7:2–5 and 15:11.

The thematic and formal similarities between 1 En. 6–11 and Mesopotamian incantations should not lead one to assume a direct genetic relationship between the two literary traditions. The following notes will make clear that the Enochic text contains a literary pattern related in some points to the literary form of Mesopotamian incantations, but also elaborated and adapted to the needs of the Jewish author writing in Aramaic. One can find a similar way of proceeding in the Aramaic Astronomical Book in relation to Mesopotamian astrological literature, some elements of which have been adapted for the description of periods of lunar visibility.[16] It is not clear whether the Jewish author used Aramaic sources influenced by the Akkadian literature, or perhaps elaborated some literary and thematic patterns that he found in the original Sumero-Akkadian texts.[17] The analysis of the list of sciences in 1 En. 8:3 allows one to affirm that the author/redactor of 1 En. 6–11 was well acquainted with the Mesopotamian conjurer and his art of exorcism (*āšipūtu*).[18] The established relationship, therefore, between the Enochic myth and cuneiform tradition in the late Persian or Hellenistic periods justifies the continuation of research in that direction.

---

see Henryk Drawnel, "The Mesopotamian Background of the Enochic Giants and Evil Spirits," *DSD* 21 (2014): 14–38.

16. For the comparison between periods of lunar visibility in tablet XIV of the *Enūma Anu Enlil* astrological series and the Aramaic calculation in 4Q208 and 4Q209, see Henryk Drawnel, *The Aramaic Astronomical Book (4Q208–4Q211) from Qumran: Text, Translation, and Commentary* (Oxford: Oxford University Press, 2011), 301–10.

17. Note the existence of an Aramaic text of uncertain origin and date written in cuneiform that contains three Aramaic incantations related to Akkadian Egalkurra incantations directed against a rival or enemy in case of slander or gossip; see Markham J. Geller, "The Aramaic Incantation in Cuneiform Script (AO 6489 = TCL 6,58)," *JEOL* 35–36 (1997–2000): 127–46.

18. It is well known that except for medicine and magic that constituted the main professional interest of the *āšipu*, cuneiform libraries from the Persian and Hellenistic periods show that the Mesopotamian conjurer busied himself with astronomy, astrology, and divination, all items attested in 4Q201 IV 1–4 (1 En. 8:3); see Henryk Drawnel, "Between Akkadian *ṭupšarrūtu* and Aramaic ספר: Some Notes on the Social Context of the Early Enochic Literature," *RevQ* 24 (2010): 373–403.

2. The Literary Form of 1 Enoch 6–11 and the Literary Pattern of the Marduk-Ea Incantation

First Enoch 6–11 is certainly a myth that makes up part of the Enochic apocalyptic writings, but its literary form and structure have not been clearly defined. Discussion on the literary characteristics of the apocalyptic literature has led to the formulation of an all-encompassing definition that is applicable to various types of apocalyptic compositions from the Second Temple period. It is, however, debatable to what extent the proposed definition corresponds to 1 En. 6–11.[19] Some scholars concentrated on the diacronic approach in order to separate different literary strata, and in the case of 1 En. 6–11 the most famous proposal is the one presented by George Nickelsburg.[20] Adapting the early analysis of some German scholars,[21] he claims that these chapters can be conveniently separated into two narrative threads, one concentrated on Shemihazah,

---

19. John J. Collins ("Introduction: Towards the Morphology of a Genre," *Semeia* 14 [1979]: 15) ascribes 1 En. 1–36 to the IIb type of the apocalyptic genre, i.e., otherworldly journeys with cosmic and/or political eschatology. It is debatable to what extent this classification corresponds to 1 En. 6–11, where the descent of the Watchers on the earth can hardly be called an "otherworldly journey." In the same volume, Collins ("The Jewish Apocalypses," 38) claims that 1 En. 17–36 contains the description of the otherworldly journeys since they take Enoch to the mythical regions at the extremities of the earth; such an interpretation does not seem to properly correspond to what an "otherworldly" journey should entail. James C. VanderKam ("Prophecy and Apocalyptics in the Ancient Near East," *CANE* 3:2089) does not classify 1 En. 1–36 as an apocalypse.

20. Concerning the literary form of the Shemihazah story, Nickelsburg stresses the verbal similarity with Gen 6–9, but it is evident that the literary structure of the biblical narrative is different, with different topics discussed as well. The Genesis account also does not know anything about the sinful nature of the Watchers, the ravages of the earth by the giants, and their successive elimination. Similar to most scholars, Nickelsburg (*1 Enoch 1: A Commentary on the Book of 1 Enoch, Chapters 1–36; 81–108,* Hermeneia [Minneapolis: Fortress, 2001], 168) is perplexed as to the definition of the literary genre of the Enochic myth. He notes that "terms such as *targum* and *midrash* are unsatisfactory ... because they are typically applied to later literary types that significantly differ from the Shemihazah story." He eventually arrives at the conclusion that the Shemihazah narrative interprets the biblical text by paraphrasing it in Aramaic. The mythic function of the text should be related to the historical times of the Diadochoi, who claimed a divine origin for themselves. The Enochic myth would be an answer to that claim in the form of a kind of parody (pp. 169–70).

21. See, e.g., Georg Beer, "Das Buch Henoch," in *Die Pseudepigraphen des Alten*

the other on Asael, with some secondary additions that have "contaminated" the original narrative. The oldest story is the one that presents the sexual sin of Shemihazah and his companions with women.[22] Although Nickelsburg's careful analysis has been influential, it does not propose convincing reasons that would explain the weaving of two parallel narratives into one story.[23] The following research indicates that there existed a literary pattern in Mesopotamian incantation literature that constituted a model for the Jewish author on the basis of which he constructed his myth about the birth and aggression of demonic beings and about ways of their elimination.

Testaments, vol. 2 of Die Apokryphen und Pseudepigraphen des Alten Testaments, ed. Emil Kautzsch (Tübingen: Mohr Siebeck, 1900), 225.

22. According to Nickelsburg (1 Enoch 1, 165–66), the oldest recoverable form of the myth is the Shemihazah story, which can be divided into three parts: (I) the crisis: (A) the conspiracy, 6:1–8; (B) the deed, 7:1a–c; (C) its results, 7:2–5; (II) the turning point: (D) the plea, 7:6 + 8:4; (E) the angelic response, 9:1–11; (III) the resolution: (F) God's response, 10:1–11:2: (1) Sariel sent to Noah, 10:1–3; (2) Michael sent, 10:11–11:2. The second literary stratum, which breaks the continuity of the Shemihazah narrative, contains the following material about Asael: (1) the teaching of Asael and other Watchers, 8:1–2; (2) the intrusion about Asael in 9:6; (3) Raphael sent to Asael, 10:4–8. The element of instruction does not fit either story: (1) the teaching of the Watchers, 7:1d–e; (2) the intrusion about the teaching of the Watchers in 8:3; (3) the intrusion about Shemihazah and mysteries in 9:8c. Finally, the functions of the angels sent by God seem to overlap: the mission to destroy the giants is first assigned to Gabriel (10:9), then to Raphael (10:15); in 10:7 Raphael is commissioned to heal the earth, while in 10:16 and 10:22 Michael destroys lawlessness and cleanses the earth.

23. Nickelsburg's explanation of the literary characteristics of the myth is unsatisfactory, for he does not find an answer to the problem of the literary genre and the synchronic structure of the myth. It is not immediately evident why the two separate narratives about Shemihazah and Asael have been intertwined into one text. The reasons for the introduction of the instruction motif are also not clear in Nickelsburg's interpretation, and the connection with the historical context of the Diadochoi is based on extremely slim evidence. Some scholars sound somewhat negative when they claim that the myth is polyvalent and can fit into different historical contexts; see John J. Collins, The Apocalyptic Imagination: An Introduction to Jewish Apocalyptic Literature, 2nd ed., Biblical Resources Series (Grand Rapids: Eerdmans, 1998), 51: "By telling the story of the Watchers rather than of the Diadochi or the priesthood, 1 En. 1–36 becomes a paradigm which is not restricted to one historical situation but can be applied whenever an analogous situation arises." Although such a statement is true as to the general application of the myth to different historical contexts, it does not say anything about the social context in which 1 En. 6–11 was composed, and which must have had a very concrete historical dimension.

2.1. The Literary Pattern of the Marduk-Ea Incantation

In his classical and still useful work about the literary characteristics of Sumero-Akkadian incantations, Adam Falkenstein divided them into four literary patterns.[24] The legitimation type contained literary formulae in which the incantation priest legitimates himself as a representative of the gods of white magic. The purpose of these formulae was to defend him from any harm inflicted by demons during the execution of his professional mission.[25] Similar to the legitimation type, the prophylactic type served to protect laypeople from dangerous attacks of demons.[26] The Marduk-Ea type contains a dialogue between the two gods of exorcism, and is most frequently used in the exorcistic rituals for the expulsion of demons or illnesses that attack humans or sometimes animals. The last type of lesser importance, called the consecration type, served to consecrate different objects used in the exorcistic rituals to purify the invalid.[27]

The Marduk-Ea[28] incantation is the most important literary pattern with a well-defined literary construction and mythological narrative, in which the narrator or the gods speak about demons in the third-person singular or plural. Falkenstein divided the incantation into four parts.[29]

---

24. His literary analysis of the incantations relies on the text witnesses from the Old Babylonian period in conjunction with the related "canonical" texts from the Neo-Assyrian period and later; see Adam Falkenstein, *Die Haupttypen der sumerischen Beschwörung, literarisch untersucht*, LSS NS 1 (Leipzig: Hinrichs, 1931), 8–15.

25. "Legitimationstyp"; see ibid., 20–35.

26. "Prophylaktischer Typ"; see ibid., 35–44.

27. "Weihungstyp"; see ibid., 76–82.

28. The names of the gods of exorcism, Ea and Marduk, the latter usually presented as Ea's son, are of Akkadian origin. In the Sumerian incantations the god of exorcism is Enki, the Sumerian counterpart of Ea. By the Ur III period Asalluḫi, depicted as "son of Enki," is often cited in incantations where he holds the position relatively subordinate to Enki. In the Old Babylonian forerunner to the Uduk-ḫul series, Asalluḫi is not yet identified with Marduk, whose later official title is "exorcist among the gods," MAŠ. MAŠ *ilī*; however, in the late form of the series, Asalluḫi is the god of exorcism as well; see Geller, *Forerunners*, 12–15. Marduk began to be identified with Asalluḫi in the Old Babylonian period. Falkenstein subsumed the dialogue between Ea and Asalluḫi under the same "Marduk-Ea" label on the basis of the later texts only. Such a labeling better corresponds to the first millennium BCE, when the contact with Aramaic literature had to take place.

29. Falkenstein in his book gives a long list of source material; the interested reader may consult the original texts listed by Falkenstein, or some recent editions of

The introduction contains two themes: one uses transitive verbal forms in the present tense, and the second one has the transitive verb in the preterite.[30] The first theme describes in a general way the activity of demons, their origin, places of their presence, and their attacks on animals and humans. This part of the introduction overlaps with the introduction found in the legitimation and prophylactic incantations.

The second part of the introduction with verbs in the preterite is unique to the Marduk-Ea incantation, and describes the attack of demons on a man, which took part in the past and is the reason for the application of the incantation.[31] The central part of the Marduk-Ea literary pattern transfers the narrative from the temporal domain to the divine realm. It contains a mythological account about the role of Marduk and his father, Ea, gods of exorcism, in the healing process.[32] When Marduk saw what

---

Sumero-Akkadian incantations series, e.g., the Udug-ḫul series published by Geller, *Forerunners*.

30. See Falkenstein, *Haupttypen*, 45–53. He puts his twofold division of the introduction into quotation marks: " 'Presentisches' und 'Präteritales' Thema" (46). He separates the two parts of the introduction on the basis of the verbal forms, but as he notes himself (46 n. 1), the difference is seen only in the case of the transitive verbs in Sumerian. For the conjugation of the Sumerian intransitive and transitive verb, see Dietz-Otto Edzard, *Sumerian Grammar*, HdO 1: Near and Middle East 71 (Leiden: Brill, 2003), 73–74, 81–91. Since the Sumerian verb in general is still poorly understood, and since it is likely that the Akkadian version of the Sumerian incantations influenced the Jewish Aramaic literature, it is better to speak about the permansive and preterite in the Akkadian verbal system.

31. Following Falkenstein, Schramm (*Compendium*, 18 and n. 18) notes that especially in late incantations the preterite theme may contain the description of the symptoms resulting from the demonic attack in the present/future tense. Since the Enochic text omits the preterite theme of the Sumerian literary pattern (see §2.2.1), the proposed distinction is of little importance for the overall comparison with the Enochic myth.

32. See Falkenstein, *Haupttypen*, 53–58. Cunningham (*Deliver Me from Evil*, 167) notes that mythological narratives, in which a junior deity notices a problem in the temporal domain and seeks advice from a senior deity, who provides the necessary solution, are attested in Sumerian incantations in each period except the Sargonic. In the earlier form of such a narrative, a junior deity sends a messenger to a senior deity; the later form speaks about the junior deity who addresses the senior deity in a temple. Falkenstein discusses these two types of mythological narrative, but the second form constitutes the basis of his literary pattern of the Marduk-Ea incantation. The comparison with 1 En. 6–11 can be made only on the basis of the later form of the Sumerian mythological dialogue.

the demons had done to the suffering man, he went into the temple of his father Ea and told him about the behavior of the demons. In his report Marduk repeats the words used in the two parts of the introduction, and then expresses his lack of knowledge as to how to remedy that situation. In response to Marduk's report, Ea politely stresses that Marduk possesses the same knowledge as that of his father, and then sends him out to solve the problem with a commissioning formula that uses the verb in the imperative: "Go, my son, Marduk." After this commissioning formula, Ea gives Marduk ritual instructions that will serve Marduk to expel the demons and heal the patient.[33] Ea's instructions indicate the superiority of the main god of exorcism and wisdom in relation to Marduk; they were presumably enacted in ritual during the recitation of the incantation, which united the temporal and divine domains.

Ea's ritual speech constitutes the third part of the Marduk-Ea literary pattern in which the Sumerian verbal forms are translated in bilingual incantations with the Akkadian imperative + *ma* or with the second-person singular in the durative. The ritual instruction may also contain a list of verbs in the precative that explains the positive results of the ritual for the patient. The goal of the instruction is to purify the patient and thus to free him or her from the pernicious influence of the demons. Since the suffering of the patient is not presented in the Sumerian incantations as a result of human sinfulness, the purification ceremony does not have the character of an atonement liturgy or expiatory sacrifice.[34]

The fourth part of the Marduk-Ea literary pattern usually consists of one subordinate clause with the verb in the precative form.[35] It expresses the wish that demons or illness should leave the patient, and later texts also invite the good spirits to take the place of the expelled demons.

Falkenstein noted that, because of its use in different exorcistic rituals, the Marduk-Ea incantation attracts some elements of other incantations, and all four literary parts often undergo substantial modifications. Of special interest is the inclusion of hymnic literature that describes the power

---

33. See Falkenstein, *Haupttypen*, 58–62.

34. One should also take into account that Akkadian incantation tradition, although based on the Sumerian incantation style, develops its own theological perspectives. Although in the Sumerian incantations there is no connection between the working of demons and human sinfulness, Akkadian translations suggest that human illness may be caused by human misbehavior; see Falkenstein, *Haupttypen*, 56.

35. See ibid., 62–67.

and goodness of Ea that always helps the person.[36] Additionally, the literary structure of the Marduk-Ea incantation often undergoes some substantial reworking,[37] and the introduction together with the Marduk-Ea dialogue can contain mythological developments that do not belong to the elementary literary pattern.[38] The Akkadian incantations of the first millennium BCE inherited the same literary patterns for the first time attested in the Sumerian literature.[39] When in the first part of the first millennium BCE the process of the Aramaization of the cuneiform culture began to take place, the contact between Mesopotamian incantations and Aramaic literature was made possible. It is more probable that the Jewish author had access to an Aramaic version of the Marduk-Ea incantation pattern rather than to the Akkadian incantations themselves.

2.2. The Literary Pattern of the Marduk-Ea Incantation and the Enochic Myth

The following notes concentrate on the literary and thematic common points between the two traditions. The similarities deal with the same topics already discussed, which is the violent behavior of demons in relation to the earth and humanity and ways of its elimination. Additionally, both the Marduk-Ea literary pattern and the Enochic myth are mythological narratives with a narrative plot that relates the heaven with the earth,

---

36. See ibid., 73. For an example with the text and translation, see 93–99.

37. See ibid., 68–74.

38. See ibid., 74–76.

39. Geller notes, "There is a huge gulf between Sumerian incantations and 1st millennium cultural milieu in which Aramaic was increasingly the vernacular in Mesopotamia, already by the 7th cent. BCE. This means that Sumerian is twice removed from the normal spoken language and dead for more than a millennium as a spoken language…. But scholars in the 1st millennium would have known these incantations by their Akkadian translations, with only a few specialists really understanding the Sumerian, much in the same way that most Greek texts were best known by their Latin translations in Europe. In fact, the *Utukkū Lemnūtu* series changed radically in the first millennium BCE, as I intend to show in my new edition of the canonical version of these incantations in Partitur format: instead of Enki-Asalluhi being primary, Marduk takes over the lead role in these incantations. Furthermore, by the first millennium the Marduk-Ea formula (now correctly designated) occurs in Akkadian contexts rather than in bilingual incantations, and we even have examples of a messenger coming to Marduk for advice, etc." (e-mail communication, May 21, 2013).

and human beings with supernatural demons.[40] In both texts humanity is helpless in front of the aggressive and personified evil, and the decisive instruction for solving the problem comes from a god.

The literary structure of 1 En. 6–11 corresponds, with some exceptions and modifications, to the literary structure of the Marduk-Ea incantation type. It can be divided into four main parts: (1) introduction (6:1–8:4); (2) angels' reaction and report to God (9:1–11); (3) divine instruction (10:1–14); (4) blessed future without impurity (10:15–11:2).[41] The first part, which narrates the birth of the giants, their violence, and the destructive teaching of their fathers, ends in 8:4 with a human plea for divine justice.

---

40. It is beyond doubt that the description of the Enochic giants in 1 En. 7:2–5 is modeled after the description of the evil *utukkū* in the Udug-ḫul incantation series; see Drawnel, "The Mesopotamian Background of the Enochic Giants and Evil Spirits," *DSD* 20 (2013): 270–77 (§2). The explanation of the origin of the evil spirits in 1 En. 15:9 as stemming from the bodies of the giants is a secondary etiological explanation of the origin of the demonic beings. That both the Enochic giants and the evils spirits are interpreted as the same kind of demonic beings is indicated by the identification of the two kinds of evil spirits in 1 En. 15:8–9. What is more important, however, is that the aggression of the evil spirits in 1 En. 15:11 against humanity can easily be explained against the same Mesopotamian background, namely the Udug-ḫul incantation series; see Drawnel, "Mesopotamian Background," 277–88. Thus the Greek term for "giants," which in the Greek translation of the myth denotes the sons of the Watchers, is inappropriate, for it only refers to the size of the violent demons. The correct terminology is the one preserved in the Aramaic Book of Giants from Qumran, where the term גבור should be rendered "hero" or rather "warrior," which, from the semantic point of view, properly corresponds to Mesopotamian terminology applied to the evil *utukkū*-demons; see Drawnel, "Mesopotamian Background," 288–89 (§4).

41. The monographs or scholarly articles that deal with 1 En. 6–11 usually analyze the literary strata of the myth from the diachronic perspective. Once the literary strata have been established, their literary plan is eventually discussed. When speaking about the structure of the narrative, Siam Bhayro (*The Shemihazah and Asael Narrative of 1 Enoch 6–11: Introduction, Text, Translation and Commentary with Reference to Ancient Near Eastern and Biblical Antecedents,* AOAT 322 [Münster: Ugarit-Verlag, 2005], 11–20) discusses its five (!) distinct strata, but does not mention the overall structure of 1 En. 6–11 from the synchronic perspective. This research indicates that there exists a literary pattern of the Enochic myth that is not difficult to grasp. The comparison with the Marduk-Ea incantation pattern shows the lines of development introduced by the Jewish author to the pattern inherited from Mesopotamian incantation literature. It also indicates that the division of the Enochic text into several literary strata too often relies on a poor understanding of the general structure and purpose of the myth.

The second part begins in heaven with the angels who notice bloodshed on the earth; thus the narration is transposed to the heavenly register, where the angels address God in a prayer with a request for help against the Watchers and demons. The third part constitutes God's response in the form of an instruction, while the last part contains a vision of the blessed future with human longevity and the earth purified from all impurity introduced presumably by the Watchers and their demonic sons.

While the first three parts of the myth contain structural and thematic elements related to the Marduk-Ea incantation, the fourth part does not seem at first sight to correspond to the fourth concluding part of the incantation. In a similar way, the Enochic myth includes and develops a narrative element not present in the Sumero-Akkadian literary pattern, which exclusively concentrated on the presentation of the violent activity of demons. In the Enochic myth the narrative develops the motif of the origin of demonic beings, a mythologem that in the incantation literature is present but plays only a minor role. The Watchers or sons of heaven, fathers of the demonic warriors, are depicted as corrupted by sin, which leads to impurity; and eventually the narrative is developed in order to accommodate not only the destructive activity of their sons but their pernicious activity and punishment as well. Finally, while the Marduk-Ea incantation type was recited by the enchanter in the ritual that intended to heal and purify the patient, we know next to nothing about the use of the Enochic myth in the liturgical rite. Yet it is beyond doubt that the instructions of the Enochic myth intend to heal the earth (10:7) and to purify it (10:20, 22). Hence also the healing and purifying character of the Enochic text directed against the activity of the impure spirits and their demonic descendants constitutes a common ground with the literary pattern of the Mesopotamian incantation.

Some elements in the Enochic text suggest that the adaptation of the exorcistic literary pattern served to create a universal myth concerning the origin of the demonic warriors in the context of Jewish history (Noah and the plant of righteousness), and concerning the authority of the God of Israel over demons. It also intended to demonize the main bearers of cuneiform knowledge (the Watchers/āšipu) and culture (Asael/Babylonian artisan), which were strongly related, in the declining centuries of cuneiform culture, with the Babylonian temple. The thematic and literary elements taken from Mesopotamian incantation literature suggest that the Jewish author(s) of the myth not only intended to criticize the Mesopotamian conjurer, but he (or they) also tried to occupy his position concerning dominion over demons and extensive astronomical and astrological knowledge.

2.2.1. Introduction (6:1–8:4)

The second part of the introductory narrative in the Marduk-Ea incantation is omitted in the literary pattern of 6:1–8:4. The Enochic text does not speak about a person attacked by demons, but presents a general activity of the demonic warriors who attack the produce of the land, human beings, and animals (7:2–5). The general presentation of the demons, together with the description of their height, belongs in the Sumero-Akkadian incantations to the first part of the introductory narrative. Thus one can conclude that the Jewish author intended to present not exclusively the evil activity of demons (7:2–5) but created a narrative that explained their cosmic origin (6:1–7:1) as well.[42] The cosmic origin of demons in the *Utukkū Lemnūtu* incantation series is usually mentioned in the introductory part of the legitimation or prophylactic incantations.[43] As noted by Falkenstein, the introductory part that in a general way describes demons is a common element in the literary structure of legitimation, prophylactic, and Marduk-Ea incantations. The cosmic origin of the evil against which the incantation is pronounced makes up part of the incantation literary tradition.

The birth of demons and their violent activity is found in 1 En. 6:1–2 and 7:1a–b, 2–5. These verses constitute the kernel of the myth that has

---

42. The Jewish author created a literary pattern that was applicable not to one sick person, but to the whole of humanity and nature. This universalizing tendency is present in the bilingual incantations from first-millennium Mesopotamia. In an incantation compendium published by Schramm, in incantation 1, ll. 42–45, instead of a preterite theme that would describe the attack of demons against a single man, the text speaks in general terms about the attack of demons against the earth and people in general. This means that the incantation should purify not one person but the earth and humanity in general; see Schramm, *Compendium*, 28 and 187. The same universalizing tendency is present in 1 En. 7:3–5. The late *Šurpu* series additionally indicates that the first part of the Marduk-Ea incantation literary pattern that usually has the verbs in the present tense may also take form of a past tense narrative; see, e.g., tablet vii, 1–18, where the general description of the demonic activity is set in the past tense. Thus the general presentation of demons in 1 En. 7:2–5 may well have followed the past tense narrative present in the first part of the introduction in the late Sumero-Akkadian incantations.

43. See §3 below.

thematic connections with the Marduk-Ea literary pattern.[44] The rest of
the text in the introduction most probably stems from the perspective of
the Jewish author. First Enoch 6:3–6 develops the narrative about the heavenly fathers of demons, stressing the sinful character of their sexual act (v.
3), their binding by an oath (vv. 4–5), their descent on Mount Hermon (v.
6), and their pollution (7:1c). The sinful and unclean character of sex with
women transforms the Mesopotamian tradition about the divine origin
of demons. The binding by an oath probably constitutes the first veiled
allusion to the Mesopotamian āšipu, who routinely used oath formulae in
order to conjure demons.[45] The second element added to the kernel of the

44. The comparison with the literary pattern of the Marduk-Ea incantation makes
it possible to indicate the sections of each subdivision in 1 En. 6–11 that overlap with
what one finds in the cuneiform literary pattern. In this way, the development introduced by the Jewish author is easily observable. The proposed literary analysis of the
Enochic text does not intend to separate different literary strata, similar to the proceedings of Nickelsburg and some other scholars. It is not only highly unlikely but
also unattested in the manuscripts that there existed two or three independent literary
strata eventually interwoven in the final form of 1 En. 6–11. The differences in 1 En.
6–11 in comparison with the Mesopotamian literary pattern might have easily been
introduced by one and the same redactor. They mostly do not stem from the hand of
different redactors but from the modification of the original literary pattern.

45. The act of conjuration applied in the incantations consisted in making
demons swear an oath that would lead them to leave the attacked man. Such a literary
formula does not assume the cooperation of demons with the conjurer, but it subjects demons to the sanctions that are related to the breaking of the oath. The implicit
consequences that stem from the purported oath breaking by demons is their being
subject to malediction or ban, which makes them magically inoperative; see Wolfgang
Schramm, *Bann, Bann!: Eine sumerisch-akkadische Beschwörungsserie*, GAAL 2 (Göttingen: Seminar für Keilschriftforschung, 2001), 5–8. The Akkadian verb used in the
conjurations is *tamû* in G ("to swear") or in D ("to make someone swear") stems, while
the noun is *māmītu*, "oath." Both the verb and noun stem from *wamā'um*, "to swear"
(*AHw* 3:1459), which in Aramaic corresponds to ימי, "to swear." The Aramaic fragments of 1 Enoch indicate that in 6:4 (4Q201 1 iii 1) and 6:6 (4Q201 1 iii 5) the verb
"to swear" from Aram. ימי is used, with the sons of heaven as its subject. The consequences of the oath for the sons of heaven is their ban from heaven, mutually imposed
on each other, as the use of אפרק (4Q201 1 iii 3 [6:5] and 5 [6:6]) seems to indicate; for a similar interpretation, see Bhayro, *Shemihazah and Asael Narrative*, 236.
The *aphel* of פרק in Jewish Babylonian Aramaic means "to excommunicate," while in
peal it means "to ban," in relation to the evil spirits; see Michael Sokoloff, *A Dictionary of Jewish Babylonian Aramaic of the Talmudic and Geonic Periods*, Dictionaries
of Talmud Midrash and Targum 3 (Ramat Gan: Bar Ilan University Press; Baltimore:
Johns Hopkins University Press, 2002), 483. While the Mesopotamian conjurer made

myth is the hierarchically structured list of the twenty sons of heaven (6:7), which cannot be separated from 8:1 and 8:3.[46] The Aramaic terminology about the hierarchy suggests the social context of the Babylonian temple,[47] and the Aramaic proper names indicate the connection with the types of knowledge taught by the Watchers in 8:1 and 8:3. The reference to healing practices and magic in 7:1d–e prepares the list of sciences in 8:3. Thus the text in 8:1–3 has been prepared by 6:7 and 7:1d–e, and it makes explicit the purpose of the insertion.[48] In 8:1 the Jewish author develops the critique of the Mesopotamian artisans,[49] while in 8:3 the types of knowledge taught by the Watchers unequivocally point to the Mesopotamian enchanter and scholar.[50] Thus the narrative, differently from the introductory part of the Marduk-Ea incantation, concentrated on the heavenly fathers of demons, thus serving as a hidden critique of Mesopotamian culture and its main bearers. The importance of the violent activity of demons in 7:3–5 that overlaps with the Mesopotamian literary pattern has been diminished,

---

demons swear an oath in order to expel them and make them inoffensive, the sons of heaven impose the oath on themselves in order to enter the earthly realm and make themselves efficacious in committing the great sin and in harming humanity with the birth of demons and with their teaching. Thus the action of the sons of heaven introduces exactly the opposite consequences from those expected from an exorcist.

46. It is difficult not to agree with Bhayro (*Shemihazah and Asael Narrative*, 239–40), who sees 6:7 as a preparation for the insertion of 8:1–3.

47. See Henryk Drawnel, "Professional Skills of Asael (*1 En.* 8:1) and Their Mesopotamian Background," *RB* 119 (2012): 526–29.

48. 1 En. 8:1e–g+2 (G^S) and 8:2 (G^C) speak about the tragic consequences of Asael's knowledge for humanity, which is quite understandable, for both the insertion of Asael's knowledge and that of the rest of the Watchers in 8:3 indicates how Mesopotamian culture negatively influences the rest of humanity. The accent laid on the fathers of demons as teachers necessarily led to such a conclusion. Thus humanity becomes prey to the demonic violence (7:3–4) and to the Watchers' teaching. While in the case of the demonic aggression humanity becomes a helpless victim, in the case of the Watchers' teaching it corrupts its ways. Human responsibility in the rest of the myth (chs. 9–11) is not explicitly considered, for the divine punishment is directed against the suprahuman perpetrators of violence and aggressive teaching. The flood motif in 10:2–3 resolves the problem of human responsibility for the acceptance of the Watchers' teaching, on the one hand, and serves as a purification of the earth that resulted from the demonic violence, on the other.

49. See Drawnel, "Professional Skills of Asael," 529–38.

50. See Drawnel, "Between Akkadian *ṭupšarrūtu* and Aramaic ספר," 382–96.

and consequently the rest of the narrative in chapters 9–11 treats demons only marginally.[51]

The accusation brought forth by the earth (7:6) and the cry for help issued by the human beings (8:4) constitute a secondary development in relation to the Marduk-Ea literary pattern, where neither the earth nor humanity brings an accusation against the violence of demons. In the narrative of the myth, 1 En. 7:6 signals the end of the description of demonic violence, while 8:4 subsumes the teaching of the Watchers under the same label of demonic violence against humanity. The developed form of 8:4 attested by G^{S1} and G^{S2} is dependent on 9:3, where it is part of the angelic report.

2.2.2. Angels' Reaction and Report to God (9:1–11)

After the description of the violence of the demonic warriors, both the Marduk-Ea incantation type and the Enochic myth change the register from earth to heaven. Marduk, exorcist among the gods, notices the situation on the earth and makes a report to Ea, god of wisdom and water, about the violence of demons, particularly concerning the attack of demons against a man. The Enochic myth downgrades the messenger to angelic status and multiplies the angels, most probably because of the development of the narrative in the introduction. The four angels not only notice the problem and report it to God, but are also charged by God to eliminate the multiform evil presented in the introduction: Asael, Shemihazah with the Watchers, and the demonic warriors. The fourth angel is added because of Noah and the plant of righteousness, a clear allusion to the future of Israel.

In the Marduk-Ea dialogue in the Mesopotamian incantations, Marduk has seen the suffering of the person assailed by demons, and then enters the temple ("house") of Ea, his father, and literally repeats the words from the first and second parts of the introduction. Finally, he expresses

---

51. The marginal treatment of demons in 1 En. 6–11 was probably one of the reasons for the composition of the Book of Giants, which dealt with the fate of the demonic warriors in greater detail. It certainly constitutes a development of Jewish demonology in which the demonic warriors receive names and personality, in contrast to 1 En. 6–11, where they are anonymous and undefined. The Jewish author of the Book of Giants seems to concentrate on the punishment of demons, a topic reduced in 1 En. 6–11 to a few sentences only (10:9–10, 15).

his lack of knowledge concerning the proper steps to be taken. Ea answers his son by stating that Marduk's knowledge equals that of his father, but eventually sends Marduk out to apply the ritual formulated in the next part of the incantation. One can notice without much trouble the similarity with 1 En. 9, where the four angels see much bloodshed on the earth. Although they only look out from the heavenly sanctuary (9:1), the text then states that they "enter" (9:2, G^{S1+S2}) it. The repetition of the human call for help in 9:3 introduces the reason for the angelic intervention and a legal context of the accusation. Since neither humanity nor single individuals usually intervene in the dialogue between Ea and Marduk, one has to state that the human accusation is an addition that most probably stems from Mesopotamian antiwitchcraft incantations, where the patient accuses his persecutors.[52] The Watchers practice magic, divination, and

---

52. The opponents of the Mesopotamian conjurer on the cosmic levels are demons, while on the human level he contends with a witch or sorcerer. It is therefore not surprising that in the Enochic myth the Watchers, identified by their professional teaching with the Mesopotamian *āšipu*, father demons and practice sorcery, which is a clear distortion of their principal professional function in Mesopotamian polytheistic society. The association, however, between witchcraft and the *āšipu* may stem from the antiwitchcraft professional literature in Mesopotamia. What we know about black magic and demons in Mesopotamia was penned by the professional conjurer, and the negative presentation of the witch there seems antithetically mirrored in the positive role of the *āšipu*; see the comment by Tzvi Abusch, "The Demonic Image of the Witch in Standard Babylonian Literature: The Reworking of Popular Concepts by Learned Exorcists," in *Mesopotamian Witchcraft: Toward A History and Understanding of Babylonian Witchcraft Beliefs and Literature*, ed. Tzvi Abusch, Ancient Magic and Divination 5 (Leiden: Brill, 2002), 7: "Although witch and *āšipu* are opponents, they nonetheless are almost mirror-images of each other insofar as they use many of the same techniques, though presumably in the service of conflicting social goals and norms." The witch plays the most important role as the main practitioner of destructive magic, yet in the first millennium BCE the male *kaššāpu* comes to prominence as well; see Yitschak Sefati and Jacob Klein, "The Role of Women in Mesopotamian Witchcraft," in *Sex and Gender in the Ancient Near East: Proceedings of the 47th Rencontre Assyriologique Internationale, Helsinki, July 2–6, 2001*, ed. Simo Parpola and Robert M. Whiting, CRRAI 47/2 (Helsinki: Neo-Assyrian Text Corpus Project, 2002), 576–86. As noted by Abusch ("Demonic Image of the Witch," 20), the demonization of the witch in Mesopotamian antiwitchcraft rituals leads to the combination of two ceremonies: one against witchcraft, the other against demons: "Two forms of the witch—the witch in human form and in demonic form—are brought together. In the combining of the two ceremonies, we have a merger of anti-witchcraft incantations involving judgment and burning, with general anti-demon incantations involving rites of burn-

especially witchcraft[53] in the introduction and in 9:8 (G^S), then as the consequence there comes the human legal intervention in 9:3 (8:4 [G^{S1+2}]), which constitutes a purposeful expansion of the literary pattern of the Marduk-Ea incantation.

It is normal that the angels address God in an intercessory prayer—they are not on the same footing with God as Marduk in relation to Ea. On the other hand, one should notice that both the Marduk-Ea formula and the angelic prayer begin with an apostrophe to the god who receives the report. While in the Sumerian incantation the apostrophe consist in one exclamation only ("My father!"), in the Enochic text it develops into a praise of God (9:4–5). The development into a prayer is quite natural, for incantations often make a recourse to prayers when addressing a god. The first part of the prayer (9:4–5) extols God and his majesty, but the second part (9:6–10), similar to the Marduk-Ea incantation, makes a report to God based on the introduction. First, the teaching of Asael is reported (9:6; see 8:1), then the sin of Shemihazah and his companions is described (9:7–8; see 6:1–2; 7:1a-c), followed by the birth of the demonic warriors (9:9; see 7:2). In 9:8 Shemihazah's group shows to women all kind of sins, which may be an allusion to 7:1d-e and 8:3; the teaching of hate-producing charms in 9:8 (G^S) expands on the information already given in 7:1 (4Q202 1 ii 19) and 8:3 (4Q201 1 iv 2), where the Watchers are accused of witchcraft. The cry of humanity that reaches the heavenly gates (9:10) is the consequence of 9:3. The recalling of the themes from the introduction is not as literal as in the Mesopotamian literary pattern, but nevertheless the applied literary strategy is identical.

The last verse in the angelic prayer (9:11) recalls Marduk's perplexity as what to do in that situation. In the Marduk-Ea incantation, Marduk expressly states that he does not know what to do and how to proceed in order to heal the patient. The angels in 9:11 stress that God knows everything but do not say what to do in such a situation, which, differently than in the Marduk-Ea incantation, amounts to an accusation. Nevertheless,

---

ing, dousing, and expulsion." Such a merger attested in Mesopotamian incantation literature finds its reflex in the Enochic myth where judgment, burning, and expulsion are applied to the Watchers and demons. For the relationship between the punishment of Asael and other Watchers with Mesopotamian antiwitchcraft literature, see Henryk Drawnel, "The Punishment of Asael (*1 En.* 10:4–8) and Mesopotamian Anti-Witchcraft Literature," *RevQ* 25 (2012): 369–94.

53. 4Q202 1 ii 19 (1 *En.* 7:1); 4Q201 1 iv 1–4; and 4Q202 1 iii 2, 4 (1 *En.* 8:3).

the angelic statement is also a request for instruction from God and an expression of their own ignorance. In the Marduk-Ea incantation, before instructing Marduk what to do, Ea praises Marduk's wisdom and equates his knowledge with the knowledge of his father. Such a statement about the angels issued from God in the Enochic text would sound quite unnatural, and consequently has been omitted. After the angelic complaint in 9:11, God immediately proceeds to instruct the angels (10:1–14).

The kernel of chapter 9 can be reduced to the following sections: the angel(s) notice(s) the problem and enter(s) the sanctuary (9:1–2); they (he) address(es) God (9:4–5); the report of the birth of the demonic warriors (9:8a–c); lack of knowledge as how to proceed (9:11).

2.2.3. Divine Instruction (10:1–14)

Once Marduk ends his report about the attack of the demons, a short narrative sentence says that Ea answers his son. Then there comes the praise of Marduk by Ea, who stresses that Marduk's knowledge equals that of his father. Finally, the father sends out his son: "Go, my son, Marduk." This messenger formula ends Ea's praise of Marduk and begins Ea's speech, which lasts until the end of the incantation. The speech is a ritual instruction with verbs in the imperative that explain the ritual proceedings, and with verbs in the precative that describe the intended result of the incantation, that is, the purification of the patient. In the ritual, water is often applied, which is quite natural since Ea, the main instructor, is the god of water in Mesopotamian religion.

The Enochic text in 10:1–14 contains not one but four commissioning formulae, and the verbs are found in the imperative and future tense. After the end of the angelic prayer, the text has a short narrative in which God speaks and sends out Sariel to the son of Lamech. When compared with the Marduk-Ea incantation, it is immediately clear that 10:1 is a short narrative introduction to God's speech, but the praise of Marduk's knowledge by Ea has been omitted, for in the preceding prayer only God is the God of knowledge; additionally, the angels are not on an equal footing with God, differently from the Marduk-Ea divine relationship. As in the Marduk-Ea incantation, God's speech begins with a short sentence ("and to … he said") followed by the messenger formula: "Go, [Sariel]!" (10:2, G^S);[54] "go,

---

54. For the Aramaic "Sariel" as the name of the fourth angel, see 4Q202 III 7

Raphael!" (10:4, G^S); "go, Gabriel!" (10:9, G^S); "go, Michael!" (10:11). Similar to the Marduk-Ea incantation, God in the list of imperatives instructs his four messengers what to do and how to proceed; there are four of them because God has to deal with Noah, Asael, the Watchers, and Shemihazah and the demons. The message to the son of Lamech (10:2–3) is a new development, not prepared in the preceding narrative thread of the Enochic myth, and clearly related to the preoccupation of the Jewish author about the fate of Israel. It also introduces the motif of the flood, which, when compared with the Marduk-Ea ritual instruction, reminds the reader of the use of water for the purification of the patient. The goal of the flood is, however, the destruction of the earth (10:2), but since the flood is part of the fourfold instruction, it is also one of the elements that leads to the purification of the earth (cf. 10:20, 22). Although such an interpretation is congruous with the context, the destructive character of the flood in 10:2 is clearly a foreign element in the structure of the myth. It makes the healing rites of the three angelic messengers futile. It may only be justified as the response to 8:2, where humanity corrupts its way as a consequence of Asael's teaching. Both elements, however (human sin and destruction of the whole earth), are not dependent of the Mesopotamian incantation pattern.

The shortest instruction, and probably the oldest one, is directed to Gabriel (10:9), and it exclusively deals with the elimination of the demons. The Watchers' request for a long life for their sons in 10:10 is the consequence of the introduction (6:1–8:4), where the sons of heaven are presented as fathers of the demonic warriors (7:1–2). The instructions directed against the Watchers (10:11–13) are similar to those directed against Asael (10:4–8), and the thematic motifs present in them indicate a relationship with Mesopotamian antiwitchcraft incantations.[55] This is most probably the reason for the lack of ritual instructions with the use of the *materia magica*, characteristic to the Marduk-Ea incantation. The reference to Mesopotamian antiwitchcraft literature also explains the reduction of the instruction to limit the demons to one verse only (10:9). The narrative thread that concentrates on the fathers of demons in 6:1–8:4 makes such an adjustment of the Mesopotamian incantation pattern understandable. The text in 10:14 is probably a redactional expansion that links the judgment of the Watchers with that of an unspecified individual.

(1 En. 9:1) in J. T. Milik, *The Books of Enoch: Aramaic Fragments of Qumrân Cave 4* (Oxford: Clarendon, 1976), 170.

55. See Drawnel, "Punishment of Asael," 378–91.

2.2.4. Blessed Future without Impurity (10:15–11:2)

In the Marduk-Ea incantation, after the messenger formula Ea continues his speech concerning the ritual to heal the patient until the end of the incantation. One subordinate clause with the verb in the precative constitutes the fourth part of the incantation literary structure. The clause states that the demons or illness should leave the patient, and sometimes an additional sentence invites the personal god or good spirits to take the place of the expelled demons.

The fourth and last part of the Enochic myth (10:15–11:2) constitutes the continuation of God's speech, which, however, should be considered not as part of the instruction directed to Raphael (10:11–14) but as an encompassing vision of all the consequences of God's instruction directed to his four angels. The use of the verbs in the future tense continues from the first part of God's speech (10:1–14), where it expressed the intended results of the angelic proceedings. Verses 15–16 and 20 preserve the imperative form of the instruction from the preceding section, but they are redactional additions that link the previsions about the future with the preceding instruction. Verse 15 is an expansion of the punishment of the demons in verse 9. The destruction of all injustice is linked in verse 16 with the plant of righteousness, a clear development related to verse 3; the command to purify the earth in verse 20 is related to the purification of the earth stated in verse 22. The remaining part of God's speech can be divided into two parts: fruitfulness of humanity and nature (10:17–19); and worship of God, purification of the earth, and open storehouses of blessings (10:21–11:2). The first part (10:17–19), which speaks about the long life and fruitfulness for humanity together with the blessing for the trees, vine, and olive trees, is not expressly prepared by the preceding three parts of the myth, except perhaps for 7:3–4, where demons destroy the produce of human hands and kill men. The same section, 10:17–19, seems to develop the idea expressed in 10:16c–d, where the plant of righteousness, a reference to Israel, will appear and be blessed together with the deeds of righteousness. It does not seem to be related to the content and purpose of the Marduk-Ea incantation.

The last part of the Enochic myth (10:15–11:2) certainly does not correspond to the fourth, concluding part of the Marduk-Ea incantation, expressed usually by one sentence only. Since God's speech in 10:2–14 continues in 10:15–11:2, the latter section also belongs to the speech. The verbs in the future tense indicate the formal relation with the preceding section (10:1–14) and describe the positive consequences of the punishment imparted upon the demonic warriors and Watchers.[56] In the Marduk-Ea incantation the ritual instructions are formulated in the imperative, as in 1 En. 10:2–14, but the consequences of the applied ritual are in the same speech expressed by the precative, both in Sumerian and Akkadian. With natural consequences for the interpretation of the text, the Enochic Aramaic text seems to have substituted the imperfect for the precative form, which usually expresses a wish or an indirect command.

In the Marduk-Ea incantation, Ea's ritual speech expressed the intended consequences of the incantations that led to the purification of the patient. The Enochic vision of the blessed future in 10:22 indicates that the earth will be purified from all defilement (μίασμα), impurity (ἀκαθαρσία), wrath (ὀργή), and plague (μάστιξ). It is not difficult to link these terms with the activity of the Watchers: defilement (μιαίνεσθαι, 7:1), impurity (ἀκαθαρσία, 10:11), wrath (ὀργή, 8:3),[57] plague (synonym πληγή, 10:7). Since the defilement and impurity of the Watchers are closely bound with their fornication with the women, their demonic descendants are also considered to be impure. The purification of the earth, therefore, includes liberation from demonic violence, in the creation of which the Watchers are directly involved. Thus the section 10:21–11:2 seems to overlap with the intended consequences of the ritual section in the Marduk-Ea incantation. While in the latter composition only one patient is cleansed from the harmful activity of demons, the Jewish author extended the consequences of God's instruction (10:1–14) to all the inhabitants of the earth (10:21) and to all the human generations (11:2). While the cleansed patient would return under the protection of his personal god, the Enochic author introduces the perspective of the conversion of all the nations of the earth to God (10:21), which clearly corresponds to his polemics against the Mesopotamian polytheistic culture and its main bearers. Thus the universal perspective in 10:21–11:2 expresses the purpose of the adaptation of the Mesopotamian literary pattern. The God of Israel is the one who holds authority over demons and with the help of his angels purifies the earth from all demonic activity.

---

56. The Aramaic fragments from Qumran confirm that the verbal forms in 10:17–19 and 10:21–11:1 stand in the imperfect form; see 4Q201 1 vi 3–6 in Milik, *Books of Enoch*, 162; 10:17–19 = 4Q204 1 v 5–8 in Milik, *Books of Enoch*, 189.

57. Note, however, that the Greek term in 8:3 is plural and seems to have a more restricted meaning there; see Drawnel, *Aramaic Astronomical Book*, 63–64.

3. From an Incantation to a Universal Myth

The first three parts of the Marduk-Ea incantation overlap with the literary structure of the Enochic myth; the latter, however, is not an incantation but a myth that explains the origin of demonic presence on the earth and indicates the God of Israel as the one who controls the destructive forces of evil and brings healing and purification to humanity and the earth.[58] The fourth part of the myth is a universalizing general vision of the blessed and purified earth and humanity. The first introductory part contains a substantial departure from the introductory section of the Sumero-Akkadian incantation, and causes the rest of the changes in the remaining parts of the literary pattern. By presenting the sons of heaven as sinful spiritual beings, the Jewish author introduced the perspective that dominates the rest of the narrative. It is nevertheless clear that the main idea that the birth of the demonic warriors stems from the sexual union of the sons of heaven with the daughters of earth has not been invented by the Jewish author. The birth of demons, according to the mythologem found in incantation literature, stems from the sexual union of the divinized heaven with the (sometimes) divinized earth.

The reference to the birth of demons in Mesopotamian incantation literature is part of a general pattern according to which the cosmic origin of the exorcised evil is often presented at the beginning of the incanta-

---

58. Lauri Honko ("The Problem of Defining Myth," in *Sacred Narrative: Readings in the Theory of Myth,* ed. Alan Dundes [Berkeley: University of California Press, 1984], 49) defines myth as a literary category in the following way: "Myth, the story of the gods, a religious account of the beginning of the world, the creation, fundamental events, the exemplary deeds of the gods as a result of which the world, nature and culture were created together with all the parts thereof and given their order, which still obtains. A myth expresses and confirms society's religious values and norms, it provides a pattern of behaviour to be imitated, testifies to the efficacy of ritual with its practical ends and establishes the sanctity of cult." Such an equilibrated definition attracts attention to a deep inner relationship between the social context in which the myth is created and its relationship to the cult. The comparison of the Enochic myth with Mesopotamian incantation literature, which is part of liturgical proceedings, indicates how strongly the Enochic myth is immersed in the religious and social context within which the author functioned, and from which he drew his creative inspiration that gave rise to a new synthesis about the origin of the evil beings, sin and impurity, and ways of their elimination.

tion.[59] In the case of the incantations against the evil *utukkū*, the reference to the cosmic origin of demons usually appears in the first, introductory part of the incantation literary pattern that describes the violent activity of demons against humanity, animals, and nature. The origin of the demonic world is often depicted as stemming from sexual intercourse between two primeval Sumerian gods, An and Ki. The reference to these two deities means that demons originate in the embryonic cosmos, before the present world order, as described in the Enuma Elish epos, was set. According to the earliest Sumerian mythology, the two divine principles, heaven (An) and earth (Ki), existing in the primeval world, were not yet separated. They copulate and bring forth life in the cosmos, with An being a male element, while Ki is a female.[60] In the Udug-ḫul incantation series, the evil *Utukkū* are often described as the "seed of Anu" and the "offspring of the earth." The Sumero-Akkadian composition does not always use the determinative dingir before the names of the two divinities; this ambiguity between the cosmic interpretation of the two elements and their divine status is also present in the early Sumerian compositions.[61] The terms "seed" (*riḫûtu*)[62] and "to spawn, to beget" (*rehû*), applied to the birth of demons do not leave any doubt as to the sexual character of the divine union that gave origin to the demonic world.[63] In the first millennium BCE, demons are also associated with the netherworld,[64] hence the chthonic goddess Ereshkigal is sometimes presented as their mother. The following examples taken from the Udug-ḫul series illustrate the divine birth of demons.

They are the offspring of earth (*i-lit-ti* KI-*tì*) spawned (*re-hu-u*) by the seed of Anu (*šá re-hu-ut* ᵈ*a-nim*) (*UL* 5:10). The attentive Watcher-demon is always pursuing something, fashioned in the netherworld (*bi-nu* KI-*tì*),

---

59. See n. 6.

60. For the cosmic hierogamy related to the primeval theogony and the birth of life on earth, see J. van Dijk, "Le motif cosmique dans la pensée sumérienne," *AcOr* 28 (1964): 34–57.

61. See ibid., 47.

62. Lit. "semen, sperm"; see *CAD* 14:341–43.

63. The term *ilittu*, "offspring, progeny," is also used in relation to the evil *utukkū*.

64. Cf. "Evil Utukku-demon, Alû, ghost, and sheriff-demon have emerged from the netherworld [KI-tì], and they came out from the midst of the distant mountain [kur-idim], the Holy Mound [du6-kù]" (*UL* 7:69–70). The term "earth," both in Sumerian (ki) and Akkadian (*erṣetu*), may denote the surface of the earth, where humanity lives, and the underworld, abode of the dead, chthonic deities, and demons; see Horowitz, *Mesopotamian Cosmic Geography*, 272–74.

but spawned in heaven (*re-ḫu-ut* AN-*e*) (*UL* 5:142–143). The "heroes" are twice seven, who, in a single spawning (*šá re-ḫu-ut-su-nu iš-ta-at*), were born (*ib-ba-nu-ú*) of Anu's seed (*re-ḫu-ut* ^d*a-nim*) (*UL* 5:151–152).

While cold and chills weaken everything, the evil Utukku-demons are spawned (*re-ḫu-u*) from the seed of Anu (*šá re-ḫu-ut* ^d*a-nim*); Namtaru (Fate), beloved son of Enlil, is born (*i-lit-ti*) of Ereshkigal (*UL* 5:1–3). Whoever is spawned (*šá re-ḫu-ut*) by Anu's seed are children who are offspring (*i-lit-ti*) of the netherworld (KI-*ti*) (*UL* 4:1).

The Poem of Erra presents the origin of demonic beings in a similar way: "When Anu, king of the gods, sowed his seed [*ir-ḫe-e-ma*] in the Earth [*er-ṣe-tu*], she bore him [*ul-da-áš-šum-ma*] seven gods, he called them the Seven [^d*Sibitti*]" (Erra I 28–29).[65] "Lord An copulated with the thriving Earth and she has borne him a warrior without fear—Asakku" (*Lugal-e* I 26–27).[66]

Thus the Mesopotamian incantations and myths locate the birth of demons by the two primordial deities in the hoary past. The depiction of demonic giants in 1 En. 7:2–5 and 15:11 makes clear that the Jewish author based his description of the violent demonic beings on the violent nature of the *utukkū lemnūtu* in the series Udug-ḫul-a-meš (Akk. *Utukkū Lemnūtu*). It is therefore not surprising that when he presented the origin of the demonic warriors as stemming from a sexual union of the sons of heaven with the daughters of men (1 En. 6:1–7:1), the Enochic author was inspired not so much by the biblical text (Gen 6:1–2, 4),[67] but by the mythological explanation of the origin of demons in Mesopotamian literature.[68]

---

65. Luigi Cagni, *L'epopea di Erra*, StSem 34 (Rome: Istituto di Studi del Vicino Oriente, 1969), 60.

66. J. van Dijk, *Lugal ud me-lám-bi nir-ǦÁL: Le récit épique et didactique des Travaux de Ninurta, du Déluge et de la Nouvelle Création*, 2 vols. (Leiden: Brill, 1983), 1:55.

67. Although the vocabulary of Gen 6:1–2, 4 partially overlaps with 1 En. 6–7, it does not describe the violent activity of the גבורים found in 1 En. 7:2–5 and 15:11. It is therefore inappropriate to identify the short Genesis narrative with 1 En. 6–7 because the גבורים in the Genesis text are not presented there as demonic beings. Additionally, the "sons of God" are not presented as sinful spiritual beings.

68. It appears that the mythological character of 1 En. 6–11 is formulated already at the beginning of the account in 6:1 by the expression ἐν ἐκείνας ταῖς ἡμέραις (G^C; Ethiopic), "in those days"; cf. Gen 6:4 (applied to the Nephilim). The Enochic verse implies a short distance from the creation of humankind, for it says that the sons of man began to grow in number. For the Sumerian expression u4-ri-a, "on that day,"

The giants are offspring of the heavenly fathers and earthly mothers, a mythological motif slightly modified in relation to the Sumerian mythology, and developed into a short mythological narrative (1 En. 6:1–7:2). The modification results from different theological categories in Judaism that excluded the reference to the god Heaven and goddess Earth, yet the male/female distribution between the heaven and earth is preserved, although attested in two different Greek manuscripts. The Watchers are called "sons of heaven" (6:2, υἱοὶ οὐρανοῦ, G^C; Ethiopic),[69] while the daughters of men are "of the earth" (6:2, τῆς γῆς, G^S),[70] and the marital dimension of the relationship has been introduced by the use of the idiom "to take wife" (7:1, λαμβάνω γυναῖκας, G^{C+S}; Ethiopic). Differently from the Sumerian mythology that depicts the relationship between An and Ki as a cosmic hierogamy,[71] the sexual relationship between the sons of heaven and daughters of the earth is termed a "great sin" (6:3, ἁμαρτία μεγάλη, G^{C+S}; Ethiopic), an unmistakable reference to fornication, that causes the pollution of the Watchers (7:1, μιαίνεσθαι, G^{C+S}). The impurity of the Watchers implies the impurity of their demonic descendants and of their teaching with which they strike the earth and which they teach their demonic children (10:7 G^C).[72]

The introduction of these two negative categories ("great sin" and "pollution") implies a partial modification of the original Mesopotamian

---

in the mythological context of the creation of the world and humanity, see van Dijk, "Motif cosmique," 16–34.

69. Note that Gen 6:4 speaks about the "sons of God" (בני האלהים), which is a considerable change in relation to the Enochic text. The antithesis between heaven and earth has thus been blurred. Additionally, the Genesis text suggests a positive relationship to God, while in the Enochic text the sons of heaven are sinful and impure; hence any relationship with God is excluded.

70. Even without the expression τῆς γῆς in 6:2 (G^S), the contrast between the heavenly beings and earthly women is clear enough to be understood. The contrast between the heavenly and earthly realms bound in a sexual relationship is later developed in 15:3–7, but the stress is laid on the incompatibility of the two modes of existence.

71. See van Dijk, *Lugal*, 1:45–46. Although TCL XVI 53 does not mention the birth of demons in this context, some other mythological texts do; see the Poem of Erra, I 28–29, cited above.

72. Against R. H. Charles, *The Ethiopic Version of the Book of Enoch*, Anecdota Oxoniensia, Semitic Series 11 (Oxford: Clarendon, 1906), 27 n. 6, the reading πατάσσω in 10:7 (G^C) should not be discarded as secondary or corrupt; to the contrary, as a *lectio difficilior* it should be preserved against the smoothed-out text of G^S.

tradition that did not consider the birth of demons in the "sin" category.
It remains, however, beyond doubt that both the Mesopotamian mythological tradition and the Enochic myth depict the birth of demons as the
result of the sexual union between the earthly and heavenly spheres. The
narrative thread of the Enochic myth concentrates, however, not on the
violence of demons, a typical topic in the introductory part of the Sumero-
Akkadian incantations. The violence of demons is presented in 7:3–5, but
they play only a minor role in the following narrative. The Enochic author
develops the following topics: the sinfulness of the sons of heaven (6:3),
their binding by an oath (6:4–5), their descent on Mount Hermon (6:6),
and the list of their leaders (6:7). It becomes therefore immediately clear
that the Enochic author concentrates on the heavenly fathers of demons,
especially on their sinful character and inner hierarchical organization.
It seems that the presentation of the Watchers in 6:1–7:1c constitutes the
first step for further identification of the Watchers with the Mesopotamian
āšipu and with the Mesopotamian artisans working within the organiza-
tional structure of the temple. The binding of the spiritual beings by an
oath (6:4) alludes to the role of the Mesopotamian conjurer who expelled
demons by making them swear an oath that caused them to depart.[73] The
division of the sons of heaven into groups of ten (6:7) with a headman at
the helm of each group recalls the division of the workforce in the Mesopotamian temple in the Neo-Babylonian and Persian periods.[74]

Thus it is evident that the explanation of the origin of demons was
reduced in importance, while the sons of heaven took the most prominent
place in the narrative, so that their future condemnation may implicitly
entail not only the punishment of sinful spiritual beings but also an accusation against the Mesopotamian temple and its personnel, the last bastion
of polytheistic cuneiform culture. The content of 1 En. 8:3 links the sons
of heaven with the Mesopotamian āšipu, while the knowledge of Asael
in 8:1 recalls the Mesopotamian artisan, with some terms suggesting an
overlapping with the profession of the āšipu. Such a development of the
narrative thread leads not only to the composition of the angelic report to
God (9:1–11), but also to God's instruction how to eliminate the lawless
ones (10:1–14), where the main accent is laid on the elimination of the
sons of heaven, while the punishment of the demonic giants is reduced

73. See n. 45.
74. See Drawnel, "Professional Skills of Asael," 526–29.

to minimum (10:9). On the other hand, the sons of heaven are presented as sinful and polluted, which leads to the presentation of their didactic activity as an aggression against humanity (10:7, G^C). Thus the activity of the sons of heaven is equated with the evil activity of their demonic sons, and they themselves are presented as a distinct category of supernatural beings, against whom an elimination ritual has to be applied.

The comparison with the literary pattern of the Marduk-Ea incantation clearly indicates that the role of Marduk as exorcist among the gods was substituted by the angel Gabriel, who is sent to destroy the demonic sons of the sons of heaven. The role of Raphael and Michael is an extension of the exorcistic function of Gabriel caused by the narrative thread that concentrates on the punishment of the sons of heaven. The role played by Sariel is rather that of a prophetic messenger with an instruction directed to Noah in order to assure his survival.[75] It is also clear that the role of Ea, the main god of exorcism, was taken over by the God of Israel, who instructs the angels what to do in order to eliminate the evil and sinful spirits from the earth. Such a change is also perfectly understandable within the structure of the Enochic myth, and it has clear theological consequences.

Basing the literary structure and main thematic motifs on the literary pattern of the Marduk-Ea incantation, the Enochic author once again made recourse to the type of Mesopotamian literature traditionally associated with the āšipu. The intellectual model of a priest, exorcist, and scientist cultivated in the last centuries of the cuneiform tradition constituted a challenge to the Jewish educated class living in Mesopotamia.[76] The theological perspective that was created due to the creation of the Enochic myth and Enochic astronomy presented the God of Israel as the one who not only reveals the mystery of the created universe through the intermediary of his angels. At the same time the Jewish, probably

---

75. See Nickelsburg, *1 Enoch 1*, 220–21.

76. Concerning the broad learning of the Mesopotamian exorcist in the Persian and Hellenistic periods, see Markham J. Geller, *Ancient Babylonian Medicine: Theory and Practice* (Chichester: Wiley-Blackwell, 2010), 163: "Probably modeled on the influence and interests of the magi, Babylonian exorcists gradually take over the practice and study of magic and medicine from this time on, and in many ways the exorcists appear to dominate the intellectual scene in Hellenistic Babylonia. They were expected to have knowledge of divination, astrology, lexicography, medicine, and magic, judging by colophons of late tablets and the professional interests of the scribes who copied them."

priestly, author explained the origin of demons and ascribed the role of the main exorcist to the God of Israel. His goal was, however, not a mere exposition of God's authority over demons, but also a polemical stance directed against the main representative of Mesopotamian polytheistic culture and religion. The priestly *āšipu* was demonized and presented as a representative of black, not white, magic, and harmful to humanity and to the earth. Thus by instructing his angels how to eliminate the demonic giants, God also orders the punishment of the sons of heaven so that his authority over the polytheistic culture and religion is established and leads to their removal. The framework of a judicial process with the accusation brought forth by humanity has its roots in Mesopotamian antiwitchcraft procedures, directed in the Enochic myth against Asael and Shemihazah, two paradigms for a Mesopotamian artisan and a Mesopotamian scholar.

4. Later Developments

The Enochic myth was most probably written in Mesopotamia for the Jewish audience living in Mesopotamia. When the myth was brought to the land of Israel, the sons of heaven were reduced to a warning example against fornication,[77] their professional function being poorly understood outside the Mesopotamian context.[78] On the other hand, the etiological explanation of the birth of the demonic warriors was much more pro-

---

77. See, e.g., Jub. 7:20–25, where the Watchers are examples of fornication and uncleanness. The giants cause bloodshed and injustice, and consequently humanity is also corrupt, which altogether causes the obliteration of all living creatures by the flood.

78. Note, however, that in Jub. 10:12 the angels teach Noah the healing character of the earth's plants that are to be used against the diseases and deceptions of demons. This is a clear antithetical development of 1 En. 7:1 and 8:3, where the Watchers teach the women the knowledge of roots and plants. Since these two Enochic verses are closely connected with Mesopotamian healing practices of the *āšipu* (see Drawnel, *Aramaic Astronomical Book*, 63–64), Jub. 10:12 should probably be seen as an appropriation of the Mesopotamian healing practices. Against Armin Lange ("The Essene Position on Magic and Divination," in *Legal Texts and Legal Issues: Proceedings of the Second Meeting of the International Organization for Qumran Studies, Cambridge 1995*, ed. Moshe Bernstein, Florentino García Martínez, and John Kampen; STDJ 23 [Leiden: Brill, 1997], 384), one has to state that neither 1 En. 8:3 nor the Jubilees text shows any contact with ancient Greek medicine.

ductive. It gave rise to the further development of demonology, where the "spirits of the bastards" constitute a well-defined class of evil spirits.[79] The authority of the God of Israel over demons in the Enochic myth most probably stems from the Jewish author's attempt to take the place of the much denigrated *āšipu* who, with the recourse to the authority of Ea and Marduk, gods of exorcism, was able to pursue his medical and exorcistic career. Once the etiology of the violent demons was created and the God of Israel became instrumental in the elimination of the sinful and violent spiritual beings, exorcism became part of Jewish religious tradition and lost all negative connotations related to its polytheistic context. In a rather universal myth, the reference to Mount Hermon and Jared in 1 En. 6:6 and to Noah in 10:2–3 firmly anchors the angelic vicissitudes in the context of Jewish religious tradition.

4.1. The Jewish Exorcist and Scientist

Thus one may assume that the Enochic myth is a proof for the existence of a new class of priestly specialist in postexilic Judaism modeled after his much denigrated Mesopotamian model.[80] The new specialist made reference in his healing practice to the authority of the God of Israel as the one who controls the evil spirits. This encouraged the creation of the exorcistic

---

79. For the analysis of the terminology concerning the spirits of the bastards and their Enochic etiology at Qumran, see Philip S. Alexander, "The Demonology of the Dead Sea Scrolls," in *The Dead Sea Scrolls after Fifty Years: A Comprehensive Assessment*, ed. Peter W. Flint and James C. VanderKam, 2 vols. (Leiden: Brill, 1999), 2:331–53, esp. 333, 337–41.

80. The following reconstruction of the professional characteristics of the Enochic author are based on the interpretation of 1 En. 6–11 in the light of the Mesopotamian incantation literature that is closely related with cult and the priestly *āšipu*. It is unlikely that the author of 1 En. 6–11 produced his piece of mythological narrative only as a pure intellectual enterprise without an attempt to influence not only his audience but his reality and his way of explaining it in the liturgical context. Reflecting on the meaning of the myth, Honko ("Problem of Defining Myth," 49) notes, "The reenactment of a creative event, for example, a healing wrought by a god in the beginning of time, is the common aim of myth and ritual. In this way the event is transferred to the present and its result, i.e. the healing of a sick person, can be achieved once more here and now. In this way, too, the world order, which was created in the primeval era and which is reflected in myths, preserves its value as an exemplar and model for the people of today."

literature attested in the Qumran scrolls,[81] and to the use of the name of the God of Israel in exorcistic practices.[82] Following the example of his Mesopotamian counterpart, this specialist associated his ways of eliminating the evil spirits with God in order to enhance their healing capacity. God's commissioning formula, "Go, Raphael," was probably applied by the Jewish exorcist to himself, for it was the conjurer who in Mesopotamian tradition was obliged to carry out the ritual transmitted by Ea to his son Marduk. Additionally, the same Jewish specialist was interested in the working of the universe, discovering its hidden laws and time structure.[83] Thus the knowledge eventually codified in the Aramaic Astronomical Book came into being. Astrology became also an element of his specialization, although the attested literary forms are quite fragmentary and preclude an unequivocal conclusion as to their inspiration. The introduction of Enoch in 1 En. 12 in a later stage of the literary development of the text indicates that the antediluvian hero came to represent in the mythological world the learned Jewish exorcist and sage who modeled the literary person partially after his own religious interests, and partially after the prediluvian *apkallu* Utu-abzu, listed in tablet III of the incantation series *bīt mēseri* that makes part of the written lore of *āšipūtu*.[84] The mytholo-

---

81. 4Q510–511 are poetical texts intended to provide protection against harm caused by demons and evil spirits, see Bilha Nitzan, "Magical Poetry," in *Qumran Prayer and Religious Poetry,* trans. Jonathan Chipman, STDJ 12 (Leiden: Brill, 1994), 227–72. 4Q444 and 6Q18 seem also to be religious poetry of an apotropaic character; see Esther Eshel, "Genres of Magical Texts in the Dead Sea Scrolls," in *Die Dämonen— Demons: Die Dämonologie der israelitisch-jüdischen und frühchristlichen Literatur im Kontext ihrer Umwelt—The Demonology of Israelite-Jewish and Early Christian Literature in Context of Their Environment,* ed. Armin Lange, Hermann Lichtenberger, and K. F. Diethard Römheld (Tübingen: Mohr Siebeck, 2003), 395–415, esp. 409–13. 4Q560, 8Q5, and 11QPsAp^a are closer to the incantation literary genre; see Eshel, "Genres of Magical Texts," 396–402; and Émile Puech, "Les deux derniers psaumes davidiques du rituel d'exorcisme, 11QPsAp^a IV 4–V 14," in *The Dead Sea Scrolls: Forty Years of Research,* ed. Devorah Dimant and Uriel Rappaport, STDJ 10 (Brill: Leiden, 1992), 64–89. These texts are paleographically dated to the period around the turn of the eras.

82. See 11Q11 III 4.

83. Note that 4Q510 frag. 1 2 speaks about the God of knowledge, and in 4Q510 frag. 1 4 it is the *maskil* who recites the hymn; cf. also 4Q511 frag. 2 i 1.

84. Rykle Borger ("Die Beschwörungsserie *bīt mēseri* und die Himmelfahrt Henochs," *JNES* 33 [1974]: 183–96, esp. 192–93) was the first to show the similarity between Enoch and the Mesopotamian Utu-abzu. Note, however, that the Watchers

gem according to which Utu-abzu, the seventh of the antediluvian *purādu*-fishes, ascended to heaven is found in the same type of Mesopotamian incantation literature that gave rise to the literary structure and thematic ideas in 1 En. 6–11. Since the antediluvian *apkallu* were often presented in Mesopotamian art as performing the exorcism,[85] and because of their own profession the *āšipū* often identified with the antediluvian mythical beings, it comes as no surprise that the new ideal wise man, Enoch, had to resemble one of them, the one who ascended to heaven.

One may assume that in this way the exorcistic practices that belonged to the sphere of liturgy[86] have been transferred from the context of Mesopotamian religion, and their execution was set under the tutelage of the God of Israel. The purification of the earth described in 10:21–11:2 as a final goal of God's exorcistic instruction recalls the role of the Levitical priest, who in the book of Leviticus deals with purity and impurity of the people[87] The identification of the Jewish author of the Enochic myth with

---

in 1 En. 6–11 are not modeled after the Mesopotamian *apkallu*, as claimed by some scholars. Although Helge S. Kvanvig (*Roots of Apocalyptic: The Mesopotamian Background of the Enoch Figure and of the Son of Man*, WMANT 61 [Neukirchen-Vluyn: Neukirchener Verlag, 1988], 160–213) discussed Mesopotamian antediluvian traditions in detail and compared them with 1 Enoch, he exclusively concentrated on Mesopotamian mythological texts, without looking into their social context; the *bīt mēseri* was unequivocally related to the *āšipu*. Thus he was not able to find a proper interpretive approach, as also the case in his latest research; see Kvanvig, *Primeval History: Babylonian, Biblical, and Enochic. An Intertexual Reading*, JSJSup 149 (Leiden: Brill, 2011); and Henryk Drawnel, review of *Primeval History: Babylonian, Biblical, and Enochic. An Intertextual Reading*, by H. S. Kvanvig, *Biblical Annals* 2 (2012): 355–61. Some modern Assyriologists who attempt to interpret 1 Enoch fall into the same trap; see esp. Amar Annus, "On the Origin of Watchers: A Comparative Study of the Antediluvian Wisdom in Mesopotamian and Jewish Tradition," *JSP* 19 (2010): 277–320. The latter work shows a rather poor understanding of the Ethiopic and Greek text of 1 Enoch and an overabundance of often loosely linked Akkadian texts and traditions.

85. Borger ("Beschwörungsserie *bīt mēseri*," 192) notes that tablet III of the *bīt mēseri* series speaks about the seven sages as seven statues (or rather paintings) that are painted with gypsum and black paste, drawn on the side wall of the chamber.

86. The ascription of Mesopotamian incantations as belonging either to magic or religion is debated and depends on the definition of these two terms. Cunningham (*Deliver Me from Evil*, 183) points out that incantation's principal concern is mediation between the human and divine domain, and in this function the incantation complements temples as the primary place of mediation between the human and divine. Hence he classifies them as belonging to the religious system, not to magic.

87. Different purification rites in Leviticus are linked with the Levitical priests,

a Levitical priest living in Mesopotamia appears to be a plausible theory, proposed for the first time many years ago.[88]

4.2. Exorcism in the Synoptic Gospels

This research has shown that the literary structure of 1 En. 6–11 is related to the literary form of the Marduk-Ea incantation.[89] The Enochic myth also provides the reader with the first etiology of the sinful spirits and demons, and ways of their elimination, in Second Temple literature.[90] It also proves a heightened interest of the Jewish writer in demonic spirit elimination already in the third century BCE. The myth is not an example of a practical exorcism, in which the magical practitioner plays the most important role. However, the analysis of its literary background shows how the Jewish author modified the literary pattern belonging to Meso-potamian exorcistic literature with the preservation of the main thematic thrust of the original pattern. The Enochic myth still explains the cosmic origin of the exorcised evil and ways of its elimination. Leaving aside the book of Tobit and its disputed dating together with traces of the belief in the demonic world in the Old Testament,[91] the myth is the earliest exam-ple of Jewish religious literature engaged in the universal cleansing of the earth from the demonic presence.

The question concerning the historical and religious background of Jesus's exorcisms in the Synoptic Gospels has usually been answered by recourse to Greek magical papyri from Egypt,[92] Qumran texts, Flavius

---

who also declare as clean (*piel* of טהר) those healed from leprosy; see Lev 13:17, 23, 28, 34, 37.

88. See Kvanvig, *Roots of Apocalyptic*, 135–43.

89. The following notes present only some directions for further research accord-ing to the interpretive lines of 1 En. 6–11 delineated in this research.

90. Concerning the Mesopotamian inspiration for the description of the demonic giants in 1 En. 7:2–5 and 15:11, see Drawnel, "Mesopotamian Background."

91. For the discussion of the demonic world in the OT and some possible links with Mesopotamian culture, see Karel van der Toorn, "The Theology of Demons in Mesopotamia and Israel: Popular Belief and Scholarly Speculation," in *Dämonen—Demons*, ed. Lange et al., 61–83. Although the demonic world is present in the OT, one can hardly speak about exorcistic literature in the OT.

92. Greek magical papyri, which stem from Greco-Roman Egypt, are dated to between the second century BCE and the fifth century CE; see Hans Dieter Betz, ed., *The Greek Magical Papyri in Translation: Including the Demotic Spells* (Chicago: Uni-

Josephus, two first-century rabbis, and some witnesses from Greek literature.[93] All these cases prove that exorcism was known and practiced in Israel, yet they provide an explanation neither for the causes that led to the spread of the practice of exorcism in Israel, nor for the origin of the religious and mythological framework related with the practice of exorcism. The interpretation of 1 En. 6–11 proposed in this research indicates the theological centrality of the God of Israel in the elimination of the sinful and unclean spirits from the earth. In this sense the Enochic myth lays a theological fundament for the practice of exorcism within the context of the Jewish religion in the Second Temple period. The exorcisms of Jesus Christ function well within the theological pattern created by the Enochic author. They constitute an element of establishing the kingdom of God on earth, and as such confirm God's authority over the unclean spirits, so powerfully expressed in the Enochic myth. In the following notes I briefly discuss some possible points of influence of the Enochic myth on the presentation of Jesus's exorcisms in the Synoptic Gospels. Any direct influence is excluded.

The evangelists stress that Jesus's exorcisms were made with authority (ἐξουσία; Mark 1:27; Luke 4:36). When he chooses his disciples, he confers upon them the authority to expel demons (Mark 3:15; Matt 10:1). He also does not make recourse to any higher authority when performing the exorcisms.[94] One cannot overlook in this context that the Enochic myth

---

versity of Chicago Press, 1986), xli. For an example of the explanation of Jesus's exorcisms on the basis of Greek magical literature, see Samson Eitrem, *Some Notes on the Demonology in the New Testament*, 2nd ed., SO 20 (Oslo: Universitetsforlaget, 1966).

93. For an overview of attested cases of exorcists and exorcism in the ancient world, see Amanda Witmer, *Jesus, the Galilean Exorcist: His Exorcisms in Social and Political Context*, LNTS 459, LHJS 10 (London: Bloomsbury T&T Clark, 2012), 22–60. Witmer completely omits any reference to Mesopotamian evidence.

94. On two occasions Jesus states that he expels demons by the finger of God (Luke 11:20; cf. Exod 8:15) or by the spirit of God (Matt 12:28). The Matthean text presents Jesus as the harbinger of the Spirit, the first agent of God's kingdom. Comparing the Matthean verse with the Enochic myth, one has to state that the role of the three spirits who in 1 En. 10:4–13 are instrumental in the elimination of the sons of heaven is a much more evident example of the exorcistic mission of the supernatural beings sent by God. On the other hand, by indicating the agency of God's Spirit in his exorcism, Jesus takes the place reserved in the Enochic myth to God, who uses the intermediary of his messengers in order to liberate the earth from the sinful and violent spirits.

stresses the authority of God over the sinful spirits. According to 1 En. 9:5, only God possesses all the authority; he also confers to Shemihazah the authority to rule over other angels (9:7).[95] The commissioning of the four angels (10:1–14) indicates the same authority exercised over the angels in removing the perpetrators of sin and violence. It is the God of Israel who through his agents imprisons the Watchers and destroys the demonic warriors in 1 En. 6–11. With his authority, Jesus achieves in his exorcisms what the supreme authority of God realized in the Enochic myth: the liberation of humanity from violent oppression by demonic forces.[96] While in the Synoptic Gospels the conflict goes on and is close to its final stage,[97] in the Enochic myth the spiritual forces are either destroyed (1 En. 10:9) or made inoperative until the time of judgment (1 En. 10:4–8, 11–13).[98]

According to Matt 12:28 (Luke 11:20), Jesus's exorcism is the kingdom of God in operation.[99] It is impossible not to compare this statement with 1 En. 10:21–11:2, where the result of the expulsion of the sinful spirits and demons is the conversion of all nations to God, divine blessing imparted upon humankind, together with the rule of truth and peace. While in the gospel the expulsion of demons is a sure sign of the presence of the kingdom of God, in the Enochic text the rule of truth and peace is projected

---

95. Note that the conferral of the authority to rule over the angels must have taken place before the sin with the women, for only the next verse (9:8) speaks about the fornication with the women.

96. It is worthwhile noting that in 1 En. 10:9 God orders Gabriel to destroy (imperative of ἀπόλλυμι) the demonic warriors. The exorcised unclean demon in the synagogue addresses Jesus with a question: "Have you come to destroy [infinitive of ἀπόλλυμι] us?" (Luke 4:34). Thus it is not difficult to notice that both the Enochic text and the Gospel of Luke speak about the destruction of the demonic forces. While in the Enochic text the angel Gabriel is sent by God to destroy the demonic warriors, the demon in the gospel unequivocally points to Jesus as the one who intends to destroy the unclean spirits.

97. In Luke 10:28 the effects of the mission of Jesus's disciples are summarized in terms of the fall of Satan. Their mission marks the victory over Satan's power or influence.

98. In 1 En. 10:11–13 first comes the binding of the Watchers and then the judgment. This twofold punishment is often cited as the background for the outcry of the demons in Matt 8:29 who state that Jesus came to torment them "before the time," which would mean before the final judgment; cf. Graham H. Twelftree, *Jesus the Exorcist: A Contribution to the Study of the Historical Jesus*, WUNT 2/54 (Tübingen: Mohr Siebeck, 1993), 223.

99. See ibid., 217–18.

into the future, but it too is the result of the elimination of the demonic world.

In Mark 1:27 those who witness Jesus's exorcism call it "a new teaching—with authority!"[100] Since Jesus teaches in the Capernaum synagogue as the one with authority (Mark 1:22), exegetes usually link the statement about the exorcism as "a new teaching" with Jesus's words of teaching in the synagogue. Thus his exorcism would serve as a sign confirming his teaching and would stem from the redactional work of Mark.[101] Since, however, 1 En. 9:11 suggests that knowledge is necessary for the elimination of the sinful Watchers and demons, the successful exorcism must be based on divinely revealed knowledge. Additionally, the relationship between 1 En. 8:3 and the knowledge of the āšipu indicates that the Jewish author was conscious of the vast amount of knowledge, not exclusively of exorcistic character, related with the practice of healing by the expulsion of the evil spirits. The exorcism in Mark 1:27, therefore, understood as a new teaching with authority, does not seem to serve as a sign confirming the truth of Jesus's words, but rather suggests the intrinsic connection between exorcism and transmission of knowledge keenly felt by Jesus's contemporaries. It seems therefore more probable to see the connection between teaching and exorcism in Mark 1:27 as stemming from the Palestinian tradition of the early church inherited by Mark.[102]

---

100. In Mark 1:27 different textual readings make it unclear whether "with authority" modifies Jesus's teaching or his exorcism. It is of little importance for the discussion here, however, for the Markan text unequivocally identifies Jesus's teaching with his exorcism.

101. See Twelftree, *Jesus the Exorcist*, 59 and n. 16.

102. According to Twelftree (ibid., 59), the Markan redaction of 1:27b–28 makes Mark responsible for associating Jesus the exorcist with Jesus the teacher, possibly after the pattern of the wandering Cynics and rabbis. Such a connection would be suggested by the mention of the synagogue in Mark's tradition. The relationship between knowledge and exorcism in 1 En. 6–11 makes such a supposition unnecessary. Some exegetes (e.g., Rudolf Pesch, "Ein Tag vollmächtigen Wirkens Jesu in Kapharnaum (Mk 1,21–34.35–39)," *BibLeb* 9 [1968]: 114–28, esp. 127) identify (!) the exorcism as a teaching.

Table 1. Thematic Kernel of 1 Enoch 6–11 in Relation to the Marduk-Ea
Literary Pattern

	Marduk-Ea Literary Pattern	1 Enoch 6–11
I/1	General description of demonic activity; cosmic origin of the exorcised evil	6:1–2; 7:1a–b; 7:2–5
I/2	Attack of demons on a man; description of the symptoms	Omitted
II/1	Marduk notices the problem and speaks with Ea	9:1–2, 4–5, 8a–c, 11
II/2	Ea praises Marduk's wisdom	Omitted
III	Ea's instruction how to remove the evil	10:9
III	Expected positive results	10:21–11:2
IV	Concluding sentence (expected positive results)	Omitted

Table 2. The Comparison of 1 Enoch 6–11 with the Literary Pattern of
the Marduk-Ea Incantation

Marduk-Ea Literary Pattern		1 Enoch 6–11	
I/1. Introduction—present tense verbal forms	General description of the demonic activity; cosmic birth of the exorcised evil	Birth of demons; demonic attack on humanity, animals, and nature	6:1–2; 7:1a–b; 7:2–5
	———————	Sinful character of the sexual union, oath, descent, list of names, pollution, teaching, accusation	6:3–8; 7:1c–e; 8:1–3; 7:6+8:4

I/2. Introduction— preterite verbal forms	Attack on a man and description of the symptoms	Omitted	
II. Marduk-Ea dialogue	Marduk sees the demonic attack	The angels see the demonic attack	9:1
	He enters the house (= the temple)	They enter (the house = the sanctuary)	9:2
	———————	The angelic report about the accusation of dying humanity	9:3, 10
	My father!	Praise of God	9:4–5
	Marduk reports to Ea (repetition of I/1 and I/2)	Angelic report to God (repetition of 8:1; 6:1–2; 7:1a-c; 7:2; 7:1d-e; 8:3)	9:6–9
	Marduk: "I do not know what to do"	Angels: "You know everything, but do not tell us what to do"	9:11
	Ea equates his knowledge with that of Marduk	Omitted	
	Narration	Narration	10:1
	Commissioning formula, "Go, my son, Marduk"	Commissioning formula, "Go, Sariel..., Raphael..., Gabriel..., Michael"	10:2, 4, 9, 11
	———————	Message to Noah	10:2–3
III. Ritual instruction	Ea's speech: Healing ritual	God's speech: Healing and elimination procedures (verbs in imperative and imperfect)	10:4–8, 9–10, 11–14
	———————	God's speech: instruction (verbs in imperative)	10:15–16, 20

		God's speech: bless-ing of humanity and nature (verbs in imperfect)	10:17–19
	Ea's speech: Expected positive results: purification of the patient, protection of the personal god (verbs in precative)	God's speech: Future positive results: purification of the earth, conversion, and blessing (verbs in imperfect)	10:21–11:2
IV. Conclusion	Ea's speech: Demons or illness should leave the man (verbs in precative)	Omitted	

Enoch, Jesus, and Priestly Tradition

Joseph L. Angel

The study of divine agents and ideal mediating figures in early Jewish literature has played a fundamental role in the clarification of the rich world of
conceptual resources available to the earliest articulators of the status and
significance of Jesus.[1] Jewish traditions about the figure Enoch in particular have long been recognized as providing a close analogue to the Christ
of the New Testament. As Philip G. Davis observes:

> Each of these individuals is presented as a decisive revealer, making
> known to humanity all the requirements of righteousness and the
> coming eschatological events; each is said to have been removed from
> the world in miraculous freedom from death; each is taken to be in a
> position to intercede actively with God; and each is to have a decisive
> influence on the last day.[2]

While direct influence has proven difficult to demonstrate, such striking points of contact suggest that the traditions surrounding the figure of
Enoch could have provided early Christians with a significant model for
interpreting the person and work of Jesus Christ.

In the present study, I would like to focus on a neglected aspect of
comparison between the figures of Enoch and Jesus, namely, the portrayal of each personage as fulfilling an exalted priestly role. In step with
the topic of our meeting, the discussion will concentrate upon the Syn-

---

1. See, e.g., the recent survey of Larry W. Hurtado, "Monotheism, Principal
Angels, and the Background of Christology," in *The Oxford Handbook of the Dead
Sea Scrolls*, ed. Timothy H. Lim and John J. Collins (Oxford: Oxford University Press,
2010), 546–64.

2. Philip G. Davis, "Divine Agents, Mediators, and New Testament Christology,"
JTS 45 (1994): 495–96.

optic and Enochic (and closely related) traditions and the relationships between them. As will soon become clear, I am concerned not simply with the figure Enoch in relation to Jesus, but also with the trajectories implied by the applications and transformations of traditions associated with Enoch to separate ideal figures, especially some of those depicted in the Qumran corpus. The objective is not so much to pursue the question of direct influence but rather to spotlight some trajectories emanating from the centrality of priestly tradition and symbolism in Enochic writings and Second Temple period Judaism more broadly. In particular, I contend that such an approach may lead to a fuller awareness of the generally underappreciated Jewish priestly background underlying certain passages in the Synoptic Gospels.

The paper will proceed in three parts. I begin with a brief discussion of some of the assumptions behind my use of the term "priestly." I then offer some preliminary remarks about how traditions regarding priests and priesthood have played into the construction of the composite figures Enoch and Jesus within Enochic and Synoptic tradition, respectively. Finally, I turn to the Jewish background of some of the seemingly priestly qualities attributed to Jesus within Synoptic tradition. In particular, I am concerned with two sacerdotal functions: atoning for and forgiving/ removing sin, and teaching torah/divine wisdom. In connection with the latter, I shall present a brief analysis of the enigmatic logion of Matt 11:25–30 in light of some texts closely related to the early Enochic stream of tradition. While the Matthean passage is often viewed as espousing a "Wisdom Christology," at home within the realm of contemporary Jewish wisdom traditions, my discussion will proceed through the lens of the priestly matters discussed in the initial sections.

What Is "Priestly"?

Since neither of the bodies of tradition with which we are concerned openly names Enoch or Jesus a priest, it will be worthwhile to begin by discussing what is meant by the term "priestly." Presently, I wish to emphasize three points. First, as is well known, historical developments in the Second Temple period engendered an unprecedented rise in the power and prestige of the Jerusalem priesthood. In step with this development, we encounter a variety of contemporary texts reflecting a range of fervent opinions regarding the proper behavior and role of priests in society. Whether from a standpoint that is critical or approving of the status quo, these compositions craft ideal patterns of priestly conduct and exemplary priestly figures. In doing so, they often expand the traditional scriptural portrait of the priest, which includes mostly cultic, but also judicial, instructional, and other responsibilities, and attribute to him the key social roles of external figures (such as king, sage, or scribe)—a literary phenomenon that may be referred to as "priestly magnetism."[3] The high priest is indeed depicted variously as a paragon of wisdom, holiness, and virtue, and as chief expositor of the law and executor of justice.[4] Moreover, his authority to govern is often deemed as a given and as scripturally authorized,[5] and the notion of an ideal eschatological polity headed by a messianic high priest takes root.

Second, there is widespread evidence that the notion of priestly identity was not strictly limited to those of Aaronite or Zadokite descent in Second Temple Judaism.[6] For groups such as the Pharisees, the Essenes, the Qumran community, and the Jesus movement, the appropriation of priestly boundaries and/or behavior served as a platform for claims to special covenantal status before God. Each of these groups can be described as priestly in the sense that they assumed a metaphoric priestly identity, employing the symbols of the priesthood/temple in order to make available the essentially priestly experience of the divine presence beyond the temple building.[7] The willingness to envision the sacerdotal role as independent of Aaronite or Zadokite lineage in this period is further demon-

---

3. See Michael E. Stone, "Ideal Figures and Social Context: Priest and Sage in the Early Second Temple Age," in *Ancient Israelite Religion: Essays in Honor of Frank Moore Cross,* ed. Patrick D. Miller Jr., Paul D. Hanson, and S. Dean McBride (Philadelphia: Fortress, 1987), 582. He defines the literary phenomenon of magnetism generally as "the tendency of certain ideal figures to attract broad and significant characteristics."

4. See, e.g., Sir 45:6–22; 50:1–21; Aramaic Levi Document; Jub. 31; 1QSb IV; Hecataeus Ab. apud Diodorus, *Bibliotheca Historica* 40.3; Let. Aris. 96–99; Josephus, *Ag. Ap.* 2.185–187.

5. See, e.g., LXX Exod 19:6 with Arie van der Kooij, "The Greek Bible and Jewish Concepts of Royal Priesthood and Priestly Monarchy," in *Jewish Perspectives on Hellenistic Rulers,* ed. Tessa Rajak et al. (Berkeley: University of California Press, 2007), 255–64.

6. See Martha Himmelfarb, *A Kingdom of Priests: Ancestry and Merit in Ancient Judaism* (Philadelphia: University of Pennsylvania Press, 2006).

7. See, e.g., Martha Himmelfarb, "'A Kingdom of Priests': The Democratization of the Priesthood in the Literature of Second Temple Judaism," *Journal of Jewish Thought and Philosophy* 6 (1997): 89–104; and, more thoroughly, Himmelfarb, *Kingdom of Priests.*

strated by the heightened speculation regarding heavenly and primordial priesthoods that emerges in contemporary texts (Songs of the Sabbath Sacrifice, Jubilees, 11QMelch, etc.).

My third and final point concerns the practical method by which we might identify texts that do not explicitly refer to priests as containing "priestly" content. For this particular issue it will be helpful to make use of the linguistic term *scenario*, which has been utilized recently in a study by Wally Cirafesi dedicated to the identification of priestly qualities of Jesus in the Fourth Gospel, as well as by Cynthia Westfall in her study of messianic themes in Hebrews and the General Epistles.[8] According to Westfall, scenario denotes:

> "An extended domain of reference," or associated bundles of information that lie behind a text. A scenario includes setting, situations, specific items, and "role" slots. For example, a restaurant scenario includes a waiter, customers, cooks/chefs, menus, food, tables, and chairs. Mentioning the scenario "restaurant" will activate roles and items in a restaurant, and mentioning a partial description of the items or roles in a restaurant, such as a waiter taking an order, will activate a restaurant scenario.[9]

Cirafesi notes further that "scenarios imply a certain level of shared information between the author and his or her recipients. Thus, when an author recounts an individual engaging in certain actions that are commonly known of, say, priests (e.g., torah teaching or the offering of sacrifices), one may rightly label the scenario 'priestly.'"[10] To this I would add the application of scriptural language or symbols that would have been recognized widely as associated with priests or priesthood (ציץ, קדש, הקדשים, etc.). Furthermore, given the expanded roles and definition of priesthood during the Second Temple period, a text need not refer to tra-

---

8. Wally V. Cirafesi, "The Priestly Portrait of Jesus in the Gospel of John in the Light of 1QS, 1QSa and 1QSb," *JGRChJ* 8 (2011–2012): 83–105; Cynthia Long Westfall, "Messianic Themes of Temple, Enthronement, and Victory in Hebrews and the General Epistles," in *The Messiah in the Old and New Testaments,* ed. Stanley E. Porter, MNTS (Grand Rapids: Eerdmans, 2007), 210–29.

9. Westfall, "Messianic Themes," 212–13. The phrase "extended domain of reference" derives from Anthony J. Sanford and Simon C. Garrod, *Understanding Written Language* (Chichester: Wiley, 1981), 110.

10. Cirafesi, "Priestly Portrait of Jesus," 86.

ditional scriptural functions of priests (such as torah instruction or sacrifice) to be considered as espousing a priestly scenario.

For my present purpose, it is important to note that while modern scholars may indeed be adept at identifying priestly scenarios in early Jewish and Christian literature, the intentions of ancient authors in creating such constructs are not always clear and certainly not uniform. So, for example, it is possible for an author to set forth a priestly scenario in order to intentionally attribute priestly identity to a figure or make a larger point centered on priesthood. This appears to be the case in the Book of the Watchers and its implicit portrayal of Enoch as a priest. However, it is also possible for an author to construct a priestly scenario without such a directly related purpose. This, I shall argue, is the case in some Synoptic portrayals of Jesus, where the appearance of priestly elements probably does not stem from an intention to portray Jesus as a priest, but rather to enhance the portrait of the ideal Messiah and Son of God.

THE PRIESTLY CREDENTIALS OF ENOCH AND JESUS

Enoch

Both Enoch and Jesus represent complex and multifaceted ideal figures of the Second Temple period. Given the central significance of the temple and its priesthood in that era, it is no surprise that both tradents of Enochic lore and early Christian authors at times found it suitable to depict their respective heroes in priestly terms. In the case of Enochic tradition, priestly identity is a recurring motif that displays remarkable longevity. As Philip Alexander notes, "Enoch in *Jubilees* in the second century B.C.E. is a high priest. Almost a thousand years later he retains that role in the Heikhalot texts, though in a rather different setting."[11] He presumably marks Jubilees as the starting point of the Enoch-as-high-priest tradition since this work makes explicit mention of the patriarch's cultic function in Eden.[12] It is commonly recognized, however, that the earlier Book of

---

11. Philip S. Alexander, "From Son of Adam to Second God: Transformations of the Biblical Enoch," in *Biblical Figures outside the Bible*, ed. Michael E. Stone and Theodore A. Bergren (Harrisburg, PA: Trinity Press International, 1998), 107.

12. According to Jub. 4:25, Enoch "burned the evening incense of the sanctuary which is acceptable before the Lord on the mountain" (trans. James C. VanderKam, *The Book of Jubilees*, CSCO 511, Scriptores Aethiopici 88 [Leuven: Peeters, 1989], 28).

the Watchers presents a scenario that already indicates Enoch's priestly identity.[13] Since this topic has been treated at length elsewhere, I will limit myself here to a brief summary of some of the key arguments put forward in previous scholarship.

One indication of a priestly scenario pertains to Enoch's physical location. The Book of the Watchers conceives of the heavenly realm as the "eternal sanctuary" and the angels as priestly ministrants.[14] In Enoch's ascent to heaven (1 En. 14), the upper realm is described in terms that relate rather precisely to the three major architectural sections of the earthly temple.[15] That Enoch is permitted access to the celestial holy of holies, where he beholds the "Great Glory" sitting upon a throne, while the angel-priests are denied this privilege (14:20–15:1), perhaps points to the patriarch's high priestly status.[16] Another indication pertains to some of the functions attributed to Enoch. While it has been noticed that Enoch fulfills a number of seemingly distinct roles in early Enochic literature (sage, scribe, eschatological witness, priest, etc.), Andrei Orlov rightly notes that "some roles of the patriarch have a composite nature, often encompassing several functions that can be linked to his other roles.... it is sometimes very difficult to delineate strictly their boundaries, as some of their functions can be interchangeable."[17] In line with this observation, several scholars have pointed out that while Enoch is explicitly called "scribe" but never priest in Book of the Watchers, the background of the scribal function and title

---

This would comport with Aaron's role in Exod 30:7–8. See also Jub. 21:10, which refers to "the words of Enoch" in Abraham's instructions to Isaac regarding matters of sacrificial cult. Cf. James C. VanderKam, *Enoch: A Man for All Generations* (Columbia: University of South Carolina Press, 1995), 117, who describes the priestly duties of Enoch here as a new element in "Enoch's expanding portfolio." See also the comments of Michael E. Stone, *Ancient Judaism: New Visions and Views* (Grand Rapids: Eerdmans, 2011), 44.

13. See e.g., the survey of Andrei Orlov, *The Enoch-Metatron Tradition*, TSAJ 107 (Tübingen: Mohr Siebeck, 2005), 70–76, which notes the positions of David Suter, George W. E. Nickelsburg, Martha Himmelfarb, David Halperin, Crispin Fletcher-Louis, and several other scholars.

14. See, e.g., George W. E. Nickelsburg, *1 Enoch 1: A Commentary on the Book of 1 Enoch, Chapters 1–36; 81–108*, Hermeneia (Minneapolis: Fortress, 2001), 207–11.

15. See Martha Himmelfarb, *Ascent to Heaven in Jewish and Christian Apocalypses* (New York: Oxford University Press, 1993), 14.

16. See, e.g., David Halperin, *The Faces of the Chariot: Early Responses to Ezekiel's Vision*, TSAJ 16 (Tübingen: Mohr Siebeck, 1988), 81–82.

17. Orlov, *Enoch-Metatron Tradition*, 40–41.

in this period is primarily priestly and thus not to be disentangled from his standing as priest.[18] Moreover, his role as intercessor for the Watchers is most naturally understood as a priestly function.[19] Finally, it is often noted that a priestly scenario in the Book of the Watchers is suggested by the many parallels with the story of the priest-scribe Ezra, who also deals with the marriage of a class of holy individuals to a group of women forbidden to them, and the resulting defilement.[20] While some have seen the critique of the angel-priests in the Book of the Watchers as a veiled indictment of the Zadokite establishment, others have argued that the Book of the Watchers' criticisms would have been at home within the Jerusalem temple milieu.[21]

Whatever the social setting behind the Book of the Watchers, this work's portrayal of Enoch as priest-scribe who ascended to the innermost chamber of the heavenly temple continued to impact later speculation about the patriarch, which reflects something of a coherent evolution of tradition. Thus, for example, whereas 1 En. 14 places Enoch before the throne of the Great Glory, in the Parables of Enoch he is himself given a throne of glory (e.g., 1 En. 45:3; 62:5; 69:27–29). The patriarch's priestly status is further developed, of course, not only in Jubilees but also in 2 Enoch (see esp. 22:8–10) and the much later 3 Enoch (see, e.g., 3 En. 15B).

Even more significant for my present purpose is that the image of Enoch in the Book of the Watchers did not simply inspire more speculation about the figure Enoch alone. Evidence suggests that certain authors of the Second Temple period appropriated various motifs and mythemes (including the specifically sacerdotal interests) associated with Enoch in the literary construction of separate ideal figures. A clear example is provided by the Aramaic Levi Document, whose portrait of the ancient hero Levi as ascending to the heavenly temple in a dream vision in order to be

---

18. See, e.g., Helge S. Kvanvig, *Roots of Apocalyptic: The Mesopotamian Background of the Enoch Figure and the Son of Man,* WMANT 61 (Neukirchen-Vluyn: Neukirchener Verlag, 1988), 99–103; Himmelfarb, *Ascent,* 23–25; and the unpublished paper of Steven D. Fraade, "'They Shall Teach Your Statutes to Jacob': Priest, Scribe, and Sage in Second Temple Times." I thank Professor Fraade for sharing his work with me.

19. Cf., e.g., Exod 28:29; Heb 7:25; Philo, *Spec. Laws* 1.116.

20. For further parallels, see George W. E. Nickelsburg, "Enoch, Levi, and Peter: Recipients of Revelation in Upper Galilee," *JBL* 100 (1981): 585.

21. See, e.g., the collection of articles on Enochians and Zadokites in *Hen* 24 (2002).

commissioned by God as high priest is modeled upon the image of Enoch in 1 En. 12–16.[22] A closely related Qumran Aramaic text (4Q541) and its depiction of a universal eschatological priestly savior will be important for the discussion below. An example of a different nature is provided by the Qumran Hodayot. In recent years, scholars have increasingly appreciated the special influence that traditions about Enoch have had on this sectarian liturgical collection. Following a line of thought initiated by George Nickelsburg, Angela Kim Harkins recently demonstrated how the so-called Teacher Hymns (1QH[a] XII–XVI) appropriate an impressive accumulation of allusions to traditions from the Book of the Watchers in order to construct the voice of the speaker, an extraordinary individual with access to divine knowledge.[23] Reminiscent of Enoch, this figure has been lifted up by God to an eternal height so that he might "walk to and fro" (ואתהלכה; cf. Gen 5:22, 24) on a limitless plain, and take up a "position" (מעמד),[24] presumably in the heavenly sanctuary, "with the host of the holy ones," and commune with the "children of heaven" (1QH[a] XI 21–23).[25] Another study by Eric Miller has highlighted intriguing parallels between

---

22. See Nickelsburg's comments, which are largely based on the evidence of T. Levi 2–7 ("Enoch, Levi, and Peter," 588–90). J. T. Milik (*The Books of Enoch: Aramaic Fragments of Qumrân Cave 4* [Oxford: Clarendon, 1976], 23–24) plausibly suggests that 4QLevi[a] ar (4Q213 frags. 3–4) displays knowledge of the Book of the Watchers.

23. See Angela Kim Harkins, "Reading the Qumran Hodayot in Light of the Traditions Associated with Enoch," *Hen* 32 (2010): 359–400; Harkins, *Reading with an "I" to the Heavens: Looking at the Qumran Hodayot through the Lens of Visionary Traditions,* Ekstasis (Berlin: de Gruyter, 2012). Nickelsburg's article is "The Qumranic Transformation of a Cosmological and Eschatological Tradition (1QH 4:29–40)," in *The Madrid Qumran Congress: Proceedings of the International Congress on the Dead Sea Scrolls, Madrid 18–21 March, 1991,* ed. Julio C. Trebolle Barrera and Luis Vegas Montaner, 2 vols., STDJ 11 (Leiden: Brill, 1992), 2:649–59.

24. Cf. 1 En. 12:4, where the word στάσις probably translates a term equivalent ot מעמד in the sense of "priestly course." See Nickelsburg, *1 Enoch 1,* 271.

25. On the resonance of this passage with cultic language applied to the Levites in 1 Chr 23:28 and 2 Chr 35:15, see Esther G. Chazon, "Human and Angelic Prayer in Light of the Dead Sea Scrolls," in *Liturgical Perspectives: Prayer and Poetry in Light of the Dead Sea Scrolls: Proceedings of the Fifth International Symposium of the Orion Center for the Study of the Dead Sea Scrolls and Associated Literature, 19–23 January, 2000,* ed. Esther G. Chazon, STDJ 48 (Leiden: Brill, 2003), 35–47, esp. 43–44. Throughout this study, translations as well as column and line numbers of 1QH[a] follow Hartmut Stegemann, Eileen Schuller, and Carol Newsom, *1QHodayot[a] with Incorporation of 1QHodayot[b] and 4QHodayot[a–f],* DJD 40 (Oxford: Clarendon, 2009).

the figure Enoch and the mysterious speaker of the so-called Self-Glorification Hymn, who is most often understood by scholars as some sort of priestly figure (see below).[26] Noting the unique nature of this figure's claims—his outranking of the angels, his exaltation vis-à-vis enthronement, and his incomparable wisdom and judgment—Eric Miller finds the closest analogue to be the Son of Man of the Parables, and even suggests that the speaker is to be identified as Enoch himself. I shall return to this text as well as to the Teacher Hymns in more detail below, for in this study I am concerned not only with the figure Enoch himself but also with the trajectories implied by the applications and transformations of traditions associated with Enoch to separate ideal figures.

Jesus

Unsurprisingly, scholarly attention to priestly Christology within the New Testament canon has been directed to Hebrews, and, to a lesser degree, the Gospel of John.[27] With regard to the Synoptic tradition, however, little has been said. Indeed, an influential trend in scholarship views the presentation of Jesus in the Synoptics as entirely divorced from a priestly background. For example, in his investigation of messianic models available to Jesus in the first century, James D. G. Dunn observes that "we can dismiss at once … the priest Messiah. There is no indication whatsoever that this was ever canvassed as a possibility or seen as an option in the case of Jesus."[28] Jürgen Becker remarks that no scholar has "ever been able to dem-

---

26. Eric Miller, "The Self-Glorification Hymn Reexamined," *Hen* 31 (2009): 307–24.

27. Several studies over the past few decades have treated the priestly themes and Christology of John. See, e.g., Cirafesi, "Priestly Portrait of Jesus"; John Paul Heil, "Jesus as the Unique High Priest in the Gospel of John," *CBQ* 57 (1995): 729–45; Helen K. Bond, "Discarding the Seamless Robe: The High Priesthood of Jesus in John's Gospel," in *Israel's God and Rebecca's Children: Christology and Community in Early Judaism and Christianity: Essays in Honor of Larry W. Hurtado and Alan F. Segal,* ed. David B. Capes et al. (Waco, TX: Baylor University Press, 2007), 183–94. For an earlier study, see Ceslas Spicq, "L'origine johannique de la conception du Christ–prêtre dans l'Épître aux Hébreux," in *Aux sources de la tradition chrétienne: Mélanges offerts à M. Maurice Goguel,* ed. Oscar Cullmann and P. H. Menoud (Neuchâtel: Delachaux & Niestle, 1950), 258–69. The literature on Hebrews is, of course, too voluminous to note.

28. James D. G. Dunn, "Messianic Ideas and Their Influence on the Jesus of History," in *The Messiah: Developments in Earliest Judaism and Christianity,* ed. James H.

onstrate a relationship between Jesus and Israel's priesthood. If anything is incontrovertible from the Jesus material, it is that there is not the slightest connection between Jesus and the theological self-understanding of the Jerusalem priesthood."[29] Presumably at least a couple of core assumptions have determined such stark proclamations: (1) Jesus's seemingly negative attitude toward the Jerusalem temple and its cult would appear to speak against a priestly self-understanding. (2) Since by all accounts Jesus was not a Levite, it is assumed that he could not have thought of himself or been thought of by others as a priest.[30] However, each of these assumptions may be challenged in the light of known conceptions and applications of priestly identity within Jesus's Jewish context.

First, if it is granted that Jesus was critical of the current Jerusalem temple establishment, this does not mean that he rejected the institution in principle. The Dead Sea Scrolls, for example, attest that Jews of this era could simultaneously reject the current temple establishment and adopt priestly categories as an expression of the apex of spiritual achievement (1QS VIII–IX; 4Q174; 4Q511 frag. 35, etc.) as well as the culmination of eschatological hopes (1QM II; 11QMelch; 11QT[a] XXIX 9; New Jerusalem; cf. Revelation). Indeed, as Bruce Chilton and others have argued, Jesus's conflict with the temple establishment is better understood in terms of disagreement about certain core principles of the cult than outright rejection.[31]

Second, while Jesus's non-Levitical descent possibly constituted a reason for the avoidance of an overt portrayal as messianic high priest in the Synoptics, it should not be thought to preclude the possibility that he has "absorbed" eschatological priestly functions.[32] One thinks immediately

---

Charlesworth (Minneapolis: Fortress, 1992), 373; Cf. Dunn, *Jesus Remembered: Christianity in the Making* (Grand Rapids: Eerdmans, 2003), 654.

29. Jürgen Becker, *Jesus of Nazareth* (Berlin: de Gruyter, 1998), 215.

30. Crispin Fletcher-Louis ("Jesus as the High Priestly Messiah: Part 1," *JSHJ* 4 [2006]: 156) identifies an additional factor: "a deeply felt antipathy to anything that smacks of a high church spirituality" in certain strands of modern scholarly tradition.

31. See, e.g., Bruce Chilton, *The Temple of Jesus: His Sacrificial Program within a Cultural History of Sacrifice* (University Park: Pennsylvania State University Press, 1992).

32. If the Messiah of Aaron and Israel of the Damascus Document (CD XII 23; XIV 19; XIX 19; cf. XX 1) is understood as a single figure, then there is precedent for such a combination. Cf. the association of Davidic qualities or themes with priestly figures in Sir 50:1–4, 21; 45:12, 15; Aramaic Levi Document 66–67; 1 Macc 14:4–15; etc. On the Messiah of Aaron and Israel as a single figure, see, e.g., Géza G. Xeravits,

of the author of Hebrews, who, noting Jesus's non-Levitical roots, aligns his priesthood with that of Melchizedek. There are, indeed, good indications that the understanding of Jesus as messianic high priest preceded and developed independently of Hebrews.[33] Harold Attridge observes that the two major roles of the celestial high priestly Jesus, intercession and self-sacrifice, are widely attributed to Jesus in early Christian literature, including some passages in the Synoptics (e.g., Matt 10:32; Mark 10:45). He thus raises the possibility that the author of Hebrews "was inspired by one or both of these priestly *functions* traditionally ascribed to Christ, to apply the *title* High Priest to Jesus."[34] Further, some scholars would argue that an exalted high priestly self-consciousness can be traced back to Jesus himself. They see evidence for this in the Synoptic tradition, when, after being asked by the acting high priest about his messianic status, Jesus explicitly appeals to Ps 110: "I am; and 'you will see the Son of Man seated at the right hand of the Power,' and 'coming with the clouds of heaven'" (Mark 14:62; cf. 12:35 parr.). Within this context, Jesus's scriptural citation may be viewed as self-referential and is perhaps meant to clarify his belief that he (*not* Caiaphas) is the true messianic priest and king of Israel.[35]

King, Priest, Prophet: Positive Eschatological Protagonists in the Qumran Library, STDJ 47 (Leiden: Brill, 2003), 221–25. To be sure, the grammar of the phrase may also be read as referring to two figures. This was noted already in 1922 by Louis Ginzberg, *An Unknown Jewish Sect* (New York: Jewish Theological Seminary, 1976), esp. 227–28. See also, e.g., James C. VanderKam, "Messianism in the Scrolls," in *The Community of the Renewed Covenant: The Notre Dame Symposium on the Dead Sea Scrolls,* ed. Eugene Ulrich and James C. VanderKam, Christianity and Judaism in Antiquity 10 (Notre Dame, IN: University of Notre Dame Press, 1993), 211–34, esp. 230.

33. See Daniel Stökl, "Yom Kippur in the Apocalyptic *imaginaire* and the Roots of Jesus' High Priesthood," in *Transformations of the Inner Self in Ancient Religions,* ed. Jan Assmann and Guy G. Stroumsa, SHR 83 (Leiden: Brill, 1999), 349–66, esp. 362. The preexistence of the notion is implied by certain texts of the early second century (e.g., Ignatius, *Phld.* 9:1; Polycarp, *Phil.* 12:2; Mart. Pol. 14:3) that refer to Jesus as high priest independently of Hebrews. Moreover, the sudden introduction of the concept in Heb 2:17 has been seen as an indication that the idea was familiar and needed no explanation.

34. Harold W. Attridge, *The Epistle to the Hebrews: A Commentary on the Epistle to the Hebrews,* Hermeneia (Philadelphia: Fortress, 1989), 102. To be sure, he rejects this option in favor of roots in Jewish notions of angelic priesthood. Cf. the conclusions of Eric F. Mason, *"You Are a Priest Forever": Second Temple Jewish Messianism and the Priestly Christology of the Epistle to the Hebrews,* STDJ 74 (Leiden: Brill, 2008).

35. So Oscar Cullmann, *The Christology of the New Testament,* trans. Shirley C.

Whether one accepts this interpretation of Jesus's words or not, when one approaches the Synoptic tradition with a more accurate view of the fluid appropriation of priestly symbolism within late Second Temple Palestine, it becomes possible to recognize how certain depictions of Jesus in the gospels relate to early Jewish traditions about the messianic or otherwise exalted priest. Cases for a priestly self-awareness of Jesus have been made in the extensive scholarship of Margaret Barker and Crispin Fletcher-Louis, both of whom take into account some possible interactions with Enochic tradition.[36] In what follows, I will not attempt an exhaustive review of this evidence, nor do I wish to address the question of whether the historical Jesus thought of himself as an eschatological sacerdotalist. Rather, I will focus instead on some of the most convincing evidence to suggest that the Synoptic authors were influenced, whether indirectly or directly, by priestly material from Enochic and closely related tradition in their multifaceted depiction of Jesus. In particular, I am interested in the Jewish background of the power of Jesus to atone for and forgive sins, and his role as revealer and teacher of the divine will.

THE JEWISH BACKGROUND OF JESUS'S PRIESTLY FUNCTIONS

Atonement and Removal/Forgiveness of Sin

The association of the Israelite priesthood with the power to atone for sin is well known from the Hebrew Bible (e.g., Lev 16). Other scriptural passages appear to associate the priesthood with removal/forgiveness of sin as well. Thus, in Exod 28:36–38, it is charged that Aaron should wear the frontlet so that he "may take away [נשא] any sin [עון] arising from the holy things." And in Lev 10:17 we are told that Aaron's sons are given

---

Guthrie and Charles A. M. Hall, rev. ed., NTL (Philadelphia: Westminster, 1963), 87–89; Margaret Barker, *The Risen Lord: The Jesus of History as the Christ of Faith* (Edinburgh: T&T Clark, 1996); Fletcher-Louis, "Jesus: Part 1," 173–74.

36. See, e.g., Barker, *Risen Lord*; Fletcher-Louis, "Jesus: Part 1"; Fletcher-Louis, "Jesus as the High Priestly Messiah: Part 2," *JSHJ* 5 (2007): 57–79. Cf. Fletcher-Louis, "The Revelation of the Sacral Son of Man: The Genre, History of Religions Context and the Meaning of the Transfiguration," in *Auferstehung—Resurrection: The Fourth Durham-Tübingen Symposium: Resurrection, Exaltation, and Transformation in Old Testament, Ancient Judaism, and Early Christianity*, ed. Friedrich Avemarie and Hermann Lichtenberger, WUNT 135 (Tübingen: Mohr Siebeck, 2001), 247–98.

the sin offering in order to "remove the sin of the congregation" (לשאת את עון העדה).[37]

More relevant for the Synoptic image of Jesus are the numerous Second Temple period texts that ascribe these important sacerdotal functions on a cosmic scale to exalted and/or eschatological priestly figures. In 1 En. 10, for example, the angel Michael likely serves as high priest when he is ordered to "cleanse the earth … from all impurities" so that "all the sons of men will become righteous."[38] The Book of the Watchers does not portray Enoch as specifically atoning, but he intercedes on behalf of the Watchers so "that they might have forgiveness" for their sins (1 En. 13:4–7). In the light of scriptural associations (e.g., Exod 30:7–10; Num 16:46–48), Enoch's offering of "the incense of the sanctuary" in Jub. 4 may imply that the patriarch is envisaged as performing an ongoing role of intercession and atonement. In a striking passage in 2 En. 64, the patriarch, who has been invested as high priest in chapter 18, is located at the site of the eschatological temple (Akhuzan), and described as "the one who carried away the sins of humankind."

It is worth mentioning a few other ideal priestly figures who assume similar functions in the Qumran corpus. In CD XIV 19 the phrase [מש]יח אהרן וישראל is followed by the words עונם יכפר. Whether the verb is taken as active or passive (and whether the phrase refers to one or two messiahs),[39] the appearance of the priestly messiah accords with atonement for sin. According to the War Scroll (1QM II 1–5), the eschatological priest will preside over the reconstituted temple cult, the ultimate object of which is atonement (לכפר בעד כול עדתו). The heavenly Melchizedek, reminiscent of Michael, brings about release "from the debt of all their iniquities" and "atones on behalf of the sons of]light[" on the eschatological Yom Kippur (11Q13 II 6–8). We might also mention the atoning function of the Qumran community in its capacity as a "temple of men" (1QS VIII 6, 10; IX 4).

---

37. The significance of these passages for understanding Jesus has been underscored by Margaret Barker, *The Revelation of Jesus Christ* (Edinburgh: T&T Clark, 2000), 46. She is followed by Fletcher-Louis, "Jesus: Part 2," 73, who notes that despite the ambiguity of these passages in their original historical and literary context, they still "offer clear precedent for Jesus' words in Mk 2:10."

38. So Nickelsburg, *1 Enoch 1*, 227–28.

39. See Joseph Angel, *Otherworldly and Eschatological Priesthood in the Dead Sea Scrolls*, STDJ 86 (Leiden: Brill, 2010), 195–96; and n. 32 above.

Of still more immediate interest for the illumination of Jesus's atoning function in the Synoptics are a group of Qumran texts that apply terminology and themes associated with the servant of Deutero-Isaiah to
eschatological or exalted priestly figures. The most significant of these
is 4QApocryphon of Levi^b? (4Q541), an Aramaic manuscript dating to
about 100 BCE[40] that preserves a composition closely related to the complex of Aramaic traditions about Levi and his descendants so popular at
Qumran that have been shown to be closely related to Enochic tradition.[41]
The manuscript consists of twenty-four fragments, two of which (frags. 9
and 24) preserve complete or nearly complete lines. Fragment 9 provides a
clear reference to a universal eschatological savior:

> (2) [And he will transmit to them] his [wi]sdom. And he will atone for all
> the children of his generation [ויכפר על כול בני דרה]; and he will be sent
> to all the children (3) of his [peop]le [עמ[ה] וישתלח לכול בני]. His word
> is like a word of the heavens, and his teaching is like the will of God. His
> eternal sun will shine; (4) and fire will burn in all the ends of the earth.
> And on the darkness it will shine; then the darkness will disappear (5)
> [fr]om the earth and the cloud from the dry land. They will speak many
> words against him, and a number of (6) [lie]s. And they will invent fables
> against him, and they will speak all manner of infamies against him. Evil
> will overturn his generation. (7) [...] will be; and because falsehood and
> violence will be its setting, and the people will go astray in his days; and
> they will be confounded.[42]

On the basis of striking parallels with the Testament of Levi (esp.
ch. 18), the setting of eschatological struggle, and especially the atoning
function mentioned in line 2, scholars agree that this text describes a
messianic priest.[43] I shall address this figure's role as revealer/teacher of

---

40. For the official edition of 4Q541 and its dating, see Émile Puech, *Qumran
Grotte 4.XXII: Textes araméens, première partie: 4Q529–549*, DJD 31 (Oxford: Clarendon, 2001), 213–56.

41. See Michael E. Stone, "Enoch, Aramaic Levi, and Sectarian Origins," *JSJ* 19
(1988): 159–70. Cf. Henryk. Drawnel, "Priestly Education in the *Aramaic Levi Document* (Visions of Levi) and *Aramaic Astronomical Book* (4Q208–211)," *RevQ* 88 (2006):
547–74.

42. This translation is an adaptation of that offered by George J. Brooke, "The
Apocryphon of Levi^d? and the Messianic Servant High Priest," in *The Dead Sea Scrolls
and the New Testament* (Minneapolis: Fortress, 2005), 144.

43. See Émile Puech, "Fragments d'un apocryphe de Lévi et le personage escha-

divine wisdom below. Presently, two points about how he is portrayed are of interest. First, from the above fragment as well as others (esp. frag. 24, which includes obscure references to hanging and "the nail[?]" [צצא], and frags. 4 and 6, which refer to physical violence), the trajectory of this figure's experience—his universal significance, the association of his mission with the removal of darkness, ridicule and abuse, perhaps violent suffering, even death, and positive results for others—appears to be modeled on that of Isaiah's servant. This is corroborated by extensive linguistic and thematic links with the Servant Songs, such as the Hebraism מכאוביכה in 4Q541 6 3 (cf. Isa 53:3–4, איש מכאבות ... ומכאבינו סבלם), or the function of the protagonist as global teacher and illuminator in frag. 9 I 3–4 (cf. Isa 42:6; 49:6; LXX 51:4–5).[44] Several scholars have thus seen evidence in 4Q541 for the notion of a suffering messiah in pre-Christian Judaism.[45] If this is correct, it is notable that this earliest available individualistic interpretation of the servant passages takes a specifically priestly direction.

The second point concerns the atoning function of the priest mentioned in line 2: "And he will atone for all the children of his generation" (ויכפר על כול בני דרה). While this passage does not detail how the atonement will be effectuated, most scholars assume that it involves sacrifice (akin, e.g., to the depiction in 1QM II). Thus John Collins observes that the protagonist "makes atonement by means of the sacrificial cult. He does not atone by his suffering and death, as is the case with Isaiah's servant."[46] There is, however, a more likely alternative. Largely on the basis of the immediately following phrase, "and he will be sent to all the children of his [peop]le" (וישתלח לכול בני עמ[ה]), Daniel Stökl argues that this is one of several early Jewish and Christian texts to apply the image of the scapegoat of the Yom Kippur ritual to a human figure.[47] He

---

tologique: 4QTestLévi[c–d](?) et 4QAj," in Trebolle Barrera and Montaner, *Madrid Qumran Congress*, 2:449–501; and more recently Puech, DJD 31, 213–56.

44. For impressive lists of further connections, see Puech, "Fragments"; Puech, DJD 31; and Brooke, "*Apocryphon of Levi[d]?*"

45. See Jean Starcky, "Les quatres étapes du messianisme à Qumrân," *RB* 70 (1963): 492. He is followed by both Puech and Brooke. Of course, this view is not without its detractors. See esp. John J. Collins, *The Scepter and the Star*, 2nd ed. (Grand Rapids: Eerdmans, 2010), 142–45.

46. Collins, *Scepter and Star*, 144.

47. See Daniel Stökl, "Fasting with Jews, Thinking with Scapegoats: Some Remarks on Yom Kippur in Early Judaism and Christianity, in particular 4Q541, Barnabas 7,

notes that while the *hithpael* form of the root שׁלח is extremely rare in ancient Hebrew and Aramaic (and this is its only appearance in an Aramaic work), it at the same time appears in the *terminus technicus* for the scapegoat in rabbinic literature, שׂעיר המשׁתלח(ה). Stökl thus believes that within the context of 4Q541 9 and especially following the verb ויכפר, the verb וישׁתלח would have immediately evoked the image of the scapegoat.[48] This is supported by the fact that the sequence of atoning and then sending matches that of Lev 16:20–22, where the act of "atoning" is followed by the "sending out" of the scapegoat.[49] Stökl's reading seems preferable, and one may conclude plausibly that the eschatological priest, like Isaiah's servant (Isa 53:11), is indeed portrayed as bearing the sins of the people and making atonement through his person. The most likely temporal setting for this would be the eschatological Day of Atonement (cf. 11Q13 for the corresponding celestial perspective). If the tradition of the abuse and killing of the scapegoat in tannaitic tradition is to be related to the possible abuse and murder of the earthly protagonist in 4Q541, then this atonement could be the outcome of his suffering and death.

Another relevant text is the Self-Glorification Hymn (hereafter SGH).[50] Even though this composition is not concerned with atone-

---

Matthew 27 and Acts 27," in *The Day of Atonement: Its Interpretations in Early Jewish and Christian Traditions*, ed. Thomas Hieke and Tobias Nicklas, TBN 15 (Leiden: Brill, 2012), 165–87.

48. We must not overlook that 4Q541 predates the earliest rabbinic writings by some three hundred years. Even so, given the appearance of rabbinic traditions about the scapegoat in earlier texts, such as Barn. 7, it is not implausible to suggest that rabbinic scapegoat traditions, including the phrase שׂעיר המשׁתלח, constituted a real part of Second Temple Judaism. For important methodological reflections on the use of rabbinic texts to illuminate Qumran texts (and vice versa), see Steven D. Fraade, *Legal Fictions: Studies of Law and Narrative in the Discursive Worlds of Ancient Jewish Sectarians and Sages*, JSJSup 147 (Leiden: Brill, 2011).

49. The objection that the text portrays the priestly protagonist as being sent to the people of his generation rather than to the desert as in Leviticus evaporates once it is realized that both the Mishnah and Barn. 7 preserve the tradition that the scapegoat is to pass *through* the people in order to get to the desert. Moreover, the tradition found both in m. Yoma 6:4 and Barn. 7:6–9 that the people abuse the scapegoat may relate to the possible suffering of the priest in 4Q541. See Stökl, "Fasting with Jews."

50. Four witnesses to SGH are extant; they have been characterized as constituting two different recensions: a portion of a Cave 4 manuscript originally thought to be part of a version of the War Scroll, commonly referred to as "Recension B" (4Q491 frag. 11 i), and portions of three Hodayot manuscripts, commonly referred to as "Recension A"

ment in its extant portions, it is worth mentioning presently due to its application of servant imagery to an ideal priestly figure. (In addition, it shall be important for the discussion regarding the background of Matt 11:25–30 below.) Amid the speaker's claims to divine status and incomparable glory, he somewhat surprisingly refers to his rejection and humiliation by others: "[W]ho has been accounted despicable like me? … Who bea[rs] sorrows like me?" (מ]יא לבוז נחשב ביא … מיא יש[א] צערים[כמוני; 4Q491 frag. 11 i 9–10). These sentiments draw upon the image of the suffering servant of Isa 53:3: "He was despised, and we esteemed him not" (נבזה ולא חשבנהו).[51] The identity of this mysterious figure has been a perennial flashpoint in scholarship. Numerous proposals have been put forward, but based on the comparative evidence the most likely explanation is that he is an extraordinary priest.[52] The most commonly cited argument in favor of this identification is the speaker's emphasis on his role as teacher, "No teaching compares [to my teaching]" (4Q491 frag. 11 i 16–17), which lines up with that of exalted human or angelic priestly figures not only in 4Q541 but also in Jub. 31:15, 1QSb III–IV, the Songs of the Sabbath Sacrifice (4Q400 frag. 1 i 17), and 4QInstruction (4Q418 frag. 81 12). Other details such as the speaker's possession of glory (כבוד) and a position among the angels in the holy abode (מעון קודש) are best seen as markers of sacerdotal identity, especially in light of the unequivocal centrality of priestly identity and the symbol of the temple in the liturgical exaltation expressed in other Qumran texts, such as 4Q511 frag. 35, 1QSb III–IV, and the Sabbath Songs.[53]

(4Q427 7, 1QHᵃ XXV 34–XXVII 3, and 4Q471b + 4Q431 frag. 1). These labels were first introduced by Esther Eshel, "4Q471b: A Self-Glorification Hymn," RevQ 17 (1996): 189–91; cf. Eshel, "Self-Glorification Hymn," in Qumran Cave 4.XX: Poetical and Liturgical Texts, Part 2, Esther Chazon et al., DJD 29 (Oxford: Clarendon, 1999), 422.

51. Cf. Eshel's reading of 4Q471b frags. 1–3 2–3, [ומי]נבזה כמונ[י ומי] כמוני חדל[ו אישים], over against Isa 53:3, נבזה וחדל אישים (DJD 29, 421–32).

52. Among numerous other studies, the following argue for a priestly identification of the speaker: Collins, Scepter and Star, 146–64, esp. 146–49; Eshel, DJD 29, 426–27; Crispin H. T. Fletcher-Louis, All the Glory of Adam: Liturgical Anthropology in the Dead Sea Scrolls, STDJ 42 (Leiden: Brill, 2002), 199–216. See also Johannes Zimmermann, Messianische Texte aus Qumran: Königliche, priesterliche und prophetische Messiasvorstellungen in den Schriftfunden von Qumran, WUNT 2/104 (Tübingen: Mohr Siebeck, 1998), 308.

53. For elaboration of these points see Joseph Angel, "The Liturgical-Eschatological Priest of the Self-Glorification Hymn," RevQ 96 (2010): 585–605.

Many scholars have commented on the similarity between the speaker of SGH and that of the Teacher Hymns of the Hodayot.[54] Like the former, the latter is concerned with conveying heavenly wisdom: "Through me you have illumined the face of many.... For you have made me understand your wonderful mysteries" (1QH^a XII 28–29). Moreover, akin to the speaker of SGH, he enjoys a position among the angels; he has been lifted by God "to an eternal height" so that he occupies a station "with the host of the holy ones" (1QH^a XI 21–23). At the same time, however, he has suffered rejection by his contemporaries and expresses this with special appeal to Isaiah's servant. For example, in 1QH^a XII 23–24 he speaks of "those who have contempt for me" and "have no regard for m[e]" (... בוזי [י]לא יחשבונ), also echoing Isa 53:3, נבזה ולא חשבנהו.[55]

These similarities have led a number of scholars to identify the speaker of SGH with the purported author of the Teacher Hymns, the historical Teacher of Righteousness, who is elsewhere explicitly identified as a priest.[56] Other scholars have highlighted several *differences* between the tone of the Teacher Hymns and SGH and conclude that they are not spoken by the same person. For example, John Collins observes that the apparent claim of heavenly enthronement in SGH surpasses any claims made in the Hodayot, and argues that it is more suitable to identify this figure as an eschatological priest, such as the יורה הצדק (CD VI 11), the דורש התורה (4QFlor), or the protagonist of 4Q541. But even he does not discount the possibility that the image of the Teacher of Righteousness was an underlying inspiration: "To some degree, this future figure is analogous to the historical Teacher, and the historical figure prefigures the one who will teach righteousness at the end of days."[57]

Philip Alexander, among others, has added an important element to the discussion. While accepting authorship by the historical Teacher as anticipation of "the eschatological high priest who would finally and per-

54. See, e.g., the discussion of Collins, *Scepter and Star*, 156–58.

55. For several more examples, see Michael O. Wise, *The First Messiah* (San Francisco: HarperCollins, 1999), 290.

56. The notion that the Teacher of Righteousness authored the Teacher Hymns is far from universally accepted. See, e.g., Angela Kim Harkins, "Who Is the Teacher of the Teacher Hymns? Re-examining the Teacher Hymns Hypothesis Fifty Years Later," in *A Teacher for All Generations: Essays in Honor of James C. VanderKam*, ed. Eric Mason, 2 vols., JSJSup 153 (Leiden: Brill, 2012), 1:449–67.

57. Collins, *Scepter and Star*, 159.

manently achieve angelic priestly status in all its fullness at the end of days," he also notes that the text "fizzes with real experience."[58] SGH, he argues, is a mystical text of ascent that was actively used by the Qumran community. The performance of SGH would have served not only to establish the priestly (and prophetic) credentials of each successive liturgical leader (*maskil*), but also to encourage the liturgical community to experience a heavenly glorification akin to that of the speaker.

Regardless of whether one construes the voice of SGH as that of the historical Teacher, the end-time priest, a present member of the community, the Enochic Son of Man (who, interestingly, is also depicted in the image of Isaiah's servant)[59] as Miller has claimed, or some combination of these options, this text constitutes, alongside 4Q541, important evidence for the application of the image of the suffering servant to an individual ideal priest in pre-Christian Judaism.

In light of the fact that pre-Christian Judaism knew of an individualistic understanding of Isaiah's servant in terms of the eschatological priest, it is suitable to ask whether the application of servant imagery to Jesus is similarly tinged with a priestly background. To be sure, the extent to which the image of the servant of Isaiah influenced early Christian authors (and even Jesus himself) has been hotly debated.[60] George Brooke has addressed the question specifically in light of the priest-servant eschatology of 4Q540–541. He finds that

> Despite the possibility that the Servant passages play only a limited role in the New Testament because of their dominant association in certain Jewish eschatology with the eschatological priest [as this sacerdotal association would not be compatible with Jesus's non-Levitical descent], nevertheless some New Testament writings reflect a concern ... to use the Servant materials and redirect them to enhance the picture of Jesus, the Davidic Messiah, or to adjust other aspects of some forms of Jewish

---

58. Philip S. Alexander, *The Mystical Texts*, LSTS 61 (London: T&T Clark, 2006), 85–91.

59. See George W. E. Nickelsburg and James C. VanderKam, *1 Enoch 2: A Commentary on the Book of 1 Enoch, Chapters 37–82*, Hermeneia (Minneapolis: Fortress, 2012), 113–20.

60. See, e.g., Marinus de Jonge, *Jesus, the Servant-Messiah* (New Haven: Yale University Press, 1991).

cultic practice and expectation to describe the character and effect of
Jesus, especially his death.[61]

In other words, despite the fact that Jesus was not of Levitical stock, Jewish
traditions about the messianic priest-servant in some way lie beneath the
understanding of Jesus's identity and purpose in certain New Testament
writings (specifically, he looks at Hebrews, John, Luke-Acts, and Mark).
The image of the servant-priest was thus profitably exploited as "the tena-
cious expression of an aspiration worth negotiating with and refining."[62]

Since we are concerned here with the Synoptic tradition, it will be
instructive to observe how this dynamic may operate within Mark.[63] Certain nuances in the narrative indicate that Jesus's occupation as servant is
envisaged as fulfilling a specifically cultic atoning function. First, at his
baptism, the image of the heavens "tearing apart" ($\sigma\chi\iota\zeta o\mu\acute{\epsilon}\nu o\nu\varsigma$; 1:10) intentionally anticipates the tearing apart ($\dot{\epsilon}\sigma\chi\acute{\iota}\sigma\theta\eta$) of the veil of the temple
at the moment of his death (15:38; cf. T. Levi 10:3). Jesus's vocation as
servant, ratified in the very next verse by the heavenly voice that cites a
combination of Ps 2:7 and Isa 42:1 (Mark 1:11), is thus understood as the
vocation to die a death that will render the holy of holies, the seat of the
divine presence on earth (entered only on the Day of Atonement by the
high priest), accessible once and for all. This detail may be read together
with the clearest Markan reflection on the saving purpose of Jesus's death:
"For the Son of Man came not to be served but to serve, and to give his life
a ransom for many [$\lambda\acute{\nu}\tau\rho o\nu~\dot{\alpha}\nu\tau\grave{\iota}~\pi o\lambda\lambda\tilde{\omega}\nu$]" (10:45). While direct linguistic
connections with Isa 53 are lacking here, the ideas in the two passages are
similar, and the Hebrew Bible passage surely lies in the background of the
verse.[64] As the servant's life is "given over" to death, the Son of Man "gives"
his life. As the servant "serves many well," the Son of Man comes to serve.
As the servant, reminiscent of the scapegoat, "bears the sins of many," the
Son of Man gives his life as "a ransom for many." While the connotation
of the word $\lambda\acute{\nu}\tau\rho o\nu$ is not entirely clear, comparative evidence suggests that

---

61. Brooke, "*Apocryphon of Levi^d*," 153.

62. Ibid., 157.

63. This paragraph expands upon the comments in ibid., 156.

64. See, e.g., Rikk E. Watts, "Jesus' Death, Isaiah 53, and Mark 10:45: A Crux
Revisited," in *Jesus and the Suffering Servant: Isaiah 53 and Christian Origins*, ed. William H. Bellinger Jr. and William R. Farmer (Harrisburg, PA: Trinity Press International, 1998), 125–51.

its most likely meaning in this context is "expiation" or "propitiation."[65] A related chain of ideas appears also in Mark 14:24, "This is my blood of the covenant, which is poured out for many." Adela Yarbro Collins suggests that this verse constitutes a combination of sacrificial terminology with the poem about the servant in Isa 53.[66] Indeed, the image of Jesus here is close to the servant of Isa 53:12 who "pours out his soul to death" and "bears the sins of many." Matthew 26:28, by adding the words "for the forgiveness of sins" (εἰς ἄφεσιν ἁμαρτιῶν) to the Markan *Vorlage*, clarifies what is implicit already in Mark—the interpretation of Jesus's death as a metaphorical atoning sacrifice. To these details may be added the Barabbas episode, which, certainly in Matthew, but likely also in the Markan telling, applies the typology of the two goats of the scapegoat ritual to the ultimate moment of the rejection of Jesus—the decision to release Barabbas and crucify Jesus.[67]

The parallels with 4Q541 are intriguing. Like the protagonist of that text, Jesus is said to execute an eschatological atoning function. While no literary dependence is evident and priestly identity is never overtly attributed to Jesus, the constellation of the motifs of universal atonement, suffering, and rejection and the application of Isaiah's servant imagery suggests that contemporary Jewish tradition about the messianic servant-priest indeed lies somewhere in the background of the gospel's conception of the significance of Jesus's suffering and death.

Parenthetically, I would like to note that the story of the healing of the paralytic in Mark 2 appears to paint a related portrait. The scribes (followed by some modern scholars) seem to hear Jesus's proclamation, "My son, your sins are forgiven" (τέκνον, ἀφίενταί σου αἱ ἁμαρτίαι; v. 5), as a blasphemous claim to the power of absolution, a power thought to be reserved for God alone. E. P. Sanders and others have argued that the utilization of

---

65. See Adela Yarbro Collins, *Mark: A Commentary,* Hermeneia (Minneapolis: Fortress, 2007), 499–504; Yarbro Collins, "The Signification of Mark 10:45 among Gentile Christians," *HTR* 90 (1997): 371–82.

66. Adela Yarbro Collins, "Finding Meaning in the Death of Jesus," *JR* 78 (1998): 175–96.

67. See Jennifer K. Berenson Maclean, "Barabbas, the Scapegoat Ritual, and the Development of the Passion Narrative," *HTR* 100 (2007): 309–34. Cf. Stökl, "Fasting with Jews," who sees evidence of the scapegoat typology in Matthew, but not in Mark. It is noteworthy that in the Barabbas episode Jesus is associated with the goat for the Lord rather than the scapegoat. On the application of both images to Jesus by early Christian authors, see Berenson Maclean, "Barabbas."

the passive voice is better read as an announcement that forgiveness has been achieved; Jesus is merely claiming to be privy to God's actions.[68] In Jesus's day the function of mediating forgiveness for sins would have been the domain of the Jerusalem priesthood. And since Jesus's language is similar to that of Leviticus, where the priest shall atone for the sin (ἁμαρτία) of Israel, and it will be forgiven (ἀφεθήσεται) them (Lev 4:20; cf. 4:26, 31, 35; 5:6; 10, 13, 16, 18, 26; and Num 15:25–26),[69] the cause of the tension with the scribes indeed could be the perception that Jesus was challenging the established institutions and procedures of the one God by arrogating to himself priestly prerogatives. In the continuation, however, Jesus neither affirms nor denies that he himself has the power to forgive sins. Rather, he appeals to the authority of the mysterious Son of Man: "So that you may know that the Son of Man has authority [ἐξουσία] on earth to forgive sins" (v. 10). While it may be debated how those listening to Jesus within such a historical setting might have understood this cryptic statement, readers of the gospel are surely to perceive that Jesus is identified with the messianic figure of Dan 7 and that his authority to forgive sins is rooted in his exalted status as God's chief agent on earth.

Since the political authority (ἐξουσία) bestowed upon the figure in Dan 7:13–14 seems distant from the authority (ἐξουσία) to forgive sins on earth, it is commonly asserted that Mark 2:10 represents a radically new interpretation of Daniel's Son of Man that emerged after the death of Jesus.[70] It is worth noting, however, the suggestion of Crispin Fletcher-Louis that within the essentially temple-centered world of Jewish apocalyptic literature, the figure of Dan 7:13 would have been perceived as Israel's true messianic high priest:

> His coming to God with the clouds evokes the Day of Atonement when the high priest enters God's presence surrounded by clouds of incense.... Where it used to be the king, as the representative of the nation, to whom God then delegated all (cosmic and historical) authority, now it is Israel's high priest who receives, sacramentally so to speak, that authority on Israel's behalf.... As near-contemporary texts show, on his return to the people from the inner sanctuary the high priest is a plenipotentiary of God's own power and Glory: he comes from "heaven" back to "earth."

---

68. See E. P. Sanders, *Jesus and Judaism* (London: SCM, 1985), 273–74.
69. Note also Exod 28:36–38 and Lev 10:17, already cited above; and see n. 37.
70. See, e.g., Yarbro Collins, *Mark*, 186–89.

The implicit liturgical scene fits the text's life-setting: the day that the high priest fully comes to God is Yom Kippur and this is also the day that provides a cosmic purification of a world that has been defiled by pagan impurities.[71]

This is not the place to offer an evaluation of this intriguing suggestion, which deserves closer attention than it has hitherto received. If it is correct, however, then Mark 2:10 need not be considered a radical post-Easter theological development. The Son of Man's power of absolution would be a natural outgrowth of his status as the true high priest of Israel.[72] However, even if one is inclined to reject this reading in favor of the more common interpretation, the Son of Man's authority to remove sin from the earth finds its best analogue in priestly figures such as Melchizedek of 11Q13, who has the power to relieve the sons of light from the "burden of all their iniquities" on the eschatological Yom Kippur, the protagonist of 4Q541, or Enoch in 2 En. 64:5. Again, it seems that pre-Christian priestly tradition lies in the background of the gospel's portrayal of Jesus.

Teaching Divine Wisdom

The portrayal of Jesus as an eschatological teacher of the divine way, who, in contrast with his contemporary rivals, instructs with "authority" (Mark 1:27; cf. Luke 4:32; Matt 21:23–27), is prominent in Synoptic tradition. Jesus is at times referred to simply as "Teacher," and in Matt 23:10 he explicitly connects his vocation as instructor to his status as Messiah: "One is your instructor, the Messiah." Perhaps for some of the reasons stated above, scholars have been reluctant to associate Jesus's eschatological teaching function with a priestly background, even though the function of teaching divine knowledge in the end time was considered a major hallmark of the priestly messiah's vocation (4Q541; cf. T. Levi 18; 1QSb IV; CD VI 11; 4Q175 [Testimonia]), and even though the association of exalted priestly figures with the mediation of divine wisdom is well known

---

71. Fletcher-Louis, "Jesus: Part 2," 58. Cf. Fletcher-Louis, "The High Priest as Divine Mediator in the Hebrew Bible: Dan 7.13 as a Test Case," in *Society of Biblical Literature 1997 Seminar Papers*, SBLSP 36 (Atlanta: Scholars Press, 1997), 161–93. Many elements of his approach to Dan 7 are anticipated by André Lacocque, *The Book of Daniel*, trans. David Pellauer (London: SPCK, 1979), 124–25.

72. See Fletcher-Louis, "Jesus: Part 2," 71–74.

in Second Temple literature (e.g., Sir 50; 4Q418 frag. 81; Let. Aris. 94–97). Detailed examination of the different nuances of the teaching role of Jesus in the gospels and their complex backgrounds is of course far beyond the scope of this paper. In the present section I would like to focus on the background of one particular saying of Jesus, Matt 11:25–30, and consider some possible points of contact with priestly traditions, especially some of those that have been mentioned earlier in this study.

Matthew 11:25–30 is typically viewed as comprising two separate sayings.[73] The first is a thanksgiving for revelation derived from Q (vv. 25–27). The formal features of this prayer as well as its apocalyptic tone have reminded scholars especially of the Qumran Hodayot.[74] The second is an invitation to find rest in the easy yoke, which draws from contemporary Jewish wisdom tradition and is ascribed to M (vv. 28–30). For my present purpose, I will concentrate on the portrait of Jesus to emerge from the present form of the text as a whole. The passage reads as follows.

> [25] At that time Jesus said, "I thank you, Father, Lord of heaven and earth, because you have hidden these things from the wise and the intelligent and have revealed them to infants; [26] yes, Father, for such was your gracious will. [27] All things have been handed over to me by my Father; and no one knows the Son except the Father, and no one knows the Father except the Son and anyone to whom the Son chooses to reveal him.
>
> [28] "Come to me, all you that are weary and are carrying heavy burdens, and I will give you rest. [29] Take my yoke upon you, and learn from me; for I am gentle and humble in heart, and you will find rest for your souls. [30] For my yoke is easy, and my burden is light." (NRSV)

Before inquiring about the possible priestly background of this difficult passage, I must address a few matters of interpretation. These verses appear at the heart of Matt 11–12, which centers on the two intimately related themes of Jesus's status as Messiah and his rejection by the Jewish leadership.[75] Within the narrative setting, "these things" (11:25) most likely

---

73. See, e.g., Celia Deutsch, *Hidden Wisdom and the Easy Yoke: Wisdom, Torah and Discipleship in Matthew 11.25–30*, JSNTS 18 (Sheffield: JSOT Press, 1987).

74. See, e.g., David Flusser, with R. Steven Notley, *The Sage from Galilee: Rediscovering Jesus's Genius* (Grand Rapids: Eerdmans, 2007), 101–3.

75. See Donald Verseput, *The Rejection of the Humble Messianic King: A Study of the Composition of Matthew 11–12*, European University Studies, Series 23, Theology, 291 (Frankfurt: Lang, 1986); Lena Lybaek, *New and Old in Matthew 11–13: Normativ-*

refers to the apprehension of the unfolding of God's plan in Jesus's works (11:2, 19). That this revelation belongs to the "infants" rather than the wise appears to reverse typical wisdom thinking. Who are the infants? W. D. Davies and Dale Allison Jr. point out that the word νήπιος is sometimes used in the LXX to denote the righteous.[76] They assume such a usage here, which would be akin to the attribution of the term "simple ones" (פתאים) to the elect community in certain Qumran writings (e.g., 1QH[a] X 10–11, where the simple receive wisdom from the "Teacher" [cf. Prov 8:5]). In light of the fact that God is actively revealing and hiding in this passage, we should indeed probably think of a limited group of chosen ones.[77] In Matt 11:27, we learn that Jesus is not only the revealed but also the revealer; as the Son of God he is the absolutely unique conduit of the knowledge of God to the elect. The similarity of this conception of revelation with that found in parts of 1 Enoch and 4QInstruction has been duly recognized in more recent scholarship.[78] Notably, Celia Deutsch and others have argued for a background in the Parables of Enoch and its portrayal of the Son of Man not only as a revealer, the source of the "secrets of wisdom," but also as part of the content of revelation himself.[79]

The rich christological statement of Matt 11:25–27 is given practical substance by the juxtaposition of the paraenetic appeal to take up the yoke of Jesus in verses 28–30.[80] Whereas in the former section the contrast is

---

ity in the Development of Three Theological Themes, FRLANT 198 (Göttingen: Vandenhoeck & Ruprecht, 2002).

76. W. D. Davies and Dale Allison Jr., *A Critical and Exegetical Commentary on the Gospel according to Saint Matthew,* 3 vols., ICC (Edinburgh: T&T Clark, 1988–1995), 2:275.

77. This appears to be the case also in Matt 13, where God allows only certain eyes and ears to perceive. Cf. Grant Macaskill, *Revealed Wisdom and Inaugurated Eschatology in Ancient Judaism and Early Christianity,* JSJSup 115 (Leiden: Brill, 2007), 145–46.

78. See esp. ibid., passim.

79. Of particular interest for Deutsch is Q's apparent appropriation of the wisdom myth of 1 En. 42:1–3, where concealed Wisdom seeks to descend from heaven and reveal herself to humanity. Deutsch (*Hidden Wisdom,* 103) argues that the Matthean passage intentionally presents Jesus in strikingly similar terms.

80. Ulrich Luz (*Matthew 8–20,* trans. James E. Crouch, Hermeneia [Minneapolis: Fortress, 2001], 176) articulates the results of the juxtaposition beautifully: "The revelation of the Father and the Son happens when, and only when, the Son of God calls his own to follow him on the way of obedience. Revelation, salvation, knowledge of God happen in life, in concrete praxis, not prior to and outside it…. For him grace and praxis belong together as the content and form of the same substance."

between the wise and the infants, who by grace receive revelation, in the latter the contrast is between two ways of life, that of "heavy burdens" over against that of the easy yoke. Given the characterization of the Pharisees as laying heavy burdens upon people's shoulders in Matt 23:4, as well as the surrounding context (esp. the Sabbath conflicts of ch. 12), the passage is likely contrasting Pharisaic teaching with the path set forth by Jesus. This reading is also supported by the use of the term "yoke," which is associated with torah /wisdom in an assortment of Jewish texts from the period (see esp. Sir 51; m. 'Abot 3:5). Earlier in the gospel, the torah of the new law-giver is said not only to fulfill but to surpass the torah of Moses (Matt 5:17–48). Here the divine origin and kind nature of Jesus's yoke distinguishes it from the fundamentally flawed teachings of rival experts in the law.

Commentators have long recognized the strong sapiential currents in Matt 11:28-30. In particular it has been proposed that these verses draw from Sir 51:23-27 (and 6:18-22, 28-30), an invitation to take up the "yoke" of wisdom associated with "finding rest" from "toil."[81] That Jesus here speaks of "my" yoke as opposed to wisdom's yoke is taken by many scholars as a deliberate alteration in order to construct a Wisdom Christology, according to which Jesus in not simply a teacher of wisdom, but personified Wisdom herself. Given that Jesus is probably identified as Wisdom in Matt 11:19 ("wisdom is vindicated by her deeds"), this may well be the case.[82]

While the sapiential allusions in Matt 11:28-30 seem clear, we should not overlook that the description of Jesus as "gentle and humble in heart" stands in some tension with the portrait of Wisdom in texts such as Sirach

---

81. See the influential study of M. Jack Suggs, *Wisdom, Christology and Law in Matthew's Gospel* (Cambridge: Harvard University Press, 1970). See also Deutsch, *Hidden Wisdom*.

82. If this interaction with Sirach is indeed direct and intentional (disputed by Graham Stanton, *A Gospel for a New People: Studies in Matthew* [Edinburgh: T&T Clark, 1992], 369, among others), it is worth recalling the thoroughly priestly associations of Wisdom/Torah in Sirach. In ch. 24 personified Wisdom officiates in the temple like an angel of the presence, and in ch. 50 Wisdom is embodied by the high priest Simon II. See Robert Hayward, "Sacrifice and World Order: Some Observations on Ben Sira's Attitude to the Temple Service," in *Sacrifice and Redemption: Durham Essays in Theology*, ed. Stephen W. Sykes (Cambridge: Cambridge University Press, 1991), 22–34, esp. 23–24. Thus, even though the most obvious accent in Matt 11:25-30 is on the sonship of Jesus, the traditional association of priesthood with Wisdom remains in the background.

and Proverbs. These adjectives are indeed more evocative of the image of Isaiah's servant and should be read in light of the extended citation of Isa 42:1–4 in Matt 12:17–21. In that passage, Jesus is identified with the servant who "will not wrangle or cry aloud." Nor will he "break a bruised reed or smoldering wick," likely a reference to the therapeutic and compassionate nature of Jesus's ministry.[83] Macaskill articulates well how these references relate to Matt 11:29:

> As one not driven by his own rights and by self-interest, the servant treats with tenderness those who are imperfect. So, too, in 11:29, it is as the one who is gentle and lowly that Jesus promises the tender treatment of all who would come to him. The reader of Matthew's gospel … surely cannot see anything but the forsaking of status and rights in the application of the adjective ταπεινὸς to Jesus in 11:29.[84]

Graham Stanton argues similarly and goes so far as to declare that the invitation to the easy yoke is issued not by "Jesus as Sophia, but Jesus as the humble Servant of God on whom God's Spirit rests."[85] I do not think that this is a case where we must choose one option over the other. It is much more likely in my view that we have here a convergence of wisdom and servant traditions. It is interesting to note the similar combination of wisdom and servant imagery in the Son of Man of the Parables, especially in light of Deutsch's claim about the background of Matt 11:25–27 in the Parables.[86]

The Priestly Background of Matt 11:25–30

The convergence of the motif of eschatological revelation of divine wisdom with the image of the servant also brings to mind several of the priestly texts discussed above. For example, the links between Jesus and the servant-priest of 4Q541 go beyond those noted above, and include also the parallel role of eschatological illuminator. In 4Q541 frag. 9 i 3, the

---

83. So Lidija Novakovic, *Messiah, the Healer of the Sick: A Study of Jesus as the Son of David in the Gospel of Matthew,* WUNT 2/170 (Tübingen: Mohr Siebeck, 2003), 142–44.

84. Macaskill, *Revealed Wisdom,* 154.

85. Graham Stanton, "Matthew 11:28–30: Comfortable Words?" *ExpTim* 94 (1982): 6.

86. See n. 79.

priest's "teaching" is in accord with God's will, his "word" is heavenly, and he apparently transmits "his [w]isdom" to his contemporaries.[87] The shining of "his eternal sun" and the disappearance of darkness accords with the eschatological triumph of righteousness over wickedness. Of particular interest in relation to Matthew is the hostility and rejection experienced by this figure. The people of his generation "will speak many words against him, and a number of [lie]s. And they will invent fables against him, and they will speak all manner of infamies against him" (frag. 9 i 5-6). This may be compared with the verses immediately prior to Matt 11:25–30, where the Son of Man is accused of being a drunkard and an associate of sinners, and where those who have rejected the "deeds of power" done in their midst are excoriated.[88]

In many ways, the speaker of the Teacher Hymns provides a closer analogy to the portrait of Jesus in Matt 11:25–30. Whereas 4Q541 is a third person narrative set in the eschatological future, the speaker of the Teacher Hymns offers thanks to God, in the first person, for a revelation that has already occurred. The similarity between the opening words of Jesus's thanksgiving (ἐξομολογοῦμαί σοι πάτερ ... ὅτι) and the common Hodayot introductory formula אודכה אדוני כיא is commonly recognized. In terms of content, Matt 11:25–27 is most frequently compared to 1QHª XII 28–29:

> Through me you have illuminated the face of the Many [ובי האירותה
> פני רבים], and have shown your infinite power. For you have given
> me knowledge of your marvelous mysteries, and have shown yourself
> mighty with me in the midst of your marvelous council, doing wonders
> before the Many for the sake of your glory.

Akin to Jesus, the speaker announces his enjoyment of a unique relationship with God resulting in the gift of divine knowledge, which he has conveyed to the elect community. One need not necessarily posit authorship by the Teacher of Righteousness to recognize a priestly scenario in this pas-

---

87. Other fragments, which likely refer to this same figure, mention a wise man (חכים, 4Q541 2 ii 6) with knowledge of deep things (ומתבונן בעמיק[י]ן, 3:1) who utters riddles (וממלל אוחידואן, 2 i 7).

88. Without positing a direct relationship between these texts, it is also interesting to note that whereas in 4Q541 frag. 9 i 6, "Evil will *overturn* his generation," (דרה באיש יאפיך), in Matt 11:23–24 Jesus declares that Capernaum is destined to suffer a fate worse than Sodom's (cf. Gen 19:25: ויהפך את־הערים האל).

sage. The phrase "to illuminate the face of the Many" appears in only one other context in the Dead Sea Scrolls corpus, the blessing of the eschatological high priest in 1QSb IV. There it is the priestly messiah, portrayed as an angel of the presence serving in the heavenly temple, who is said to bring "a light [...] to the world with knowledge and to illuminate the face of the Many [פני רבים ולהאיר]" (1QSb IV 25–27).[89] The speaker in our Hodayot passage thus claims to have fulfilled already one of the major functions of the priestly messiah.[90]

Further intriguing parallels with Matthew emerge when it is recognized that the composition preserved in 1QH^a XII is a thanksgiving hymn that focuses on contrasting the divine teaching of the speaker with the flawed instruction of rival experts, likely including Pharisees—"lying interpreters and deceitful seers" who "exchange your law ... for slippery words" (XII 10-11).[91] As I have noted above, the contrast of Jesus's yoke with Pharisaic teaching is a key element of Matt 11:28–30. As in Matt 11:28, in 1QH^a XII 12 the false teachings of rivals are portrayed metaphorically as physically oppressive and harmful. Moreover, akin to Matt 11–12, the hodayah is peppered with complaints pertaining to rejection and hostility. This experience is expressed with appeal to the language of Isaiah's servant: "I have been rejected by them. They have no regard for me" (XII 9; cf. ll. 23–24). It is interesting to note another contextual similarity. Just as Matt 11:25–30 is immediately preceded by a promise of destruction to the Galilean villages that have rejected Jesus, 1QH^a XII 26 promises "destruction to all the peoples of the lands, in order to cut off in judgment all who transgress your word." There are, then, striking parallels between Matthew 11 and 1QH^a XII in the realms of content, context, and form.

---

89. Cf. the analogous duty of the מבקר in CD XIII 7 to "instruct the Many in the deeds of God" and "teach them his mighty marvels, and recount to them the eternal events with their explanations." The מבקר is best understood as a priestly or Levitical figure. See, e.g., Steven D. Fraade, "Shifting from Priestly to Non-priestly Legal Authority: A Comparison of the Damascus Document and the Midrash Sifra," in *Legal Fictions*, 193–210, esp. nn. 12–13.

90. Compare the implied relationship between the מורה הצדק and his typological, eschatological counterpart the יורה הצדק באחרית הימים (CD VI 11), who is best understood as an eschatological priest. For further discussion, see Angel, *Otherworldly and Eschatological Priesthood*, 180–95.

91. For the identification of these rivals as Pharisees, see, e.g., Alex P. Jassen, *Mediating the Divine: Prophecy and Revelation in the Dead Sea Scrolls and Second Temple Judaism*, STDJ 68 (Leiden: Brill, 2007), 283–85.

Finally, a few observations about the exalted priest of SGH in relation to Matt 11:25–30. The hymn is spoken in the first person, but unlike
Matt 11:25–27 and 1QH^a XII, it is not an expression of thanksgiving for
revelation. The supremely high self-consciousness of the speaker, who has
exceeded the ranking of angels, goes beyond the claims of the speaker of
the Teacher Hymns and is more similar to Jesus the Son or the Son of Man
in the Parables. Yet, as we have seen, despite this special status he refers to
his rejection and humiliation by others in terms of Isaiah's servant.

As I noted above, the speaker of SGH emphasizes the incomparability
of his teaching and the "flow of his lips." While he does not mention the
identity of his students or the effects of his extraordinary teaching upon
them, these details are clarified by the so-called Canticle of the Righteous,
which immediately follows SGH in both recensions.[92] Here the elect liturgical community is called to praise by the exalted speaker. Comparison
of the language attributed to the speaker in SGH with that applied to the
community shows a special affinity between the two parties—the one mirrors the other. While the speaker is labeled "beloved of the king" (ידיד
המלך), the community is referred to as "favored/beloved ones" (ידידים).[93]
While the speaker enjoys a position "in the glory of the holy [dwe]lling"
(בכבוד [מע]ון קודש), the community is bidden to give praise to God "in
the holy dwelling" (במעון הקודש).[94] Moreover, the speaker and the community apparently share in the three interrelated experiences of suffering,
heavenly exaltation, and access to divine knowledge.[95] From this mirror
imagery emerges the following: the speaker, by summoning the community to worship, is evidently leading them to an experience of heavenly
glorification comparable to his own. Within this particular framework it is
interesting to note the community's blessing for revelation: "Bless the one
who wonderfully does majestic deeds … seal[ing] mysteries and revealing hidden things, raising those who stumble" (4Q427 frag. 7 i 18–19).
Later on in the hymn the community proclaims nothing less than possession of the knowledge of God himself: "We have known you, God of righ-

92. See n. 50.

93. See 4Q427 frag. 7 i 10 (vis-à-vis 4Q471 frags. 1–3 7) and 4Q427 frag. 7 i 13.

94. See 4Q491c frag. 11 14–15 and 20.

95. So Paola Augusta de Souza Nogueira, "Ecstatic Worship in the Self-Glorifica-
tion Hymn," in *Wisdom and Apocalypticism in the Dead Sea Scrolls and in the Biblical
Tradition,* ed. F. García Martínez, BETL 168 (Leuven: Leuven University Press and
Peeters, 2003), 385–94, esp. 391–92.

teousness, and we have become enlightened" (ידענוכה אל הצדק והשכלנו;
4Q427 frag. 7 ii 14). If, as seems likely, the community's knowledge of God is the product of the incomparable teaching of the speaker, then the parallel with Matt 11 is especially close—the supremely exalted teacher has revealed knowledge of God himself to the elect.

What type of conclusion may one draw in light of the relationships charted above? First, it is important to acknowledge that while my analysis has focused on drawing attention to points of similarity, this should not lead us to undervalue the substantial differences in form and content between Matthew and the Qumran texts. Indeed, despite some intriguing points of contact, it cannot be shown that Matt 11:25–30 drew directly from 4Q541, 1QH[a] XII, or SGH. Moreover, there does not appear to be any intention to portray Jesus as a specifically priestly revealer; rather his status as Son, who reveals due to his exclusive relationship with the Father, appears to be the dominant image of this passage.[96] At the same time, the lines of contact between the texts are close enough in my opinion to show that Matt 11:25–30 is at home among Second Temple Jewish traditions associating the apocalyptic revelation of divine wisdom specifically with an eschatological priestly figure who encounters hostility from rival teachers, rejection by the people, and is cast in the image of Isaiah's servant. This is especially apparent in light of the comparison with 1QH[a] XII, which is characterized not only by the Hodayot form and the application of the servant imagery, but also the motifs of thanksgiving for the gift of revelation, mediation of revelation to an elect remnant over against the majority of faithless Israel, contrast of the harmful nature of Pharisaic teaching over against the salvific nature of the Teacher's divine instruction, rejection and hostility from the people at large, and announcement of destruction for nonbelievers. The constellation of similar form and motifs in Matthew suggests that traditions about an eschatological priestly teacher of the kind expressed in the Qumran texts indeed lie beneath the portrait of Jesus the Son of God in Matt 11:25–30.

---

96. See, e.g., Jack D. Kingsbury, *Matthew: Structure, Christology, and Kingdom* (Philadelphia: Fortress, 1986), 64. Note also the Moses typology suggested by Dale Allison Jr., "Two Notes on a Key Text: Matthew 11:25–30," *JTS* 39 (1988): 477–85; Allison, *The New Moses: A Matthean Typology* (Edinburgh: T&T Clark, 1993).

CONCLUSION: ENOCH, JESUS, AND PRIESTLY TRADITION

It is a testimony to both the central significance and the fluidity of priestly tradition in Second Temple Judaism that the non-Levites Enoch and Jesus attract priestly roles and identity in the literature. As we have seen, portrayals of the primordial patriarch Enoch in sacerdotal terms in the early Enochic corpus most likely did not directly influence the image of Jesus in the Synoptic Gospels. However, the texts that scholars have shown do appropriate various motifs and attributes associated with Enoch in the literary construction of separate ideal priestly figures have been more relevant in illuminating the priestly background of certain portrayals of Jesus in the Synoptics. In particular, the image of the atoning servant-priest of 4Q541 provides significant background for the depiction of Jesus's universal atoning function. Moreover, the same protagonist of 4Q541 as well as the speaker of the Teacher Hymns and the speaker of SGH provide important background for the portrait of Jesus as eschatological teacher/revealer of divine wisdom presented in Matt 11:25–30. While it is tempting to posit that the Synoptic authors were aware of or perhaps even drew upon some of these traditions in their construction of the figure of Jesus, in no case does the evidence permit the conclusion of direct literary influence. The significance of these texts for comprehending the Synoptic portrayal of Jesus remains in their illumination of a specific trajectory of thinking about priests and priesthood in which the gospels also apparently participate. As we might expect, however, in line with the specific concern of the gospels to spotlight other aspects of Jesus's identity, the priestly elements attributed to Jesus remain beneath the surface.

Jesus among Wisdom's Representatives: 4QInstruction

Benjamin Wold

How wisdom reaches human beings is presented in various ways in early Jewish tradition. When revealed, and this by different means and figures, it is usually accessible only to an elect community. The role that righteous individuals play is well known, and their portrayal as representing or mediating wisdom may be more or less unique. 4QInstruction, an early-second-century BCE document preserved in at least six copies at Qumran (1Q26; 4Q415–4Q418, 4Q423), has attracted considerable attention because of its interest in revealed wisdom. However, much more may be said about who accesses revealed wisdom in the document and the means by which it is attained. The aim here is to assess first-person language in 4QInstruction as a window to exalted figures who represent wisdom, and to do so in relationship to other constructs and particularly to the Gospels of Matthew and Luke.

How wisdom reaches human beings in Matthew and Luke is similar but by no means monolithic. When Jesus prays in Matt 11:25–30, he thanks the Father because he has "hidden these things from the wise and understanding and revealed them to babes" (ὅτι ἔκρυψας ταῦτα ἀπὸ σοφῶν καὶ συνετῶν καὶ ἀπεκάλυψας αὐτὰ νηπίοις). Yet Jesus claims a unique relationship to the Father, as Son, thereby limiting the possibility that wisdom can reach humanity by any other means. Indeed, this is explicit in Jesus's declaration that "no one knows the Son except the Father, and no one knows the Father except the Son and any one to whom the Son chooses to reveal him" (11:27).

Although Jesus is the quintessential expression of wisdom in the gospels, the degree to which this is expressed varies. In Luke 7:35 (= Q 7:35) we read, "Wisdom is vindicated by all of her children" (καὶ ἐδικαιώθη ἡ σοφία ἀπὸ πάντων τῶν τέκνων αὐτῆς). "Children" here is likely a reference to Jesus and John and as such draws attention to wisdom itself, so that it is not just Jesus who functions to disseminate wisdom; alongside Jesus, John the Baptist and the disciples can also have such a role, which is seen to be sanctioned by God. Similarly, when Matt 11:19 preserves this same passage, although the evangelist writes about "deeds" rather than "children" (ἐδικαιώθη ἡ σοφία ἀπὸ τῶν ἔργων αὐτῆς), this appears to reflect wisdom's identification with Jesus and John the Baptist (cf. Matt 11:18 and Luke 7:33 and the charge against John the Baptist). Therefore, Q 7:35 portrays Jesus, John, and the disciples as representatives of wisdom.

Within the Synoptic tradition, particularly Matthew and Luke, there is a contrast between the more and less exclusive ways that wisdom is available to Jesus. Matthew 8:20 portrays the Son of Man as having nowhere to lay his head, a statement that seemingly alludes to embodied and personified wisdom dwelling with humanity.[1] In Luke 11:31 the comparison with Solomon ("something greater than Solomon is here") evokes wisdom imagery and echoes a failure to acknowledge the superior wisdom that Jesus preaches. In Luke 21:15 Jesus promises to give wisdom to his disciples for them to use against their opponents.[2]

To different degrees, Jesus is presented in the gospels as enjoying more or less exclusive relationships with wisdom, the far end of the spectrum being his portrayal as Wisdom. When situating Jesus as an exemplary of wisdom among other figures from the period, one finds that the Enochic tradition offers viewpoints on the ways that wisdom reaches humanity. The dissemination of wisdom in Enochic tradition may place emphasis on Enoch, but this is not depicted in an exclusionary way. Enoch is a source of wisdom that was passed down to Methuselah and ultimately to his descendants and beyond (1 En. 82; 91; 105:1–2). The Enochic community is the rightful bearer of revealed wisdom; the descendants of Methuselah are the legitimate heirs of revelation. An analogy in the Matthean passage

---

1. A saying that has often been compared to 1 En. 42:1–2: "Wisdom found no place where she might dwell; then a dwelling place was assigned her in the heavens, Wisdom went forth to make her dwelling among the children of men, and found no dwelling place. Wisdom returned to her place, and took her seat among the angels." The translation is adapted from George W. E. Nickelsburg and James C. VanderKam, *1 Enoch: The Hermeneia Translation,* rev. ed. (Minneapolis: Fortress, 2012).

2. In Matthew there is no explicit narrative of the disciples performing exorcisms, whereas in Luke there are.

(11:25–30) is the claim that some will inherit the wisdom Jesus embodies; this claim translates into claims of legitimacy for a community as the locus of wisdom.

How 4QInstruction deciphers wisdom reaching an elect community remains, at several points, unclear. Assessing how wisdom is revealed, and to whom, in 4QInstruction is particularly pertinent because this document is such an early witness to an "apocalyptic" worldview. How authority is constructed in 4QInstruction hinges on how one interprets the revelation of wisdom. Authority constructs may be seen to compete or complement one another, or progress on from one another in an evolutionary way. Assessing authority vis-à-vis revealed wisdom in 4QInstruction permits reflection not only on this single document and its place among others, but more importantly on differing degrees to which revelation comes to humanity, or groups of human beings, by more or less exclusive means.

Crucial to understanding how wisdom is revealed in 4QInstruction are the very first lines of the document, and yet whether these are even preserved among the manuscripts is debatable. Eibert Tigchelaar suggests that 4Q418 frags. 222 + 221 + 220 preserve the opening lines of 4QInstruction, which is significant because first-person speech may be found in these fragments.[3] Should this first-person speech be compared to that of Enoch's source of knowledge, found frequently in reference to visions of heaven, wisdom written in heaven, and words of angels? Tigchelaar describes Enoch as a heavenly conduit to heaven and the wisest of men (1 En. 92:1), and considers that Enoch's role in 1 En. 92:1 is similar to that of wisdom in 4QInstruction, but that Wisdom is the one who speaks in the opening of 4QInstruction (1 En. 42:1–2).[4]

----

3. Eibert J. C. Tigchelaar, *To Increase Learning for the Understanding Ones: Reading and Reconstructing the Fragmentary Early Jewish Sapiential Text 4QInstruction*, STDJ 44 (Leiden: Brill, 2001), 245; Tigchelaar is less committed in "Towards a Reconstruction of the Beginning of 4QInstruction (4Q416 Fragment 1 and Parallels)," in *The Wisdom Texts from Qumran and the Development of Sapiential Thought*, ed. Charlotte Hempel, Armin Lange, and Hermann Lichtenberger, BETL 159 (Leuven: Peeters, 2002), 123, "since the fragment does not overlap with 4Q416 1, and does not provide any plausible textual joins, this identification is no more than a possibility." Émile Puech ("Les fragments eschatologiques de *4QInstruction* [4Q416 1 et 4Q418 69 ii, 81–81a, 127]," *RevQ* 22 [2005]: 90) reconstructs a reference to a maskil in 4Q416 frag. 1.

4. Tigchelaar, "Wisdom and Counter-Wisdom in 4QInstruction, Mysteries, and

There is reason to think that the author connects himself explicitly with his speech in 4QInstruction rather than personified Wisdom. 4Q418 frags. 222 + 221 preserve first-person forms that are self-referential;[5] moreover, if they are to be located in the first column of the document, then 4Q418 frag. 238 and its reference to a *maskil* should be tentatively located along with them.[6] Taken together, the first-person addresses and reference to a *maskil* indicate that from the outset the author refers to his own role increasing learning for the understanding ones. These fragments may be transcribed and translated as follows:[7]

4Q418 frags. 222 + 221

[בֹ]ל[בֹּ vacat דֹבֹרֹתֹי ooolֹ0ֹ8[לכ	]	1
שמ]עה רוחי ומזל שפתי א[ל	]	2

1 Enoch," in *The Early Enoch Literature,* ed. Gabriele Boccaccini and John J. Collins, JSJSup 121 (Leiden: Brill, 2007), 190–91.

5. The letters *waw* and *yod* are indistinguishable in this hand, and yet in frags. 222 + 221 the most convincing reading is that several *yod*s are first-person pronouns; see DJD 34, 436–38, with the editors' note at 437: "Palaeographic considerations do not especially favour either *yod* or *waw*." The right stroke, or "head," of the *yod* in 4Q418 is often times fuller than that of a *waw*; if this is an indication, then a *yod* is favored here. Cf. Frank M. Cross, "The Development of the Jewish Scripts," in *The Bible and the Ancient Near East: Essays in Honor of W. F. Albright,* ed. G. Ernest Wright (Garden City, NY: Doubleday, 1965), 133–202.

6. Tigchelaar ("Wisdom and Counter-Wisdom," 186) notes, "because of their [4Q418 frags. 220, 221, 222, 238] physical similarity … I suggest that they be placed close to one another."

7. Cf. ibid., 187.

8. Line 1: before דברתי the editors read]בֹּןֹ הֹ[, and having examined the fragment along with Torleif Elgvin, with the use of an electronic microscope and infrared imaging, I have been able to rule out this reading. The remains of a diagonal stroke from the top left down and to the right where the *he* should be suggests rather the possibility of a *shin* or *samek*. The word to follow is not בנ for several reasons: (1) the bottom horizontal stroke is too long, and there is the trace of ink at the top of the line that appears to be the remains of an upper horizontal line; this indicates that either בכ or בב are to be read here; (2) the space that follows these two letters appears to be a long *vacat* due to the absence of ink traces where they would be expected; (3) in the likelihood that this is a *vacat,* the scribe who copied 4Q418 is highly skilled and there are no instances of him using a *nun* where a final *nun* is required. The space between the first remaining letter of this line and the *bet* may be a break or possibly a *lamed*; 4Q418 frag. 204 2 preserves בלבב, which is possible here.

[ ]   3   [להוכיח פּוֹשעים וְלֹהֹבִין]

[ ]   4   [דּעֹז̇] [○]○[ ] כֹ̇יֹא בֹּ]

[ ]   5   ]○[לֹ[

[ ]   1   [הֹמה ולֹוֹאֹ] [פִי]

[ ]   2   [ ] נֹבִֿיאים ולהבין כֹּוֹל פּוֹתִיִים]

[ ]   3   להו]סֹיף לקח למבינים *vacat* [

[ ]   4   [נא ז̇דעו משפטִי ואז תבד̇לוֹ בֹ]ין

[ ]   5   וֹ]תתבוננו לדעת טוֹב]

1   [ ]in the heart. *vacat* I spoke and ...[
2   [he]ar *my* spirit and the outpouring of *my* lips, do not[
3   [ ]to reprove transgressor and to gain understand[ing
4   [ ] know[ ] [ ] for in [

1   [ ] them, and no [ ]mouth of/my mouth[
2   [ ] prophets, and to give insight to all the simple ones[
3   [and to] increase learning for the understanding ones *vacat* [
4   [ ] and know *my* judgments, and then you will distinguish betwe[en
5   [and] you will understand to know good[

4Q418 frag. 238

[ ]   1   ואני [מֹשכיל זֹא]

[ ]   2   אֹ] וֹימעשה]

[ ]   3   התבו]נֹן בנהיי עֹ]ולם

[ ]   4   יֹ]מֹֹ̇י נצח ○[

[ ]   5   [יום [

1   [*and I the*] *maskil* ... [
2   [ ] and ⁱⁿ deed[
3   [cons]ider by those who have been fore[ver
4   [d]ays everlasting [

One may observe similarities between 4Q418 238 and the Songs of the Sage (4Q510 4, "and I, the Instructor," ואני משכיל) and the Hodayot (1QH^a XX 14–16, אני משכיל), where the author clearly calls himself *maskil* and refers to himself in the first-person.[9] When we compare 4Q418 222 + 221 and 238 with other documents from Qumran that are concerned with the figure of the *maskil*, we find that they share common terms and expressions that are infrequent elsewhere. The chart below sets these three fragments from 4QInstruction alongside Qumran literature that mentions a *maskil*:[10]

Maskil and Related Language in 4QInstruction 4Q418 frags. 222 + 221, 238	Language Found in the Context of References to *Maskil* in Qumran Texts
משכיל in opening address	4QS^b IX 1 (מדרש למשכיל) 1QH^a XXV 34 "Recension A" of the Self-Glorification Hymn (למשכיל מזמור) 4Q298 frags. 1–2 I 1 (דברי משכיל)
Self-referential use of משכיל + first-person pronouns	4Q510 frag. 1 4 (אני משכיל) 1QH^a XX 14–16 (אני משכיל)
להבין כול פותיים	1QH^a V 2–3 (להבין פיתאים)
מזל שפתי	4Q511 frags. 63–64 II 4
מזל שפתי + משפטי	4Q471^c frags. 1–4 5–7
להוסיף לקח	4Q298 frags. 3–4 II (הוסיפו לקח); cf. 4Q418 frag. 81 17

---

9. Loren T. Stuckenbruck, "Pseudepigraphy and First Person Discourse in the Dead Sea Documents: From the Aramaic Texts to the Writings of the *Yaḥad*," in *The Dead Sea Scrolls and Contemporary Culture,* ed. Adolfo D. Roitman, Lawrence H. Schiffman, and Shani Tzoref; STDJ 93 (Leiden: Brill, 2011), 293–326, esp. 300.

10. Benjamin G. Wold, *The Mystery of Existence: The Construction of Authority in 4QInstruction* (forthcoming). I discuss the maskil of 4QInstruction in reference to the maskil in Daniel, Rule of the Community, Treatise on the Two Spirits, Rule of the Blessings, Hodayot, Songs of the Sage, Self-Glorification Hymn, Words of the Maskil to All the Sons of Dawn, and Songs of the Sabbath Sacrifice.

The phrase מזל שפתי is not found in the Hebrew Bible, nor is it found in use along with משפטי outside of recensions of the Self-Glorification Hymn.[11] In one line of this hymn (4Q471b frags. 1–4 5–7a) we read:

> Who is like me among the angels? [Who will oppose me when I open my mouth? and the flow] of my lips [מזל שפתי] endure? Who can match me in [speech and compare with my judgment [במשפטי]? For I] am a friend of the king, and of angels.

The similarity of these rare expressions found in both the Self-Glorification Hymn and in 4Q418 frags. 222 + 221 suggests that this language relates to the authority of the speaker based upon the acquisition of heavenly wisdom. Moreover, in 4QSongs of the Sage, the *maskil* speaks to his audience and describes his own speech with the expression מזל שפתי ("outpouring of my lips," 4Q511 frags. 63–64 ii 4).[12] That this expression is found only on these occasions and in relationship to exalted individuals suggests that the expression in these fragments of 4Q418 is similarly related to an exalted figure. As we shall see further below, 4Q418 frag. 81 likely also begins with the expression "outpouring of lips," which is significant for the assessment of the *maskil* in 4QInstruction.

If 4QInstruction does indeed begin with a reference to a *maskil* who accesses heavenly wisdom (i.e., רז נהיה), then what are his character and function? That the *maskil* of the Self-Glorification Hymn is an egomaniac is well known, and so it would be fair to query whether the *maskil* of 4QInstruction also shares his narcissistic qualities. To answer this question we can turn to the three other occurrences of משכיל in 4QInstruction (4Q416 frag. 2 ii 15; 4Q417 frag. 2 i 25; 4Q418 frag. 81 17). However, before exam-

---

11. There are four witnesses to the Self-Glorification Hymn, and they have frequently been discussed as constituting two different recensions: Recension A (4Q427 frag. 7, 1QHᵃ XXV 34–XXVII 3, and 4Q471b + 4Q431 i); Recension B (4Q491c frag. 1 = 4Q491 frag. 11 col. i). Recension A are three portions of the Hodayot MSS, Recension B was originally thought to be part of the War Scroll; cf. Brian Schultz, *Conquering the World: The War Scroll (1QM) Reconsidered,* STDJ 76 (Leiden: Brill, 2009), 375–76; and Joseph Angel, "The Liturgical-Eschatological Priest of the *Self-Glorification Hymn*," *RevQ* 96 (2010): 585–605, esp. 585–86. Émile Puech suggests an alternative to recensions in "L'hymne de la glorification du Maître de 4Q431," in *Prayer and Poetry in the Dead Sea Scrolls and Related Literature,* ed. Jeremy Penner, Ken M. Penner, and Cecilia Wassen, STDJ 98 (Leiden: Brill, 2012), 377–408.

12. Note the similarity with 1QS IX 4–5: ותרומת שפתים למשפט כניחוח צדק.

ining these references, I want to examine a somewhat obscure observation that may also hold a clue about the character of the *maskil*.

The author of 4QInstruction typically writes with the singular address "you" and exhorts his audience with statements such as, "you, O understanding one." There are a few instances of masculine plural addresses, and in one fragment there appears to be an address to a woman (second-person feminine singular form, 4Q415 frag. 2 ii). More importantly for my observation, there are a few instances of first-person plural address ("we") and use of first-person plural pronouns ("our"). In 4Q418 frag. 55 and 4Q417 frag. 2 ii the author includes himself with his audience.

> 4Q418 frag. 55 3–4
>
> And] with *toil* we *will contemplate* [נכרה] *its* ways [i.e., the רז
> נהיה]. We will *have/give* rest [נרגיע] [...] But vigilance *shall
> be* in our heart [*at all times*] and *assurance* in our ways. *vacat*

> 4Q417 frags. 1 ii + 23 5
>
> [...] stumble in it, and in *our* reproach [וֹבֹח[רפת]נוֹ], cover
> your face, and in the iniquity of imprisonment [ובאולתֿיֿ
> מאסיר]...

The "we" expressions found in these two passages portray the author, along with the *maven*, as pursuing the רז נהיה and sharing reproach. By including himself in the activities of the *maven*, the author gives us insights into his status and how he perceives his relationship to his audience. He seeks wisdom with them, and he is also imperfect like them. This evidence suggests that our *maskil* conceives of his relationship with the addressees in a more egalitarian way than in the Self-Glorification Hymn. Moreover, there is a third possible use of "we" that I shall refer to in the discussion of the *maskil* elsewhere in the document (4Q418 frag. 81 20).

The three remaining references to משכיל in 4QInstruction further demonstrate the type of relationship the instructor shares with the instructed.[13] The most controversial, and yet pivotal, occurrence is found

---

13. Charlotte Hempel ("The Qumran Sapiential Texts and the Rule Books," in *The Wisdom Texts from Qumran and the Development of Sapiential Thought*, ed. Charlotte Hempel, Armin Lange, and Hermann Lichtenberger, BETL 159 [Leuven: Peeters, 2002], 287) understands these three occurrences of משכיל as participles rather than nouns.

in 4Q416 frag. 2 ii in a context that is highly ambiguous. The pronouns throughout this section are notoriously difficult to render and their referents difficult to identify. For the present topic lines 15–16 are particularly relevant.

4Q416 frag. 2 ii 12b–17 (par. 4Q417 frags. 1 ii + 23; 4Q418 frags. 8, 21, 22; 4Q418a)[14]

12b ‏[...]ל̇ א̇ם ברצונו תחזיק עבודתו וחכמת אוטו
13 ‏[ש̇ש̇   ]oo[תיעצנו] והייתה]ל̇ו לבן בכור וחמל עליכה כאיש על יחידו
14 ‏[   ] כי אתה עבדו ובחי̇[רו וא̇תה אל תבטח למה תש̇נ̇א̇ ואל תשקור ממדהכה
15 ‏[ואתה דמה ל̇י לעב̇ד משכי̇]ל וגם אל תשפל נפשכה לאשר לא ישוה בכה ואז תהי̇[ה]
16 ‏[ל̇י לא̇ב   ] לאשר אין כוחכה אל תגע פן תכשל וחרפתכה תרבה מו̇א̇דה
17 ‏[אל תמ]כ̇ור נ̇פשכה בהון טוב היותכה עבד ברוח וחנם תעבו̇ד נוגשכה ובמחיר

12b [...] if in *his* goodwill you hold fast,
and serve *him*, and the wisdom of *his* אוט,
13 [...] and you will council him;
And you will be to *him* as a firstborn son,
And *he* will have compassion upon you,
as a man upon his only child;
14 [For you are *his* servant and *his* chosen] one,
and do not trust in what you hate,
and do not be concerned about [stay on watch for] your own destruction,
15 [And you, be like *me*, a servant of a Maski]l,
And also, do not lower your soul to one not equal with you,
And then you will be 16 [to *me* as a father,
] to one who has not your strength do not strike,

---

14. Note that square brackets are not hypothetical reconstructions but rather indicate that 4Q416 frag. 2 ii has been supplemented by parallels. In the case of ll. 15–16 these readings are found, respectively, in 4Q417 frags. 1 ii + 23 19 and 4Q418 frag. 21 2.

lest you stumble and multiply your shame greatly,
17 [do not] sell your soul for wealth,
it is good for you to be a servant in the spirit,
and to serve your oppressor freely, and by a price….

The editors, as well as other translators, have interpreted the third-person masculine pronouns found in lines 12–14 (in italics above) as referring to the creditor (נושה) found in lines 4–5 (not transcribed above).[15] By line 12 the topic, or nuance, of instruction has transitioned from that found in the preceding lines. That this is the case may be adduced from line 12, where it is not at all clear that the *creditor*'s "goodwill" is in mind, as this expression would suggest that the *maven* follows in the creditor's way. The identification of the creditor as a positive figure, which is needed in order to interpret pronominal suffixes in lines 12–14 as referring to him, is unlikely. The referent in these lines, I believe, is God. 4QInstruction clearly understands that the wicked and righteous are differentiated (4Q418 frag. 81 1–2). There are two clear options: either the creditor belongs to the author's own group, or he should be identified with the segment of humanity described as רוח בשר.[16] If lines 4–5 are straightforwardly concerned with borrowing and paying back money, it is unconvincing that this is taking place within the community. After all, this is the same creditor about whom the *maven* is admonished: "for no price exchange [תמר] your holy spirit" (l. 6). The creditor should not be seen as belonging to the righteous community, and nothing in the context suggests that he does. Indeed, if borrowing is taking place within the community, then it is surprising that there is no instruction directed to the wealthy on lending to members of the community who are impoverished. Although the addressees may well come from different segments of society, none of them is said to enjoy material wealth in the present, which is made clear by the insistence of the author that the *maven* is poor.

The broken stich in line 13, "[…] and you will council him," cannot be read in reference to God (or the creditor).[17] It is presumably by wisdom

15. See DJD 34, 93.
16. The *opinio communis* is that 4QInstruction is a nonsectarian, or perhaps "presectarian," composition; as such, financial relationships derived from views on how the Essenes conducted their monetary affairs are not operative here.
17. The average number of letter spaces in each line of this column is about 62, indicating that about half of the line is missing.

gained (l. 12) that the addressee counsels others. The act of gaining wisdom
and offering others counsel is part of the elevated status of the addressee.
Therefore, the *maven* is compared to a firstborn (cf. 4Q418 frag. 81 5), and
only, son who receives fatherly care. Moreover, the addressee holds the
status of a chosen one and servant of God (l. 14a). A series of admonitions
follows, the first of which is not to trust "in what you hate" (l. 14b). Given
the interest of the document in the righteous not associating with the iniq-
uitous (cf. esp. 4Q417 frag. 1 i 7 and 4Q418 frag. 81 1–2), this would be
another formulation of the same teaching. In the stich to follow (l. 14c),
the admonition may relate to the addressee paying no mind to his own
mortality, an exhortation that would make sense if he is to inherit eternal
glory and not associate with the "flesh."

Daniel Harrington and John Strugnell translate line 15a as, "But
become thou to him like a wise servant."[18] The editors comment, though,
that the expression עבד משכיל may be translated either as "servant of
an *intelligent man*" or "wise servant."[19] דמה should be understood as an
imperative and not as a participle ("you are like").[20] Whether לו or לי
should be read here must be adduced from the context.[21] If it is לו, since
the creditor is not in view, the option remaining is that God is the referent.
The *maven* has already been told that he is a servant (l. 14); therefore an
admonition to be a wise servant to God would not be out of place if it were
not for the comparison in the following line (l. 16). That is, the addressee
certainly cannot be like a father to God! Therefore, reading first-person
pronouns in lines 15–16 is one of the few ways to make sense of the pronouns in the context.

---

18. John Strugnell, Daniel J. Harrington, S.J., and Torleif Elgvin, *Qumran Cave
4.XXXIV: Sapiential Texts, Part 2: 4QInstruction (Mûsār lĕ Mēvîn): 4Q415ff. with a
Re-edition of 1Q26*, DJD 34 (Oxford: Clarendon, 1999), 93; on 244 the editors comment, "4Q417 2 ii 19 read probably דמה לו but לי דמה could be possible too," and "the
expression [עבד משכיל] might mean 'servant of an intelligent man' "; cf. *DSSSE* 2:851,
"And you, be for him like a wise servant."

19. DJD 34, 244; cf. Prov 14:35 (רצון־מלך לעבד משכיל) and 17:2 (עבד־משכיל
ימשל בבן מביש); משכיל is used as a *hiphil* verb. The expression עבד משכיל is found
in Hebrew Sirach on several occasions (see 7:21, "let your soul love intelligent slaves";
10:25, "free citizens will serve a wise servant").

20. In this scroll, if it were a participle the orthography expected would be דומה.

21. There are many instances in these lines where the letters *waw* and *yod* are
indistinguishable; in the immediately preceding context of 4Q416 frag. 2 ii, see l. 10
בלו; l. 11 תנו, זראה, בזני; and even אוטו.

The exhortation for the *maven* to be like the *maskil* expresses that he should seek the רז נהיה and achieve wisdom to the same degree as the author. While the instructor enjoys the status of *maskil*, the *maven* too is able to serve in the same capacity. Perhaps this is a role that is open to anyone in the community, one that could be achieved or to which one could be appointed. If the former then this would be by pursuit of heavenly knowledge—thus the urgent concern to exhort the addressees to pursue and seek the רז נהיה.[22] The addressee's elevated status in relationship to wisdom is the author's interest and is why in the stich to follow he admonishes him not to lower himself to one who is not equal. Indeed, the very next line (l. 16) envisages that the *maven* can reach a position in which he becomes a father (תהיה לי לאב).[23] As the *maven* arrives to a position of leadership and enjoys the role of instructor, he is exhorted how to behave: do not strike the weak, in your poverty do not be sidetracked by the pursuit of wealth, be a servant in the spirit, and serve even those who oppress you. The *maskil* is raising a disciple who may suffer at the hands of his oppressors, but who will become a servant-leader to his own community. Moreover, the *maskil* himself apparently embodies his own vision of servant-instructor when he is willing to accept the elevation of his disciple to a position of authority (viz. "father").

Another place where משכיל occurs is in 4Q417 frag. 2 i 25. The surrounding context is unclear; what remains is: "[...] son of a *maskil* [בֹן משכיל], understand by your mysteries, and the foundation [...]." "Son of a *maskil*" has been taken as a possible expression for both the instructor[24] and for the *maven*.[25] If משכיל is read as a noun, the expression "son of a *maskil*" draws attention to the relationship that the *maven* enjoys with the instructor. They relate to one another as "father" and "son," and yet these are not necessarily static roles, as we have already seen (4Q416 frag. 2 ii 16).

---

22. The elevation of the righteous to *maskilim* is well known from Dan 12:3: והמשכילים יזהרו כזהר הרקיע ומצדיקי הרבים ככובים לעולם ועד.

23. In the composite text, it is 4Q417 frags. 1 ii + 23 20 that preserves ואז תהיה לי, and the short downward stroke and filled-in head in this manuscript suggest preference for reading *yod* rather than *waw*.

24. Tigchelaar, "Towards a Reconstruction," 123.

25. Hempel, "Qumran Sapiential Texts," 287, similar to בן מבין; cf. Sir 47:12, where it is used adjectively: "After him a wise son [בן משכיל] rose up."

The final occurrence of משכיל in 4Q418 frag. 81 17 makes clear that multiple *maskilim* are present in 4QInstruction. This reference is found in a passage consisting of the partial remains of six lines:[26]

15 ואתה מבין אם בחכמת ידים המשילכה זדע]ת

16 אוט לכול הולכי אדם ומשם תפקוד טרפכה ו]

17 התבונן מודה ומיד כול משכילכה הוסף לקח]

18 הוצא מחסורכה לכול דורשי חפץ ואז תבין]

19 תמלא ושבעתה ברוב טוב ומחכמת ידיכה]

20 כי אל פלג נחלת]ם בכו[ל]ֹ חי] וכול חכמי לב השכלנֹ]ו

15 And you, understanding one, if over manual craftsmanship he has placed you in charge, and knowled[ge

16 אוט to all *the ways of* humankind (?), and from there [i.e., אוט] you are appointed your sustenance and[

17 grow in understanding exceedingly, and from the hand of each of your instructors increase learning[

18 make your lacking evident to all pleasure seekers and then you shall establish[

19 you shall fill, and you will be satisfied in the abundance of good things, and your craftsmanship[

20 for God apportioned [their] inheritance [in ever]y[living thing] and *we* have taught all those wise of heart.

The instruction of lines 15–20 here and the preceding lines (4Q418 frag. 81 1–14; see further below) are similar in that they both are concerned to instruct a *maven* how to serve in a position of authority and relate to others in the community. The difference between them is that one *maven* enjoys an exalted status (ll. 1–14) while the other is an overseer of manual labor (l. 15). The meaning of line 16 is not entirely clear; perhaps it refers to sustenance in relationship to the industry the *maven* has been placed in authority over.[27] Line 17 is the only instance in the document where more than one *maskil* is referred to (כול משכילכה is collective). The author is

---

26. The first 14 lines, and an unknown number of preceding lines, preserve a passage that should be distinguished from the lines that follow (ll. 15–20), since the phrase "and you, understanding one," in l. 15 is used frequently in 4QInstruction to begin a new section.

27. DJD 34, 309–10.

not the only *maskil*; others may serve in this role, and each of them may impart knowledge to the understanding ones. Similarly, in 4Q418 frag. 221 3 we saw that the "I" describes the *maskil* in his role "increasing learning for the understanding ones." One last observation that returns to the use of the first-person plural in 4QInstruction: the translation of line 20 as "*we* have taught all those wise of heart" makes good sense in light of the multiple *maskilim* here.[28] The "we" is composed of the one instructing and others who through their pursuit of wisdom serve as instructors.

Before I conclude on the role of the *maskil* in 4QInstruction, several comments on the first fourteen lines of 4Q418 frag. 81 are in order. 4Q418 frag. 81 1–14 are among the most discussed in the entire document. Nearly every interpreter agrees that the one addressed in these lines is, in one way or another, an exalted figure. This exalted figure leads the community in blessing angels; he is called "most holy" and a firstborn; special insight and authority have been opened to him; and he turns away wrath from the "men of good pleasure." These lines read:

Transcription:[29]

0	[במזל]
1	שפתיכה פתח מקור לברך קדושים ואתה כמקור עולם הלל ○ מא[ז] הבדילך מכול
2	רוח בשר ואתה הבדל מכול אשר שנא והנזר מכול תעבות נפֹשֹ כי[א] הוא עשה כול
3	ויורישם איש נחלתו והוא חלקכה ונחלתכה בתוך בני אדם] ובנ[חֹלתו המשילכֹ/מֹה ואתה
4	בזה כבדהו בהתחדשכה לו כאשר שמכה לקודש קדושים] לכול]תבל ובכול] מ[לֹ]אכיו[
5	הפיל גורלכה וכבודכה הרבה מואדה וישימכה לו בכור בֹ] [לֹ] כי אמר אברככה]

---

28. Strugnell and Harrington (DJD 34, 311) find here a possible defective spelling of the *hiphil* (השכלו instead of השכילו), and comment: "One might instead read השכלנו 'we have taught the wise,' which meets the requirements of the traces materially, grammatically, and orthographically; but a move to the 1st plural verb would be unexpected in this fragment."

29. See esp. DJD 34, 300–301; Tigchelaar, *To Increase Learning*, 230–31; Jean-Sébastien Rey, *4QInstruction: Sagesse et eschatologie*, STDJ 81 (Leiden: Brill, 2010), 307–8.

6   וטובתי֯ לכה אתן ואתה להלוא לכה טוֹבוֹ ובאמונתוֹ הלך[

7   מעשיכה ואתה דְרוֹש משפטיו מיד כול יריבכֹֹה בכול מזֹ[oֹ]

8   אהבהו ובחסד עוֹלֹם וברחמים על כול שומרי דברו זֹקנאתוֹ[

9   ואתה שכֹלֹ[פ]תח לכה ובאוצרו המשילכה ואיפת אמת פיקד[ה

10   אתכה המה ובידכה להשיב אף מאנשי רצון ולפקוד עֹלֹ[ן

11   עמכה בֹטֹרם תקח נחלתכה מידו כבד קדושיו ובט[רם

12   פתח[מ]קֹוֹר כול קדוֹשים וכול הנקרא לשמו קדושֹי[ם

13   עם כול קצֹים הדרֹ֯ פארתו למטעת עוֹ[לם

14   ] oֹ[ ] תבֹלֹ בֹוֹ י֯תהלכו כול נוחלי ארץ כי בשמ[ים

Translation:[30]

0 [… by the pouring out of] [1] your lips open up a spring to bless the
     holy ones.
And you, as an everlasting spring, praise his [name,
sin]ce he separated you from every [2] fleshly spirit;

And you, keep separate from everything that he hates,
and keep apart from all the abominations of the soul;
[Fo]r he has made everyone,
[3] and has given to each man his own inheritance,
but he is your portion and your inheritance among the children of
     humankind,
[and over] his [in]heritance he has set you in authority.

And you, [4] honor him in this: by consecrating yourself to him,
just as he has appointed you as a most holy one [over all the] earth,
and among all [his a]n[gels] [5] he has cast your lot,
and has magnified your glory greatly,
he has appointed you for himself as a firstborn among [ ]
[saying, "I will bless you] [6] "and I will give my good things to you."

And you, do his good things not belong to you?
In faithfulness to him walk continually
[   ] [7] your deeds?

---

30. Cf. division into stichoi by Rey, *4QInstruction*, 309–10.

And you, seek his justice from the hand of each of your opponents,
and with all [   ] [8] love him,
and with eternal lovingkindness,
and with mercy for all those who keep his words,
and his zeal [   ]

[9] And you, he has [op]ened up insight for you,
and he has placed you in authority over his treasure,
and a true measure is appoint[ed
[   ] [10] are with you,
and it is in your hand to turn away anger from the men of good plea-
    sure,
and to appoint upon[   ] [11] your people.

Before you take your inheritance from his hand, glorify his holy ones,
and bef[ore] [12] open [a spring *of* all the ho]ly ones,
and every one who is called by his name,
holy [ones] [13] during all periods,
the majesty of his glory for an ever[lasting] plantation
[   ] [14] [   ] of the world,
in it all those who will inherit the land walk,
for in he[aven   ]....

When these lines are set alongside other remaining passages of 4QInstruc-
tion, it is clear that the exalted figure instructed in 4Q418 frag. 81 enjoys
a different role and status in comparison with others in the community.
This has led most to understand that the teachings in the document are
directed to different people in the group or different segments of society.
But who exactly is our *maskil* teaching and what are they to do? There are
priestly predicates in 4Q418 frag. 81, and yet they do not straightforwardly
indicate that the addressee is of priestly descent. That priests are in view
has been challenged, and one interpretation that is gaining traction is that
this passage is democratizing priestly roles.[31] In light of the possibility that
the instructor is a *maskil*, I would take this one step further and say that
4Q418 frag. 81 contains instruction from a maskil about how a maven is

---

31. See esp. Joseph Angel, *Otherworldly and Eschatological Priesthood in the Dead
Sea Scrolls*, STDJ 86 (Leiden: Brill, 2010), 76–77.

to act in the role of maskil—just like him. Moreover, the *maskil* derives authority to teach about mysteries from his present participation with the angels, and when he teaches others how to act in this role, he exhorts them to bless and glorify the angels.[32] The author is not simply looking forward to a future and eschatological participation in another world; in 4QInstruction the *maskilim* enjoy a relationship to the heavenly realm in the present insofar as they relate to angelic beings when seeking the רז נהיה.

CONCLUSIONS

In the opening column of 4QInstruction the sender presents himself as a *maskil*. As he addresses himself to his audience he speaks to them in the first-person. When the other occurrences of משכיל are examined in light of the opening address, they too may be interpreted as referring to a *maskil*. The purpose of the speaker's instruction is to address disciples who are being trained to act in the same or a similar role as him. However, not every *maskil* is identical. Although each *maskil* is a leader, this may vary from looking after manual labor and caring for possessions to leading others in liturgy, study, and the pursuit of the mystery of existence (רז נהיה). The exalted status of the *maven* in 4Q418 frag. 81 may reflect the pinnacle of this vocation.

That 4QInstruction is interested in a range of mundane daily life issues as well as worship and participation with the angels may be explained by the variety of ways one might act as a *maskil* (or various stages of development). The role of a *maskil* is to act as a community leader. Therefore there is interest to teach (about how to teach) women, wives, and daughters in one manuscript of 4QInstruction. The *maven* does not stand outside society—he also marries and has children. The insistence that he is poor, a leitmotif of the document, is a reminder that occurs within the context of training up a leader for the community.

The reminder and description of the *maven's* poverty is part of the broader way that the role of *maskil* is conceived. Poverty language has several nuances that include material poverty as well as a humble status that transcends financial matters. The speaker's character is somewhat modest.

---

32. Perhaps what distinguishes the addressees from the spirit of flesh (רוח בשר) in these lines is accessing heavenly revelation. 4QInstruction does not mention torah, although, like Enochic literature, torah is used nonexplicitly; and it may be that the type of wisdom that one acquires is crucial.

When contrasted with the exalted speaker of the Self-Glorification Hymn, this becomes even more pronounced. The *maskil* of 4QInstruction may refer to his own judgments and the outpouring of his lips, but this reflects his role as mediator between the heavenly and his own community or just the other understanding ones. The *maskil* has a special role in accessing heavenly mysteries and knowledge.

4Q418 frag. 81 describes the addressee as being placed in authority over God's treasure and inheritance. He is a firstborn son and his lot is cast with the angels. 4Q416 frag. 2 ii encourages the *maven* to stand firm and serve God, and promises that by doing so he will become like a firstborn son. The speaker teaches that if he is diligent and acts accordingly he will become like him: a servant of a *maskil*. 4Q418 frag. 81 addresses the faithful *maven* who is the "servant of a *maskil*," while 4Q416 frag. 2 ii leads along the path to help him arrive there.

When this assessment of 4QInstruction is set alongside formal apocalypses in which a righteous individual ascends to the heavens, it is possible to take a somewhat more egalitarian view of revealed wisdom. While there are competing views of who the speaker of the Self-Glorification Hymn may be (and differing assessments on this point are not offered here), in the case that the figure is human, then its construction of authority may be more closely aligned with these formal apocalypses. The one who disseminates revealed wisdom may hold a more or less unique status. 4QInstruction is active in broadening conceptions in regard to who in the elect community may participate in accessing and mediating revealed wisdom. Unfortunately any thoroughgoing assessment of 4QInstruction's "cross talk" falters when it encounters issues of dating.

In 4Q418 frag. 81 the exalted figure enjoys a status as firstborn son, and yet this claim to sonship appears not to be the claim to as unique a relationship to wisdom, as some have thought. When in Jesus's prayer in Matt 11:25–30 he claims a unique relationship to the Father, as Son, the limitations on possible other ways that wisdom can reach humanity is more pronounced than in 4QInstruction. Luke 7:35 (// Matt 11:19) portrays wisdom being disseminated by Jesus, John the Baptist, and the disciples, and thus shares with 4QInstruction the view that wisdom may reach humanity vis-à-vis multiple figures.

When Jesus is presented in the gospels as enjoying more and less exclusive relationships with wisdom, these varying degrees are also apparent in an examination of 4QInstruction alongside the Self-Glorification Hymn in their presentation of a *maskil*. The claim that there are those who fall heir to the wisdom that Jesus or Enoch embodies—and thus claims of legitimacy for a community as the locus of wisdom—does not resonate entirely with 4QInstruction, where the *maskil* is anonymous and trains others to participate in this role. 4QInstruction, Enochic tradition, and the gospels all relate exalted figures and the dissemination of wisdom to claims of authority and legitimacy.

THE VENERATION MOTIF IN THE TEMPTATION
NARRATIVE OF THE GOSPEL OF MATTHEW:
LESSONS FROM THE ENOCHIC TRADITION

Andrei A. Orlov

INTRODUCTION

The story of Jesus's temptation in the wilderness found in the Synoptic Gospels baffles the reader with a plethora of apocalyptic motifs.[1] Some features in Matthew's version of Jesus's encounter with Satan in the desert

---

1. Scholars believe that the stories of Jesus's temptation by Satan found in the Gospel of Matthew and the Gospel of Luke originated from Q. See Terence L. Donaldson, *Jesus on the Mountain: A Study in Matthean Theology*, JSNTSup 8 (Sheffield: JSOT Press, 1985), 242–43; W. D. Davies and Dale C. Allison Jr., *The Gospel according to Saint Matthew*, 3 vols., ICC (Edinburgh: T&T Clark, 1988–1997), 1:351; Christopher M. Tuckett, "The Temptation Narrative in Q," in *The Four Gospels: Festschrift Frans Neirynck*, ed. Frans Van Segbroeck et al., 3 vols., BETL 100 (Leuven: Peeters, 1992), 1:479–507. Both Matthew and Luke are also informed by the temptation narrative found in the Gospel of Mark. That both Matthew and Luke start with the temptation in the wilderness might suggest that both of them were influenced by Mark's account. Cf. Nicholas H. Taylor, "The Temptation of Jesus on the Mountain: A Palestinian Christian Polemic against Agrippa I," *JSNT* 83 (2001): 27–49, esp. 33. The Gospel of Matthew then follows this first temptation with the second one in the temple, and the third on the mountain. In contrast to the Gospel of Matthew, the Gospel of Luke places as second a temptation from a high place, then concludes with the temptation in the temple. Matthew and Luke thus exhibit some differences in the order of the temptations. The majority of scholars think that the Gospel of Matthew attests the original order of the temptation narrative, while the Gospel of Luke represents the inversion of this original order. Cf., e.g., Jacques Dupont, *Les tentations de Jésus au désert*, StudNeot 4 (Brugge: Desclée de Brouwer, 1968), 290; Joseph A. Fitzmyer, *The Gospel according to Luke*, 2 vols., AB 28 (Garden City, NY: Doubleday, 1981–1985), 1:507–8; Donaldson, *Jesus on the Mountain*, 88; Davies and Allison, *Matthew*, 1:364.

seem to contain more explicit references to apocalyptic traditions than do Mark and Luke.[2] Mark and Luke, who take the forty-day period to encompass the whole process of temptation,[3] seem to use the traditional allusion to the forty years of the Israelites' ordeal in the wilderness. Yet Matthew's emphasis on the initiatory forty-day fasting that is followed by the appearance of Satan might suggest that the fast serves here as a tool for inducing a visionary experience.[4] The canonical stories of two famous visionaries of the Hebrew Bible, Moses and Elijah, contain passages referring specifically to the period of forty days. Exodus 24:18 tells of Moses abiding forty days and forty nights at the top of Mount Sinai.[5] First Kings 19:8 refers to the story of Elijah's being sustained by angels for forty days[6] during his journey to Mount Horeb.[7] In both accounts, as in Matthew, the motif of the

---

2. This intense presence of apocalyptic motifs in the temptation narrative reflects the general tendency of the gospel. Some scholars, such as Donald Hagner ("Apocalyptic Motifs in the Gospel of Matthew: Continuity and Discontinuity," *HBT* 7 [1985]: 53), have argued that in the Gospel of Matthew, "the apocalyptic perspective holds a much more prominent place than in any of the other Gospels."

3. Luke, like Mark, states that Satan's temptation of Jesus in the wilderness lasted for forty days. In contrast, Matthew's account seems to emphasize the length of Jesus's fast by claiming that he *fasted* forty days and forty nights. Davies and Allison (*Matthew*, 1:359) note, "In Matthew all temptation appears to come only after the fast; in Luke Jesus is tempted during the forty day period. Matthew's version, in which the forty days go with the fasting, is closer to Exod 32.28."

4. Luigi Schiavo ("The Temptation of Jesus: The Eschatological Battle and the New Ethic of the First Followers of Jesus in Q," *JSNT* 25 [2002]: 144–45) suggests, "The expression that opens the account of the temptation of Jesus [in Q] ἤγετο ἐν τῷ πνεύματι ('he was led/taken up by the spirit') characterizes the narrative as a transcendental experience of religious ecstasy. The verb, which always appears in the passive, indicates an action that comes from outside. The expression at Q 4.1, ἤγετο ἐν τῷ πνεύματι, albeit with literary variations, occurs in various texts of the New Testament and intertestamental literature [1 En. 71.1, 5; Asc. Isa. 6.9; Rev. 1.10; 4.2; 17.3; 21.10; Mt. 4.1; Ezek. 3.14], always in relation to accounts of visions."

5. "Moses entered the cloud, and went up on the mountain. Moses was on the mountain for forty days and forty nights" (NRSV).

6. "He got up, and ate and drank; then he went in the strength of that food forty days and forty nights to Horeb the mount of God" (NRSV).

7. For the discussion of the forty-day motif, see Susan R. Garrett, *The Temptations of Jesus in Mark's Gospel* (Grand Rapids: Eerdmans, 1998), 57; Birger Gerhardsson, *The Testing of God's Son (Matt 4:1–11 and Par.): An Analysis of an Early Christian Midrash*, trans. John Toy, ConBNT 2 (Lund: Gleerup, 1966), 41–43; Henry Ansgar Kelly, "The Devil in the Desert," *CBQ* 26 (1964): 196.

forty-day fast appears along with the theme of the encounter on a mountain, signifying a visionary experience on high.

If we accept the transformational value of fasting in Matthew's account, the fast may have served to induce the vision, not of God, but of Satan.[8] The depiction could have a polemical flavor in attempting to challenge or deconstruct traditional apocalyptic settings.

---

8. Regarding Satan and Satan's traditions, see Gary A. Anderson, "The Exaltation of Adam and the Fall of Satan," in *Literature on Adam and Eve: Collected Essays,* ed. Gary A. Anderson, Michael E. Stone, and Johannes Tromp; SVTP 15 (Brill: Leiden, 2000), 83–110; Cilliers Breytenbach and Peggy L. Day, "Satan," *DDD,* 726–32; Joseph Dan, "Samael and the Problem of Jewish Gnosticism," in *Perspectives on Jewish Thought and Mysticism,* ed. Alfred L. Ivry, Elliot R. Wolfson and Allan Arkush (Amsterdam: Harwood Academic, 1998), 257–76; Peggy L. Day, *An Adversary in Heaven: Śāṭān in the Hebrew Bible,* HSM 43 (Atlanta: Scholars Press, 1988); Neil Forsyth, *The Old Enemy: Satan and the Combat Myth* (Princeton: Princeton University Press, 1987); Harry E. Gaylord, "How Satanael Lost His '-el,'" *JJS* 33 (1982): 303–9; Victor P. Hamilton, "Satan," *ABD* 5:985–98; Henry Ansgar Kelly, *Towards the Death of Satan: The Growth and Decline of Christian Demonology* (London: Chapman, 1968); Kelly, *Satan: A Biography* (Cambridge: Cambridge University Press, 2006); Rivkah Schärf Kluger, *Satan in the Old Testament,* Studies in Jungian Thought 7 (Evanston, IL: Northwestern University Press, 1967); Adolphe Lods, "Les origines de la figure de satan, ses fonctions à la cour céleste," in *Mélanges syriens offerts à Monsieur René Dussaud,* ed. J.-Adrien Blanchet, Franz Cumont, and Georges Contenau; 2 vols. (Paris: Geuthner, 1939), 2:649–60; Elaine H. Pagels, "The Social History of Satan, the 'Intimate Enemy': A Preliminary Sketch," *HTR* 84 (1991): 105–28; Pagels, "The Social History of Satan, 2: Satan in the New Testament Gospels," *JAAR* 62 (1994): 17–58; Pagels, *The Origin of Satan* (New York: Vintage, 1996); Pagels, "The Social History of Satan, 3: John of Patmos and Ignatius of Antioch: Contrasting Visions of 'God's People,'" *HTR* 99 (2006): 487–505; Constantinos A. Patrides, "The Salvation of Satan," *JHI* 28 (1967): 467–78; Jeffrey Burton Russell, *Satan: The Early Christian Tradition* (Ithaca, NY: Cornell University Press, 1981); Michael Schneider, "The Myth of the Satan in the *Book of Bahir,*" *Kabbalah* 20 (2009): 287–343 [in Hebrew]; Rainer Stichel, "Die Verführung der Stammeltern durch Satanael nach der Kurzfassung der slavischen Baruch-Apocalypse," in *Kulturelle Traditionen in Bulgarien,* ed. Reinhard Lauer and Peter Schreiner, AAWG 177 (Göttingen: Vandenhoeck & Ruprecht, 1989), 116–28; Michael E. Stone, *Adam's Contract with Satan: The Legend of the Cheirograph of Adam* (Bloomington: Indiana University Press, 2002); Stone, "'Be You a Lyre for Me': Identity or Manipulation in Eden," in *The Exegetical Encounter between Jews and Christians in Late Antiquity,* ed. Emmanouela Grypeou and Helen Spurling, Jewish and Christian Perspective Series 18 (Leiden: Brill, 2009), 87–99.

340   ORLOV

The apocalyptic thrust in Matthew's version of the temptation story
has been noted by scholars.[9] Some studies have even suggested that the
narrative mimics or even offers a polemic against the apocalyptic ascent
and vision trends.[10] Many details of the account also reveal a connection
to the protological typologies prominent in Jewish apocalyptic accounts.
The aim of this study is to explore more closely the connections in Matthew's version of the temptation narrative with extrabiblical apocalyptic
traditions, especially those found in the Enochic materials.

ADAMIC TRADITIONS AND THE TEMPTATION NARRATIVE

Scholars have long recognized that the story of Jesus's temptation in the
Synoptic Gospels seems to be influenced by an Adamic typology.[11] Some
studies suggested that the chain of pivotal Adamic themes known from
biblical and extrabiblical accounts is already introduced in the terse narration of Jesus's temptation in the Gospel of Mark.[12] For example, Joachim

---

9. See, e.g., Davies and Allison, *Matthew*, 1:364; David C. Sim, *Apocalyptic Eschatology in the Gospel of Matthew* (Cambridge: Cambridge University Press, 1996).

10. See my chapter entitled "Satan and the Visionary: Apocalyptic Roles of the
Adversary in the Temptation Narrative of the Gospel of Matthew," in *Dark Mirrors:
Azazel and Satanael in Early Jewish Demonology* (Albany: State University of New
York Press, 2011), 107–12.

11. Some early Christian interpreters saw the temptation of Jesus as the reversal
of Adam's sins. Cf., e.g., Justin, *Dial.* 103; Irenaeus, *Haer.* 5.21.2. On this see Dale
C. Allison Jr., "Behind the Temptations of Jesus: Q 4:1–13 and Mark 1:12–13," in
Authenticating the Activities of Jesus, ed. Bruce Chilton and Craig A. Evans, NTTS 28.2
(Leiden: Brill, 2002), 196.

12. Wilhelm August Schultze, "Der Heilige und die wilden Tiere: Zur Exegese
von Mc 1 13b," *ZNW* 46 (1955): 280–83; André Feuillet, "L'épisode de la tentation
d'après l'évangile selon saint Marc I,12–13," *EstBib* 19 (1960): 49–73; Joachim Jere-
mias, "Ἀδάμ," *TDNT* 1:141–43; Jeremias, "Nachwort zum Artikel von H.-G. Leder,"
ZNW 54 (1963): 278–79; Antonio Vargas-Machuca, "La tentación de Jesús según
Mc. 1,12–13 ¿Hecho real o relato de tipo haggádico?" *EstEcl* 48 (1973): 163–90; Petr
Pokorný, "The Temptation Stories and Their Intention," *NTS* 20 (1973–1974): 115–27;
Joachim Gnilka, *Das Evangelium nach Markus*, 2 vols., EKKNT 2.1–2 (Zurich: Ben-
ziger; Neukirchen-Vluyn: Neukirchener Verlag, 1978–1979), 1:58; Robert A. Guelich,
Mark 1–8:26, WBC 34A (Dallas: Word, 1989), 38–39; Richard J. Bauckham, "Jesus
and the Wild Animals (Mark 1:13): A Christological Image for an Ecological Age," in
*Jesus of Nazareth: Lord and Christ: Essays on the Historical Jesus and New Testament
Christology*, ed. Joel B. Green and Max Turner (Grand Rapids: Eerdmans, 1994), 3–21;

Jeremias draws attention to the phrase in Mark 1:12 that Jesus "was with the wild beasts" (ἦν μετὰ τῶν θηρίων). In Jeremias's opinion, this phrase is reminiscent of the protoplast (Adam), who lived among wild animals in paradise according to Gen 2:19. Jeremias suggests that Jesus might be envisioned, in the Gospel of Mark, as an eschatological Adam who restores peace between humans and animals.[13] He proposes that Mark's account sets forth a belief that "paradise is restored, the time of salvation is dawning; that is what ἦν μετὰ τῶν θηρίων means. Because the temptation has been overcome and Satan has been vanquished, the gate to paradise is again opened."[14] Jeremias also discerns the Adamic typology in the saying that the angels did Jesus "table service" (διηκόνουν αὐτῷ); in his view:

> This feature, too, is part of the idea of paradise and can only be understood in that light. Just as, according to the Midrash, Adam lived on angels' food in paradise, so the angels give Jesus nourishment. The table-service of angels is a symbol of the restored communion between man and God.[15]

Richard Bauckham also sees a cluster of Adamic motifs in Mark's version of the temptation story and argues that it envisions Jesus "as the eschatological Adam who, having resisted Satan, instead of succumbing to temptation as Adam did, then restores paradise: he is at peace with the animals and the angels serve him."[16] From this perspective, Jesus's temptation by Satan plays a pivotal role in the unfolding of the Adamic typological appropriations.[17] Dale Allison draws attention to another possible

---

Jeffrey Gibson, *Temptations of Jesus in Early Christianity*, JSNTSup 112 (Sheffield: Sheffield Academic, 1995), 65–66; Allison, "Behind the Temptations of Jesus," 196–99.

13. Joachim Jeremias, *New Testament Theology*, trans. John Bowden (New York: Scribner's Sons, 1971), 69. The theme of alienation between humanity and animals looms large already in the book of Jubilees. It receives further development in the Primary Adam Books, in which Eve and Seth encounter a hostile beast.

14. Jeremias, *New Testament Theology*, 69–70.

15. Ibid., 70.

16. Bauckham, "Jesus and the Wild Animals," 6.

17. In this respect, Davies and Allison (*Matthew*, 1:356) remark, "In Mk 1.12–13 Jesus is probably the last Adam (cf. Rom 5.12–21; 1 Cor 15.42–50; Justin, *Dial.* 103; Gosp. Philip 71.16–21; Irenaeus. *Adv. haer.* 5.21.2). He, like the first Adam, is tempted by Satan. But unlike his anti-type, he does not succumb, and the result is the recovery of paradise (cf. T. Levi 18.10): the wild beasts are tamed and once again a man dwells with angels and is served by them."

connection with the protoplast story by wondering whether Mark's "forty days" is also part of his Adamic typology. He notices that, according to Jub. 3:9, Adam was placed in Eden forty days after he was created, and in the Primary Adam Books, Adam does penance for forty days.[18]

In Matthew and Luke, the Adamic typology hinted at in Mark receives further conceptual development. Moreover, not only the temptation narrative, but other parts of Matthew and Luke become affected by the panoply of Adamic motifs. It has been suggested, for example, that "perhaps Luke prefaced his temptation account with a genealogy that concludes with Adam (Luke 3:38) because the evangelist viewed Jesus' victory over temptation as a reversal of Adam's failure."[19] Similarly, Matthew's Gospel continues the appropriation and development of the Adamic typology in the unfolding story of Jesus's temptations. It appears that the most concentrated presence of Adamic motifs can be found in the third temptation in which Satan asks Jesus to prostrate himself before him. This cultic motif of worship appears to be reaffirmed at the end of the temptation narrative, which tells that angels approached Jesus and served him.

In the search for the conceptual roots of this veneration motif, scholars have often turned to the account of Adam's elevation and veneration by angels, found in various versions of the so-called Primary Adam Books. Although known macroforms of the Primary Adam Books survive only in their later medieval versions, these later Christian compilations undoubtedly contain early Jewish conceptual seeds that might also stand behind the veneration motif in the gospels' temptation story.

One particular theme found in the Primary Adam Books deserves special attention, namely, the account of the protoplast's creation and his introduction into the angelic community. During this initiation, Adam is ordered to venerate the Deity, and then God commands the angelic hosts to venerate the protoplast. Further, although some angels agree to venerate Adam, Satan refuses to bow down before the first human. This cluster of motifs is intriguing as it recalls that which is found in Matthew. In the gospel, the tempter asks Jesus to prostrate himself, suggesting literally that he will "fall down" (πεσών) before Satan. Here Matthew seems to hew more closely to the Adamic blueprint than Luke, since in Luke πεσών is missing. Here one again encounters an example of Matthean Adamic Christology

---

18. Allison, "Behind the Temptations of Jesus," 198.
19. Ibid., 196 n. 6.

that depicts Jesus as the last Adam. The presence of such conceptualiza-
tion in Matthew is not unusual since implicit and explicit comparisons
between Adam and Jesus are already made in the earliest Christian materials, including the Pauline epistles and the Gospel of Mark. Thus scholars
have suggested that the understanding of Jesus as the last Adam can be
found as early as Rom 5, which predates Matthew. Moreover, some studies
propose that the Pauline material might constitute the conceptual basis for
the Adamic typology found in the Synoptic Gospels. Thus, for example,
Dale Allison argues,

> if the Jesus of Mark 1:12–13 undoes the work of Adam, then one is inevi-
> tably reminded of Paul's Christology, in which Adam's disobedience and
> its attendant effects are contrasted with Jesus's obedience and its atten-
> dant effects (Rom 5:12–21; 1Cor 15:21–23, 45–49). Indeed, one wonders,
> given the other intriguing connections between Mark and Paul, whether
> Mark 1:12–13 was composed under Paul's influence.[20]

Satan's request for veneration also can be a part of the evangelists' Adam
Christology: Satan, who lost his celestial status by refusing to venerate the
first Adam, is now attempting to reverse the situation by asking the last
Adam to bow down.

Although the tradition of Satan's request for worship is also found
in Luke, Matthew appears to reinforce this veneration theme further by
adding the peculiar terminology of prostration and by concluding his
temptation story with the appearance of servicing angels. It is possible that
these embellishments are intended to affirm the traditions of devotion
to and exaltation of the last Adam that are constructed both negatively
and positively by invoking the memory of the first Adam's veneration.[21]

---

20. Ibid., 199.

21. The suggestion that the veneration motif found in the temptation story might
be connected to the theme of worship of Jesus in Matthew is hinted by the usage of
the verb προσκυνέω. Larry Hurtado (*How on Earth Did Jesus Become a God? Historical
Questions about Earliest Devotion to Jesus* [Grand Rapids: Eerdmans, 2005], 143) suggests that the "pattern of preference for προσκυνέω, with its strong associations with
cultic worship, suggests that Matthew has chosen to make these scenes all function
as foreshadowings of the exalted reverence of Jesus familiar to his Christian readers
in their collective worship.... The net effect of Matthew's numerous omissions and
insertions of προσκυνέω in cases where Jesus is the recipient of homage is a consistent
pattern. It is not simply a matter of preference of one somewhat synonymous word

Scholars have noted wide usage of the formulae of worship and veneration in the Gospel of Matthew that appears to be more consistent than in the other Synoptic Gospels.[22] In view of this tendency, the Adamic tradition of veneration of humanity might also be perceived in other parts of Matthew, including the magi story narrated earlier in the gospel. It is noteworthy that both the temptation and the magi narratives contain identical terminology of worship. First, in the magi story one can see repeated usage of the verb προσκυνέω (cf. Matt 2:2, 8, 11), which is also prominent in the temptation story (Matt 4:9, 10). In both accounts this terminology appears to have a cultic significance.[23] Also, both in the magi story and in the third Matthean temptation of Jesus, one can find a distinctive juxtaposition of the expression "falling down" (πεσόντες/πεσών) with the formulae of worship (προσεκύνησαν/προσκυνήσῃς).[24]

The story of the magi speaks of mysterious visitors from the East who came to pay homage to the newborn king of the Jews. Some details of the account suggest that one might have here not simply the story of veneration by foreign guests, but possibly the theme of angelic reverence. Some scholars have pointed to the angelological details of the narrative. For

for others. Matthew reserves the word προσκυνέω for the reverence of Jesus given by disciples and those who are presented as sincerely intending to give him homage. As Günther Bornkamm, Gerhard Barth, and Heinz Joachim Held concluded from their analysis of scenes where Jesus is the recipient of the gesture in Matthew, προσκυνέω is used 'only in the sense of genuine worship of Jesus.' "

22. Hurtado (ibid., 142–43), in his analysis of usage of the verb προσκυνέω in the New Testament, which both Matthew and Luke use in their temptation narratives (Matt 4:9; Luke 4:7), suggests that "the term προσκυνέω is a recurrent feature of Matthew's narrative vocabulary, with thirteen occurrences, a frequency exceeded only by the twenty-four uses in Revelation among the New Testament writings." In the gospels προσκυνέω "appears twice in Mark, three times in Luke (in two passages), eight times in John (in three passages), and thirteen times in Matthew (in nine distinguishable passages)" (142).

23. Cf. Matt 2:2: ἤλθομεν προσκυνῆσαι αὐτῷ; Matt 2:8: ὅπως κἀγὼ ἐλθὼν προσκυνήσω αὐτῷ. With respect to these formulae, scholars note that in some LXX passages "ἔρχομαι followed by προσκυνέω denotes a cultic action" (Davies and Allison, Matthew, 1:236). Similarly, in the temptation narrative, προσκυνέω is also placed in the cultic context. Cf., e.g., Matt 4:10: Κύριον τὸν θεόν σου προσκυνήσεις καὶ αὐτῷ μόνῳ λατρεύσεις.

24. Cf. Matt 2:11: καὶ πεσόντες προσεκύνησαν αὐτῷ; Matt 4:9: πεσὼν προσκυνήσῃς μοι. Scholars note that similar terminological constellations occur also in Ps 72:11; Dan 3:5–7; Josephus, Ant. 7.95; 9.11; Acts 10:25; 1 Cor 14:25; Rev 4:10; 7:11; 22:8. Concerning this, see Davies and Allison, Matthew, 1:248.

example, it has been observed that the mysterious star, which assists the magi in their journey to the Messiah, appears to be an angel, more specifically a guiding angel whose function is to lead the foreign visitors to Jesus.[25] Other features of the story are also intriguing, as they, like the details of the temptation narrative, seem to betray some traces of apocalyptic traditions. It is also possible that, here, as in the temptation story, one can see a cluster of Adamic motifs. The baby Jesus, for instance, might be depicted as an eschatological counterpart of the first human, and, just as in the creation of the protoplast, which in the Primary Adam Books is marked by angelic veneration, the entrance of the last Adam into the world is also celebrated by a similar ritual of obeisance.

Let us now explore more closely other possible Adamic allusions in the story of the magi. First, the origin of the magi from the East (ἀπὸ ἀνατολῶν) might show a possible connection with Eden, a garden that according to biblical testimonies was planted in the East.[26] Gifts of the magi, including frankincense and myrrh, which were traditionally used in antiquity as ingredients of incense,[27] bring to mind Adam's sacrifices, which according

---

25. Dale C. Allison Jr., "The Magi's Angel (Matt. 2:2, 9–10)," in *Studies in Matthew: Interpretation Past and Present*, ed. Dale C. Allison Jr. (Grand Rapids: Baker Academic, 2005), 17–41. Cf. also Allison, "What Was the Star That Guided the Magi?" *BRev* 9.6 (1993): 24; Bogdan G. Bucur, *Angelomorphic Pneumatology: Clement of Alexandria and Other Early Christian Witnesses*, VCSup 95 (Leiden: Brill, 2009), 93.

26. Cf. Gen 2:8: "And the LORD God planted a garden in Eden, in the east; and there he put the man whom he had formed" (NRSV).

27. With respect to the cultic functions of frankincense and myrrh, as ingredients in incense, Dale Allison (*Matthew: A Shorter Commentary* [London: T&T Clark, 2004], 27) notes that "**frankincense** was an odoriferous gum resin from various trees and bushes which had a cultic usage in the ancient world. According to Exod 30.34–8, it was a prescribed ingredient of sacred incense. According to Lev 24.7, it was to be offered with the bread of the Presence. According to Lev 2.1–2, 14–6; 6.14–8, it was added to cereal offerings.... **myrrh** was a fragrant gum resin from trees ... a component of holy anointing oil, and an ingredient in incense." The magis' gifts also include gold, a material which is mentioned in the description of Eden in Gen 2:11. In relation to this, Gordon Wenham ("Sanctuary Symbolism in the Garden of Eden Story," in *The Period of the Bible*, division A of *Proceedings of the Ninth World Congress of Jewish Studies, Jerusalem, August 4–12, 1985* [Jerusalem: World Union of Jewish Studies, 1986], 22) observes that "if Eden is seen as a super sanctuary, this reference to gold can hardly be accidental for the most sacred items of tabernacle furniture were made of or covered with 'pure gold.'" With respect to the connections between gold of Eden and the materials used for decoration of the tabernacle and priestly vestments in

to Jewish extrabiblical lore, the protoplast was offering in the garden of Eden in fulfillment of his sacerdotal duties. Such sacrifices are mentioned in Jub. 3:27, a passage depicting Adam as a protological high priest[28] who burns incense in paradise.[29] In view of the possible cultic flavor of the magi story, Jesus might be understood there not simply as the last Adam but as a priestly eschatological Adam in a fashion reminiscent of the book of Jubilees. In the context of these traditions, the magi could be understood as visitors, possibly even angelic visitors, from the garden of Eden, once planted in the East, who are bringing to a new priest the sacerdotal

---

the book of Exodus, see also David Chilton, *Paradise Restored: A Biblical Theology of Dominion* (Fort Worth, TX: Dominion, 1985).

28. Jacques van Ruiten argues that, in Jubilees, "the Garden of Eden is seen as a Temple, or, more precisely as a part of the Temple: the room which is in the rear of the Temple, where the ark of the covenant of the Lord is placed, and which is often called 'Holy of Holies.'" Such an understanding of Eden as the temple presupposes the protoplast's role as a sacerdotal servant. In relation to this, van Ruiten suggests that, according to the author of Jubilees, Adam is acting as a prototypical priest as he burns incense at the gate of the garden of Eden. Van Ruiten puts this description in parallel with a tradition found in Exodus, which tells that the incense was burned in front of the holy of holies; see van Ruiten, "Visions of the Temple in the Book of Jubilees," in *Gemeinde ohne Tempel/Community without Temple: Zur Substituierung und Transformation des Jerusalemer Tempels und seines Kults im Alten Testament, antiken Judentum und frühen Christentum*, ed. Beate Ego, Armin Lange, and Peter Pilhofer; WUNT 118 (Tübingen: Mohr Siebeck, 1999), 215–28; and van Ruiten, "Eden and the Temple: The Rewriting of Genesis 2:4–3:24 in the Book of Jubilees," in *Paradise Interpreted: Representations of Biblical Paradise in Judaism and Christianity*, ed. Gerard P. Luttikhuizen, TBN 2 (Leiden: Brill, 1999), 76.

29. Jub. 3:27 reads: "On that day, as he was leaving the Garden of Eden, he burned incense as a pleasing fragrance—frankincense, galbanum, stacte, and aromatic spices—in the early morning when the sun rose at the time when he covered his shame"; trans. James C. VanderKam, *The Book of Jubilees*, 2 vols., CSCO 510–511, Scriptores Aethiopici 87–88 (Leuven: Peeters, 1989), 2:20. Regarding the Edenic incense, see also 1 En. 29:2: "And there I saw ... vessels of the fragrance of incense and myrrh"; trans. Michael A. Knibb, *The Ethiopic Book of Enoch: A New Edition in the Light of the Aramaic Dead Sea Fragments*, 2 vols. (Oxford: Clarendon, 1978), 2:117–18; Sir 24:15: "like cassia and camel's thorn I gave forth perfume, and like choice myrrh I spread my fragrance, like galbanum, onycha, and stacte, and like the odor of incense in the tent" (NRSV); Armenian LAE 29:3 reads: "Adam replied and said to the angels, 'I beseech you, let (me) be a little, so that I may take sweet incenses with me from the Garden, so that when I go out of here, I may offer sweet incenses to God, and offerings, so that, perhaps, God will hearken to us'"; trans. in *A Synopsis of the Books of Adam and Eve*, ed. Gary A. Anderson and Michael E. Stone, 2nd ed., EJL 17 (Atlanta: Scholars Press, 1999), 72E.

tools used in the distant past by Adam.[30] This exegetical connection is not implausible given that some later Christian materials, including Cave of Treasures, often associate the gifts of the magi with Adam's sacrifices.[31]

Moreover, it appears that other details of the magi narrative, including the peculiar juxtaposition of its antagonistic figure with the theme of worship, again bring to mind the protoplast story reflected in various versions of the Primary Adam Books, with its motifs of angelic veneration and Satan's refusal to worship the first human. Recall that Matthew connects the main antagonist of the magi story, Herod, with the theme of veneration by telling that the evil king promised to worship the messianic child.[32]

The magi narrative demonstrates that the veneration motifs play an important role in the overarching theological framework of Matthew's Gospel. The cultic significance of the veneration motif can be further illustrated in Matthew's transfiguration story in chapter 17.[33] There, at the end of Jesus's transfiguration on the mountain, the already familiar veneration motif is evoked again when the disciples, overwhelmed with the vision, throw themselves down with their faces to the ground.[34] It is noteworthy

---

30. Previous studies have identified the connection between the magi story and the birth of a priestly child (Noah, Melchizedek, Moses) in some Jewish accounts. In the gifts that the magi brought to the child, these studies see the sacerdotal items. Thus, e.g., Crispin H. T. Fletcher-Louis (*All the Glory of Adam: Liturgical Anthropology in the Dead Sea Scrolls*, STDJ 42 [Leiden: Brill, 2002], 53) observes that "it is noteworthy that at the birth of Jesus, of course, there is signaled the child's priestly identity in the gift of gold, frankincense and myrrh (cf. Exod 30:23; 28:5, 6, 8 etc.) from the magi (Matt 2:11)."

31. Concerning this tradition, Davies and Allison (*Matthew*, 1:251) note that "of the many legends that later came to surround the magi and their gifts, one of the most pleasing is found in the so-called *Cave of Treasures* (6th cent. A.D.). Adam, we are told, had many treasures in paradise, and when he was expelled therefrom he took what he could with him—gold, frankincense, and myrrh. Upon his death, Adam's sons hid their father's treasures in a cave, where they lay undisturbed until the magi, on their way to Bethlehem, entered the cave to get gifts for the Son of God. In this legend, Matthew's story has become the vehicle for a very Pauline idea, namely, that Jesus is the second Adam."

32. Cf. Matt 2:8: Πορευθέντες ἐξετάσατε ἀκριβῶς περὶ τοῦ παιδίου· ἐπὰν δὲ εὕρητε ἀπαγγείλατέ μοι, ὅπως κἀγὼ ἐλθὼν προσκυνήσω αὐτῷ.

33. Matt 17:6: καὶ ἀκούσαντες οἱ μαθηταὶ ἔπεσαν ἐπὶ πρόσωπον αὐτῶν καὶ ἐφοβήθησαν σφόδρα.

34. The motif of the disciples' veneration is reminiscent of the one performed by the magi. Thus Davies and Allison (*Matthew*, 1:248) note that "the magi do not simply

that this depiction of the disciples' prostration at Jesus's transfiguration is strikingly absent from both Mark and Luke. In Matthew this motif seems to fit nicely in the chain of previous veneration occurrences, thus evoking the memory of both the falling down of the magi and Satan's quest for prostration—traditions likewise absent from other Synoptic accounts.[35]

ENOCHIC TRADITIONS AND THE TEMPTATION NARRATIVE

Although previous studies have investigated the cluster of Adamic allusions in the Synoptic versions of the temptation narrative, they have been often reluctant to explore the formative influences of the Enochic tradition. It is possible that the motif of angelic veneration of humanity reflected in the Gospel of Matthew has its true origins not in the Adamic tradition but in early Enochic lore, a portentous mediatorial trend in which the early Jewish angelology received its most profound symbolic expression. So, in 2 Enoch, which is often viewed by scholars as being contemporary with or possibly even earlier than the Gospel of Matthew,[36] one can find a clus-

---

bend their knees (cf. 17.14; 18.29). They fall down on their faces. This is noteworthy because there was a tendency in Judaism to think prostration proper only in the worship of God (cf. Philo, *Leg. Gai.* 116; *Decal.* 64; Mt 4.9–10; Acts 10.25–6; Rev 19.10; 22.8–9)." Robert Gundry (*Matthew: A Commentary on His Handbook for a Mixed Church under Persecution* [Grand Rapids: Eerdmans, 1994], 31) notes that "they [the magi] knelt down before him with heads to the ground."

35. Another unique Matthean occurrence of this motif is in Matt 18:26, in which one can find a familiar constellation of πεσών and προσεκύνει. Gundry (*Matthew*, 31–32) observes that, besides the magi story, "Matthew inserts the same combination of falling down and worshiping in 4:9 and uses it in unique material at 18:26." He further notes that, "in particular, πεσόντες sharpens Matthew's point, for in 4:9 falling down will accompany worship in the alternatives of worshiping God and worshiping Satan, and without parallel it describes the response of the disciples who witnessed the transfiguration (17:6)."

36. The general scholarly consensus holds that the apocalypse was composed before the destruction of the Second Temple in 70 CE. Already in his first systematic exploration of the text published in 1896, R. H. Charles used references to the temple practices found in the Slavonic apocalypse as main proofs for his hypothesis of the early date of the apocalypse, which he placed in the first century CE before the destruction of the Second Temple. Charles and scholars after him noted that the text gives no indication that the catastrophe of the destruction of the temple had already occurred at the time of the book's composition. Critical readers of the pseudepigraphon would have some difficulties finding any explicit expression of feelings of sad-

ter of intriguing conceptual developments connected with the theme of angelic veneration. The first part of this Jewish apocalypse depicts Enoch's ascent to heaven. Second Enoch 21–22 narrates the final stage of the patriarch's celestial journey, during which the seventh antediluvian hero is brought by his angelic guides to the edge of the seventh heaven. At the Deity's command, the archangel Gabriel invites the patriarch to be a permanent servant of God. Enoch agrees and the archangel carries him to the glorious face of God, where the patriarch does obeisance to the Deity. God then personally repeats the invitation to Enoch to stand before him forever. After this invitation, another archangel, Michael, brings the patriarch to the front of the face of the Lord. The Lord then tells his angels, sounding them out: "Let Enoch join in and stand in front of my face forever!" In response to the Deity's command, the angels do obeisance to Enoch.[37]

ness or mourning about the loss of the sanctuary. Affirmations of the value of animal sacrifice and Enoch's halakic instructions found in 2 En. 59 also appear to be fashioned not in the "preservationist," mishnaic-like mode but rather as if they reflected sacrificial practices that still existed when the author was writing his book. There is also an intensive and consistent effort on the part of the author to legitimize the central place of worship, which through the reference to the place Achuzan—a cryptic name for the Temple Mount in Jerusalem—is explicitly connected in 2 Enoch with the Jerusalem temple. Further, the Slavonic apocalypse also contains a direct command to visit the temple three times a day, advice that would be difficult to fulfill if the sanctuary had been already destroyed. On the date of 2 Enoch see R. H. Charles and W. R. Morfill, *The Book of the Secrets of Enoch* (Oxford: Clarendon, 1896), xxvi; R. H. Charles and Nevill Forbes, "The Book of the Secrets of Enoch," in *The Apocrypha and Pseudepigrapha of the Old Testament,* ed. R. H. Charles, 2 vols. (Oxford: Clarendon, 1913), 2:429; Milik, *Books of Enoch,* 114; Christfried Böttrich, *Das slavische Henochbuch,* JSHRZ 5/7 (Gütersloh: Gütersloher Verlaghaus, 1995), 813; Andrei Orlov, *The Enoch-Metatron Tradition,* TSAJ 107 (Tübingen: Mohr Siebeck, 2005), 323–28; Orlov, "The Sacerdotal Traditions of 2 Enoch and the Date of the Text," in *New Perspectives on 2 Enoch: No Longer Slavonic Only,* ed. Andrei Orlov and Gabriele Boccaccini, Studia Judaeoslavica 4 (Leiden: Brill, 2012), 103–16.

37. Francis I. Andersen, "2 (Slavonic Apocalypse of) Enoch," *OTP* 1:138. The tradition of the angelic veneration of Enoch is attested to in both recensions of 2 Enoch. Cf. 2 En. 22:6–7 in MS J (longer recension): "And the Lord said to his servants, sounding them out, 'Let Enoch join in and stand in front of my face forever!' And the Lord's glorious ones did obeisance and said, 'Let Enoch yield in accordance with your word, O Lord!'" (ibid.). See 2 En. 22:6–7 in MS A (shorter recension): "The Lord said, 'Let Enoch come up and stand in front of my face forever!" And the glorious ones did obeisance and said, 'Let him come up!'" (ibid., 139).

Scholars have noted that 2 En. 21–22 is reminiscent of the account of Adam's elevation and his veneration by angels found in Armenian, Georgian, and Latin versions of the Primary Adam Books, in which the archangel Michael is depicted as bringing the first human being into the divine presence, forcing him to bow down before God.[38] In the Primary Adam Books, the Deity then commands all the angels to bow down to the protoplast.[39] The results of this order are mixed. Some angels agree to venerate Adam, while others, including Satan, refuse to do obeisance.[40] Michael Stone notes that, along with the motifs of Adam's elevation and his veneration by angels, the author of 2 Enoch also appears to be aware of the motif of angelic disobedience and refusal to venerate the first human. Stone draws attention to the phrase "sounding them out," found in 2 En. 22:6, which another translator of the Slavonic text rendered as "making a trial of them."[41] Stone suggests that the expression "sounding them out" or "making a trial of them" implies here that it is the angels' obedience that is

---

38. Latin LAE 13:2: "When God blew into you the breath of life and your coun-tenance and likeness were made in the image of God, Michael led you and made you worship in the sight of God." Armenian LAE 13:2: "When God breathed his spirit into you, you received the likeness of his image. Thereupon, Michael came and made you bow down before God" (Anderson and Stone, Synopsis of Adam and Eve, 16E).

39. Latin LAE 13:2–14:1: "The Lord God then said: 'Behold, Adam, I have made you in our image and likeness.' Having gone forth Michael called all the angels saying: 'Worship the image of the Lord God, just as the Lord God has commanded.'" Armenian LAE 13:2–14:1: "God said to Michael, 'Behold I have made Adam in the likeness of my image.' Then Michael summoned all the angels, and God said to them, 'Come, bow down to god whom I made'" (Anderson and Stone, Synopsis of Adam and Eve, 16E).

40. Latin LAE 14:2–15:1: "Michael himself worshipped first, then he called me and said: 'Worship the image of God Jehovah.' I answered: 'I do not have it within me to worship Adam.' When Michael compelled me to worship, I said to him: 'Why do you compel me? I will not worship him who is lower and later than me. I am prior to that creature. Before he was made, I had already been made. He ought to worship me.' Hearing this, other angels who were under me were unwilling to worship him." Arme-nian LAE 14:2–15:1: "Michael bowed first. He called me and said. 'You too, bow down to Adam.' I said, 'Go away, Michael! I shall not bow [down] to him who is posterior to me, for I am former. Why is it proper [for me] to bow down to him?' The other angels, too, who were with me, heard this, and my words seemed pleasing to them and they did not prostrate themselves to you, Adam" (Anderson and Stone, Synopsis of Adam and Eve, 16E–17E).

41. Charles and Morfill, Book of Secrets, 28.

being tested.[42] Stone concludes that 2 En. 21–22 is reminiscent of the traditions found in Armenian, Georgian, and Latin versions of the Primary Adam Books.[43]

Scholars have also observed striking structural similarities between the veneration accounts in 2 Enoch and those in Armenian, Georgian, and Latin versions of the Primary Adam Books. The accounts include three chief events:

1. Installation on high. In the Primary Adam Books Adam is created and situated in heaven; in 2 Enoch the seventh antediluvian patriarch is brought to heaven.

---

42. Michael E. Stone, "The Fall of Satan and Adam's Penance: Three Notes on the *Books of Adam and Eve*," in *Literature on Adam and Eve*, ed. Anderson et al., 47.

43. The tradition of the angelic veneration of humanity was forgotten in later Enochic lore. Often these later developments help us to clarify the obscure details of the early tradition by providing additional insight into the distorted mosaic of their patterns. Third Enoch is also cognizant of the tradition of the angelic veneration portraying the celestial citizens bowing down, as in the Slavonic apocalypse, before the translated seventh antediluvian hero. Sefer Hekhalot 4:1–10 depicts Rabbi Ishmael questioning his celestial guide Metatron about his name "Youth": "R. Ishmael said: I said to Metatron: '... you are greater than all the princes, more exalted than all the angels, more beloved than all the ministers ... why, then, do they call you "Youth" in the heavenly heights?' He answered: 'Because I am Enoch, the son of Jared ... the Holy One, blessed be he, appointed me in the height as a prince and a ruler among the ministering angels. Then three of ministering angels, Uzzah, Azzah, and Azael, came and laid charges against me in the heavenly height. They said before the Holy One, blessed be He, "Lord of the Universe, did not the primeval ones give you good advice when they said, Do not create man!" ... And once they all arose and went to meet me and prostrated themselves before me, saying Happy are you, and happy your parents, because your Creator has favored you. Because I am young in their company and mere youth among them in days and months and years—therefore they call me 'Youth' " (trans. Philip S. Alexander, "3 (Hebrew Apocalypse of) Enoch," *OTP* 1:258–59. Commenting on this passage, Gary Anderson suggests that if "we remove those layers of the tradition that are clearly secondary ... we are left with a story that is almost identical to the analog we have traced in the Adam and Eve literature and II Enoch"; see Anderson, "Exaltation of Adam," 107. Anderson further notes (108) that the acclamation of Enoch as "Youth" in *Sefer Hekhalot* is intriguing because the reason 3 Enoch supplies this title is deceptively simple and straightforward: "Because I am young in their company and a mere youth among them in days and months and years—therefore they call me 'Youth' "; Anderson proposes that the title might point to its Adamic provenance since the explanation for the epithet "youth" recalls the reason for the angelic refusal to worship Adam in LAE on the basis of his inferiority to them by way of his age.

2. Veneration of the Deity. In the Primary Adam Books Adam does obeisance to God; in 2 Enoch the seventh antediluvian hero does obeisance to the Deity.

3. Initiation into the celestial community: angelic veneration of the protagonist and Satan's refusal to bow down. In the Primary Adam Books, God commands the angels to bow down. All the angels do obeisance. Satan and his angels disobey. In 2 Enoch the angelic rebellion is assumed. God tests whether this time the angels will obey.[44]

It is noteworthy that both 2 Enoch and the Primary Adam Books operate with a double veneration: first, the human protagonists, Enoch and Adam, are asked to bow down before the Deity; and second, they are themselves venerated by the angels, an event that signifies their acceptance into the community of celestial citizens.

Keeping in mind these conceptual developments, we now turn our attention to the temptation narrative in the Gospel of Matthew. Here one can discern the already familiar patterns manifested in 2 Enoch and the Primary Adam Books. Like Enoch and Adam, Jesus first is brought to the elevated place represented by the divine mountain. He is then asked to venerate Satan, an idolatrous pseudorepresentation of the Deity. Finally, the Matthean version of the temptation narrative portrays Jesus's initiation into the community of angels who came to offer their services. In view of these similarities, it is possible that the tradition of veneration reflected in 2 Enoch, which is believed by some scholars to be written before the destruction of the Second Temple, and therefore before the composition of the Gospel of Matthew, might exercise formative influence not only on the protoplast stories in the Primary Adam Books but also on the story of Jesus's temptation in Matthew.[45]

APOCALYPTIC FEATURES OF THE TEMPTATION NARRATIVE

If the author of the Gospel of Matthew was indeed cognizant of the apocalyptic traditions similar to those found in 2 Enoch, it is apparent

---

44. Stone, "Fall of Satan," 48.

45. In this respect, it should be noted that scholars have demonstrated that 2 Enoch has more parallels with the Gospel of Matthew than with any other book in the New Testament; see Christfried Böttrich, *Weltweisheit, Menschheitsethik, Urkult: Studien zum slavischen Henochbuch,* WUNT 2/50 (Tübingen: Mohr Siebeck, 1992), 219–21.

that Christian authors were not just blindly appropriating these currents; rather, they attempted to deconstruct these themes by assigning some familiar attributes and duties of the angels and the Deity to the ominous mediator, Satan. We should now direct our attention to these paradoxical reformulations of the apocalyptic motifs.

Satan as Jesus's Psychopomp and *Angelus Interpres*

Jewish apocalyptic accounts often depict the transportation of human visionaries into the upper realms with the help of angelic guides. In view of these apocalyptic currents, it is striking that, in the temptation narrative, Satan serves as a psychopomp of Jesus and transports him to high, possibly even the highest, places.[46] In apocalyptic literature, angels or archangels often serve as visionaries' psychopomps. For example, in 2 Enoch, the seventh antediluvian patriarch is taken to heaven by two angels. In the same apocalyptic account, Melchizedek is transported on the wings of Gabriel to the garden of Eden.[47] In the temptation narrative, Satan seems to be fulfilling similar functions of a transporting angel.[48] It is important that in both cases Satan is transporting Jesus not to hell but to "high places," first to the top of the temple in the Holy City and then to the highest mountain. Some scholars believe that the mountain here represents the place of divine abode, as in some other apocalyptic texts. Satan's apocalyptic roles are puzzling and might represent an attempt to deconstruct familiar apocalyptic motifs.

It is also noteworthy that in both Matthew and Luke, Satan serves not merely as a psychopomp but also as an *angelus interpres* who literally "leads

---

46. Davies and Allison (*Matthew*, 1:364) discuss the visionary mold of these traditions of transportation, noting, "Whether we are to think of a visionary experience (so Theodore of Mopsuestia in PG 66:721a and other Antiochene theologians) or of a miraculous teleportation (cf. Acts 8.39–40; 2 Bar. 6.3; Apoc. Zeph. frag, in Clement of Alexandria, *Strom.* 5.11.77; Liv. Pro. Hab. 4–7; and the Catholic stories of bilocating saints, such as those about St. Martin de Porres) is unclear (cf. 2 Cor 12.2!), although 4.8 ('and he showed him all the kingdoms of the world') may argue for the former possibility."

47. Concerning the transportation of Jesus in the temptation narrative, also see also Schiavo, "Temptation of Jesus," 147–48.

48. With respect to this, Schiavo (ibid., 147) notes that "on his journey, Jesus is also accompanied, but this time by the Devil, a fallen angel, whose function is to lead him and show him his dominion and power on earth."

up" (ἀναγαγὼν αὐτόν) the visionary and "shows him" (δείκνυσιν αὐτῷ/ἔδειξεν αὐτῷ) the visionary reality, thus fulfilling the traditional functions of the interpreting angels in Jewish apocalyptic and mystical accounts. The interaction between the seer and his demonic guide also reveals influences of Mosaic typology. Scholars have noted terminological similarities between the temptation narrative and Deut 34:1–4,[49] in which God serves as an *angelus interpres* during Moses's vision on Mount Nebo, showing (ἔδειξεν) the prophet the promised land and giving him an explanation of it.[50] Yet the *angelus interpres* traditions found in Matthew an attempt to transcend the "Mosaic" biblical makeup by enhancing the story with details of extrabiblical apocalyptic accounts.

The Progression to the Highest Place

It has been observed that, in comparison with Luke, Matthew's order of Jesus's temptations attests to the seer's gradual upward progression as he goes from the lower places to higher places, from the desert to a pinnacle in the temple and finally to a sacred mountain.[51] This dynamic is reminiscent of heavenly journeys that depict visionaries' progress from lower to higher heavens.[52] Often these visionary accounts portray the seer's initiation, occurring at the highest point of his journey. It is noteworthy, then, that it is in the third and final temptation in Matthew that the cluster of

---

49. "Then Moses went up from the plains of Moab to Mount Nebo, to the top of Pisgah, which is opposite Jericho, and the LORD showed him the whole land: Gilead as far as Dan, all Naphtali, the land of Ephraim and Manasseh, all the land of Judah as far as the Western Sea, the Negeb, and the Plain—that is, the valley of Jericho, the city of palm trees—as far as Zoar. The LORD said to him, 'This is the land of which I swore to Abraham, to Isaac, and to Jacob, saying, "I will give it to your descendants"; I have let you see it with your eyes, but you shall not cross over there' " (NRSV).

50. Jacques Dupont, "L'arrière-fond biblique du récit des tentations de Jésus," *NTS* 3 (1957): 297.

51. Thus, for example, Davies and Allison (*Matthew*, 352) observe that "the three temptations exhibit a spatial progression, from a low place to a high place. The first takes place in the desert, the second on a pinnacle in the temple, the third on a mountain from which all the kingdoms of the world can be seen. This progression corresponds to the dramatic tension which comes to a climax with the third temptation."

52. Schiavo ("Temptation of Jesus," 147) argues that "there is no doubt that the account of the temptation can be read in the wider context of the heavenly journey. With regard to the way the experience is prepared and the nature of the experience, it appears truly to be a journey, even if its content is quite different."

veneration motifs is introduced at the highest point. It again brings to mind the seventh antediluvian patriarch's journey in 2 Enoch, in which the seer's arrival to the highest heaven is peaked by angelic veneration.

The third Matthean temptation takes place on a mountain. Several scholars have remarked that the mountain might allude to the place of divine presence and dominion. Here, however, strangely enough, it becomes the exalted place from which Satan asks Jesus to venerate him. In the Enochic and Mosaic traditions, the high mountain often serves as one of the technical designations of the *Kavod*. For example, 1 En. 25:3 identifies the high mountain as a location of the throne of God.[53] In the Exagoge of Ezekiel the Tragedian, Moses is identified with the *Kavod* on the mountain.[54] If indeed Matthew has in mind the mountain of the *Kavod*, Satan's ability to show Jesus all the kingdoms of the world and their splendor might be a reference to the celestial curtain or *pargod*, the sacred veil of the divine presence, which in 3 En. 45 is described as an entity that literally "shows" all generations and all kingdoms at the same time.[55] As already demonstrated in my previous essay on the cosmological temple, these revelatory functions of the *pargod* are also reflected in the Apocalypse of Abraham in which the horizontal heavenly curtain

---

53. 1 En. 25:3 reads: "And he answered me, saying: 'This high mountain which you saw, whose summit is like the throne of the Lord, is the throne where the Holy and Great One, the Lord of Glory, the Eternal King, will sit when he comes down to visit the earth for good'" (trans. Knibb, *Ethiopic Book of Enoch*, 2:113).

54. Ezek. Trag. 67–90 reads: "Moses: I had a vision of a great throne on the top of Mount Sinai and it reached till the folds of heaven. A noble man was sitting on it, with a crown and a large scepter in his left hand. He beckoned to me with his right hand, so I approached and stood before the throne. He gave me the scepter and instructed me to sit on the great throne. Then he gave me a royal crown and got up from the throne. I beheld the whole earth all around and saw beneath the earth and above the heavens. A multitude of stars fell before my knees and I counted them all. They paraded past me like a battalion of men. Then I awoke from my sleep in fear"; trans. Howard Jacobson, *The Exagoge of Ezekiel* (Cambridge: Cambridge University Press, 1983), 54–55.

55. Thus, e.g., in 3 En. 45:1–4 one can find the following tradition about the *pargod*: "R. Ishmael said: Metatron said to me: Come and I will show you the curtain of the Omnipresent One which is spread before the Holy One, blessed be he, and on which are printed all the generations of the world and their deeds, whether done or to be done, till the last generation ... the kings of Judah and their generations, their deeds and their acts; the kings of Israel and their generations, their deeds and their acts; the kings of the gentiles and their generations, their deeds and their acts" (trans. Alexander, "3 Enoch," 295–98).

associated with the firmament unveils to Abraham the whole course of human history.[56] Scholars have noted striking similarities between the presentation of revelations in the Apocalypse of Abraham and the temptation narrative.[57] Although some attestations to the *pargod* symbolism are found in later rabbinic and *hekhalot* accounts, the early roots of these developments can be traced to the apocalyptic imagery of the heavenly tablets in Mesopotamian and early Enochic materials. Several Second Temple Jewish materials testify that these media of revelation, as in the later *pargod* tradition, are able to communicate to the seer the totality of historical and physical reality.[58]

The Transformation of the Seer

I have already demonstrated that, in the temptation story, Satan fulfills several functions traditionally ascribed to angelic figures, such as offices of the psychopomp and the *angelus interpres*. Yet the elusive adversary is able to mimic not only the duties of angelic figures but also the Deity himself. It is therefore possible that, in the Matthean account, Satan is portrayed as an idolatrous negative replica of the divine *Kavod*.

Previous studies have often missed the transformational thrust of the veneration themes found in the temptation story. Nevertheless, already in

---

56. Regarding this, see also Andrei Orlov, *Heavenly Priesthood in the Apocalypse of Abraham* (Cambridge: Cambridge University Press, 2013), 159–78.

57. Thus, e.g., Schiavo ("Temptation of Jesus," 147–48) notes, "In the *Apocalypse of Abraham* ... Abraham is led in the body by an angel to the throne of God.... From there, Abraham sees heaven with the throne of God, before his descent to the earth and the history of the world until the judgment. The similarity between this text and Q 4.1–13 is striking: Jesus, like Abraham, is transported bodily, on a journey to the sky. From up there, he contemplates the temple and the earth (earthly kingdoms)."

58. Thus, e.g., according to 4Q180 frag. 1 1–3, "all ages" are engraved on the heavenly tablets; it reads: "Interpretation concerning the ages which God has made: An age to conclude [all that there is] and all that will be. Before creating them he determined [their] operations [according to the precise sequence of the ages,] one age after another age. And this is engraved on the [heavenly] tablets [for the sons of men,] [for] /[a]ll/ the ages of their dominion" (trans. in *DSSSE* 1:371). Furthermore, according to 1 En. 81:1–2, by looking at the heavenly tablets, the seventh antediluvian hero was able to learn about every human action: "And he said to me: 'O Enoch, look at the book of the tablets of heaven, and read what is written upon them, and learn *every individual act.*' And I looked at everything in the tablets of heaven, and I read everything which was written, and I noted everything" (trans. Knibb, *Ethiopic Book of Enoch*, 2:186).

2 Enoch and in the story of Adam's veneration in the Primary Adam Books in which the human seers are ordered to bow down to the Deity, the hero's veneration of God appears to coincide with his transition into a new onto- logical state. Satan's request for veneration has affinities with this cluster of transformational motifs. What is important here is that Satan requests veneration while standing on the mountain, the location interpreted by scholars as a reference to the place of the divine presence. Satan's presence on the mountain appears to be envisioned in the temptation narrative as a counterpart of divine habitation. Is it possible, then, that Satan positions himself here as the negative counterpart of *Kavod*?

In Jewish apocalyptic accounts the ritual of prostration before the divine *Kavod* often plays a pivotal role in the transformation of a seer into a celestial being, or even his identification with the divine form.[59] In the course of this initiation, a visionary often acquires the nature of the object of his veneration, including the luminosity that signals his identification with the radiant manifestation of the Deity.

In the light of these traditions, it is possible to detect a similar trans- formational motif in the temptation narrative. One encounters here an example of negative transformational mysticism; by forcing Jesus to bow down, the tempter wants the seer to become identified with Satan's form, in opposition to the visionaries of Jewish apocalyptic writings who, through their prostration before the divine Face, become identified with the divine *Kavod*.

The Standing One

The transformation of human seers in the apocalyptic accounts often leads to their inclusion into the celestial retinue. This new office presumes unceasing service, uninterrupted with rest. In the rabbinic tradition, the citizens of heaven are predestined to stand forever, as there is no sitting in heaven.[60] Apocalyptic and mystical accounts, therefore, often identify an angelic state with a standing posture. Thus, in the aforementioned account

---

59. On this tradition see Orlov, *Enoch-Metatron Tradition*, 165–76.

60. Cf. b. Ḥag. 15a: "It is taught as a tradition that on high there is no sitting and no emulation, and no back, and no weariness" (trans. Israel Epstein, *The Babylonian Talmud: Ḥagiga* [London: Soncino, 1959]); and Merkavah Rabbah, in Peter Schäfer, Margarete Schlüter, and Hans Georg von Mutius, eds., *Synopse zur Hekhalot-Literatur*, TSAJ 2 (Tübingen: Mohr Siebeck, 1981), 246: "He said: the sages taught: above there

of Enoch's transformation into an angelic being in 2 En. 21–22, one can find repeated references to the seer's standing position. Moreover, both the angels and the Deity promise to the seventh antediluvian hero that he will be standing before God's presence forever. Scholars believe that these promises represent the first known attestations that hint at the future office of Enoch-Metatron as the שר הפנים—the prince of the divine presence, a special angelic servant whose role is to stand forever in front of the Deity.[61] It is noteworthy that not only Matthew but also Luke contain references to Jesus's standing and installation to this position by his angelic psycho-pomp Satan.[62] This tradition is reminiscent of Enoch's installation in the Slavonic apocalypse, in which he was also placed in this standing position by his angelic guide.

It appears that both in 2 Enoch and in the temptation story the instal-lation of the seer as a "standing one" might be connected with the Mosaic typology.[63] The tradition of Moses's standing plays an important role already in the biblical materials. Thus in Exod 33 the Lord commands Moses to stand near him: "There is a place by me where you shall stand on the rock." A similar command also is found in Deut 5:31, in which God again orders Moses to stand with him: "But you, stand here by me, and I will tell you all the commandments, the statutes and the ordinances, that you shall teach them." The motif of standing also plays a significant part in

---

is no standing, and no sitting, no jealousy and no rivalry, and no duplicity and no affliction."

61. Hugo Odeberg may have been the first scholar to discover the characteristics of the prince of the presence in the longer recension of 2 Enoch. He demonstrated, in his synopsis of the parallel passages from 2 and 3 Enoch, that the phrase "stand before my face forever," found in the Slavonic apocalypse, does not serve there merely as a typical Hebraism "to be in the presence," but establishes the angelic status of Enoch as Metatron, the Prince of the Presence; see *3 Enoch or the Hebrew Book of Enoch* (1928; repr., New York: Ktav, 1973), 55. Charles Gieschen's research also reinforces this posi-tion; he argues (*Angelomorphic Christology: Antecedents and Early Evidence*, AGAJU 42 [Leiden: Brill, 1998], 158 n. 17) that Enoch's "standing" in front of the face of the Lord forever conclusively indicates the status of a principal angel. He further observes that "those who stand immediately before the throne are usually the principal angels, i.e., the Angels of the Presence."

62. Matt 4:5: καὶ ἔστησεν αὐτὸν ἐπὶ τὸ πτερύγιον τοῦ ἱεροῦ; Luke 4:9: καὶ ἔστησεν ἐπὶ τὸ πτερύγιον τοῦ ἱεροῦ.

63. Concerning the Mosaic typology in the Gospel of Matthew, see Dale C. Alli-son Jr., *The New Moses: A Matthean Typology* (Minneapolis: Fortress, 1994).

extrabiblical Mosaic accounts, including the Exagoge of Ezekiel the Tragedian, in which Moses is portrayed as standing before the divine throne.[64]

In view of the aforementioned developments in 2 Enoch and the Exagoge, it is possible that Jesus's standing position on high reflects a cluster of
apocalyptic motifs. Yet in the Synoptic accounts of Jesus's temptation, this
tradition receives a new polemical meaning since the seer's installation is
performed by the main antagonist of the story, Satan.

As I conclude this section of this study, let me draw attention to the
structure of the second Matthean temptation in which Satan asks Jesus to
throw himself down, and in which the motif of the seer's installation to
the standing position occurs. It has been noted that the third temptation
appears to reflect three events found also in 2 Enoch and in the Primary
Adam Books: first, the installation of the seer by his psychopomp; second,
the seer's veneration of the Deity; and third, the angelic veneration of the
seer. In 2 Enoch, after the seventh antediluvian hero is brought by his psychopomp to the highest place, he first bows down before the Deity and
then is exalted by the angels through their veneration. The same pattern is
present in the Primary Adam Books in which the archangel Michael first
"presents" Adam before the Deity,[65] then Adam bows down before God,[66]
followed by his exaltation through angelic obeisance.[67] In light of these
developments, it is intriguing that the structure of the second Matthean
(and the third Lukan) temptation might reflect a similar structure. The
seer is first installed to the high place by his psychopomp.[68] Then he is
asked to throw himself down.[69] Then his psychopomp cites Scriptures
to assure the seer that he will be elevated by the angels.[70] As this story

---

64. Jacobson, *Exagoge of Ezekiel*, 54.

65. Georgian LAE 13:2: "And Michael came; he presented you" (trans. Anderson
and Stone, *Synopsis of Adam and Eve*, 16E).

66. Georgian LAE 13:2: "and made you bow down before God" (trans. Anderson
and Stone, *Synopsis of Adam and Eve*, 16E).

67. Georgian LAE 14:1–2: "Then Michael came; he summoned all the troops of
angels and told them, 'Bow down before the likeness and the image of the divinity.'
And then, when Michael summoned them and all had bowed down to you, he summoned me also" (trans. Anderson and Stone, *Synopsis of Adam and Eve*, 16E).

68. Matt 4:5: "Then the devil took him to the holy city and placed him on the pinnacle of the temple" (NRSV).

69. Matt 4:6a: "saying to him, 'If you are the Son of God, throw yourself down'"
(NRSV).

70. Matt 4:6b: "for it is written, 'He will command his angels concerning you,'

unfolds, one can see three narrative steps, which involve first installation, second denigration, and finally angelic exaltation. In view of these correspondences, it is possible that the second temptation anticipates the events of the third temptation by foreshadowing its threefold structure.

CONCLUSION

The polemical nature of Matthew's appropriations of the apocalyptic traditions in the temptation story remains one of the enigmas of this biblical text. At the same time, this overwhelming deconstructive thrust helps illuminate the puzzling form of the veneration motifs in this portion of Matthew's Gospel. Like other apocalyptic themes, the veneration themes are also deconstructed: the exalted human protagonist refuses to venerate a pseudorepresentation of the Deity and the angelic hosts in their turn too do not explicitly bow down to the hero. This striking reworking brings us again to the function of the veneration motifs not only in the temptation story but in the whole gospel. Although scholars have argued that the veneration motifs in the temptation story, and especially Jesus's refusal to venerate Satan, are closely connected with the theme of idolatry, it appears that some other, even more important conceptual ramifications might also be at play. Thus, both in 2 Enoch and in the Primary Adam Books, the angelic veneration plays a portentous role in the construction of a unique upper identity of the apocalyptic heroes, often revealing the process of their deification.[71] In these texts, angelic veneration shepherds the human protagonists into their new supra-angelic ontology when they become depicted as "icons" or "faces" of the Deity, the conditions often established both via angelic obeisance and the seers' own venerations of the Deity. Yet, in the temptation story, the divinity of the human protagonist is affirmed in a new paradoxical way, not through the veneration motifs, but through their deconstruction. This new way of establishing the hero's upper iden-

---

and 'On their hands they will bear you up, so that you will not dash your foot against a stone'" (NRSV).

71. Thus the deification of Adam is especially evident in the Armenian LAE 14:1: "Then Michael summoned all the angels, and God said to them, 'Come, bow down to god whom I made'" (trans. Anderson and Stone, *Synopsis of Adam and Eve*, 16E). Second Enoch also underlines the supra-angelic status of its hero when it tells him that he is above the angels by being placed closer to the Deity than Gabriel and, by revelation, closer to the mysteries of creation that God never revealed to the angels.

tity appears to be novel, and yet one is able to detect similar developments in the later Jewish "two powers in heaven" debates, with their emphasis on the deconstruction of the veneration motifs. Although in the Primary Adam Books it is Satan who opposes veneration of humanity, in the later "two powers in heaven" developments this function of opposition is often transferred to the Deity himself. In these later accounts, it is God who opposes veneration of the newly created protoplast and shows to angelic hosts that his beloved creature does not deserve the obeisance reserved now solely for the Creator.[72] Yet, in the midst of these debates, which

---

72. Jarl Fossum's research demonstrates that the motif of the God's opposition to the veneration of Adam by the angels appears in several forms in the rabbinic literature. Fossum ("The Adorable Adam of the Mystics and the Rebuttals of the Rabbis," in *Geschichte-Tradition-Reflexion: Festschrift für Martin Hengel zum 70. Geburtstag*, ed. Hubert Cancik, Hermann Lichtenberger, and Peter Schäfer; 3 vols. [Tübingen: Mohr Siebeck, 1996], 1:529–39) differentiates three major forms of this tradition: "(1) The angels mistake Adam for God and want to exclaim 'Holy' before him, whereupon God lets sleep fall upon Adam so it becomes clear that the latter is human; (2) all creatures mistake Adam for their creator and wish to bow before him, but Adam teaches them to render all honor to God as their true creator; (3) the angels mistake Adam for God and wish to exclaim 'Holy' before him, whereupon God reduces Adam's size." An important similarity can be detected between these Adamic traditions and the Metatron accounts. In b. Ḥag. 15a, for instance, God punished Metatron with sixty fiery lashes. Alan Segal (*Two Powers in Heaven: Early Rabbinic Reports about Christianity and Gnosticism*, SJLA 25 [Leiden: Brill, 1977], 112) observes that "just as Metatron needed correction for the false impression he gave Aher, so Adam needs correction for the false impression given the angels." Indeed, in the Adamic "two powers" accounts, the protoplast is disciplined in various ways, including the reduction of his stature. Thus from Gen. Rab. 8:10 one can learn that when God created man in his own image "the ministering angels mistook him [for a divine being] and wished to exclaim 'Holy' before Him.... What did the Holy One, blessed be He, do? He caused sleep to fall upon him, and so all knew that he was [only a mortal] man" (trans. from Harry Freedman and Maurice Simon, eds. *Midrash Rabbah*, 10 vols. [London: Soncino, 1961], 1:61). In the Alphabet of Rabbi Akiva the angels' erroneous behavior is explained through reference to Adam's gigantic body: "This teaches that initially Adam was created from the earth to the firmament. When the ministering angels saw him, they were shocked and excited by him. At that time they all stood before the Holy One, blessed be He, and said to Him; 'Master of the Universe! There are two powers in the world, one in heaven and one on earth.' What did the Holy One, blessed be He, do then? He placed His hand on him, and decreased him, setting him at one thousand cubits"; trans. Moshe Idel, "Enoch Is Metatron," *Imm* 24/25 (1990): 226. For the Hebrew text, see Shlomo Aharon Wertheimer, *Batei Midrashot*, ed. Abraham Joseph Wertheimer, 2nd ed., 2 vols. (Jerusalem: Ktav Yad we-Sefer, 1989), 2:333–477. Pesiqta de Rab Kahana 1:1 reflects the

might be interpreted as attempts to limit the possibility for theosis, one can find one of the most profound exaltations of humanity ever recorded in Jewish lore—a tradition that portrays the seventh antediluvian patriarch as יהוה הקטן, a lesser representation of the Deity.[73] Here, as in the temptation narrative of Matthew's Gospel, a deconstruction of the veneration motifs opens new paradoxical horizons for the deification of humankind.

---

same tradition: "Said R. Aibu, 'At that moment the first man's stature was cut down and diminished to one hundred cubits'"; trans. Jacob Neusner, *Pesiqta de Rab Kahana*, 2 vols. (Atlanta: Scholars Press, 1987), 1:1.

73. Regarding Enoch-Metatron's title יהוה הקטן, see Orlov, *Enoch-Metatron Tradition*, 136–43.

BIBLIOGRAPHY

Aalen, Sverre. "St Luke's Gospel and the Last Chapters of I Enoch." *NTS* 13 (1966–1967): 1–13.

Abegg, Martin G., Jr., James E. Bowley, and Edward M. Cook. *The Dead Sea Scrolls Concordance*. 3 vols. Leiden: Brill, 2003–2010.

Abusch, Tzvi. "The Demonic Image of the Witch in Standard Babylonian Literature: The Reworking of Popular Concepts by Learned Exorcists." Pages 3–25 in *Mesopotamian Witchcraft: Toward a History and Understanding of Babylonian Witchcraft Beliefs and Literature*. Edited by Tzvi Abusch. Ancient Magic and Divination 5. Leiden: Brill, 2002.

Abusch, Tzvi, and Daniel Schwemer. "Das Abwehrzauber-Ritual Maqlû ('Verbrennung')." Pages 128–86 in *Omina, Orakel, Rituale und Beschwörungen*. Edited by Bernd Janowski and Gernot Wilhelm. TUAT NF 4. Gütersloh: Gütersloher Verlagshaus, 2008.

Adams, Edward. *The Stars Will Fall from Heaven: Cosmic Catastrophe in the New Testament and Its World*. LNTS 347. London: T&T Clark, 2007.

Adamczewski, Bartosz. *Q or Not Q? The So-Called Triple, Double and Single Traditions in the Synoptic Gospels*. Frankfurt: Lang, 2010.

Aland, Kurt, ed. *Synopsis Quattuor Evangeliorum*. 13th ed. 1985. Repr., Stuttgart: Deutsche Bibelgesellschaft, 1990.

Alexander, Philip S. "3 (Hebrew Apocalypse of) Enoch." *OTP* 1:223–315.

———. "Contextualizing the Demonology of the Testament of Solomon." Pages 613–35 in *Die Dämonen—Demons: Die Dämonologie der israelitisch-jüdischen und frühchristlichen Literatur im Kontext ihrer Umwelt—The Demonology of Israelite-Jewish and Early Christian Literature in Context of Their Environment*. Edited by Armin Lange, Hermann Lichtenberger, and K. F. Diethard Römheld. Tübingen: Mohr Siebeck, 2003.

———. "The Demonology of the Dead Sea Scrolls." Pages 331–53 in vol. 2 of *The Dead Sea Scrolls after Fifty Years: A Comprehensive Assessment*.

Edited by Peter W. Flint and James C. VanderKam. 2 vols. Leiden: Brill, 1999.

———. "From Son of Adam to Second God: Transformations of the Biblical Enoch." Pages 87–122 in *Biblical Figures outside the Bible*. Edited by Michael E. Stone and Theodore A. Bergren. Harrisburg, PA: Trinity Press International, 1998.

———. *The Mystical Texts*. LSTS 61. London: T&T Clark, 2006.

———. "'Wrestling against Wickedness in High Places': Magic in the Worldview of the Qumran Community." Pages 318–37 in *The Scrolls and the Scriptures: Qumran Fifty Years After*. Edited by Stanley E. Porter and Craig A. Evans. JSPSup 26. Sheffield: Sheffield Academic, 1997.

Allison, Dale C., Jr. "Behind the Temptations of Jesus: Q 4:1–13 and Mark 1:12–13." Pages 195–213 in *Authenticating the Activities of Jesus*. Edited by Bruce Chilton and Craig A. Evans. NTTS 28.2. Leiden: Brill, 2002.

———. "The Magi's Angel (Matt. 2:2, 9–10)." Pages 17–41 in *Studies in Matthew: Interpretation Past and Present*. Grand Rapids: Baker Academic, 2005.

———. *The New Moses: A Matthean Typology*. Minneapolis: Fortress, 1994.

———. "The Scriptural Background of a Matthean Legend: Ezekiel 37, Zechariah 14, and Matthew 27." Pages 153–81 in *Life beyond Death in Matthew's Gospel: Religious Metaphor or Bodily Reality?* Edited by Wim Weren, Huub van de Sandt, and Joseph Verheyden. BTS 13. Leuven: Peeters, 2011.

———. *Studies in Matthew: Interpretation Past and Present*. Grand Rapids: Baker Academic, 2005.

———. *Testament of Abraham*. CEJL. Berlin: de Gruyter, 2003.

———. "Two Notes on a Key Text: Matthew 11:25–30." *JTS* 39 (1988): 477–85.

———. "What Was the Star That Guided the Magi?" *BRev* 9.6 (1993): 20–24.

———, ed. *Matthew: A Shorter Commentary*. London: T&T Clark, 2004.

Andersen, Francis I. "2 (Slavonic Apocalypse of) Enoch." *OTP* 1:91–221.

Anderson, Gary A. "The Exaltation of Adam and the Fall of Satan." Pages 83–110 in *Literature on Adam and Eve: Collected Essays*. Edited by Gary A. Anderson, Michael E. Stone, and Johannes Tromp. SVTP 15. Leiden: Brill, 2000.

Anderson, Gary A., and Michael E. Stone, trans. and eds. *A Synopsis of the Books of Adam and Eve*. 2nd ed. EJL 17. Atlanta: Scholars Press, 1999.

Anderson, Janice Capel. "Matthew: Gender and Reading." Pages 25–51 in *A Feminist Companion to Matthew*. Edited by Amy-Jill Levine. FCNTECW 1. Cleveland: Pilgrim, 2001.

Angel, Joseph. "The Liturgical-Eschatological Priest of the *Self-Glorification Hymn*." *RevQ* 96/1 (2010): 585–605.

———. *Otherworldly and Eschatological Priesthood in the Dead Sea Scrolls*. STDJ 86. Leiden: Brill, 2010.

Annus, Amar. "On the Origin of Watchers: A Comparative Study of the Antediluvian Wisdom in Mesopotamian and Jewish Tradition." *JSP* 19 (2010): 277–320.

Ashton, John. *The Religion of Paul the Apostle*. New Haven: Yale University Press, 2000.

Astell, Ann W. "In the Bosom of Abraham: Saint Bonaventure, Lazarus, and the Houses of Hospitality." Pages 139–52 in *Crisis, Call, and Leadership in the Abrahamic Traditions*. Edited by Peter Ochs and William Stacy Johnson. New York: Palgrave Macmillan, 2009.

Attridge, Harold W. *The Epistle to the Hebrews: A Commentary on the Epistle to the Hebrews*. Hermeneia. Philadelphia: Fortress, 1989.

Avigad, Nahman, and Yigael Yadin. *A Genesis Apocryphon: A Scroll from the Wilderness of Judaea*. Jerusalem: Magnes, 1956.

Baggott, Jim. *Farewell to Reality: How Modern Physics Has Betrayed the Search for Scientific Truth*. London: Constable & Robinson, 2013.

Bampfylde, Gillian. "The Prince of the Host in the Book of Daniel and the Dead Sea Scrolls." *JSJ* 14 (1983): 129–34.

Barker, Margaret. *The Revelation of Jesus Christ*. Edinburgh: T&T Clark, 2000.

———. *The Risen Lord: The Jesus of History as the Christ of Faith*. Edinburgh: T&T Clark, 1996.

Barr, James. "'Determination' and the Definite Article in Biblical Hebrew." *JSS* 34 (1989): 307–35.

Barthes, Roland. "Death of the Author." Pages 142–54 in *Image, Music, Text*. Translated by Stephen Heath. London: Fontana, 1977.

Batluck, Mark. "Religious Experience in New Testament Research." *CurBR* 9 (2010): 339–63.

Bauckham, Richard J. "The Ascension of Isaiah: Genre, Unity and Date." Pages 363–90 in *The Fate of the Dead: Studies on the Jewish and Christian Apocalypses*. NovTSup 93. Leiden: Brill, 1998.

———. "Jesus and the Wild Animals (Mark 1:13): A Christological Image for an Ecological Age." Pages 3–21 in *Jesus of Nazareth: Lord and*

Christ: Essays on the Historical Jesus and New Testament Christology.
Edited by Joel B. Green and Max Turner. Grand Rapids: Eerdmans,
1994.

———. "The Rich Man and Lazarus: The Parable and the Parallels." *NTS*
37 (1991): 225–46.

Baynes, Leslie. "*Enoch* and *Jubilees* in the Canon of the Ethiopian Orthodox Church." Pages 799–818 in vol. 2 of *A Teacher for All Generations:
Essays in Honor of James C. VanderKam.* Edited by Eric F. Mason. 2
vols. JSJSup 153. Leiden: Brill, 2012.

Becker, Jürgen. *Jesus of Nazareth.* Berlin: de Gruyter, 1998.

Beckwith, Roger T. *Calendar and Chronology, Jewish and Christian: Biblical, Intertestamental and Patristic Studies.* Leiden: Brill, 2001.

Beer, Georg. "Das Buch Henoch." Pages 217–310 in *Die Pseudepigraphen
des Alten Testaments.* Vol. 2 of *Die Apokryphen und Pseudepigraphen
des Alten Testaments.* Edited by Emil Kautzsch. Tübingen: Mohr Siebeck, 1900.

Bellah, Robert N. "The Heritage of the Axial Age: Resource or Burden?"
Pages 447–67 in *The Axial Age and Its Consequences.* Edited by Robert
N. Bellah and Hans Jonas. Cambridge: Harvard University Press, 2012.

———. *Religion in Human Evolution: From the Paleolithic to the Axial Age.*
Cambridge: Harvard University Press, 2011.

———. "Religious Evolution." *American Sociological Review* 29 (1964):
358–74.

———. "What Is Axial about the Axial Age?" *Archives Européennes de Sociologie* 46 (2005): 69–89.

Benoit, Pierre, J. T. Milik, and Roland de Vaux, eds. *Les grottes de
Murabba'ât.* 2 vols. DJD 2. Oxford: Clarendon, 1961.

Berenson Maclean, Jennifer K. "Barabbas, the Scapegoat Ritual, and the
Development of the Passion Narrative." *HTR* 100 (2007): 309–34.

Bernstein, Moshe J. "Divine Titles and Epithets and the Sources of the
Genesis Apocryphon." *JBL* 128 (2009): 291–310.

Betz, Hans D., ed. *The Greek Magical Papyri in Translation: Including the
Demotic Spells.* Chicago: University of Chicago Press, 1986.

Bhayro, Siam. *The Shemihazah and Asael Narrative of 1 Enoch 6–11: Intro-
duction, Text, Translation and Commentary with Reference to Ancient
Near Eastern and Biblical Antecedents.* AOAT 322. Münster: Ugarit-
Verlag, 2005.

Bietenhard, Hans. *Die himmlische Welt im Urchristentum und Spätjudentum.* Tübingen: Mohr Siebeck, 1951.

Black, Matthew. *The Book of Enoch or 1 Enoch: A New English Edition with Commentary and Textual Notes.* SVTP 7. Leiden: Brill, 1985.

Blackmore, Susan. *Consciousness: An Introduction.* London: Hodder & Stoughton; New York: Oxford University Press, 2003.

Boccaccini, Gabriele. *Roots of Rabbinic Judaism.* Grand Rapids: Eerdmans, 2002.

———, ed. *Enoch and the Messiah Son of Man: Revisiting the Book of Parables.* Grand Rapids: Eerdmans, 2007.

———, ed. *Il messia tra memoria e attesa.* Brescia: Morcelliana, 2005.

Boccaccini, Gabriele, and Piero Stefani. *Dallo stesso grembo: Le origini del cristianesimo e del giudaismo rabbinico.* Bologna: Dehoniane, 2012.

Bond, Helen K. "Discarding the Seamless Robe: The High Priesthood of Jesus in John's Gospel." Pages 183–94 in *Israel's God and Rebecca's Children: Christology and Community in Early Judaism and Christianity: Essays in Honor of Larry W. Hurtado and Alan F. Segal.* Edited by David B. Capes, April D. DeConick, Helen K. Bond, and Troy Miller. Waco, TX: Baylor University Press, 2007.

Borger, Rykle. "Die Beschwörungsserie *bīt mēseri* und die Himmelfahrt Henochs." *JNES* 33 (1974): 183–96.

Boring, M. Eugene. *Introduction to the New Testament: History, Literature, Theology.* Louisville: Westminster John Knox, 2012.

Botterweck, G. Johannes, Helmer Ringgren, and Heinz-Josef Fabry, eds. *Theological Dictionary of the Old Testament.* Translated by John T. Willis, Geoffrey W. Bromiley, David E. Green, and Douglas W. Stott. 15 vols. Grand Rapids: Eerdmans, 1974–2006.

Böttrich, Christfried. *Das slavische Henochbuch.* JSHRZ 5/7. Gütersloh: Gütersloher Verlagshaus, 1995.

———. *Weltweisheit, Menschheitsethik, Urkult: Studien zum slavischen Henochbuch.* WUNT 2/50. Tübingen: Mohr Siebeck, 1992.

Bourguignon, Erika. *Psychological Anthropology: An Introduction to Human Nature and Cultural Differences.* New York: Holt, Rinehart & Winston, 1979.

Boustan, Ra'anan S. "Angels in the Architecture: Temple Art and the Poetics of Praise in the Songs of the Sabbath Sacrifice." Pages 195–212 in *Heavenly Realms and Earthly Realities in Late Antique Religions.* Edited by Ra'anan S. Boustan and Annette Yoshiko Reed. Cambridge: Cambridge University Press, 2004.

Bovon, François. *Luke 2: A Commentary on the Gospel of Luke 9:51–19:27.* Translated by Donald S. Deer. Hermeneia. Minneapolis: Fortress, 2013.

Box, G. H. *The Ezra-Apocalypse, Being Chapters 3–14 of the Book Commonly Known as 4 Ezra (or II Esdras)*. London: Pitman, 1912.

Breytenbach, Cilliers, and Peggy L. Day. "Satan." *DDD* 726–32.

Brin, Gershon. *The Concept of Time in the Bible and The Dead Sea scrolls*. STDJ 39. Leiden: Brill, 2001.

Brodie, Thomas L. *The Birthing of the New Testament: The Intertextual Development of the New Testament Writings*. NTM 1. Sheffield: Sheffield Phoenix, 2004.

Brooke, George J. "The *Apocryphon of Levib*? and the Messianic Servant High Priest." Pages 140–57 in *The Dead Sea Scrolls and the New Testament*. Minneapolis: Fortress, 2005.

———. Review of *Angels at Qumran: A Comparative Study of 1 Enoch 1–36, 72–108 and Sectarian Writings from Qumran*, by Maxwell J. Davidson. *JQR* 86 (1995): 186–89.

Brower, Kent. "Jesus and the Lustful Eye: Glancing at Matthew 5:28." *EvQ* 76 (2004): 291–309.

Bucur, Bogdan G. "The Angelic Spirit in Early Christianity: Justin, the Martyr and Philosopher." *JR* 88 (2008): 190–208.

———. *Angelomorphic Pneumatology: Clement of Alexandria and Other Early Christian Witnesses*. VCSup 95. Leiden: Brill, 2009.

———. "Hierarchy, Prophecy, and the Angelomorphic Spirit: A Contribution to the Study of the Book of Revelation's *Wirkungsgeschichte*." *JBL* 127 (2008): 173–94.

———. "Revisiting Christian Oeyen: 'The Other Clement' on Father, Son, and the Angelomorphic Spirit." *VC* 61 (2007): 381–413.

———. "The Son of God and the Angelomorphic Holy Spirit: A Rereading of the *Shepherd's* Christology." *ZNW* 98 (2007): 120–42.

Bultmann, Rudolf. *Theology of the New Testament*. Translated by Kendrick Grobel. 2 vols. New York: Scribner's Sons, 1951–1955.

Burkett, Delbert. *The Son of Man Debate: A History and Evaluation*. SNTSMS 107. Cambridge: Cambridge University Press, 1999.

Cagni, Luigi. *L'epopea di Erra*. StSem 34. Rome: Istituto di Studi del Vicino Oriente, 1969.

Carlson, P. M. "Clues, Red Herrings, and Other Plot Devices." Pages 160–65 in *Writing Mysteries*. Edited by Sue Grafton. 2nd ed. Cincinnati: Writer's Digest, 2002.

Carroll, John T. *Luke: A Commentary*. NTL. Louisville: Westminster John Knox, 2012.

Casey, Maurice. *An Aramaic Approach to Q: Sources for the Gospels of Matthew and Luke*. SNTSMS 122. Cambridge: Cambridge University Press, 2002.

———. "Aramaic Idiom and the Son of Man Problem: A Response to Owen and Shepherd." *JSNT* 25 (2002): 3–32.

———. *Aramaic Sources of Mark's Gospel*. SNTSMS 102. Cambridge: Cambridge University Press, 1998.

———. *The Solution to the "Son of Man" Problem*. LNTS 343. London: T&T Clark, 2007.

Chalmers, David J. *The Conscious Mind*. Oxford: Oxford University Press, 1996.

Chambers, J. K., and Peter Trudgill. *Dialectology*. 2nd ed. CTL. Cambridge: Cambridge University Press, 1998.

Charles, R. H. *The Book of Enoch or 1 Enoch*. Oxford: Clarendon, 1913.

———. *The Ethiopic Version of the Book of Enoch*. Anecdota Oxoniensia, Semitic Series 11. Oxford: Clarendon, 1906.

Charles, R. H., and Nevill Forbes. "The Book of the Secrets of Enoch." Pages 425–69 in vol. 2 of *The Apocrypha and Pseudepigrapha of the Old Testament*. Edited by R. H. Charles. 2 vols. Oxford: Clarendon, 1913.

Charles, R. H., and W. R. Morfill. *The Book of the Secrets of Enoch*. Oxford: Clarendon, 1896.

Charlesworth, James H., ed. *Old Testament Pseudepigrapha*. 2 vols. Garden City, NY: Doubleday, 1983–1985.

Charlesworth, James H., and Darrell L. Bock, eds. *Parables of Enoch: A Paradigm Shift*. JCTCRS 11. London: Bloomsbury T&T Clark, 2013.

Charlesworth, James H., and Blake A. Jurgens. "Select Bibliography on 'the Son of Man' and the *Parables of Enoch*." Pages 373–90 in *Parables of Enoch: A Paradigm Shift*. Edited by James H. Charlesworth and Darrell L. Bock. JCTCRS 11. London: Bloomsbury T&T Clark, 2013.

Charlesworth, James H., and Carol A. Newsom, eds. *Angelic Liturgy: Songs of the Sabbath Sacrifice*. Vol. 4B of *The Dead Sea Scrolls: Hebrew, Aramaic, and Greek Texts with English Translations*. PTSDSSP 4B. Tübingen: Mohr Siebeck; Louisville: Westminster John Knox, 1999.

Chazon, Esther G. "Human and Angelic Prayer in Light of the Dead Sea Scrolls." Pages 35–47 in *Liturgical Perspectives: Prayer and Poetry in Light of the Dead Sea Scrolls: Proceedings of the Fifth International Symposium of the Orion Center for the Study of the Dead Sea Scrolls and*

Associated Literature, 19–23 January, 2000. Edited by E. G. Chazon, R. A. Clements, and Avital Pinnick. STDJ 48. Leiden: Brill, 2003.

Chazon, Esther, Torleif Elgvin, Esther Eshel, Daniel Falk, Bilha Nitzan, Elisha Qimron, Eileen Schuller, David Seely, Eibert Tigchelaar, and Moshe Weinfeld. *Qumran Cave 4.XX: Poetical and Liturgical Texts, Part 2.* DJD 29. Oxford: Clarendon, 1999.

Chesnutt, Randall D. "*Oxyrhynchus Papyrus* 2069 and the Composition History of *1 Enoch.*" *JBL* 129 (2010): 485–505.

Chialà, Sabino. *Libro delle parabole.* Brescia: Paideia, 1997.

———. "The Son of Man: The Evolution of an Expression." Pages 153–78 in *Enoch and the Messiah Son of Man: Revisiting the Book of Parables.* Edited by Gabriele Boccaccini. Grand Rapids: Eerdmans, 2007.

Chilton, Bruce. *The Temple of Jesus: His Sacrificial Program within a Cultural History of Sacrifice.* University Park: Pennsylvania State University Press, 1992.

Chilton, David. *Paradise Restored: A Biblical Theology of Dominion.* Fort Worth, TX: Dominion, 1985.

Cirafesi, Wally V. "The Priestly Portrait of Jesus in the Gospel of John in the Light of 1QS, 1QSa and 1QSb." *JGRChJ* 8 (2011–2012): 83–105.

Clark-Soles, Jaime. *Death and the Afterlife in the New Testament.* New York: T&T Clark, 2006.

Clines, David J., ed. *The Dictionary of Classical Hebrew.* 8 vols. Sheffield: Sheffield Academic, 1993–2011.

Coblentz Bautch, Kelley. "Heavenly Beings Brought Low: A Study of Angels and the Netherworld." Pages 59–75 in *Angels: The Concept of Celestial Beings: Origins, Development and Reception.* Edited by Friedrich V. Reiterer, Tobias Nicklas, and Karin Schöpflin. Deuterocanonical and Canonical Literature Yearbook 2007. Berlin: de Gruyter, 2007.

———. "Putting Angels in Their Place: Developments in Second Temple Angelology." Pages 174–88 in *"With Wisdom as a Robe": Qumran and Other Jewish Studies in Honour of Ida Fröhlich.* Edited by Károly Dobos and Miklós Kőszeghy. HBM 21. Sheffield: Sheffield Phoenix, 2009.

———. *A Study of the Geography of 1 Enoch 17–19: "No One Has Seen What I Have Seen."* JSJSup 81. Leiden: Brill, 2003.

Collins, John J. *The Apocalyptic Imagination: An Introduction to Jewish Apocalyptic Literature.* 2nd ed. Biblical Resources Series. Grand Rapids: Eerdmans, 1998.

———. *The Apocalyptic Vision of the Book of Daniel.* HSM 16. Missoula, MT: Scholars Press, 1977.

———. *Apocalypticism in the Dead Sea Scrolls*. London: Routledge, 1997.

———. *Daniel: A Commentary*. Hermeneia. Minneapolis: Fortress, 1993.

———. "Enoch and the Son of Man: A Response to Sabino Chialà and Helge Kvanvig." Pages 216–27 in *Enoch and the Messiah Son of Man: Revisiting the Book of Parables*. Edited by Gabriele Boccaccini. Grand Rapids: Eerdmans, 2007.

———. "Enochic Judaism: An Assessment." Pages 219–34 in *The Dead Sea Scrolls and Contemporary Culture*. Edited by Adolfo D. Roitman, Lawrence H. Schiffman, and Shani Tzoref. Leiden: Brill, 2011.

———. "Genre, Ideology, and Social Movements in Jewish Apocalypticism." Pages 25–51 in *Mysteries and Revelations: Apocalyptic Studies since the Uppsala Colloquium*. Edited by John J. Collins and James H. Charlesworth. JSPSup 9. Sheffield: Sheffield University Press, 1991.

———. "How Distinctive Was Enochic Judaism?" *Meghillot: Studies in the Dead Sea Scrolls* 5–6 (2007): 17*–34*.

———. "Introduction: Towards the Morphology of a Genre." *Semeia* 14 (1979): 1–20.

———. "The Jewish Apocalypses." *Semeia* 14 (1979): 21–59.

———. *The Scepter and the Star: The Messiahs of the Dead Sea Scrolls and Other Ancient Literature*. 2nd ed. Grand Rapids: Eerdmans, 2010.

———. "The Sibylline Oracles." *OTP* 1:317–472.

Comfort, Philip. "Two Illustrations of Scribal Gap Filling in Luke 16:19." Pages 111–13 in *Translating the New Testament: Text, Translation, Theology*. Edited by Stanley E. Porter and Mark J. Boda. MNTS. Grand Rapids: Eerdmans, 2009.

Conybeare, F. C. *Christian Demonology*. Repr., Piscataway, NJ: Gorgias, 2007.

Cotton, Hannah M., and Ada Yardeni, eds. *Aramaic, Hebrew and Greek Documentary Texts from Naḥal Ḥever and Other Sites, with an Appendix Containing Alleged Qumran Texts (Seiyâl Collection II)*. DJD 27. Oxford: Clarendon, 1997.

Couliano, Ioan P. *Out of This World: Otherworldly Journeys from Gilgamesh to Albert Einstein*. London: Shambhala, 1991.

Craffert, Pieter F. *The Life of a Galilean Shaman: Jesus of Nazareth in Anthropological-Historical Perspective*. Matrix: The Bible in Mediterranean Perspective 3. Eugene, OR: Wipf & Stock, 2008.

———. "'Seeing' a Body into Being: Reflections on Scholarly Interpretations of the Nature and Reality of Jesus' Resurrected Body." *R&T* 9 (2002): 89–107.

————. "Shamanism and the Shamanic Complex." *BTB* 41 (2011): 151–61.

Cross, Frank M. "The Development of the Jewish Scripts." Pages 133–202 in *The Bible and the Ancient Near East: Essays in Honor of W. F. Albright*. Edited by G. E. Wright. Garden City, NY: Doubleday, 1961.

Cullmann, Oscar. *The Christology of the New Testament*. Translated by Shirley C. Guthrie and Charles A. M. Hall. Rev. ed. NTL. Philadelphia: Westminster, 1963.

Cummings, John T. "The Tassel of His Cloak: Mark, Luke, Matthew—and Zechariah." Pages 47–61 in *Papers on the Gospels*. Vol. 2 of *Studia Biblica 1978, Sixth International Congress on Biblical Studies, Oxford 3–7 April 1978*. Edited by E. A. Livingstone. JSNTSup 2. Sheffield: JSOT Press, 1980.

Cunningham, Graham. *"Deliver Me from Evil": Mesopotamian Incantations 2500–1500 BC*. StPohl, Series Maior 17. Rome: Pontifical Biblical Institute, 1997.

Dalman, Gustaf. *Words of Jesus*. Translated by D. M. Kay. Edinburgh: T&T Clark, 1902.

Dan, Joseph. "Samael and the Problem of Jewish Gnosticism." Pages 257–76 in *Perspectives on Jewish Thought and Mysticism*. Edited by Alfred L. Ivry, Elliot R. Wolfson, and Allan Arkush. Amsterdam: Harwood Academic, 1998.

Davidsen, Ole. *The Narrative Jesus: A Semiotic Reading of Mark's Gospel*. Aarhus: Aarhus University Press, 1993.

Davidson, Maxwell J. *Angels at Qumran: A Comparative Study of 1 Enoch 1–36, 72–108 and Sectarian Writings from Qumran*. JSPSup 11. Sheffield: Sheffield Academic, 1992.

Davies, W. D., and Dale C. Allison Jr. *A Critical and Exegetical Commentary on the Gospel according to Saint Matthew*. 3 vols. ICC. London: T&T Clark, 1988–1997.

Davila, James R. "The Ancient Jewish Apocalypses and the *Hekhalot* Literature." Pages 105–25 in *Paradise Now: Essays on Early Jewish and Christian Mysticism*. Edited by April D. DeConick. SymS 11. Atlanta: Society of Biblical Literature, 2006.

————. *Descenders to the Chariot: The People behind the Hekhalot Literature*. JSJSup 70. Leiden: Brill, 2001.

————. *Liturgical Works*. Eerdmans Commentaries on the Dead Sea Scrolls. Grand Rapids: Eerdmans, 2000.

————. "Ritual in the Jewish Pseudepigrapha." Pages 158–83 in *Anthro-*

pology and Biblical Studies: Avenues of Approach. Edited by Louise J. Lawrence and Mario I. Aguilar. Leiden: Deo, 2004.

Davis, Philip G. "Divine Agents, Mediators, and New Testament Christology." *JTS* 45 (1994): 479–503.

Day, Peggy L. *An Adversary in Heaven: Śāṭān in the Hebrew Bible.* HSM 43. Atlanta: Scholars Press, 1988.

De Armas, Frederick A. "Cervantes and the Italian Renaissance." Pages 32–57 in *The Cambridge Companion to Cervantes.* Edited by Anthony J. Cascardi. Cambridge: Cambridge University Press, 2002.

Deines, Roland. "Not the Law but the Messiah: Law and Righteousness in the Gospel of Matthew—An Ongoing Debate." Pages 53–84 in *Built upon the Rock: Studies in the Gospel of Matthew.* Edited by D. M. Gurtner and J. Nolland. Grand Rapids: Eerdmans, 2008.

Deltgen, Florian. *"Bewegung" als historischer und soziologischer Begriff: Versuch einer theoretischen Präzisierung.* Cologne: Gouder, 1969.

Dennett, Daniel C. *Consciousness Explained.* Boston: Little, Brown, 1991.

Deutsch, Celia. *Hidden Wisdom and the Easy Yoke: Wisdom, Torah and Discipleship in Matthew 11.25–30.* JSNTSup 18. Sheffield: JSOT Press, 1987.

Dietrich, Manfred, Oswald Loretz, and Joaquín Sanmartín, eds. *Die keilalphabetischen Texte aus Ugarit.* AOAT 24.1. Neukirchen-Vluyn: Neukirchener Verlag, 1976.

Dietrich, Manfred, Oswald Loretz, and Joaquín Sanmartín, eds. *The Cuneiform Alphabetic Texts from Ugarit, Ras Ibn Hani, and Other Places.* Münster: Ugarit-Verlag, 1995.

Dijk, J. van. *Lugal ud me-lám-bi nir-ĞÁL: Le récit épique et didactique des Travaux de Ninurta, du Déluge et de la Nouvelle Création.* 2 vols. Leiden: Brill, 1983.

———. "Le motif cosmique dans la pensée sumérienne." *AcOr* 28 (1964): 1–59.

Dillmann, August. *Lexicon linguae Aethiopicae cum indice Latino.* Leipzig: Weigel, 1865.

Dodds, Eric Robertson. *The Greeks and the Irrational.* 1951. Repr., Berkeley: University of California Press, 1963.

Donaldson, Terence L. *Jesus on the Mountain: A Study in Matthean Theology.* JSNTSup 8. Sheffield: JSOT Press, 1985.

———. *Paul and the Gentiles: Remapping the Apostle's Convictional World.* Minneapolis: Fortress, 1997.

Donner, Herbert, and Wolfgang Röllig. *Kanaanäische und aramäische Inschriften.* 2nd ed. 3 vols. Wiesbaden: Harrassowitz, 1966–1969.

Doran, Robert. "Pseudo-Eupolemus." *OTP* 2:873–82.

Drawnel, Henryk. *The Aramaic Astronomical Book (4Q208–4Q211) from Qumran: Text, Translation, and Commentary.* Oxford: Oxford University Press, 2011.

———. "Between Akkadian *ṭupšarrūtu* and Aramaic ספר: Some Notes on the Social Context of the Early Enochic Literature." *RevQ* 24 (2010): 373–403.

———. "The Mesopotamian Background of the Enochic Giants and Evil Spirits." *DSD* 21 (2014): 14–38.

———. "Priestly Education in the Aramaic Levi Document (Visions of Levi) and Aramaic Astronomical Book (4Q208–211)." *RevQ* 88 (2006): 547–74.

———. "Professional Skills of Asael (*1 En.* 8:1) and Their Mesopotamian Background." *RB* 119 (2012): 518–42.

———. "The Punishment of Asael (*1 En.* 10:4–8) and Mesopotamian Anti-Witchcraft Literature." *RevQ* 25 (2012): 369–94.

———. Review of *Primeval History: Babylonian, Biblical, and Enochic. An Intertextual Reading,* by H. S. Kvanvig. *Biblical Annals* 2 (2012): 355–61.

Dunn, James D. G. *Christology in the Making: An Inquiry into the Origins of the Doctrine of the Incarnation.* 2nd ed. London: SCM, 1989.

———. *Jesus Remembered: Christianity in the Making.* Grand Rapids: Eerdmans, 2003.

———. "Messianic Ideas and Their Influence on the Jesus of History." Pages 365–81 in *The Messiah: Developments in Earliest Judaism and Christianity.* Edited by James H. Charlesworth. Minneapolis: Fortress, 1992.

Dupont, Jacques. "Ľarrière-fond biblique du récit des tentations de Jésus." *NTS* 3 (1957): 287–304.

———. *Les tentations de Jésus au desert.* StudNeot 4. Brugge: Desclée de Brouwer, 1968.

Ebertz, Michael. *Das Charisma des Gekreuzigten: Zur Soziologie der Jesusbewegung.* WUNT 45. Tübingen: Mohr Siebeck, 1987.

Edzard, Dietz-Otto. *Sumerian Grammar.* HdO, section 1: Near and Middle East 71. Leiden: Brill, 2003.

Ego, Beate. "Textual Variants as a Result of Enculturation: The Banishment of the Demon in Tobit." Pages 371–78 in *Septuagint Research: Issues and Challenges in the Study of the Greek Jewish Scriptures.* SCS

53. Edited by Wolfgang Kraus and R. Glenn Wooden. Atlanta: Society of Biblical Literature, 2006.

Eitrem, Samson. *Some Notes on the Demonology in the New Testament.* 2nd ed. SO 20. Oslo: Universitetsforlaget, 1966.

Ellens, J. Harold. *The Son of Man in the Gospel of John.* New Testament Monograph 28. Sheffield: Sheffield Phoenix Press, 2010.

Epstein, Isidore. *The Babylonian Talmud: Ḥagiga.* London: Soncino, 1959.

Erho, Ted M., and Loren T. Stuckenbruck. "A Manuscript History of Ethiopic Enoch." *JSP* 23 (2013): 87–133.

Eshel, Esther. "4Q471b: A Self-Glorification Hymn." *RevQ* 17 (1996): 189–91.

———. "Genres of Magical Texts in the Dead Sea Scrolls." Pages 395–415 in *Die Dämonen—Demons: Die Dämonologie der israelitisch-jüdischen und frühchristlichen Literatur im Kontext ihrer Umwelt—The Demonology of Israelite-Jewish and Early Christian Literature in Context of Their Environment.* Edited by Armin Lange, Hermann Lichtenberger, and K. F. Diethard Römheld. Tübingen: Mohr Siebeck, 2003.

Fabian, Johannes. "Charisma and Cultural Change." *CSSH* 11 (1969): 155–73.

Falk, Robert P., and William Beare. "Parody." Pages 600–602 in *Princeton Encyclopedia of Poetry and Poetics.* Edited by Alex Preminger. Enl. ed. Princeton: Princeton University Press, 1974.

Falkenstein, Adam. *Die Haupttypen der sumerischen Beschwörung, literarisch untersucht.* LSS NF 1. Leipzig: Hinrichs, 1931.

Feuillet, André. "L'épisode de la tentation d'après l'Évangile selon saint Marc I,12–13." *EstBib* 19 (1960): 49–73.

Fitzmyer, Joseph A. *The Genesis Apocryphon of Qumran Cave 1 [1Q20]: A Commentary.* 3rd ed. BibOr 18B. Rome: Pontifical Biblical Institute, 2004.

———. "The New Testament Title 'Son of Man' Philologically Considered." Pages 143–60 in *A Wandering Aramean: Collected Aramaic Essays.* SBLMS 25. Missoula, MT: Scholars Press, 1979.

———. *The Gospel according to Luke.* 2 vols. AB 28, 28A. Garden City, NY: Doubleday, 1981–1985.

Fitzmyer, Joseph A., and Daniel J. Harrington. *A Manual of Palestinian Aramaic Texts.* BibOr 34. Rome: Biblical Institute Press, 1978.

Fletcher-Louis, Crispin H. T. *All the Glory of Adam: Liturgical Anthropology in the Dead Sea Scrolls.* STDJ 42. Leiden: Brill, 2002.

376 BIBLIOGRAPHY

——. "The High Priest as Divine Mediator in the Hebrew Bible: Dan 7.13 as a Test Case." Pages 161–93 in *Society of Biblical Literature 1997 Seminar Papers*. SBLSP 36. Atlanta: Scholars Press, 1997.

——. "Jesus as the High Priestly Messiah: Parts 1 and 2." *JSHJ* 4 (2006): 155–75; 5 (2007): 57–79.

——. *Luke-Acts: Angels, Christology and Soteriology*. WUNT 2/94. Tübingen: Mohr Siebeck, 1997.

——. "Religious Experience and the Apocalypses." Pages 125–44 in *Inquiry into Religious Experience in Early Judaism and Early Christianity*. Vol. 1 of *Experientia*. Edited by Frances Flannery, Colleen Shantz, and Rodney A. Werline. SymS 40. Atlanta: Society of Biblical Literature, 2008.

——. "The Revelation of the Sacral Son of Man: The Genre, History of Religions Context and the Meaning of the Transfiguration." Pages 247–98 in *Auferstehung—Resurrection: The Fourth Durham-Tübingen Symposium: Resurrection, Exaltation, and Transformation in Old Testament, Ancient Judaism, and Early Christianity*. Edited by Friedrich Avemarie and Hermann Lichtenberger. WUNT 135. Tübingen: Mohr Siebeck, 2001.

Flusser, David, with R. Steven Notley. *The Sage from Galilee: Rediscovering Jesus' Genius*. Grand Rapids: Eerdmans, 2007.

Forsyth, Neil. *The Old Enemy: Satan and the Combat Myth*. Princeton: Princeton University Press, 1987.

Fossum, Jarl. "The Adorable Adam of the Mystics and the Rebuttals of the Rabbis." Pages 529–39 in vol. 1 of *Geschichte-Tradition-Reflexion: Festschrift für Martin Hengel zum 70. Geburtstag*. Edited by Hubert Cancik, Hermann Lichtenberger, and Peter Schäfer. 3 vols. Tübingen: Mohr Siebeck, 1996.

Foster, Benjamin R. *Before the Muses: An Anthology of Akkadian Literature*. 3rd ed. Bethesda, MD: CDL, 2005.

Fowler, Alastair. *Kinds of Literature: An Introduction to the Theory of Genres and Modes*. Oxford: Oxford University Press, 1982.

Fraade, Steven D. *Legal Fictions: Studies of Law and Narrative in the Discursive Worlds of Ancient Jewish Sectarians and Sages*. JSJSup 147. Leiden: Brill, 2011.

Frankfurter, David. "Master-Demons, Local Spirits, and Demonology in the Roman Mediterranean World: An Afterword to Rita Lucarelli." *JANER* 11 (2011): 126–31.

Freedman, Harry, and Maurice Simon, eds. *Midrash Rabbah.* 10 vols. London: Soncino, 1961.

Frieden, Ken. "Language of Demonic Possession: Keyword Analysis." Pages 41–52 in *The Daemonic Imagination: Biblical Text and Secular Story.* Edited by Robert Detweiler and William G. Doty. AARSR 60. Atlanta: Scholars Press, 1990.

Fröhlich, Ida. "Invoke at Any Time." *BN* 137 (2008): 41–74.

García Martínez, Florentino, and Eibert J. C. Tigchelaar, eds. *The Dead Sea Scrolls Study Edition.* 2 vols. Leiden: Brill; Grand Rapids: Eerdmans, 1997–1998.

Garrett, Susan R. *No Ordinary Angel: Celestial Spirits and Christian Claims about Jesus.* New Haven: Yale University Press, 2008.

———. *The Temptations of Jesus in Mark's Gospel.* Grand Rapids: Eerdmans, 1998.

Gaylord, Harry E. "How Satanael Lost His '-el.'" *JJS* 33 (1982): 303–9.

Geertz, Armin W. "Brain, Body and Culture: A Biocultural Theory of Religion." *MTSR* 22 (2010): 304–21.

Geller, Markham J. *Ancient Babylonian Medicine: Theory and Practice.* Chichester: Wiley-Blackwell, 2010.

———. "The Aramaic Incantation in Cuneiform Script (AO 6489 = TCL 6,58)." *JEOL* 35–36 (1997–2000): 127–46.

———. *Evil Demons: Canonical Utukkū Lemnūtu Incantations.* SAACT 5. Helsinki: Neo-Assyrian Text Corpus Project, 2007.

———. *Forerunners to Udug-hul: Sumerian Exorcistic Incantations.* FAOS 12. Freiburg: Steiner, 1985.

———. "Incantations within Akkadian Medical Texts." Pages 389–99 in *The Babylonian World.* Edited by Gwendolyn Leick. New York: Routledge, 2007.

———. "The Last Wedge." *ZA* 87 (1997): 43–86.

Gerhardsson, Birger. *The Testing of God's Son (Matt 4:1–11 and Par.): An Analysis of an Early Christian Midrash.* Translated by John Toy. ConBNT 2. Lund: Gleerup, 1966.

Gibson, Jeffrey. *Temptations of Jesus in Early Christianity.* JSNTSup 112. Sheffield: Sheffield Academic, 1995.

Gieschen, Charles A. *Angelomorphic Christology: Antecedents and Early Evidence.* AGAJU 42. Leiden: Brill, 1998.

Gigot, Francis E. "Abraham, Bosom of." Pages 55–56 in vol. 1 of *The Catholic Encyclopedia.* Edited by Charles G. Herbermann, Edward A. Pace,

Condé B. Pallen, Thomas J. Shahan, and John J. Wynne. 15 vols. New York: Appleton, 1907–1912.

Ginzberg, Louis. *An Unknown Jewish Sect.* New York: Jewish Theological Seminary, 1976.

Gnilka, Joachim. *Das Evangelium nach Markus.* 2 vols. EKKNT 2. Zurich: Benziger; Neukirchen-Vluyn: Neukirchener Verlag, 1978–1979.

Goodacre, Mark. *The Case against Q: Studies in Markan Priority and the Synoptic Problem.* Harrisburg, PA: Trinity Press International, 2002.

———. *Goulder and the Gospels: An Examination of a New Paradigm.* JSNTSup 133. Sheffield: Sheffield University Press, 1996.

Goulder, Michael. *Luke: A New Paradigm.* 2 vols. JSNTSup 20. Sheffield: Sheffield University Press, 1989.

Grabbe, Lester L. *Ancient Israel: What Do We Know and How Do We Know It?* London: T&T Clark, 2007.

———. *Judaic Religion in the Second Temple Period: Belief and Practice from the Exile to Yavneh.* London: Routledge, 2000.

———. "Omri and Son, Incorporated: The Business of History." Pages 61–83 in *Congress Volume, Helsinki 2010.* Edited by Martti Nissinen. VTSup 148. Leiden: Brill, 2012.

Grayson, A. Kirk. *Assyrian Rulers of the Early First Millennium BC II (858–745 BC).* RIMA 3. Toronto: University of Toronto Press, 1996.

Grébaut, Sylvain. *Supplément au Lexicon Linguae Aethiopicae de August Dillmann (1865) et Édition du Lexique de Juste d'Urbin (1850–1855).* Paris: Imprimerie Nationale, 1952.

Greenfield, Jonas C., and Elisha Qimron. "The Genesis Apocryphon Col. XII." Pages 70–77 in *Studies in Qumran Aramaic.* Edited by Takamitsu Muraoka. AbrNSup 3. Leuven: Peeters, 1992.

Greimas, Algirdas Julien. *Du sens II: Essais sémiotiques.* Paris: Seuil, 1983.

Greimas, Algirdas Julien, and Joseph Courtés. *Sémiotique: Dictionnarie raisonné de la théorie du langage.* Paris: Hachette, 1979.

Grensted, Laurence W. "The Use of Enoch in St. Luke xvi. 19–31." *ExpTim* 26 (1914–1915): 333–34.

Gressmann, Hugo. *Vom reichen Mann und armen Lazarus: Eine literargeschichtliche Studie.* Abhandlungen der Königlichen Preussischen Akademie der Wissenschaften 7. Berlin: Königliche Akademie der Wissenschaften, 1918.

Grierson, Fiona. "The Testament of Moses." *JSP* 17 (2008): 265–80.

Grobel, Kendrick. " '…Whose Name Was Neves.' " *NTS* 10 (1963–1964): 373–82.

Guelich, Robert A. *Mark 1–8:26.* WBC 34A. Dallas: Word, 1989.

Gundry, Robert. *Matthew: A Commentary on His Handbook for a Mixed Church under Persecution.* Grand Rapids: Eerdmans, 1994.

Hägerland, Tobias. *Jesus and the Forgiveness of Sins.* SNTSMS 150. Cambridge: Cambridge University Press, 2012.

Hagner, Donald A. "Apocalyptic Motifs in the Gospel of Matthew: Continuity and Discontinuity." *HBT* 7 (1985): 53–82.

———. *Matthew 1–13.* WBC 33A. Dallas: Word, 1993.

Hall, Robert G. "Isaiah's Ascent to See the Beloved: An Ancient Jewish Source for the Ascension of Isaiah?" *JBL* 113 (1994): 463–84.

Hallbäck, Geert. "The Early Jesus: Gospel Genres and Types of Authority." Pages 135–45 in *The New Testament in Its Hellenistic Context: Proceedings of a Conference of New Testament Scholars, held at Skálholt.* Edited by Gunnlaugur A. Jónsson, Einar Sigurbjörnsson, and Pétur Pétursson. Studia Theologica Islandica 10. Reykjavík: Gudfraedistofnun—Skálholtsútgáfan, 1996.

———. "Den fortidige Jesus: Om evangelierne og Acta som historieskrivning." Pages 186–99 in *Bibel og historieskrivning.* Edited by Geert Hallbäck and John Strange. Copenhagen: Museum Tusculanum, 1999.

Halperin, David. *The Faces of the Chariot: Early Responses to Ezekiel's Vision.* TSAJ 16. Tübingen: Mohr Siebeck, 1988.

Hannah, Darrell D. *Michael and Christ: Michael Traditions and Angel Christology in Early Christianity.* WUNT 2/109. Tübingen: Mohr Siebeck, 1999.

Harkins, Angela Kim. "Reading the Qumran Hodayot in Light of the Traditions Associated with Enoch." *Hen* 32 (2010): 359–400.

———. *Reading with an "I" to the Heavens: Looking at the Qumran Hodayot through the Lens of Visionary Traditions.* Ekstasis. Berlin: de Gruyter, 2012.

———. "Who Is the Teacher of the Teacher Hymns? Re-examining the Teacher Hymns Hypothesis Fifty Years Later." Pages 449–67 in vol. 1 of *A Teacher for All Generations: Essays in Honor of James C. VanderKam.* Edited by Eric F. Mason. 2 vols. JSJSup 153. Leiden: Brill, 2012.

Harnack, Adolf von. *Entstehung und Entwicklung der Kirchenverfassung und des Kirchenrechts in den ersten zwei Jahrhunderten.* Leipzig: Hinrichs, 1910.

———. *Die Mission und Ausbreitung des Christentums in den ersten drei Jahrhunderten.* Leipzig: Hinrichs, 1902.

———. "Kirchliche Verfassung und kirchliches Recht im I. und II. Jahrhundert," *Protestantische Realenzyklopädie für Theologie und Kirche* 20 (1908): 508–46.

Harrington, Daniel J. *The Gospel of Matthew.* SP 1. Collegeville, MN: Liturgical Press, 1991.

———. "Pseudo-Philo." *OTP* 2:297–377.

Hartman, Lars. *Asking for a Meaning: A Study of 1 Enoch 1–5.* ConBNT 12. Lund: Gleerup, 1979.

Haupt, Paul. "Abraham's Bosom." *AJP* 42 (1921): 162–67.

Hays, Richard B. *Echoes of Scripture in the Letters of Paul.* New Haven: Yale University Press, 1989.

Hayward, Robert. "Sacrifice and World Order: Some Observations on Ben Sira's Attitude to the Temple Service." Pages 22–34 in *Sacrifice and Redemption: Durham Essays in Theology.* Edited by Stephen W. Sykes. Cambridge: Cambridge University Press, 1991.

Heil, John Paul. "Jesus as the Unique High Priest in the Gospel of John." *CBQ* 57 (1995): 729–45.

———. *The Meal Scenes in Luke-Acts: An Audience-Oriented Approach.* SBLMS 52. Atlanta: Society of Biblical Literature, 1999.

Hempel, Charlotte. "The Qumran Sapiential Texts and the Rule Books." Pages 277–95 in *The Wisdom Texts from Qumran and the Development of Sapiential Thought.* Edited by Charlotte Hempel, Armin Lange, and Hermann Lichtenberger. BETL 159. Leuven: Peeters, 2002.

Himmelfarb, Martha. *Ascent to Heaven in Jewish and Christian Apocalypses.* Oxford: Oxford University Press, 1993.

———. *A Kingdom of Priests: Ancestry and Merit in Ancient Judaism.* Philadelphia: University of Pennsylvania Press, 2006.

———. "'A Kingdom of Priests': The Democratization of the Priesthood in the Literature of Second Temple Judaism." *Journal of Jewish Thought and Philosophy* 6 (1997): 89–104.

Hock, Ronald F. "Lazarus and Micyllus: Greco-Roman Backgrounds to Luke 16:19–31." *JBL* 106 (1987): 447–63.

Hoffmann, Andreas Gottlieb. *Das Buch Henoch in vollständiger Uebersetzung mit fortlaufendem Commentar, ausführlicher Einleitung und erläuternden Excursen.* Part 2: *Uebersetzung und Commentar aus Kp. 56–105, nebst Excursen.* Jena: Croeker, 1838.

Hoftijzer, Jacob, and Karen Jongeling. *Dictionary of North-West Semitic Inscriptions.* 2 vols. Leiden: Brill, 1995.

Hogeterp, Albert L. A. *Expectations of the End: A Comparative Traditio-Historical Study of Eschatological, Apocalyptic, and Messianic Ideas in the Dead Sea Scrolls and the New Testament*. STDJ 83. Leiden: Brill, 2009.

Holl, Karl. *Enthusiasmus und Bussgewalt beim griechischen Mönchtum: Eine Studie zu Symeon dem neuen Theologen*. Leipzig: Hinrichs, 1898.

———. "Der Kirchenbegriff bei Paulus in seinem Verhältnis zu dem der Urgemeinde." Pages 44–67 in vol. 2 of *Gesammelte Aufsätze zur Kirchengeschichte*. 2 vols. Tübingen: Mohr Siebeck, 1928.

Holladay, Carl R. *Theios Aner in Hellenistic Judaism: A Critique of the Use of the Category in New Testament Christology*. SBLDS 40. Missoula, MT: Scholars Press, 1977.

Hollander, John. *The Figure of Echo: A Mode of Allusion in Milton and After*. Berkeley: University of California Press, 1981.

Honko, Lauri. "The Problem of Defining Myth." Pages 41–52 in *Sacred Narrative: Readings in the Theory of Myth*. Edited by Alan Dundes. Berkeley: University of California Press, 1984.

Horowitz, Wayne. *Mesopotamian Cosmic Geography*. MC 8. Winona Lake, IN: Eisenbrauns, 1998.

Hultgård, Anders, and Stig Norin, eds. *Le jour de Dieu—Der Tag Gottes*. WUNT 245. Tübingen: Mohr Siebeck, 2009.

Humphrey, Edith. "God and Angels." Pages 35–60 in *Jesus among Friends and Enemies: A Historical and Literary Introduction to Jesus in the Gospels*. Edited by Chris Keith and Larry W. Hurtado. Grand Rapids: Baker Academic, 2011.

Hurtado, Larry W. *How on Earth Did Jesus Become a God? Historical Questions about Earliest Devotion to Jesus*. Grand Rapids: Eerdmans, 2005.

———. "Monotheism, Principal Angels, and the Background of Christology." Pages 546–64 in *The Oxford Handbook of the Dead Sea Scrolls*. Edited by Timothy H. Lim and John J. Collins. Oxford: Oxford University Press, 2010.

Hurtado, Larry W., and Paul L. Owen. *"Who Is This Son of Man?": The Latest Scholarship on a Puzzling Expression of the Historical Jesus*. LNTS 390. London: T&T Clark, 2011.

Huxley, Aldous. *Perennial Philosophy*. London: Harper & Brothers, 1946.

Idel, Moshe. "Enoch Is Metatron." *Imm* 24/25 (1990): 220–40.

Ingelaere, Jean-Claude. "Les jours du Seigneur dans l'Évangile selon Matthieu." Pages 92–98 in *Le jour de Dieu—Der Tag Gottes*. Edited by

Anders Hultgård and Stig Norin. WUNT 245. Tübingen: Mohr Siebeck, 2009.

Isaac, Ephraim. "1 (Ethiopic Apocalypse of) Enoch." *OTP* 1:5–90.

Jacobson, Howard. *The Exagoge of Ezekiel.* Cambridge: Cambridge University Press, 1983.

Jassen, Alex P. *Mediating the Divine: Prophecy and Revelation in the Dead Sea Scrolls and Second Temple Judaism.* STDJ 68. Leiden: Brill, 2007.

Jeremias, Joachim. "Nachwort zum Artikel von H.-G. Leder." *ZNW* 54 (1963): 278–79.

———. *New Testament Theology.* Translated by John Bowden. New York: Scribner's Sons, 1971.

Jonge, Marinus de. *Jesus, the Servant-Messiah.* New Haven: Yale University Press, 1991.

Josephus, Flavius. *The Genuine Works of Flavius Josephus.* Translated by William Whiston. 2 vols. Chester: Shaw/Shoemaker 1801–1819.

Juvenal and Persius. Translated by G. G. Ramsay. LCL. London: Heinemann, 1920.

Juvenal and Persius. Translated by Susanna Morton Braund. Rev. ed. LCL. Cambridge: Harvard University Press, 2004.

Kaler, Michael. "Talking about Religious Experience at Nag Hammadi." *BSR* 42 (2013): 2–7.

Kelly, Henry Ansgar. "The Devil in the Desert." *CBQ* 26 (1964): 190–220.

———. *Satan: A Biography.* Cambridge: Cambridge University Press, 2006.

———. *Towards the Death of Satan: The Growth and Decline of Christian Demonology.* London: Chapman, 1968.

Kingsbury, Jack D. *Matthew as Story.* Philadelphia: Fortress, 1988.

———. *Matthew: Structure, Christology, Kingdom.* Philadelphia: Fortress, 1975.

Kjeldstadli, Knut. *Fortida er ikke hva den en gang var: En innføring i historiefaget.* Oslo: Universitetsforlaget, 1999.

Klostergaard Petersen, Anders. "1 Maccabees from an Axial Age Perspective." In *Die Makkabäer/The Maccabees.* Edited by Michael Tilly, Stefan Krauter, and Predrag Bukovec. WUNT. Tübingen: Mohr Siebeck, 2016.

———. "At the End of the Road—Reflections on a Popular Scholarly Metaphor." Pages 45–72 in *The Formation of the Early Church.* Edited by Jostein Ådna. WUNT 83. Tübingen: Mohr Siebeck, 2005.

———. "Attaining Divine Perfection through Different Forms of Imitation." *Numen* 60 (2013): 7–38.

————. "The Diversity of Apologetics: From Genre to a Mode of Thinking." Pages 15–41 in *Critique and Apologetics: Jews, Christians and Pagans in Antiquity*. Edited by Anders-Christian Jacobsen, Jörg Ulrich, and David Brakke. Early Christianity in the Context of Antiquity 4. Frankfurt: Lang, 2009.

————. "The Emergence of Historiography: An Axial Age Perspective." Pages 63–92 in *History and Religion: Writing a Religious Past*. Edited by Bernd-Christian Otto, Susanne Rau, and Jörg Rüpke. RVV 68. Berlin: de Gruyter, 2015.

————. "Finding a Basis for Interpreting New Testament Ethos." Pages 53–81 in *Early Christian Ethics in Interaction with Jewish and Greco-Roman Contexts*. Edited by Jan Willem van Henten and Joseph Verheyden. STR 17. Leiden: Brill, 2013.

————. "From Morse to Matthew." In *Contextualising Rewritten Scripture: Different Approaches to the Rewriting of Scripture and the Attribution of Authority to Rewritings*. Edited by Anders Klostergaard Petersen. Leiden: Brill, 2016.

————. "Konstruktionen von Geschlecht und Sexualität im Neuen Testament." *ZNW* 30 (2012): 12–23.

————. "Paulus—en antikarismatisk karismatiker." Pages 45–65 in *Fra Buddha til Beckham—karisma og suggestion i sport og religion*. Edited by Poul Götke, Jonas Havelund, and Kristian Rasmussen. Odense: University of Southern Denmark Press, 2005.

————. "The Riverrun of Rewriting Scripture: From Textual Cannibalism to Scriptural Completion." *JSJ* 43 (2012): 475–96.

————. "Textual Fidelity, Elaboration, Supersession or Encroachment? Typological Reflections on the Phenomenon of Rewritten Scripture." Pages 13–48 in *Rewritten Bible after Fifty Years: Texts, Terms, or Techniques? A Last Dialogue with Geza Vermes*. Edited by Joszéf Zsengellér. JSJSup 166. Leiden: Brill, 2014.

Kluger, Rivkah Schärf. *Satan in the Old Testament*. Studies in Jungian Thought. Evanston: Northwestern University Press, 1967.

Knibb, Michael A. *The Ethiopic Book of Enoch: A New Edition in the Light of the Aramaic Dead Sea Fragments*. 2 vols. Oxford: Clarendon, 1978.

————. "The Translation of 1 Enoch 70:1: Some Methodological Issues." Pages 340–54 in *Biblical Hebrew, Biblical Texts: Essays in Memory of Michael P. Weitzman*. Edited by Ada Rapoport-Albert and Gillian Greenberg. JSOTSup 333. Sheffield: Sheffield Academic, 2001.

Koester, Helmut. *Ancient Christian Gospels: Their History and Development*. Philadelphia: Trinity Press, 1990.

Kolenkow, Anitra B. "The Angelology of the Testament of Abraham." Pages 153–62 in *Studies in the Testament of Abraham*. Edited by George W. E. Nickelsburg. SCS 6. Missoula, MT: Scholars Press, 1976.

Kooij, Arie van der. "The Greek Bible and Jewish Concepts of Royal Priesthood and Priestly Monarchy." Pages 255–64 in *Jewish Perspectives on Hellenistic Rulers*. Edited by Tessa Rajak Sarah Pearce, James Aitken, and Jennifer Dines. Berkeley: University of California Press, 2007.

Krahmalkov, Charles R. *Phoenician-Punic Dictionary*. OLA 90, Studia Phoenicia 15. Leuven: Peeters, 2000.

Kreitzer, Larry. "Luke 16:19–31 and 1 Enoch 22." *ExpTim* 103 (1992): 139–42.

Krippner, Stanley. "Altered States of Consciousness." Pages 1–5 in *The Highest State of Consciousness*. Edited by John White. Garden City, NY: Doubleday, 1972.

Kristeva, Julia. *Desire in Language: A Semiotic Approach to Literature and Art*. Translated by T. Gora, A. Jardine, and L. S. Roudiez. Oxford: Blackwell, 1980.

Kuschel, Karl-Josef. *Geboren vor aller Zeit: Der Streit um Christi Ursprung*. Munich: Piper, 1990.

Kvanvig, Helge S. *Primeval History: Babylonian, Biblical, and Enochic. An Intertextual Reading*. JSJSup 149. Leiden: Brill, 2011.

———. *Roots of Apocalyptic: The Mesopotamian Background of the Enoch Figure and of the Son of Man*. WMANT 61. Neukirchen-Vluyn: Neukirchener Verlag, 1988.

Lacocque, André. *The Book of Daniel*. Translated by David Pellauer. London: SPCK, 1979.

Lakoff, George, and Mark Johnson. *Philosophy in the Flesh: The Embodied Mind and Its Challenge to Western Thought*. New York: Basic Books, 1999.

Lambdin, Thomas Oden. *Introduction to Classical Ethiopic (Geʿez)*. HSS 24. Missoula, MT: Scholars Press, 1978.

Lambert, W. G. "The Classification of Incantations." Pages 93–98 in *Proceedings of the 51st Rencontre Assyriologique Internationale Held at the Oriental Institute of the University of Chicago, July 18–22, 2005*. Edited by Robert D. Biggs, Jennie Myers, and Martha T. Roth. SAOC 62. Chicago: Oriental Institute of the University of Chicago, 2008.

Lange, Armin. "The Essene Position on Magic and Divination." Pages 377–435 in *Legal Texts and Legal Issues: Proceedings of the Second Meeting of the International Organization for Qumran Studies, Cambridge 1995*. Edited by Moshe Bernstein, Florentino García Martínez, and John Kampen. STDJ 23. Leiden: Brill, 1997.

Langton, Edward. "What Are Demons?" *London Quarterly and Holborn Review* 23 (1954): 26–32.

Laurence, Richard. *The Book of Enoch the Prophet: An Apocryphal Production, Supposed for Ages to Have Been Lost; but Discovered at the Close of the Last Century in Abyssinia; Now First Translated from an Ethiopian Ms. in the Bodleian Library*. Oxford: Parker, 1821; 2nd ed. 1833.

Lawlor, Hugh Jackson. "Early Citations from the Book of Enoch." *Journal of Philology* 25 (1897): 164–225.

Lehtipuu, Outi. *The Afterlife Imagery in Luke's Story of the Rich Man and Lazarus*. NovTSup 123. Leiden: Brill, 2007.

Leslau, Wolf. *Comparative Dictionary of Ge'ez (Classical Ethiopic)*. Wiesbaden: Harrassowitz, 1987.

Levison, John R. "The Angelic Spirit in Early Judaism." Pages 464–93 in *Society of Biblical Literature 1995 Seminar Papers*. SBLSP 34. Atlanta: Society of Biblical Literature, 1995.

———. "The Pluriform Foundation of Christian Pneumatology." Pages 66–85 in *Advents of the Spirit: An Introduction to the Current Study of Pneumatology*. Edited by Bradford E. Hinze and D. Lyle Dabney. Milwaukee: Marquette University Press, 2001.

———. "The Prophetic Spirit as an Angel according to Philo." *HTR* 88 (1995): 189–207.

———. *The Spirit in First-Century Judaism*. AGAJU 29. Leiden: Brill, 1997.

Lewis, Naphtali. *The Documents from the Bar Kokhba Period in the Cave of Letters: Greek Papyri*. Aramaic and Nabatean Signatures and Subscriptions. Jerusalem: Israel Exploration Society, 1989.

LiDonnici, Lynn R., and Andrea Lieber, eds. *Heavenly Tablets: Interpretation, Identity and Tradition in Ancient Judaism*. JSJSup 119. Leiden: Brill, 2007.

Lindars, Barnabas. *Jesus Son of Man: A Fresh Examination of the Son of Man Sayings in the Gospels in the Light of Recent Research*. London: SPCK, 1983.

Lods, Adolphe. "Les origines de la figure de Satan, ses fonctions à la cour céleste." Pages 649–60 in vol. 2 of *Mélanges syriens offerts à Monsieur*

René Dussaud. Edited by J.-Adrien Blanchet, Franz Cumont, and Georges Contenau. 2 vols. Paris: Geuthner, 1939.

Lucarelli, Rita. "Demonology during the Late Pharaonic and Greco-Roman Periods in Egypt." *JANER* 11 (2011): 109–25.

Luck, Georg. "Theurgy and Forms of Worship in Neo-Platonism." Pages 185–225 in *Religion, Science, and Magic: In Concert and in Conflict*. Edited by Jacob Neusner, Ernest S. Frerichs, and Paul Virgil McCracken Flesher. New York: Oxford University Press, 1989.

Luz, Ulrich. *Matthew 1–7: A Commentary*. Translated by James E. Crouch. Hermeneia. Minneapolis: Fortress, 2007.

———. *Matthew 8–20: A Commentary*. Translated by James E. Crouch. Hermeneia. Minneapolis: Fortress, 2001.

———. *Matthew 21–28: A Commentary*. Translated by James E. Crouch. Hermeneia. Minneapolis: Fortress, 2005.

Lybaek, Lena. *New and Old in Matthew 11–13: Normativity in the Development of Three Theological Themes*. FRLANT 198. Göttingen: Vandenhoeck & Ruprecht, 2002.

Lyons, Christopher. *Definiteness*. CTL. Cambridge: Cambridge University Press, 1999.

Macaskill, Grant. "Matthew and the *Parables of Enoch*." Pages 218–30 in *The Parables of Enoch: A Paradigm Shift*. Edited by James H. Charlesworth and Darrell L. Bock. JCTCRS 11. London: Bloomsbury T&T Clark, 2013.

———. *Revealed Wisdom and Inaugurated Eschatology in Ancient Judaism and Early Christianity*. JSJSup 115. Leiden: Brill, 2007.

Mach, Michael. *Entwicklungsstadien des jüdischen Engelglaubens in vorrabbinischer Zeit*. TSAJ 34. Tübingen: Mohr Siebeck, 1992.

Maldonatus, Johannes. *Commentarii in Quatuor Evangelistas*. Edited by J. M. Raich. Illustrium Theologorum in Sacras Novi Testamenti Scripturas Commentarii II. Moguntiae: Sumptibus Francisci Kirchheim, 1874.

Marguerat, Daniel. *Le jugement dans l'Evangile de Matthieu*. 2nd ed. MdB 6. Geneva: Labor et Fides, 1995.

Marshall, I. Howard. *The Gospel of Luke: A Commentary on the Greek Text*. NIGTC. Grand Rapids: Eerdmans, 1978.

Martin, Dale B. "When Did Angels Become Demons?" *JBL* 129 (2010): 657–77.

Mason, Eric F. "Biblical and Nonbiblical Traditions in Jude and 2 Peter: Sources, Usage, and the Question of Canon." Pages 181–200 in *Read-*

ing 1–2 Peter and Jude: A Resource for Students. Edited by Eric F. Mason and Troy W. Martin. RBS 77. Atlanta: Society of Biblical Literature, 2014.

———. *"You Are a Priest Forever": Second Temple Jewish Messianism and the Priestly Christology of the Epistle to the Hebrews.* STDJ 74. Leiden: Brill, 2008.

Mathews, Mark D. "The Function of Imputed Speech in the Apocalypse of John." *CBQ* 74 (2012): 319–38.

Mayer, Werner R. *Untersuchungen zur Formensprache der babylonischen "Gebetsbeschwörungen."* StPohl, Series Maior 5. Rome: Pontifical Biblical Institute, 1976.

McVann, Mark. "Dwelling among the Tombs: Discourse, Discipleship, and the Gospel of Mark 4:35–5:43." PhD diss. Emory University, 1984.

Meier, Gerhard. *Die assyrische Beschwörungssammlung Maqlû.* AfOB 2. Berlin: Weidner, 1937.

Merkur, Dan. "Cultivating Visions through Exegetical Meditations." Pages 62–91 in *With Letters of Light: Studies in the Dead Sea Scrolls, Early Jewish Apocalypticism, Magic, and Mysticism in Honor of Rachel Elior.* Edited by Daphna V. Arbel and Andrei A. Orlov. Ekstasis 2. Berlin: de Gruyter, 2010.

———. "The Visionary Practices of Jewish Apocalyptists." *Psychoanalytic Study of Society* 14 (1989): 119–48.

Metzger, James A. *Consumption and Wealth in Luke's Travel Narrative.* BibInt 88. Leiden: Brill, 2007.

Michalak, Aleksander R. *Angels as Warriors in Late Second Temple Jewish Literature.* WUNT 2/330. Tübingen: Mohr Siebeck, 2012.

Milik, J. T. *The Books of Enoch: Aramaic Fragments of Qumrân Cave 4.* Oxford: Clarendon, 1976.

Miller, Eric. "The Self-Glorification Hymn Reexamined." *Hen* 31 (2009): 307–24.

Mödritzer, Helmut. *Stigma und Charisma im Neuen Testament und seiner Umwelt: Zur Soziologie des Urchristentums.* NTOA 28. Freibourg: Universitätsverlag; Göttingen: Vandenhoeck & Ruprecht, 1994.

Moor, Johannes C. de, ed. *A Bilingual Concordance to the Targum of the Prophets.* 21 vols. Leiden: Brill, 1995–2005.

Mühlmann, Wilhelm Emil. *Homo Creator: Abhandlungen zur Soziologie, Anthropologie und Ethnologie.* Wiesbaden: Harrassowitz, 1962.

———. *Rassen, Ethnien und Kulturen.* Berlin: Neuwied, 1964.

Mühlmann, Wilhelm Emil, and Ernst W. Müller. *Kulturanthropologie.* Berlin: Kiepenheuer und Witsch, 1966.

Murphy, Frederick. *Apocalypticism in the Bible and Its World: A Comprehensive Introduction.* Grand Rapids: Baker Academic, 2012.

Murray, Robert. "The Origin of Aramaic ʿîr, Angel." *Or* 53 (1984): 303–17.

Nestle, Eberhard, Erwin Nestle, Barbara and Kurt Aland, Johannes Karavidopoulos, Carlo M. Martini, and Bruce M. Metzger. *Novum Testamentum Graece.* 27th ed. Stuttgart: Deutsche Bibelgesellschaft, 1993.

Neusner, Jacob, trans. *Pesiqta de Rab Kahana.* 2 vols. Atlanta: Scholars Press, 1987.

Neusner, Jacob, William Scott Green, and Ernest S. Frerichs, eds. *Judaisms and Their Messiahs at the Turn of the Christian Era.* Cambridge: Cambridge University Press, 1987.

Newberg, Andrew B., Eugene G. D'Aquili, and Vince Rause. *Why God Won't Go Away: Brain Science and the Biology of Belief.* New York: Ballantine, 2001.

Newsom, Carol A. " 'Sectually Explicit' Literature from Qumran." Pages 167–87 in *The Hebrew Bible and Its Interpreters.* BJSUCSD 1. Edited by William Henry Propp, Baruch Halpern, and David Noel Freedman. Winona Lake, IN: Eisenbrauns, 1990.

———. *Songs of the Sabbath Sacrifice: A Critical Edition.* HSS 27. Atlanta: Scholars Press, 1985.

Newsom, Carol A., and James H. Charlesworth. "Angelic Liturgy: Songs of the Sabbath Sacrifice (4Q400–4Q407, 11Q17, Mas1k)." Pages 1–137 in *Angelic Liturgy: Songs of the Sabbath Sacrifice.* Edited by James H. Charlesworth and Carol A. Newsom. Vol. 4B of *The Dead Sea Scrolls: Hebrew, Aramaic, and Greek Texts with English Translations.* Edited by James H. Charlesworth. Tübingen: Mohr Siebeck; Louisville: Westminster John Knox, 1999.

Nickelsburg, George W. E. *1 Enoch 1: A Commentary on the Book of 1 Enoch, Chapters 1–36; 81–108.* Hermeneia. Minneapolis: Fortress, 2001.

———. "Enoch, Levi, and Peter: Recipients of Revelation in Upper Galilee." *JBL* 100 (1981): 575–600.

———. "Four Worlds That Are 'Other' in the Enochic Book of Parables." Pages 55–77 in *Other Worlds and Their Relation to This World: Early Jewish and Ancient Christian Traditions.* Edited by Tobias Nicklas, Joseph Verheyden, Erik M. M. Eynikel, and Florentino García Martínez. JSJSup 143. Leiden: Brill, 2010.

———. *Jewish Literature between the Bible and the Mishnah: A Historical and Literary Introduction.* 2nd ed. Minneapolis: Fortress, 2005.

———. "Patriarchs Who Worry about Their Wives: A Haggadic Tendency in the Genesis Apocryphon." Pages 177–99 in vol. 1 of *George W. E. Nickelsburg in Perspective: An Ongoing Dialogue of Learning.* Edited by Jacob Neusner and Alan J. Avery-Peck. 2 vols. JSJSup 80. Leiden: Brill, 2003.

———. "The Qumranic Transformation of a Cosmological and Eschatological Tradition (1QH 4:29–40)." Pages 649–59 in vol. 2 of *The Madrid Qumran Congress: Proceedings of the International Congress on the Dead Sea Scrolls, Madrid 18–21 March, 1991.* Edited by Julio Trebolle Barrera and Luis Vegas Montaner. 2 vols. STDJ 11. Leiden: Brill, 1992.

———. "Revisiting the Rich and the Poor in 1 Enoch 92–105 and the Gospel according to Luke." Pages 547–71 in vol. 2 of *George W. E. Nickelsburg in Perspective: An Ongoing Dialogue of Learning.* Edited by Jacob Neusner and Alan J. Avery-Peck. 2 vols. JSJSup 80. Leiden: Brill, 2003.

———. "Riches, the Rich, and God's Judgment in 1 Enoch 92–105 and the Gospel according to Luke." Pages 521–46 in vol. 2 of *George W. E. Nickelsburg in Perspective: An Ongoing Dialogue of Learning.* Edited by Jacob Neusner and Alan J. Avery-Peck. 2 vols. JSJSup 80. Leiden: Brill, 2003.

Nickelsburg, George W. E., and James C. VanderKam. *1 Enoch: A New Translation.* Minneapolis: Fortress, 2004.

Nickelsburg, George W. E., and James C. VanderKam. *1 Enoch: The Hermeneia Translation.* Rev. ed. Minneapolis: Fortress, 2012.

Nickelsburg, George W. E., and James C. VanderKam. *1 Enoch 2: A Commentary on the Book of 1 Enoch, Chapters 37–82.* Hermeneia. Minneapolis: Fortress, 2012.

Nicklas, Tobias. "Angels in Early Christian Narratives on the Resurrection of Jesus: Canonical and Apocryphal Texts." Pages 293–311 in *Angels: The Concept of Celestial Beings: Origins, Development and Reception.* Edited by Friedrich V. Reiterer, Tobias Nicklas, and Karin Schöpflin. Deuterocanonical and Cognate Literature Yearbook 2007. Berlin: de Gruyter, 2007.

———. "Resurrection in the Gospels of Matthew and Peter: Some Developments." Pages 27–41 in *Life beyond Death in Matthew's Gospel: Reli-*

gious Metaphor or Bodily Reality? Edited by Wim Weren, Huub van de Sandt, and Joseph Verheyden. BTS 13. Leuven: Peeters, 2011.

Nitzan, Bilha. "Magical Poetry." Pages 227–72 in *Qumran Prayer and Religious Poetry.* Translated by Jonathan Chipman. STDJ 12. Leiden: Brill, 1994.

Noffke, Eric. *Giovanni Battista: Un profeta esseno? L'opera e il messaggio di Giovanni nel suo contesto storico.* Turin: Claudiana, 2008.

Norin, Stig. "Der Tag Gottes im Alten Testament: Jenseits der Spekulationen—Was ist übrig?" Pages 33–42 in *Le jour de Dieu—Der Tag Gottes.* Edited by Anders Hultgård and Stig Norin. WUNT 245. Tübingen: Mohr Siebeck, 2009.

Novakovic, Lidija. *Messiah, the Healer of the Sick: A Study of Jesus as the Son of David in the Gospel of Matthew.* WUNT 2/170. Tübingen: Mohr Siebeck, 2003.

Odeberg, Hugo. *3 Enoch or the Hebrew Book of Enoch.* 1928. Repr., New York: Ktav, 1973.

Oelsner, Joachim. "Incantations in Southern Mesopotamia—From Clay Tablets to Magical Bowls (Thoughts on the Decline of the Babylonian Culture)." Pages 31–52 in *Officina Magica: Essays on the Practice of Magic in Antiquity.* Edited by Shaul Shaked. Institute of Jewish Studies: Studies in Judaica 4. Leiden: Brill, 2005.

O'Kane, Martin. "'The Bosom of Abraham' (Luke 16:22): Father Abraham in the Visual Imagination." *BibInt* 15 (2007): 485–518.

Olmo Lete, Gregorio del, and Joaquín Sanmartín. *A Dictionary of the Ugaritic Language in the Alphabetic Tradition.* Translated by Wilfred G. E. Watson. HdO I/67, Parts 1–2. Leiden: Brill, 2003.

Olson, Daniel C. *Enoch: A New Translation: The Ethiopic Book of Enoch, or 1 Enoch, Translated with Annotations and Cross-References.* North Richland Hills, TX: BIBAL, 2004.

———. "Enoch and the Son of Man in the Epilogue of the Parables." *JSP* 9 (18) (1998): 27–38.

———. "'Enoch and the Son of Man' Revisited: Further Reflections on the Text and Translation of 1 Enoch 70.1–2." *JSP* 18 (2009): 233–40.

Olyan, Saul M. *A Thousand Thousands Served Him: Exegesis and the Naming of Angels in Ancient Judaism.* TSAJ 36. Tübingen: Mohr Siebeck, 1993.

Oomen, Tharaileth Koshy. "Charisma, Social Structure and Social Changes." *CSSH* 10 (1967): 85–99.

Orlov, Andrei A. *Dark Mirrors: Azazel and Satanael in Early Jewish Demonology*. Albany: State University of New York Press, 2011.

——. *The Enoch-Metatron Tradition*. TSAJ 107. Tübingen: Mohr Siebeck, 2005.

——. *Heavenly Priesthood in the Apocalypse of Abraham*. Cambridge: Cambridge University Press, 2013.

——. "The Sacerdotal Traditions of 2 Enoch and the Date of the Text." Pages 103–16 in *New Perspectives on 2 Enoch: No Longer Slavonic Only*. Edited by Andrei Orlov and Gabriele Boccaccini. Studia Judaeoslavica 4. Leiden: Brill, 2012.

Orr, Mary. *Intertextuality: Debates and Contexts*. Cambridge: Polity, 2003.

Oswald, Wolfgang. "Zukunftserwartung und Gerichtsankündigung: Zur Pragmatik der prophetischen Rede vom Tag Jhwhs." Pages 19–29 in *Le jour de Dieu—Der Tag Gottes*. Edited by Anders Hultgård and Stig Norin. WUNT 245. Tübingen: Mohr Siebeck, 2009.

Overman, J. Andrew. *Church and Community in Crisis: The Gospel according to Matthew*. Valley Forge, PA: Trinity Press International, 1996.

Owen, Paul L. "Problems with Casey's 'Solution.'" Pages 28–49 in *"Who Is This Son of Man?": The Latest Scholarship on a Puzzling Expression of the Historical Jesus*. Edited by Larry W. Hurtado and Paul L. Owen. LNTS 390. London: T&T Clark, 2011.

Owen, Paul, and David Shepherd. "Speaking up for Qumran, Dalman and the Son of Man: Was *Bar Enasha* a Common Term for 'Man' in the Time of Jesus?" *JSNT* 81 (2001): 81–122.

Pagels, Elaine H. *The Origin of Satan*. New York: Vintage, 1996.

——. "The Social History of Satan, the 'Intimate Enemy': A Preliminary Sketch." *HTR* 84 (1991): 105–28.

——. "The Social History of Satan, 2: Satan in the New Testament Gospels." *JAAR* 62 (1994): 17–58.

——. "The Social History of Satan, 3: John of Patmos and Ignatius of Antioch: Contrasting Visions of 'God's People.'" *HTR* 99 (2006): 487–505.

Pankoke, Eckart. *Soziale Bewegung, soziale Frage, soziale Politik: Grundfragen der deutschen Sozialwissenschaft im 19. Jahrhundert*. Stuttgart: Klett, 1970.

Patella, Michael. *The Death of Jesus: The Diabolical Force and the Ministering Angel (Luke 23, 44–49)*. CahRB 43. Paris: Gabalda, 1999.

Patrides, Constantinos A. "The Salvation of Satan." *JHI* 28 (1967): 467–78.

Pesch, Rudolf. "Ein Tag vollmächtigen Wirkens Jesu in Kapharnaum (Mk 1,21–34.35–39)." *BibLeb* 9 (1968): 114–28.

Peters, Dorothy M. *Noah Traditions in the Dead Sea Scrolls: Conversations and Controversies of Antiquity.* EJL 26. Atlanta: Society of Biblical Literature, 2008.

Philonenko, Marc. "Au jour du jugement: Origine et diffusion d'une formule eschatologique (contribution d'une sociolecte esseno-qoumrânien)." Pages 101–5 in *Le jour de Dieu—Der Tag Gottes.* Edited by Anders Hultgård and Stig Norin. WUNT 245. Tübingen: Mohr Siebeck, 2009.

Pierce, Chad. *Spirits and the Proclamation of Christ: 1 Peter 3:18–22 in Light of Sin and Punishment Traditions in Early Jewish and Christian Literature.* WUNT 2/305. Tübingen: Mohr Siebeck, 2011.

Pilch, John J. "Altered States of Consciousness: A 'Kitbashed' Model." *BTB* 26 (1996): 133–38.

———. "The Ascension of Jesus: A Social Scientific Perspective." Pages 75–82 in *Kultur, Politik, Religion, Sprache—Text.* Vol. 2 of *Kontexte der Schrift: Für Wolfgang Stegemann zum 60. Geburtstag.* Edited by Christian Strecker. Stuttgart: Kohlhammer, 2005.

Plato. Translated by Harold North Fowler, W. R. M. Lamb, R. G. Bury, and Paul Shorey. 12 vols. LCL. Cambridge: Harvard University Press, 1914–1937.

Platt, Thomas Pell, ed. *Novum Testamentum Domini nostri et Salvatoris Jesu Christi Aethiopice.* Leipzig: Officina G. Drugulini, 1899.

Plutarch's Lives. Translated by Bernadotte Perrin. 11 vols. LCL. Cambridge: Harvard University Press, 1914–1926.

Pokorný, Petr. "The Temptation Stories and Their Intention." *NTS* 20 (1973–1974): 115–27.

Puech, Émile. "Les deux derniers psaumes davidiques du rituel d'exorcisme: 11QPsApa IV 4–V 14." Pages 64–89 in *The Dead Sea Scrolls: Forty Years of Research.* Edited by Devorah Dimant and Uriel Rappaport. STDJ 10. Brill: Leiden, 1992.

———. "Fragments d'un apocryphe de Lévi et le personage eschatologique: 4QTestLévi[c-d](?) 4QAJa." Pages 449–501 in vol. 2 of *The Madrid Qumran Congress: Proceedings of the International Congress on the Dead Sea Scrolls, Madrid 18–21 March, 1991.* Edited by Julio Trebolle Barrera and Luis Vegas Montaner. 2 vols. STDJ 11.2. Leiden: Brill, 1992.

———. "Les fragments eschatologiques de *4QInstruction* (4Q416 1 et 4Q418 69 ii, 81–81a, 127)." *RevQ* 22 (2005): 89–119.

———. "L'hymne de la glorification du Maître de 4Q431." Pages 377–408 in *Prayer and Poetry in the Dead Sea Scrolls and Related Literature: Essays in Honor of Eileen Schuler on the Occasion of Her 65th Birthday.* Edited by Jeremy Penner, Ken M. Penner, and Cecilia Wassen. STDJ 98. Leiden: Brill, 2012.

———. *Qumrân Grotte 4.XXII: Textes araméens, première partie: 4Q529–549.* DJD 31. Oxford: Clarendon, 2001.

Qimron, Elisha. "Toward a New Edition of 1QGenesis Apocryphon." Pages 106–9 in *The Provo International Conference on the Dead Sea Scrolls: Technological Innovations, New Texts, and Reformulated Issues.* Edited by Donald W. Parry and Eugene Ulrich. STDJ 30. Leiden: Brill, 1999.

Rebiger, Bill. "Angels in Rabbinic Literature." Pages 629–44 in *Angels: The Concept of Celestial Beings: Origins, Development and Reception.* Edited by Friedrich V. Reiterer, Tobias Nicklas, and Karin Schöpflin. Deuterocanonical and Cognate Literature Yearbook 2007. Berlin: de Gruyter, 2007.

Reed, Annette Yoshiko. *Fallen Angels and the History of Judaism and Christianity.* Cambridge: Cambridge University Press, 2005.

Reiner, Erica. *Šurpu: A Collection of Sumerian and Akkadian Incantations.* AfOB 11. Graz: Weidner, 1958.

Rey, Jean-Sébastien. *4QInstruction: Sagesse et eschatologie.* STDJ 81. Leiden: Brill, 2010.

Reynolds, Benjamin E. *The Apocalyptic Son of Man in the Gospel of John.* WUNT 249. Tübingen: Mohr Siebeck, 2008.

———. "The Use of the Son of Man Idiom in the Gospel of John." Pages 101–29 in *"Who Is This Son of Man?": The Latest Scholarship on a Puzzling Expression of the Historical Jesus.* Edited by Larry W. Hurtado and Paul L. Owen. LNTS 390. London: T&T Clark, 2011.

Richter, Amy E. *Enoch and the Gospel of Matthew.* PTMS. Eugene, OR: Pickwick, 2012.

Robinson, James M., Paul Hoffmann, and John S. Kloppenborg, eds. *The Critical Edition of Q: Synopsis Including the Gospels of Matthew and Luke, Mark and Thomas with English, German, and French Translations of Q and Thomas.* Hermeneia. Minneapolis: Fortress, 2000.

Rowland, Christopher, and Christopher Morray-Jones. *The Mystery of God: Early Jewish Mysticism and the New Testament.* CRINT 12. Leiden: Brill, 2009.

Ruiten, Jacques van. "Eden and the Temple: The Rewriting of Genesis 2:4–3:24 in the Book of Jubilees." Pages 63–94 in *Paradise Interpreted: Representations of Biblical Paradise in Judaism and Christianity*. Edited by Gerard P. Luttikhuizen. TBN 2. Leiden: Brill, 1999.

———. "Visions of the Temple in the Book of Jubilees." Pages 215–28 in *Gemeinde ohne Tempel/Community without Temple: Zur Substituierung und Transformation des Jerusalemer Tempels und seines Kults im Alten Testament, antiken Judentum und frühen Christentum*. Edited by Beate Ego, Armin Lange, and Peter Pilhofer. WUNT 118. Tübingen: Mohr Siebeck, 1999.

Runciman, Walter Garrison. *Sociology in Its Place*. Cambridge: Cambridge University Press, 1970.

Russell, Jeffrey Burton. *Satan: The Early Christian Tradition*. Ithaca, NY: Cornell University Press, 1981.

Sacchi, Paolo. "The 2005 Camaldoli Seminar on the Parables of Enoch: Summary and Prospects for Future Research." Pages 499–512 in *Enoch and the Messiah Son of Man: Revisiting the Parables of Enoch*. Edited by Gabriele Boccaccini. Grand Rapids: Eerdmans, 2007.

———. *Gesù e la sua gente*. Cinisello Balsamo: San Paolo, 2003.

———. *Jewish Apocalyptic and Its History*. Translated by William J. Short. JSPSup 20. Sheffield: Sheffield Academic, 1996.

Sacy, Antoine Isaac Silvestre de. "Notice du Livre d'Enoch." *Magasin Encyclopédique, ou Journal des Sciences, des Lettres et des Arts* 6.1 (1800): 369–98.

Saldarini, Anthony. "Absent Women in Matthew's Households." Pages 157–70 in *A Feminist Companion to Matthew*. Edited by Amy-Jill Levine. FCNTECW 1. Sheffield: Sheffield Academic, 2001.

Sanders, Ed Parish. *Jesus and Judaism*. London: SCM, 1985.

Sanders, Jack T. *The New Testament Christological Hymns: Their Historical Religious Background*. SNTSMS 15. Cambridge: Cambridge University Press, 1971.

Sandmel, Samuel. "Parallelomania." *JBL* 81 (1962): 1–13.

Sanford, Anthony J., and Simon C. Garrod. *Understanding Written Language*. Chichester: Wiley, 1981.

Sasson, Jack M., ed. *Civilizations of the Ancient Near East*. 4 vols. New York: Scribner's Sons, 1995.

Saussure, Ferdinand de. *Course in General Linguistics*. Translated by Roy Harris. 3rd ed. Chicago: Open Court, 1972.

Schäfer, Peter, Margarete Schlüter, and Hans Georg von Mutius, eds. *Synopse zur Hekhalot-Literatur.* TSAJ 2. Tübingen: Mohr Siebeck, 1981.

Schäfer, Peter. *The Hidden and Manifest God: Some Major Themes in Early Jewish Mysticism.* Translated by Aubrey Pomerance. Albany: State University of New York Press, 1992.

Schiavo, Luigi. "The Temptation of Jesus: The Eschatological Battle and the New Ethic of the First Followers of Jesus in Q." *JSNT* 25 (2002): 141–64.

Schmidt, Nathaniel. "The Son of Man in the Book of Daniel." *JBL* 19 (1900): 22–28.

Schneweis, Emil. *Angels and Demons according to Lactantius.* Washington, DC: Catholic University of America Press, 1944.

Schneider, Michael. "The Myth of the Satan in the Book of Bahir." *Kabbalah* 20 (2009): 287–343 [in Hebrew].

Schramm, Wolfgang. *Bann, Bann! Eine sumerisch-akkadische Beschwörungsserie.* GAAL 2. Göttingen: Seminar für Keilschriftforschung, 2001.

———. *Ein Compendium sumerisch-akkadischer Beschwörungen.* Göttinger Beiträge zum Alten Orient 2. Göttingen: Universitätsverlag, 2008.

Schultz, Brian. *Conquering the World: The War Scroll (1QM) Reconsidered.* STDJ 76. Leiden: Brill, 2009.

Schulze, Wilhelm August. "Der Heilige und die wilden Tiere: Zur Exegese von Mc 1 13b." *ZNW* 46 (1955): 280–83.

Schwartz, Jeffrey M., Henry P. Stapp, and Mario Beauregard. "Quantum Physics in Neuroscience and Psychology: A Neurophysical Model of Mind-Brain Interaction." *Philosophical Transactions of the Royal Society B: Biological Sciences* 360 (2005): 2–19.

Sedley, David. "The Ideal of Godlikeness." Pages 309–28 in *Plato 2: Ethics, Politics, Religion, and the Soul.* Edited by Gail Fine. Oxford: Oxford University Press, 1999.

Sefati, Yitschak, and Jacob Klein. "The Role of Women in Mesopotamian Witchcraft." Pages 569–87 in vol. 1 of *Sex and Gender in the Ancient Near East: Proceedings of the 47th Rencontre Assyriologique Internationale, Helsinki, July 2–6, 2001.* Edited by Simo Parpola and Robert M. Whiting. 2 vols. CRRAI 47. Helsinki: Neo-Assyrian Text Corpus Project, 2002.

Segal, Alan. *Two Powers in Heaven: Early Rabbinic Reports about Christianity and Gnosticism.* SJLA 25. Leiden: Brill, 1977.

Segal, Michael. *The Book of Jubilees.* JSJSup 117. Leiden: Brill, 2007.

Setzer, Claudia. *Resurrection of the Body in Early Judaism and Christianity: Doctrine, Community, and Self-Definition*. Leiden: Brill, 2004.

Shakespeare, William. *Shakespeare's Sonnets*. Edited by Stephen Booth. Yale Nota Bene Edition. New Haven: Yale University Press, 2000.

Sharf, Robert H. "The Rhetoric of Experience and the Study of Religion." *Journal of Consciousness Studies* 7 (2000): 267–87.

Shepherd, David. "Re-Solving the Son of Man 'Problem' in Aramaic." Pages 50–60 in *"Who Is This 'Son of Man'?": The Latest Scholarship on a Puzzling Expression of the Historical Jesus*. Edited by Larry W. Hurtado and Paul L. Owen. LNTS 390. New York: T&T Clark, 2011.

Sim, David C. *Apocalyptic Eschatology in the Gospel of Matthew*. SNTSMS 88. Cambridge: Cambridge University Press, 1996.

———. "Matthew 22.13a and 1 Enoch 10.4a: A Case of Literary Dependence." *JSNT* 47 (1992): 3–19.

Smith, Dennis E. *From Symposium to Eucharist: The Banquet in the Early Christian World*. Minneapolis: Fortress, 2003.

———. "The Messianic Banquet Reconsidered." Pages 64–73 in *The Future of Early Christianity: Essays in Honor of Helmut Koester*. Edited by Birger A. Pearson. Minneapolis: Fortress, 1991.

———. "Table Fellowship as a Literary Motif in the Gospel of Luke." *JBL* 106 (1987): 613–38.

Smith, Morton. "Ascent to the Heavens and the Beginning of Christianity." *ErJb* 50 (1981): 403–29.

Sohm, Rudolph. *Die geschichtlichen Grundlagen*. Vol. 1 of *Kirchenrecht*. Berlin: von Duncker & Humblot, 1892.

Sokoloff, Michael. *A Dictionary of Jewish Babylonian Aramaic of the Talmudic and Geonic Periods*. Dictionaries of Talmud Midrash and Targum 3. Ramat Gan: Bar Ilan University Press; Baltimore: Johns Hopkins University Press, 2002.

Solms-Rödelheim, Max Ernst Graf zu. "Max Webers Religionssoziologie heute: Zum 40. Todestag des Forschers." *Deutsche Rundschau* 86 (1960): 524–30.

Souza Nogueira, Paolo Augusto de. "Ecstatic Worship in the Self-Glorification Hymn." Pages 385–94 in *Wisdom and Apocalypticism in the Dead Sea Scrolls and in the Biblical Tradition*. Edited by Florentino García Martínez. BETL 168. Leuven: Leuven University Press and Peeters, 2003.

Spicq, Ceslas. "L'origine johannique de la conception du Christ-prêtre dans l'Épître aux Hébreux." Pages 258–69 in *Aux sources de la tradi-*

tion chrétienne: Mélanges offerts à M. Maurice Goguel. Edited by Oscar Cullmann and P. H. Menoud. Neuchâtel: Delachaux & Niestlé, 1950.

Stanton, Graham. *A Gospel for a New People: Studies in Matthew.* London: T&T Clark, 1992.

———. "Matthew 11:28–30: Comfortable Words?" *ExpTim* 94 (1982): 3–8.

Starcky, Jean. "Les quatres étapes du messianisme à Qumrân." *RB* 70 (1963): 481–505.

Stegemann, Hartmut, and Eileen Schuller, with translation of texts by Carol Newsom. *1QHodayot^a with Incorporation of 1QHodayot^b and 4QHodayot^{a-f}.* DJD 40. Oxford: Clarendon, 2009.

Stevens, Heidi. "Catching a Red Herring: What's the Origin of This Ubiquitous Phrase?" *Chicago Tribune,* Lifestyles. http://tinyurl.com/SBL3544a.

Stichel, Rainer. "Die Verführung der Stammeltern durch Satanael nach der Kurzfassung der slavischen Baruch-Apocalypse." Pages 116–28 in *Kulturelle Traditionen in Bulgarien.* Edited Reinhard Lauer and Peter Schreiner. AAWG 177. Göttingen: Vandenhoeck & Ruprecht, 1989.

Stökl, Daniel. "Fasting with Jews, Thinking with Scapegoats: Some Remarks on Yom Kippur in Early Judaism and Christianity, in particular 4Q541, Barnabas 7, Matthew 27 and Acts 27." Pages 165–87 in *The Day of Atonement: Its Interpretations in Early Jewish and Christian Traditions.* Edited by Thomas Hieke and Tobias Nicklas. TBN 15. Leiden: Brill, 2012.

———. "Yom Kippur in the Apocalyptic *imaginaire* and the Roots of Jesus' High Priesthood." Pages 349–66 in *Transformations of the Inner Self in Ancient Religions.* Edited by Jan Assmann and Guy G. Stroumsa. SHR 83. Leiden: Brill, 1999.

Stone, Michael E. *Adam's Contract with Satan: The Legend of the Cheirograph of Adam.* Bloomington: Indiana University Press, 2002.

———. *Ancient Judaism: New Visions and Views.* Grand Rapids: Eerdmans, 2011.

———. " 'Be You a Lyre for Me': Identity or Manipulation in Eden." Pages 87–99 in *The Exegetical Encounter between Jews and Christians in Late Antiquity.* Edited by Emmanouela Grypeou and Helen Spurling. Jewish and Christian Perspectives Series 18. Leiden: Brill, 2009.

———. "Enoch, Aramaic Levi, and Sectarian Origins." *JSJ* 19 (1988): 159–70.

———. "The Fall of Satan and Adam's Penance: Three Notes on the Books of Adam and Eve." Pages 43–56 in *Literature on Adam and Eve: Col-*

lected Essays. Edited by Gary A. Anderson, Michael E. Stone, and Johannes Tromp. SVTP 15. Brill: Leiden, 2000.

———. Features of the Eschatology of IV Ezra. HSS 35. Atlanta: Scholars Press, 1989.

———. Fourth Ezra: A Commentary on the Book of Fourth Ezra. Hermeneia. Minneapolis: Fortress, 1990.

———. "Ideal Figures and Social Context: Priest and Sage in the Early Second Temple Age." Pages 575–86 in Ancient Israelite Religion: Essays in Honor of Frank Moore Cross. Edited by Patrick D. Miller Jr., Paul D. Hanson, and S. Dean McBride. Philadelphia: Fortress, 1987.

———. "A Reconsideration of Apocalyptic Visions." HTR 96 (2003): 167–80.

Strugnell, John, Daniel J. Harrington, S.J., and Torleif Elgvin. Qumran Cave 4.XXIV: Sapiential Texts, Part 2: 4QInstruction (Mûsār lĕ Mēvîn): 4Q415ff. with a Re-edition of 1Q26. DJD 34. Oxford: Clarendon, 1999.

Stuckenbruck, Loren T. 1 Enoch 91–108. CEJL. Berlin: de Gruyter, 2007.

———. Angel Veneration and Christology. WUNT 2/70. Tübingen: Mohr Siebeck, 1995.

———. "The 'Angels' and 'Giants' of Genesis 6:1–4 in Second and Third Century BCE Jewish Interpretation: Reflections on the Posture of Early Apocalyptic Traditions." DSD 7 (2000): 354–77.

———. "The Book of Enoch: Its Reception in Second Temple Jewish and in Christian Tradition." Early Christianity 4 (2013): 7–40.

———. The Book of Giants from Qumran: Texts, Translation, and Commentary. TSAJ 63. Tübingen: Mohr Siebeck, 1997.

———. "Conflicting Stories: The Spirit Origin of Jesus' Birth." Pages 142–60 in The Myth of Rebellious Angels: Studies in Second Temple Judaism and New Testament Texts. WUNT 335. Tübingen: Mohr Siebeck, 2014.

———. "The Human Being and Demonic Invasion: Therapeutic Models in Ancient Jewish and Christian Texts." Pages 161–86 in The Myth of Rebellious Angels: Studies in Second Temple Judaism and New Testament Texts. WUNT 335. Tübingen: Mohr Siebeck, 2014.

———. "The Other World in the Epistle of Enoch." Pages 79–93 in Other Worlds and Their Relation to This World: Early Jewish and Ancient Christian Traditions. Edited by Tobias Nicklas, Joseph Verheyden, Erik M. M. Eynikel, and Florentino García Martínez. JSJSup 143. Leiden: Brill, 2010.

———. "The Parables of Enoch according to George Nickelsburg and Michael Knibb: A Summary and Discussion of Some Remaining

Questions." Pages 65–71 in *Enoch and the Messiah Son of Man: Revisiting the Book of Parables*. Edited by Gabriele Boccaccini. Grand Rapids: Eerdmans, 2007.

———. "Pseudepigraphy and First Person Discourse in the Dead Sea Documents: From the Aramaic Texts to the Writings of the *Yaḥad*." Pages 293–326 in *The Dead Sea Scrolls and Contemporary Culture*. Edited by Adolfo D. Roitman, Lawrence H. Schiffman, and Shani Tzoref. STDJ 93. Leiden: Brill, 2011.

Stuckenbruck, Loren T., and Mark D. Mathews. "The Apocalypse of John, *1 Enoch*, and the Question of Influence." Pages 281–325 in *The Myth of Rebellious Angels: Studies in Second Temple Judaism and New Testament Texts*. WUNT 335. Tübingen: Mohr Siebeck, 2014.

Suggs, M. Jack. *Wisdom, Christology, and Law in Matthew's Gospel*. Cambridge: Harvard University Press, 1970.

Sullivan, Kevin. *Wrestling with Angels: A Study of the Relationship between Angels and Humans in Ancient Jewish Literature and the New Testament*. AGAJU 55. Leiden: Brill, 2004.

Suter, David W. "Fallen Angel, Fallen Priest: The Problem of Family Purity in 1 Enoch 6–16." *HUCA* 50 (1979): 115–35.

———. "*Māšāl* in the Similitudes of Enoch." *JBL* 100 (1981): 193–212.

———. *Tradition and Composition in the Parables of Enoch*. SBLDS 47. Missoula, MT: Scholars Press, 1979.

Tart, Charles T. "On the Scientific Study of Nonphysical Worlds." Pages 214–19 in *Body, Mind, Spirit: Exploring the Parapsychology of Spirituality*. Edited by Charles T. Tart. Charlottesville: Hampton Roads, 1997.

Taves, Ann. *Religious Experience Reconsidered: A Building-Block Approach to the Study of Religion and Other Special Things*. Princeton: Princeton University Press, 2009.

Taylor, Nicholas H. "The Temptation of Jesus on the Mountain: A Palestinian Christian Polemic against Agrippa I." *JSNT* 83 (2001): 27–49.

Tigchelaar, Eibert J. C. *To Increase Learning for the Understanding Ones: Reading and Reconstructing the Fragmentary Early Jewish Sapiential Text 4QInstruction*. STDJ 44. Leiden: Brill, 2001.

———. "Towards a Reconstruction of the Beginning of 4QInstruction (4Q416 Fragment 1 and Parallels)." Pages 99–126 in *The Wisdom Texts from Qumran and the Development of Sapiential Thought*. Edited by Charlotte Hempel, Armin Lange, and Hermann Lichtenberger. BETL 159. Leuven: Peeters, 2002.

——. "Wisdom and Counter-Wisdom in 4QInstruction, Mysteries, and 1 Enoch." Pages 177–93 in *The Early Enoch Literature*. Edited by Gabriele Boccaccini and John J. Collins. JSJSup 121. Leiden: Brill, 2007.

Tiller, Patrick A. *A Commentary on the Animal Apocalypse of 1 Enoch*. EJL 4. Atlanta: Scholars Press, 1993.

Toorn, Karel van der. "The Theology of Demons in Mesopotamia and Israel: Popular Belief and Scholarly Speculation." Pages 61–83 in *Die Dämonen—Demons: Die Dämonologie der israelitisch-jüdischen und frühchristlichen Literatur im Kontext ihrer Umwelt—The Demonology of Israelite-Jewish and Early Christian Literature in Context of Their Environment*. Edited by Armin Lange, Hermann Lichtenberger, and K. F. Diethard Römheld. Tübingen: Mohr Siebeck, 2003.

Tromp, Johannes. *The Life of Adam and Eve in Greek: A Critical Edition*. PVTG 6. Leiden: Brill, 2005.

Tucker, Robert C. "The Theory of Charismatic Leadership." *Daedalus* 97 (1968): 731–56.

Tuckett, Christopher M. "The Temptation Narrative in Q." Pages 479–507 in vol. 1 of *The Four Gospels: Festschrift Frans Neirynck*. Edited by Frans Van Segbroeck, Christopher M. Tuckett. Gilbert Van Belle, and Joseph Verheyden. 3 vols. BETL 100. Leuven: Peeters, 1992.

Twelftree, Graham H. *Jesus the Exorcist: A Contribution to the Study of the Historical Jesus*. WUNT 2/54. Tübingen: Mohr Siebeck, 1993.

Uhlig, Siegbert. *Das äthiopische Henochbuch*. JSHRZ 5/6. Gütersloh: Gütersloher Verlagshaus, 1984.

Urbach, Ephraim E. *The Sages: Their Concepts and Beliefs*. Translated by Israel Abrahams. Jerusalem: Magnes, 1975.

VanderKam, James C. "1 Enoch, Enochic Motifs, and Enoch in Early Christian Literature." Pages 33–101 in *The Jewish Apocalyptic Heritage of Early Christianity*. Edited by James C. VanderKam, and William Adler. CRINT 3/4. Assen: Van Gorcum; Minneapolis: Fortress, 1996.

——. "The Angel of the Presence." *DSD* 7 (2000): 378–93.

——, trans. *The Book of Jubilees*. CSCO 510–511, Scriptores Aethiopici 87–88. Leuven: Peeters, 1989.

——. *Enoch: A Man for All Generations*. Columbia: University of South Carolina Press, 1995.

——. *Enoch and the Growth of an Apocalyptic Tradition*. CBQMS 16. Washington DC: Catholic Biblical Association, 1984.

——. "Messianism in the Scrolls." Pages 211–34 in *The Community of the Renewed Covenant: The Notre Dame Symposium on the Dead Sea*

Scrolls. Edited by Eugene Ulrich and James C. VanderKam. Christianity and Judaism in Antiquity 10. Notre Dame: University of Notre Dame Press, 1993.

———. "Prophecy and Apocalyptics in the Ancient Near East." *CANE* 3:2083–94.

———. "Righteous One, Messiah, Chosen One, and Son of Man in 1 Enoch 37–71." Pages 169–91 in *The Messiah: Developments in Earliest Judaism and Christianity.* Edited by James H. Charlesworth. First Princeton Symposium on Judaism and Christian Origins. Minneapolis: Fortress, 1992.

Vargas-Machuca, Antonio. "La tentación de Jesús según Mc. 1,12–13 ¿Hecho real o relato de tipo haggádico?" *EstEcl* 48 (1973): 163–90.

Vermes, Geza. "Appendix E: The Use of נש בר/נשא בר in Jewish Aramaic." Pages 310–30 in *An Aramaic Approach to the Gospels and Acts,* by Matthew Black. 3rd ed. Oxford: Clarendon, 1967.

Verseput, Donald. *The Rejection of the Humble Messianic King: A Study of the Composition of Matthew 11–12.* European University Studies, Series 23, Theology, 291. Frankfurt: Lang, 1986.

Walck, Leslie W. "The *Parables of Enoch* and the Synoptic Gospels." Pages 231–68 in *The Parables of Enoch: A Paradigm Shift.* Edited by James H. Charlesworth and Darrell A. Bock. JCTCRS 11. London: Bloomsbury T&T Clark, 2013.

———. *The Son of Man in the Parables of Enoch and in Matthew.* JCTCRS 9. London: T&T Clark, 2011.

———. "The Son of Man in the Parables of Enoch and the Gospels." Pages 299–337 in *Enoch and the Messiah Son of Man: Revisiting the Book of Parables.* Edited by Gabriele Boccaccini. Grand Rapids: Eerdmans, 2007.

Wassen, Cecilia. "Angels in the Dead Sea Scrolls." Pages 499–520 in *Angels: The Concept of Celestial Beings: Origins, Development and Reception.* Edited by Friedrich V. Reiterer, Tobias Nicklas, and Karin Schöpflin. Deuterocanonical and Cognate Literature Yearbook 2007. Berlin: de Gruyter, 2007.

Watts, Rikk E. "Jesus' Death, Isaiah 53, and Mark 10:45: A Crux Revisited." Pages 125–51 in *Jesus and the Suffering Servant: Isaiah 53 and Christian Origins.* Edited by William H. Bellinger Jr. and William R. Farmer. Harrisburg, PA: Trinity Press International, 1998.

Weber, Max. *Gesammelte Aufsätze zur Wissenschaftslehre.* Tübingen: Mohr Siebeck, 1968.

———. *Wirtschaft und Gesellschaft: Grundriss der verstehenden Soziologie*. 1956. Repr., Tübingen: Mohr Siebeck, 1972.

Wenham, Gordon J. "Sanctuary Symbolism in the Garden of Eden Story." Pages 19–25 in *The Period of the Bible*. Division A of *Proceedings of the Ninth World Congress of Jewish Studies, Jerusalem, August 4–12, 1985*. Jerusalem: World Union of Jewish Studies, 1986.

Wertheimer, Shlomo Aharon. *Batei Midrashot*. Edited by Abraham Joseph Wertheimer. 2nd ed. 2 vols. Jerusalem: Ktav Yad we-Sefer, 1989.

West, Martin L. *The East Face of Helicon: West Asiatic Elements in Greek Poetry and Myth*. Oxford: Oxford University Press, 1997.

Westfall, Cynthia Long. "Messianic Themes of Temple, Enthronement, and Victory in Hebrews and the General Epistles." Pages 210–29 in *The Messiah in the Old and New Testaments*. Edited by Stanley E. Porter. MNTS. Grand Rapids: Eerdmans, 2007.

Williams, Peter J. "Expressing Definiteness in Aramaic: A Response to Casey's Theory concerning the Son of Man Saying." Pages 61–77 in *"Who Is This 'Son of Man'?": The Latest Scholarship on a Puzzling Expression of the Historical Jesus*. Edited by Larry W. Hurtado and Paul L. Owen. LNTS 390. New York: T&T Clark, 2011.

Willner, Ann Ruth, and Dorothy Willner. "The Rise and Role of Charismatic Leaders." *Annals of the American Academy of Political and Social Sciences* 358 (1965): 77–88.

Wilson, Bryan R. *The Noble Savages: The Primitive Origins of Charisma and Its Contemporary Survival*. Berkeley: University of California Press, 1975.

Winckelmann, Johann. "Exkurs zur weltgeschichtlichen Stellung des antiken Judentums." Pages 219–23 in *Max Webers Studie über das antike Judentum: Interpretation und Kritik*. Edited by Wolfgang Schluchter. Frankfurt: Suhrkamp, 1981.

Wise, Michael O. *The First Messiah: Investigating the Savior before Jesus*. San Francisco: HarperCollins, 1999.

Witmer, Amanda. *Jesus, the Galilean Exorcist: His Exorcisms in Social and Political Context*. LNTS 459; LHJS 10. London: Bloomsbury T&T Clark, 2012.

Woit, Peter. *Not Even Wrong: The Failure of String Theory and the Search for Unity in Physical Law*. New York: Basic Books, 2006.

Wold, Benjamin G. *The Mystery of Existence: The Construction of Authority in 4QInstruction*. Forthcoming.

Worsley, Peter. *The Trumpet Shall Sound: A Study of "Cargo" Cults in Melanesia*. New York: Schocken Books, 1968.

Wright, Archie T. *The Origin of Evil Spirits*. WUNT 2/198. Tübingen: Mohr Siebeck, 2005.

Wright, J. Edward. *The Early History of Heaven*. New York: Oxford University Press, 2000.

Wyatt, Nicholas. "Qeteb." *DDD* 673–74.

Xeravits, Géza G. *King, Priest, Prophet: Positive Eschatological Protagonists in the Qumran Library*. STDJ 47. Leiden: Brill, 2003.

Yadin, Yigael, and Yaakov Meshorer. *Masada I: The Yigael Yadin Excavations 1963–1965. Final Reports: The Aramaic and Hebrew Ostraca and Jar Inscriptions. The Coins of Masada*. Jerusalem: Israel Exploration Society, 1989.

Yarbro Collins, Adela. "Finding Meaning in the Death of Jesus." *JR* 78 (1998): 175–96.

———. *Mark: A Commentary*. Hermeneia. Minneapolis: Fortress, 2007.

———. "The Signification of Mark 10:45 among Gentile Christians." *HTR* 90 (1997): 371–82.

Zimmermann, Johannes. *Messianische Texte aus Qumran: Königliche, priesterliche und prophetische Messiasvorstellungen in den Schriftfunden von Qumran*. WUNT 2/104. Tübingen: Mohr Siebeck, 1998.

Contributors

Joseph L. Angel is Associate Professor of Bible at the Department of Jewish Studies of Yeshiva University, New York. His focus is on ancient Judaism, especially on religion and history in the Second Temple period. He is the author of *Otherworldly and Eschatological Priesthood in the Dead Sea Scrolls* (Brill, 2010). His other publications include articles on ancient Jewish magic, the Second Temple of Jerusalem, and Qumran liturgy, as well as commentaries on Second Temple–period texts such as the Damascus Document and "New Jerusalem."

Daniel Assefa is Director of the Capuchin Franciscan Research and Retreat Center in Addis Abeba, Ethiopia. He holds a PhD in Biblical Theology from the Catholic Institute of Paris and teaches Sacred Scriptures at Capuchin Franciscan Institute of Philosophy and Theology in Addis Ababa. Having published a number of academic articles, he is the author of *L'Apocalypse des Animaux (1 Hen 85–90) une propagande militaire? Approches narrative, historico-critique, perspectives theologiques* (Brill, 2007).

Leslie Baynes is Associate Professor at the Department of Religious Studies at Missouri State University. She is the author of *The Heavenly Book Motif in Judeo-Christian Apocalypses 200 BCE–200 CE* (Brill, 2012) and has published many academic articles and essays, including pieces on C. S. Lewis in venues such as *The Journal of Inklings Studies* and *The Wall Street Journal*.

Kelley Coblentz Bautch is an Associate Professor of Religious and Theological Studies at St. Edward's University in Austin, Texas. She is author of *A Study of the Geography of 1 Enoch 17–19: "No One Has Seen What I Have Seen"* (Brill, 2003) and coeditor of *Fallen Angels Traditions: Second Temple Developments and Reception History* (Catholic Biblical Association of America, 2014) and *The Watchers in Jewish and Christian Traditions*

(Fortress, 2014); she has also published many academic articles in the fields of Second Temple Judaism and early Christianity.

Gabriele Boccaccini is Professor of Second Temple Judaism and New Testament at the University of Michigan and the founding director of the Enoch Seminar. He is the author and editor/coeditor of numerous books, including *Middle Judaism* (Fortress, 1992); *Beyond the Essene Hypothesis* (Eerdmans, 1998); *Roots of Rabbinic Judaism* (Eerdmans, 2002); *Enoch and Qumran Origins* (Eerdmans, 2005); *Enoch and the Messiah Son of Man* (Eerdmans, 2007); *Enoch and the Mosaic Torah* (Eerdmans, 2009); *New Perspectives on 2 Enoch* (Brill, 2012); *4 Ezra and 2 Baruch: Reconstruction after the Fall* (Brill, 2013); *The Seleucid and Hasmonean Periods and the Apocalyptic Worldview* (T&T Clark, 2016); and *Paul the Jew* (Fortress, 2016).

Henryk Drawnel is Associate Professor at the Institute of Biblical Studies of the Catholic University of Lublin, Poland. His monograph publications include *The Aramaic Astronomical Book (4Q208–4Q211) from Qumran: Text, Translation, and Commentary* (Oxford University Press, 2011) and *An Aramaic Wisdom Text from Qumran: A New Interpretation of the Levi Document* (Brill, 2004); he is the author of many academic studies on Second Temple Jewish literature and the New Testament.

André Gagné is an Associate Professor in Theological Studies at the Concordia University in Montreal, Canada. He is the coeditor of *En marge du canon: Études sur les écrits apocryphes juifs et chrétiens* (Cerf, 2012); *Le Vivant qui fait vivre: Esprit, éthique et résurrection dans le Nouveau Testament; Mélanges offerts à la professeure Odette Mainville* (Médiaspaul, 2011); *The Construction of Religious Identities* (Peeters, 2016); and *The Global Impact of Religious Violence* (Wipf & Stock, forthcoming). In addition, he is the author of many articles on the Gospel of Thomas.

Lester L. Grabbe is Emeritus Professor at the University of Hull, UK, where he taught Old Testament and Early Judaism. He is the author of a number of books, including *An Introduction to Second Temple Judaism: History and Religion of the Jews in the Time of Nehemiah, the Maccabees, Hillel, and Jesus* (T&T Clark, 2010); *A History of the Jews and Judaism in the Second Temple Period* (2 vols.; T&T Clark, 2004, 2011); and *An Introduction to Early Judaism* (T&T Clark, 2010). Having recently edited and coedited several volumes, including *Open-Mindedness in the Bible and*

Beyond: A Volume of Studies in Honour of Bob Becking (T&T Clark, 2015), *The Temple in Text and Tradition: A Festschrift in Honour of Robert Hayward* (T&T Clark, 2016), and *Enquire of the Former Age: Ancient Historiography and Writing the History of Israel* (T&T Clark, 2011), he has published many articles on Jewish wisdom and apocalyptic literature, as well as on the history of Judaism during the Second Temple period.

Daniel M. Gurtner is Ernest and Mildred Hogan Professor of New Testament Interpretation at the Southern Baptist Theological Seminary in Louisville, Kentucky. His authored books include *Studies on the Text of the New Testament and Early Christianity* (Brill, 2015); *From Creation to New Creation: Biblical Theology and Exegesis* (Hendrickson, 2013); and *Exodus: A Commentary on the Greek Text of Codex Vaticanus* (Brill, 2013); he is also coeditor of *Jesus, Matthew's Gospel and Early Christianity: Studies in Memory of Graham N. Stanton* (T&T Clark, 2013).

Andrei A. Orlov is a Professor of Theology at Marquette University, Michigan. He is the author of several books, including *Resurrection of the Fallen Adam: Ascension, Transfiguration, and Deification of the Righteous in Early Jewish Mysticism* [Russian] (RSUH, 2014) and *Divine Scapegoats: Demonic Mimesis in Early Jewish Mysticism* (State University of New York Press, 2015), and he has published over forty articles in edited volumes, dictionaries, and scholarly journals such as *Journal for the Study of Judaism*, *Journal for the Study of the Pseudepigrapha*, *Henoch*, *Biblica*, and *Journal of Jewish Studies*.

Anders Klostergaard Petersen is Professor in the Department for the Study of Religion at Aarhus University. He is author and coeditor of a number of books as well as about 450 book chapters, articles, reviews, and the like on late Second Temple Judaism, Greco-Roman religion and philosophy, early Christ-religion, and matters pertaining to method, theory, and biocultural evolution. Among his most recent and forthcoming publications are coedited volumes on *Ancient Philosophy and Religion: Religio-philosophical Discourses within the Graeco-Roman, Jewish and Early Christian World* (Brill, 2016); *Contextualising Rewritten Scripture: Wrestling with Authorithy* (Brill 2017); and *Divination and Magic and Their Interactions* (Brill, 2017).

Loren T. Stuckenbruck is Professor of New Testament (with emphasis on Second Temple Judaism) at the Ludwig-Maximilians-Universität München. He is the author of *Angel Veneration and Christology* (Mohr Siebeck, 1995); *The Book of Giants from Qumran* (Mohr Siebeck, 1997); *1 Enoch 91–108* (de Gruyter, 2007); *The Myth of Rebellious Angels* (Mohr Siebeck, 2014); and the coeditor and author of numerous books and academic articles.

Benjamin Wold is an Associate Professor in Early Judaism and Christianity at the Department of Religions and Theology at Trinity College Dublin, Ireland. His academic articles have focused on Dead Sea Scrolls, the Synoptic Gospels, the book of Revelation, conceptualizations of "evil" (dualism, demonology), and the phenomenon of ancient "apocalypticism." He has published *Women, Men and Angels* (Mohr Siebeck, 2005) and is coeditor of *Dualism, the Devil, and Demons* (Mohr Siebeck, 2014).

Archie T. Wright is an Associate Professor at the School of Divinity of Regent University in Virginia Beach. He is the author of *The Origin of Evil Spirits: The Reception of Genesis 6:1–4 in Early Jewish Literature* (rev. ed., Fortress, 2015) and the coeditor of *Spirit and Scripture: Exploring a Pneumatic Hermeneutic* (T&T Clark, 2012) and the forthcoming *Early Jewish Literature: Introduction and Reader* (Eerdmans). He has also published numerous article-length studies on early Jewish and Christian texts.

INDEX OF ANCIENT SOURCES

INDEX OF MODERN AUTHORS

CPSIA information can be obtained at www.ICGtesting.com
Printed in the USA
BVOW02s0045120916

461699BV00001B/1/P